Vegetarian Dis

Rose Elliot is one of Britai[n's] vegetarian cookery. She is the books and her original and imaginative style has made her a favourite among vegetarians and non-vegetarians alike. Her recipes range from creations of subtle sophistication to simple and cheap dishes for the novice cook and those on a tight budget.

Rose Elliot became a cookery writer by accident. She was planning to take a degree in history when she met and married her husband and became involved in cooking, entertaining and bringing up a family. For many years she has tried out all her recipes at home, the very best of which she has included in her books.

Also by Rose Elliot

SIMPLY DELICIOUS
NOT JUST A LOAD OF OLD LENTILS
THE BEAN BOOK
BEANFEAST
YOUR VERY GOOD HEALTH
GOURMET VEGETARIAN COOKING
VEGETARIAN MOTHER AND BABY BOOK
CHEAP AND EASY

ROSE ELLIOT

Vegetarian Dishes of the World

FONTANA/Collins

First published by William Collins Sons & Co. Ltd 1981
First issued in Fontana Paperbacks 1982 under the title *A Foreign Flavour*
Third impression 1985
Reissued in 1988 under its original title, *Vegetarian Dishes of the World*

Printed and bound in Great Britain by
William Collins Sons & Co. Ltd, Glasgow

For Katy, Margaret and Claire

Contents

Introduction

Although I was brought up as a vegetarian, when I started to cook for people who were used to eating meat I found that, unlike me, they did not relish with delight the thought of nut roast. So I began to look for alternatives which they would enjoy more. I soon realized that nearly every country has in its cuisine at least one or two traditional dishes that do not contain meat or fish yet which are still good to look at, good to eat and very satisfying. Over the years I have gradually built up a collection of these recipes and this book is the result; it contains over 250 recipes from more than 30 different countries.

From Britain there are a couple of traditional cheese dishes, including Welsh rabbit; a creamy leek pie and pease pudding, which I've included because although really intended as an accompaniment to meat it is nutritious enough to eat as a main course, and probably often was when times were hard. It's good with vegetables and one of the piquant sauces – mint sauce or apple sauce – which Britain does so well. But the real strength of the British contribution lies in the baking – there are some excellent breads, scones and cakes, including Madeira cake and Dundee cake – and some quite surprisingly superb puddings such as trifle, gooseberry fool and *crème brûlée*, which sounds and tastes as though it ought to be French, but isn't.

France itself has any number of delectable vegetarian dishes. The French just seem to have the knack of putting together a few simple, yet high quality ingredients and finishing up with something that's exactly right. Add to this a love of and respect for vegetables and you come up with such wonderful mixtures as red cabbage cooked with butter, chestnuts and red wine, or aubergines stuffed with mushrooms, parsley and cheese. This book contains many examples of this type of flair as well as those great French vegetarian classics, omelettes, soufflés and savoury flans with their mouthwatering combination of crisp pastry and creamy filling. Then there are the dishes which to me exemplify the thrifty, inventive side of French cookery, the light stuffed pancakes and the golden puffed up savoury choux pastry ring, or *gougère*, which help make the precious vegetables go further. Finally there are one or two slightly frivolous cakes and some good simple puddings.

Italy, with its pizza, pasta and rice dishes, is another country which has a great deal to offer the vegetarian and it's just the type of food that is so useful and popular – cheap and tasty, quick to make and quick to eat. I've often thought it strange that the Italian cuisine, which is the oldest in Europe, should in many ways be the one with the most contemporary appeal and practicality. There is certainly plenty of scope for the vegetarian: as well as cereal and pasta dishes there are also vegetable dishes, including a rich-tasting aubergine casserole and stuffed onions; then there's that cheesy golden bake, *gnocchi alla Romana*, as well as delicate spinach *gnocchi* and some tasty fritters. From Italy also come some refreshing puddings including again the one with perhaps the most appeal for today, ice cream.

German cookery is rather like that of Great Britain in that it seems to be very much orientated towards meat, but there are some interesting vegetable dishes and I particularly like the German way of mixing fruit with vegetables – haricot beans or carrots with apples, fried potato cake with cranberry or apple sauce. The Germans also have a split pea purée rather like the British pease pudding except that they add vegetables which makes a good variation. And they use dried fruits for a compote which makes a pleasant winter pudding.

Austria does not seem to be a very rich source of vegetarian dishes – here again the emphasis is on meat – but the Austrians do have a good way of serving those light little cheesy dumplings, *gnocchi*, in a velvety mushroom sauce, and also of course that marvellous almond and raspberry tart, *Linzertorte*.

Much of the cookery of Spain and Portugal includes fish or meat in one form or another but I have allowed myself the indulgence of including a vegetarian version of perhaps the most famous Spanish dish of all, paella. Although fish is usually among the ingredients, it's a very variable dish and so I hope a vegetarian version will be considered valid. As well as this there is that well-known cold Spanish soup, gazpacho, and some simple stuffed vegetables, also a red kidney bean dish from Portugal; and from Spain perhaps one of the most luxurious puddings of all, chocolate and orange mousse.

Some useful cheese dishes are to be found in both Holland and Switzerland, including one of the best cheese dishes of all, surely a classic, cheese fondue. I have attributed this to Switzerland, although I believe a rather similar dish is made in Holland and in my recipe I have perhaps rather cheekily suggested Dutch Edam cheese as a good alternative to more expensive Gruyère and Emmenthal! Also from Switzerland come what I consider to be a particularly successful cheese flan, a couple of vegetable dishes and a moist fruit bread.

The main contribution from Scandinavia seems to be in the puddings section. From Denmark there's red fruit pudding made from raspberries and redcurrants, and the rice and almond pudding which is traditionally served at Christmas; there's apricot and almond pudding from Sweden, ways with rhubarb and prunes from Norway and with apples from Finland. But the Scandinavians also have some unusual ways of serving vegetables to make them a bit special. I especially like the two Finnish mushroom recipes and the Norwegian cabbage and new potatoes. And then of course there are open sandwiches – ideal for a buffet meal – and also Danish pastries, for which I've developed a wheatmeal version.

Although the countries of Eastern Europe are not vegetarian, they do have a number of national dishes that do not contain meat and so are ideal for vegetarians. In Rumania, for instance, there is a mixed vegetable stew called *ghiveci* and while this can sometimes contain meat it by no means always does, and so I have given an all-vegetable version of that, also a protein-rich cheesy dip. Then from Bulgaria there are a couple of stews, one based on lentils and the other made from red kidney beans; from Hungary come a couple of vegetable stews enlivened with soured cream and paprika, and from Poland a vegetable and bean salad which is pretty to look at and very filling.

Russian cookery offers the vegetarian an ingenious dip with smoky mock caviar; then there's beetroot soup, or borsch, and to eat with it some little curd cheese tartlets, *vatrushki*, and a protein-rich pudding, that traditional Easter dish made from curd or cream cheese, called *pashka*.

I love the easy-going, inventive feel of American cookery; it's exciting and it's fun. The Americans seem to be particularly good with salads – to them we owe coleslaw and Waldorf salad, also some cooked vegetable dishes, including glazed sweet potatoes and sweetcorn fritters; and perhaps the best chilled soup of all, vichyssoise, which was invented by a chef in America although admittedly he was French. But then one of the strengths of American cookery seems to be the way it can contain the cuisines of so many different nationalities yet retain a recognizable character of its own. There are also some substantial puddings; I've included those American favourites, cheese cake and pumpkin pie and also a less well-known flan, raisin and sour cream pie.

In the cookery of South America and the Caribbean there are several vegetarian dishes; a red bean rice dish from the Caribbean, as well as pumpkin soup and banana fritters, and from South America chilled avocado soup and that creamy avocado dip, *guacamole*; also an unusual hot potato salad with a peanut and chilli dressing which sounds strange but works well. In South America, as in India, unleavened breads play an important part in the diet; here they are called tortillas and usually made from maize flour. You will find a recipe for making these and two recipes for stuffing and baking them like pancakes, and also how to·make them into *tostadas* by frying them and using them as a base for salad mixtures.

The national cereal of North Africa is couscous, which consists of pellets of semolina (or other grains) and is served with spicy sauces. These sauces generally contain meat of some type, but nearly always have chick peas in the mixture too, which in fact provide excellent protein without the meat when eaten with the couscous. I have therefore given a vegetarian version based on chick peas, vegetables and spices. Cooling side salads are served with couscous meals and there are some typical mixtures in the salads section.

I think the Middle East offers some of the best vegetarian dishes of all. There are dreamy dips – smooth chick pea *hummus*, of course – as well as some less well-known ones made from aubergine and sesame cream and from dried beans. These make first courses or fillings for sandwiches or for the pocket-shaped Middle Eastern bread, pitta, of which I've evolved a wholewheat version. Then there are some unusual salads, among them the famous bulgur wheat, tomato and parsley one called *tabbouleh*, and a cold cooked spinach one which sounds odd but which is particularly cooling on a hot day. But perhaps the most important Middle Eastern contribution to vegetarian cookery is the stuffed vegetables that look so appetizing: tomatoes stuffed with rice, little stuffed aubergines, stuffed vine leaves baked in tomato sauce. There are some splendid pies, too; I think the spinach pie, with its smooth filling and flaky crust is one of the best. And when it comes to puddings, there's an easy uncooked yoghurt tart, a honey cheese cake and a chilled ground rice and rosewater pudding which are nutritious and therefore useful in menu planning, as well as being good to eat.

India has a large proportion of vegetarians in its population and so is as you might expect one of the best sources of vegetarian food – and what colourful, tasty food it is! I think there are few foods as appetizing as a really well-cooked curry or spicy rice dish and you will find a number of recipes for these including *khitchari*, that mixture of lentils and rice from which our present-day kedgeree originated. The Indians are also excellent at making unleavened breads and these are lovely for eating not only with curries, but also with salads and dips as a change from ordinary bread. One of these unleavened bread mixtures is also rolled out thinly, wrapped around a vegetable filling then deep-fried to make *samosas*, little Indian pastries.

China is another country which has plenty to offer the vegetarian. The Chinese were making their own versions of textured protein from wheat flour long before it was ever thought of in the West. I have included a sweet and sour way with this wheat protein, also a recipe using that other high-protein vegetable product, *tofu*, which is made from soya beans and which you can sometimes buy very cheaply in Chinese shops. There are also a couple of the crunchy stir-fried vegetable dishes that the Chinese do so well.

I think most people like to try something new sometimes and there are occasions when even the most dedicated meat eater feels like a change, so I hope this book will prove interesting and helpful and that you will be tempted to cook the recipes and will enjoy the results.

Note on Measurements

Throughout this book I've given both metric and Imperial measurements. As long as you keep to either one set of measurements or the other in a recipe you should find that all is well. I have used the standard equivalents, listed below, but as you will see, for some of the Imperial measurements there are two possible metric equivalents and sometimes I have used one and sometimes the other, depending on which is the more accurate for a particular recipe. This mainly applies to sauces and pastries, where proportions are important.

With liquids I have generally used pints and fractions of a pint as the Imperial equivalent to millilitres, but again, in one or two recipes, where accuracy is particularly important, or where there is no near fractional equivalent, I've used fluid ounces as the equivalent. Measuring liquids is easy with a good measuring jug marked in millilitres, pints and fluid ounces.

The tablespoons and teaspoons used in the recipes are standard size, 15 ml and 5 ml respectively, and level unless otherwise stated.

The eggs used are always standard, size 3.

Grams (g)	Ounces (oz)	Millilitres (ml)	Fluid ounces (fl oz)
25	1	25	1
40	1½	50	2
50	2	75	3
60	2½	125	4
75	3	150	5 (¼ pint)
100	4 } (¼ pound)	175	6
125	4 } (¼ pound)	200	7
150	5	225	8
175	6	250	10 } (½ pint)
200	7	275	10 } (½ pint)
225	8 (½ pound)	300	11

15

Grams (g)	Ounces (oz)	Millilitres (ml)	Fluid ounces (fl oz)
250	9	350	12
275	10	375	13
300	11	400	15 } (¾ pint)
350	12 (¾ pound)	425	16 } (¾ pint)
375	13	450	16
400	14	475	17
425	15	500	18
450	16 (1 pound)	550	20 } (1 pint)
475	17	575	20 } (1 pint)
500	18	850	(1½ pints)
700	24 (1½ pounds)	1000 (1 litre)	35
1000 (1 kilo)	2–2¼ pounds	1·2 litres	(2 pints)

Oven Temperatures

Temperature	Centigrade (°C)	Fahrenheit (°F)	Gas Mark
	70	150	
	80	175	
	100	200	
Very Cool	110	225	¼
	120	250	½
	140	275	1
Cool	150	300	2
Warm	160	325	3
Moderate	180	350	4
Fairly Hot	190	375	5
	200	400	6
Hot	220	425	7
	230	450	8
Very Hot	240	475	9
	260	500	9

Equivalents for North American Readers

Ingredients

Aubergine	Egg plant
Beetroot	Beet
Biscuits	Cookies
Black treacle	Molasses
Caster sugar	Fine sugar
Cornflour	Cornstarch
Courgette	Zucchini
Double cream	Heavy cream
Grill	Broiler
Hazel nuts	Filberts
Icing sugar	Confectioner's sugar
Marmite	Savita
Marrow	Squash/very large zucchini
Single cream	Light cream
Spanish onion	Bermuda onion
Spring onion	Scallion

Measurements

1 pint (20 fl oz/575 ml)	2¼ cups
25 g (1 oz) chopped nuts	2 tablespoons
25 g (1 oz) fat/butter/margarine	2 tablespoons
25 g (1 oz) flour	2 tablespoons
25 g (1 oz) grated cheese	4 tablespoons
25 g (1 oz) caster sugar	2 tablespoons
450 g (1 lb) fresh breadcrumbs	8 cups
450 g (1 lb) large beans	3 cups
450 g (1 lb) small beans	2 cups
450 g (1 lb) bulgur wheat	2 cups
450 g (1 lb) cottage/cream/curd cheese	2 cups

450 g (1 lb) grated whole nuts	4 cups
450 g (1 lb) macaroni	3 cups
450 g (1 lb) mashed potato	2 cups
450 g (1 lb) cooked/uncooked rice	2 cups
450 g (1 lb) semolina	2 cups
450 g (1 lb) wholewheat flour	4 cups

Centimetres to Inches

Centimetres	Inches
6 mm	$\frac{1}{4}$ in
1 cm	$\frac{1}{2}$ in
2·5 cm	1 in
5 cm	2 in
7·5 cm	3 in
10 cm	4 in
12·5 cm	5 in
15 cm	6 in
18 cm	7 in
20 cm	8 in
23 cm	9 in
25 cm	10 in
28 cm	11 in
30 cm	12 in

Note on Special Ingredients

Most of the recipes are self-explanatory and nearly all the ingredients are easy to get; when something scarce or exotic is called for I've tried to give substitutes where possible so that even if you can't get it you can still make the dish. But here are just one or two notes that might be helpful.

Fats and Oils

You will notice that I generally suggest butter in the recipes because very often that is the fat traditionally used and therefore the one which gives the most authentic flavour. You could substitute a pure vegetable margarine if you prefer and of course make it an unsaturated one if you wish.

It's difficult to decide whether butter or polyunsaturated margarine is better from the health point of view because opinions differ depending on which expert you consult. I must admit that I'm veering towards margarine although I do still use butter sometimes at the table and in some cookery. I also use corn oil, which is low in saturated fat, for frying, and olive oil, which is neutral, for salad dressings. If you want to use a white fat (high in saturated fat) for pastry, choose a pure vegetable one.

Whatever your feelings about the butter versus polyunsaturated margarine controversy, I think the most important thing is to keep a check on the amount of *any* fat used in cooking (including cream and egg yolks) and try to plan a day's – and a week's – meals carefully, balancing eggs, cheese and fats with plenty of cereal and vegetable protein, low-fat cheeses such as cottage cheese and quark (a lovely smooth white cheese which is readily available and which I find very useful) and yoghurt, vegetables and salad.

Flour

The flour I normally use is plain 100% wholewheat, which I find excellent for nearly all my cooking. If you're new to wholewheat flour it's often helpful to start with to mix it with a proportion of plain unbleached white flour; I've given suggestions for this in the recipes where applicable. I also use unbleached plain white flour for all sauces which require a flour thickening.

You will notice in the recipes where wholewheat flour is sifted I say 'add the sifted flour and the residue of bran left in the sieve' or similar. People sometimes ask me why I bother to sift the flour and then add the bran that's been sifted out. The flour is sifted to aerate it and make it light, not to remove the bran, so, having sifted the flour the bran can then be put back.

Sugar

This is another controversial subject and my own feelings are that it's not so much the colour of the sugar that makes a dish healthy or not, but the quantity used. Brown sugar 'feels' healthier to use but I've found this tends to make me a bit more lavish with it! I use brown sugar in breads and in cakes such as Dundee cake, parkin and chocolate brownies, also sometimes in shortbreads and cookies. But there are times when I prefer to use a small quantity of caster sugar or honey because they give the dish a better flavour and appearance. This is particularly true, I feel, when a delicate vanilla flavour is called for and for this I think there is nothing better than vanilla sugar which is so easy to make. All you do is break a vanilla pod in half and bury the halves in a canister of caster sugar, topping up the sugar as it is used.

Salt

I'm afraid I'm very addicted to sea salt which I know is more expensive than ordinary table salt but I like it because it's natural and pure. The trouble is it also makes food taste so much better that once you've used it it spoils you for anything else.

Herbs and Spices

It's often the use of a herb or spice that makes food taste of a particular country: dill immediately gives a Scandinavian or Eastern European flavour, paprika a Hungarian one. I've tried, however, to keep the recipes as simple and straightforward as possible (while still, I hope, keeping their authenticity) and the only spice that I think you could have difficulty in obtaining is fresh ginger root (unless there is a large Asian community where you live). But it's much easier to find than it used to be and I've discovered that the root will keep beautifully in the deep freeze, just wrapped in foil or polythene. You can grate it straight from the freezer, so it's worth buying up a few knobbly pieces of root when you see it or if you have to go some distance to get it.

Pulses

These days it's not usually difficult to find dried beans, peas and lentils and I've been delighted to see dried red kidney beans, chick peas and continental lentils appearing in my local super-market alongside the more familiar split red lentils and butter beans. Instructions for using these pulses appear in the individual recipes but as a general rule it's worth remembering that if you rinse pulses after soaking, before cooking, it helps to make them more digestible. Also it's best not to add salt to the cooking water as this can toughen the skin before the inside is cooked. In the recipes I've given approximate cooking times for the pulses but these can vary according to how long the pulses have been stored so it's best to keep an eye on them and adjust the timing a little if necessary; do make sure the pulses are thoroughly cooked. I've gone into this whole question of pulse cookery in detail in *The Bean Book*.

RED KIDNEY BEANS – A WARNING

You may have heard that, under certain conditions, it can be dangerous to eat red kidney beans. The toxic factor is most probably a haemagglutinin which may lead to acute gastroenteritis if not destroyed by adequate cooking. Soaking and rinsing the beans prior to cooking reduces the haemagglutinins by two thirds (to about the level present in other dried beans, soaked or un-soaked). The danger can be eliminated entirely by *ensuring that the beans are allowed to boil vigorously for 10 minutes* before lowering the heat and letting the beans cook gently until tender. It is safe to use a slow cooker *provided they are boiled for 10 minutes* as above, before being put into the slow cooker.

Menu Planning

Planning a vegetarian meal is not complicated or difficult – all you have to do is to decide on your source of protein, just like you would with meat or fish, and build the rest of the meal around that. So you could have something like, say, cheese soufflé with new potatoes and French beans followed by a refreshing pudding like tangy orange salad. If you wanted a first course as well you could have a salady one, like stuffed tomato salad or mushrooms *à la Grecque*, or a dip such as mock caviar with crisp Melba toast, or a vegetable purée soup, like French tomato soup or lettuce soup – as you can see there is plenty of scope!

Other examples of this type of simple menu planning based around a protein-rich main course are: Caribbean courgettes stuffed with cheese and onion, with tomato sauce, new potatoes (or cooked rice) and spinach or baby carrots, preceded by pumpkin soup (also from the Caribbean) if you like, and perhaps followed by exotic fruit salad or banana fritters. Or from Italy, gorgeous tomato and mushroom pizza with green salad, with perhaps stuffed cucumber as a starter and pineapple sorbet for pudding. There are plenty of high-protein dishes like these in the book and plenty of scope for many different combinations. Although I've given suggestions for more than one course, if you want to be simpler and more economical the first courses and puddings can of course be left out as long as you've included some protein in the main course.

I think, however, that part of the pleasure of vegetarian cookery and a great deal of satisfaction, as far as I'm concerned, comes from the fact that it gives the opportunity to be very fluid and creative in meal planning. This also enables you to enjoy dishes that you probably wouldn't otherwise. Take for instance luscious French red cabbage stuffed with chestnuts and baked in red wine. This really makes a lovely main dish but it only contains

23

a minimal amount of protein; however there's no reason why the protein should always be in the main dish. You can make a beautifully balanced meal by serving a protein-rich first course, such as the creamy chick pea and vegetable salad *aigroissade*, with warm rolls; or little individual cheese soufflés which make a wonderfully impressive starter; or a nutritious dip, like goat cheese and herb spread, or *hummus*, with fingers of hot buttered or Melba toast.

You could boost the protein level still further if you wanted to by concluding the meal with a pudding like little coffee custards or *coeurs à la crème*, or biscuits and cheese. Another way of introducing protein into a meal is by including it in a vegetable dish, such as potatoes Anna layered with grated cheese or green salad with Gruyère cheese or haricot bean salad.

Here are some of the ways in which you can provide protein for the meal when it is not in the main dish.

1. *Serve a protein starter* such as lentil soup with crusty rolls, French onion soup, or chilled cucumber soup; or tomatoes stuffed with cheese, individual cheese soufflés or individual asparagus tartlets.

2. *Offer a milk-based or cheesy sauce with the meal* – this is particularly good with some of the stuffed vegetable dishes such as the tomatoes à la Provençale or stuffed onions.

3. *Have grated cheese for people to add to their meal* – this is a useful and simple way of increasing the protein with some pasta dishes or vegetable stews such as ratatouille or the mixed vegetable stew from Bulgaria.

4. *Garnish the dish with slices of hardboiled egg* – again, if you like egg, this is a good simple way of adding protein to some vegetable casseroles, salads, curries or rice dishes.

5. *Serve the meal with rice and even add some nuts, sunflower seeds or sesame seeds to the rice to increase the protein further* – this works well with vegetable mixtures like the red peppers with tomatoes and onions and some of the stuffed vegetable dishes.

6. *Have a protein-rich vegetable or salad with the meal* – this is a nice easy way of adding nourishment. Potatoes Anna, layered with cheese, are good, or jacket potatoes with a dollop of

curd cheese or smooth low-fat cheese like quark (see page 19), or the German haricot beans with apples. Or, green salad with Gruyère cheese, haricot bean salad or tomato, cheese and olive salad are all excellent and go with lots of different dishes.

7. *Provide protein with a nutritious pudding* – perhaps this is one time when you can indulge with a relatively easy conscience! Examples of such puddings are ice cream (home-made with egg custard), yoghurt tart, *crème brûlée*, coffee *ricotta* pudding, cheese cake, special ground rice pudding or even biscuits and cheese – and possibly also one of the protein-rich dips – or bowls of assorted nuts and raisins.

As you will see some of these ideas are really very simple, others take more time and organization, but I think you'll agree the idea is quite feasible and practical and it really is fun to experiment with creative menus.

Here are just a few examples of how this planning works – there are lots more ideas with the recipes.

Stuffed tomato salad – fondue with French bread – pear bread (*birnbrot*).

Chick pea soup – paella with Spanish green salad – chocolate and orange mousse.

Individual cheese soufflés – aubergines *à la duxelles* with wine sauce – *gratin dauphinoise* – French beans – fresh peach salad.

Bean pâté with fingers of hot toast – stuffed vine leaves – tomato salad – Greek honey pie.

Avocados with vinaigrette – mushroom soufflé – green salad – *Linzertorte*.

Aubergine and sesame pâté or mock caviar with hot toast – Russian beetroot soup with little cheese tartlets – fresh fruit.

French onion soup – tomatoes à la Provençale with noodles and French beans – *crème brûlée*.

Hummus – tomatoes stuffed with rice – green salad with Gruyère cheese (or you could serve cheese sauce) – orange fruit salad.

Red cabbage and chestnut casserole – jacket potatoes filled with low-fat quark or soured cream and chopped chives – little coffee custards.

Chilled cucumber soup – red pepper stew with brown rice – green salad with Gruyère – chilled yoghurt.

Biriani – curry sauce – tomato side salad – chopped hardboiled eggs, roasted peanuts, poppadums, mango chutney – special ground rice pudding.

Small portions haricot bean salad with bread and butter – ratatouille with potatoes Anna (with layers of cheese) – crêpes suzette.

If you follow the suggestions I've given in the book you certainly needn't worry about missing out on any essential nutrients. The dairy foods, cheese, eggs, milk and milk products such as yoghurt are as rich in protein as meat, whilst the other forms of protein, nuts and seeds, pulses and cereals, are all nourishing if you mix ingredients from two or more of the categories at the same meal – I've given lots of suggestions with the individual recipes. If you want to go into this question of vegetarian nutrition more deeply you will find I've explained it in more detail in my book *Not Just a Load of Old Lentils* and also in *The Bean Book*. But honestly, there really isn't a problem and you needn't worry that you'll be undernourished!

Soups

A bowl of home-made soup makes a very welcoming start to a meal. It can even become the main part of the meal if it's a filling soup: one of our favourite weekend lunches in winter is a good lentil soup with hot rolls and cheese and fresh fruit. There are other hearty soups to choose from besides lentil; French onion soup, with its cheesy bread topping is another favourite, and vivid beetroot soup from Russia is cheering to look at as well as filling to eat on a cold day.

For serving before other more substantial dishes there are some lighter soups made from puréed vegetables, fresh-tasting and delicious, as well as some chilled soups. I know some people find the idea of chilled soups rather strange, but they make a beautifully refreshing start to a summer meal. Both the chilled avocado soup and the chilled cucumber soup are also very easy to do if you've got a liquidizer.

Personally I consider a liquidizer to be almost essential for soup making, but you could use a Mouli-légumes for nearly all the soups in this section if you prefer.

In most of the soups the thickening comes from the vegetables themselves after they have been puréed. This usually seems to be sufficient, especially if a little potato is included in the ingredients. Quite often I liquidize half or three-quarters of the mixture to give the soup a thick, smooth base, and leave the rest as it is to supply some texture and add interest, but this is something you can vary according to how you feel and the effect you want to achieve.

You will notice in the recipes that sometimes I suggest using vegetable stock, sometimes just water and sometimes a choice. I think some soups, like French onion soup, for instance, need stock to give a good flavour; you can use home-made stock, or vegetarian stock cubes or powder from a health shop. There are other soups, however, particularly the simple vegetable soups, for which I don't think it is so important to use stock, and

27

sometimes I think you can even get a better effect by just using water which allows the full flavour of the vegetables to come through, so don't feel guilty if you haven't got any stock.

I've also found it a mistake to think that the longer soups cook the tastier they'll be. This may be true of meat soups, but with vegetable soups once the vegetables are tender there's no point in further cooking and the soup tastes fresher if it's not over-cooked.

Soups are fun to serve because it doesn't take much extra trouble to make them look really pretty. A few fresh green herbs snipped over a pale soup, a swirl of cream on a deep-coloured tomato or beetroot soup or some crunchy little cubes of fried bread topping a smooth-textured soup take only moments and make the soup look and taste extra good.

BEETROOT SOUP

This soup looks very warming and appetizing, its rich ruby red
swirled with soured cream. Although borsch, to give it its Russian
name, is usually made with beef stock and may contain meat as
well, there are numerous versions throughout Russia, the only
consistent ingredient being beetroot. So I don't think my vegetarian one is too far-fetched. In Russia borsch is often accompanied by little cottage or curd cheese tartlets, *vatrushki*,
which turn it into a complete lunch or supper.

2 large onions	450 g (1 lb) cooked beetroot
2 large carrots	(not beetroot in vinegar)
2 stalks celery	Sea salt
125 g (4 oz) cabbage	Sugar
2 tablespoons vegetable oil	150 ml (5 fl oz) carton
1 litre (1¾ pints) water or	soured cream (optional)
vegetable stock	Fresh dill or chives (optional)
225 g (8 oz) can tomatoes	

Serves 4–6

Peel and chop the onions; scrape and dice the carrots and slice
the celery and cabbage. Heat the oil in a good-sized saucepan and
add the prepared vegetables; stir them so that they all get coated
with the oil, then leave them to fry over a gentle heat for about
10 minutes, stirring from time to time. Stir in the water or
vegetable stock and tomatoes, bring up to the boil, then cover the
saucepan and leave the soup to simmer for about 20 minutes
until all the vegetables are tender. (I sometimes use a pressure-
cooker for this in which case it takes about 5 minutes.)

While this is happening rub the peel off the beetroot and cut
them into dice. Add the beetroot to the soup and season well with
salt and a little sugar. Bring the soup up to the boil again and let
it simmer gently for 3–4 minutes. You can serve the borsch like
this, but I prefer to liquidize about half of it, which makes the
soup slightly thicker while still retaining a nice texture. If using

the soured cream whisk it lightly with a fork to make it creamy. then swirl a little into each bowl. Sprinkle with chopped dill if you've got some; or you can use chopped chives.

CHEESE AND ONION SOUP   ITALY

Although the ingredients used in this soup are very similar to those of French onion soup, the result is quite different because it is white with a smooth texture, and the cheese is stirred in just before serving to thicken and flavour it. If you've got time to do them it's very nice with some crunchy cubes of fried bread on top. It's a filling, protein-rich soup, lovely before a salad meal, or buttery pasta and green salad.

700 g (1½ lb) onions	125-175 g (4-6 oz) grated cheese
850 ml (1½ pints) water	25 g (1 oz) Parmesan cheese
25 g (1 oz) butter	Croûtons of crunchy fried
Sea salt	bread
Freshly ground black pepper	

Serves 4

Peel and chop onions, then put them into a large saucepan with the water and simmer them gently until tender – 15–20 minutes. Liquidize the soup, then return it to the rinsed out saucepan and add the butter and a little seasoning. When you're ready to serve the soup reheat it until bubbling hot. Take it off the heat and stir in the cheeses. Check the seasoning and serve the soup immediately.

If you reheat the soup once the cheese has been added don't let it boil or it might get stringy. Also be careful not to overseason the soup before you add the cheese because the cheese will make it taste saltier.

CHESTNUT SOUP

ITALY

The starchy texture and slightly sweet flavour of chestnuts go well with hot vegetables and make this a very warming winter soup. You can use fresh chestnuts if you've got time to prepare them but I must admit I usually use the dried ones which you can get easily now in health shops and some supermarkets.

700 g (1½ lb) fresh chestnuts
  or 225 g (8 oz) dried
  chestnuts.
1 large onion
2 large carrots
1 turnip
2 celery stalks
25 g (1 oz) butter
1 litre (1¾ pints) stock or water
1 tablespoon chopped parsley
Sea salt
Freshly ground black pepper

Serves 4–6

If you're using fresh chestnuts make a little cut in them with a sharp knife, then simmer them in boiling water until the cut opens – about 10 minutes. Remove the skins with a sharp, pointed knife – keep the chestnuts in the water until you're ready to peel them because the skins will firm up as they cool. If you're using dried chestnuts soak them in cold water for an hour or so then simmer them gently in plenty of water until they're really tender. I find this takes a good hour or more. Drain the cooked dried chestnuts, saving the liquid.

Peel and chop the onion, carrots and turnip; wash and dice the celery. Melt the butter in a large saucepan and fry the onion for 5 minutes, then add the rest of the vegetables and cook for a further 5 minutes before pouring in the stock. (If you're using dried chestnuts, make the reserved cooking liquid up to a litre (1¾ pints) with water or stock and use this.) Simmer the soup for about 40 minutes until the chestnuts and vegetables are tender. Stir in the parsley and season the soup with salt and pepper.

CHICK PEA SOUP
SPAIN

I think chick peas have a very special savoury sort of flavour, and here they are used to make a tasty soup. If possible you need to allow time for them to soak before cooking as this does speed up the cooking time. This is a useful soup for serving before the Spanish paella or stuffed peppers because it supplies plenty of protein.

225 g (8 oz) chick peas – you can get these easily from health shops
1 onion
2 carrots
50 g (2 oz) butter

1 tablespoon lemon juice
1 bay leaf
Sea salt
Freshly ground black pepper
A few croûtons of fried bread

Serves 4

Soak the chick peas in cold water for several hours or overnight, then drain and rinse them. Put them into a saucepan with plenty of cold water and simmer gently until they are tender – this can take as long as an hour or even more. Then drain the chick peas, keeping the liquid. Measure this and make it up to 1·2 litres (2 pints) with some water or stock.

Peel and chop the onion; scrape the carrots and cut them up into dice. Melt half the butter in a large saucepan and fry the onion and carrot for 5 minutes, letting them get golden brown. Stir them often so that they don't stick, then add the chick peas, liquid, lemon juice and the bay leaf and simmer the soup gently until the vegetables are tender – about 20 minutes. Take out the bay leaf and liquidize the soup. Put it into a clean saucepan, stir in the remaining butter and season to taste. Serve topped with croûtons of fried bread.

CHILLED AVOCADO SOUP   SOUTH AMERICA

This soup is a good way of making two avocados feed six people. It's very easy to make (with a liquidizer) and comes out a creamy very pale green colour. It's best not to make it more than about 45 minutes in advance in case it discolours.

2 large ripe avocado pears –
  make sure they feel slightly
  soft all over when you hold
  them in the palm of your
  hand
1 tablespoon lemon juice

850 ml (1½ pints) ice-cold
  creamy milk
Sea salt
Freshly ground black pepper
2 tablespoons chopped chives

Serves 6

Cut the avocados in half, then twist the two halves apart and remove the stones. Carefully peel off the skin. Cut the avocados into chunks and put these into the liquidizer goblet with the lemon juice and milk. Blend at medium speed until the mixture is smooth. Season with salt and pepper. Put the soup into the fridge to chill until it's needed; if there's room it's a good idea to put the soup bowls in too.

When you're ready to serve ladle the soup into the bowls and sprinkle generously with chopped chives.

CHILLED CHERRY SOUP   HUNGARY

No one finds it odd to start a meal with melon and really a fruit soup is only taking this a stage further! Anyway, this black cherry soup looks so delicious with its topping of soured cream that I don't think you'll have much trouble persuading people to try it. I usually use frozen or canned morello cherries but of course fresh ones would be better if you can get them.

450 g (1 lb) frozen or fresh
   morello cherries
850 ml (1½ pints) water
225 g (8 oz) caster sugar
   (or use two 425 g (15 oz) cans
   black cherries and omit
   the above)

2 tablespoons arrowroot
150 ml (¼ pint) dry red wine
A little lemon juice (optional)
A little soured cream

Serves 6

Stone the cherries by halving them and digging out the stones with a sharp knife; or use a cherry stoner if you've got one.

If you're using fresh or frozen cherries put them into a saucepan with the water and sugar and heat gently to dissolve the sugar, then bring them up to the boil and simmer gently until tender. If you're using canned cherries just stone them, put them into a saucepan and bring them up to the boil. Mix the arrowroot with a little cold water to make a smooth paste, then stir a ladleful of the hot cherry liquid into the arrowroot mixture. When blended add it to the saucepan and simmer for 2–3 minutes. Take the saucepan off the heat and pour the soup into a bowl. When it's cool stir in the wine, then chill it before serving. Taste and add a little more sugar if necessary or possibly a drop or two of lemon juice if you've used canned cherries and need to sharpen the flavour slightly; it should be sweet but refreshing. Swirl soured cream on top before serving.

CHILLED CUCUMBER SOUP   BULGARIA

Yoghurt, cucumber, walnuts and dill sound like rather a strange mixture but actually the combination of smooth creamy yoghurt and chewy walnut with refreshing cucumber and dill works well and this soup makes a lovely protein-rich starter for a summer meal.

1 large cucumber
1 garlic clove, peeled and
  crushed in a little salt
425 ml (15 fl oz) natural
  yoghurt
25 g (1 oz) walnut pieces
Sea salt

Freshly ground black pepper
1 tablespoon chopped fresh dill
  weed or parsley (or 1 teaspoon dried dill weed and
  2 teaspoons chopped fresh
  parsley)

Serves 4

Peel the cucumber (if you leave the skin on it can make the soup taste rather bitter), then cut it into rough chunks. Put the chunks into the liquidizer with the garlic, yoghurt, walnuts, about half a teaspoonful of sea salt and a grinding of pepper and blend until you've got a smoothish purée. Taste the mixture and add some more salt and pepper if you think it needs it, then pour the soup into a bowl and chill it thoroughly.

To serve the soup ladle it into individual bowls and sprinkle each with the chopped green herbs.

CHILLED CUCUMBER SOUP   TURKEY

This soup is rather similar to the preceding one but milder in flavour – no walnuts, garlic or dill, just mint and parsley. It's very refreshing and delicious in hot weather and also beautifully low in calories, so ideal for slimmers.

1 cucumber
425 ml (15 fl oz) natural
  yoghurt
8 sprigs of mint

4 sprigs of parsley
1 teaspoon sea salt
4 sprigs of mint to garnish

Serves 4

Peel the cucumber, then cut it into rough chunks. Put the chunks into the liquidizer goblet with the yoghurt. Wash the mint and parsley and remove the stalks; add the leaves to the cucumber and yoghurt together with the salt. Blend at medium speed until you've got a smooth purée. Transfer the purée to a bowl and place it in the fridge until it's really cold. Check the seasoning and add more salt if necessary – chilling tends to dull the flavour – then serve the soup in individual bowls with a sprig of mint floating on top.

If you want a richer-tasting soup for a special occasion you can replace some of the yoghurt with single ceam but it's not so good for slimmers then!

GAZPACHO   SPAIN

Most people know of this chilled Spanish 'salad soup' and there are many versions of it. The method I've evolved is very quick and easy: you just liquidize canned tomatoes then stir in chopped fresh vegetables and herbs. If you keep a can of tomatoes in the fridge in the summer you can make this soup in a matter of moments. It's nice served with some crunchy cubes of fried bread.

1 large onion, peeled and cut into rough chunks
2 large garlic cloves, peeled and crushed in a little salt
792 g (1 lb 12 oz) can tomatoes
4 tablespoons olive oil
2 teaspoons wine vinegar
1½ teaspoons sea salt
Freshly ground black pepper

About 10 cm (4 in) cucumber
1 small green or red pepper
1 tablespoon chopped fresh chives
1 tablespoon chopped fresh mint
A few cubes of bread fried in oil

Serves 6

Put the onion and garlic into the liquidizer goblet together with the tomatoes, olive oil, vinegar, salt and a grinding of pepper and blend to a purée. (If you haven't got a liquidizer, grate the onion finely and pass the tomatoes through a vegetable mill, then mix them together and add the garlic, oil, vinegar and seasoning.) Chill the mixture.

Just before you want to serve the soup dice the cucumber and de-seed and finely chop the pepper. Stir the cucumber and pepper pieces into the soup, together with the freshly chopped herbs, then ladle the soup into individual bowls and hand round the croûtons of fried bread separately.

GREEN SPLIT PEA SOUP   HOLLAND

I must admit that this soup is a bit of an adaptation because it usually contains pork and sausages which are cut up and added at the end, but we think this vegetarian version tastes good and it makes a lovely warming winter soup. It's useful for serving before a main course when you want to add more protein to the meal but it's also nice for lunch or supper with just some wholewheat bread, cheese and fruit.

175 g (6 oz) green split peas –
   you can get these at health
   shops and you needn't soak
   them before cooking
1·2 litres (2 pints) water
1 onion
2 medium-sized potatoes

2 celery stalks
2 small leeks
½ teaspoon dried savory or
   marjoram
Sea salt
Freshly ground black pepper

Serves 4

Wash the split peas and put them into a large saucepan with the water. Peel and slice the onion and potatoes; wash and slice the celery and leeks. Add all these vegetables to the saucepan. Bring up to the boil and simmer gently until the peas are tender – about 40 minutes. Stir in the savory or marjoram and season the soup carefully with salt and pepper. You can serve the soup as it is but I think it's best to liquidize it or to liquidize half of it to make a good base and leave the remainder to give some texture.

LENTIL SOUP

MIDDLE EAST

I think this is one of the most comforting soups of all and as you don't have to prepare lots of vegetables it's also one of the easiest to make. It takes about 5 minutes to get everything into the saucepan, followed by 15–20 minutes gentle simmering, then a quick blend in the liquidizer and it's ready. Quite often when we get in late and the childen are milling around me in a hungry way I make the soup in a pressure cooker which cuts the cooking time to 5 minutes. (If you do use a pressure cooker, add a couple of tablespoons of oil to the mixture to prevent the water from frothing up as it comes to the boil.)

It makes quite a filling meal on its own with bread and fruit, or serve it before the low-protein Middle Eastern dishes such as rice-stuffed tomatoes or stuffed vine leaves to make a well balanced meal.

225 g (8 oz) split red lentils
1·2 litres (2 pints) stock or water
1 large onion, peeled and chopped

2 garlic cloves, peeled and crushed
1 teaspoon ground cumin
25 g (1 oz) butter
Salt and pepper

Serves 4

Wash the lentils, then put them into a large saucepan with the stock or water, onion, garlic and cumin; bring up to the boil and simmer gently for 15–20 minutes until the lentils are cooked. Liquidize the soup until smooth, then add the butter and seasoning to taste and re-heat the soup gently. This makes a thickish soup but you can of course thin it down with a little milk or water if you want to.

LETTUCE SOUP   FRANCE

I like this soup because it's such a good way of using up those outer lettuce leaves you feel so guilty about throwing away. It's also got a nice fresh summery flavour. For a special occasion it's lovely with the single cream added but for everyday you can leave it out and use extra milk instead.

1 onion	400 ml (¾ pint) milk
450 g (1 lb) potatoes	150 ml (5 fl oz) single cream
Outside leaves of 2 or 3	Sea salt
lettuces	Freshly ground black pepper
25 g (1 oz) butter	Nutmeg
575 ml (1 pint) water	

Serves 4

Peel and chop the onion and potatoes. Wash the lettuce leaves and cut them up. Melt the butter in a large saucepan and fry the onion and potato gently for 5 minutes, but don't brown them. Then add the lettuce leaves and stir them for a minute or two so that they get all buttery. Add the water and milk and let the soup simmer gently for 15–20 minutes, until the vegetables are cooked.

Liquidize the soup and stir in the cream if you're using it. Season it with salt, pepper and a grating of nutmeg. Reheat it but don't let it boil after you've added the cream.

MUSHROOM SOUP   GERMANY

You can vary the character of this soup according to the type of mushrooms you use. Open mushrooms, or wild field mushrooms make a dark, richly-flavoured soup, while little white button mushrooms give a delicate, pale, creamy result. In either case, if you want to make the soup really special, add a tablespoonful of sherry at the end.

39

225 g (8 oz) mushrooms
Small piece of onion, peeled
1 bay leaf
1 garlic clove, peeled and
  sliced
A few parsley stalks
575 ml (1 pint) stock
50 g (2 oz) butter

40 g (1½ oz) flour
About 575 ml (1 pint) milk
Sea salt
Freshly ground black pepper
Nutmeg
Cayenne pepper
1 tablespoon sherry (optional)

Serves 4

Wash the mushrooms and remove the stalks. If you're using field mushrooms take off the skins too – but this isn't necessary with cultivated mushrooms. Put the stalks (and skins if you've removed them) into a medium-sized saucepan together with the piece of onion, bay leaf, garlic, parsley stalks and stock and bring up to the boil, then leave to simmer for 10 minutes to extract the flavours. Strain the liquid into a measuring jug and make the quantity up to 850 ml (1½ pints) with the milk. (You won't need the mushroom stalks, etc.)

Melt three-quarters of the butter in the saucepan and stir in the flour. After a moment or two, when it looks bubbly, pour in a quarter of the milk mixture and stir over a fairly high heat until it has thickened. Repeat the process with the rest of the milk in three more batches. Now chop or slice the mushrooms, fry them lightly in the remaining butter and add them to the thickened milk, together with salt, pepper, a grating of nutmeg, a pinch of cayenne pepper and the sherry if you're using it. Let the soup simmer for 3-4 minutes to give the flavours a chance to blend before serving.

ONION SOUP   FRANCE

Although French onion soup is usually made with brown meat stock, I've found that it's possible to make a surprisingly rich-tasting vegetarian version. The important part is the preliminary careful frying of the onions in the butter – and the sherry, if you can spare it, makes all the difference too. This soup is splendid served as a protein-rich starter before a light vegetable main course; it's also filling enough to make a lovely late night supper with just a little fruit to follow.

700 g (1½ lb) onions	Sea salt
40 g (1½ oz) butter	Freshly ground black pepper
1 tablespoon flour	Slices of wholemeal or French
850 ml (1½ pints) vegetable	bread
stock or water	125–175 g (4-6 oz) grated
3 tablespoons cheap sherry	cheese

Serves 4

Peel the onions and slice them into fairly fine rings. Melt the butter in a large saucepan and fry the onions slowly for 15–20 minutes until they're golden, stirring them from time to time, then mix in the flour and cook for a few seconds before adding the stock or water, sherry and a seasoning of salt and pepper. Bring the mixture up to the boil, then let it simmer gently with the lid on the saucepan for 30 minutes. Just before the soup is ready warm heatproof soup bowls and lightly toast a slice of bread for each; put the toast roughly broken into the bowls. Prepare a moderately hot grill. When the soup is ready check the seasoning, then ladle it into the bowls, scatter the grated cheese on top and place the bowls under the grill to melt the cheese; serve immediately.

If you have a large grill I find it's a help to stand the bowls on a metal tray or baking sheet – then they're easier to withdraw from the grill when ready. Alternatively you can put all the soup in a large ovenproof dish or soup tureen – in this case you'll probably need to use the oven to melt the cheese. Or another way of doing it is to prepare the bread and cheese separately under the grill and then pop it on top of the soup just before you serve it!

POTATO SOUP

FRANCE

This is a velvety soup with a delicate creamy flavour. You can make it even better by adding a little cream at the end for special occasions but it's very good just as it is.

225 g (8 oz) onions
350 g (12 oz) potatoes
25 g (1 oz) butter
275 ml (½ pint) milk

575 ml (1 pint) water
Sea salt
Freshly ground black pepper
Fresh chives (optional)

Serves 4

Peel and chop the onion; peel the potatoes and cut them into small dice. Melt the butter in a large saucepan and put in the onion; fry it for 5 minutes, stirring often. Don't let it brown. Add the potato and cook for a further 2–3 minutes until the potato looks nice and buttery, then stir in the milk and water and a teaspoon of sea salt. Bring the soup up to the boil and let it simmer gently for 20–30 minutes, until the vegetables are tender. Liquidize the soup to a smooth creamy consistency then return it to the rinsed out saucepan and check the seasoning. Reheat the soup gently. It's nice served with a scattering of chopped chives on top to provide a little colour.

PUMPKIN SOUP

JAMAICA

Pumpkin makes a very delicious soup, golden in colour with a delicate yet distinctive flavour. It's lovely sprinkled with chopped parsley and served with garlic bread at Hallowe'en.

1 kilo (2¼ lb) pumpkin (this weight includes the skin and pips)

1 litre (1¾ pints) stock
Sea salt
Freshly ground black pepper

2 large onions
2 large garlic cloves
25 g (1 oz) butter

Serves 6

150 ml (5 fl oz) single cream
  or top of the milk
Fresh parsley

Cut the skin off the pumpkin and scoop out the seeds; cut the flesh into even-sized pieces. Peel and chop the onion; peel and crush the garlic.

Melt the butter in a heavy saucepan and cook the chopped onions for about 5 minutes, then put in the garlic and pumpkin and cook for a further 5 minutes. Add the stock and some salt and pepper; bring to the boil and simmer until the pumpkin is tender – this takes about 15 or 20 minutes. Sieve or liquidize the soup then stir in the single cream or top of the milk. Reheat the soup gently. Serve in individual bowls with some chopped parsley on top.

TOMATO SOUP

FRANCE

This is a lovely light soup with a buttery tomato flavour. I think it's best when you can make it with fresh tomatoes in the late summer but I use canned tomatoes in the winter and it's still very good.

1 onion
350 g (12 oz) potatoes
25 g (1 oz) butter
450 g (1 lb) tomatoes or a
  425 g (15 oz) can
1·2 litres (2 pints) water
Sea salt

Freshly ground black pepper
Sugar
Chopped fresh green herbs –
  basil is best if you can get it,
  otherwise use chives or
  parsley

Serves 4 6

Peel and chop the onion; peel and cube the potatoes. Melt the butter in a large saucepan and fry the onion for about 5 minutes, until it's beginning to soften, but not brown, then put in the potato and stir over the heat for a minute or two until it is well coated with butter. With fresh tomatoes wash and quarter them – there's no need to skin them as the soup is first liquidized then strained at the end. If you're using canned tomatoes drain them and keep the juice. Add the tomatoes to the vegetables in the saucepan, mix them round and then pour in the water, or reserved tomato juice and water to make 1·2 litres (2 pints) in all. Bring up to the boil and let the soup simmer for 20–30 minutes, until the vegetables are tender. Liquidize the soup then pour it through a sieve into a clean saucepan. Season it with salt, pepper and about half a teaspoonful of sugar which helps to bring out the flavour of the tomatoes. Reheat and serve with a sprinkling of finely chopped fresh green herbs on top.

VICHYSSOISE   USA

I've often thought it surprising that you can make such good chilled soup from what are really winter vegetables – leeks and potatoes! It's rather a pity really that these vegetables start coming into season just when the days are getting crisp and you're thinking more of soups to warm you up than cool you down. But vichyssoise is so creamy and delicious that it always seems to be popular. If the weather gets really cold you can always serve it hot, when I think it's every bit as good.

1 onion, peeled and chopped	Sea salt
25 g (1 oz) butter	575 ml (1 pint) milk
225 g (8 oz) potatoes	Freshly ground black pepper
700 g (1½ lb) leeks	150 ml (5 fl oz) single cream
575 ml (1 pint) water	2 tablespoons chopped chives

Serves 6

Fry the onion in the butter for about 5 minutes in a large saucepan but don't let it get at all brown. While it's cooking peel the potatoes and cut them into smallish chunks. Cut the roots and most of the green top off the leeks, slit them down the side, open them out and rinse them thoroughly under the cold tap then cut them up into small rings. Add the potato and leek to the onion and mix so that everything gets coated in the butter, then let it all cook gently for a further 4–5 minutes but be very careful you don't let it brown. Stir in the water and a teaspoonful of sea salt and bring up to the boil; then put a lid on the saucepan and leave the soup to simmer for 20–30 minutes until the vegetables are tender. Liquidize the soup, adding some of the milk if you like, to make the process easier, then tip the soup into a bowl or jug which will fit your fridge and add the remaining milk. Taste and season the soup then chill it.

You can stir the cream into the soup before you serve it, or swirl some over the top of each bowlful then sprinkle with the chopped chives. It looks very pretty – palest green with the darker chives on top. It's a good idea to check the seasoning after you've chilled the soup and add some more salt and pepper if necessary, as chilling seems to dull the flavour a little.

WATERCRESS SOUP FRANCE

I think this is one of the best soups because it's got such a lovely flavour and the ingredients are easy to get and don't take much preparation. My own special tip is to cook only the watercress stalks with the potatoes and add the chopped leaves at the end, just before you serve the soup. This makes the soup look and taste very fresh and inviting.

2 bunches of watercress	275 ml ($\frac{1}{2}$ pint) milk
1 onion	Sea salt
450 g (1 lb) potatoes	150 ml (5 fl oz) single cream
25 g (1 oz) butter	or top of the milk
575 ml (1 pint) water	

Serves 6

Wash the watercress carefully, then separate the tough stalks from the leaves; chop the stalks roughly. Peel and slice the onion and potatoes. Melt the butter in a large saucepan and add the onion; cook gently for 5 minutes (but don't brown it), put in the potato and watercress stalks (keep the leaves on one side for later). Stir the vegetables over a gentle heat for a minute or two so that they all get coated with the butter, then pour in the water and milk, bring the mixture up to the boil and let it simmer gently for about 15 minutes or until the potato is soft. Put the soup in the liquidizer goblet together with the watercress leaves and a little salt and blend until smooth. Stir in the cream or top of the milk and check the seasoning; reheat the soup gently.

Although the cream gives the final touch to the recipe and makes it suitable for extra special occasions, you can make a nice everyday version without it – just increase the quantity of milk to 400 ml ($\frac{3}{4}$ pint).

YELLOW SPLIT PEA SOUP   CZECHOSLOVAKIA

This is quite a simple soup but it has a good flavour and is lovely on a cold day. The split pea purée is thickened slightly with some butter and flour which gives the soup a nice smooth texture and a buttery flavour.

225 g (8 oz) yellow split peas

1·7 litres (3 pints) water

25 g (1 oz) butter

1 large or 2 medium onions, peeled and finely chopped

1 garlic clove, peeled and crushed

25 g (1 oz) wholewheat flour

Sea salt

Freshly ground black pepper

Serves 4–6

Put the split peas into a saucepan with the water; let them simmer gently for 40–50 minutes until they're tender then liquidize them. Melt the butter in the rinsed out saucepan and fry the onion until it's golden, then stir in the garlic and flour. Cook for a minute or two, then gradually pour in the split pea purée, stirring until you have a smooth mixture. Let the soup simmer for 5–10 minutes to cook the flour, then season with salt and pepper to taste. This makes quite a thick soup; if you want it thinner you can always add more liquid.

You will need to use a large saucepan for boiling the split peas because of the way they bubble up as they cook. Adding a couple of tablespoonfuls of oil to the cooking water helps, or if your saucepan isn't quite big enough you can cook the peas using only 1·2 litres (2 pints) of water and add the rest when you liquidize the soup.

Sauces and Salad Dressings

These sauces and salad dressings are the ones which I find useful in practice and which go with the foods in this book. Some of them such as the milk-based white sauces and cheese sauce, also the sweet pouring egg custard, are an easy and delicious way of including more protein in the meal. Others, particularly the fruit sauces and the English mint sauce are good for adding piquancy and colour to the meal and seem to go with many vegetarian dishes just as well as the meat ones with which they are traditionally served.

APPLE SAUCE   GREAT BRITAIN

This sauce is also very popular in Germany where it's often served with crisp potato fritters – a delightful combination. It's also good with bean and lentil dishes.

225 g (8 oz) cooking apples   Sea salt
15 g (½ oz) butter
25–50 g (1–2 oz) granulated
  sugar

Serves 4–6

Peel and core the apples then cut them up into smallish pieces. Put the apple into a heavy-based saucepan with the butter and 25 g (1 oz) sugar. Cover the saucepan and set it over a fairly gentle heat for about 10 minutes, until the apple has softened and collapsed to a soft purée. Beat the mixture a bit with a wooden spoon then taste it and add a little more sugar and some salt if necessary. I think this sauce is nicest served warm.

CHEESE SAUCE   FRANCE

This cheese sauce, *sauce Mornay*, is useful both for incorporating into other dishes before baking or grilling them and for serving with vegetables to make them into more of a meal. Strictly speaking this sauce should be made with half Gruyère cheese and half Parmesan. The Gruyère makes it creamy and the Parmesan gives it a good flavour, but both are expensive and for day-to-day cooking I use a cheaper substitute plus a good seasoning of mustard, cayenne and freshly ground black pepper.

25 g (1 oz) butter
25 g (1 oz) plain white flour
1 bay leaf
250 ml ($\frac{1}{2}$ pint) milk
50 g (2 oz) grated cheese –
   Cheddar, or I like double
   Gloucester as it's creamy-

tasting and gives the sauce a
  pretty colour
1 teaspoon mustard powder
Cayenne pepper
Sea salt
Freshly ground black pepper

Makes 250 ml ($\frac{1}{2}$ pint)

Melt the butter in a medium-sized saucepan and stir in the flour; cook for a few seconds until the flour bubbles round the edges, then add the bay leaf, turn up the heat and pour in about one-third of the milk. Stir hard until the sauce is very thick and smooth, then repeat the process twice with the remaining milk so that you finish with a smooth, medium-thick sauce. Take the saucepan off the heat and beat in the grated cheese, mustard, a tiny pinch of cayenne pepper and salt and pepper to taste. Don't let it get too hot once the cheese has been added or it may go stringy and spoil.

CRANBERRY SAUCE
USA

Red cranberry sauce with its sweet yet slightly astringent taste is one of the most delicious parts of the traditional American Thanksgiving dinner, and of our British Christmas, of course. It goes surprisingly well with vegetable dishes such as the German potato fritters and the sweetcorn pudding from the USA.

175 g (6 oz) cranberries
4 tablespoons water
75 g (3 oz) sugar

Sort out the cranberries and remove any bruised ones; take off any little stems. Wash the berries and put them into a saucepan with the water. Cook gently until the berries begin to 'pop' and are tender – 7–10 minutes on rather a high heat. Add the sugar and simmer for a further few minutes. This makes quite a thick mixture, you can thin it with a little more water (or some red wine) if you like.

CURRY SAUCE INDIA

This spicy sauce is useful for serving with Indian rice dishes like *biriani* or with the spicy little Indian pastries, *samosas*. It also provides the basis of a quick curry – you just add some vegetables, simmer them in the sauce until they're tender then serve with fluffy boiled rice.

1 large onion	1 teaspoon ground cumin
2 tablespoons oil, butter or *ghee*	2 teaspoons ground coriander
1–2 garlic cloves, peeled and crushed	1 bay leaf
	275 ml (½ pint) water
225 g (8 oz) can tomatoes	Sea salt
½ teaspoon ground ginger	Freshly ground black pepper

Serves 4–6

Peel and chop the onion and fry it in the butter, oil or *ghee* in a fairly large saucepan for 10 minutes, until it's tender but not browned. Add the garlic, tomatoes, spices and bay leaf to the onion, mixing them around so that they all get coated with the fat. Pour in the water and bring up to the boil, then turn the heat down, partially cover the saucepan and leave the mixture to simmer for about 20 minutes. Taste and season with salt and pepper. Take out the bay leaf and liquidize the sauce if you want it smooth; or serve it as it is if you would like some texture.

POURING EGG CUSTARD   ENGLAND

This is a sweet sauce, a real egg custard that is delicious with puddings when you don't want to have cream; it's useful too because it's a way of adding protein to the meal.

2 eggs
25 g (1 oz) caster sugar – or use vanilla sugar if you've got it

275 ml (½ pint) milk
A little extra vanilla flavouring

Serves 4–6

Whisk the eggs in a medium-sized bowl. Put the sugar into a saucepan with the milk and bring just to the boil, then pour on to the beaten eggs. Strain this mixture back into the saucepan and stir over the heat for a minute or two until the sauce thickens. This will happen very quickly and you need to be ready to take the saucepan off the heat immediately. If, in spite of all your care, it does overheat and curdle, I've found it's usually all right again if I liquidize it, just like one would any lumpy sauce! Flavour with a few drops more vanilla if you like. It's also nice flavoured with grated orange or lemon rind. Serve this sauce hot or cold.

GRAVY   GREAT BRITAIN

I have to admit that this is not quite a traditional British gravy because that's usually made with the fat and juices from meat, but I hope you'll agree that this vegetarian version is also very tasty. You can buy vegetarian stock cubes and powder from health shops and these make a good basis for the gravy; so does Marmite or one of the other vegetable yeast extracts. The preliminary browning of the flour is important because this gives the gravy a lovely nutty flavour and dark colour.

1 onion

2 tablespoons vegetable oil

25 g (1 oz) flour

1 garlic clove

575 ml (1 pint) well-flavoured
  stock

A bouquet garni or a bay leaf
  and ¼ teaspoon mixed herbs

Sea salt

Freshly ground black pepper

Serves 6

Peel and finely chop the onion and fry it in a saucepan in the oil
for 5 minutes, then stir in the flour and continue to cook until
the flour and onion are well browned. Add the garlic, stock
and the bouquet garni or bay leaf and herbs. Bring up to the boil
and let the mixture simmer for 10–15 minutes without a lid on the
saucepan. Take out the bouquet garni or the bay leaf and season
the gravy well with salt and pepper. You can serve the gravy as it
is, with the bits of onion in it, or sieve or liquidize it to give a
smooth consistency. For a special occasion it's delicious with a
tablespoon of sherry stirred in.

MAYONNAISE
FRANCE

If you use a liquidizer to make mayonnaise it really is a quick
and easy process. I find that mayonnaise keeps very well in a jar
in the fridge.

1 whole egg

¼ teaspoon salt

¼ teaspoon dry mustard

2 or 3 grindings of black
  pepper

2 teaspoons wine vinegar

2 teaspoons lemon juice

200 ml (7 fl oz) olive oil or a
  mixture of olive oil and
  other good quality oil such
  as corn oil or sunflower oil

Makes 200 ml (7 fl oz)

Break the egg straight into the liquidizer and add the salt,
mustard, pepper, vinegar and lemon juice. Blend for a minute

at medium speed until everything is well mixed, then turn the speed up to high and gradually add the oil, drop by drop, through the hole in the lid of the liquidizer goblet. When you've added about half the oil you will hear the sound change to a 'glug-glug' noise and then you can add the rest of the oil more quickly, in a thin stream. If the consistency of the mayonnaise seems a bit on the thick side you can thin it with a little boiling water or some milk.

MINT SAUCE
ENGLAND

Sharp-tasting yet sweet as well, mint sauce is lovely for serving with many lentil and bean dishes. It's particularly good with pease pudding.

Enough fresh mint leaves to make 2 tablespoons when chopped	1 tablespoon sugar
	1 tablespoon boiling water
	4 tablespoons cider vinegar

Serves 4–6

If you've got a liquidizer just wash the mint leaves and take off any stalks, then put the leaves into the goblet with all the other ingredients and blend until the mint is all chopped. Pour into a jug to serve.

If you'd rather make the sauce by hand, wash and chop the mint leaves, then put them into a bowl, add the sugar, boiling water and cider vinegar and mix well.

TOMATO SAUCE
ITALY

With canned tomatoes and a liquidizer this sauce really couldn't be easier and is one of my standbys. I find it best not to let the tomatoes cook for very long; this way the sauce seems to have a much fresher flavour.

1 onion	425 g (15 oz) can tomatoes
2 tablespoons vegetable oil	Sea salt
1 garlic clove	Freshly ground black pepper

Serves 4–6

Peel and chop the onion and fry it gently in the oil in a medium-sized saucepan until it's soft but not browned – about 10 minutes. Peel the garlic, crush it in a little salt with the blade of a knife and add it to the onions along with the tomatoes.

Liquidize or sieve the mixture, then put it back in the saucepan and reheat it. Taste the sauce and season with salt and pepper.

That's the basic recipe but you can vary it in lots of ways. Try putting a bay leaf with the onions to draw out its lovely flavour as the onions soften, or add a little chopped or dried basil, thyme or powdered cinnamon to the finished sauce; or stir a couple of tablespoons of red wine into the liquidized mixture before you reheat it. Another addition which I sometimes make, and which I'm rather ashamed to admit, is a little Heinz tomato ketchup; used discreetly it perks up the flavour without being at all obvious!

VINAIGRETTE

FRANCE

The secret of a good vinaigrette lies almost entirely in the ingredients. If you use a really top quality olive oil, wine vinegar, sea salt and freshly ground black pepper and remember the proportions three or four parts oil to one of vinegar you really can't fail!

| 1 tablespoon wine vinegar – I think red wine vinegar has the best flavour | 3 or 4 tablespoons olive oil Sea salt Freshly ground black pepper |

Serves 4–6

Mix together the vinegar and 3 tablespoons of oil. Add a good seasoning of salt and pepper – remember the dressing will be weakened by being put with other ingredients so it needs to be well seasoned. Taste the dressing and if it's too vinegary add the remaining oil until you get the flavour just right. Pour the dressing into a small jug and stir it again before you serve it. This is also nice with a tablespoon of chopped herbs added, or a little mustard, depending on what you're going to serve it with. It's fun to experiment once you've got the basic mixture right.

WHITE SAUCE AND VARIATIONS   FRANCE

Strictly speaking a proper *sauce Béchamel* is made from milk which has been delicately flavoured by being heated in a saucepan with a clove, a piece of onion, a slice of carrot and a bay leaf, covered and left to infuse and then strained. I must admit that for normal cookery I generally use ordinary milk plus a bay leaf, and rely on good seasoning for the flavouring, but if you do go to the trouble to infuse the milk first, the sauce will be that much more delicate and delicious.

When making a sauce I always used to let it simmer for 10 or 15 minutes after I'd added the milk, to cook the flour. This was a nuisance because it was all too easy to burn it and also one had to remember to make the sauce a bit on the thin side to allow for it to reduce. Then one day when I hadn't got my milk measured out properly I added it in 2 or 3 instalments and I found the sauce had no floury-taste and needed no extra simmering. I realized that if you add the milk in batches and let the sauce thicken over a good heat before adding more, by the time you've added all the milk the flour has cooked and the process is much quicker. So I always make sauces by this 'batch' method now.

Sauce making is easy if you can remember the basic quantities. I find it difficult to hold figures in my head so I remember just one quantity and relate everything to that. 25 g (1 oz) each of butter and plain (white) flour and 250 ml ($\frac{1}{2}$ pint) liquid makes a medium-thick sauce – the type you would use to cover cauliflower or stuffed pancakes, commonly called a coating sauce. If you want it thicker or thinner you simply decrease or increase the quantity of milk: 400 ml (¾ pint) milk gives a thickish pouring sauce, 575 ml (1 pint) gives a thin pouring sauce.

25 g (1 oz) butter or margarine	1 bay leaf
25 g (1 oz) plain white flour	Sea salt
250 ml (½ pint) milk – ordinary milk or milk that you have flavoured as above	Freshly ground black pepper Nutmeg

Makes 250 ml (½ pint)

Put the butter or margarine into a medium-sized saucepan and melt it gently over quite a low heat, then stir in the flour and add the bay leaf. Let the flour cook for a few seconds, then turn up the heat, pour in one-third of the milk and stir vigorously until you've got a very thick, smooth sauce, then add another third of the milk. At first the sauce will look lumpy but don't worry, continue stirring over a high heat and soon the sauce will be beautifully smooth again.

Repeat the process with your final batch of milk, then when the sauce is smooth turn down the heat and season the sauce with salt, pepper and a grating of nutmeg. It's now ready to serve, but if you want to make it look extra good and glossy for a special occasion you can beat in about 15 g (½ oz) extra butter at the last minute.

If you're making the sauce in advance and want to prevent a skin forming you can dot this extra butter over the surface, then beat it in when you reheat it. Alternatively a circle of damp greaseproof paper pressed down on to the surface of the sauce also stops it getting a skin.

MUSHROOM SAUCE

This is good with vegetables and for serving with pasta and

gnocchi. To make it, wash and finely slice 125 g (4 oz) button mushrooms and add them to the basic Béchamel sauce. Some people fry the mushrooms lightly in butter before adding them to the sauce but I prefer the less rich version I've given.

WHITE ONION SAUCE

Another useful variation, good when you want to add more flavour to a meal. Make it by peeling and finely chopping an onion; fry the onion in the butter before adding the flour. I I think this is nice flavoured with a pinch of ground cloves.

PARSLEY SAUCE

For this fresh-tasting variation add 1 or 2 tablespoons of finely chopped parsley to the Béchamel sauce. Or, an easier way, take the stalks off a few sprigs of parsley and put the sprigs into the liquidizer with the sauce; blend for a few seconds.

WINE SAUCE   FRANCE

This sauce always makes a meal taste special. You can either use a cheap wine for the sauce or buy a little extra to have with the meal and use some to make the sauce.

400 ml ($\frac{3}{4}$ pint) stock	2–3 parsley stalks
400 ml ($\frac{3}{4}$ pint) red wine	1 tablespoon redcurrant jelly
1 bay leaf	Sea salt
A piece of onion, peeled	Freshly ground black pepper
1 garlic clove, peeled and sliced	40 g ($1\frac{1}{2}$ oz) butter, softened
A pinch of dried thyme	20 g ($\frac{3}{4}$ oz) flour
$\frac{1}{2}$ teaspoon black peppercorns	

Serves 6

Put the stock and red wine into a saucepan with the bay leaf, onion, garlic, thyme, peppercorns and parsley stalks and bring to the boil. Let the mixture boil vigorously for 10–15 minutes so that the amount of liquid reduces to half. Strain the liquid into a clean saucepan and mix in the redcurrant jelly and some salt and pepper. Next make a *beurre manié:* mash half the butter with the flour to make a paste and add this, in small pieces, to the still-warm sauce, mixing well after you've added each piece. Put the sauce back over the heat and stir it gently until it has thickened slightly. Then let the sauce simmer gently for a few minutes to cook the flour. Check the seasoning again and beat the remaining butter into the sauce just before serving to make it look glossy and appetizing.

If you want to prepare the sauce in advance, after you've added the *beurre manié* and simmered the sauce for a few minutes, take it off the heat and dot the remaining butter over the top of the sauce to prevent a skin forming. When you're ready heat the sauce gently and stir the butter in.

Dips and Spreads

These dips and spreads are really the vegetarian alternative to pâtés and meat pastes. If you serve them with something crisp like fingers of hot buttered toast they make a delicious first course; or for a party you can spread them on little crackers and garnish them with pieces of olive, gherkin or parsley.

One of these dips with a bowl of home-made soup and some hot rolls or toast makes a welcoming late supper or winter lunch. In the summer they're also nice served very cold from the fridge with some crisp salad.

Some of the dips contain protein which makes them useful for serving as a starter when you want to increase the nourishment of a meal, or for putting in sandwiches for packed lunches.

As with soups, I think you really need a liquidizer for making dips; you can get such a deliciously smooth and creamy texture that way.

In my view dips should have a slightly salty, tangy flavour to whet the appetite, so they need careful seasoning, and it's worth using good quality olive oil and wine vinegar if possible.

The sesame cream or *tahini* that's used in two of the recipes can be bought from health shops. It's very nourishing indeed, and an excellent source of calcium. It's quite expensive but it keeps for ages.

AÏOLI WITH CRUDITÉS FRANCE

Crisp raw vegetables dipped in smooth garlic-flavoured mayonnaise make a delicious starter or can become a complete salad meal with a lentil or vegetable soup and some wholewheat bread or rolls.

If you want to serve aïoli but hesitate on account of all the calories it contains you might like to do what I usually do and use half mayonnaise and half natural yoghurt; or add some garlic to the dressing given for the Russian cucumber salad with soured cream and hardboiled eggs and use that instead of the mayonnaise. It tastes surprisingly like mayonnaise but contains no oil.

The *crudités* can be a gloriously colourful selection of whatever fresh vegetables are available: crunchy red radishes served whole with some of the green part still attached; bright orange carrot cut into matchsticks; red or green pepper de-seeded and cut into strips; tiny crimson cubes of raw beetroot; sprigs of pearly cauliflower; small very fresh mushrooms; baby green Brussels sprouts served whole or bigger ones (as long as they're firm) cut into halves or quarters; spring onions, shiny white and just trimmed; pieces of crunchy fennel bulb; juicy cucumber in chunks; crisp leaves of chicory or sticks of celery; quarters of firm red tomatoes.

For the crudités
A selection of vegetables as above; about 4 or 5 different types.

For the aïoli:

1 egg	$\frac{1}{4}$ teaspoon pepper
2–4 garlic cloves, peeled and crushed	2 teaspoons wine vinegar
	2 teaspoons lemon juice
$\frac{1}{4}$ teaspoon sea salt	200 ml (7 fl oz) salad oil
$\frac{1}{4}$ teaspoon dry mustard	

Serves 4–6

Break the egg into the liquidizer goblet and add the garlic, salt, mustard, pepper, vinegar and lemon juice. Blend at medium speed for about 1 minute. Then turn the speed to high and gradually add the oil, drop by drop, through the top of the goblet lid. When about half the oil has been added and you hear the sound of the mixture change you can add the oil more quickly in a thin stream. If the mixture is very thick you can thin it by stirring in a little hot water; or if you're doing the yoghurt version add this now, stirring it gently into the mayonnaise. Spoon the aïoli into a bowl and stand it on a large plate or small tray with the *crudités* arranged around it. People can then help themselves to a spoonful of the aïoli and some of the vegetables and eat them together.

AUBERGINE AND SESAME PÂTÉ   MIDDLE EAST

In this pâté, *baba ghannooj*, the intense, subtle flavour of the aubergine goes well with the rich, earthy taste of the sesame cream and the texture is substantial without being at all heavy. I think it's nice with fingers of crisp toast or some warm pitta bread. It makes a good light lunch dish after lentil soup.

2 medium aubergines – about 450 g (1 lb)	Freshly ground black pepper
2 heaped tablespoons sesame cream *(tahini)*	Crisp lettuce leaves
1 tablespoon lemon juice	Olive oil
1 large garlic clove, peeled and crushed	Sesame seeds, if available
Sea salt	Fresh parsley and chives
	Fingers of hot wholewheat toast or some warm pitta bread

Serves 4–6

Prick the aubergines, then place them on a baking sheet and bake in a fairly hot oven – say 200°C (400°F), gas mark 6. But don't heat it specially; the aubergines will bake with something else and adapt to any temperature from about 160°C (325°F), gas mark 3 to 230°C (450°F), gas mark 8. They'll take about 20–30 minutes, depending on the temperature, and are done when they can be pierced easily with the point of a sharp knife. Let them cool, then remove the stalks. Chop the aubergine flesh as finely as you can then mix it with all the other ingredients, or put the aubergine into the liquidizer goblet with the sesame cream, lemon juice and garlic and blend until fairly smooth. You will probably have to do this in several short bursts, stopping the machine and stirring the mixture in between, as it is fairly thick. Season the mixture with salt and pepper, then chill it.

To serve, spoon the pâté into little dishes and smooth the tops, or arrange a bed of lettuce leaves on small plates and spoon it on top. Pour a little olive oil over the pâté, sprinkle with some whole sesame seeds, if you have them, and snip some parsley and chives over the top of everything. Hand round hot fingers of whole-wheat toast or warm pitta bread.

AVOCADO DIP   MEXICO

In Mexico this creamy pale green avocado mixture, *guacamole*, would probably be served as a sauce or as a filling for tortillas but we think it makes a lovely starter either served on a base of crisp lettuce heart or with some crunchy Melba toast. It's also another good way of making two avocados feed six people.

2 large ripe avocado pears	Freshly ground black pepper
2 tablespoons lemon juice	Paprika pepper
1 garlic clove	Crisp lettuce leaves or Melba
Sea salt	toast
Tabasco sauce	

Serves 6

Cut the avocados in half, twist the halves in opposite directions to separate them and remove the stones. Carefully peel off the

67

skins – they should come away quite easily if the avocados are really ripe. Put the avocado into a bowl, sprinkle it with lemon juice and mash it with a fork. Peel the garlic and crush it in a little salt with the blade of a knife; add the garlic to the avocado together with a drop or two of Tabasco (go carefully as it's hot) and some pepper. Taste and add more salt, pepper and Tabasco as necessary. Either spoon the *guacamole* on to a plate, decorate the top with the prongs of a fork and sprinkle with paprika pepper to give a nice touch of scarlet against the pale green, or arrange lettuce leaves on small individual plates and spoon the *guacamole* on top.

Guacamole is best made just before you need it; don't keep it waiting more than 1 hour or the avocado will begin to discolour.

BEAN PÂTÉ
MIDDLE EAST

You're supposed to use *ful medames* or dried broad beans for this dip but these are hard to get and I find it tastes good with other types of bean. British field beans have the right earthy sort of flavour and so have continental lentils, which I like best of all for this recipe because you don't need to sieve them like the beans. This is a protein-rich dish, so it makes a useful starter before a salad or vegetable meal. It is also good as a sandwich filling or as a spread for little biscuits.

175 g (6 oz) *ful medames*
  beans, British field beans
  or continental (whole) lentils
2 tablespoons olive oil
1 tablespoon lemon juice
1 garlic clove, peeled and
  crushed
1 tablespoon finely chopped
  parsley

Sea salt
Freshly ground black pepper
Sugar
4 black olives
Fingers of hot brown toast
Butter

Serves 4

68

Cover the beans generously with boiling water and leave them to soak for 4–5 hours if possible (not so long if you're using lentils), then drain and rinse them, put them into a good-sized saucepan with plenty of cold water and simmer them over a gentle heat until they're tender – $1\frac{1}{4}$–$1\frac{1}{2}$ hours for beans, 30–45 minutes for lentils. Drain the beans or lentils, reserving the liquid. Pass the beans through a vegetable mill or mash the lentils with a fork, then mix in the olive oil, lemon juice, garlic, parsley, salt and pepper and, if necessary, enough of the reserved cooking liquid to make a thick creamy pâté. Taste the mixture and add a little sugar if you think it needs it.

Spoon the pâté into 4 small ramekin dishes, smooth the surface and decorate each with an olive. Serve the pâté chilled and hand round fingers of hot toast for people to spread first with butter and then with the pâté.

CREAM CHEESE AND SOURED CREAM DIP

USA

An American friend gave me this recipe which she serves on Thanksgiving Day as a first course. Like the aïoli, it's superb with a colourful selection of crisp fresh vegetables for dipping into the creamy mixture. The recipe as I've given it makes a luxurious-tasting dip; for an even richer version you could use cream cheese (which was used in the original recipe); alternatively, for a less calorific dip, you could use natural yoghurt in place of the soured cream.

For the dip:

225 g (8 oz) low-fat quark
Two 150 g (5 fl oz) cartons
  soured cream
1 garlic clove, peeled and
  crushed

2 tablespoons finely chopped
  chives
Sea salt
Freshly ground black pepper

For the crudités:

A selection of about 5 different vegetables of contrasting colours, like those described for the aïoli on page 65.

Serves 6

Put the quark into a bowl and break it up with a fork, then stir in the soured cream, garlic and chives and mix to a smooth consistency. Season with salt and pepper. Spoon the dip into a serving dish and chill it until required. Arrange the colourful vegetables around the dip and let everyone help themselves to a spoonful of the creamy mixture and some crisp *crudités*.

GOAT CHEESE AND HERB SPREAD   RUMANIA

If you can't get goat cheese I find that crumbly white Wensleydale makes a good alternative, although it's not as salty. You can serve this spread in a pâté dish or if you want to be more Rumanian heap it up into a cone shape in the centre of a serving dish and surround it with tangy black olives, whole radishes, crunchy spring onions and quartered tomatoes.

125 g (4 oz) brynza or feta
   cheese (or use crumbly
   white Wensleydale)
125 g (4 oz) unsalted butter,
   softened
1 tablespoon chopped chives

1 tablespoon chopped green
   fennel, if available
1 tablespoon chopped parsley
Pinch each of paprika and
   caraway seeds

Serves 4 as a starter

Crumble the cheese finely. Put the butter into a bowl and cream it with a wooden spoon, then gradually beat in the crumbled cheese and the herbs and spices. Chill the spread, then serve it as suggested above or use it as a sandwich filling or a topping for savoury biscuits.

70

HUMMUS   MIDDLE EAST

If I, as a vegetarian, told you that one of my favourite dishes
consisted of a purée of chick peas and sesame cream you might
well be forgiven for thinking it was some strange vegetarian
concoction, certainly too adventurous to be tried. Yet the dish
I've described is of course *hummus*, one of the best known and
most popular dips in the Middle East. It's interesting too,
because it contains two complementary proteins and therefore
represents excellent nourishment as well as being delectable.
The sesame cream, *tahini*, can be bought from health shops.
It tastes like rather earthy, slightly bitter peanut butter, but once
you come to appreciate the flavour it's very more-ish.

225 g (8 oz) chick peas
8 tablespoons olive oil
3 garlic cloves, peeled and
  crushed
4 tablespoons lemon juice

4 tablespoons sesame cream
  (*tahini*)
Sea salt
Paprika pepper
Lemon wedges

Serves 4 as a main meal, 8 as a starter

Soak the chick peas in plenty of cold water for several hours,
then drain and rinse them. Put them into a saucepan, cover them
with fresh cold water and simmer them for 1–1½ hours until they're
tender, then drain them, keeping the cooking water. You can pass
the chick peas through a vegetable mill, then mix in half the olive
oil and all the other ingredients, but I find the easiest way to
make *hummus* is to use the liquidizer. Put the chick peas into the
goblet with half the olive oil, the garlic, lemon juice, sesame cream
and some salt and blend to a smooth, fairly thick purée. You may
need to add some of the cooking liquid to enable the liquidizer
to cope with this process and to bring the *hummus* to a nice
creamy consistency. Chill the *hummus*, then serve it on a flat dish,
with the rest of the olive oil spooned over the top and a good
sprinkling of paprika. Garnish with lemon wedges. Or, if you're
serving the *hummus* as a starter, it's probably easiest to cope with
if you put individual portions on to medium-sized plates and top

each one with some olive oil and paprika. Serve it with extra olive oil and plenty of soft bread – pitta bread if you can buy or make it (see page 330); this is the usual accompaniment in the Middle East.

LIPTAUER CHEESE   HUNGARY

This mixture of cottage cheese, soft butter and flavourings is popular in Austria, Hungary, Yugoslavia and Holland. It makes a good starter with hot fingers of toast. You don't need extra butter with it and it's quick to spread, so it's also good in sandwiches or on little cracker biscuits.

50 g (2 oz) butter, softened
225 g (8 oz) low-fat quark or
  cottage cheese
1 teaspoon paprika pepper

1 teaspoon chopped capers
1 tablespoon chopped chives
½ teaspoon French mustard
Salt and pepper

Serves 4–6

Beat the butter until it's soft and light, then gradually mix in the quark or cottage cheese and continue to beat until it's well blended. Add the paprika, capers, chives and mustard, then season to taste with salt and a grinding or two of black pepper. Put the mixture into a small bowl or pottery crock and serve it chilled; peop` can take a portion from the bowl and eat it with hot toast.

MOCK CAVIAR   RUSSIA

This always popular Russian dip is made from aubergines. It has a luscious, slightly smoky taste and a lovely creamy consistency which goes beautifully with rye bread or wholewheat toast. It makes an unusual starter for when you're entertaining adventurous friends!

1 large aubergine – about 450 g (1 lb)	3 tablespoons olive oil
	1 tablespoon lemon juice
1 large garlic clove, peeled and crushed	Sea salt
	Freshly ground black pepper

Serves 4–6

Before you make this dip you need to char the aubergine – this gives the dip its slightly smoky flavour. The easiest way to do it is to put the aubergine on the prongs of a fork and turn it over a gas flame until the skin is black and the inside is soft. Or you can place it under a hot grill or in the oven, turning it round from time to time so that it gets evenly burnt. Then carefully scrape off the skin (you don't need this!) and mash, chop or liquidize the aubergine. Put this purée into a bowl and stir in the garlic, oil, lemon juice and a seasoning of salt and pepper. Mix everything well together, then spoon the mixture into a small dish – or individual dishes – and chill until required.

Salads

The salads in this section can be divided into two types, those which contain protein and those which don't, and I've mentioned this in the individual recipes. Most of the protein salads can be made into complete meals, perhaps with some bread and another lighter salad, like green or tomato salad to accompany them. The butter bean salad from the Middle East, the haricot bean salad, chick pea and vegetable mayonnaise and *salade Niçoise* from France and the vegetable and bean salad from Poland are all examples of this type of substantial salad; there are others too. These protein salads are also useful for serving as a first course if the main dish is something which is rather low in protein, like a vegetable casserole; alternatively they can be served with the main dish as a side salad. The tomato, cheese and olive salad and the green salad with Gruyère cheese are particularly useful for this.

The non-protein salads make excellent side salads too, and these I serve alongside main dishes which contain plenty of protein, such as cheese flans or stuffed pancakes. They are often quicker to prepare than a cooked vegetable and very refreshing. Some of these salads also make good first courses before a substantial main dish; I particularly like the stuffed tomato salad, from Switzerland, which is good before a fondue, and the spicy mushrooms *à la Grecque*, from France, which are good before something like a soufflé.

AVOCADO AND CARROT SALAD   MIDDLE EAST

This mixture of pale green buttery avocado, crisp orange carrot and sweet raisins is very pleasant. If you serve the salad with some bread and butter and soft cheese or hardboiled egg wedges it makes a good lunch or supper.

1 large ripe avocado pear	Juice of 1 orange
A little fresh lemon juice	50 g (2 oz) seedless raisins,
225 g (8 oz) coarsely grated	washed
carrot	Parsley sprigs

Serves 2 as a salad, 4 as a starter

Cut the avocado pear in half, twist the halves in opposite directions to separate them, then remove the stone. Carefully peel off the outer skin of the avocado halves, using a sharp pointed knife to prise it up – it should then come away quite easily if the avocado pear is really ripe. Cut the avocado into long, thin slices and sprinkle them with lemon juice, making sure that the cut surfaces are completely coated.

Mix together the grated carrot, orange juice and raisins. Arrange the avocado slices on individual plates, top with the grated carrot mixture and garnish with parsley sprigs.

BEETROOT AND HORSERADISH SALAD   AUSTRIA

A curiously pleasant mixture of flavours and textures, this salad makes a good accompaniment to cold savoury dishes.

700 g (1½ lb) cooked beetroot	1 tablespoon sugar
1 eating apple	2 tablespoons wine vinegar
1 teaspoon caraway seeds	1–2 tablespoons horseradish
	sauce

Serves 4

Peel and dice the beetroot and the apple. Put them into a bowl with the caraway seeds, sugar, vinegar and horseradish sauce and mix them all together lightly. Chill before serving.

BULGUR WHEAT, TOMATO AND PARSLEY SALAD   MIDDLE EAST

In this Middle Eastern salad, *tabbouleh*, parsley is used rather like a vegetable to provide the basis of the dish, and it's surprising what a big bunch you'll need to weigh 125 g (4 oz). If you haven't got enough I find you can use a bunch of watercress or some tender young spinach leaves instead. The bulgur wheat is quite easy to get in health shops.

225 g (8 oz) bulgur wheat
125 g (4 oz) parsley
25 g (1 oz) mint leaves
1 onion
3 tomatoes
2 tablespoons olive oil

Juice of 1 lemon
1 garlic clove, peeled and
   crushed in a little salt
Sea salt
Freshly ground black pepper

Serves 4

Cover the wheat with boiling water and leave it to soak for 15 minutes, then drain it thoroughly and put it into a bowl. Meanwhile wash the parsley and mint and chop them up fairly finely; peel and chop the onion and tomatoes, then add them to the wheat, together with the oil, lemon juice and garlic. Mix everything together and season with salt and pepper to taste.

Spoon the mixture on to a flat serving dish and press it down with the back of a spoon. Serve it chilled. You can sprinkle a little extra olive oil over the top if you like to make it look shiny. Or serve it simply, in a salad bowl or heaped up on crisp lettuce leaves.

BUTTER BEAN SALAD

MIDDLE EAST

Serve this substantial, protein-rich dish with a fresh vegetable salad such as the Middle Eastern cabbage salad or a platter of lettuce and juicy sliced tomato for a complete meal, along with soft wholemeal bread rolls or pitta bread.

175 g (6 oz) butter beans
6 spring onions
2 tablespoons chopped fresh
  parsley

1 tablespoon lemon juice
3 tablespoons olive oil
Sea salt
Freshly ground black pepper

Serves 4

Cover the butter beans with water and leave them to soak for several hours if possible. Then drain and rinse the beans and simmer them gently in plenty of water until they're tender; drain them thoroughly (the liquid makes good stock). Put the beans into a bowl.

Wash and trim the spring onions, retaining as much of the green part as seems reasonable, then chop them up and add them to the butter beans, along with the parsley, lemon juice, oil and a seasoning of salt and pepper. Stir the mixture gently, being careful not to break up the beans, then leave it to cool. I think the salad is nicest served really cold.

CABBAGE SALAD WITH MINT AND POMEGRANATE

MIDDLE EAST

Those large white cabbages make a good basis for winter salads when lettuce is scarce and expensive, but I think they need additional ingredients to make them really interesting. Here in this Middle Eastern salad the cabbage is flavoured with mint and topped with a flush of red pomegranate seeds. When you can't get fresh mint I find you can get a good flavour by omitting some of the lemon juice from the recipe and replacing it with the same amount of mint sauce – this makes a nice dressing for other salads, too.

450 g (1 lb) hard white cabbage (about a quarter of a small/medium white cabbage)	3 tablespoons oil
	Freshly ground black pepper
	2 tablespoons chopped fresh mint
1 garlic clove	1 pomegranate
Sea salt	A few sprigs of fresh mint if available
2 tablespoons lemon juice	

Serves 4–6

Cut the cabbage into fine shreds with a sharp knife. Put these into a colander, rinse them under the cold tap then drain them well. Peel the garlic and crush it in a little salt with the blade of a knife; put it into a large bowl and gradually add the lemon juice, oil and a grinding of black pepper, stirring until it's all well blended. Put the cabbage into the bowl together with the mint and mix everything gently so that the cabbage all gets coated with the dressing and the mint gets distributed throughout.

Next prepare the pomegranate; cut it in half and carefully ease out the juicy red seeds using the point of a sharp knife or a pointed skewer or cocktail stick – catch the juice on a plate as you work. Arrange the cabbage salad on a shallow dish with the pomegranate seeds and juice poured over the top. Garnish with a few sprigs of fresh mint if available.

If you prepare the cabbage an hour or more before you need it you will find that it will soften considerably in the dressing; do not add the pomegranate until just before serving.

CAULIFLOWER AND APPLE SALAD   USA

This is useful for serving as a side salad with cooked dishes, particularly those containing cheese, and it's quick and easy to make.

1 small cauliflower   Juice of 1 orange
2 large sweet apples   Sea salt

Serves 4

Wash the cauliflower then break it into florets and slice fairly finely. Dice the apples, discarding the cores. Mix the cauliflower and apple together in a large bowl; pour in the orange juice and turn the salad so that everything gets coated with the juice. Season with a very little salt if you like.

You can add a tablespoonful or so of oil to the dressing if you like but I think orange juice makes a very refreshing dressing on its own.

CELERIAC SALAD   FRANCE

Celeriac, that knobbly root with the delicious celery flavour, makes a good salad. In some ways I prefer it to celery itself, although the texture is not as crisp. It's very nice prepared the French way in a mustardy vinaigrette, and makes a pleasant side salad to accompany either a hot or cold protein dish.

1 smallish celeriac – about   1 tablespoon wine vinegar
   450 g (1 lb)   3 tablespoons olive oil
½ teaspoon mustard powder   1 bunch of watercress, washed
½ teaspoon sugar   and trimmed
¼ teaspoon sea salt   Paprika pepper
Freshly ground black pepper

Serves 4

Peel the celeriac and cut it into quarters. Keep the pieces under cold water while you make the dressing as celeriac quickly discolours. Put the mustard, sugar and salt into a shallow dish with a good grinding of black pepper and add the vinegar. Mix to a paste then gradually stir in the oil. Grate the celeriac straight into the dish, turning it over in the dressing as you do so to coat it well and prevent it from discolouring. I think it's best to use a fairly coarse grater as it gives the salad a nice texture. Taste the mixture and add a little more seasoning if you think it needs it. If possible leave it for 30 minutes or so to give the celeriac a chance to soak up the flavour of the dressing, then pile it into a serving dish, arrange the watercress round the edge and sprinkle the top with a little red paprika pepper.

CHICK PEA AND VEGETABLE MAYONNAISE   FRANCE

This combination of chick peas, cooked tender young vegetables and smooth garlic-flavoured mayonnaise, called *aigroissade*, is delicious. It makes a beautiful protein-rich starter or main salad dish with just some crisp lettuce or watercress. You can use all mayonnaise for the dressing but I prefer this lighter version.

175 g (6 oz) chick peas
700 g (1½ lb) tender new
   vegetables – potatoes,
   carrots, french beans,
   shelled broadbeans –
   cooked, drained and cooled
400 g (14 oz) can artichoke
   hearts, drained

1–2 large garlic cloves, crushed
6 rounded tablespoons mayonnaise
6 rounded tablespoons natural yoghurt
Sea salt
Freshly ground black pepper
A little chopped fresh parsley

Serves 4 as a main meal, 6–8 as a starter

Cover the chick peas with cold water and leave them to soak for

82

several hours, then drain and rinse them, put them into a saucepan
with a good covering of water and simmer them for about 1–1½
hours, until they're tender. Drain the chick peas thoroughly –
the cooking water makes good stock for soups and sauces.

Cut the cooked vegetables and the artichoke hearts into chunky
pieces and put them into a bowl with the chick peas. Mix together
the garlic, mayonnaise and yoghurt then add this to the vegetables
in the bowl, turning them over gently until they're all coated
with the creamy mixture. Season carefully with salt and pepper.
Cool, then chill the salad. Serve it heaped up in a serving dish,
or spoon the salad on to crisp lettuce leaves arranged on individual plates. Sprinkle the top with chopped parsley to give a
pleasant colour contrast. It's nice with warm soft rolls, French
bread or pitta bread.

COLESLAW
USA

'Cole' is the general term for all members of the cabbage family
and coleslaw is a delicious cabbage salad mixture. It's best made
with firm white 'salad' cabbage in the winter and in the summer a
compact, hearty cabbage such as Primo. If it's made an hour or so
in advance the cabbage will soften a little which makes it easier to
eat. It's useful as a side salad.

350 g (12 oz) white cabbage
2 medium carrots
1 small onion
Serves 4

3–4 tablespoons mayonnaise
Sea salt
Freshly ground black pepper

Wash and very finely shred the cabbage; scrape or peel and
coarsely grate the carrots; skin and finely slice the onion. Put all
the prepared vegetables into a bowl and stir in the mayonnaise
so that you have a nice creamy mixture. Season the salad with a
little salt and pepper.

This is the basic coleslaw but you can vary it by adding other ingredients such as chopped red or green peppers, raisins, chopped dates, roasted peanuts, sunflower seeds, cress, sprouted seeds, sliced apple or other fruits and green herbs. You can also use half mayonnaise and half natural yoghurt for a less rich, lower-calorie version.

CUCUMBER SALAD WITH SOURED CREAM AND HARDBOILED EGGS
RUSSIA

This refreshing salad makes a useful protein-rich starter accompanied by thinly sliced brown bread and butter. Traditionally the dressing is made with soured cream, but yoghurt can also be used for a low-calorie dressing which incidently makes an excellent slimmer's substitute for mayonnaise.

1 large cucumber
Sea salt
Whites of 4 hardboiled eggs
1 tablespoon chopped fresh dill weed or ½ teaspoon dried dill and 2 teaspoons chopped parsley
4 crisp nicely shaped lettuce leaves

For the dressing
Yolks of 4 hardboiled eggs
2 teaspoons wine vinegar
1 teaspoon caster sugar
1 teaspoon mustard powder
Sea salt
Freshly ground black pepper
150 ml (5 fl oz) carton soured cream or natural yoghurt

Serves 4

Wash the cucumber and remove the peel if you want to, then slice the cucumber into thin rounds, put them into a colander, sprinkle with salt and put a weight on top. Leave them for 30 minutes to draw out the excess water. Meanwhile chop the egg whites and leave them on one side. Make the dressing: put the egg yolks into a medium-sized bowl with the vinegar, sugar, mustard and some salt and pepper and mash them all together. Add a little of the soured cream or yoghurt and mix well to make a

84

smooth creamy consistency; gradually add the remainder, beating well. Taste and season. Drain the cucumber rings and mix them with the egg white and dill; chill if possible.

When ready to serve arrange a lettuce leaf on each serving dish, divide the cucumber mixture between them and spoon the dressing over the top.

STUFFED CUCUMBER SALAD ITALY

This is an unusual dish with a fresh, tangy flavour. It makes a good protein-rich starter or can be the basis of a simple lunch. It's nice served with thin slices of brown bread and butter and if you don't like onions use chopped chives or spring onion green instead.

1 large cucumber	1 tablespoon olive oil
150 ml (¼ pint) water	½ teaspoon mustard powder
2 tablespoons wine vinegar	1 small onion, peeled and
Sea salt	chopped
Freshly ground black pepper	Sprigs of watercress
2 hardboiled eggs	A few radishes

Serves 2 as a salad meal, 4 as a starter

Trim the cucumber then cut it into 4 equal-sized chunks. Peel the chunks then halve them lengthwise and with a teaspoon scoop out the seeds to leave a cavity for the stuffing – you won't need the seeds. Put the pieces of cucumber into a saucepan with the water, wine vinegar and a little salt and pepper and bring up to the boil, then put a lid on the saucepan and leave the cucumber to simmer gently for about 5–7 minutes until it feels tender when pierced with a knife. There won't be much liquid left in the saucepan so watch it towards the end of the cooking time. Drain and cool the cucumber.

To make the filling shell the eggs and mash them with a fork, then mix in the olive oil, mustard, onion and salt and pepper to taste. Arrange the cucumber in a serving dish and spoon the filling neatly into the cavities. Decorate the dish with the watercress and radishes.

CUCUMBER AND YOGHURT SALAD MIDDLE EAST

The combination of cucumber, yoghurt and herbs is very refreshing, making this a good salad to serve on a hot day, either accompanying a main dish, or as a starter.

1 cucumber
Sea salt
1 tablespoon chopped fresh
  parsley
1 tablespoon chopped fresh
  chives
2 teaspoons chopped fresh dill
  or fennel if available

275 ml (10 fl oz) natural
  yoghurt
Freshly ground black pepper
1 crisp lettuce heart, cut into
  4 or 6 pieces, one for each
  person; or warm wholewheat
  rolls

Serves 4–6

Wash the cucumber and slice it finely or grate it fairly coarsely. Put the pieces into a colander, sprinkle them with salt, place a weight on top and leave for about 30 minutes to draw out the excess moisture. Then squeeze the cucumber to extract as much liquid as possible and place it in a large bowl. Stir in all the other ingredients and season with pepper and some more salt if you think it's necessary.

This salad is nicest served really cold so put it into the fridge to chill for an hour or so if you can. You can serve each portion of the salad spooned over a crisp wedge of lettuce heart, or put it into small bowls and accompany it with fresh warm wholewheat rolls.

FENNEL AND CUCUMBER SALAD   ITALY

Raw fennel, with its crisp texture and slightly aniseed flavour, combines well with cool juicy cucumber and makes a refreshing first course or side salad.

1 cucumber

Sea salt

2 fennel bulbs

6 crisp lettuce leaves

1 tablespoon olive oil

1 tablespoon chopped fresh mint

1 teaspoon caster sugar

For the dressing:

1 tablespoon lemon juice

Serves 4–6

Wash the cucumber then cut it into small dice and put these into a colander, sprinkling each layer with a little salt. Put a saucer on top and weigh it down with something heavy: leave for about 30 minutes, then pat dry. Meanwhile wash the fennel and trim off the root ends and tough stalks, but keep any tender stems and little bits of feathery leaf, then cut the fennel into neat slices and put them into a bowl.

Mix up a dressing: put the lemon juice, oil, mint and sugar into a bowl and beat them together until blended. Add the cucumber and the dressing to the fennel and mix everything together gently so that it all gets coated with the dressing. Taste and add a bit more salt if necessary (you may not need to because of the preliminary salting of the cucumber). Arrange the lettuce leaves in the base of a salad bowl, or put one on each individual serving dish, and spoon the salad on top.

GREEN SALAD

FRANCE

A well-made green salad goes with so many dishes; it's quick and easy to do and ideal for entertaining because you can serve it instead of a vegetable and then don't have to worry about last minute cooking. You can serve it with the main dish or, as is often done in France, afterwards, as a palate-cleansing course on its own, before the cheese.

1 large lettuce
1 bunch watercress

For the dressing:
1 garlic clove
1 tablespoon wine vinegar –
   red or white

3 tablespoons olive oil
Sea salt
Freshly ground black pepper
Fresh green herbs – parsley
   and chives, and others such
   as tarragon, chervil, lovage
   and fennel as available

Serves 4

Wash the lettuce and watercress, discarding tough stalks and damaged leaves. Dry the salad in a salad shaker, salad spin-drier or by patting gently in a clean tea-towel. Keep the salad in a polythene bag in the base of the refrigerator until you're almost ready to serve it. Meanwhile make the dressing – you can make it in a screw-top jar but I think it's easier to put the ingredients directly into the salad bowl and mix it in that. Peel the garlic, and either cut it in half and rub the salad bowl thoroughly with the cut surfaces, if you like a delicate garlic flavour, or for a stronger taste, crush the garlic to a paste in a little salt with the blade of a knife, and put it into the salad bowl. Add the vinegar, oil, some salt and pepper and mix well with the salad servers or a wooden spoon. Scatter the herbs on top of the dressing and leave in a cool place until just before the meal, then put in the lettuce and watercress, tearing them into manageable pieces as you go. Turn the salad in the dressing at the last moment so that it won't go soggy – I usually do this at the table.

A green salad is easy to make but its success depends on the quality of the ingredients: really crisp lettuce and watercress, the best wine vinegar and olive oil, sea salt and freshly ground black pepper. Make sure that you dry the salad carefully or the water clinging to it will dilute the dressing and spoil it.

GREEN SALAD   SPAIN

This Spanish-style green salad makes a useful accompaniment to dishes such as the paella and the Portuguese kidney bean stew.

1 large lettuce	Freshly ground black pepper
1 bunch watercress	1 large tomato
1 tablespoon lemon juice	1 large onion, preferably
1 tablespoon olive oil	Spanish
Sea salt	A few olives

Serves 4

Wash the lettuce and watercress, discarding any damaged leaves and tough stems; dry the salad in a salad drier or by patting it gently in a clean tea-towel. Tear the lettuce leaves into even-sized pieces and put them into a bowl with the watercress.

Make the dressing by mixing together the lemon juice, olive oil and a seasoning of salt and pepper. Add this to the lettuce and watercress in the bowl and turn the salad gently, so that all the leaves get coated in the dressing and are glossy-looking; arrange the salad in a mound on a large plate. Slice the tomato into thin rounds; peel and thinly slice the onion; arrange these on top of the green salad, together with a few olives. Serve at once.

GREEN SALAD WITH GRUYÈRE CHEESE

This delicious variation on the basic green salad makes a useful accompaniment to a low-protein main dish such as vegetable rice or stuffed peppers. Traditionally Gruyère cheese is used, but it's also nice with other smooth, firm cheeses such as Edam or Gouda.

1 lettuce
1 bunch watercress
125–175 g (4–6 oz) Gruyère
  cheese

For the dressing:
1 garlic clove
1 tablespoon wine vinegar

3 tablespoons olive oil
Sea salt
Freshly ground black pepper
1 tablespoon chopped fresh
  summer savory if available,
  otherwise use chives or
  tarragon

Serves 4

Wash the lettuce and watercress and shake them dry, then if possible put them into a polythene bag and pop it in the fridge to chill for a while. Cut the cheese into little dice and leave on one side. Peel the garlic clove, and crush it in a little salt with the blade of a knife and put it into the salad bowl together with the vinegar, oil, a little sea salt and a grinding of pepper and mix them round with the salad servers. Sprinkle the herbs on top and leave until just before the meal, then put in the lettuce and watercress, breaking them up with your fingers, and the cubes of cheese. Just before serving turn the salad over with the servers so that it all gets coated with the dressing.

HARICOT BEAN SALAD

FRANCE

Served with one or two other salad dishes, such as a green salad and a tomato salad, and some nice soft wholewheat rolls, this makes a delicious main dish for a light meal. It's also good as a starter. The important thing is to cook the beans so that they're just right: catch them when they're tender but before they start to break up, because they get firmer as they cool and if they're at all underdone it makes for a very chewy salad. I think the mustard and sugar in the dressing go well with the beans but it's really the chopped fresh herbs which make all the difference and enable you to vary the flavour. If you can't get any fresh green herbs, one or two chopped spring onions (including as much of the green part as possible) are also good.

225 g (8 oz) dried haricot beans
1 teaspoon caster sugar
1 teaspoon mustard powder
1 tablespoon wine vinegar
4 tablespoons olive oil
Sea salt

Freshly ground black pepper
3 tablespoons chopped
  fresh green herbs; parsley,
  chives, mint, chervil,
  tarragon or fennel

Serves 4

Soak the beans in plenty of cold water for 2–3 hours if possible, then drain and rinse them, put them into a saucepan with plenty of cold water and let them simmer gently for 1–1¼ hours or until they're very tender but not soggy. Drain. Put the sugar, mustard, vinegar and oil into a salad bowl and mix together; season with salt and pepper, then stir in most of the herbs and the hot beans. Turn the beans gently in the dressing so that they all get well coated. Leave them to get cold, then chill them. Serve sprinkled with the remaining herbs.

LENTIL SALAD   FRANCE

You need continental (whole) lentils for this salad because they hold their shape when they're cooked. Combined with a good fruity olive oil, lemon juice and some crisp onion rings they make a delicious salad. If you serve it with some bread – soft wholewheat rolls, French bread or pitta bread – and a lettuce or other green salad it makes a complete meal.

225 g (8 oz) continental lentils	Sea salt
1 tablespoon lemon juice	Freshly ground black pepper
3 tablespoons olive oil	1 onion

Serves 4

Soak the lentils in water for a couple of hours or so if possible, then drain and rinse them, put them into a saucepan with fresh water and simmer them gently until tender – about 45 minutes. Drain the lentils thoroughly (keep the cooking liquid, it makes good stock) and put them into a bowl with the lemon juice, olive oil and some salt and pepper. Peel the onion and cut it into thin rounds then add these to the lentils and mix everything gently together. Cool, then chill the salad. It looks nice in a white bowl which contrasts with the rich brown lentils.

MUSHROOM SALAD   FINLAND

This salad differs from mushrooms *à la Grecque* in that the mushrooms are not cooked, so you need to use very fresh white button mushrooms. It makes a pleasant starter particularly if accompanied by soft warm wholewheat rolls.

225 g (8 oz) fresh white button
mushrooms
1 tablespoon lemon juice
Sea salt
Freshly ground black pepper

2 tablespoons lightly whipped
double cream, soured cream
or natural yoghurt
Lettuce leaves
Fresh chives

Serves 4 as a starter

Wash the mushrooms, then pat them dry and slice thinly. Put
the slices into a bowl and sprinkle them with lemon juice and
some salt and pepper. Add the double cream, soured cream or
natural yoghurt and stir gently. Chill, then check the seasoning.
To serve the salad, spoon it on to lettuce leaves on individual
plates and sprinkle some chopped chives over the top.

The mushrooms will give off some liquid after you've sprinkled
them with the lemon juice and salt and this will blend with the
cream to make a thin dressing. If you would prefer a thicker
dressing, sprinkle the lemon juice and salt on the mushrooms an
hour or so before the meal, then drain off the juice which will
have accumulated and fold the mushrooms through the cream
just before serving them, checking the seasoning. (The mushroom
liquid makes good stock.)

MUSHROOMS À LA GRECQUE   FRANCE

These coriander-flavoured mushrooms make an excellent starter
before a non-spicy main meal.

450 g (1 lb) small white button
mushrooms
4 tablespoons olive oil
2 teaspoons ground coriander
1 bay leaf
2 garlic cloves, peeled and
crushed

2 tablespoons lemon juice
Freshly ground black pepper
Sea salt
Lettuce leaves
Fresh parsley

Serves 4

Wash the mushrooms, halving or quartering any larger ones, then fry them in the olive oil with the coriander, bay leaf and garlic for about 2 minutes, stirring all the time. Turn the mushrooms straight into a large bowl to prevent further cooking, then add the lemon juice and a grinding of black pepper. Leave the mixture to cool, then chill it. Check the seasoning before serving the mushrooms piled up on lettuce leaves on individual plates and sprinkled with chopped parsley. They're also nice served in a bowl as part of a selection of different salads for a buffet lunch or supper.

SALADE NIÇOISE   FRANCE

I don't suppose purists would call this a *salade Niçoise* at all as it doesn't contain tuna fish and anchovies. But as there's no exact recipe and it's open to many variations I'm putting forward my vegetarian version which is a mixture of the other usual ingredients – tomatoes, cooked French beans, black olives and hardboiled eggs – all bound together in a good vinaigrette and served in a glossy, colourful heap. It makes a very filling starter or an excellent main lunch dish with soft warm wholewheat rolls or crunchy French bread.

1 large lettuce	*For the dressing:*
450 g (1 lb) tomatoes	1 large garlic clove, peeled
6 hardboiled eggs	and crushed
450 g (1 lb) cooked French	2 tablespoons wine vinegar
beans	6 tablespoons olive oil
12 black olives	Sea salt
2 tablespoons chopped fresh	Freshly ground black pepper
parsley	

Serves 4

Wash the lettuce and dry it in a salad shaker or by patting it dry with a clean tea-towel. Spread the leaves out on a flat serving dish. Slice the tomatoes, quarter the hardboiled eggs and cut the green beans into even-sized lengths. Put them all into a bowl together with the olives and parsley.

Next make the dressing: put the garlic into a bowl and gradually mix in the wine vinegar, then add the oil and some salt and pepper and beat it all together until it's smooth. Pour the dressing over the bean and tomato mixture and turn it gently so that it all gets coated with the dressing but doesn't get broken up. Heap the salad on top of the lettuce leaves and serve at once.

ORANGE AND RADISH SALAD   NORTH AFRICA

Bright red radishes and golden segments of orange make a colourful salad. I find it's a useful salad for early summer when lettuce is still scarce but the first radishes have appeared and there are plenty of juicy oranges in the shops.

2 bunches of radishes   Sea salt
6 large oranges   1 bunch of watercress

Serves 4

Wash the radishes then cut them into rings. Using a sharp knife cut the skin and pith from the oranges and then cut the segments away from the white skin. Mix the oranges with the radishes and season to taste with a very little salt. Chill, then serve the salad in a border of watercress.

POTATO SALAD   USA

For this salad you need firm potatoes which won't break up and go mushy when you mix them with the mayonnaise. In the summer new potatoes are ideal but in the winter I use King Edwards or Desirée. As with the chick pea and vegetable salad, and the Waldorf salad, I prefer to use a mixture of mayonnaise and yoghurt which is lighter and less fattening, but of course you could use just mayonnaise. You could also use the dressing given for the Russian cucumber salad with soured cream and hardboiled eggs.

700 g (1½ lb) new potatoes or
  firm-cooking old potatoes
Sea salt
2 rounded tablespoons
  mayonnaise

2 rounded tablespoons yoghurt
2 tablespoons fresh green
  herbs – parsley, chives,
  tarragon, fennel – whatever
  is available

Serves 4

Scrub the potatoes then cook them in their skins in boiling, salted water until they're tender. Let them get cool enough to handle then slip the skins off using a small pointed knife. (Cooking the potatoes in their skins like this really does make a surprising difference to the flavour.) Cut the potatoes into chunky pieces and put them into a bowl with the mayonnaise, yoghurt and herbs. Turn the mixture gently with a spoon until all the potatoes are coated with the dressing but be careful not to break them up. Check the seasoning, adding pepper and salt if necessary.

Cool, then chill the mixture and serve it heaped up on a dish: it looks good in a shallow glass one or on a base of crisp lettuce on a flat plate.

HOT POTATO SALAD WITH PEANUT DRESSING SOUTH AMERICA

This is one of those dishes which sounds very strange but tastes really good. It's a mixture of hot and cold, bland and spicy, and it is rich in protein too. You can use ordinary salted peanuts but if you can get the plain roasted kind from a health shop they're better.

225 g (8 oz) roasted peanuts	700 g (1½ lb) potatoes
150 ml (¼ pint) milk	1 lettuce
50 g (2 oz) finely grated cheese	1 bunch of watercress
½–1 teaspoon chilli powder, or	4 tomatoes
a small green chilli	1 onion

Serves 4

First put the peanuts and milk into the liquidizer goblet and blend until they're thick and fairly smooth – add a little more milk if necessary to give the consistency of whipped cream. Turn the mixture into a bowl and stir in the grated cheese. Add chilli powder to taste, or, if you're using a fresh chilli remove and discard the seeds and chop the flesh very finely – add it to the mixture a little at a time, tasting to get the right degree of hotness.

Peel the potatoes and cut them into even-sized pieces, then boil them in salted water until they're just tender; drain. Wash the lettuce, watercress and tomatoes; peel the onion. Slice the onion and tomatoes into thin rounds.

To serve pile the hot potatoes into the centre of a serving dish (or individual plates) and arrange the lettuce, watercress, tomatoes and onion round the edge. Spoon the peanut sauce over the potatoes and serve at once.

RED BEAN SALAD   USA

This salad looks particularly appetizing, with its shiny red beans and slivers of white onion. You can make it taste spicier if you want to by adding some chilli powder and cumin to the dressing. It makes a lovely lunch with home-made wholewheat bread and some lettuce and watercress.

225 g (8 oz) red kidney beans,
  soaked, cooked (see p. 22)
  and drained;
  or use 2 cans of beans,
  drained
1 small onion, peeled and cut
  into thin slices
Fresh parsley if available

1 garlic clove, peeled and
  crushed
Sea salt
Freshly ground black pepper
1 tablespoon tomato purée
1 tablespoon red wine vinegar
3 tablespoons olive oil

For the dressing:
½ teaspoon mustard powder
½ teaspoon sugar

Serves 4

Put the beans into a bowl with the onion. For the dressing put
the mustard, sugar and garlic into a small bowl with a little
salt and a grinding of pepper. Mix to a paste with the tomato
purée and vinegar then gradually add the oil and stir until
everything is blended. Pour this dressing over the beans, turning
them gently until they're all coated with it and look glossy.
Check the seasoning and add more salt, pepper and sugar if
necessary.

This salad looks pretty in a glass or white china bowl with
chopped parsley sprinkled over the top.

RED CABBAGE SALAD   POLAND

This is a useful winter salad and the warm mauve colour is
cheerful on a cold day.

  It makes a nice side salad or accompaniment to a protein-
rich dish such as a cheese flan. Because of its unusual colour
it's also a good salad to include when you're making several for a
buffet lunch or supper.

You can leave out the caraway seeds if you don't like them
though they do give a lovely spicy flavour. I don't think the

raisins are very authentic in this salad but we like them and I'm giving you the version I usually make – you can leave them out, too, if you prefer!

450 g (1 lb) red cabbage
2 eating apples
50 g (2 oz) raisins
1 tablespoon lemon juice or red wine vinegar

2–3 tablespoons oil
2–3 teaspoons caraway seeds
Sea salt
Freshly ground black pepper

Serves 4

Wash the cabbage then grate or shred it as finely as you can. I think it's best grated because then it makes a nice soft mixture which blends well with the other ingredients and isn't too chewy. Cut the apples into small dice discarding the cores and wash the raisins, then add these to the cabbage together with the lemon juice or vinegar, oil, caraway seeds and a little salt and pepper. Stir well so that everything is thoroughly mixed together.

RICE AND ARTICHOKE HEART SALAD
FRANCE

This makes a complete meal if you serve it with one or two other vegetable salads such as a bowl of crisp lettuce and herbs and a juicy tomato salad. If you serve it with the green salad with Gruyére cheese or the tomato salad with cheese and olives they will supply the extra protein needed; or the salad can be garnished with wedges of hardboiled egg. Alternatively you could start or end the meal with a protein dish such as a lentil soup or home-made ice cream.

225 g (8 oz) long-grain brown
rice
575 ml (1 pint) water
Sea salt
400 g (14 oz) can artichoke
hearts, drained
1 garlic clove
1 tablespoon wine vinegar
3 tablespoons olive oil

Freshly ground black pepper
1 tablespoon chopped fresh
parsley
1 tablespoon chopped fresh
chives
Extra parsley to garnish
3 hardboiled eggs, quartered
(optional)

Serves 4

Wash the rice then put it into a heavy-based saucepan with the water and half a teaspoon of salt and bring to the boil, then put a lid on the saucepan, turn the heat down low and leave the rice to cook very gently for 40–45 minutes. You should find that the rice is tender and all the water has been absorbed. If there is still a little water, put the lid back on the saucepan and leave it to stand (off the heat) for 10–15 minutes.

While the rice is cooking cut the artichoke hearts into slices and peel the garlic and crush it in a little salt with the blade of a knife. Put the garlic into a small bowl and mix in the vinegar, olive oil and a grinding of pepper, then stir this mixture gently into the hot rice, together with the parsley, chives and sliced artichoke hearts, using a fork to avoid mashing the rice. Check the seasoning – rice can take quite a lot of salt – then leave the mixture to cool.

Serve the salad heaped upon a shallow dish with a sprinkling of chopped parsley on top and the hardboiled eggs, if you're using them, tucked round the edge.

SPINACH SALAD USA

This is different from the Middle Eastern spinach salad because here tender young spinach leaves are used uncooked and they make a surprisingly good mixture. In this recipe from the USA they're combined with tomatoes and button mushrooms and tossed in a garlic-flavoured French dressing.

225 g (8 oz) very fresh tender
   spinach
2 tomatoes
125 g (4 oz) fresh white button
   mushrooms

1 tablespoon red wine vinegar
3 tablespoons olive oil
Freshly ground black pepper
Sugar

For the dressing:
1 garlic clove
Sea salt

Serves 4

Wash the spinach thoroughly then dry it in a salad drier or clean tea-towel and tear it into rough pieces, discarding any tough stems. Wash and chop the tomatoes and mushrooms.

Peel the garlic then crush it in a little salt with the blade of a knife. Put the garlic into a large bowl – you can use the bowl in which you're going to serve the salad – and add the vinegar, mixing it with the garlic to make a paste, then gradually add the oil. Season with a little pepper and a pinch of sugar, then put in the spinach, tomatoes and mushrooms and turn them lightly so that they all get coated with the dressing and look glossy. Serve at once.

COLD SPINACH SALAD   MIDDLE EAST

I know some people find the idea of a salad made from cold cooked spinach very off-putting, but I think the mixture of the soft, dark green spinach, the fruity olive oil and the sharp-tasting lemon juice is delicious. There are versions of this salad throughout the Middle East. Yoghurt can be included in the dressing or served with the salad, as in this recipe; cooked chick peas can be added, providing a pleasant contrast of colour and texture as well as protein. I also like it with a topping of slivered almonds fried golden and crisp in butter.

1 kg (2¼ lb) spinach	1 garlic clove
1 tablespoon lemon juice	275 ml (½ pint) natural yoghurt
3 tablespoons olive oil	Fresh mint, parsley or chives;
Sea salt	or 50 g (2 oz) slivered
Freshly ground black pepper	almonds fried in butter

Serves 4

Wash the spinach well then cook it in just the water clinging to it. When it's done drain it thoroughly and leave to cool. Chop the cold spinach and put it into a bowl with the lemon juice, olive oil, some salt and pepper and turn it gently so that the oil and lemon juice get well distributed.

Peel and crush the garlic then mix it with the yoghurt and add some salt and pepper. Put the spinach salad on to a flat plate and spoon some of the yoghurt mixture on top; garnish with chopped green herbs or fried almonds. Serve the rest of the yoghurt separately.

THREE-BEAN SALAD   USA

This attractive salad shows off the contrasting shapes and colours of three different types of bean: red kidney beans, haricot or other white beans and chick peas. Other beans could of course be used; the aim is to get as much variety as possible. It's advisable to soak and cook the red kidney beans separately as the colour can stain the others slightly pink, but you can cook them all in one saucepan if you wish.

125 g (4 oz) red kidney beans
125 g (4 oz) haricot or other
   white beans
125 g (4 oz) chick peas
2 tablespoons chopped fresh
   green herbs

2 tablespoons wine vinegar
6 tablespoons olive oil
Sea salt
Freshly ground black pepper

Serves 4 as a main meal, 6–8 as a starter

Soak the red kidney beans in water in one bowl and the other two types together in another, then drain, rinse and cook them in fresh water until they're tender, again keeping the red ones separate if possible. Drain the beans well, put them all into a bowl together and add the herbs (you don't need to cool the beans). Mix the vinegar, oil and some salt and pepper in a small bowl, then stir this dressing into the bean mixture, turning the beans until they're coated with it and all look glossy. Leave the mixture to cool, stirring it from time to time, then chill it.

Three-bean salad looks pretty served in a shallow glass bowl or white dish to show off the colours of the beans, or it can be spooned over crisp lettuce leaves and garnished with extra chopped fresh green herbs if you prefer.

TOMATO SALAD   FRANCE

One of the joys of late summer is getting firm, fragrant, orange-red tomatoes and then using them extravagantly, as in this juicy salad which I like to serve with pasta dishes.

700 g (1½ lb) tomatoes	1 tablespoon olive oil
1 small onion	Sea salt
1 teaspoon red wine vinegar	Freshly ground black pepper

Serves 4

Wash the tomatoes and cut them into slices. Peel and finely slice the onion. Put the tomato and onion into a bowl and gently stir in the vinegar, oil and salt and pepper to taste. Serve as soon as possible.

TOMATO, CHEESE AND OLIVE SALAD   FRANCE

If you serve this as a side salad with a plain pasta or rice dish it will supply the extra protein; accompanied by bread or rolls it also makes a delicious lunch, simple yet good. The type of cheese you use is up to you; the Brie or Camembert are delicious but I find a cheaper white cheese like Caerphilly is very good too.

450 g (1 lb) firm tomatoes	Sea salt
1 onion	Freshly ground black pepper
8 black olives	175 g (6 oz) soft white cheese
2 tablespoons olive oil	such as Brie or Camembert
1 tablespoon wine vinegar	or use Caerphilly

Serves 4 as a side salad, 2–3 for lunch

Wash the tomatoes and cut them into fairly thin slices; peel and finely slice the onion. Put them into a bowl with the olives, oil, vinegar and some salt and pepper and mix them lightly together. Just before you want to serve it cut up the cheese and add it to the salad. This looks good in a shallow glass bowl or white china dish. If possible don't make it more than about 30 minutes in advance or the juices will run and it could be a bit too wet.

STUFFED TOMATO SALAD   SWITZERLAND

Stuffed tomato salad from Switzerland makes a refreshing starter in late summer when tomatoes are large and cheap; or it can make a light salad lunch after a substantial soup.

6 good-sized tomatoes – about 450 g (1 lb)
Sea salt
2 eating apples
4 stalks of crisp, tender celery
1 tablespoon mayonnaise
1 tablespoon natural yoghurt
Freshly ground black pepper
Lettuce leaves

Serves 6

Halve the tomatoes round their middles and, using a teaspoon, scoop out the centres – you won't need them for this recipe. Sprinkle a little salt inside each tomato half and leave them upside down on a plate or in a colander to drain off any excess liquid.

Wash the apples and celery then cut them into small dice and add the mayonnaise, yoghurt and a little salt and pepper to taste. Arrange the tomatoes, right way up, on a base of lettuce. Spoon the celery and apple mixture into the tomato halves, piling it up attractively.

VEGETABLE AND BEAN SALAD   POLAND

This salad, *salata mehania* from Poland, makes a lovely filling
meal. It's nice with home-made brown bread or pitta bread.
You can really use any dried beans but I prefer the red kidney
beans as they're nice and colourful.

125 g (4 oz) frozen peas
125 g (4 oz) frozen green beans
125 g (4 oz) red kidney beans,
  soaked, cooked and drained,
  or use a 424 g (15 oz) can
225 g (8 oz) cooked potatoes,
  cubed
125 g (4 oz) fresh firm button
  mushrooms
1 celery heart
225 g (8 oz) firm cabbage,
  red or white

2 tablespoons chopped chives,
  if available
1 garlic clove
Sea salt
Freshly ground black pepper
½ teaspoon mustard powder
½ teaspoon sugar
1 tablespoon wine vinegar
3 tablespoons olive oil

Serves 4–6

Cook the peas and green beans together in a little fast-boiling
salted water until they're just tender, then drain them. Put them
into a bowl with the kidney beans and potatoes. Wash and slice
the mushrooms and celery; wash and shred the cabbage and
add these all to the bowl, together with the chives.

Peel the garlic and crush it in a little salt, then put it into a small
bowl and add a grinding of pepper, the mustard, sugar and vinegar.
Mix well, then gradually stir in the oil. Put this dressing over the
vegetables in the bowl and turn them lightly so that they all get
coated with it and look glossy and appetizing. Serve the salad in a
glass bowl or on a base of crisp lettuce on a flat plate.

WALDORF SALAD   USA

This salad contains a very pleasant mixture of flavours and textures: crisp celery, sweet apple and crunchy walnuts bound together in a creamy mayonnaise (I use half mayonnaise, half natural yoghurt). The only problem is the colour which can be rather dull so I try to use red-skinned apples which don't need peeling. Accompanied by crisp lettuce leaves, Waldorf salad makes an excellent lunch, and is also delicious as a protein-rich starter.

1 celery heart – about 225 g (8 oz) after it's been trimmed
2 red-skinned apples – about 225 g (8 oz)
125–175 g (4–6 oz) walnuts, roughly chopped
3–4 rounded tablespoons mayonnaise
3–4 rounded tablespoons natural yoghurt
Sea salt

Serves 4 as a main salad, 6–8 as a starter

Wash the celery thoroughly then slice it fairly finely. Quarter the apples and remove the cores, then cut the quarters into dice. Put the apple and celery into a bowl and add the walnuts. Stir in enough mayonnaise and yoghurt to bind everything lightly and give a creamy consistency. Taste and season with a little salt if necessary. The salad looks nice piled up in a shallow glass bowl and garnished with a few extra pieces of walnut, or heaped on to crisp lettuce leaves.

If you don't like the slightly bitter flavour of walnuts you can of course use other nuts for this salad. My family likes it best made with whole roasted hazel nuts: I spread 175 g (6 oz) of hazel nuts on a dry baking tray and roast them in a moderate oven – 180°C (350°F), gas mark 4 – for about 20 minutes or until the skins will rub off easily, then I cool them and remove the skins by rubbing the nuts gently in a soft dry cloth before mixing them with the apple and celery. You could also used roasted peanuts or toasted flaked almonds.

Accompanying Vegetables

These recipes are for the vegetables that you serve alongside the main dish, and some of them make good hot starters, too. They are mostly fairly simple ideas for making ordinary vegetables a bit different, or for preparing some of the more exotic vegetables like okra, fennel, pumpkin and sweet potatoes that you can sometimes find these days. One or two of the recipes contain protein – the Brussels sprouts with cheese, haricot beans with apples and potatoes Anna, for instance – which makes them another useful way of increasing the nourishment of a meal.

BRUSSELS SPROUTS WITH CHEESE   HOLLAND

This is really a very simple way with Brussels sprouts but it's useful if you want to add a little extra protein to the meal. It's also good for a dinner party because it means you don't have to deal with the sprouts at the last minute.

700 g (1½ lb) Brussels sprouts
Sea salt
A little butter

125–175 g (4–6 oz) finely
grated Edam cheese
Freshly ground black pepper

Serves 4

Set the oven to 160°C (325°F), gas mark 3. Wash and trim the sprouts. Leave them whole if they're tiny, otherwise halve or quarter them – that way they cook well and don't get soggy. Put 1 cm (½ in) water and a little salt into a saucepan and bring to the boil; add the sprouts, bring up to the boil again and cook for 2 minutes. Drain the sprouts immediately. Grease an ovenproof dish quite generously with butter and put in the sprouts; sprinkle the grated cheese over them and grind over a little pepper. Dot with a little more butter, cover with foil or a lid and bake the sprouts in the oven for about 20 minutes until the cheese has melted and they're piping hot.

If you want to keep the sprouts warm for longer I find they will stay nice and fresh-looking for quite a long time if you prepare them as above and put them in a lower oven – say 140–150°C (275–300°F), gas mark 1–2.

CABBAGE WITH SOURED CREAM   NORWAY

If you cook cabbage until it's just tender, then drain it well and stir in some soured cream you get a delicious mixture: simple, yet good enough for a special occasion. In Norway some caraway seeds would probably be added too, but these are optional.

111

700–900 g (1½–2 lb) firm
  cabbage, washed and
  shredded
Sea salt
150 ml (5 fl oz) soured
  cream

Freshly ground black
  pepper
1 teaspoon caraway seeds
  (optional)

Serves 4

Put about 2·5 cm (1 in) water into a large saucepan, together
with a teaspoonful of salt, bring up to the boil, then add the
cabbage. Let the cabbage simmer gently, with a lid on the saucepan, for about 7–10 minutes, until it is just tender. Drain the
cabbage well and stir in the soured cream, a good grinding of
pepper and the caraway seeds if you're using them. Taste and
add a little more salt if necessary. Reheat for a minute or two,
just to warm through the cream, then serve.

STIR-FRIED CHINESE CABBAGE CHINA

Chinese cabbage, or 'Chinese leaves' as it's sometimes called,
is quite often found in the shops now and makes a lovely cooked
vegetable dish that's very quickly prepared. I like to stir-fry the
cabbage in the Chinese way; it's good with either an ordinary
Western-style meal or as part of a Chinese meal.

1 Chinese cabbage,
  about 700 g (1½ lb)
1 small onion, peeled and
  chopped
2 tablespoons oil
1 garlic clove, crushed
1 piece of fresh ginger, if
  available, peeled and
  grated to make 1 teaspoonful:

or use ½ teaspoon
  ordinary powdered ginger
1 teaspoon soy sauce
½ teaspoon cornflour
1 tablespoon cold water
Sugar
Sea salt
Freshly ground black pepper

Serves 4

Wash the cabbage and shred it – not too finely. Fry the onion in the oil in a large saucepan for about 7 minutes without browning it, then add the garlic and ginger and fry for a further 2 or 3 minutes. Take the saucepan off the heat and leave on one side until just before you want to serve the cabbage. Mix the soy sauce, cornflour and water together in a small cup and keep these on one side too.

When you're ready for the cabbage, reheat the onion in the large saucepan. When it's really hot put in the cabbage and fry it over a fairly high heat for about 2 minutes, stirring all the time. It will quickly soften. Give the cornflour mixture a quick stir then pour it into the saucepan with the cabbage and stir over the heat for about 30 seconds until the juices have thickened. Check the seasoning, adding a little sugar, salt and pepper if necessary, then serve immediately. The cabbage should still be rather crisp and crunchy.

CARROTS WITH APPLES GERMANY

Fruit, both dried and fresh, is used a good deal in German cookery, with some delicious sweet-sour mixtures. Here the soft slightly sharp cooking apples contrast well with the firm sweet carrots. Like the haricots with apples, this is a useful recipe to serve with a dish which would normally require an apple sauce.

700 g (1½ lb) carrots	Sea salt
900 g (2 lb) cooking apples	Freshly ground black pepper
1 large onion	Sugar
2 tablespoons oil	

Serves 4

Peel the carrots and cut them into even-sized pieces; cook them in a little boiling, salted water until they're nearly tender, then drain them, reserving the cooking liquid. While this is happening, peel and slice the apples and the onion. Add the

113

apple to the cooked, drained carrot in the saucepan, together with 4 tablespoons of the reserved cooking liquid and cook over a gentle heat, with a lid on the saucepan, for 5–7 minutes, until the apple has reduced to a soft pulp. Meanwhile fry the onion in the oil until it's crisp and beginning to brown. Taste the carrot and apple mixture and add salt, pepper and sugar to taste.

Serve the carrot and apple with the fried onion poured over the top.

CARROTS À LA VICHY FRANCE

Although you're supposed to use new baby carrots for this recipe I find it's a marvellous way of making older carrots taste extra special. Some people use Vichy water for cooking the carrots or put a pinch of bicarbonate of soda in with them to give a more authentic-tasting result but I don't think this makes much difference and I just use ordinary tap water. Personally I think it's the butter, sugar and chopped parsley that work the magic, not the water!

450 g (1 lb) carrots
75 ml ($\frac{1}{8}$ pint) water
1 tablespoon caster sugar

15 g ($\frac{1}{2}$ oz) butter
Sea salt
Fresh parsley

Serves 4

Scrape the carrots then cut them into matchsticks. Put the water, sugar, butter and salt into a heavy-based saucepan and bring to the boil, then add the carrots and put a lid on the saucepan. Simmer very gently for about 10–15 minutes, until the carrots are tender and all the water has been absorbed. Watch them carefully towards the end to make sure they don't burn. Serve them sprinkled with a little chopped parsley.

114

CAULIFLOWER IN TOMATO SAUCE   GREECE

This is an easy and attractive way of cooking cauliflower and the sauce means that you don't have to serve a gravy as well.

1 onion, peeled and chopped	Sea salt
2 tablespoons oil	Freshly ground black pepper
1 garlic clove, peeled and crushed	1 medium cauliflower, washed and broken into florets
425 g (15 oz) can tomatoes	
275 ml (½ pint) water	Fresh parsley if available

Serves 4

Cook the onion gently in the oil for 10 minutes until it's soft but not browned, then put it into the liquidizer with the garlic, tomatoes and water and blend to a purée. Put this purée into a fairly large saucepan and add some salt and pepper. Bring the mixture up to the boil then put in the cauliflower and simmer gently, with a lid on the saucepan, for 10–15 minutes, until the cauliflower is just tender. You can take the cauliflower out of the saucepan using a perforated spoon and serve the sauce separately, but I usually serve them together with a little chopped parsley sprinkled over the top.

COURGETTES WITH FRESH HERBS   FRANCE

This is a good way to serve courgettes early in the season when they're young and tender and you want to make the most of their delicate flavour.

700 g (1½ lb) young courgettes	1 tablespoon finely chopped fresh chives
Sea salt	
25 g (1 oz) butter	Freshly ground black pepper
1 tablespoon finely chopped fresh parsley	

Serves 4-6

Wash the courgettes and trim the ends. Cut the courgettes into 6 mm ($\frac{1}{4}$ in) slices then cook them in 1 cm ($\frac{1}{2}$ in) boiling salted water for 5–7 minutes, until they're just tender but not soggy. Drain the courgettes well and add the butter, parsley, chives, pepper and a little more salt to taste if necessary.

FENNEL BAKED WITH CHEESE   ITALY

It's quite easy to find crisp white bulbs of Florentine fennel in the shops these days and it makes an interesting vegetable dish. It's very nice steamed and served simply with just a little butter and black pepper or you can boil it then bake it with cheese, as in this recipe, which gives a tasty golden result.

2 large bulbs of fennel – about 700 g (1½ lb) together	25 g (1 oz) butter
275 ml (½ pint) water	Freshly ground black pepper
Sea salt	50 g (2 oz) grated cheese

Serves 4–6

Set the oven to 200°C (400°F), gas mark 6. Trim the fennel and slice the bulbs into quarters or eighths. Put the water and a little salt into a saucepan; bring to the boil then put in the fennel and simmer for 20–30 minutes until the fennel is tender. Take the fennel out of the saucepan with a draining spoon and put it into a shallow greased dish. While you're doing this let the water in which the fennel was cooked boil away vigorously until it has reduced to just a couple of tablespoons or so of well-flavoured liquid. Pour this liquid over the fennel, then dot with the butter, grind some pepper over the top and finally sprinkle with the grated cheese. Bake the fennel, uncovered, for 20–30 minutes, until it's heated through and golden brown on top.

The cheese in this dish adds protein of course and so makes it useful for serving when you want to increase the food value of a meal – you could use more cheese if you want to – 125 g (4 oz) or even 175 g (6 oz).

HARICOT BEANS WITH APPLES   GERMANY

You might think this is an unlikely combination, but it works well. The apples collapse, bathing the beans in a soft sweet-sour sauce and making this an ideal mixture for serving with a dish which would normally require an apple sauce. The recipe can also be made with pears but I think it's nicest with apples. Obviously with the protein-rich beans it's useful for serving with a low-protein main dish. I like it with the crisp German potato cakes or the Swiss *rösti*.

225 g (8 oz) haricot beans	2 tablespoons caster sugar
450 g (1 lb) cooking apples	Sea salt
50 g (2 oz) butter or margarine	Freshly ground black pepper

Serves 4

Cover the beans with plenty of cold water and leave them to soak for several hours or overnight. Then drain off the water and rinse the beans under cold running water; put them into a large saucepan, cover them generously with cold water and simmer gently until they're tender – about 1 hour. Drain off the cooking liquor – it won't be needed for this recipe but as it's nutritious it's worth keeping for soups or sauces.

Peel, core and dice the apples. Melt the fat in a fairly large saucepan and fry the apples gently in it, without browning, until they're soft. Then add the beans and cook gently until they're heated through. Stir in the sugar and salt and pepper to taste.

MUSHROOMS IN SOURED CREAM   FINLAND

In Finland and Sweden whole families go into the woods in the autumn to gather baskets of fresh earthy-smelling mushrooms and they have quite a number of different ways of cooking them. This is one of the simplest but it makes a luxurious vegetable dish to go with a plainer main course, or it can be served as a delicious starter, in little individual dishes, with fingers of hot toast.

1 medium onion	150 ml (5 fl oz) carton
450 g (1 lb) mushrooms –	soured cream
field ones if you have them,	Sea salt
or else button ones	Freshly ground black pepper
25 g (1 oz) butter	Fresh parsley

Serves 2–3 as a vegetable, 4–6 as a starter

Peel and finely chop the onion; wash the mushrooms. If you're using wild mushrooms, remove the stalk and peel off the skin – this is not necessary with cultivated mushrooms. Cut the mushrooms into even-sized pieces. Melt the butter in a fairly large saucepan and fry the onion, without browning, for about 5 minutes, then add the prepared mushrooms and cook for a further 4–5 minutes until they are tender. If they make a lot of liquid boil them vigorously for a minute or two without a lid on the saucepan to evaporate it. Then stir in the soured cream and salt and pepper and heat through gently. Spoon at once into a warmed dish or individual containers and sprinkle with chopped parsley.

SPICY OKRA INDIA

You can sometimes get okra in Indian shops where it may be called *bhindi* or ladies' fingers. It's an intriguing vegetable, a plump green pod which has a soft, glutinous texture and delicate flavour when it's cooked. You can usually get canned okra at specialist food shops and delicatessens. Prepared like this it's nice as an accompaniment to curries or Caribbean rice dishes.

225 g (½ lb) fresh okra; or
   425 g (15 oz) can okra in
   brine
1 medium onion, peeled and
   chopped
25 g (1 oz) butter
225 g (8 oz) can tomatoes

1 garlic clove, peeled and
   crushed
2 teaspoons ground coriander
3 teaspoons garam masala
Sea salt
Freshly ground black pepper
2 teaspoons lemon juice

Serves 4

Top and tail the fresh okra or drain off the liquid if you're using the canned variety. Fry the onion in the butter for about 10 minutes until it's soft and golden, then add the tomatoes, garlic, coriander, garam masala and a little salt – not too much if you're using canned okra. Bring up to the boil then put in the okra and let it simmer gently for 15–20 minutes (until it's tender) if it's fresh, or about 5 minutes for canned. Check the seasoning and add more salt if necessary and a little lemon juice to taste.

CREAMED ONIONS AND PEAS   USA

An American friend gave me the recipe for this creamy vegetable dish which she serves her family at Thanksgiving. It's useful for serving when you want to add extra protein to a meal.

350 g (12 oz) baby onions –
   the type sold for pickling
Sea salt
450 g (1 lb) frozen peas
40 g (1½ oz) butter

40 g (1½ oz) flour
400 ml (¾ pint) milk
Freshly ground black pepper
Nutmeg
Ground cloves

Serves 6

Peel the onions with a small sharp, pointed knife then boil them in a little salted water for 15–20 minutes until they're almost tender; drain them, reserving the liquid. De-frost the peas by putting them in a colander and rinsing them under hot water.

Melt the butter in a large saucepan and add the flour; cook for a minute or two then stir in the milk in three batches, over a high heat, stirring each time until the mixture is smooth before adding more. When all the milk has been incorporated and you have a smooth sauce taste it and season with salt, pepper, some grated nutmeg and a pinch of ground cloves. Carefully stir in the onions and peas and cook gently for 5 minutes to heat them through. Serve at once.

SUGAR-GLAZED PARSNIPS   FRANCE

This French way of cooking parsnips gently with butter, sugar and just a little liquid leaves them glistening in a buttery syrup which enhances their natural sweetness and makes them delicious. You can cook other root vegetables besides parsnips in this way: carrots, turnips and swedes are all good and so are sweet potatoes.

700 g (1½ lb) parsnips	1 tablespoon soft brown sugar
175 ml (6 fl oz) water or stock	½ teaspoon sea salt
25 g (1 oz) butter	Freshly ground black pepper

Serves 4

Peel the parsnips and cut them into small even-sized pieces, discarding the central 'core' if it is at all tough, though it should be all right if the parsnips are small. Put the parsnips into a heavy-based saucepan with the liquid, butter, sugar, salt and a grinding of black pepper, cover with a lid and simmer over a gentle heat for about 20 minutes until the pieces of parsnip are tender and the liquid reduced to a syrupy glaze.

PEAS BRAISED WITH LETTUCE FRANCE

If you can get fresh young peas they are superb cooked like this:
sweet, tender and juicy. But it's also a marvellous way of making
frozen peas taste really good – and it's so simple to do.

450 g (1 lb) frozen peas or
    900 g (2 lb) fresh peas
About 6 outer lettuce leaves
25 g (1 oz) butter

2–3 sprigs of mint or parsley
    if available
½ teaspoon sea salt
½ teaspoon caster sugar

Serves 4

Put the frozen peas into a colander and run them under the hot
tap to rinse off the ice. Or, if you're using fresh peas, shell them
then rinse them in cold water. Wash the lettuce leaves then tear
them roughly and put them in a heavy-based saucepan. Put the
peas in on top, then the butter, in pieces, and the mint or parsley,
salt and sugar. Cover the saucepan with a lid and set it over a
moderate heat; when you hear it start to bubble turn the heat
down a bit and let it cook gently until the peas are tender – 5
minutes for frozen peas, 15–20 minutes for fresh. Remove the
parsley or mint sprigs before serving.

I find you don't need to add any water if the lettuce leaves are
freshly washed when they're put into the saucepan and they
really give the peas a lovely flavour. You can also add some
spring onions – just the white part – to make a pleasant variation.

POTATOES ANNA FRANCE

This is another useful potato dish which will cook slowly in the
oven and won't spoil. It's rather like the creamy potato dish,
gratin dauphinoise, except that it's turned out like a cake for
serving. You don't have to add cheese, but I often do because it
improves the flavour and increases the protein content of the

dish making it useful to serve with something like ratatouille, making a complete meal.

50 g (2 oz) butter	Salt and pepper
700 g (1½ lb) waxy potatoes such as Desirée	Fresh parsley
150 g (6 oz) grated cheese (optional)	

Serves 4–6

First line an 18 cm (7 in) cake tin by pressing a piece of foil into the base, extending it up the sides a little. Set the oven to 160°C (325°F), gas mark 3.

Melt the butter in a small saucepan, then use some of it to brush the inside of the foil-lined cake tin. Peel the potatoes, then slice them into thin rounds using a mandolin or the slicing edge of a grater. Put the rounds into a colander and rinse them thoroughly under cold water, then drain them and pat them dry with a clean cloth. Arrange a layer of potato in the base of the tin then sprinkle it with some of the grated cheese and a little salt and pepper; then add another layer of potato and continue in this way until it is all used up, ending with a generous layer of grated cheese. Pour the remaining butter over the top and cover with foil. Bake in the oven for about 2 hours, or until the potato can be pierced easily with the point of a knife. Pour off any excess butter, then slip a knife round the sides of the tin to loosen the potato. Invert the tin over a warmed plate and turn the potato out. Remove the foil. Sprinkle a little chopped parsley over the top of the potato.

BAKED POTATOES   GREAT BRITAIN

There are two ways of doing baked potatoes. You can rub the skins with fat or oil before you bake them, which makes the skin soft and flavoursome; or you can just wash them, prick them and bake them as they are (with the skins still wet), in a hot oven, and this way the skins will get lovely and crisp and crunchy. So you can use one method or the other depending on what people prefer and which goes best with the particular meal you're making.

4 medium unblemished   A little oil or butter if liked
   potatoes – about 175 g (6 oz)
   each

Serves 4

Set the oven to 230°C (450°F), gas mark 8. Scrub the potatoes and cut out any blemishes if necessary. Make two or three small cuts or fork pricks on each potato to allow the steam to escape. Rub each potato in a little oil or butter if you're using this, then put them in a baking tin and place them in the oven. Bake the potatoes for 1–1¼ hours until they feel tender when squeezed slightly. Serve them at once, particularly if you want them crisp.

I find the skins get soft if you try to keep the potatoes waiting and it's no good reducing the oven heat – they have to remain at this high temperature to retain their crispness. If you're going to have to keep them waiting it's best to do the soft-skinned variety. These can be cooked at a lower temperature, too, if more convenient – anything from 160°C (325°F), gas mark 3 is all right but of course then they take longer to cook.

Baked potatoes can really make the basis of a simple meal. Of course they're delicious served with grated cheese and a bowl of mixed salad, or you can make quite a festive meal by offering a choice of salads and several different toppings for the potatoes such as *hummus* and the soured cream dip or the goat cheese and herb spread, and bowls of different-coloured grated cheeses – a white one, such as Wensleydale, with for instance orange Leicester and golden Cheddar as well as cottage cheese.

POTATOES BAKED WITH CREAM FRANCE

In this dish, *gratin dauphinoise,* potatoes are sliced very thinly, layered in a shallow casserole with cream and butter and baked in a slow oven until they're meltingly tender. I find it a useful dish for entertaining because it doesn't need any last-minute attention and will keep warm in the oven for a long time without spoiling.

If you want to increase the protein content of a meal you can add some layers of grated cheese, preferably Gruyère, but I think the flavour is better without. Incidentally you can make a nice economical family version by using creamy milk instead of the single cream and my own favourite but unauthentic variation is to substitute tomato juice for the cream. This gives a tasty, less rich result which is very useful for a meal when you want plainly cooked potatoes to contrast with a creamy first course or pudding.

1 garlic clove, peeled and halved	Sea salt
25 g (1 oz) butter	Freshly ground black pepper
700 g (1½ lb) waxy potatoes – the red-skinned Desirée are good	Nutmeg
	275 ml (10 fl oz) single cream

Serves 4–6

First prepare a shallow ovenproof dish by rubbing the inside with the cut clove of garlic then greasing it generously with about half the butter. Set the oven to 160°C (325°F), gas mark 3.

Next peel the potatoes, then slice them very finely, using a mandolin or the slicing edge of a grater. Put the potato slices into a colander and rinse them thoroughly under the cold tap to remove some of the starch; pat them dry on kitchen paper or a tea-towel. Arrange a layer of the potato slices in the prepared dish, season with salt, pepper and a little grating of nutmeg, then add another layer of potato slices, continuing in this way

124

until all the potato is used. Pour the cream evenly over the top and dot with the remaining butter. Cover with a piece of foil and bake in the preheated oven for 1½–2 hours, until the potatoes feel tender when pierced with the point of a knife – sometimes this takes the full two hours so you need to allow this amount of time when planning the meal. Remove the foil and serve the potatoes straight from the dish.

Usually I find I'm baking this dish in the oven with other things and so have to compromise a little over the temperature; it's all right at a hotter temperature if it's near the bottom of the oven.

NEW POTATOES BAKED IN BUTTER NORWAY

This is such an easy way to cook new potatoes but it really seems to conserve their delicate flavour and they come out tender and buttery. In Norway they would probably be garnished with a sprinkling of chopped fresh dill, which is a very popular flavouring in Scandinavia, but chopped parsley or chives will do just as well.

700 g (1½ lb) baby new potatoes – try to choose ones that are all the same size, the smaller the better

40 g (1½ oz) butter
1 teaspoon sea salt
Freshly ground black pepper
Fresh dill, parsley or chives

Serves 4

Set the oven to 160°C (325°F), gas mark 3. Scrape the potatoes or just scrub them thoroughly and leave the skins on. Put them into an ovenproof casserole with the butter, salt and a little grinding of black pepper. Cover the casserole and place it in the oven for about 45 minutes, or until the potatoes are tender when pierced with a sharp knife. Serve the potatoes sprinkled with chopped herbs.

If you want to cook something else in the oven and need to have it hotter, I find the potatoes are all right if they're put near the bottom.

ROAST POTATOES   GREAT BRITAIN

Quite a number of vegetarian dishes have a fairly soft consistency and so I think need to be served with something crisp. These crunchy golden potatoes are a popular and delicious way of providing that textural contrast.

900 g (2 lb) potatoes   Vegetable oil – I like corn oil
Sea salt   best for this

Serves 4

Set the oven to 220°C (425°F), gas mark 7. Peel the potatoes and cut them into even-sized pieces. With medium-sized potatoes I usually cut them into about four pieces as I think it's nicer to have two or three small crisp potatoes than one larger one. Cook the potatoes in boiling, salted water for 5–6 minutes, then drain them thoroughly.

While the potatoes are boiling put the oil in the oven to heat: pour about 6 mm (¼ in) corn oil into a roasting tin and place it towards the top of the oven. Put the hot, drained potatoes into the hot oil – if the oil is really hot enough it should hiss and splutter as they go in. Turn the potatoes over in the oil so that they get well coated in it then put the tin back in the oven. After about 25–30 minutes have a look at the potatoes and if they're nice and golden underneath turn them over to give the other side a chance to crisp. I find they take about 45 minutes. If they seem to be racing along and you're afraid they'll be done before you're ready, turn the oven down to 160°C (325°F), gas mark 3 and this

will keep them in good condition until you're ready. Drain the
potatoes with a perforated spoon and serve them in a hot dish.

PUMPKIN BAKED WITH BUTTER AND GARLIC

FRANCE

Pumpkins are a vegetable I find difficult to resist. I don't know
whether it's something to do with the time of the year and the
magic of Hallowe'en, or whether it's their glorious warm apricot
colour and pretty rounded shape, but I always seem to end up
buying one. This is my favourite way of cooking pumpkin as a
vegetable (it's also good for vegetable marrow).

700 g (1½ lb) pumpkin or
  vegetable marrow, weighed
  after skin and seeds have
  been removed
1 large garlic clove or 2
  small ones

Sea salt
50 g (2 oz) butter
Freshly ground black pepper

Serves 4

Set the oven to 180°C (350°F), gas mark 4. Cut the pumpkin or
marrow into smallish even-sized pieces. Peel the garlic and
crush it into a paste with a little salt, then mix it with the butter.
Use half this garlic butter to grease an ovenproof dish generously,
then put in the pumpkin or marrow and top with the remaining
butter and a good grinding of black pepper. Cover and bake in
the oven for about 40 minutes or until the pumpkin or marrow
is tender, stirring it once or twice during the cooking so that the
butter gets to all the pieces.

STEWED RED CABBAGE

GERMANY

This is a useful vegetable dish because you can more or less forget it while it cooks. It doesn't need any last minute attention; it turns out moist and juicy so you don't need gravy and it can also be reheated if necessary and still tastes good. It's a lovely warming dish for winter but it's also good cold, as a salad.

There are similar recipes for red cabbage in many other European countries and in Scandinavia. In France chestnuts are sometimes added and I've given a recipe for this delicious variation in the stews and casseroles section of the book. In Russia the red cabbage might be served with soured cream which is a lovely addition and in Denmark red cabbage is part of the traditional Christmas feast.

700 g (1½ lb) red cabbage
2 large onions
2 large cooking apples
3 tablespoons oil

50 g (2 oz) raisins or sultanas
1 tablespoon sea salt
1 tablespoon brown sugar
1–2 tablespoons lemon juice

· *Serves 6*

Prepare the cabbage by shredding it fairly finely with a sharp knife, discarding the hard core. Put the cabbage into a large saucepan, cover it with cold water and bring it up to the boil then take it off the heat and turn it into a colander to drain.

Meanwhile peel and chop the onions and apples and fry them lightly in a large saucepan for 5–10 minutes. Add the cabbage together with the raisins or sultanas, salt, sugar and lemon juice. Stir well so that the cabbage gets coated with the oil and everything gets mixed together, then put a lid on the saucepan and leave the cabbage to cook very gently for 1½ hours, stirring from time to time, until it's very tender. Or you can put the cabbage into an ovenproof casserole, cover with a lid and bake it in the oven, at 160°C (325°F), gas mark 3, for about 2 hours.

You can make the cabbage spicier if you want to by adding

128

some cinnamon, caraway seeds or cloves to the basic mixture – lots of variations are possible.

SALSIFY WITH PARSLEY, BUTTER AND LEMON

Salsify – and its close relative, scorzonera – look like long, rather dirty roots when you see them in the shops, but when they're peeled and cooked they have a most delicate flavour which I think makes them ideal as a hot first course. They're also nice served in a well-flavoured cheesy sauce and baked in little individual dishes; or mixed with a good vinaigrette while still warm and served cold as a first course or salad.

1 kilo (2¼ lb) salsify or scorzonera – this might seem a lot but you lose a great deal in peeling	Sea salt
	25 g (1 oz) butter
	2 tablespoons chopped fresh parsley
Lemon juice	Freshly ground black pepper

Serves 4–6

Peel the roots, keeping them under cold water to preserve the colour. Cut them into 2·5 cm (1 in) pieces and put them straight into a bowl of cold water with a tablespoonful of lemon juice, again to help keep them white. When they're all prepared, bring 2·5 cm (1 in) of salted water to the boil in a large saucepan and cook them for about 10 minutes, or until just tender.

Drain and add the butter, a tablespoonful of lemon juice, the parsley and salt and pepper to taste. Heat gently to melt the butter then serve at once. Some thinly sliced wholewheat bread and butter is nice with it.

CREAMED SPINACH

SWEDEN

People who don't normally like spinach might enjoy it done this way because the creamy sauce takes off the acidity and makes it less sharp-tasting. This is a useful dish for when you want to add protein to a meal; you could increase the protein content further by garnishing the creamy spinach with chopped hardboiled egg, which is the Finnish way of serving it.

450 g (1 lb) spinach	Sea salt
25 g (1 oz) butter	Freshly ground black pepper
25 g (1 oz) flour	Nutmeg
275 ml (½ pint) milk	

Serves 4

Wash the spinach very thoroughly: I find the easiest way to do this is to put it into a big bowl full of cold water and swish it round with my hands, then take it out and repeat the process twice with fresh water each time. Put the spinach into a large saucepan. If you have just washed it you won't need to put any water in the saucepan as the spinach will be wet enough not to burn. Cook the spinach over a moderate heat. Have a lid on the saucepan but keep pushing the spinach down into the sauce-pan with a fish slice, chopping it a bit as it gets softer. It will take about 10 minutes to get really tender. Drain the spinach very well – the easiest way is to turn it into a colander and press it with a spoon to squeeze out all the liquid.

While the spinach is cooking make a sauce. Melt the butter in a medium-sized saucepan and add the flour, cook for a minute or two without browning then add a third of the milk and stir over a high heat until the mixture is thick and smooth; repeat with the rest of the milk, adding it in two batches. When all the milk is in and the sauce is thick and smooth take it off the heat and season it with salt, pepper and some grated nutmeg.

Mix the sauce with the spinach and check the seasoning;

you'll probably need to add some more. I think spinach needs plenty of pepper. Reheat the mixture gently, stirring all the time.

BAKED CREAMED SWEDES SWEDEN

This is a useful vegetable dish because you can get it ready in advance and just heat it through in the oven when you want it. The crunchy breadcrumb topping contrasts well with the soft creamy swede.

900 g (2 lb swede)	Freshly ground black pepper
25 g (1 oz) butter	Nutmeg
2 tablespoons creamy milk	Soft breadcrumbs
Sea salt	A little extra butter

Serves 4

Peel the swede and cut it into even-sized pieces. Put the pieces into a large saucepan, almost cover them with cold water and then cook gently, with a lid on the saucepan, until tender. Drain off all the water, then return the saucepan to the heat for a minute or two to dry the swede a little. Mash the swede until it's smooth, adding the butter, milk and seasoning and beating well. Lightly grease an ovenproof dish – a shallow one is best as it gives you plenty of crispy topping – and spoon the swede mixture into it, smoothing the surface.

Sprinkle the top fairly generously with soft crumbs and dot with a few little pieces of butter. All this can be done in advance; before the meal bake the casserole in a moderate oven – 180°C (350°F), gas mark 4 – for about 40 minutes, until the inside is heated through and the top golden brown and crisp.

GLAZED SWEET POTATOES

USA

You can sometimes find sweet potatoes at the greengrocer's. They look like large ordinary red-skinned potatoes and have a sweet, chestnutty flavour which I love. You can prick them and bake them in the oven like a jacket potato; par-boil and roast them as you would ordinary potatoes or glaze them as in this American recipe. This brings out the sweetness of the potatoes in a delicious way. Done like this they're good with Caribbean dishes and with the sort of dishes which you'd normally serve with redcurrant jelly or a sweet chutney. They're also very nice just on their own, with some crisp salad.

700 g (1½ lb) sweet potatoes –
  if they're very large the
  greengrocer may sell you a
  piece of potato

25 g (1 oz) butter
25 g (1 oz) brown sugar
2 tablespoons lemon juice
Sea salt

Serves 4

Scrub the potatoes, cut them into even-sized pieces then put them in a saucepan, cover with water and boil gently until tender – about 15–20 minutes. Drain them and peel off the skins. Set the oven to 200°C (400°F), gas mark 6. Use half the butter to grease a shallow ovenproof dish generously; then arrange the potato pieces in the dish and sprinkle them with the sugar, lemon juice and a little salt, dot with the remaining butter and place them, uncovered, in the oven. Bake them for 40–50 minutes, until they're golden brown and glazed, turning them over once or twice during the cooking time.

Vegetable Bakes, Stews and Casseroles

There are some very colourful and delicious mixtures in this section from quite a number of different countries ranging from Great Britain, France, Portugal and Italy to Russia, Hungary and Rumania. Some of these recipes were really originally intended for serving as an accompaniment to meat, but I think they are substantial and delicious enough to be main dishes in their own right with a side salad or cooked vegetables and rice or potatoes.

You will notice that a number of the dishes – the red cabbage and chestnut casserole, ratatouille, the red peppers with tomatoes and onions and the mixed vegetable stew – while being colourful and delicious, don't contain protein, so you need to introduce this into the meal. One way is to serve these stews with fluffy brown rice which has had some cheese or crunchy nuts or sunflower seeds forked into it; alternatively potatoes Anna made with layers of cheese in it is good or you could of course serve a protein starter or pudding, as I've suggested in the section on menu planning. I've also given suggestions with each individual recipe.

ASPARAGUS PUDDING   ITALY

This savoury pudding is called a *sformato* in Italy and is a cross
between a soufflé and a savoury loaf. I think it's best to serve it
straight from the dish and it's nice with something crisp – hot
garlic bread if you're serving it as a first course, triangles of fried
bread or crunchy golden roast potatoes and a good tomato sauce
for a main course.

50 g (2 oz) butter	3 eggs
50 g (2 oz) flour	Two 300 g (10½ oz) cans cut
275 ml (½ pint) milk	green asparagus
2–3 tablespoons grated	1 tablespoon chopped fresh
Parmesan cheese	parsley
Sea salt	Triangles of fried bread
Freshly ground black pepper	

Serves 4 as a main dish, 6 as a starter

Set the oven to 180°C (350°F), gas mark 4. Make a sauce: melt
the butter and stir in the flour; when it's blended add the milk in
three batches, keeping the heat up high and stirring well each
time until the mixture thickens before adding any more. Take the
saucepan off the heat and add the grated Parmesan cheese and
salt and pepper to taste.

Whisk the eggs. Drain the asparagus – you won't need the
liquid for this recipe. Mix the eggs into the sauce then gently stir
in the asparagus and parsley. Check the seasoning, then pour the
mixture into a lightly greased shallow ovenproof dish. Put the
dish into a baking tin containing about 2·5 cm (1 in) of very hot
water and place it in the centre of the oven. Bake for about 1 hour
or until the mixture is set and serve with triangles of fried bread.

AUBERGINE BAKE   ITALY

I love aubergines, with their shiny purple skins and strange subtle flavour, and this Italian dish, *parmigiana*, is one of my favourite ways of cooking them. With crusty bread and a green salad it makes a good lunch or supper, or with creamy mashed potatoes or fluffy brown rice and a cooked green vegetable it is substantial enough to make a main meal.

450 g (1 lb) aubergines
Sea salt
Vegetable oil
450 g (1 lb) onions, peeled
  and sliced
1 glass red wine – you can
  leave this out but it's lovely
  if you've got it
3 large garlic cloves, peeled
  and crushed

792 g (1 lb 12 oz) can
  tomatoes
Freshly ground black pepper
175 g (6 oz) cheese – sliced
  mozzarella plus some
  grated Parmesan if you
  want to be really authentic
  but Cheshire or Lancashire
  are a good cheaper
  substitute

Serves 4

Wash the aubergines and slice them thinly, discarding stalk ends. Put the slices into a colander and sprinkle them with salt. Place a plate and weight on top and leave for half an hour for the bitter juices to be drawn out. Then wash the slices under cold water and pat them dry. Preheat the oven to 180 C (350 F), gas mark 4.

Heat about 4 tablespoons of oil in a large saucepan and fry the onions for about 10 minutes until they're softened but not brown, then remove from the heat and stir in the wine, if you're using it, and the garlic and tomatoes. Season with salt and pepper. Heat some more oil in a frying pan and quickly fry the aubergine slices until they're soft and lightly browned – you may have to do this in two or more batches. Drain the aubergines then lay half of them in the base of a shallow ovenproof dish. Spread with half the tomato mixture, then with half the cheese. Repeat the layers,

136

ending with grated cheese, then bake it for about 1½ hours until crisp, golden brown and bubbly. Serve immediately.

CAULIFLOWER, EGG AND POTATO BAKE

In Russia soured cream would probably be used for this bake but as this makes it both expensive and rather rich I use a well-flavoured cheese sauce instead, and the result is a filling dish rather like a substantial cauliflower cheese. If you don't like eggs you could put in a layer of sliced fried mushrooms instead – you'll need about 225 g (8 oz).

700 g (1½ lb) even-sized
  smallish potatoes
Sea salt
1 medium-sized
  cauliflower

850 ml (1½ pints) cheese sauce
6 hardboiled eggs, sliced
Dried crumbs
A little butter for
  topping

Serves 4–6

Scrub the potatoes then cook them in their skins in boiling salted water until they're tender; drain and cool them, then slip off the skins with a sharp knife. (Cooking the potatoes in their skins like this makes a big difference to the flavour.) Cut the potatoes into slices. Wash the cauliflower, break it into even-sized sprigs and cook these in a little boiling salted water for about 7 minutes until they're just tender; drain well. Set the oven to 190 C (375 F), gas mark 5.

Grease a large shallow ovenproof dish with butter, then place a layer of the potato slices in the base, followed by some of the sauce, then the cauliflower and the egg slices, then some more sauce. Continue like this until everything has been used, ending if possible with layers of potato and sauce. Sprinkle the top with dried crumbs, dot with a little butter and bake for about 50 minutes, until heated through and golden brown on top.

All this needs as an accompaniment is some lightly cooked

greens – little firm sprouts are ideal, or some buttered cabbage or spinach.

CHOP SUEY   CHINA

Although the list of ingredients always makes this dish look rather daunting it's actually very easy to make. You get all the preparation done in advance so you only have to cook the vegetables quickly at the last minute.

1 onion
1 garlic clove
1 piece of fresh root ginger, about 2·5 cm (1 in) if possible; otherwise use ½ teaspoon ground ginger
225 g (8 oz) fresh or canned bean sprouts
125 g (4 oz) button mushrooms
1 small pepper, preferably red
432 g (15½ oz) can sliced pineapple in its own juice

225 g (8 oz) can wheat protein from health shops or Chinese stores
1 teaspoon soy sauce
1 tablespoon tomato ketchup
1 teaspoon sugar
1 tablespoon cheap sherry
2 tablespoons water
1 egg
Sea salt
A little oil

Serves 4

Peel and chop the onion; peel and crush the garlic, peel and grate the ginger. Wash the bean sprouts if fresh. Wash and slice the mushrooms and the pepper. discarding the seeds from the pepper. Drain the pineapple and the wheat protein; cut both into small pieces. In a cup mix together the soy sauce, tomato ketchup, sugar, sherry and water. Break the egg into a bowl and whisk it with a little salt.

When you're ready to make the meal, heat 2 tablespoons of oil in a large saucepan and fry the onion for 5 minutes, then stir in the garlic and ginger and cook for a few seconds before adding the bean sprouts, mushrooms, pepper, pineapple and wheat protein. Stir and fry over quite a high heat for about 2 minutes, then add the mixture from the cup and stir well. Leave this to cook for just a minute or so while you quickly make an omelette with the beaten egg. Keep the omelette flat. To serve the chop suey pile it up on a hot dish and lay the omelette on top.

Serve with lots of hot, well-cooked rice and some other Chinese dishes if you like.

GREEN PEPPER AND TOMATO STEW   HUNGARY

This spicy Hungarian stew, called *Lecso*, is rather similar to the Italian *peperonata* but it's made with green peppers and has a generous seasoning of paprika. You can serve it Hungarian style with a fried egg on top, but I think it's nicer with fluffy brown rice or warm crusty bread and soft cheese.

450 g (1 lb) green peppers,
   de-seeded and roughly
   chopped
2 medium onions
3 tablespoons vegetable oil

2 garlic cloves, crushed
2 tablespoons paprika
425 g (15 oz) can tomatoes
Salt and pepper

Serves 4

Slice the peppers into even-sized pieces, discarding seeds and stalk. Peel and chop the onions, then fry them in the oil in a large saucepan for about 5 minutes until golden brown. Remove from the heat and stir in the garlic, paprika, peppers, tomatoes and a seasoning of salt and pepper. Cover and cook gently for about 30 minutes until all the vegetables are tender. Check seasoning and serve.

KIDNEY BEANS WITH TOMATOES, ONIONS AND CUMIN

PORTUGAL

This Portuguese mixture of glossy red kidney beans, tomatoes, onions and cumin is spicy and delicious.

225 g (8 oz) red kidney beans
6 tablespoons olive oil
Sea salt
Freshly ground black pepper

1 large onion
2 teaspoons cumin seeds
225 g (8 oz) can tomatoes

Serves 4

Soak the kidney beans for 2–3 hours in plenty of cold water then drain and rinse them. Put them into a saucepan with enough cold water to come about 2·5 cm (1 in) above them and add 4 tablespoons of the olive oil. Simmer the beans gently, with a lid on the saucepan, until they're very tender and most of the water has gone. Season them with salt and pepper.

While the beans are cooking peel and chop the onion and fry it lightly in the remaining 2 tablespoons of oil. Cook the onion for about 10 minutes, until is is soft but not brown, then add the cumin seeds and stir them for a minute or two before putting in the tomatoes and some salt and pepper. Let the mixture simmer for about 10 minutes to give all the flavours a chance to blend, then take it off the heat and mix it gently with the beans. Reheat as necessary and serve with fluffy brown rice or warm wholewheat bread and a crisp green salad.

LENTIL AND RED PEPPER STEW

BULGARIA

You can make this stew with all lentils or all beans but I think with this half-and-half mixture you get the best of both; the lentils thicken the sauce and give it body while the beans supply extra interest and texture. One of the nicest things about this is its colour – it comes out a heart-warming vivid red and is really welcoming on a chilly day. Serve it with a dollop of soured cream, some crunchy jacket potatoes and a green side salad; or try creamy mashed potatoes and a cooked green vegetable.

125 g (4 oz) red lentils	1 litre (2 pints) unsalted stock
125 g (4 oz) haricot beans	or water
2 large onions	4 tablespoons tomato purée
700 g (1½ lb) red peppers –	Sea salt
about 4 large ones	Sugar
40 g (1½ oz) butter	

Serves 4

Put the lentils and beans into a bowl and cover generously with cold water; leave them to soak for several hours or overnight, then drain and rinse them.

Peel and chop the onions; slice the peppers, discarding the cores and seeds. Melt the butter in a large saucepan and fry the onion for about 10 minutes to soften it, then add the red peppers and cook for a further 4–5 minutes before stirring in the drained lentils and beans and the stock or water. Bring the mixture up to the boil and let it simmer gently, with a lid half on the saucepan, until the beans are tender – 1–1¼ hours.

Then mix in the tomato purée, and some salt and sugar to taste, as necessary. If the stew still seems a bit runny, turn up the heat and boil it for a few minutes without the lid on until it's the right consistency.

MIXED VEGETABLE STEW RUMANIA

Unlike so many stews, this one, *ghiveci*, does not have to contain meat but may be just a gloriously colourful mixture of every sort of vegetable you can find. You can really use whatever is available.

In the early autumn I make it with the first of the parsnips, celery and leeks and the last of the vegetable marrows and serve it with jacket potatoes, baked in a hot oven so they've got lovely crunchy skins. As the season progresses I replace the marrow with swede or turnip and at the end of the cooking time I may stir in some cooked butter beans, kidney beans or even, I'm ashamed to admit, some baked beans to make it more filling for the cold weather.

When preparing the vegetables try to cut them up into the sort of sizes which will make them all cook in about the same amount of time.

2 tablespoons oil
2 large onions, peeled and
 sliced
2 celery stalks, washed and
 chopped
225 g (8 oz) carrots, scraped
 and sliced
225 (8 oz) parsnips, peeled
 and diced
225 g (8 oz) vegetable marrow,
 de-seeded, peeled if
 necessary and cut into
 chunks
450 g (1 lb) leeks, washed,

trimmed and cut into
 2·5 cm (1 in) pieces
3 large tomatoes, skinned
 and quartered
450 g (1 lb) potatoes, peeled
 and cut into chunks
25 g (1 oz) flour
575 ml (1 pint) water or stock
2 tablespoons tomato purée
2 bay leaves
1 garlic clove, peeled and
 crushed
Sea salt
Freshly ground black pepper

Serves 4

Heat the oil in a large saucepan and fry the onion for 5 minutes, then put in the celery, carrots, parsnips, marrow, leeks, tomatoes and potatoes and cook for a further 4–5 minutes, turning them often to prevent sticking. Then sprinkle the flour over the vegetables and mix gently to distribute it. Pour in the water or stock, stirring, and add the tomato purée, bay leaves, garlic and a seasoning of salt and pepper. Bring the mixture up to the boil then turn the heat down and leave the stew to simmer very gently, with a lid on the saucepan, for about 25–30 minutes or until the potatoes and other vegetables are tender. Taste the mixture and add more seasoning if necessary.

I often serve this with a bowl of grated cheese or roasted sun-flower seeds (just sunflower seeds spread on a baking sheet and baked for about 10 minutes in a moderate oven) for people to help themselves and sprinkle over the top of their portion – but really it's very nice just as it is because it's delicately flavoured with all the vegetables. If you don't serve the cheese or sunflower seeds, though, you need to add protein to the meal, and I think the best way is to serve a pudding such as yoghurt, cheese cake or even *pashka* – or just finish with biscuits and cheese.

MUSHROOMS AND TOFU   CHINA

Tofu, or bean curd, is creamy white and extremely high in protein. It is sold in small squares in Chinese shops and other delicatessens. If you can't get it you could use a small can of wheat protein – available from health shops – for this recipe but the result won't be quite the same. If you can get dried Chinese mushrooms they give the dish an excellent flavour, but you can use ordinary fresh mushrooms instead.

6 dried Chinese mushrooms or use 125 g (4 oz) fresh mushrooms
8 squares of *tofu*
Vegetable oil for shallow frying – sesame oil if possible
1 onion, peeled and chopped
Garlic clove, peeled and crushed
1 piece of fresh root ginger

about 2·5 cm (1 in) long, peeled and grated
½ teaspoon soy sauce
½ teaspoon vegetarian stock powder or crumbled stock cube
2 tablespoons water or liquid drained from the dried mushrooms
50 g (2 oz) flaked almonds

Serves 2 or 4 with other Chinese dishes

If you're using dried mushrooms, rinse them under the tap then put them into a small bowl, cover them with boiling water and leave them for 1 hour. Drain the mushrooms, reserving the liquid.

Cut the mushrooms into pieces; if you're using fresh mushrooms wash and slice them. Cut the *tofu* into smallish cubes, heat a little oil in a large saucepan and fry the *tofu* quickly until it is lightly browned on all sides. Take it out of the oil and keep it warm. Heat a little more oil in the saucepan and fry the onions for about 7 minutes, then add the garlic, ginger and mushrooms and fry for about 2 minutes, until the mushrooms are just tender. Stir in the soy sauce, stock powder and water or mushroom liquid. Let the mixture bubble for a moment or two, then put in the *tofu* and cook gently for about 2 minutes, just to reheat the *tofu* and give it a chance to absorb the flavours of the sauce. Sprinkle the almonds over the mixture just before serving it.

Serve this with fluffy cooked rice and Chinese cabbage; or include it as part of a selection of Chinese dishes, adding chop suey and fried wheat protein in sweet and sour sauce as well.

PEASE PUDDING

GREAT BRITAIN

Pease pudding is one of the few traditional British dishes which are vegetarian. Mrs Beeton describes it as 'an exceedingly nice accompaniment to boiled beef' but I think it also makes a very good main dish in its own right. It's quick to make, high in fibre and protein, low in fat and cholesterol and very economical too. We like it with crisp roast potatoes, a vegetable such as sprouts, a savoury brown gravy and some mint or apple sauce which gives a pleasant sharpness that's just right with the sweet-tasting peas.

450 g (1 lb) yellow split peas
2 large onions
40 g (1 ½ oz) butter or
  margarine

Sea salt
Freshly ground black pepper

Serves 4

If possible soak the peas in cold water for a couple of hours or so this speeds up the cooking time – then drain and rinse them, put them into a large saucepan with a good covering of cold water and simmer them gently, with the lid half on the saucepan, until they're tender. I find the cooking time of split peas seems to vary quite a bit; sometimes they're done in 30 minutes, other times they can take as long as an hour. Watch the water level and add more if necessary as they cook; when they're done drain off any excess – they should be soft but not soggy.

While this is happening, peel and chop the onions and fry them gently in the butter until they're soft and golden – 10 minutes. Add the onion to the split peas and season with salt and pepper. You can serve the mixture straight away or keep it warm in a covered casserole in a low oven.

You can vary pease pudding in quite a few ways. It's nice with some grated lemon rind added, or some chopped marjoram or sage. Caraway, cumin and fennel seeds also go well with it – add them to the onion when it's nearly done – and a pinch of ground cloves is nice, too.

POTATO BAKE   HOLLAND

A simple savoury dish that's useful for children's suppers because it's quick to make and popular. It's nice with a juicy salad or with grilled tomatoes and a green vegetable. A parsley or tomato sauce goes well with it too.

900 g (2 lb) potatoes
25 g (1 oz) butter or vegetable margarine
25 g (1 oz) grated Parmesan cheese
125 g (4 oz) grated Edam cheese

2 eggs
275 ml ($\frac{1}{2}$ pint) top of the milk or creamy milk
Sea salt
Freshly ground black pepper

Serves 4

Set the oven to 190°C (375°F), gas mark 5. Peel the potatoes, cut

145

them into even-sized pieces and boil them in salted water until they're tender, then drain and mash them. Add the butter or margarine, the Parmesan cheese and half the Edam cheese and mix well. Beat together the eggs and milk and gradually add this to the potato mixture, stirring well. Season with salt and pepper. Spoon the mixture into a shallow ovenproof dish, scatter the remaining grated cheese on top and bake for 30–40 minutes, until slightly puffed up and golden brown.

POTATO AND MUSHROOM STEW WITH SOURED CREAM   HUNGARY

A Hungarian stew or *paprikas*, as it's called, doesn't always contain meat but can be based on vegetables, as in this version which makes a lovely vegetarian main dish. The protein can be supplied by serving a protein starter, side salad or pudding or by garnishing the *paprikas* with wedges of hardboiled eggs or grated cheese.

900 g (2 lb) potatoes	look for Hungarian 'rose'
1 medium onion	paprika
1 garlic clove	25 g (1 oz) flour
175 g (6 oz) button	400 ml (¾ pint) stock
mushrooms	Sea salt
3 tablespoons oil	Black pepper
1 tablespoon mild paprika –	150 ml (5 fl oz) soured cream
	or natural yoghurt

Serves 4

Peel the potatoes and cut them into even-sized chunks, peel and chop the onion, crush the garlic, wash the mushrooms and cut them into halves or quarters if necessary. Heat the oil in a large saucepan and fry the onion for about 5 minutes until golden, then stir in the garlic, potatoes, paprika and flour and cook for a further minute or two. Add the stock and bring up to the boil.

146

Put a lid on the saucepan and leave it over a gentle heat for about 20 minutes, until the potatoes are very nearly tender, then put in the mushrooms and cook for a further 3–4 minutes.

Put the soured cream or yoghurt into a small bowl and gradually add to it a ladleful of the liquid from the saucepan; mix well then pour this into the saucepan and heat gently until the mixture is very hot. Season to taste. Serve immediately.

RATATOUILLE
FRANCE

In the late summer when courgettes, aubergines, peppers and tomatoes are cheap and plentiful, ratatouille makes the basis of a delicious vegetarian meal. You can serve it with lots of plain fluffy brown rice and a crisp green salad with fresh herbs in it, with a protein starter like individual cheese soufflés or a pudding such as little coffee custards, ice cream or crisp wholewheat biscuits and Brie cheese.

450 g (1 lb) courgettes or marrow	2 large garlic cloves
	2 red peppers
450 g (1 lb) aubergines	4 tomatoes
Kitchen salt	Sea salt
2 large onions	Freshly ground
Olive oil or vegetable oil – or a mixture	black pepper
	Fresh parsley

Serves 4

Cut the courgettes or marrow and the aubergines into small dice. Put them into a colander and sprinkle with kitchen salt. Place a plate with a weight on it on top and leave for at least half an hour for any bitter liquids to be drawn out of the aubergines and excess moisture out of the courgettes.

Peel and slice the onions and fry them in a little oil in a big saucepan until they're beginning to get soft, then add the garlic. Slice the peppers and remove the seeds; add the sliced pepper to the saucepan together with the aubergine and courgette. Cook gently with a lid on the pan for about 30 minutes, then add the tomatoes, skinned and chopped, and cook for another 30 minutes. Season with salt and pepper and sprinkle with chopped parsley.

When marrows are good and cheap I quite often make this with double the amount of marrow and no aubergine.

RED CABBAGE AND CHESTNUT CASSEROLE
FRANCE

Real warming winter food this, a rich burgundy-coloured casserole of succulent red cabbage and sweet-tasting chestnuts cooked with butter, onions and red wine. It's lovely served as a main dish with jacket potatoes which have been split and filled with soured cream and chopped chives. If there's any over it's very good cold as a salad. I rather lazily tend to use dried chestnuts but you could use fresh ones. You'll need about 450 g (1 lb) for this recipe. Prepare them in the way I've described on page 31 and add them to the casserole with the wine and seasoning.

125 g (4 oz) dried chestnuts
1 large onion
50 g (2 oz) butter
700 g (1½ lb) red cabbage

275 ml (½ pint) cheap red wine
Sea salt
Freshly ground black pepper
Sugar

Serves 3–4

Cover the chestnuts with plenty of cold water and leave them to soak for several hours. After that cook them gently until they're tender – this will take 1–1½ hours and you'll need to watch the level of the water and probably add some more so that they don't burn dry. Drain the chestnuts.

Set the oven to 150°C (300°F), gas mark 2. Peel and chop the onion and fry it in the butter for 10 minutes; while it's cooking wash and shred the cabbage, then add this to the onion and turn it so that it gets coated with the butter. Stir in the chestnuts, wine and some salt and pepper. Bring the mixture up to the boil, then transfer it to an ovenproof casserole, cover with a lid and bake slowly for 2–3 hours, until the cabbage is very tender. Check the seasoning – you'll probably need to add more salt and pepper and some sugar to bring out the flavour.

This dish can be made in advance and reheated – in fact I think this actually improves the flavour – and it can also be cooked at the bottom of a hotter oven if you want to bake jacket potatoes at the same time.

RED KIDNEY BEAN STEW   BULGARIA

This warm-coloured stew is lovely with buttery brown rice, baked potatoes or creamy mashed potatoes and a lightly cooked green vegetable. For a short cut you can use two cans of red kidney beans; this makes it a very quick dish to make.

175 g (6 oz) dried red kidney beans	Sea salt
450 g (1 lb) onions	Freshly ground black pepper
50 g (2 oz) butter	Sugar
Two 425 g (15 oz) cans tomatoes	

Serves 4

Soak the kidney beans for 2–3 hours in plenty of cold water then drain and rinse them. Put the beans into a saucepan with a good covering of cold water, boil vigorously for 10 minutes, simmer them gently until they're tender, then drain.

While the beans are cooking peel and chop the onions and fry them in the butter in a good-sized saucepan for about 10 minutes until they're soft but not browned. Add the tomatoes and beans to the onions with a good seasoning of salt, pepper and a little sugar if necessary. Let the mixture simmer gently for 10–15 minutes, then serve.

RED PEPPERS WITH TOMATOES AND ONIONS ITALY

Although this Italian dish, *peperonata*, doesn't contain protein, you can build some nice meals around it. It's lovely served with rice, noodles or potatoes and protein can be introduced in the starter, side salad or pudding.

450 g (1 lb) red peppers	crushed in a little salt
450 g (1 lb) onions	(optional)
4 tablespoons oil	Sea salt
425 g (15 oz) can tomatoes	Freshly ground black pepper
1 garlic clove, peeled and	

Serves 4

Cut the peppers into even-sized pieces, discarding seeds, stalk and core. Peel and slice the onions.

Heat the oil in a large saucepan and fry the onions for about 5 minutes until they're beginning to soften, then add the peppers and cook for a couple of minutes more, stirring so that they all get coated with the fat. Mix in the tomatoes, garlic if you're using it and some salt and pepper. Let the mixture simmer gently for about 30 minutes, stirring it from time to time, until all the vegetables are tender.

Some people let it cook to an almost purée-like consistency, but personally I prefer not to cook it this long as I think the flavour is fresher and sweeter and the texture more interesting if it's slightly under-done.

SWEETCORN PUDDING USA

Really this is another of those dishes that's supposed to be served as an accompaniment to meat, but I think you'll agree it also makes a good main dish in its own right. I like to serve it with sprouts, gravy, roast potatoes and cranberry sauce – rather a bizarre-sounding combination, I know, but it works.

275 ml (½ pint) milk
25 g (1 oz) butter
125 g (4 oz) bread, weighed
  with the crusts removed
330 g (11½ oz) can sweetcorn
  kernels, drained
1 egg or 2 egg yolks

1 tablespoon chopped fresh
  parsley
½ teaspoon paprika
Sea salt
Freshly ground black pepper
A little grated cheese

Serves 3–4

Set the oven to 190°C (375°F), gas mark 5. Put the milk and butter into a saucepan and heat gently until the butter has melted. Remove from the heat and with your fingers crumble the bread into the milk – don't worry if there are some lumpy pieces. Leave on one side for a few minutes to allow the bread to soften, then mix it round and add the sweetcorn, egg, parsley, paprika and salt and pepper to taste. Spoon the mixture into a greased oven-proof dish and sprinkle with grated cheese. Bake the pudding for 35–40 minutes until set and golden brown.

TIAN FRANCE

This is a baked vegetable casserole, rather like a savoury loaf except that it is served from the dish. It takes its name from the earthenware casserole dish in which it is cooked in Provence and it can be made from any green vegetable, although spinach or chard are the most usual with courgettes sometimes added too. It can be served hot or cold. If you're having it hot, try it with crunchy roast potatoes, tomato sauce and a colourful vegetable such as carrots. Cold it's nice with some garlic mayonnaise, tomato salad and hot French bread.

175 g (6 oz) long-grain
brown rice

Just under 575 ml (1 pint)
water

Sea salt

450 g (1 lb) spinach

2 tablespoons olive oil

2–3 garlic cloves, peeled and
crushed

1 tablespoon chopped fresh
parsley

125 g (4 oz) grated cheese

2 eggs

Freshly ground black pepper

2–3 tablespoons dried crumbs

2–3 tablespoons grated
Parmesan cheese

2 tablespoons olive oil

Serves 4

Wash the rice then put it into the saucepan with the water and a teaspoonful of salt, bring it up to the boil then turn the heat down and leave the rice to cook very slowly, with a lid on the saucepan, for 40–45 minutes, until it's tender and all the liquid has been absorbed. (If there's still some water left in the saucepan just leave it to stand off the heat but with the lid on for 10–15 minutes, after which you should find it has been absorbed.)

Set the oven to 200 C (400 F), gas mark 6. Wash the spinach thoroughly in three changes of water, then chop it up – you can use the stalks too. Heat the olive oil in a large saucepan and put in the spinach; turn it in the hot oil for 2–3 minutes until it has softened slightly and is all glossy-looking from the oil. Take it off the heat and add the rice, garlic, parsley and grated cheese. Beat in the eggs and mix everything together, seasoning it with salt and a good grinding of pepper. Spoon the mixture into a shallow oven-proof dish and sprinkle the crumbs, Parmesan and olive oil on top. Bake without a lid for 30–40 minutes until it's puffed up and golden brown and crispy on top.

YELLOW SPLIT PEA PURÉE WITH VEGETABLES   GERMANY

In Germany this would probably be served as an accompaniment to meat, like the British pease pudding, but I think it makes a good main dish with jacket potatoes.

350 g (12 oz) yellow split peas
1 litre (1¾ pints) water
3 onions, sliced
2 carrots, sliced
1 leek, sliced
2 celery stalks, sliced

½ teaspoonful mint or
   marjoram
4 teaspoons lemon juice
Sea salt and freshly ground
   black pepper
50 g (2 oz) butter

Serves 4

Soak the split peas in cold water for an hour or two or overnight, then rinse them and put them into a pan with the water, half the sliced onion and all the other vegetables and the herbs and let it simmer gently until the split peas are soft and the vegetables tender – this takes 30–40 minutes – then sieve or liquidize. Add the lemon juice, season with salt and pepper and turn the mixture into a shallow heatproof dish. Set the oven to 180°C (350°F), gas mark 4 or preheat the grill, set fairly high. Fry the remaining onion in the butter until it's beginning to soften, then pour the onion and butter over the top of the split pea purée and put it into the oven for about 20–30 minutes or under the grill until the top is slightly crusted looking and the onion crisp and brown.

Stuffed Vegetables

I love stuffed vegetable dishes because they always look festive and special and I think they're ideal for entertaining. Some of them, particularly the aubergines *à la duxelles*, the stuffed aubergines in Béchamel sauce, the red cabbage stuffed with chestnuts, the stuffed courgette bake and the stuffed onions make good main courses. Others are more suitable for serving as a first course – I think the stuffed tomatoes and stuffed vine leaves are particularly good for this.

Some of these stuffed vegetables contain a fair amount of protein but others don't, so you need to look at the recipe and plan the meal accordingly. If you want to serve one of the low-protein stuffed vegetables you can add nourishment to the meal very simply by serving the vegetables with a well-flavoured cheese sauce or with the green salad with Gruyère cheese. Or of course you can have a protein-rich starter or pudding – *hummus* or the Middle Eastern bean pâté are particularly good with the Grecian recipes, with ground rice and rosewater pudding, yoghurt tart or honey cheese cake as suggestions for pudding; or for the French recipes, *coeurs à la crème* or little coffee custards; and coffee *ricotta* or ice cream after the Italian ones.

With the exception of the red cabbage, which needs a good deep saucepan or flameproof dish big enough to hold the whole cabbage, the stuffed vegetables need to be cooked in a large shallow ovenproof dish. I find one measuring about 28 cm × 18 cm (11 in × 7 in) is just right for recipes serving 4 people, while when I'm doing them for 6 people I use an oval Pyrex one measuring about 39 cm × 27 cm (15½ in × 10½ in). It looks vast and institutional when it's empty but it's just right and looks super when it's filled with delicious vegetables bursting with tasty stuffing. I've also seen some lovely large shallow French ovenproof dishes in deep muted shades and one of these would look even better.

155

STUFFED AUBERGINES IN BÉCHAMEL SAUCE GREECE

Really, minced meat should be used for this recipe and you might feel that the lentils I've suggested are rather a corruption. But as lentils are used so much in Middle Eastern cookery I don't think they're too far-fetched, and they do make a tasty and satisfying dish.

3 medium aubergines – about 700 g (1½ lb) in all
Kitchen salt
3–4 tablespoons oil
2 medium onions, peeled and chopped
3 tablespoons tomato purée
3 garlic cloves, peeled and crushed in a little salt
175 g (6 oz) split red lentils
225 ml (8 fl oz) water
2 tablespoons chopped fresh parsley

75 g (3 oz) grated cheese
Sea salt
Freshly ground black pepper
50 g (2 oz) grated cheese
A little sugar

For the sauce:
25 g (1 oz) butter
25 g (1 oz) flour
400 ml (¾ pint) milk
1 egg
Nutmeg

Serves 6

Cut the aubergines in half lengthwise then scoop out the centres to leave space for the stuffing and chop up the scooped-out flesh. Sprinkle the aubergine flesh and the inside of the skins with kitchen salt; leave for half an hour, then squeeze out the bitter brown juice, rinse the aubergine flesh and skins under the tap and dry. Heat 3 tablespoons of oil in a frying pan and fry the aubergine skins for about 5 minutes on each side to soften them; drain them and put into a shallow ovenproof dish. Set the oven to 180°C (350°F), gas mark 4. Fry the onion in the same saucepan, adding a little more oil if necessary; when it is soft but not brown – about 10 minutes – add the aubergine flesh, tomato purée, garlic, lentils and water and cook for about 20–30 minutes until the lentils are done. Remove from the heat, add the parsley and grated cheese and season carefully to taste. Divide the filling between the aubergine skins, piling it up well.

Make the Béchamel sauce: melt the butter in a saucepan and stir in the flour then add a third of the milk and stir over a high heat until the mixture is smooth and thick; repeat the process twice more using the rest of the milk. Remove from the heat and beat in the egg and salt, pepper and grated nutmeg to taste. Pour the sauce over and round the aubergines, sprinkle with the grated cheese and bake them in the oven for 35 minutes until they're tender and the sauce is bubbly and golden brown.

These aubergines are nice with a crisp herby green salad or a cooked green vegetable.

AUBERGINES STUFFED WITH CHEESE

YUGOSLAVIA

This is a simple but delicious way of serving aubergines. I think a tomato sauce goes well with them and also something crisp – triangles of toast or fried bread, for instance, or crunchy roast potatoes.

4 small/medium aubergines – about 700 g (1½ lb) in all
Sea salt
25 g (1 oz) butter
1 onion, peeled and finely chopped

175 g (6 oz) grated cheese
1 egg
1 tablespoon chopped fresh parsley
Freshly ground black pepper

Serves 4

Set the oven to 200°C (400°F), gas mark 6. Wash the aubergines and remove the stalk ends. Half fill a good-sized saucepan with cold water, add a teaspoonful of salt and bring up to the boil.

158

Cook the aubergines in the water for about 5 minutes, until they feel just barely tender when pierced with the point of a knife. Drain and cool the aubergines, then split them in half lengthways and scoop the flesh out into a bowl, leaving the skins intact.

Arrange the skins in a lightly greased shallow ovenproof dish. Mash the aubergine flesh with a fork, then stir in the onion, grated cheese, egg, parsley and salt and pepper to taste. Bake the aubergines for 30–40 minutes until they're golden brown.

STUFFED AUBERGINES À LA DUXELLES
FRANCE

If you chop up an onion and some mushrooms and cook them in a little butter until they make a thick, dry purée you have what the French call *duxelles*. It will keep in a screw top jar ready for flavouring soups and sauces, but in this recipe the whole batch is used to give the aubergines a rich mushroomy flavour.

This dish is nice served with a wine or tomato sauce, new potatoes or *gratin dauphinoise* and another vegetable. There isn't much protein in the aubergine mixture, though, so you really need to serve a protein-rich starter such as individual cheese soufflés, or round off the meal with a nourishing pudding like *coeurs à la crème* or little coffee custards.

450 g (1 lb) mushrooms
1 onion
25 g (1 oz) butter
2 medium aubergines
Sea salt
Oil
2 tablespoons chopped fresh parsley

225 g (8 oz) cottage cheese or low-fat quark
Freshly ground black pepper
50 g (2 oz) grated cheese, preferably Parmesan or a mixture of Parmesan and cheaper cooking cheese
50 g (2 oz) fine breadcrumbs

Serves 4

159

First prepare the *duxelles*: wash the mushrooms then chop them finely: peel and finely chop the onion. Put the chopped mushrooms and onion into a cloth and squeeze firmly to extract excess liquid – this can be saved and added to a soup or a sauce. Melt the butter in a large saucepan, then stir in the chopped mushroom and onion and fry, without a lid on the saucepan, until the mixture is thick, dry and purée-like – 15–20 minutes. Remove from the heat.

While the *duxelles* is cooking start preparing the aubergines: cut them in half lengthwise and scoop out the centres to form cavities for stuffing. Sprinkle the scooped-out aubergine and the insides of the skins with salt and leave them on one side for the bitter juices to be extracted. After about 30 minutes squeeze the liquid out of the aubergine, rinse it under cold water and pat dry.

Set the oven to 180°C (350°F), gas mark 4. Fry the aubergine skins on both sides in hot oil, then drain them and put them into a shallow ovenproof dish, ready for stuffing. Fry the scooped-out aubergine flesh in a couple of tablespoons of oil for about 5 minutes, then add the *duxelles*, chopped parsley, cottage cheese or quark and most of the cheese. Taste the mixture and season as necessary, then pile it into the prepared aubergine skins and sprinkle the tops with breadcrumbs and remaining grated cheese. Cover the dish with foil and bake for about 40 minutes, removing the foil for the last 10 minutes so that the crumbs get crisp.

STUFFED COURGETTE BAKE   SPAIN

In this dish courgettes are filled with a mixture of tomatoes, onion and garlic then baked in a well-flavoured cheese sauce. It's best to use fairly large courgettes as these hold the filling well.

4 medium/large courgettes –
about 700 g (1½ lb) in all
2 large onions
25 g (1 oz) butter
450 g (1 lb) tomatoes, skinned,
or a 425 g (15 oz) can
2 garlic cloves
Sea salt
Freshly ground black pepper

Serves 4

50 g (2 oz) grated cheese

For the sauce:
50 g (2 oz) butter
50 g (2 oz) flour
575 ml (1 pint) milk
50 g (2 oz) grated Parmesan or
strong tasting cheese

Set the oven to 190°C (375°F), gas mark 5. Peel the courgettes then cut them in half lengthways and scoop out the seeds – a teaspoon is good for this. Cook the courgettes in 1 cm (½ in) of boiling salted water for 5–10 minutes until they're just tender, but don't let them get soggy. Drain the courgettes very well and dry them lightly with kitchen paper or a clean cloth. Leave them on one side while you prepare the filling and make the sauce.

To make the filling, peel and chop the onions and fry them in the butter in a medium-sized saucepan for 10 minutes. Remove the seeds from the tomatoes and chop the flesh. If you're using canned tomatoes drain off the juice – you won't need it for this recipe. Peel the garlic and crush it in a little salt. Add the garlic to the onions, together with the tomatoes, and cook the mixture for a further 10–15 minutes until it is fairly thick and will hold its shape. Season with salt and pepper.

While the tomato mixture is cooking make the sauce. Melt the butter in a medium-sized saucepan and stir in the flour, cook for a moment or two, then pour in a third of the milk. Stir over a high heat until the milk is incorporated and the mixture has become very thick and smooth, then repeat with the rest of the milk, adding it in two instalments. When you have added all the milk and have a smooth sauce, take the saucepan off the heat and stir in the grated Parmesan cheese and salt and pepper to taste.

Pour half the sauce into a shallow ovenproof dish and arrange the courgette halves on top. Spoon the tomato mixture into the cavities in the courgettes, piling it up as necessary. Pour the remaining sauce over the courgettes, sprinkle the grated cheese on top and bake them just above the centre of the oven for about 40–45 minutes, until the mixture is bubbly and golden brown on top. Serve at once. They're nice with buttery new potatoes, rice or noodles and a green vegetable such as spinach, with a fresh fruity pudding to follow.

COURGETTES STUFFED WITH CHEESE AND ONION

CARIBBEAN

This is a simple dish that's quickly made but the combination of the tender courgettes and crisp cheese topping is delicious. It's a good recipe for slimmers if you cook the onions in the minimum of fat in a non-stick saucepan and use Edam cheese. On the other hand for a special occasion it's delicious with a couple of tablespoons of white wine added.

4 good-sized courgettes – about 175 g (6 oz) each	350 g (12 oz) grated cheese
	½ teaspoon dried thyme
50 g (2 oz) butter	Sea salt
2 large onions, peeled and chopped	Freshly ground black pepper
1 garlic clove, peeled and crushed	

Serves 4

Set the oven to 190°C (375°F), gas mark 5. Wash the courgettes thoroughly, then cut them in half lengthwise. Heat 5 cm (2 in) of water in a large saucepan and when it boils add the courgette halves and simmer them gently for about 3 minutes, just to soften them a little, then drain them well. Using a teaspoon,

162

scoop out the centre of the courgettes to leave a cavity for stuffing. Chop up the scooped-out courgette centre.

Melt the butter in a medium-sized saucepan and fry the onion for 5 minutes; then add the garlic and chopped courgette flesh and cook for a further 4–5 minutes. Remove the saucepan from the heat and stir in the grated cheese, thyme and seasoning to taste. Grease a shallow oblong dish and arrange the courgette halves in it. Divide the onion and cheese mixture between the courgette halves, arranging it in the cavities. Bake in the preheated oven for 20–30 minutes, until the courgettes are tender and the filling is golden and brown.

Serve with fresh tomato sauce. New potatoes and spinach or French beans go well with it.

STUFFED ONIONS   ITALY

Onions, macaroons, cheese and sultanas sound a very strange mixture but the combination of sweet and savoury really works well, like cheese and chutney or curry and banana. I like to use those big Spanish onions to make this when they come into the shops early in September.

4 large Spanish onions	50 g (2 oz) grated Parmesan
4 macaroons	cheese – or use strong cooking
75 g (3 oz) soft wholewheat	cheese
breadcrumbs	25–50 g (1–2 oz) sultanas
¼ teaspoon ground cinnamon	Sea salt
¼ teaspoon ground cloves	Freshly ground black pepper
¼ teaspoon grated nutmeg	15 g (½ oz) butter
2 eggs, beaten	

Serves 4

Rinse the onions but don't peel them. Put them into a large saucepan of water and simmer them for about 20 minutes, until

163

they feel tender when pierced with the point of a knife. (They should not be completely cooked through at this stage.) Drain the onions and let them get cool enough to handle, then remove the skins and root ends and cut the onions in half horizontally. Scoop out the centre of each half making a nice cavity for the stuffing and leaving three or four layers of onion. Arrange the onion halves in a greased shallow ovenproof dish.

Set the oven to 180°C (350°F), gas mark 4. Now make the stuffing. Chop the scooped-out onion fairly finely and put it into a bowl. Crush the macaroons – press them with a rolling pin or pop them into the liquidizer and blend for a moment or two. Add them to the onions, also the breadcrumbs, spices, eggs, cheese and sultanas and stir until everything is well mixed to a softish consistency. You might need to add a drop or two of milk but I usually find the natural juiciness of the onions together with the eggs sufficient. Season with salt and a good grinding of pepper then spoon the mixture into the onion cavities, piling them up. Put a piece of butter on top of each and bake them, uncovered, for 30 minutes.

Stuffed onions are good with a sharply flavoured cheese sauce, mashed potatoes and a cooked green vegetable.

STUFFED PEPPERS   SPAIN

In this recipe rice, mushrooms, onions and grated cheese are used to stuff peppers and then they're baked in a simple fresh tomato sauce. They're nice as a main course, served with a cooked vegetable and some buttery new potatoes.

125 g (4 oz) long-grain brown
   rice
275 ml ($\frac{1}{2}$ pint) water
Sea salt
2 medium green peppers
1 large onion, peeled and
   chopped
1 garlic clove, peeled and
   crushed in a little salt
4 tablespoons olive oil

125 g (4 oz) button
   mushrooms washed and
   finely sliced
1 teaspoon dried thyme
$\frac{1}{2}$ teaspoon mustard powder
2 teaspoons lemon juice
125 g (4 oz) grated cheese
Freshly ground black pepper
450 g (1 lb) tomatoes, peeled
   and chopped – or use a 425
   (15 oz) can

Serves 4

First cook the rice: put it into a heavy-based saucepan with
the water and a pinch of salt. Bring it up to the boil then turn
the heat down and let it cook very gently, with a lid on the
saucepan, for about 40 minutes, until the rice is tender and
has absorbed all the liquid. (The rice can be cooked well in
advance because it will keep for several days in the fridge.)

Set the oven to 180°C (350°F), gas mark 4. Halve the peppers
and remove the centre and seeds; rinse them under the cold tap.
Put the peppers into a saucepan half full of cold water and bring
them up to the boil, then take them off the heat, drain them and
leave on one side.

Fry the onion and garlic in the oil for 10 minutes. Mix half the
onion and garlic with the cooked rice and add the mushrooms,
thyme, mustard, lemon juice, grated cheese and a good seasoning
of salt and pepper.

Mix the tomatoes with the remaining onion and garlic in the
pan and add salt and pepper to taste. Pour the tomato mixture
into a shallow ovenproof dish and place the peppers on top.
Spoon the rice mixture into the peppers, piling it up well. Bake
the peppers, uncovered, for about 40 minutes, until the stuffing is
golden brown and the peppers tender.

RED CABBAGE STUFFED WITH CHESTNUTS

FRANCE

The sweetness of chestnuts goes particularly well with red cabbage and if you add butter and red wine too you get a really rich-tasting, warming dish, just right for the winter when the chestnuts and cabbage are in season. There's not much protein in the dish, though, so it's a good idea to follow it with a protein pudding like biscuits and cheese, *crème brûlée* or rice and almond pudding.

700 g (1½ lb) fresh chestnuts or 225 g (8 oz) dried chestnuts
1 small/medium red cabbage, about 1·4 kilos (3 lb)
125 g (4 oz) butter
2 large onions, peeled and chopped

1 tablespoon lemon juice
Sea salt
Freshly ground black pepper
2 carrots, peeled and sliced
1 tablespoon redcurrant jelly
275 ml (½ pint) red wine

Serves 6

First prepare the chestnuts. If you're using fresh ones slash each one with a sharp knife then simmer them in boiling water for about 10 minutes until the cuts open and you can remove the skins using a small, sharp pointed knife. Keep the rest of the chestnuts in the boiling water as you work because the skins get hard again as they cool. If you've decided to save time by using dried chestnuts, as I must admit I usually do, let them soak in some cold water for a while if possible – this isn't essential but it helps as they can be very hard sometimes – then simmer them gently in plenty of water for at least an hour, until they're tender, then drain them.

Now wash and trim the cabbage, removing any tough or damaged leaves and cutting the stalk end level. Slice a lid from the top of the cabbage and using a small sharp knife and a spoon scoop out as much of the inside of the cabbage as possible, leaving a neat, good-sized cavity for stuffing. Chop the cabbage

166

which you've scooped out fairly finely. Heat half the butter in a largish saucepan and fry half the onion for about 5 minutes, without browning, then stir in the chopped-up cabbage and cook for a further 5 minutes, with a lid on the saucepan, stirring occasionally. Add the chestnuts and half the lemon juice and season with salt and pepper. Leave on one side. Put the whole cabbage into a large saucepan half filled with cold water. Bring to the boil and simmer for 2 minutes with a lid on the saucepan. Drain and rinse the cabbage under cold water.

Melt the remaining butter in a saucepan that's large enough to hold the cabbage and fry the remaining onion and the carrots for 5 minutes. Mix the redcurrant jelly and the rest of the lemon juice with the onion and carrots, add some salt and pepper, then place the cabbage on top and carefully fill the cavity with the chestnut mixture, piling it up high. Pour the wine around the sides of the cabbage, put the saucepan over a low heat and cover with a lid. Leave it to cook very gently for about 3 hours or until the cabbage feels beautifully tender when pierced with the point of a knife.

It's easiest to serve this straight from the cooking pot and it's delicious with really light mashed potatoes.

TOMATOES STUFFED WITH CHEESE   PORTUGAL

These juicy tomatoes with their cheesy breadcrumb stuffing make a delicious hot starter or light supper dish for late summer when tomatoes are plentiful, and they're quick and easy to do.

8 large or 4 very large tomatoes – about 700 g (1½ lb) in all
Sea salt
125 g (4 oz) wholewheat breadcrumbs

225 g (8 oz) grated cheese
1 garlic clove, peeled and crushed
Freshly ground black pepper
1 tablespoon olive oil

Serves 4–5

Set the oven to 190 C (375 F), gas mark 5. Halve the tomatoes and scoop out the centres. Sprinkle a little salt inside each tomato and put them upside down on a plate to drain off any excess liquid while you make the filling. Chop the tomato centres and mix them with the breadcrumbs, grated cheese and garlic. Season with salt and pepper to taste. Arrange the tomato halves in a shallow greased dish. Pile the stuffing mixture into the tomato halves and sprinkle the olive oil on top. Bake the tomatoes for 20–30 minutes until they're tender and the filling is golden brown.

They're nice served with creamy mashed potatoes, buttered noodles or brown rice and a cooked green vegetable or crisp green salad.

STUFFED TOMATOES À LA PROVENÇALE

FRANCE

These tomatoes, with their herby, garlicky stuffing, make a very good first course but if you serve them with some buttery noodles or rice and a sharp-flavoured cheese sauce they also make an excellent lunch or supper, with a crisp green salad to accompany them.

8 large tomatoes – about 700 g
(1½ lb) in all
Sea salt
1 large onion
150 ml (¼ pint) olive oil
4 garlic cloves, peeled and
crushed

75 g (3 oz) fine fresh
wholewheat breadcrumbs
4 tablespoons chopped fresh
parsley
½ teaspoon dried thyme
Freshly ground black pepper

Serves 4

Cut a thin slice off the top of each tomato and leave these slices on one side to use as lids later. Using a teaspoon scoop out the tomato pulp to leave a cavity for stuffing (you won't need the pulp for this recipe but it can be used to flavour sauces and soups). Sprinkle the inside of each tomato with a little salt then turn them upside down on a large plate and leave them while you prepare the filling.

Peel and finely chop the onion. Heat the olive oil in a large saucepan and fry the onion until it's golden, then take it off the heat and add the garlic, breadcrumbs, herbs and a good seasoning of salt and pepper.

Set the oven to 200°C (400°F), gas mark 6. Place the tomatoes in a lightly greased baking dish; fill each with some of the stuffing mixture and arrange the reserved lids on top.

Bake them in the oven for 15–20 minutes, to heat them right through, then serve them at once.

TOMATOES STUFFED WITH RICE   GREECE

Like the stuffed tomatoes in the previous recipe these can be served either as a starter or as a main course. If you're making a meal of them I think it's a good idea to start off with a first course like *hummus* and finish with the yoghurt tart or special ground rice, all of which add protein to the meal and continue the Middle Eastern theme.

125 g (4 oz) long-grain brown rice
275 ml (½ pint) water
Sea salt
8 large tomatoes – about 700 g (1½ lb) in all
2 tablespoons olive oil
1 medium onion, peeled and chopped
2 cloves of garlic, peeled and crushed

6 tablespoons tomato purée
6 tablespoons chopped fresh parsley
2 tablespoons chopped fresh mint
Pinch of oregano
Freshly ground black pepper
150 ml (¼ pint) stock – or red wine is delicious

Serves 4

169

Put the rice into a heavy-based saucepan with the water and half a teaspoonful of salt; bring it up to the boil then turn the heat right down, put a lid on the saucepan and cook the rice very gently for about 40 minutes until it's tender and all the water has been absorbed.

While the rice is cooking prepare the tomatoes. Cut a small piece off the top of each and hollow out the centre, using a teaspoon – keep the sliced-off tomato tops to use as lids later. Sprinkle some salt inside each tomato then leave them upside down to drain.

Set the oven to 180°C (350°F), gas mark 4. Next make the stuffing. Heat the oil in a fairly large saucepan and fry the onion until beginning to soften – about 5 minutes – then add the garlic, rice, scooped-out tomato pulp, half the purée, the herbs and seasoning. Cook over a highish heat until the mixture is fairly dry. Arrange the tomatoes in a greased ovenproof dish, fill with the stuffing and put the slices back as lids. Mix the remaining tomato purée with the stock or red wine and a little salt and pepper and pour it round the tomatoes, then bake them for about 20 minutes until they're tender.

A cheesy sauce goes well with these, and a crisp green salad.

STUFFED VINE OR CABBAGE LEAVES GREECE

These *dolmades*, or little leafy parcels of rosemary-flavoured rice with nuts and raisins can be served hot or cold. If you're serving them cold – as is frequently done in Greece – you can omit the sauce and just bake them in some seasoned tomato juice or a mixture of tomato purée and stock. This is really a more authentic way of doing them but I'm giving my version which has a flour-thickened sauce because I've found this is the most popular. I also like to finish them off with a crunchy topping of crumbs and grated cheese but this isn't very Grecian either, so you might prefer just to sprinkle them with chopped parsley after cooking.

I think the *dolmades* are very much better served hot, with a crisp green salad and some dry white wine. The green salad with Gruyère cheese goes well with them and supplies some extra protein; or you could of course serve a protein-rich starter or pudding. The *dolmades* also make rather a nice unusual hot starter themselves if you bake them in individual ovenproof dishes.

36 fresh vine leaves, if available, or a small can; or about 18 cabbage leaves – Savoy, January King and Primo are all fine

1 large onion

2 tablespoons olive oil

225 g (8 oz) cooked long-grain brown rice (about 75 g (3 oz) uncooked)

1 teaspoon fresh rosemary, chopped, or ½ teaspoon dried

50 g (2 oz) chopped mixed nuts

50 g (2 oz) raisins

Sea salt

Freshly ground black pepper

50 g (2 oz) soft fresh brown breadcrumbs and

50 g (2 oz) grated cheese; or

A little fresh parsley

For the sauce:

50 g (2 oz) butter

50 g (2 oz) flour

575 ml (1 pint) water or stock

2 tablespoons tomato purée

Serves 3–4 as a main meal, 4–6 as a starter

If you're using fresh vine leaves or cabbage leaves, first of all half fill a large saucepan with water and bring it to the boil. Trim the leaves, removing the tough cabbage stalks with a 'V' shaped cut, then put them into the boiling water, cover and simmer for 2 minutes. Then drain them and run them under the cold tap to refresh them; drain well. With canned vine leaves just drain them and rinse them well under the cold tap.

Set the oven to 180°C (350°F), gas mark 4. Make the filling by peeling and chopping the onion and frying it in the olive oil for 10 minutes – don't let it brown – then stir in the rice, rosemary, nuts, raisins and salt and pepper to taste. Mix well, then put a spoonful of this filling on each leaf, fold over the edges and place the little bundles side by side in a shallow ovenproof dish. If there are some leaves over use them to fill in any gaps.

171

Make the sauce: melt the butter in a saucepan and stir in the flour, cook it for a minute or two, then mix in a little of the water, stirring vigorously over a high heat until the mixture is thick and smooth; then add a bit more water and continue like this until all the water has been used and you have a smooth, thick sauce. Then stir in the tomato purée and salt and pepper to taste. Pour this sauce over the stuffed leaves, making sure they are completely covered, then sprinkle them with the crumbs and grated cheese, if you're using them, and bake in the oven for 30 minutes. If you haven't used the crumb topping sprinkle the top of the dish with chopped parsley before serving.

Note: Pine kernels are really the correct nut to use for this dish but they are so expensive that I use this more economical mixture of chopped mixed nuts (which you can get at any supermarket) and pine-flavoured rosemary.

172

Cereals, Rice and Curry Dishes

These dishes are satisfying to make because the cereal gives a good basis to which you can add all sorts of colourful and tasty ingredients. The red bean rice from the Caribbean, the vegetarian paella from Spain and the Indian *biriani* are all examples of this, and they're very good to eat.

I use brown rice for all these recipes and I find it perfectly satisfactory but it does vary considerably from batch to batch and so it's not always easy to be sure it's going to behave in exactly the same way each time. In particular I've found that rice varies in its ability to absorb water, sometimes needing 2 cups of water to 1 cup of rice and sometimes only 1¾ cups of water, so a little experimentation is probably advisable when you buy a new type. Start with the larger amount of water and if you find there is some over at the end of the cooking time let the rice stand, off the heat, but with the lid still in place, for 10–15 minutes. Then if there is still some water left, try using less next time. My favourite long-grain brown rice for all these savoury recipes is the type with the slenderest, most pointed grains; Harmony foods do a good one which cooks up beautifully and takes between 40 and 45 minutes. You can either cook it gently with just the right amount of water and the lid on the saucepan, or boil it in lots of water in a large saucepan so that the rice moves around as it cooks. I've given instructions in the individual recipes.

The other cereals used in this section are bulgur wheat, couscous and semolina. Bulgur is a delightful grain to use. In the packet it looks rather like a very granular semolina but when you soak it in boiling water for a few minutes it quickly absorbs the water and puffs up to become light and fluffy and you then simply heat it through. As it's quick I find it more useful for emergency meals than rice and in fact it can take the place of boiled rice for serving with vegetable stews and casseroles.

173

Couscous is a form of coarse-grained semolina and rather like bulgur to look at. You have to sprinkle couscous with cold salted water and allow it time to absorb the water, then steam it for 20–30 minutes. It's nice for a change, served with a spicy sauce. If you can't get couscous you could use bulgur wheat instead.

Semolina is used in one of the recipes, the tasty cheese *gnocchi* from Italy (and also in one of the dishes in the fritter section). I know people don't always like the idea of serving semolina as a savoury dish, but *gnocchi* is cheap and tasty and well worth trying. If you can get wholewheat semolina from the health shop that is ideal – you use it in exactly the same way as ordinary semolina and it isn't too dark-looking when it's cooked.

You will notice that I suggest using *ghee* in the Indian recipes. This does give a lovely nutty flavour and makes the food taste that much more Indian, but if you haven't got any don't worry, just use butter or vegetable oil instead. If you like Indian food and make it a lot, though, you might like to make your own *ghee* which is quite easy to do and keeps for 2 or 3 months at room temperature or for months in the fridge.

To make the *ghee*, cut 225 g (8 oz) unsalted butter into rough pieces and melt it very gently, in a heavy-based saucepan. Don't let the butter brown. When it has melted stir it then let it simmer, without a lid on the saucepan, over a very low heat, for about 45 minutes or until the solids at the bottom of the melted butter turn golden brown, and the butter on top becomes transparent. Strain the *ghee* through a sieve lined with 4 layers of damp muslin. If any of the solids come through, strain the *ghee* again; it must be perfectly clear otherwise it won't keep properly.

If you store the *ghee* in the fridge, it will solidify and you will need either to stand the container in a warm place before using the *ghee*, or to melt the *ghee* in a saucepan before use, but it will taste just as good.

BIRIANI INDIA

This deliciously spicy Indian rice dish is popular in our family.
I usually serve it with lots of little bowls of extras for people to
add at the table and the children love helping themselves to
these. Favourites include chopped apple, mango chutney, diced
cucumber, roasted peanuts, raisins, desiccated coconut, sliced
onion, quarters of tomato and chopped hardboiled egg.

450 g (1 lb) long-grain brown
  rice
4 teaspoons turmeric
2 teaspoons sea salt
1·2 litres (2 pints) water
4 onions
3 tablespoons *ghee* or 75 g
  (3 oz) butter
2 teaspoons garam masala

2 teaspoons ground coriander
2 teaspoons poppy seed
2 teaspoons mustard seed
½ teaspoon chilli powder
225 g (8 oz) can tomatoes
125 g (4 oz) frozen green
  beans or canned okra·
Freshly ground black pepper

Serves 4

Put the rice, turmeric, sea salt and water into a heavy-based
saucepan and bring to the boil, then turn down the heat, put a lid
on the saucepan and leave the rice to simmer gently for 40
minutes.

While the rice is cooking peel and chop the onions and fry them
in the *ghee* or butter for 10 minutes until they're soft and golden
but not browned. Stir in the garam masala, coriander, poppy seed,
mustard seed and chilli powder and cook for 2 minutes, then
add the tomatoes and cook gently for 10 minutes. Set the oven to
180°C (350°F), gas mark 4.

When the rice has cooked for 40 minutes add the tomato
mixture to the saucepan and also the green beans or okra; mix
lightly with a fork. Season with salt and pepper. Transfer the
mixture to an ovenproof dish and bake the *biriani*, covered, for
20–30 minutes.

Biriani is nice served with curry sauce, a moist side salad and some crunchy golden poppadums. A cool, yoghurty or milky pudding goes well with it and supplies some extra protein.

BULGUR WHEAT PILAF   MIDDLE EAST

You can get bulgur wheat from health shops. It looks like a very large-grain semolina and is a pre-cooked cracked wheat. It makes a delicious pilaf and is quick and easy to use. I like it very much as a change from rice and you can make this pilaf the basis of a lovely Middle Eastern-style meal, starting with *hummus* or chilled cucumber soup and ending with the special ground rice pudding.

225 g (8 oz) bulgur wheat
575 ml (1 pint) boiling water
2 large onions
1–2 garlic cloves
1 red pepper
50 g (2 oz) butter

50 g (2 oz) raisins
Sea salt
Freshly ground black pepper
50–100 g (2–4 oz) roasted
   cashew nuts, almonds or
   pine kernels

Serves 3–4

Put the bulgur wheat into a large bowl and cover it with boiling water. Leave it on one side for 15–30 minutes; it will absorb most of the water and swell up.

While the bulgur is soaking peel and chop the onions, peel and crush the garlic and chop the pepper, discarding the seeds. Heat the butter in a large saucepan and fry the onions for 5 minutes, without browning them, then put in the garlic and pepper and fry gently for another 5 minutes. Drain the bulgur and add it to the onion mixture together with the raisins, stirring over the heat until the bulgur is well coated with butter. Season with salt and pepper to taste. Let the bulgur cook gently for 5–10 minutes until it's hot.

You can serve it at this point, but I think it's even better if you put a lid on the saucepan and let the pilaf stand for another 10–15 minutes, gently cooking in its own heat. Serve it sprinkled with the nuts. A juicy salad goes well with this dish.

Note: I find you can make the bulgur pilaf in advance and heat it through in a covered casserole in a moderate oven for about 30 minutes but it's best to add the nuts just before serving so that they retain their crispness.

BULGUR WHEAT AND CHEESE PILAF

MIDDLE EAST

The mixture of chewy garlic-flavoured bulgur wheat and soft melted cheese is very good. You don't have to add the raisins but I think this touch of sweetness is pleasant. The pilaf can be made in advance and reheated in a covered casserole in a moderate oven but don't add the cheese until just before serving.

225 g (8 oz) bulgur wheat
575 ml (1 pint) boiling water
2 large onions
50 g (2 oz) butter
1–2 cloves of garlic
1 green pepper

50 g (2 oz) raisins
Sea salt
Freshly ground black pepper
175–225 (6–8 oz) Lancashire
    cheese, cut into small dice

Serves 3–4

Put the wheat into a large bowl and pour in the boiling water; leave for 15–20 minutes to give the wheat a chance to expand. While this is happening peel and chop the onions and fry them for about 5 minutes in the butter in a large saucepan. Peel and crush the garlic; chop the pepper, discarding the seeds. Add the pepper and garlic to the onion and cook for a further 3–4 minutes.

Drain the wheat and stir this into the onion mixture, turning it over several times so that it all gets coated with the butter. Add the raisins and some salt and pepper then let the pilaf cook gently over a low heat for 5–10 minutes, until it's heated through. If you can then let it stand for 10 minutes, with a lid over the pan, steaming in its own heat, it will be even better. Heat it up again gently, then just before serving, when the pilaf is piping hot, stir in the pieces of cheese. Serve at once.

A tomato salad goes well with this followed by a fresh, fruity pudding.

CHEESE CURRY INDIA

In India the cheese for this curry would probably be made at home from yoghurt. As this is rather a laborious process I use white Lancashire cheese instead. You may feel my method is cheating a bit but I think you'll agree the spicy sauce and melting, creamy cheese make a delicious combination.

1 large onion	1 bay leaf
2 tablespoons oil, butter or ghee	275 ml (½ pint) water
1–2 cloves of garlic, peeled and crushed	225 g (8 oz) frozen peas
	Sea salt
225 g (8 oz) can tomatoes	Freshly ground black pepper
½ teaspoon ground ginger	175–225 g (6–8 oz) Lancashire cheese
1 teaspoon ground cumin	
2 teaspoons ground coriander	Hot cooked rice and mango chutney to serve

Serves 3–4

Peel or chop the onion then fry it in the butter, oil or *ghee* in a large saucepan for 10 minutes, until it's tender but not browned. Add the garlic, tomatoes, spices and bay leaf to the onions, mixing them around so that they all get coated with the fat. Pour in the water and bring up to the boil, then turn the heat down, partially cover the saucepan and leave the mixture to simmer for about 20 minutes. Then add the peas and cook for a further 3 4 minutes, just to heat them through. Season with salt and pepper. Cut the cheese into smallish dice – about 6 mm (¼ in) – and stir them into the curry just as you are about to serve it. Don't add

178

them too soon or they will melt too much and spoil the curry. Serve with hot cooked rice and mango chutney.

COUSCOUS
MOROCCO

Couscous looks rather like tiny grains of rice but it's actually made from semolina formed into little pellets. You sprinkle the pellets with salted water then steam them and serve them with a spicy vegetable stew. In Morocco couscous is cooked in a steamer called a *couscousier* but you don't really need any special equipment – I cook mine in a steamer with the vegetable stew cooking in the saucepan below. You could equally well put the couscous into a metal colander, put it on top of the saucepan of vegetables and cover with a lid or some foil.

225 g (8 oz) couscous
½ teaspoon sea salt dissolved in a cupful of warm water
A little butter or olive oil

For the vegetable stew:
1 large or 2 medium onions
3 tablespoons oil
2 large carrots
2 tomatoes, skinned and chopped
125 g (4 oz) chick peas,

soaked, cooked until tender and drained
1 teaspoon cinnamon
1 teaspoon ground cumin
1 teaspoon ground coriander
2 tablespoons tomato purée
75 g (3 oz) raisins
400 ml (¾ pint) water
1 tablespoon chopped parsley
2 teaspoons lemon juice
Sea salt
Freshly ground black pepper

Serves 3–4

First of all start preparing the couscous: spread it out on a large plate and sprinkle it with about a third of the salted water then rub the grains gently between your fingers – rather like rubbing fat into flour for pastry – to help separate the grains. Leave the

179

couscous for 10 minutes then repeat the process twice more, using the rest of the water.

While you're waiting for the couscous you can begin the stew. Peel and chop the onions and fry them in the oil in a large saucepan for 10 minutes until they're tender. Peel and dice the carrots and add them to the onions together with the tomatoes, chick peas, spices, tomato purée, raisins and water. Bring the mixture to the boil.

Line a steamer or metal colander with a piece of clean muslin or a double layer of kitchen paper and put in the couscous. Set the steamer over the saucepan containing the stew and cover with a lid or a piece of foil. Let it simmer gently for about 30 minutes, until the vegetables are cooked and the couscous is tender. Add some more water to the vegetable mixture if it is too thick and stir in the parsley, lemon juice and salt and pepper to taste.

Stir the couscous gently with a fork to make sure the grains are separate and fluffy and mix in a little butter or olive oil just to add flavour and make the couscous look shiny and appetizing.

To serve, spoon the couscous on to a large, warmed dish and pour the stew in the centre. Couscous makes a pleasant change from curry and rice. It shouldn't be too hot-tasting, just warmly and fragrantly spiced.

GNOCCHI ALLA ROMANA   ITALY

When this is brought from the oven, sizzling and golden brown, people find it difficult to believe it's made from semolina which they associate with dull school puddings. It's delicious and though you've got to allow time for the semolina mixture to get completely cold, it's not a difficult dish to make and one which you can do in stages and get ready in advance. It also freezes well.

Gnocchi should really be made with Parmesan cheese which of course gives it a lovely flavour, but when I'm making it for the family I use Cheddar spiced up with plenty of mustard powder and a pinch of cayenne pepper. For more flavour you can add some crushed garlic and/or grated onion to the basic mixture too.

This dish is lovely baked in little individual dishes and served as a first course. Or as a main dish I like to serve it with a tasty tomato sauce and either a lightly cooked green vegetable or a well-flavoured green salad. Another variation which is totally un-Italian is gnocchi with chips and parsley sauce!

Many people add semolina to milk by sprinkling it over the top of the boiling milk and stirring. I find it's all too easy to get lumps this way, so as you will see I use a different method which I find works well.

175 g (6 oz) semolina – you can buy the wholewheat variety from health shops	175 g (6 oz) grated cheese – including some Parmesan or Cheddar with 1½ teaspoons mustard powder and a pinch of cayenne
1½ teaspoons sea salt	
A good grinding of black pepper and nutmeg	
850 ml (1½ pints) milk	2 eggs
	Oil

Serves 4 as a main dish, 6–8 as a starter

Put the semolina into a large bowl with the salt, pepper and nutmeg and mix it to a cream with some of the milk. Bring the rest of the milk to the boil, then pour it into the semolina mixture, stirring all the time. Tip the semolina and milk mixture back into the saucepan and stir over a fairly high heat until it thickens. Then let the mixture simmer gently until it's very thick and has lost its very granular appearance, stirring from time to time. In Italy they say that the mixture is ready when a spoon will stand up in it unsupported. In practice I find you can only achieve this if you've happened to use a small, deep saucepan, and that 10 minutes of simmering is about right. Remove the saucepan from the heat and stir in two-thirds of the cheese (and the mustard and cayenne if you're using them) and the eggs which will cook in the heat of the mixture. Taste and add more seasoning if necessary.

Lightly oil a large plate, tray or other suitable flat surface and turn out the semolina mixture on to this, spreading it to a thickness of about 6 mm ($\frac{1}{4}$ in). Leave it to get completely cold – overnight if possible.

When the mixture is cold it should be firm enough to cut into shapes. Traditionally it should be cut into circles with a pastry cutter which makes the finished dish look very attractive and doesn't really take a moment, but squares will do if you're in a hurry. Brush a large flat ovenproof dish with oil – I use one of those big white pizza plates which is ideal – and arrange the *gnocchi* in slightly overlapping circles, like roof tiles. Brush the top of the *gnocchi* with some oil and sprinkle with the remaining grated cheese, then either bake for about 15 minutes in a fairly hot oven 200°C (400°F), gas mark 6, or put the whole dish under a hot grill for about 20 minutes, if you have a grill which is big enough. Get the *gnocchi* really crisp and golden, then serve at once.

KHITCHARI

INDIA

This is the dish from which the English kedgeree is derived. Although modern kedgeree is usually a fishy dish, the original *khitchari* was a spicy mixture of rice and lentils, ideal for vegetarians.

The usual way of making this, and the method I used to use, is to cook the lentils and rice together. But it's difficult to judge the amount of water and the timing and recently I've been cooking them separately then mixing them together and find that this gives a better result – light and slightly dry. I like *khitchari* with a juicy tomato salad and some mango chutney or lime pickle, but some people like to have some curry sauce with it too – there's a recipe for this in the sauces section of this book.

225 g (8 oz) split red lentils
700 ml (1¼ pints) water
1 bay leaf
225 g (8 oz) long-grain brown rice
Sea salt
2 large onions
2 tablespoons butter or *ghee*

Serves 4

1 garlic clove, peeled and crushed
2 teaspoons curry powder
1 teaspoon cumin seeds (optional – from health shops)
Freshly ground black pepper
1–2 teaspoons lemon juice

Put the lentils into a saucepan with the water and bay leaf and simmer them gently until the lentils are tender and have absorbed most of the water to make a thickish purée when you mix them. Take out the bay leaf. Keep the lentils warm.

While the lentils are cooking boil the rice in plenty of salted water until it's just tender – this will take 40–45 minutes – then drain and rinse it.

Peel and chop the onion and fry it in the butter or *ghee* in a small saucepan for 5 minutes, then stir in the garlic, curry powder and cumin seeds and cook for a further 5 minutes, until the onion is softened but not browned.

To assemble the dish, gently mix together the rice and lentils – use a fork for this to avoid damaging the grains of rice – then gently stir in the onion mixture. Season with salt and pepper and add a little lemon juice to taste.

You can vary *khitchari* in a number of ways. It's good with some sliced skinned tomato, chopped hardboiled eggs or fried mushrooms or green pepper stirred in just before serving.

PAELLA   SPAIN

Paella usually consists of saffron-flavoured rice with onions, tomatoes, fish and sausages, but the composition varies enormously depending on the whim of the cook and the contents of the store cupboard so I hope you won't think my vegetarian version too far-fetched. Anyway, people seem to enjoy this mixture of pale yellow saffron rice and tomatoes or green peas with its crunchy topping of golden brown flaked almonds. We like it with a fresh-tasting tomato sauce and a Spanish green salad. A chilled protein-rich pudding goes well with it – *crème brûlée* or little coffee custards, or chocolate and orange mousse if you want to continue the Spanish theme.

2 large onions
6 tablespoons olive oil
350 g (12 oz) long-grain
  brown rice
850 ml (1½ pints) water
1 packet of saffron – or 2
  packets give a more intense
  colour and flavour for a
  special occasion
2 teaspoons sea salt

Freshly ground black pepper
2 large garlic cloves, crushed
4 large carrots
1 large red pepper
4 tomatoes, skinned
125 g (4 oz) frozen peas
125 g (4 oz) flaked almonds
  toasted on a dry baking
  sheet in a moderate oven
  for 10–15 minutes

Serves 4

Peel and slice the onions. Heat the oil in a large saucepan and fry the onions for 10 minutes until they're soft but not browned. Wash and pick over the rice then add it to the onion together with the water, saffron, salt, a good grinding of pepper and the garlic. Bring the water up to the boil then turn the heat down, put a lid on the saucepan and leave the rice to cook very gently for 40 minutes. While the rice is cooking scrape the carrots and cut them into chunky dice. Cut the pepper into rings, discarding the seeds, and quarter the tomatoes. After the rice has been cooking for 20 minutes add the carrot – just put it in on top of the rice then put the lid back on the saucepan.

Ten minutes later add the pepper in the same way. After the rice has cooked for its 40 minutes put the tomatoes and peas into the saucepan. Put the lid back on and leave the rice, off the heat, for a further 15 minutes, to finish cooking slowly in its own heat. Then gently reheat the mixture, stirring with a fork to mix the

rice with all the other vegetables. Sprinkle the nuts on top of the
paella just before you serve it, so that they keep nice and crisp.

RED BEAN RICE   CARIBBEAN

This rice dish is a lovely medley of reds: tomato-coloured rice, with
pieces of bright red pepper and deep crimson kidney beans –
warming fare indeed and with a spicy taste to match! Serve it with
pumpkin soup as a starter, a well-dressed green salad as an
accompaniment and exotic fruit salad for dessert for a delicious
Caribbean meal.

125 g (4 oz) red kidney beans,
  soaked, cooked (see p. 22),
  rinsed and simmered for 1
  hour or so until tender
2 large onions, peeled and
  chopped
3 tablespoons vegetable oil
2 large garlic cloves, peeled
  and crushed

2 large red peppers, de-seeded
  and sliced
425 g (15 oz) can tomatoes
150 ml ($\frac{1}{4}$ pint) water or stock
225 g (8 oz) long-grain rice
Sea salt
3 teaspoons ground coriander
$\frac{1}{2}$–1 teaspoon chilli powder
Freshly ground black pepper

Serves 4

Drain the kidney beans; leave on one side. Peel and chop the onions
and fry them for 10 minutes until they're tender. Stir in the garlic
and red pepper and fry for a further minute or two, stirring so
that everything gets coated with the oil. Add the can of tomatoes
and the water or stock. Rinse the rice in cold water then put this
into a saucepan together with a teaspoonful of salt, the spices and
a grinding of pepper. Bring the mixture up to the boil then turn
the heat right down and leave it to cook very gently for 40–45
minutes, until the rice is tender. Take the saucepan off the heat
and leave it to stand, with the lid still on, for 10–15 minutes. Add

the red beans, mixing them in gently with a fork. Check the seasoning then reheat.

FRIED RICE

INDIA

This is a basic recipe for a spicy rice to eat with curries. It comes out a pretty bright yellow colour because of the turmeric. You can vary it by stirring in some nuts, sesame seeds or poppy seeds at the end to make it more crunchy and nutritious or you can add raisins or currants for sweetness, or chopped red or green peppers for extra colour.

225 g (8 oz) long-grain brown rice
1 tablespoon *ghee*
575 ml (1 pint) boiling water

1 teaspoon turmeric
3 cloves
1 bay leaf
Salt and pepper

Serves 4

Wash the rice thoroughly, then drain it and, if possible, leave it for half an hour or so to dry off a little.

Heat the *ghee* in a heavy-based saucepan and add the drained rice. Fry the rice over a gentle heat until it has become opaque – this will take about 5 minutes and it's best to stir the rice all the time so that it doesn't brown – then put in the boiling water, turmeric, cloves and bay leaf and a seasoning of salt and pepper. When the mixture is boiling vigorously, turn down the heat and put a lid on the saucepan. Leave the rice to cook very gently for about 45 minutes, after which it should be tender and have absorbed all the liquid. Take out the cloves and bay leaf before serving the rice. (If there is still a little water left in the saucepan let the rice stand, still covered with the lid, for a further 10–15 minutes, after which you should find all is well.)

RICE AND PEAS   ITALY

This Italian dish, *risi e bisi*, is really halfway between a risotto and a soup, with a lovely creamy consistency. It's easy to make and good served with a tomato salad and some triangles of crisp toast.

2 large onions	350 g (12 oz) frozen peas
25 g (1 oz) butter	175 g (6 oz) finely grated
350 g (12 oz) long-grain	cheese
brown rice	1 teaspoon dry mustard
1·2 litres (2 pints) water	Freshly ground black pepper
Sea salt	Grated nutmeg

Serves 4

Peel and chop the onions. Melt the butter in a large saucepan and add the onions; fry them gently for about 10 minutes until they're soft and buttery but not browned. Wash the rice and put it into the saucepan with the onion; stir in the water and a rounded tea-spoonful of salt. Bring the mixture up to the boil then put a lid on the saucepan, turn the heat down and leave the rice to cook gently for 40 minutes.

If the peas are very icy put them into a sieve and rinse them under hot water, then put them into the saucepan on top of the rice 5 minutes before it's cooked. At the end of the cooking time take the rice off the heat and leave it, with a lid on the saucepan, for 10 minutes, to finish cooking in its own heat. After this you should find that the rice and peas are both cooked but that there is still some liquid left in the saucepan.

Stir the mixture with a fork, mixing in the cheese, dry mustard and salt, pepper and nutmeg to taste. Reheat very gently then serve at once.

RICE AND PEAS WITH TOMATO SAUCE

This German dish, *Schoten*, is made from ingredients similar to those used for the Italian *risi e bisi* but the result is different. The rice and pea mixture is drier, more like a pilaf, and it's served with a tomato sauce which provides moisture and colour.

350 g (12 oz) long-grain brown rice	50 g (2 oz) butter
850 ml (1½ pints) water	1 onion, peeled and chopped
Sea salt	425 g (15 oz) can tomatoes
350 g (12 oz) frozen peas	Freshly ground black pepper

Serves 4

Wash the rice and put it into a heavy-based saucepan with the water and a rounded teaspoonful of salt. Bring it up to the boil then turn the heat down, put a lid on the saucepan and let the rice cook very gently for 40 minutes. If the peas are very frozen tip them into a sieve and put them under the hot tap for a minute, then put them on top of the rice 5 minutes before it's ready.

When the rice is cooked take it off the heat and leave it, with the lid still on the saucepan, for 10 minutes to finish steaming in its own heat. While this is happening make the sauce. Melt half the butter in a medium-sized saucepan and fry the onion for 10 minutes until it's tender. Stir in the tomatoes and cook for 2–3 minutes, then liquidize the mixture. Season with salt and pepper and reheat gently.

To finish the dish add the remaining butter to the peas and rice and stir gently with a fork. Season carefully and serve with the tomato sauce.

RISOTTO BIANCO ITALY

The proper way to make risotto is to add the liquid a little at a time, pouring in some more as each batch is absorbed. This means that you have to stand over the saucepan and with brown rice, which takes a long time to cook, it's very time-consuming. So I make risotto by cooking the rice slowly with a lid on the saucepan in the usual way, then beating it to make it creamy. You could leave out the fried mushrooms or red pepper if you want to but I think they make the risotto more interesting.

You might think that the quantity of rice I've given is rather large, but as you won't be serving potatoes and will probably just have a salad with the risotto, I think this is the right quantity. But if there's any left over it makes lovely little croquettes, rolled in crumbs and fried until crisp and golden.

2 large onions
75 g (3 oz) butter
450 g (1 lb) long-grain brown rice, washed
1·5 litres (2½ pints) water, stock or, for special occasions, replace 150 ml (¼ pint) of the liquid with white wine

Sea salt
125 g (4 oz) grated Parmesan cheese
225 oz (8 oz) mushrooms, lightly fried in a little butter; or 225 g (8 oz) red pepper, chopped and fried in oil
Freshly ground black pepper

Serves 4–6

Peel and chop the onions. Melt the butter in a heavy-based saucepan and fry the onions for 5 minutes, but don't let them brown. Add the rice and stir for a minute or two until it is well mixed with the buttery onion. Pour in the liquid and add some salt. Bring the mixture up to the boil, then put a lid on the saucepan, turn the heat right down and leave the rice to cook gently for 45 minutes. There will still be a little liquid left in the saucepan after the rice is done. Now beat the mixture with a wooden spoon to break up the grains of rice a bit and give a creamy texture.

189

Just before you serve the rice stir in the grated cheese and mushrooms or red peppers if you're using them. Check the seasoning, then take the rice to the table while it's still beautifully hot and the melting cheese all soft and creamy. Risotto is delicious with a tomato salad or a well-dressed green salad.

VEGETABLE CURRY INDIA

This vegetable curry is spicy but not 'hot'. If you want to you can make it 'hotter' by increasing the amount of chilli powder. It's lovely with plain boiled rice, or the spicy fried rice, some mango chutney and crunchy golden poppadums or chapatis. I usually serve it with a juicy side salad, too, which is cooling and refreshing.

50 g (2 oz) *ghee* or butter
1 large onion, peeled and chopped
2 garlic cloves, peeled and crushed
1 bay leaf
3 teaspoons ground coriander
3 teaspoons ground cumin
1 teaspoon ground ginger

¼ teaspoon chilli powder
225 g (8 oz) canned tomatoes
1 teaspoon sea salt
Freshly ground black pepper
575 ml (1 pint) water
350 g (12 oz) carrots
350 g (12 oz) potatoes
125 g (4 oz) peas

Serves 4

Heat the *ghee* or butter in a large saucepan and fry the onion for 7–8 minutes, then add the garlic, bay leaf and spices and stir over the heat for 2–3 minutes. Mix in the tomatoes, salt, a grinding of pepper and the water. Simmer for 5–10 minutes while you prepare the vegetables. Scrape and slice the carrots, peel the potatoes and cut them into even-sized chunks. Add the potatoes and carrots to the tomato mixture and simmer gently for 15–25 minutes, until the vegetables are almost tender, then put in the peas and simmer for a further 5 minutes. Check the seasoning before serving.

Cheese and Egg Dishes

This section contains perhaps the most classic recipes of the vegetarian repertoire, with its omelettes and soufflés from France and cheese fondue from Switzerland, all delicious and surprisingly easy to make. There are also a couple of quick bread and cheese dishes, two interesting stuffed egg bakes and two beautiful savoury choux pastry rings which make an impressive centrepiece to a special meal.

Although I know it's a straightforward chemical process that makes a soufflé rise in the oven I still feel a thrill of pride and delight when I open the oven and see a puffed up golden soufflé! And despite its simplicity a soufflé always seems to impress people and convince them you're a wonderful cook – but really if you've got the proportions right in the mixture all you need are punctual guests, good nerves and the right-sized dish. Actually regarding the first two requirements, although a soufflé really is best if you eat it as soon as it's done I have found that as long as it is fairly well cooked it will stay risen in the oven for a few extra minutes if I turn off the heat. As far as the dish is concerned you need one of the correct capacity, which I've given in the recipes, and as long as the dish is big enough it doesn't really matter, from the flavour point of view, what shape it is. But if you want to produce a flamboyant, well-risen soufflé you need a narrow, fairly tall dish and the mixture should come just level with the rim when you put it into the oven. Don't pile it up any higher, as I rather foolishly did once, or you will find half your soufflé on the floor of the oven. If you're buying a soufflé dish look out for French ones made of metal with little handles at each side at the top. They may be called by their French name of *charlotte* and the ones I've seen are not very expensive.

Of course all the dishes in this section are rich in protein so menu planning is easy and straightforward. When I'm serving eggs or cheese for the main course I try to plan for a low-fat or non-dairy starter and pudding; perhaps a vegetable purée soup or mushrooms *à la Grecque*, for instance, and a simple fruity pudding.

BAKED STUFFED EGGS

Usually stuffed eggs are served cold as a first course or part of a salad so this hot version from Russia is a pleasant variation. They're good as a first course baked in individual dishes and served with hot toast or as a main course, with fluffy boiled rice and perhaps a buttery spinach purée.

8 hardboiled eggs	Sea salt
2 large onions	Freshly ground black pepper
50 g (2 oz) butter	
1 tablespoon chopped fresh parsley	

Serves 4 as a main course, 8 as a starter

Set the oven to 180°C (350°F), gas mark 4. Cut the hardboiled eggs in half and take out the yolks; put the whites on one side. Peel and finely chop the onions. Melt the butter in a medium-sized saucepan and use some of it to brush a shallow oblong ovenproof dish which is big enough to hold all the egg whites in a single layer. Add the onion to the rest of the butter in the saucepan and fry it gently for 10 minutes, without letting it brown. Take the saucepan off the heat and add the egg yolks, mashing them into the onions until they're fairly creamy and smooth then stir in the parsley, salt and pepper. Spoon the mixture into the egg white cavities, piling it up neatly, then put the egg whites into the greased dish. Cover the dish with foil and bake in the oven for about 30 minutes, until the eggs are heated through.

These are also good with ½–1 teaspoon of dried dill, fennel or caraway seeds added to the mixture, if you like the taste.

BREAD AND CHEESE PUDDING   WALES

This is rather like a Welsh rabbit baked in one dish in the oven. It's useful if you want to make a toasted cheese dish that you can prepare in advance for cooking later. You could use cider or beer instead of the milk for a more heady result, rather like a baked fondue.

8–10 slices of wholewheat bread
Butter
350 g (12 oz) grated Caerphilly
   or double Gloucester cheese
275 ml (½ pint) milk

Serves 4

You need enough slices of bread to line the base of a shallow ovenproof dish, and the same again to make a bread topping for the cheese. Grease the dish lightly. Toast all the bread and butter it on one side. Lay half the toast in the dish, unbuttered side down, then put most of the cheese and the remaining toast on top, buttered side down, and sprinkle with the last of the grated cheese. Pour the milk over the pudding and leave it to soak for about 30 minutes – or longer if you want. Put a few little pieces of butter over the top of the pudding.

When you're ready to cook the pudding, preheat the oven to 190°C (375°F), gas mark 5, then bake for about 40 minutes, until the pudding is crusty and brown on top. This is quite rich so it's nice served fairly simply with a tomato or watercress salad.

CHEESE FONDUE   SWITZERLAND

Although fondue is very quick and easy to prepare I always think there's something rather festive and special about it – perhaps it's because everyone is dipping their bread into the communal pot of bubbling golden cheese. If you haven't got a fondue burner you can improvise with nightlights in a shallow dish with a couple of supports or a grill rack across to hold the saucepan of fondue.

Although fondue is at its best when made with dry white wine, Gruyère and Emmenthal cheeses and kirsch, I've found you can make an excellent, much cheaper version with Edam cheese and dry cider.

1 garlic clove	Sea salt
275 ml (½ pint) dry white wine or cider	Freshly ground black pepper
	Grated nutmeg
225 g (8 oz) Gruyère cheese and 225 g (8 oz) Emmenthal cheese, grated; or use 450 g (1 lb) grated Edam cheese	1 large French loaf or crusty wholewheat loaf – or half of each – cut into bite-sized pieces and warmed in the oven
1 tablespoon cornflour	
1–2 tablespoons kirsch (optional)	

Serves 4–6

Halve the garlic and rub the cut surfaces over the inside of a medium-sized saucepan (or special fondue pan). Put the wine or cider and cheese into the saucepan and heat gently, stirring all the time until the cheese has melted. Mix the cornflour to a paste with the kirsch if you're using it, or use a drop more wine or cider; pour this paste into the cheese mixture, stirring all the time until you have a lovely smooth creamy consistency. Occasionally the cheese goes all lumpy and stringy at this point. Don't despair; if you beat it vigorously for a moment or two with a rotary whisk all will be well. Season the fondue then place the saucepan over the lighted burner and let everyone start dipping their bread into the delicious mixture.

Fondue is rich so the menu planning needs some care. If you have a starter, keep this light and salady; follow the fondue with something refreshing and non-creamy like fresh peaches or pineapple sorbet.

CURRIED STUFFED EGGS   INDIA

This is a tasty dish, hardboiled eggs stuffed with a curry mixture and baked in a spicy sauce. They're lovely served with hot boiled rice, some mango chutney and crisp poppadums.

8 hardboiled eggs	1 teaspoon ground coriander
1 large onion	1 teaspoon ground ginger
3 tablespoons *ghee*, oil or butter	½ teaspoon turmeric
1 garlic clove	275 ml (½ pint) water
225 g (8 oz) can tomatoes	Sea salt
1 teaspoon ground cumin	Freshly ground black pepper

Serves 4

Halve the eggs, take out the yolks and put them into a bowl. Leave the whites on one side for the moment. Peel and finely chop the onion and fry it gently in the *ghee* for 10 minutes. Peel and crush the garlic and add it to the onion, together with the tomatoes, spices, water and some salt and pepper. Let the mixture simmer, with a lid on the saucepan, for 20 minutes, then sieve or liquidize this sauce. Check the seasoning. Set oven to 180°C (350°F), gas mark 4. Mash the egg yolks and stir in 2 or 3 tablespoons of sauce, enough to make a soft but not sloppy mixture.

Spoon the yolk mixture into the egg whites. Pour the curry sauce into a shallow ovenproof dish that's big enough to hold all the eggs in one layer, then put the eggs in on top of the sauce. Cover with foil and bake for 30 minutes just to heat the eggs through.

GOUGÈRE WITH MUSHROOMS, ONIONS AND RED WINE SAUCE

FRANCE

This is an impressive and delicious dish, a big puffed-up ring of golden choux pastry, the centre filled with button mushrooms and onions in red wine sauce. It's lovely served with baby Brussels sprouts and creamy mashed potatoes. *Gougère* is not difficult to make but it's best eaten as soon as it's ready, so you need to be able to get everyone to the table on time. Don't be put off by the long list of ingredients for the sauce; it's really quite easy to do.

For the gougère:
125 g (4 oz) butter or margarine
275 ml (½ pint) water
150 g (5 oz) plain wholewheat
   flour – or half wholewheat
   and half unbleached white
   flour
1 teaspoon sea salt
4 eggs, beaten
175 g (6 oz) grated cheese
A good pinch of cayenne pepper

For the filling:
3 onions, peeled and sliced
15 g (½ oz) butter
225 g (8 oz) baby button
   mushrooms, washed and
   left whole

Serves 6

For the sauce:
400 ml (¾ pint) stock – or water
   and a good teaspoon of
   vegetarian stock powder
400 ml (¾ pint) red wine
1 bay leaf
1 piece of onion, peeled
1 garlic clove, peeled and sliced
A good pinch of thyme
½ teaspoon black peppercorns
1–2 parsley stalks if available
1 tablespoon redcurrant jelly
Sea salt
Freshly ground black pepper
Sugar
40 g (1½ oz) soft butter
20 g (¾ oz) flour

You can make the main preparations for the various parts of this dish in advance if that is most convenient for you. To make the *gougère*, put the butter or margarine and water into a medium-sized saucepan and heat gently until the butter has melted, then turn up the heat and bring the mixture to the boil. Mix

197

the flour with the salt and quickly pour into the saucepan all at once. Stir over the heat with a wooden spoon for 1 minute, by which time the mixture will have formed a glossy ball of dough, then take the saucepan off the heat and tip the dough into a clean bowl.

Add about a quarter of the beaten egg and beat vigorously with a wooden spoon until the dough has absorbed the egg and become smooth and glossy again, then add another quarter and beat again. Repeat until all the egg has been used. I sometimes find when I'm using all wholewheat flour that the mixture will only take three-quarters of the egg; by then it is quite soft and any more would make it sloppy – it must hold its shape softly. If this happens to you don't worry; just use the extra to glaze the top before sprinkling on the cheese and baking. The reason is that wholewheat flour is not as absorbent as white and varies quite a bit from batch to batch. Stir in about two-thirds of the grated cheese, and the cayenne pepper. You can cover the mixture with a plate and leave it at this point for several hours if you wish.

To make the filling, fry the onions in the 15 g ($\frac{1}{2}$ oz) butter for 10 minutes until they're soft, then put in the mushrooms and fry for a further 3–4 minutes until they too are tender. Season with salt and pepper and leave on one side. If the mushrooms produce a great deal of liquid drain it off and use it as part of the stock for the sauce.

For the sauce put the stock and red wine into a good-sized saucepan with the bay leaf, onion, garlic, thyme, peppercorns and parsley stalks if you've got them and bring up to the boil. Let the mixture bubble away furiously without a lid for 10–15 minutes until it has reduced by half and you're left with 400 ml ($\frac{3}{4}$ pint) of liquid. Strain this liquid into a clean saucepan and stir in the redcurrant jelly and salt, pepper and sugar to taste. Make a *beurre manié*: put half the butter on a plate with the flour and mash them together with the back of a spoon to make a paste. Add this *beurre manié* to the wine mixture in several pieces, beating well after each, then put the sauce back on the heat and stir it for a minute or two until it's slightly thickened. Let it simmer for a further 4–5 minutes to cook the flour, then take the saucepan off the heat and dot the remaining butter over the surface of the sauce to prevent a skin forming. Leave on one side until you're ready to serve the *gougère*.

To finish the *gougère* preheat the oven to 200 °C (400 °F), gas mark 6. Oil a large ovenproof dish – one of those big white pizza plates is ideal if you have one but any large shallow oven-proof dish will do – and spoon the *gougère* mixture all round the edge, heaping it up into as neat a ring as possible but leaving the centre free. Sprinkle the top of the ring with the rest of the grated cheese then bake the *gougère* for 40 minutes until it is puffed up and golden brown. When the *gougère* is nearly done reheat the onions and mushrooms gently, also the sauce.

Take the *gougère* out of the oven, spoon the mushroom mixture into the centre and pour a little sauce over the mushrooms and onions – serve the rest of the sauce separately in a jug. Serve the *gougère* immediately.

You can put other things into the centre of the *gougère*; it's nice with a buttery purée of spinach in the middle and cheese sauce served separately.

COLD GOUGÈRE WITH CREAM CHEESE FILLING

FRANCE

If you make a *gougère* as in the previous recipe and bake it for longer so that it's really firm, you can split it round the middle and serve it cold, sandwiched with soft white cheese and its centre filled with crisp lettuce, tomato, watercress and spring onion salad. It makes an attractive buffet dish.

Gougère mixture as in the previous recipe.

For the filling:
700 g (1½ lb) low-fat quark or
   cream cheese
Sea salt
Freshly ground black pepper

To garnish:
1 crisp lettuce
½ bunch watercress
4 tomatoes, sliced
6 spring onions, trimmed

Serves 8–12

Make the *gougère* as described in the preceding recipe but bake it for a good hour until it is well-risen and very firm – all 'sizzling' should have ceased in the choux pastry. If it's not really firm it will collapse and be soggy inside.

Take the *gougère* out of the oven, slit it horizontally with a sharp knife and leave it on the dish to get completely cold.

It's best not to fill the *gougère* until just before you're going to serve it so that it stays as crisp as possible. Put the cheese into a bowl and mash it with a fork to break it up, then beat it until it's soft and light. Season the cheese with salt and pepper – a touch of garlic is nice too, if you like it. Carefully remove the top half of the *gougère* and spread the cheese over the bottom layer, then replace the top half. Arrange the salad in the middle of the circle. An alternative is to put the salad inside the *gougère* on top of the cheese.

OMELETTE

FRANCE

I think a well-made omelette, light and golden brown on the outside, creamy and moist within, is still one of the best and quickest convenience foods of all. It's versatile, too, because you can serve it with all sorts of different fillings. The important thing is to have the filling all ready to pop into the omelette and everyone sitting at the table before you start to cook the omelette because it's speed that's the essence of success.

For the filling:
Any of the following:
50 g (2 oz) finely grated cheese
50 g (2 oz) button mushrooms, sliced and lightly fried
50 g (2 oz) canned cut green asparagus, heated in its own liquid and drained just before using
50 g (2 oz) canned artichoke hearts, sliced, heated and drained just before using
1 tablespoon chopped fresh green herbs – parsley, chives, chervil, tarragon – whatever is available

200

For the omelette:
2 eggs
2 teaspoons cold water
Sea salt

Freshly ground black pepper
1 teaspoon oil
15 g ($\frac{1}{2}$ oz) butter

Serves 1

Beat the eggs in a bowl with the water, a pinch of salt and a grinding of pepper. Put the frying pan – a 15–18 cm (6–7 in) one is best if you've got one as it makes a nice thick omelette – over a high heat for about one minute, then turn the heat down and put in first the oil and then the butter. When the butter has melted turn up the heat again and put in the beaten egg. Immediately start moving the egg using a palette knife to push the edges of the omelette towards the centre, tipping the pan as you do so to make the liquid egg in the middle run to the edges – keep the heat up high. All this happens very quickly – the omelette should be done in under a minute. Loosen the edges of the omelette quickly with the palette knife, spoon the filling on top then tip the pan away from you so that the omelette folds over itself, then gently tip it on to a warmed plate. Serve immediately.

PIPÉRADE
FRANCE

This tasty mixture of tomatoes, peppers and onions in creamy lightly-set scrambled egg makes a good quick supper dish. It's lovely served with warm crisp French bread or wholewheat rolls.

2 onions
2 garlic cloves
1 green pepper
1 red pepper
4 tomatoes

50 g (2 oz) butter
6 eggs
Sea salt
Freshly ground black pepper
Chopped fresh parsley

Serves 4

Peel and chop the onions, peel and crush the garlic; wash, de-seed and chop the peppers, skin and chop the tomatoes. Melt the butter in a large saucepan, put in the onion and fry it for about 5 minutes without letting it brown, then mix in the garlic, peppers and tomatoes and cook for a further 5 minutes over a low heat with the lid on the saucepan.

Meanwhile beat the eggs in a small bowl with some salt and pepper. When the vegetables are tender pour the egg into the saucepan and stir gently over a low heat until the egg is lightly scrambled, but don't let it get too dry – it's best to keep the heat low all the time and take the *pipérade* off the stove while it's still runny. Check seasoning, then serve at once, sprinkled with chopped parsley and accompanied by the warm bread. Follow with fresh fruit or a fruity type of pudding.

CHEESE SOUFFLÉ   FRANCE

I think this is perhaps the best soufflé of all with its satisfying savoury flavour and lovely golden colour. The classic cheese to use is Gruyère but I find Cheddar is fine for everyday cooking whilst a red cheese such as Leicestershire or double Gloucester makes the soufflé a beautiful rich golden colour which looks very appetizing.

40 g (1½ oz) butter
40 g (1½ oz) flour
275 ml (½ pint) milk
125 g (4 oz) grated cheese
4 egg yolks

1 teaspoon mustard powder
Sea salt
Freshly ground black pepper
5 egg whites

Serves 4

Grease a 1¾ litre (3 pint) soufflé dish or tin with a little butter or oil. Melt the butter in a large saucepan and stir in the flour; cook for a few seconds than add a third of the milk. Stir the mixture over a high heat until it first goes lumpy then smooth and very thick, then add another third of the milk and repeat until you've used all the milk. Stir for a minute or two then draw the saucepan off the heat and pour the sauce into a large bowl. Let the mixture cool slightly then mix in the grated cheese, egg yolks, mustard and a good seasoning of salt and pepper. (You can cover the mixture and leave it for several hours at this stage if necessary.)

Set the oven to 190°C (375°F), gas mark 5. If you have a baking sheet place this on the shelf above the centre – it will get hot and when you put your soufflé dish on it there will be a nice blast of heat from the base to get things off to a good start. Whisk the egg whites. They should be stiff enough for you to be able to turn the bowl over without them coming out, but not so stiff that you could almost slice them with a knife, so stop in time. Mix a rounded tablespoonful of egg white into the cheese mixture to soften it then tip the rest of the egg white on top of the mixture and using the side of a flattish metal spoon cut and fold the egg whites into the cheese mixture until the egg white has all been incorporated and you have a very light airy mixture. Pour the soufflé gently into the prepared dish – ideally the mixture should come up level with the rim; it doesn't matter if it's lower but don't pile it up above the rim. Bake the soufflé for 30–35 minutes until it looks firm when you shake it slightly – you can test it if you like with a fine skewer which should come out clean.

Cheese soufflé is lovely with a green salad or simply cooked vegetables such as new potatoes and French beans; it also makes an excellent first course, followed by a vegetable-based main course such as ratatouille and garlic bread or stuffed tomatoes à la Provençale and courgettes, with a fruity pudding to follow.

If you want to make a soufflé feed 6 people, use a 2 litre (3½–4 pint) dish and increase the quantities like this: 50 g (2 oz) each of butter and flour; 400 ml (¾ pint) milk; 175 g (6 oz) grated cheese; 5 egg yolks and 6 egg whites. You will need to cook it for just a little longer, too.

INDIVIDUAL CHEESE SOUFFLÉS

FRANCE

Puffy golden individual cheese soufflés look impressive and make a lovely first course or lunch dish. They're also very practical because they only take 15–20 minutes to cook so you can get the initial preparation done in advance, receive your visitors or round up the family, then add the egg whites and put the soufflés to cook 15 or 20 minutes before you want to eat. As a starter these soufflés are ideal before one of the low-protein vegetable dishes. Or for a special lunch serve them after avocados, with a tasty green salad and fruity pudding.

25 g (1 oz) butter or margarine 125 g (4 oz) grated cheese
25 g (1 oz) flour 2 eggs, separated
150 ml (¼ pint) milk
Pinch each of mustard powder
  and cayenne pepper

Makes 3 individual soufflés

Prepare 3 individual soufflé dishes – those little white porcelain ones are ideal – by greasing lightly with oil or butter. Place a baking sheet in the centre of the oven.

Melt the butter or margarine in a medium-sized saucepan and stir in the flour; when it froths add the milk mixing well over a gentle heat for a few minutes until smooth and thick. Remove from the heat, cool slightly then add the seasoning, grated cheese and the egg yolks. (The mixture can be prepared in advance up to this stage.)

Set the oven to 190°C (375°F), gas mark 5. Whisk the egg whites until they are very stiff and able to hold their shape but not dry. Mix a heaped tablespoonful of egg white into the cheese mixture to loosen it, then add the rest and carefully incorporate it by folding the cheese mixture gently over it with a metal spoon, so that you don't flatten the egg white. Divide the mixture between the little dishes and place them in the oven on the baking sheet.

Bake for 15–20 minutes until risen and golden brown. Serve immediately; they will keep in the oven for a further few minutes if you turn off the heat but the sooner they are served the better they are.

These quantities will double satisfactorily to serve 6. To serve 4 use the basic mixture with an extra egg.

LEEK SOUFFLÉ   FRANCE

The chunky pieces of leek in this soufflé give it a lovely delicate flavour and interesting texture. Try to find really thin leeks if you can then they can be sliced into nice neat pieces which will stay firm when they're cooked.

3–4 thin leeks, weighing 350 g   275 ml (½ pint) milk
  (12 oz) before you trim them   4 egg yolks
Sea salt   Freshly ground black pepper
40 g (1½ oz) butter   Nutmeg
40 g (1½ oz) flour   5 egg whites

Serves 4

First of all prepare a 1¾ litre (3 pint) soufflé dish or tin by greasing generously. Then cut the roots and leafy green part off the leeks. Slit the leeks down one side and wash them carefully under running water, then cut them into 2·5 cm (1 in) lengths. Cook the leeks in 1 cm (½ in) boiling salted water until they're just tender – about 7–10 minutes. Drain the leeks well and keep them on one side.

Melt the butter in a medium-sized saucepan and put in the flour; cook for a few moments then add about a third of the milk. Stir all the time over a high heat until the mixture has thickened, then add another third of the milk and repeat the process until all the milk has been added and you've got a nice smooth thickish sauce. Transfer the sauce to a large bowl – this cools it slightly ready for adding the egg yolks and is more convenient later when you want to fold in the egg white. Beat in the egg yolks one by one then gently stir in the leeks. Season the mixture with salt, pepper and nutmeg – be fairly generous because the egg whites will 'dilute' the mixture. Now you can leave this mixture until just before you want to cook the soufflé – I have kept it for several hours in the fridge and it has been perfect.

When you're ready to cook the soufflé place a baking sheet on the middle shelf of the oven. Set the oven to 190°C (375°F), gas mark 5. Whisk the egg whites until they're thick and standing in soft peaks but don't let them get hard and dry. Stir a generous heaped tablespoonful of egg white into the leek sauce mixture to loosen it then tip all the egg white on top of it and gently fold it in with a metal spoon. When it has all been incorporated pour the mixture gently into your prepared dish – it should come just up to the rim. If it is lower it will still taste good even though it won't look so impressively high and puffy but if it is piled up above the rim it will overflow.

Put the soufflé on the baking sheet and bake for 30–35 minutes until it looks firm when you move the dish slightly and a skewer pushed gently down into the soufflé comes out clean. If it's done before you're quite ready turn off the oven and the soufflé will keep for 4–5 minutes longer although it won't be quite so puffy. I think this soufflé is nicest served with just one well-cooked vegetable such as buttered baby carrots, sprouts or peas.

If you want to make this soufflé serve 6 people grease a 2 litre (3½–4 pint) dish and use 50 g (2 oz) butter and flour and 400 ml (¾ pint) milk for the sauce with 5 egg yolks and 6 egg whites – cook the soufflé for a little longer.

MUSHROOM SOUFFLÉ   FRANCE

This is a delicious soufflé – when you cut it open the chunks of mushroom look most appetizing. It's nicest made with those firm white button mushrooms.

175 g (6 oz) firm white button
 mushrooms
50 g (2 oz) butter
1 garlic clove, peeled and crushed
40 g (1½ oz) flour

275 ml (½ pint) milk
4 egg yolks
Sea salt
Freshly ground black pepper
5 egg whites

Serves 4

Prepare a 1¾ litre (3 pint) soufflé dish or tin by greasing with
a little butter. Wash the mushrooms then cut them into halves
or quarters so that the pieces are all roughly the same size. Melt a
quarter of the butter in a medium-sized saucepan and put in the
mushrooms. Cook them gently without a lid on the saucepan
for about 5 minutes, then stir in the garlic.

Melt the rest of the butter in another medium-sized saucepan
and stir in the flour, then add about a third of the milk, stirring
over a high heat until the mixture has thickened, then add another
third and continue like this until it has all been added. Take the
saucepan off the heat and pour the sauce into a large bowl.
Let it cool a bit then mix in the mushrooms (drain off any excess
liquid), egg yolks and seasoning to taste. Leave on one side (for
several hours or overnight in the fridge if necessary) until you're
ready to cook the soufflé.

Put a baking sheet on the shelf above the centre of the oven and
heat to 190°C (375°F), gas mark 5. Whisk the egg whites until
they're stiff but not dry and fold them carefully into the mushroom mixture. Spoon the soufflé into the prepared dish – ideally
it should come to the top but no higher – and bake it for 30–35
minutes, until it's golden brown, well risen and it looks firm
when moved slightly. A skewer inserted should come out clean.
Serve at once. This soufflé is nice with some green beans, baked
tomatoes and creamy mashed potatoes.

If you want to expand this soufflé to serve 6 people, here are the
quantities. Use a 2 litre (3½–4 pint) dish and 60 g (2½ oz) butter,
225 g (8 oz) mushrooms, 50 g (2 oz) flour, 400 ml (¾ pint) milk,
5 egg yolks and 6 egg whites. You will need to allow a few minutes
longer for the soufflé to cook.

POTATO AND WATERCRESS SOUFFLÉ   HOLLAND

I have to admit that I've allowed myself a bit of licence here because the addition of the watercress is my own idea and you could omit it if you want to be more authentic. But I found the plain potato soufflé rather dull and so I added the watercress which I think gives the soufflé a more interesting flavour and colour. It makes a good light main dish and it's nice served as a protein-rich accompanying vegetable dish.

700 g (1½ lb) potatoes	2 bunches watercress
Sea salt	4 egg yolks
50 g (2 oz) butter	Freshly ground black pepper
150 ml (5 fl oz) milk or single cream	5 egg whites

Serves 4–6

Peel the potatoes, cut them into even-sized pieces and cook them in boiling salted water until they're tender, then drain and mash them with the butter and milk or cream. Wash the watercress carefully and remove the coarse stems, then chop the leaves fairly finely and stir them into the potato mixture together with the egg yolks and plenty of salt and pepper to taste.

You can prepare the soufflé up to this point in advance. When you're ready to cook it set the oven to 190°C (375°F), gas mark 5; grease a 1¾ litre (3 pint) soufflé dish or tin. Whisk the egg whites until they're very stiff but not dry, then fold them into the potato mixture. Spoon the soufflé into the dish and bake for 45 minutes, until it's puffed up and golden and looks firm when you move the dish slightly. Serve the soufflé at once – or within 5 minutes at the most. It's nice with home-made tomato sauce and a lightly cooked colourful vegetable such as carrots.

WELSH RABBIT

Some people say that this dish derives its name from the fact that it was served instead of rabbit when times were hard; anyway, it's one of our favourite quick supper dishes.

4 large slices wholewheat bread	3 tablespoons milk or beer
225 g (8 oz) grated Cheddar or Caerphilly cheese	Cayenne pepper
	Freshly ground black pepper

Serves 2–4

Toast the bread; arrange the slices in a grill pan or on a baking sheet which will fit under the grill. Put the grated cheese and milk or beer into a saucepan and heat them together, stirring all the time until the cheese has melted. Remove from the heat and add a pinch of cayenne pepper and a grating of black pepper. Pour the cheese mixture over the toast and pop it under a moderately hot grill for about 5 minutes, until the cheese is bubbly and lightly browned. Serve immediately.

This goes well with a tomato and onion salad or a nice crisp lettuce salad with fresh green herbs in it; alternatively serve the Welsh rabbit on its own and follow with some fresh fruit.

Fritters and Rissoles

It's surprising what a variety of dishes come into this section. There are delicious, crisp little cheesy fritters – the fried *gnocchi* and rice croquettes from Italy and the Glamorgan sausage from Wales; there are spicy lentil fritters from the Middle East and fritters made from wheat protein from China. Then from Germany and Switzerland there are potato fritters which are crisp and delicious but need to be served with some extra protein, and sweetcorn fritters from the USA.

Perhaps the most unusual recipes are the *gnocchi* which are a kind of savoury dumpling. They don't sound at all exciting but when they're served all hot and puffed up and oozing with melted butter and cheese they're delicious, excellent as either a first course or a main course.

Some of the fritters need to be dipped in crisp crumbs. I make these by cutting up a wheatmeal loaf and baking the slices in a low oven until they're really dry and crisp, then crushing them with a rolling pin, popping them into a liquidizer or putting them through an electric grater. They keep very well in an airtight jar. When it comes to coating the fritters with the crumbs, which I think is a horrid, messy job, I find the task of clearing up is greatly eased if you put the dry crumbs on a large piece of grease-proof paper and work on this. Afterwards you can simply roll up the paper with any left over crumbs and sticky eggy bits and pieces and throw it away.

GLAMORGAN SAUSAGE

WALES.

These little cheesy sausages are delicious and an excellent source of protein. They're good with salad and some chutney or with a parsley or tomato sauce and cooked vegetables. If you make the sausages tiny they're lovely as a nibble with drinks.

350 g (12 oz) Caerphilly cheese, grated
125 g (4 oz) soft wholewheat breadcrumbs
1 teaspoon mustard powder
6 tablespoons cold water
Freshly ground black pepper
A little flour
1 egg, beaten with 1 tablespoonful of cold water
Dried crumbs for cooking
Oil for shallow frying

Serves 4

Mix together the cheese, soft breadcrumbs, mustard, cold water and some pepper to taste. Gather the mixture into a ball then divide it into 8 pieces and roll each into a sausage shape on a floured board. Dip each little sausage into the beaten egg and then into dried crumbs. Heat a little oil in a frying pan and fry the sausages quickly until they're crisp, then drain them and serve immediately.

I've found that you can also make a delicious nut version of this recipe which I'm sure a Welshman wouldn't own but which we prefer. Use 225 g (8 oz) grated cheese and 125 g (4 oz) grated cashew nuts or hazel nuts with the breadcrumbs and water as above. It's nice flavoured with a little chopped rosemary.

Both this mixture and the proper version are good baked instead of fried – press the mixture into a greased ovenproof dish and bake it at 200°C (400°F), gas mark 6 for about 45 minutes. The result is rather a crisp savoury cake which can be cut up and served with a parsley or tomato sauce; it's also nice cold with chutney and salad.

FRIED GNOCCHI   ITALY

This is my version of the fried *gnocchi* or *bombolini* sold in the market in Verona. People sometimes hesitate to try them because they associate semolina with school puddings, but it's completely different and delicious in this crisp, savoury form.

125 g (4 oz) semolina –
 ordinary semolina or the
 wholewheat variety from
 health shops
575 ml (1 pint) milk
1 bay leaf
1 small onion, peeled
1½ teaspoons mustard powder
125 g (4 oz) grated Cheddar
 cheese

1 teaspoon sea salt
A good grinding of black
 pepper
1 egg, beaten with a
 tablespoonful of water
Dried crumbs
Oil for deep or shallow frying

Serves 4

Put the semolina into a medium-sized bowl and mix to a paste with a little of the milk. Heat the remaining milk with the bay leaf and onion; bring just to the boil then cover the saucepan and leave it on one side, off the heat, for 10 minutes or so for the flavours to infuse the milk. Remove the bay leaf and onion and reheat the milk. When it boils pour it over the semolina cream in the bowl, then return the mixture to the saucepan and bring to the boil, stirring all the time. Let the mixture cook for a few minutes until it's thick and has lost its granular appearance – about 10 minutes. Take the saucepan off the heat and stir in the mustard, grated cheese, salt and pepper. Taste the mixture and add more seasoning if necessary to give a tangy savoury flavour.

Turn the mixture on to a lightly oiled plate, spread it out to a thickness of about 1 cm (½in) and leave it to get completely cold. As it cools it will firm up and you will be able to cut it into small squares or other shapes. Dip the shapes first into the beaten egg then into the dry crumbs and deep or shallow fry them until they're golden brown and crisp. Drain the *gnocchi* on kitchen paper.

These are very popular with my children who like them best with chips, lemon slices and parsley sauce. They freeze very well; I open-freeze them after coating them with egg and bread-crumbs, then store them in a polythene bag. They can be shallow-fried straight from the freezer.

GNOCCHI IN MUSHROOM SAUCE   AUSTRIA

Although in Italy *gnocchi* are usually served with grated cheese on top, in France and Austria it's more common to find them covered in a sauce, as in this version.

75 g (3 oz) flour –
  wholewheat is fine
50 g (2 oz) butter
125 g (4 oz) grated
  Cheddar cheese
½ teaspoon sea salt
½ teaspoon mustard powder
2 eggs
Dried breadcrumbs
A little grated cheese

For the sauce:
50 g (2 oz) butter
50 g (2 oz) flour
1 bay leaf
575 ml (1 pint) milk
125 g (4 oz) mushrooms,
  washed and chopped
Freshly ground black pepper
Grated nutmeg

Serves 4

To make the *gnocchi* mix together the flour, butter, cheese, salt and mustard; when they're combined break in the eggs one by one and blend well with a fork to make a dough. Form the dough into walnut-sized balls on a lightly floured board. Heat half a saucepanful of salted water; when it boils drop in the little *gnocchi* and let them simmer gently for about 7 minutes, until they puff up, rise to the surface of the water and look firm. (Cut one in half to see if it's cooked and set inside.) Take the *gnocchi* out of the water with a draining spoon and put them into a lightly greased shallow ovenproof dish.

For the sauce melt the butter in a large saucepan and add the flour and bay leaf; stir for a moment or two, then add a quarter of the milk, stirring all the time over a high heat until the mixture is smooth. Then add another quarter of the milk, repeating the process until all the milk has been added and you have a smooth sauce. Take the saucepan off the heat and mix in the mushrooms and plenty of salt, pepper and nutmeg to taste. Pour the sauce over the *gnocchi* and sprinkle with dried crumbs and a little grated cheese.

When you're ready to finish the *gnocchi* set the oven to 190°C (375°F), gas mark 5 and bake them for 30–40 minutes, until they're heated through and the topping is crisp and golden.

This is good served with either a salad or a cooked green vegetable. It also makes an excellent first course if you bake small portions in individual ovenproof dishes.

RICOTTA GNOCCHI   ITALY

These little savoury dumplings are quick and easy to do and make a delicious light meal or first course with their golden cheesy topping. If it's more convenient you can make them in advance and just put them into a fairly hot oven for about 20 minutes to heat them through and brown the topping before you serve them. A green salad with a tasty dressing goes best with them I think.

75 g (3 oz) flour –
  wholewheat is fine
50 g (2 oz) butter
125 g (4 oz) grated Cheddar
  cheese – if you can include a
  little Parmesan it gives a
  lovely flavour

125 g (4 oz) *ricotta* or
  cottage cheese
½ teaspoon sea salt
½ teaspoon mustard powder
2 eggs

To finish:
A little extra flour
25 g (1 oz) butter

1 garlic clove, peeled and
 crushed in a little salt
75 g (3 oz) grated cheese

Serves 4 for supper, 6 as a first course

Put the flour into a bowl and mix in the butter, Cheddar cheese, *ricotta* cheese, salt and mustard, then break in the eggs, one by one, and mix well with a fork until everything is blended to a dough. Put walnut-sized pieces of the dough on to a lightly floured board and with your fingers form them into smooth balls, using more flour to coat them as necessary.

Half fill a large saucepan with water, add a teaspoon of salt and bring to the boil. Drop the *gnocchi* into the gently boiling water - you'll probably have to do them in 2 batches – and let them simmer gently for about 7 minutes. They will swell and rise to the surface of the water as they cook. When I think they're done I find it best to test one by cutting it in half to make sure it's cooked inside. Take the *gnocchi* out of the water with a draining spoon and put them into a lightly greased shallow ovenproof dish. When all the *gnocchi* are done melt the butter and mix it with the garlic; pour this over the *gnocchi* and sprinkle the grated cheese on top.

When you're ready to bake the *gnocchi* set the oven to 200°C (400°F), gas mark 6. Put the *gnocchi* in the oven for about 20 minutes until they're golden brown on top, then serve at once.

A variation of this recipe which I make sometimes is to fry some chopped walnuts or flaked almonds in the butter and pour them over the *gnocchi* instead of the grated cheese.

SPINACH GNOCCHI   ITALY

Spinach *gnocchi* are light and tender and when served with a topping of melted butter and cheese I think they're one of the most delicious dishes. The secret of success when making them is to let the spinach get completely cold before mixing everything together.

450 g (1 lb) spinach or 225 g
  (8 oz) frozen chopped
  spinach
75 g (3 oz) wholewheat
  flour
50 g (2 oz) butter
125 g (4 oz) grated cheese
2 eggs

½ teaspoon sea salt
½ teaspoon mustard powder
Grated nutmeg
Freshly ground black pepper

To finish
25 g (1 oz) melted butter
Grated cheese

Serves 4

Wash the spinach thoroughly then cook it without any additional water until it's tender – about 10 minutes. Drain, cool and chop the spinach. If you're using frozen spinach just let it thaw then put it into a sieve and press out as much liquid as possible.

Mix the cold spinach with the flour, butter, cheese, eggs and seasonings – it's easiest to use a fork. Form the mixture into about 20 walnut-sized balls and roll them in flour. Bring half a saucepan of salted water to the boil and drop in the *gnocchi* – you will probably have to do them in more than one batch. Let them simmer for 7–8 minutes. They will puff up and rise to the surface of the water; I think the best way to tell if they're done is to cut one in half and taste some of the middle to make sure there is no raw flavour. Put the *gnocchi* into a lightly greased ovenproof dish, dot with butter and sprinkle with grated cheese. Before you serve the *gnocchi* heat them through in a moderate oven – 180°C (350°F), gas mark 4 – for 25–30 minutes until they're piping hot and bathed in a buttery cheesy glaze.

Like the other *gnocchi* they make an excellent starter or supper dish. If you're serving them for supper some hot noodles or crusty garlic bread will go well with them – bake the garlic bread in the oven with the *gnocchi* – and a tomato salad.

SWISS FRIED POTATO CAKE   SWITZERLAND

Swiss potato cake, *rösti*, is different from the German potato pancakes because it uses cooked potato and it's made into one large cake which fills the whole frying pan. This makes a good basis for a cooked supper; protein can be introduced into the meal by serving a protein-rich side salad or by having something like yoghurt, cheese cake or biscuits and cheese for pudding.

900 g (2 lb) cooked potatoes	4 tablespoons vegetable oil
Sea salt	

Serves 4

Grate the potatoes coarsely – this is easiest to do if you chill them beforehand for a while in the fridge. Season them with salt. Heat half the oil in a large frying pan and put in all the potato, pressing it down gently with the back of a spoon. Fry the potato over a moderate heat until the underside is golden brown, then turn the cake over and cook the other side, adding the remaining oil if necessary. You may be able to turn the cake with a fish slice; alternatively you can turn it out on to a plate then tip it back into the frying pan again, crispy side uppermost. When the second side is cooked turn the potato cake out on to a hot plate and serve it in big chunky wedges.

You can vary the basic potato cake in a number of ways – it's nice with chopped herbs or spring onions added; sunflower seeds, sesame seeds and chopped hazel nuts are also good.

POTATO PANCAKES   GERMANY

These crispy little pancakes make a good quick supper dish or children's tea. It's typically German – and I think delicious – to serve them with a sharp-tasting apple or cranberry sauce, but children usually prefer them with tomato ketchup.

450 g (1 lb) potatoes, scrubbed
1 onion, peeled
Sea salt
Freshly ground black pepper

2 eggs
3 tablespoons flour
Oil for shallow frying
Cranberry or apple sauce

Serves 4

Grate the potatoes coarsely, peeled or unpeeled according to taste. Grate the onion. Mix potatoes and onion with salt and pepper, eggs and flour and stir to make a batter. Heat a little oil in a frying pan and fry tablespoonfuls of the mixture until golden and crispy, turning them over so that both sides are cooked. Drain on kitchen paper and serve immediately with the sauce and a crunchy salad.

RICE CROQUETTES

ITALY

These crisp croquettes are good for a first course if you serve them on small plates with a tomato or mushroom sauce; or, with vegetables and potato, they make a tasty supper. They're an excellent way of using up leftover risotto and I sometimes make an extra large batch specially with this in mind – you simply form the risotto into little rounds and coat them in beaten egg and dried crumbs. But if you're making the croquettes from scratch, this is the way to do them.

225 g (8 oz) long-grain
  brown rice
1 teaspoon sea salt
400 ml (¾ pint) water
1 large onion, peeled and finely
  chopped
25 g (1 oz) butter
125 g (4 oz) grated cheese
½–1 teaspoon mustard powder

1 egg
Freshly ground black pepper

To finish:
1 egg, beaten with 1 tablespoon
  of cold water
Dried crumbs
Oil for deep or shallow frying

Serves 4

Wash the rice and put it into a saucepan with the salt and water. Bring up to the boil, then turn the heat down low, put a lid on the saucepan and leave it to simmer for 40 minutes until the rice is cooked. Then take it off the heat and leave it to stand, with the lid still on the saucepan, for a further 10 minutes.

While the rice is cooking fry the onion gently in butter for 10 minutes until it's golden and soft. Stir the onion into the cooked rice together with the grated cheese, mustard and egg. Mix well and season to taste with salt and plenty of pepper. It's easier to shape the mixture into croquettes if it's cool and better still if there's time to chill it in the fridge. Dip tablespoonfuls of the mixture first into the beaten egg then into the dried crumbs, shaping them into rounds with your hands. Fry the croquettes in deep or shallow oil until they're crisp all over. Drain them on kitchen paper and serve them as soon as possible.

SPICY FRITTERS   MIDDLE EAST

This is a cheating recipe for these spicy chick pea fritters, or *felafel,* as they're called, because they're really supposed to be made from chick peas. I've given the proper chick pea version in *The Bean Book* but if, like me, you find the long cooking then the sieving of the chick peas rather time-consuming, I thought you might like to try this red lentil recipe which is just as tasty but easier to do.

350 g (12 oz) split red lentils
700 ml (1¼ pints) water
25 g (1 oz) butter or margarine
1 medium onion, peeled and grated
1½ teaspoons ground cumin
1½ teaspoons ground coriander

1 tablespoon chopped fresh parsley
1 egg
Sea salt
Freshly ground black pepper
A little wholewheat flour
Oil for shallow frying

Serves 4

221

Put the lentils and water in a medium-sized saucepan and bring to the boil, then let them simmer gently until the lentils are soft and golden and all the water has been absorbed. Mash the lentils with the butter or margarine and mix in the onion, cumin, coriander, parsley and egg. Season the mixture with plenty of salt and pepper.

Form the lentil mixture into small flat cakes on a lightly floured board – it's easier to handle if there's time to chill it in the fridge for a while first. Fry the little cakes in hot shallow oil and drain them well.

Served with pitta bread and a bowl of salad – lettuce, tomatoes, cucumber and spring onion tossed in vinaigrette – these little fritters make a tasty and filling lunch. They're also nice with garlic mayonnaise, chilled yoghurt or mango chutney; or with gravy, potatoes and a cooked vegetable they make a simple cooked meal that usually appeals to children.

SWEETCORN FRITTERS

USA

Although these fritters are usually served as an accompaniment to meat they are quite filling and make a good supper or lunch dish, with tomato sauce, mashed potato and a green vegetable. They also make an interesting first course.

330 g (11 ½ oz) can sweetcorn	Sea salt
1 egg, separated	Freshly ground black pepper
25 g (1 oz) wholewheat flour	Oil for shallow frying

Serves 3

Drain the sweetcorn, put it into a bowl with the egg yolk, flour and some salt and pepper and mix well. Whisk the egg white until it's standing in soft peaks, then gently fold it into the sweetcorn mixture. Heat a little oil in a frying pan and fry the sweetcorn mixture, a tablespoonful at a time, on both sides, until crisp.

(Stand back as you do so because the corn tends to 'pop'.) As soon as they're ready drain the fritters on kitchen paper. Keep the first ones warm while you fry the remainder, then serve them straight away.

FRIED WHEAT PROTEIN WITH SWEET AND SOUR SAUCE CHINA

We talk about 'knitted soya steaks' and textured vegetable proteins as though they were something very new and unusual, but the inventive Chinese have been using wheat protein for centuries and it's an entirely natural product which you can make from strong flour in your own home if you want to. You just make a dough with flour, a little salt and water, soak it in a bowl of cold water for 1 hour then pummel and knead it under cold running water. As you do this the white starch washes away and you're left with a firm, pliable piece of dough which you can then simmer in well-flavoured stock and use in stews and casseroles – or in this recipe.

It's quite easy to do but a bit laborious so I usually buy it in a can: you can get it at Chinese shops or from health shops where it's called meatless savoury cuts. The wheat contains good protein and I think it's delicious fried like this and served in a sweet and sour sauce. The ingredients and proportions for the sauce are those recommended by the distinguished Chinese cook and author, Kenneth Lo.

For the sauce:
2½ tablespoons soft brown sugar
2 tablespoons red wine vinegar
1½ tablespoons cornflour
1½ tablespoons tomato purée or tomato ketchup
1½ tablespoons soy sauce
1 tablespoon cheap sherry
1 tablespoon orange juice
4 tablespoons cold water

223

For the fried wheat protein:
425 g (15 oz) can and 225 g
 (8 oz) can wheat protein
1 garlic clove
Sea salt
1 egg, beaten
1 piece of fresh root ginger,

about 2·5 cm (1 in) long;
or ½ teaspoon ordinary
ground ginger
Dry crumbs
Oil for shallow frying –
sesame oil if possible

Serves 4

First prepare the sauce. Put all the ingredients into a small saucepan and mix to a smooth paste. Leave on one side while you prepare the wheat protein.

If the wheat protein has been prepared with liquid, drain this off and keep it on one side. Cut the wheat protein into chunky bite-sized pieces. Peel the garlic, crush it with a knife then mix it to a creamy paste with a little salt and put it into a smallish bowl with the beaten egg. Peel the ginger and grate it finely into the bowl with the garlic and egg, or add the ground ginger. Mix it all together. Dip the pieces of wheat protein into the egg mixture then coat them with dry crumbs. Fry the little fritters in hot shallow oil, turning them so that they're crisp all over. Drain them well on kitchen paper and keep them warm.

Now quickly finish the sauce by putting the small saucepan over a moderate heat and stirring the mixture for a couple of minutes until it has thickened. If you think it's too thick, thin it down with a little extra orange juice, water or the liquid from the canned wheat protein. Pour the sauce over the hot fritters and serve at once.

This is nice served with hot cooked rice and some Chinese vegetables – the Chinese cabbage or chop suey go well with it and so does some Chinese plum sauce which you can get at Chinese shops – or you can use ordinary chutney.

Pasta and Pancakes

Pasta and pancake dishes are warming and filling and some of them are also very quick and easy to make. They are perfect served with just a simple salad, which helps to cut down on preparation time.

For all the pasta recipes I use the wholewheat variety. It's very easy to get these days and although it looks rather dauntingly dark in the packet it cooks up much lighter and is just as quick to use as ordinary white pasta. One of the secrets of cooking wholewheat pasta successfully is to use a big saucepan and plenty of water so that the pasta can move around as it cooks. It's also helpful to add a couple of tablespoons of cooking oil to the water as this prevents the pasta from sticking together and also stops the water frothing up and boiling over. When the pasta is cooked so that it's just tender I find it best to drain it then put it back into the still hot saucepan with a knob of butter or a little olive oil. There's no need to rinse the pasta in either hot or cold water.

Although stuffed pancake dishes, which I've also included in this section, are not particularly quick to make, I do think they're quite convenient when you're busy because each part – the pancakes, the filling and the sauce – can be quickly made on its own when you can fit it in and then the whole dish can be assembled at the last minute. Actually stuffed pancakes are one of my favourite dishes for entertaining; I can make the pancakes, filling and sauce gradually during the week before and freeze them, then it doesn't take long to assemble them on the day. Also they don't spoil if they're kept covered with foil in a cool oven (150°C (300°F), gas mark 2) for quite a long time which gives me a chance to relax and enjoy myself without worrying what's going on in the oven. I take the foil off the top of the dish and turn the oven up when we start the meal to brown the top of the pancakes.

You can make excellent nutty-tasting pancakes with wholewheat flour. If you want them very light use half wholewheat flour and half white – if these are successful you might like to try them with all wholewheat which is fine as long as you take care to make the pancakes really thin.

When you're making pancakes the important thing is to have the right-sized frying pan. I have a small non-stick pan measuring 17–18 cm (6–7 in) and it's ideal because the pancakes are just the right size, and the fact that the frying pan is non-stick means I only have to add the very minimum of fat to cook the pancakes which makes them easier to control in the pan and of course less fatty when they're finished.

A large shallow ovenproof dish is best for baking the stuffed pancakes in because they are nicest if you can arrange them in one layer. I put them in the same big Pyrex dish that I use for stuffed vegetables – it measures about 39 cm × 27 cm (15½ in × 10½ in). A similar-sized porcelain or earthenware dish would be even better.

BLINI

These buckwheat yeast pancakes from Russia have a character all their own. They come out light and delectable; the buckwheat gives them a dark, nutty flavour. I think they're nicest served hot from the pan with melted butter or soured cream, accompanied by a big bowl of crunchy salad; hearty chunks of lettuce, celery, spring onions, tomatoes and fingers of carrot.

400 ml (¾ pint) milk
1 teaspoon sugar
15 g (½ oz) dried yeast
225 g (8 oz) flour
75 g (3 oz) buckwheat flour
25 g (1 oz) butter

½ teaspoon salt
2 tablespoons soured cream
3 eggs, separated
Oil for shallow frying
Soured cream or melted
    butter to serve

Serves 4

Heat two-thirds of the milk to lukewarm; add the sugar and yeast and leave in a warm place for 5 minutes to froth up. Put the flour and half the buckwheat flour into a bowl and add the yeast mixture. Beat hard until smooth then cover and put in a warm place until doubled in bulk – about 1½ hours. Add the rest of the buckwheat flour and beat the mixture again. Put back into a warm place for another 2 hours.

Melt the butter in a small pan and add the remaining milk; heat the mixture to lukewarm. Add this to the flour mixture together with the salt, soured cream and egg yolks. Beat well. Whisk the egg whites until they're standing in peaks, then fold them gently into the mixture with a metal spoon. Cover the bowl and leave for a further 30 minutes.

Heat a little oil in a frying pan; put 2 tablespoonsful of the *blini* mixture into the hot fat and fry until crisp on one side; flip the little pancake over with a spatula and cook the other side.

These pancakes can also be served as a pudding, with soured cream and/or jam, syrup or sugar.

CHICK PEAS AND VERMICELLI   ITALY

At first glance this seems a strange mixture but it works well, the firm golden chick peas contrasting with the soft creamy-coloured vermicelli, and both shiny with olive oil and pungent with garlic and Parmesan cheese. Incidentally, if you use canned chick peas for this recipe it brings it into the quick-to-make emergency meal category.

225 g (8 oz) chick peas
Sea salt
6 tablespoons olive oil
175 g (6 oz) vermicelli or fine
   wholewheat spaghetti

1–2 garlic cloves, peeled and
   crushed
Freshly ground black pepper
25–50 g (1–2 oz) grated
   Parmesan cheese

Serves 4

Cover the chick peas with cold water and leave them to soak for several hours, then drain and rinse them, put them into a saucepan with plenty of fresh water and simmer them gently until they're tender. Keep them hot. Half fill a large saucepan with cold water; add a teaspoon of salt and 2 tablespoons of the olive oil and bring to the boil. Cook the pasta in the water until it's just tender. Drain the pasta and return it to the hot saucepan with the rest of the olive oil, the garlic and salt and pepper. Drain the hot chick peas and add them to the pasta, turning the mixture gently so that everything gets coated with the oil. Serve immediately, sprinkled with grated Parmesan cheese.

   This dish is rich in protein and is lovely served with a simple tomato or green salad.

LASAGNE WITH SPINACH AND CHEESE   ITALY

An easy-to-make dish that's very tasty and filling. The exact amount of lasagne needed will depend on the brand you're using and the shape of your dish. I think it's best to try the pieces of lasagne in the dish before you cook them – arrange the pieces in a shallow square or oblong ovenproof dish so that they make a complete layer but don't overlap, and then allow the same amount again so that you will have 2 layers in the finished dish. This will probably be about 125 g (4 oz) of lasagne – if the dish you're planning to use calls for very much more than this you'll probably have to double all the other ingredients and it will then feed 6 or 8 people.

This lasagne is lovely served with a juicy tomato salad.

About 125 g (4 oz) lasagne
450 g (1 lb) spinach or 350 g
   (12 oz) chopped frozen
   spinach
Sea salt
Freshly ground black pepper

450 g (1 lb) *ricotta* or curd
   cheese or low-fat quark
25 g (1 oz) Parmesan cheese
2 eggs
175 g (6 oz) grated Edam
   cheese

Serves 3–4

Set the oven to 200°C (400°F), gas mark 6. Half fill a large saucepan with salted water. When the water is boiling put in the strips of lasagne – stand them in the water and as the ends soften gradually ease the rest of the lasagne down until it's all submerged. Simmer the lasagne gently for about 15 minutes, until it's tender, then drain it in a colander.

While the lasagne is cooking wash and pick over the spinach then put it into a large saucepan; don't add water, as that still clinging to the spinach should be sufficient. Put a lid on the saucepan and cook the spinach for about 7–10 minutes until it's tender. Drain the spinach, then chop it in the saucepan using the end of a fish slice. Season with salt and pepper. Mix the *ricotta* or curd cheese or quark with the Parmesan, eggs and salt and pepper.

Lightly grease your selected ovenproof dish and put half the spinach in the base, followed by half the cheese mixture. Spread a layer of lasagne evenly over the top, then repeat the layers. Sprinkle the grated cheese over the top. Bake the lasagne for 45 minutes, until it's golden brown on top, hot and bubbly within. Serve at once.

MACARONI CHEESE

ENGLAND

People usually laugh when I tell them I like macaroni cheese but I think it's delicious if it's well made, quite as good as some of the Italian pasta dishes which people rave about. I think the secret with macaroni cheese is to make the sauce quite thin so that you get a light, moist result. It's lovely with a juicy tomato salad or a crisp green salad. You can cook macaroni cheese in the oven or under the grill, whichever is more convenient.

125 g (4 oz) wholewheat
   short macaroni
Sea salt
40 g (1 ½ oz) butter
40 g (1 ½ oz) flour
850 ml (1 ½ pints) milk
175 g (6 oz) grated cheese,

preferably double
Gloucester which gives a
lovely colour
1 teaspoon mustard powder
Freshly ground black pepper
Dried crumbs
A little extra grated cheese

Serves 4

If you're going to bake the macaroni cheese set the oven to 200 C (400°F), gas mark 6. Half fill a large saucepan with water and add a teaspoonful of salt. Bring the water to the boil, put in the macaroni and let it simmer until it's just tender – this will be in about 10 minutes; the time given on the packet will be a guide but keep your eye on it and bite a piece when you think it's nearly done to check it. Drain the macaroni.

While the macaroni is cooking make the sauce. Melt the butter in a large saucepan and stir in the flour; let it cook over the heat for a few moments, then mix in about a fifth of the milk. Keep the heat up high and stir vigorously until the mixture is smooth, then add some more milk as before and repeat until it's all in and you have a smooth, rather thin sauce. (You may think it's *too* thin, but don't worry, it will be all right.) Take the saucepan off the heat and mix in the grated cheese, mustard powder and salt and pepper to taste.

Stir the macaroni into the sauce then pour the mixture into a lightly greased shallow ovenproof dish. Cover the top all over with the crumbs and a little grated cheese. Bake the macaroni cheese in the oven for about 40 minutes or put it under a hot grill for about 15–20 minutes until it's bubbling and golden and crisp on top.

PANCAKES STUFFED WITH ASPARAGUS

FRANCE

I'm afraid this is rather an extravagant dish, using four cans of asparagus, but for a special occasion it really makes a lovely main course that's no more expensive than good meat or fish would be.

For the pancakes:
125 g (4 oz) plain flour – I use wholewheat but you could also use a mixture of wholewheat and white
A pinch of sea salt
2 eggs
2 tablespoons vegetable oil
200 ml (7 fl oz) milk
Extra oil for frying

For the filling:
Four 300 g (10½ oz) cans cut asparagus
2 tablespoons chopped parsley

Serves 6

For the sauce:
75 g (3 oz) butter
75 g (3 oz) flour
850 ml (1½ pints) milk
1 bay leaf
1–1½ teaspoons mustard powder
175 g (6 oz) grated cheese, preferably double Gloucester
Sea salt
Freshly ground black pepper

To finish:
50g (2oz) grated cheese

First make the pancake batter: the easiest way to do this is to put all the ingredients into the liquidizer and blend until you have a smooth creamy mixture. If you do this I have found that it doesn't matter if you don't let the batter stand for 30 minutes as in the traditional method. If you haven't a liquidizer, put the flour and salt into a bowl, break in the eggs and beat, then gradually mix in the oil and milk until you've got a creamy mixture. Beat well, then leave the batter to stand for 30 minutes and beat again.

To make the pancakes brush a small frying pan with oil and set it over a moderate heat. When it is hot pour in enough pancake batter to coat the base of the pan thinly. Tip and swirl the pan so that the mixture runs all over the base. Then put the pan over the heat for 20–30 seconds until the top of the pancake is set and the underside is flecked golden brown. Flip the pancake over using a small palette knife and your fingers if necessary. Cook the other side of the pancake, then lift it out on to a plate. Brush the frying pan with more oil if necessary (I find with a non-stick frying pan I only have to do this after about every three pancakes) and make another pancake in the same way, putting it on top of the first pancake when it's done. Continue until you've finished the mixture and have a nice pile of 12 or 15 pancakes. (You can do all this well in advance if you want to.)

To make the filling drain the asparagus and mix it with the chopped parsley. This may seem a rather simple filling but it's delicious when put with the pancakes and sauce.

For the sauce, melt the butter in a large saucepan and stir in the flour, cook for a moment or two then add about a fifth of the milk and the bay leaf and stir over a good heat until the mixture is smooth and very thick. Then add another lot of milk and repeat the process until it has all been incorporated and you've got a smooth sauce. Take the saucepan off the heat, stir in the mustard and grated cheese and season the sauce carefully. If you're having some white wine with the meal a couple of tablespoons of it will make a delicious addition.

To assemble the dish put a heaped tablespoonful of asparagus on each pancake, roll the pancake neatly and place it in a large shallow greased casserole. These pancakes look best arranged in a single layer but you will need a big dish to accommodate them. When the pancakes are all in the dish pour the sauce evenly over them, removing the bay leaf when it comes to light. Sprinkle the grated cheese over the top and cover the dish with a piece of foil.

When you're ready to bake the pancakes set the oven to 180 C (350°F), gas mark 4. Bake them for about 1 hour, removing the foil about 15 minutes before the end of the cooking time to brown the cheese on top.

These pancakes are good served with *gratin dauphinoise* and either a green salad or a cooked vegetable.

PANCAKES STUFFED WITH CHEESE AND BAKED IN SPICY TOMATO SAUCE

MEXICO

When you put the spoon into this dish the creamy white filling oozes out and looks very appetizing against the golden pancakes and tomato sauce. The 'pancakes' are actually tortillas, which are very easy to make; they're not as light as pancakes but very good and very filling – you could use ordinary wholewheat pancakes instead if you prefer.

12 tortillas as described on page 332

For the filling:
700 g (1½ lb) cottage cheese, curd cheese or quark
350 g (12 oz) grated cheese
1½ teaspoons mustard powder
2 garlic cloves, peeled and crushed
Sea salt
Freshly ground black pepper

For the sauce:
1 large onion, peeled and chopped
1 tablespoon oil
1 garlic clove, peeled and crushed
792 g (1 lb 12 oz) can tomatoes
½–1 teaspoon chilli powder

To finish:
125 g (4 oz) grated cheese

Serves 6–8

Make the filling by mixing together the cottage cheese, curd cheese or quark, the grated cheese, mustard powder and garlic; add salt and pepper to taste.

Fry the onion in the oil for 10 minutes, then stir in the garlic, tomatoes, chilli powder and salt and pepper to taste. Sieve or liquidize the sauce.

Heat the oven to 190°C (375°F), gas mark 5. Grease a large shallow ovenproof dish. Spoon the filling on to the tortillas, rolling them neatly round and dividing the mixture evenly between them. Place the plump rolls side by side in the dish and pour the tomato sauce over them. Sprinkle the grated cheese on top.

Cover the dish with foil and bake the pancakes, or *enchiladas*, as they're called in Mexico, for 45 minutes, then take off the foil and leave them in the oven for a further 15 minutes or so to brown the top. They're lovely with just a lightly cooked green vegetable like sprouts, or with a green salad.

PANCAKES STUFFED WITH MUSHROOMS AND ARTICHOKE HEARTS
FRANCE

I think small open mushrooms are the best to use for this recipe because they have a lovely rich flavour when they're cooked, but you could use button mushrooms. Like the pancakes stuffed with asparagus this dish is a bit extravagant but it's a delicious mixture of tender pancakes, tasty filling and light cheesy sauce.

For the pancakes:
125 g (4 oz) plain flour – all wholewheat or half wholewheat and half white
Pinch of sea salt
2 eggs
2 tablespoons vegetable oil
200 ml (7 fl oz) milk
Extra oil for frying

For the filling:
1 onion

50 g (2 oz) butter
700 g (1½ lb) mushrooms
2 large garlic cloves, peeled and crushed
400 g (14 oz) can artichoke hearts, drained and sliced
2 tablespoons chopped parsley
4 tablespoons cream
2–3 teaspoons lemon juice
Freshly ground black pepper

234

For the sauce:
75 g (3 oz) butter
75 g (3 oz) flour
1 bay leaf
850 ml (1½ pints) milk
175 g (6 oz) grated cheese,
  preferably double
  Gloucester

1–1½ teaspoons mustard
  powder

To finish:
50 g (2 oz) grated cheese

Serves 4

Mix the batter as explained in the recipe for pancakes stuffed with asparagus, page 231 and make 12 or 15 small thin pancakes. This can be done several days in advance if convenient.

For the filling peel and finely chop the onion and fry it in the butter for 10 minutes but don't let it brown. Wash the mushrooms and pat them dry in a cloth, then halve or quarter them and add them to the butter; let them cook for 5 minutes or so until they're tender. If the mushrooms produce much water let them boil vigorously until the mixture is fairly dry. Take the saucepan off the heat and stir in the garlic, artichoke hearts, parsley and cream. Sharpen the mixture with a little lemon juice and add salt and pepper to taste.

To make the sauce melt the butter in a largish saucepan and add the flour. Cook for a moment or two then add the bay leaf and about a fifth of the milk and stir vigorously over a high heat until you have a smooth, very thick mixture. Repeat, stirring in another fifth of the milk and continue in this way until all the milk has been added and you have a smooth sauce. Take the saucepan off the heat and mix in the grated cheese, salt and pepper and enough mustard to give the mixture a nice tang. This, like the pancakes and the filling, can be made in advance.

When you're ready to assemble the dish divide the filling between the pancakes, rolling them up neatly and placing them side by side in a shallow ovenproof dish. Take the bay leaf out of the cheese sauce and pour the sauce evenly over the pancakes; sprinkle with the grated cheese. Cover the dish with foil and bake the pancakes at 180°C (350°F), gas mark 4 for about an hour, taking the foil off for about the last 15 minutes to brown the top of the dish.

The pancakes are equally good served with a cooked vegetable or a green salad, with or without potatoes.

PANCAKES STUFFED WITH SPICY RED BEANS   MEXICO

If you don't like making ordinary pancakes you might like to try this recipe which uses tortillas instead. The tortillas are very easy to make from a wholewheat flour and maize flour (or just wholewheat flour) dough; I've given the recipe and method in the bread, scones and sandwiches section.

12 tortillas, see page 332

For the filling:
1 large onion, peeled and chopped
1 tablespoon oil
2 garlic cloves, peeled and
   crushed
780 g (1 lb 11½ oz) can tomatoes
225 g (8 oz) red beans, soaked,
   cooked (see p. 22) and
   drained
½–1 teaspoon chilli powder
Sea salt
Freshly ground black pepper

Serves 6–8

For the sauce:
75 g (3 oz) butter
75 g (3 oz) flour
850 ml (1½ pints) milk
175 g (6 oz) grated cheese
1½ teaspoons mustard powder

To finish:
125 g (4 oz) grated cheese

First make the filling. Fry the onion in the oil in a large saucepan for 10 minutes, until it's soft but not browned, then stir in the garlic, tomatoes, red beans and enough chilli powder, salt and pepper to give a good flavour. Mash the beans and tomatoes a bit with the spoon to break them up.

Next make the sauce. Melt the butter in a medium-sized saucepan and stir in the flour. Cook for a moment or two then

236

pour in about a fifth of the milk. Stir over a high heat until you have a smooth, very thick mixture, then put in some more milk and continue in this way until all the milk has been added and you have a smooth sauce. Take the saucepan off the heat and mix in the grated cheese, mustard and a good seasoning of salt and pepper.

When you're ready to assemble the dish set the oven to 190°C (375°F), gas mark 5. Grease a large shallow ovenproof dish. Put some of the bean mixture on to each tortilla and roll the tortilla up neatly. Place the tortillas side by side in the dish and cover them evenly with the sauce. Sprinkle the grated cheese over the top and cover the dish with a piece of foil. Bake for 45 minutes, then remove the foil and leave the pancakes in the oven for a further 15 minutes or so to brown the top. Serve with a crisp green salad or cooked green vegetable.

PASTA AND BEANS   ITALY

You can serve this mixture as soon as it's ready or you can spoon it into a shallow ovenproof dish, sprinkle the top with bread-crumbs and grated cheese and bake until it's crisp and golden. Whichever you do I think you'll agree it's a tasty, satisfying and economical dish.

125 g (4 oz) red kidney beans
125 g (4 oz) split red lentils
1 large onion
2 tablespoons olive oil
1 garlic clove, crushed
2 tomatoes, skinned
1 litre (1¾ pints) water
125 g (4 oz) cut wholewheat
    macaroni
1 tablespoon tomato ketchup

2 tablespoons chopped parsley
1 teaspoon cinnamon powder
1 teaspoon lemon juice
Sea salt
Freshly ground black pepper

Optional topping:
Dry crumbs
50 g (2 oz) grated cheese

Serves 3–4

Put the beans and lentils into a big bowl, cover with plenty of cold water and leave for several hours if possible, then drain and rinse them. Peel and chop the onion and fry it in a large saucepan in the oil for 10 minutes. Add the garlic, tomatoes, beans and lentils and the water. Bring up to the boil, put a lid on the saucepan and leave it to simmer for 1-1¼ hours until the beans are tender. At this stage the mixture will look more like soup than anything else, but don't worry. Add the macaroni, tomato ketchup and parsley to the saucepan and let it simmer for about 10 minutes until the macaroni is tender. The mixture should still be quite moist – add a little liquid if necessary (red wine if you've got any). Then stir in the cinnamon, lemon juice and salt and pepper to taste. Serve immediately or spoon the mixture into a lightly greased shallow casserole, sprinkle with the crumbs and grated cheese and bake in a moderate oven for 30–40 minutes until golden brown.

This is lovely served with a fresh juicy salad with a good dressing.

PASTA WITH CREAM CHEESE AND WALNUTS

ITALY

Although it's quick and easy to do this dish is rich and luxurious tasting. I think it's nicest made with wholewheat pasta rings but you could use other types of pasta. Hazel nuts can be used instead of walnuts – bake them first for about 20 minutes in a moderate oven until the skins will rub off easily and the nuts underneath are golden brown.

Sea salt
1 tablespoon oil
225 g (8 oz) wholewheat pasta
 rings
15 g (½ oz) butter
350 g (12 oz) low-fat quark:
 you could use real cream
cheese but I think this
 makes the dish rather
 too rich
1 garlic clove, crushed
Freshly ground black pepper
125–175 g (4–6 oz) fresh walnuts,
 roughly chopped

Serves 4

238

Half fill a large saucepan with water; add a teaspoon of salt and the oil. Bring to the boil then put in the pasta rings and simmer them gently until they're just tender.

While the pasta rings are cooking make the cheese sauce. Melt the butter in a medium-sized saucepan over a gentle heat then add the quark or cream cheese and garlic. Stir all the time, over the heat, until the cheese has heated through and is very smooth and creamy. Season with salt and pepper.

Spoon the pasta into a hot serving dish, pour the sauce over the top and scatter with the chopped nuts. Serve with a green salad but don't put too much dressing on it as the pasta dish is rather rich.

PASTA WITH LENTILS
MIDDLE EAST

In the Middle East this would probably be made with noodles but I generally use fine wholewheat spaghetti instead. You can use either the little red split lentils or continental lentils.

For the lentils:
225 g (8 oz) split red lentils or continental lentils
1 large onion
2 tablespoons oil
2 garlic cloves
1 small green pepper or 125 g (4 oz) mushrooms
575 ml (1 pint) water
1 tablespoon tomato ketchup
1 tablespoon chopped parsley
½ teaspoon cinnamon
Sea salt
Freshly ground black pepper

For the pasta:
225 g (8 oz) noodles or wholewheat spaghetti
2 tablespoons oil

Serves 4

Wash the lentils. Peel and chop the onion and fry it in the oil in a large saucepan for 5 minutes. While this is happening peel and crush the garlic and wash, de-seed and chop the pepper or wash and chop the mushrooms. Add the garlic and pepper or mushrooms to the saucepan and cook for a further 2–3 minutes, then put in the lentils and stir them so that they get coated with the oil. Mix in the water, tomato ketchup, parsley and cinnamon; bring up to the boil then cover the saucepan and leave it to simmer gently until the lentils are cooked – from 30 minutes to an hour, depending on the type. Season with salt and pepper.

When the lentils are nearly done cook the noodles or spaghetti in plenty of boiling salted water for about 10 minutes. Drain the pasta and turn it in the oil. Serve the pasta with the lentils. A green salad goes well with this.

SPAGHETTI WITH PESTO   ITALY

Pesto looks a curious thick green mixture when it's first made, but when it's added to the hot, cooked spaghetti it really transforms it into something special with a delicious, rich flavour. You should really use fresh basil for this recipe but it's not easy to get and I find that a bunch of fresh parsley plus a good seasoning of dried basil makes a very good alternative.

225 g (8 oz) wholewheat spaghetti
Sea salt
2 tablespoons vegetable oil
2 garlic cloves, peeled and crushed
1 large bunch of fresh basil or
  a large bunch of fresh parsley
and 2–3 teaspoons dried basil
40 g (1½ oz) pine kernels
40 g (1½ oz) grated Parmesan cheese
8 tablespoons olive oil

Serves 4

Half fill a large saucepan with water and add a teaspoon of salt and the vegetable oil. Bring to the boil then gently ease in the spaghetti, pushing it down into the water as it softens. Let the spaghetti simmer gently until it's just tender – about 10 minutes. Drain the spaghetti and return it to the hot saucepan.

While the spaghetti is cooking make the *pesto*. Take the stalks off the fresh basil or parsley and put the leaves into the liquidizer goblet, together with the dried basil if you're using it and the garlic, pine kernels, Parmesan and olive oil. Blend at medium speed until you have a thick purée the consistency of softly whipped cream.

Put the pasta on to a hot serving dish and spoon the *pesto* on top; or serve the *pesto* separately and let everyone help themselves.

You'll need to serve a protein starter or pudding with this for a balanced meal – or you could offer a protein-rich salad.

Savoury Pastries, Pizzas and Pies

Savoury pastries and pies are always popular and there are some lovely vegetarian ones: light and delicious flans from France, flaky golden pies from the Middle East and cheesy pizzas from Italy which fill the kitchen with their warm fragrance as they cook and make your mouth water.

These are useful dishes for the cook because they're so adaptable. Most of them can be served either hot or cold, with salad or with cooked vegetables, for lunch or for supper. They make good starters as well as main courses and are also splendid picnic food.

The pies and flans in this section are made from three basic types of pastry. For the pies there's a light crumbly shortcrust pastry made from wholewheat flour, and a quick flaky pastry which uses half wholewheat and half white flour; and for the flans I use a wholewheat shortcrust which cooks crisply.

One of the main problems when making savoury flans is to get the pastry crisp while keeping the filling light and moist. Over the years I've tried all sorts of different ways of achieving this but the best method and the one which I always use now was discovered by a friend, a super cook, who very kindly let me into the secret of her very crisp flans. All you do is simply to brush the flan case all over with a little very hot oil as soon as you take it out of the oven; and if there's time it helps if you pre-cook the custard part of the flan before pouring it into the flan case – I've explained this is in the recipes where applicable. It also helps if you use a metal flan dish, although the method I've described works well even with a porcelain one. And in my experience there's no need to fiddle around with pieces of greaseproof paper and baking beans. Pricking the base of the flan with a fork before baking is all I ever do and seems to be completely adequate. I do think it helps, though, if you put a baking sheet on the oven shelf and heat it up with the oven, then stand the flan dish on this to get it off to a good start.

These are filling dishes and most of them contain a good quantity of protein so a vegetable starter and a fruity pudding go well with them.

INDIVIDUAL ASPARAGUS TARTS   FRANCE

These light creamy little tarts make a very good starter for a
dinner party; they're also nice with salad for lunch. They would
be lovely made in individual flan dishes if you've got them.
Otherwise use patty tins or any small ovenproof containers.

For the pastry:
150 g (6 oz) plain wholewheat
    flour
1 teaspoon baking powder
Pinch of salt
75 g (3 oz) butter
5–6 teaspoons cold water
2 tablespoons oil

For the filling:
1 onion, peeled and finely
    chopped

1 small garlic clove, peeled
    and crushed
25 g (1 oz) butter
4 egg yolks or 2 whole eggs
275 ml ($\frac{1}{2}$ pint) milk or single
    cream
Sea salt
Freshly ground black pepper
Grated nutmeg
300 g (10$\frac{1}{2}$ oz) can cut
    asparagus, drained

Serves 6

Place a baking sheet in the centre of the oven and set the temperature to 200°C (400°F), gas mark 6. To make the pastry sift
the flour, baking powder and salt into a bowl, including also
the bran left in the sieve. Rub in the butter with your fingertips
until the mixture looks like breadcrumbs, then stir in enough
water to make a dough. Roll out the pastry on a lightly floured
board and use it to line 6 individual patty tins. Prick the bases
all over and place the tins on the baking sheet in the oven. Bake
for 10–15 minutes until crisp and golden brown. Have the 2
tablespoons of oil very hot and brush this over the tarts as soon
as you take them out of the oven. Turn the oven setting down to
180°C (350°F), gas mark 4.

Fry the onion and garlic in the butter over a gentle heat for 10
minutes, but don't let them brown. Take the saucepan off the

heat. Whisk together the eggs and milk or cream then add these to the onion and garlic and cook very gently, stirring all the time until the mixture thickens. Season with salt and pepper and add some grated nutmeg to taste. Arrange the asparagus in the flans and then pour in the egg mixture, dividing it equally between them.

Bake the flans in the preheated oven for about 20 minutes until the filling is set. Serve them hot or warm.

CHEESE PIE GREECE

This is a beautiful flaky golden pie with a creamy mild-tasting cheese filling. In Greece the crust would be made from phyllo pastry and the filling from feta and mitzithra cheeses but as these ingredients are not easy to get I make it with a quick flaky pastry, and a mixture of cottage cheese, curd cheese or quark and Lancashire cheese for the filling. I also sometimes add some lightly fried onion which gives extra flavour. You might think all this is very unauthentic but it still makes a lovely pie! It's nice as a hot starter or as a main meal with a cooked vegetable, such as the cauliflower in tomato sauce. If you want to try making the pie with phyllo pastry see page 260.

For the pastry:
250 g (9 oz) plain flour – I use half wholewheat and half white flour
225 g (8 oz) butter, hard from the fridge
Cold water to mix

For the filling:
450 g (1 lb) cottage cheese, curd cheese or quark
225 g (8 oz) Lancashire cheese, grated
50 g (2 oz) flour
150 ml (5 fl oz) natural yoghurt
3 eggs
Sea salt
Freshly ground black pepper

Serves 6

246

First make the pastry – you need to do this an hour or so in advance to give it a chance to chill before you use it. Sift the flours into a bowl adding also any residue of bran left in the sieve, then grate in the hard butter using a coarse grater. Very lightly mix the butter with the flour using a fork and making sure that there are no large lumps of butter clinging together. Stir in enough cold water to make a soft manageable dough – it should be the same consistency as scone dough. Wrap the dough in a piece of greaseproof paper and put it into the fridge to chill for at least an hour.

Meanwhile you can make the filling for the pie. Put the cottage cheese, curd cheese or quark into a large bowl and stir in all the other ingredients, beating them together until you've got a nice creamy mixture. Season with salt and pepper. (If you want to add some onion to the pie chop 1 or 2 onions, fry them in a little butter and add them to the mixture when they're tender.)

Set the oven to 200°C (400°F), gas mark 6. Roll out two-thirds of the pastry and use it to line a pie dish. Dampen the edges with cold water. Fill with the cheese mixture then roll out the remaining pastry and put that on top, pressing the edges together. Trim and decorate the pie, making two or three holes in the top to allow the steam to escape. Bake the pie for 35 minutes, until it's golden brown. Serve it while it's all hot and light and flaky.

If you want to freeze this pie I think it's best to do so after cooking. To serve, remove the coverings and let the pie defrost for about 3 hours. Heat the pie through before serving it.

LITTLE CHEESE TARTLETS   RUSSIA

In Russia these little tartlets, *vatrushki*, are usually served either on their own as a first course or as an accompaniment to beetroot soup. I think they make a lovely first course if you serve them hot from the oven and offer a bowl of soured cream and chopped dill for people to spoon over the tartlets. They are also very good with the beetroot soup, turning it into a meal, but it's quite an unusual combination, best saved for those with adventurous palates!

For the filling:
225 g (8 oz) cottage cheese, curd cheese or quark
1 egg
Sea salt
Freshly ground black pepper

For the pastry:
200 g (8 oz) plain wholewheat flour

2 teaspoons baking powder
100 g (4 oz) butter or margarine and white vegetable fat mixed
2 tablespoons cold water

For the glaze:
1 egg beaten with ½ teaspoon salt

Serves 4 for lunch or supper. 4–6 as a starter

Set the oven to 220°C (425°F), gas mark 7. Make the filling by mixing the cottage cheese, curd cheese or quark with the egg and seasoning with salt and pepper.

Sift the flour, baking powder and a pinch of salt into a bowl and rub in the fat until the mixture resembles fine breadcrumbs, then add the water and mix to a dough. Roll the pastry out fairly thinly on a lightly floured board and cut into 16 or 18 7·5 cm (3 in) rounds. Put a heaped teaspoonful of the cheese mixture on to each round. Press the edges of the rounds up towards the centre to make a rim. Brush the tartlets over with the beaten egg glaze then bake them for about 20 minutes until set, puffed up and golden brown. They're nicest served immediately.

CHEESE AND ONION TART   SWITZERLAND

This is a good tart and the layer of little cubes of cheese seems to help keep the pastry nice and crisp. The proper cheeses, Gruyère and Emmenthal, are expensive and I generally use Edam instead – it gives a very similar result.

100 g (4 oz) plain flour – I
  generally use all
  wholewheat but you could
  use half wholewheat and
  half white
Pinch of salt
50 g (2 oz) butter
1 tablespoon cold water
1 tablespoon oil

For the filling:
1 medium onion
25 g (1 oz) butter
75 g (3 oz) Gruyère cheese and
  75 g (3 oz) Emmenthal
  cheese; or use all Edam cheese
2 eggs
150 ml (¼ pint) single cream
  or top of the milk
Sea salt
Freshly ground black pepper
Grated nutmeg

Serves 4–5

Put a baking sheet in the centre of the oven, then set the temperature to 200°C (400°F), gas mark 6. Sift the flour and salt into a bowl; rub in the butter until the mixture resembles fine breadcrumbs, then add the cold water and mix to a dough. On a lightly floured board roll the pastry out to fit a 20–23 cm (8–9 in) flan dish or tin. Press the pastry gently into place, trim the edges and prick the base. Cook the flan case on the baking sheet in the preheated oven for 15 minutes until it's crisp, then take the flan out of the oven. Have the tablespoon of oil smoking hot in a saucepan and as soon as you take the flan out of the oven brush it all over with the very hot oil – this will help to keep the pastry crisp.

While the flan case is cooking make the filling. Peel and chop the onion and fry it gently in the butter for 10 minutes until it's soft but not browned. Cut the cheeses into 6 mm (¼ in) dice. In a small bowl beat together the eggs and cream and season them with salt, pepper and nutmeg. Scatter half the cheese over the base of the cooked flan, put the onions on top and then the rest of the cheese; finally gently pour in the egg mixture. Bake the flan for 30–35 minutes until it's puffed up and golden. Serve hot.

This makes a good lunch with a juicy tomato salad and some fresh fruit to follow.

LEEK FLAN

FRANCE

Leeks make a delicious flan, delicate in flavour and colour, and there are many versions of this dish. I like to use soured cream or yoghurt because I think its sharp creaminess contrasts well with the slight sweetness of the leeks.

For the flan:
100 g (4 oz) plain wholewheat
   flour
Pinch of salt
50 g (2 oz) butter
1 tablespoon cold water
1 tablespoon oil

For the filling:
900 g (2 lb) leeks
25 g (1 oz) butter
150 ml (5 fl oz) soured cream
   or natural yoghurt
4 egg yolks or 2 whole eggs
Sea salt
Freshly ground black pepper

Serves 4

Put a baking sheet in the centre of the oven then set the temperature to 200°C (400°F), gas mark 6. Sift the flour and salt into a bowl, adding also the residue of bran left in the sieve, and rub in the butter until the mixture looks like breadcrumbs. Then add the water and mix to a dough. Roll out the pastry on a lightly floured board and use it to line a 20–23 cm (8–9 in) lightly greased flan tin. Prick the base of the flan with a fork, then put the flan case on the baking sheet in the oven and bake it for about 15 minutes until set and golden. Just before the flan is ready heat the tablespoon of oil in a small saucepan then take the flan out of the oven and immediately brush the surface over with the oil. Reduce the oven heat to 180°C (350°F), gas mark 4.

To make the filling cut the roots and most of the green leaves off the leeks; then slit them down the side and open up the layers under cold running water to wash away the grit. Slice the leeks fairly finely. Melt the butter in a large saucepan and put in the leeks; let them cook over a gentle heat for 10–15 minutes, with a lid on the saucepan, until they're tender. Stir them often and don't let them brown or it will spoil the flavour.

When the leeks are ready take them off the heat and stir in the soured cream. Whisk the eggs and add them to the creamy leek mixture together with seasoning to taste. Pour the mixture into the flan case and bake in the preheated oven for about 30 minutes, until the filling is set.

Serve the flan hot or warm with some cooked vegetables such as baby carrots, French beans and perhaps a good home-made tomato sauce, or serve it with a juicy tomato salad. It's also nice cold but I think it's at its best when warm.

LEEK PIE   ENGLAND

This pie from Cornwall is rather similar to the French *flamiche*. Both these pies usually contain small quantities of crumbled bacon but you can also make a very good vegetarian version, rich and creamy tasting. You could use a little of the bacon-flavoured soya protein, 'smoky snaps' with the leeks if you like, or sprinkle them with Parmesan cheese to add extra flavour.

My method of making the pie differs a little from the traditional one. Instead of baking the leeks under the pie crust then carefully removing it and pouring in the cream, which is very tricky if the pastry is light and crumbly, I find it best to boil the leeks first then mix them with the cream, cover with pastry and bake for about 20–25 minutes until the pastry is golden and the filling set.

For the filling:
1 kilo (2¼ lb) leeks
25 g (1 oz) grated Parmesan cheese; or 25–50 g (1–2 oz) 'smoky snaps'
150 ml (¼ pint) Cornish cream (or use double cream) or low-fat quark if you want a less rich, healthier dish
2 eggs, beaten
Sea salt
Freshly ground black pepper

For the pastry:
175 g (6 oz) plain wholewheat flour
1½ teaspoons baking powder
125 g (4 oz) white fat and margarine, mixed
1 tablespoon cold water
A little beaten egg (optional)

Serves 4

251

Wash the leeks and cut them into 2·5 cm (1 in) pieces. Put them into a large saucepan, cover them with cold water and bring to the boil. Simmer the leeks gently for 10–15 minutes, until they're tender, then drain them very well in a colander, using a spoon to press out all the water.

While the leeks are cooking make the pastry. Sift the flour and baking powder into a bowl adding also the residue of bran left in the sieve. Rub in the fat until the mixture resembles fine breadcrumbs then add the water and form the mixture into a dough. On a lightly floured board roll the pastry out big enough to fit your pie dish. Set the oven to 200°C (400°F), gas mark 6.

Mix the leeks with the Parmesan cheese or 'smoky snaps', the cream or low-fat quark, eggs, and salt and pepper to taste. Put the mixture into the pie dish and cover with the pastry, trimming it to fit and decorating it as you fancy. Brush it over with a little beaten egg if you want a shiny finish. Bake the pie for 20–25 minutes until the pastry is golden brown and cooked. Serve it immediately with cooked vegetables. The cream makes this a rich dish so I think it's best to serve a fresh salady starter or simple vegetable purée soup and fruity pudding.

MUSHROOM FLAN   FRANCE

Creamy, light and delicately flavoured, I think this is my favourite flan. It is delicious for a special lunch or supper. As it is rich I try to plan the rest of the meal accordingly: a simple cooked vegetable or salad to accompany the flan and a fresh-tasting fruity pudding to follow it.

For the pastry:
100 g (4 oz) plain wholewheat
   flour
Pinch of salt

50 g (2 oz) butter
1 tablespoon cold water
1 tablespoon oil

For the filling:

1 onion
1 garlic clove
50 g (2 oz) butter
225 g (8 oz) button
   mushrooms
1 heaped tablespoon
   chopped parsley

4 egg yolks or 2 whole eggs
150 ml ($\frac{1}{4}$ pint) single cream
   or milk for everyday
Sea salt
Freshly ground black pepper
Grated nutmeg

Serves 4–6

Place a baking sheet in the centre of the oven and set the temperature to 200°C (400°F), gas mark 6. Next make the pastry. Sift the flour and salt into a bowl and add the residue of bran left in the sieve. Rub the butter into the flour until the mixture looks like breadcrumbs then add the water and mix to a dough. Roll out the pastry and use to line a 20–23 cm (8–9 in) flan tin. Prick the base then put the flan into the oven on the baking sheet and bake for about 15 minutes, until it's cooked and golden. Heat the oil in a saucepan and immediately brush the surface of the flan with very hot oil. Reduce the oven heat to 180°C (350°F), gas mark 4.

While the flan is cooking make the filling. Peel and chop the onion, peel and crush the garlic and cook them together in the butter for 10 minutes, until the onion is soft but not browned. Meanwhile wash and slice the mushrooms; add these to the onion and garlic and fry for a further 3 minutes or so without a lid on the saucepan, then stir in the chopped parsley. Put the egg yolks into a medium-sized bowl and whisk them with the cream or milk. Add this to the mushroom mixture and season with salt and pepper to taste. Heat the mixture gently, stirring all the time, until it begins to thicken. This will happen quickly but don't worry even if it gets really very thick because it will be all right once it's baked.

Pour the mushroom mixture into the cooked flan case – it doesn't matter if the pastry is still hot – and bake in the oven for about 30 minutes, until the creamy mixture is set. Serve hot or warm.

ONION FLAN   FRANCE

This is a good flan with a creamy onion filling and crisp pastry base. I usually make it with milk but of course for special occasions it's lovely made with single cream instead – or a mixture.

For the pastry:

100 g (4 oz) plain wholewheat
  flour
Pinch of salt
50 g (2 oz) butter
1 tablespoon cold water
1 tablespoon oil

For the filling:

450 g (1 lb) onions, peeled
  and thinly sliced

Serves 4–6

25 g (1 oz) butter
4 egg yolks or 2 whole eggs
150 ml ($\frac{1}{4}$ pint) milk or
  single cream
50 g (2 oz) grated cheese
$\frac{1}{4}$ teaspoon mustard powder
Sea salt
Freshly ground black pepper
1 tomato, sliced, to decorate
  the top

Put a baking sheet in the centre of the oven and set the temperature to 200°C (400°F), gas mark 6. Sieve the flour and salt into a bowl, adding also the residue of bran left in the sieve. Cut the butter into small pieces and rub these into the flour with your fingertips so that the mixture looks like fine breadcrumbs; then mix in the water. Press the mixture lightly together to make a dough. Roll the pastry out on a lightly floured board and use it to line a 20–23 cm (8–9 in) flan tin. Trim the edges neatly and prick the base thoroughly all over. Put the flan on the baking sheet in the oven and bake it for 15 minutes, until it's crisp and golden brown. Just before you take the flan out of the oven heat the oil until it's smoking hot, then brush the surface of the flan all over with oil as soon as you take it out of the oven. Turn the oven down to 180°C (350°F), gas mark 4.

To make the filling fry the onions lightly in the butter until they're soft and golden – about 10 minutes. Whisk together the eggs or egg yolks and the milk or cream then add these to the onions in the saucepan and stir over a gentle heat until the mixture thickens. Take the saucepan off the heat and mix in the grated cheese, mustard and salt and pepper to taste. Pour this mixture into the flan case. Arrange the tomato slices on top. Put the flan into the oven on the baking sheet and bake for about 30 minutes, until the filling is set.

This flan is delicious served hot with some tender French beans or courgettes or a crisp salad. It also makes a good protein-rich starter before a vegetable-based main course.

PIZZA

ITALY

Pizza makes a very good vegetarian meal. It's filling and tasty and looks and smells so appetizing with its topping of red tomatoes, golden cheese and black olives, and its mouth-watering aroma of home-made bread. Although it sounds complicated pizza isn't really too difficult or time-consuming to make and only needs a crunchy green salad to accompany it.

The quantity given here is enough to fill two of those large white pizza dishes and feeds 4–8 people depending on how hungry they are. Instead of pizza dishes you could use two big baking sheets or four 18 cm (7 in) sandwich tins. Although mozzarella cheese is the authentic one it's expensive and not always easy to get, and I find Lancashire a very good substitute.

For the dough:
½ teaspoon sugar
2 teaspoons dried yeast
100 ml (4 fl oz) warm water
275 g (10 oz) plain wholewheat or wheatmeal flour
Pinch of salt
40 g (1½ oz) soft butter or margarine
1 egg

For the topping:
2 large onions
2 tablespoons oil
792 g (1 lb 2 oz) can tomatoes
125 g (4 oz) mozzarella or Lancashire cheese
Sea salt
Freshly ground black pepper
8–12 black olives, stoned and halved
A little olive oil

Serves 4–8

to make the dough first put the sugar, yeast and warm water into a small bowl and mix them briefly with a fork. Leave on one side for about 10 minutes for the yeast to froth up. While this is happening put the flour and salt into a bowl and rub in the butter or margarine. Add the yeast to the flour, also the egg, mixing them with your hands to make a dough. It should be soft enough to knead without effort but firm and pliable. Add a tiny bit more flour or water if necessary to adjust the consistency, then turn the dough on to a clean board or working surface and knead for about 5 minutes. Put the kneaded dough into a bowl, cover with a clean damp cloth then put the bowl under a polythene carrier bag if you have one and leave in a warm place to double in size – this takes 45–60 minutes.

While you're waiting for the dough make the topping. Peel and slice the onions and fry them gently in the oil for about 10 minutes until they're soft but not browned. Drain and chop the tomatoes, reserving the juice; cut the cheese into thin slices.

When the dough has doubled in size punch it down with your hand and turn it out on to a lightly floured board. Knead the dough briefly, then divide it into two or four pieces and roll each out to fit your plate or tin. Brush the plates or tins with oil and lay the dough on them, pressing it down and tucking in the edges to fit. Cover the top of the dough with the chopped tomatoes, adding a little of the juice as necessary to moisten, then arrange the fried onions and sliced cheese on top and decorate with the olives. Sprinkle a little oil over the top of the pizza and brush some over the edges of the dough. Season with salt and pepper.

Set the oven to 200°C (400°F), gas mark 6. Put the pizzas (uncovered) on one side to 'prove' for 15 minutes while the oven is heating up. I stand mine on top of the cooker so that they get the benefit of the heat from the oven as it warms up, but this isn't essential. Bake the pizzas for 15-20 minutes until the base is puffed up and the cheesy topping all golden brown and delicious-looking.

Pizza freezes very well. Place the uncooked pizza in the freezer and open-freeze until firm, then wrap it in foil or polythene.

To use the pizza, remove the coverings, leave for 15–30 minutes to defrost while the oven heats up and then bake as usual.

MUSHROOM PIZZA

Make this as above, but omit the olives. Instead arrange on top of the pizza 125 g (4 oz) washed and finely sliced button mushrooms, brushed lightly with olive oil.

HERBY PIZZA

Sprinkle the top of the tomato pizza with plenty of dried oregano or marjoram; drip a little extra olive oil over the top to moisten the herbs.

GREEN PEPPER PIZZA

Wash and de-seed a large green or red pepper. Cut the pepper into strips and fry these with the onions, adding them to the saucepan after 5 minutes. Arrange the slices on top of the pizza with the onions – you can make a very pretty pizza with a lattice of pepper strips on top.

ARTICHOKE PIZZA

Finely slice 3 or 4 canned artichoke hearts; arrange the slices on top of the tomato mixture. Omit the olives but keep the fried onions.

QUICK NON-YEAST PIZZA   ITALY

This pizza, *pizza al tegame,* is made from a flour and baking powder dough cooked in a frying pan in a little hot oil then finished off under the grill or in the oven. It's very useful for those emergencies when you find yourself having to rustle up food unexpectedly, because it's quick to make and uses basic store-cupboard ingredients. It's a dish I often make when we're holidaying in our caravan with more limited cooking facilities than usual but heartier appetites!

For the pizza base:
225 g (8 oz) plain wholewheat
  flour
2 teaspoons baking powder
½ teaspoon salt
2 tablespoons oil
6–8 tablespoons cold water

For the topping:
1 large onion
2 tablespoons oil
1 garlic clove, peeled and
  crushed

Two 425 g (15 oz) cans
  tomatoes
1 teaspoon marjoram
Sea salt
Freshly ground black pepper
125 g (4 oz) cheese, sliced,
  preferably white Cheshire
  or Lancashire but any firm
  cooking cheese will do in
  an emergency
Oil for shallow frying

Serves 4

Sift the flour, baking powder and salt into a bowl, adding the residue of bran from the sieve as well. Mix in the oil and enough water to make a soft but not sticky dough. Knead the dough lightly on a floured board then leave it to rest for a minute or two while you make the pizza topping.

Peel and chop the onion and fry it in the oil in a large saucepan for 10 minutes, until it's soft but not browned, then stir in the garlic. Drain the juice from the tomatoes – you won't need it for this recipe but it's useful for soups, sauces and for the non-cream version of the potato dish on page 124. Add the tomatoes to the onion and garlic, breaking them up a bit with the spoon. Stir in the marjoram and salt and pepper to taste; then keep this mixture warm while you finish making the base.

Divide the dough into two pieces and roll each one into a circle to fit your frying pan – probably about 20 cm (8 in). Heat a little oil in the frying pan and fry the first pizza over a moderate heat. When the underside is cooked, turn it over and fry the other side, then carefully remove the pizza and put it on to a dish or tin which will fit under the grill. Spread half the tomato mixture over the pizza, then arrange half the cheese slices on top. Put the pizza under the grill for a few minutes, just to heat up the topping and melt the cheese. Keep it warm while you make the other pizza in the same way.

A quick salad like a watercress salad or a cabbage and apple salad goes well with this and can be prepared while you're waiting for the pizzas to cook. It's also nice with frozen peas.

SAMOSAS INDIA

These little Indian pastries with their spicy vegetable filling are delicious for a main meal with some Indian curry sauce and perhaps a curried vegetable or side salad. They are also nice cold with some yoghurt or mayonnaise to dip them into and a crisp salad.

For the filling:
1 large onion
1 large garlic clove
25 g (1 oz) *ghee* or butter
1 teaspoon mustard seed
1 teaspoon ground ginger
1 teaspoon ground cumin
1 teaspoon ground coriander
900 g (2 lb) cooked mixed
  vegetables: potatoes, carrots
  and frozen peas, or whatever
  is available

Sea salt
Freshly ground black pepper

For the pastry:
200 g (8 oz) plain
  wholewheat flour
½ teaspoon sea salt
½ teaspoon baking powder
50 g (2 oz) *ghee* or butter
6–7 tablespoons cold water
Oil for deep or shallow frying

Serves 6

First make the filling. Peel and chop the onion, peel and crush the garlic. Fry them gently in the fat for 10 minutes then stir in the spices. Mix well, then add the cooked vegetables and turn these gently with a spoon so that they all get coated with the spicy onion and oil. Season with salt and pepper then let the mixture cool.

To make the pastry sift the flour, salt and baking powder into a bowl, together with any residue of bran, and rub in the butter or *ghee* and enough water to make a soft but not sticky dough. Knead the dough for 5 minutes, then divide it into 16 pieces. Roll each piece into a ball then use a rolling pin to roll each into a circle about 15 cm (6 in) in diameter. Cut the circles in half to get 32 half circles. Put a heaped teaspoonful of the filling on to each half circle of pastry, dampen the edges with a pastry brush dipped in cold water and fold the corners over to make a little triangular-shaped packet, pressing the edges well together. When all the *samosas* are ready, deep or shallow fry them a few at a time until they are golden and crisp. Drain them well and serve them hot or cold.

SPINACH PIE   MIDDLE EAST

This combination of crisp golden pastry, buttery spinach and soft white cheese is very delicious. Like the cheese pie from Greece this should really be made with phyllo pastry which you can sometimes get in delicatessens and shops specializing in foreign foods. It's not always easy to obtain but if you do get some you'll need about 225 g ($\frac{1}{2}$ lb) for the pie. Brush the pie dish with melted butter and lay a piece of the pastry in it, then brush this with more butter and put another piece on top. Repeat this until you have used half the pastry and then put in your filling. Cover the filling with more layers of pastry and melted butter as before. Trim the pie and brush more melted butter over the top. Bake the pie as for the flaky pastry version given below. You need to work fairly fast with phyllo pastry as it hardens as the air gets to it – it's a good idea to keep the pieces you're not actually using in a polythene bag until required.

If you're using the flaky pastry version you need to get organized in advance to allow time for the pastry to chill and rest.

For the pastry:
250 g (9 oz) plain flour – I
   use half wholewheat, half
   white for this pastry or an
   81% or 85% flour from the
   health shop
Pinch of salt
225 g (8 oz) butter, hard
   from the fridge
Cold water to mix

For the filling:
900 g (2 lb) fresh spinach or
   450 g (1 lb) frozen chopped
   spinach

1 large onion
Olive oil
1 garlic clove
Chopped mixed fresh herbs as
   available: parsley, chives,
   thyme
150 g (6 oz) Cheshire or
   Wensleydale cheese,
   crumbled
Sea salt
Freshly ground black pepper
A little beaten egg (optional)

Serves 4 as a main course, 6 as a starter

First make the pastry. Sift the flour and salt into a large bowl and grate in the butter. Add enough cold water to make a manageable dough – it should be pliable but not sticky. Roll the dough into a ball, wrap it in greaseproof paper and put it in the fridge for 2 hours.

Next make the filling – this too can be done in advance. If you're using fresh spinach wash it thoroughly and cook it in a dry saucepan until it's tender, then drain and chop it. If you're using frozen spinach, put it into a colander and leave it to defrost then drain off the excess water; press the spinach with a spoon to squeeze out as much water as possible. Peel and chop the onion and fry it in a little oil in a fairly large saucepan for about 10 minutes until it is tender, then take the saucepan off the heat and stir in the garlic, spinach, herbs, cheese and salt and pepper to taste. Leave the mixture to cool.

When you're ready to finish and cook the pie, set the oven to

230°C (450°F), gas mark 8. Roll out two-thirds of the pastry on a lightly floured board and gently lay the pastry in a deep pie dish. Spoon the filling into the pastry-lined dish. Roll out the remaining piece of pastry and use this to cover the top of the pie. Trim the pastry and crimp or fork the edge. Brush the top of the pie with some beaten egg if you want a shiny finish. Bake the pie for 20 minutes then turn the heat down to 200 C (400°F), gas mark 6 and cook for a further 20 minutes.

This pie makes a delicious main course if you serve it with creamy mashed potato and a brightly coloured vegetable such as carrots. Or serve it on its own as a warming and welcoming first course before one of the lighter main dishes.

The pie can be frozen; I think it's best to freeze it before glazing and cooking. Thaw the pie for 2–3 hours then glaze it with beaten egg, if you want to, and cook as usual.

Puddings

Most people like to finish a meal with a pudding – and most adults probably feel slightly guilty about eating them! For this reason I have included quite a number of light, fruity puddings that round things off nicely without being either too rich or fattening.

One nice thing about vegetarian cooking though is that it gives you the opportunity to plan a meal to take full advantage of the pudding course if you wish. You can have a simple first course such as a puréed vegetable soup, followed by a plain but tasty main course based on rice or vegetables, such as paella or tomatoes à la Provençale with noodles and French beans, then finish the meal with a flourish by serving something like a real trifle, luscious home-made ice cream with meringues, or gorgeous crêpes suzette. Or you could offer one of the tarts from the next section of this book if you want a more substantial pudding.

Some of these puddings are rich in protein, a point worth exploiting when you're planning a meal. Remember, protein is just as good if you eat it in the pudding course as in the main course; serving a nutritious pudding after a high protein main course means you're probably eating more protein than you need and the excess is just used for energy, like carbohydrates, which is wasteful. Vegetarian cookery gives you the flexibility to utilize protein economically if you wish.

APPLE SNOW   FINLAND

This is a useful pudding to serve after a filling meal because it's
light and refreshing, but it's also nourishing because of the egg
whites.

450 g (1 lb) cooking apples
125 g (4 oz) granulated sugar
2 egg whites
A little grated lemon rind

Serves 4

Peel, core and slice the apples then put them into a heavy-
based saucepan with the sugar and cook them over a gentle heat,
with a lid on the saucepan, until they're soft and purée-like.
If the apples have produced a great deal of liquid take the
lid off the saucepan and cook them for a few minutes more to
thicken them up but watch them carefully and stir them often
so that they don't burn. Cool the apples then sieve or liquidize
them.

Whisk the egg whites until they're stiff but not dry then fold
them into the apple purée. Grate enough lemon rind into the
mixture to give a refreshing tang. Divide between four individual
bowls and serve chilled. It's nice with some crisp biscuits –
macaroons go well with it.

APRICOT AND ALMOND PUDDING   SWEDEN

This easy-to-make dish from Sweden is actually halfway between
a pudding and a cake – a light, gooey almond-flavoured sponge
with apricots baked into the middle. It's best eaten warm, with
pouring cream if you like; or cold, when it can be decorated with
some piped whipped cream and toasted flaked almonds if you
want to make it extra special. You can use either canned apricots

or soaked dried apricots. If you're using the latter I think it's worth getting the best quality whole (stoned) ones if possible. It's best to use a loose-based cake tin if you have one; otherwise use an ordinary deep tin lined with foil.

125 g (4 oz) soft vegetable margarine	125 g (4 oz) ground almonds
125 g (4 oz) caster or Barbados sugar	125 g (4 oz) dried apricots, soaked and cooked until tender, or use a 425 g (15 oz) can apricot halves
2 eggs	
50 g (2 oz) plain wholewheat flour	A few flaked almonds

Serves 4

Lightly grease and flour a 20 cm (8 in) loose-based cake tin; set the oven to 160°C (325°F), gas mark 3. Put the margarine and sugar into a bowl and cream them until they're light, then add the eggs and beat again. Add the flour and ground almonds and beat the mixture until it's very light and fluffy. Put half the mixture into the base of the cake tin. Drain the apricots and arrange them on top of the almond mixture, then spread remaining mixture on top and scatter with a few flaked almonds. Bake the pudding for 60–70 minutes, until it is set and golden brown. Cool in the tin, then slip a knife round the edges, ease the pudding out of the tin and serve.

BANANA FRITTERS WITH LIME   CARIBBEAN

The recipe for these puffy banana fritters was given to me by a friend in the Caribbean and they make an interesting and unusual pudding. The only snag is they really need to be fried just before you serve them, so it means getting up from the table to do them, but they don't take long if you have everything ready in advance. I've found you can even shallow fry them if you prefer and they're still puffy and good.

50 g (2 oz) plain wholewheat
 flour
Pinch of baking powder
Pinch of salt
3 firm, ripe bananas
½ teaspoon Angostura bitters,
 if available

4 teaspoons milk
1 egg white
Fat for deep or shallow frying
Slices of lime or lemon
Soft brown sugar

Serves 4

Sift the flour, baking powder and salt into a bowl, adding also
the residue of bran left in the sieve. Peel the bananas and mash
them with a fork, then add them to the flour, together with the
Angostura bitters and milk. (You can do all this in advance.)

When you're ready to finish the fritters, whisk the egg white
until it's standing in soft peaks and fold it into the banana mixture.
Drop tablespoonfuls of the mixture into hot deep or shallow fat
and fry them until they're browned on one side, then turn them
over to fry the other side. Take the fritters out with a perforated
spoon and drain them on kitchen paper; then transfer them to a
hot dish and serve them at once, garnished with the lime or
lemon slices. Serve the soft brown sugar separately for people to
help themselves.

CHOCOLATE AND ORANGE MOUSSE   SPAIN

This is a wickedly delicious pudding; smooth dark chocolate
flavoured with the sharp freshness of orange. It's also very easy to
make.

225 g (8 oz) dark chocolate
2 tablespoons orange juice
Grated rind of 1 orange
1 tablespoon orange liqueur
 such as Curaçao – or use
 brandy

4 eggs, separated
A little whipped cream
A few toasted almonds or
 chocolate curls

Serves 6

Break up the chocolate and put it into a bowl. Set the bowl over a saucepan of boiling water, or pop it into a moderate oven for about 10 minutes until the chocolate has melted. Stir the orange juice and rind into the melted chocolate, then the liqueur or brandy and the egg yolks. Whisk the egg whites until they're standing in soft peaks then gently fold them into the chocolate mixture using a metal spoon and a cutting and folding motion. Spoon the mixture into six little dishes – it looks very nice in those little white individual soufflé dishes. Put the mousse into the fridge for at least 2 hours to chill and set. You can leave it overnight if this is convenient.

It's lovely served just as it is, or you can garnish it with some whipped cream and toasted flaked almonds or chocolate curls. To make the chocolate curls just run a potato peeler down the flat side of a bar of chocolate.

Chocolate mousse is good after Spanish vegetable rice or any cereal or vegetable-based dish.

COEURS À LA CRÈME   FRANCE

Hearts of creamy white cheese surrounded by shiny red strawberries make a beautiful summer pudding that's rich in protein and ideal for serving after something like ratatouille and rice. You need to start making the hearts the night before you want to serve the pudding. The quantities I've given are right for five of those white heart-shaped china dishes you can get with little holes in the base. Alternatively you can make some holes in the base of cream, yoghurt or small cottage cheese cartons and use these; I've also used a colander successfully. And if you can't get muslin to line the moulds, fine net curtain makes a good substitute.

450 g (1 lb) curd cheese, quark
or cottage cheese – if you're
using cottage cheese push it
through a sieve to make it
smooth

150 ml (5 fl oz) double cream
2 tablespoons caster sugar
350 g (12 oz) strawberries
A little extra caster sugar

Serves 5

Put the cheese into a large bowl, mix it with the cream and sugar and beat with a wooden spoon until the mixture thickens and holds its shape. Line your white china dishes, yoghurt, cream or cottage cheese pots, or colander, with muslin, then spoon in the creamy mixture and smooth the surface. Stand the containers or the colander on a plate to catch the liquid which will drain off and place them in the fridge overnight.

Next day wash and hull the strawberries, halving or quartering any larger ones as necessary. Then sprinkle them lightly with sugar and leave on one side.

To serve, turn the creamy cheese mixture out on to a large plate and carefully peel off the muslin. Arrange the strawberries round the cheese or cheeses.

Don't assemble this dish until just before you need it or the juice from the strawberries can spoil the look of it. It's a good way of making a few strawberries go further when they're expensive.

If you're slimming I've found you can make this dish equally well using natural yoghurt instead of cream. The result is very similar though not so creamy-tasting, and I find if I use 450 g (1 lb) low-fat quark or cottage cheese, 150 ml (5 fl oz) natural yoghurt and 3–4 tablespoons caster sugar, the mixture fills four white china hearts, not five as it does when made with double cream. The yoghurt version also gives off a little more liquid as it drains and settles in the fridge.

LITTLE COFFEE CUSTARDS

FRANCE

These little dishes of velvety, chilled coffee custard make a lovely pudding, simple, quick to make, yet luxurious tasting. They are splendid for serving when you want to increase the protein content of a meal. I've given a rather economical version of this pudding; for a special occasion it's superb with single cream replacing some or all of the milk. You can top the custards with a whirl of cream or with a baby meringue, which gives a pleasant crispness.

4 eggs
1 tablespoon good quality
   instant coffee
275 ml (½ pint) milk

50 g (2 oz) caster sugar
A little whipped cream
   or 4 baby meringues (optional)

Serves 4

Set the oven to 150°C (300°F), gas mark 2. Break the eggs into a medium-sized bowl and whisk them until they're frothy. Put the instant coffee, milk and sugar into a small saucepan and heat almost to boiling point. Remove the saucepan from the heat and gradually add the milk to the beaten eggs, stirring all the time. Strain the mixture into a jug then pour it into four little fireproof dishes – little white ramekins are ideal. Cover each dish with a piece of foil. Stand the dishes in a baking tin filled with 2·5 cm (1 in) very hot water. Place the tin in the oven and bake the custards for 45–50 minutes, or until they are firmly set and a knife put into the centre comes out clean. Cool the custards, keeping the foil over them, which prevents a hard skin from forming, then put them into the fridge. Serve the little custards straight from the fridge so that they're beautifully cold and refreshing; garnish them with whipped cream or baby meringues if you like.

COFFEE RICOTTA PUDDING
ITALY

A very easy to make, protein-rich pudding. It's lovely served after one of the vegetable casseroles or cereal main dishes, or after a low-protein pasta dish.

2 teaspoons best quality instant coffee, continental type
1 tablespoon water, rum or Tia Maria
450 g (1 lb) *ricotta* cheese, curd cheese, quark or cottage cheese – if you're using cottage cheese try to get the type with the softest, finest curds
50 g (2 oz) caster sugar

Serves 4

Dissolve the coffee by mixing it with the water, rum or Tia Maria. If the cheese is very lumpy it might be best to push it through a sieve, otherwise put it straight into a bowl. Add the coffee mixture and sugar to the cheese, stirring until everything is combined. Spoon into small dishes; serve chilled. It's nice with macaroons or other small crunchy biscuuts.

CRÈME BRÛLÉE
ENGLAND

Although this pudding sounds French it is in fact English and originated at Trinity College, Cambridge. It's a useful pudding to serve when you want to add protein to the meal. At its richest and most luxurious it's made entirely with single cream but you can also make a less extravagant version using a mixture of single cream and milk, or even just milk. You can also use two whole eggs instead of the egg yolks, but the mixture is not as smooth tasting.

271

400 ml (¾ pint) milk
150 ml (5 fl oz) single cream
40 g (1½ oz) sugar
4 egg yolks or 2 whole eggs

A vanilla pod or a few drops
   of vanilla essence
A little icing sugar

Serves 6

Put the milk and cream into a saucepan and bring up to the boil,
then take off the heat. In a medium-sized bowl beat together the
sugar and egg yolks or eggs then add the milk, stirring. Strain the
mixture back into the saucepan or into the top of a double
saucepan and add the vanilla pod or a few drops of vanilla
essence. Stir the mixture over a gentle heat for a few minutes
until it thickens, then take it off the heat, remove the vanilla
pod (this can of course be washed, dried and used again and again)
and pour the custard into little individual heatproof dishes.
Let the custard get completely cold. Two or three hours before
you want to serve them, sift a little icing sugar over the top of each
custard so that they are covered completely but not too thickly.
Place the custard under a hot grill for about 5 minutes to melt and
lightly brown the sugar. Cool, then chill the puddings in the
fridge and serve them nice and cold.

CRÊPES SUZETTE

FRANCE

Crêpes suzette sound so complicated and people are always
terribly impressed by them, but they're really not at all difficult
to make and you can do all the main preparation well in advance.

For the pancakes:
125 g (4 oz) plain flour – I
   use all wholewheat or half
   wholewheat, half white
Pinch of salt

2 tablespoons vegetable oil
2 eggs
200 ml (7 fl oz) milk
Extra oil for frying

272

For the orange sauce:
125 g (4 oz) butter
150 g (5 oz) caster sugar
Grated rind and juice of 3
  small-medium oranges

Grated rind and juice of 1 lemon
2 tablespoons orange liqueur
  such as Curaçao if available
4 tablespoons brandy

Serves 4–6

First of all make the pancakes. If you want to you can do this a
day or two in advance and keep the pancakes covered in the
fridge, or even further in advance if you've got a deep freeze.
To make the batter either put all the ingredients into the liquidizer
goblet and blend until smooth and creamy: or sift the flour and
salt into a bowl, make a well in the middle, put in the oil and eggs
and gradually beat in the milk until everything is well mixed.
If you've made the batter by hand let it stand for 30 minutes,
then beat it again before you use it.

To cook the pancakes set a small frying pan over a moderate
heat and brush the base with a thin film of oil. Pour a little
batter into the hot frying pan, tilting and turning it so that the
batter runs quickly all over the base and coats it thinly. When the
underside of the pancake is golden brown and the top of the
pancake is just set – about 20–30 seconds – turn it over using a
palette knife and your fingers and cook the second side – this
only takes a few seconds. Take the pancake out and put it on to a
plate. Brush the frying pan with a little more oil (unless you're
using a non-stick frying pan which only needs oiling after
about every 3 or 4 pancakes) and make another pancake in the
same way. Continue until all the batter is used and you have
a pile of about 14 thin pancakes. Cover them and keep them
in a cool place until needed.

You can assemble the dish an hour or so in advance. Put the
butter, sugar, grated rinds and juices, and the orange liqueur
if you're using it, into a large frying pan or shallow flameproof
dish that you can take to the table, and heat gently to melt the
butter and sugar. Turn off the heat, then dip the pancakes in this
mixture, one by one, coating each side of the pancake then folding

273

it in half and in half again, so that it's a triangle shape. As each pancake is done push it to the side of the frying pan. When all the pancakes have been dipped leave them in the frying pan or dish until you're almost ready to eat them then put the frying pan over the heat to warm through the sauce and the pancakes. When they're ready, turn up the heat high for about 1 minute to make the sauce very hot, quickly pour in the brandy and set it alight with a taper or by tilting the frying pan down towards the gas flame. You can take it to the table at this point, burning away. The flame will die out in a few seconds, when all the fat has been burnt. Serve immediately.

This is a protein-rich pudding that's delicious after a light main course.

DRIED FRUIT COMPOTE   GERMANY

A dried fruit compote has an intense, intriguing flavour which comes from the slow simmering of the fruits and which I think is delicious. It's a very useful winter pudding. You can buy 250 g (9 oz) packets of mixed dried fruits or you may be able to buy them loose in a health shop. If you prefer to make up your own selection you can buy dried apricots, apple rings, peaches, pears and prunes separately and mix them as you wish. Leave out the ginger in the recipe if you don't like it; I don't think it's authentically German but it makes this recipe taste unusual and specially good.

450 g (1 lb) mixed dried fruit
2 or 3 thin strips of lemon rind
1 or 2 pieces of stem ginger, finely chopped
4 tablespoons syrup from the jar

A little softly whipped cream
Crisp shortbread or almond biscuits to serve

Serves 4

274

Wash the dried fruit then put it into a bowl, cover generously with boiling water and leave to soak for a few hours. Transfer fruit and liquid to a large saucepan and add the lemon rind, and a little extra water if necessary to bring the level of the liquid just up to the fruit. Bring to the boil then leave it to simmer very gently for 30 minutes with a lid on the saucepan. The fruit should be very tender and the liquid reduced to a glossy-looking syrup. Remove the lemon rind and add the ginger and ginger syrup. Leave to cool, then chill the mixture. Serve in individual dishes.

I like this with a spoonful of softly whipped cream on top; some pouring cream or chilled vanilla custard sauce would also be nice.

EXOTIC FRUIT SALAD   SOUTH AMERICA

I like to use a can of pink guavas as the basis of this salad because they're such a beautiful colour and they give the mixture a rather exotic appearance and flavour. Kiwi fruit, or Chinese gooseberries, are quite easy to get these days – they sometimes appear in my local supermarket and are about the size of a large egg with a brown, slightly furry-looking skin. When you cut them open they're an amazing, gorgeous green and enhance any fruit salad mixture. But if you can't get them just use extra pineapple or banana or a small can of mangoes instead – or a fresh mango if you can get it.

410 g (14½ oz) can guavas   2 large ripe bananas
1 ripe pineapple   2–3 kiwi fruit

Serves 6

Put the syrup from the guavas into a bowl. Cut the pieces of guava into halves or quarters, then add these to the bowl of syrup. Slice the leaves and prickly skin off the pineapple and dice

275

the flesh, removing the hard centre core. Peel and slice the bananas. Using a sharp knife peel the skin off the kiwi fruit – like peeling an apple – then slice the fruit into thin rounds. Mix all the fruits together and chill the salad before serving. If you need more liquid add a little fresh orange juice.

This salad is nice served with crisp coconut biscuits.

FRESH FRUIT SALAD   ITALY

This mixture of fresh figs, with their exotic-looking purple and red flesh, oranges, peaches and plums, makes an Italian-style fruit salad reminiscent of hot sun and blue seas. If you can't get fresh figs you could use canned ones or substitute something like black grapes or strawberries instead.

4 large oranges	450 g (1 lb) ripe plums
4 large peaches	4 fresh figs

Serves 6

Cut the peel and pith from the oranges then cut out the segments of flesh, leaving the skin behind. Do this over a bowl to catch any juice. Put the orange segments into the bowl. Peel the peaches as you would tomatoes, by covering them with boiling water, leaving for 1 minute then draining; slip the point of a knife under the skin and ease it off. Cut the peaches into small pieces, discarding the stones. Halve, stone and cut up the plums, and slice the figs. Add them all to the bowl and mix everything gently together, stirring in a little extra orange juice to moisten if necessary. Chill well before serving.

VARIATIONS
A fruit salad makes one of the most delicious puddings and of course the mixture of fruits can be varied according to what's

available. Another summer version would be peaches, melon, oranges or strawberries; in the autumn those sweet, crisp green grapes, oranges, new-season apples and plums. In the winter, oranges, pineapples, Cox's orange pippins and black grapes are delicious; in the spring, sweet juicy pears, oranges, apples and green grapes.

You can make fruit salad more substantial if you want to by serving it with crisp biscuits or sponge fingers and some whipped cream or chilled pouring egg custard, or brandy snaps filled with cream.

FRUITY MUESLI SWITZERLAND

Most people think of this as a breakfast dish consisting mainly of oats and other cereals. But when Dr Bircher-Benner invented it for his patients in his clinic in Zurich at the turn of the century it was really a fruit dish and as such it makes a delicious pudding, light and nourishing. If you use condensed milk, which is the type Dr Bircher-Benner used, it gives the muesli a delectable, almost jellied consistency and sweet taste.

4 tablespoons sweetened
  condensed milk
4 tablespoons lemon juice
4 level tablespoons rolled oats

4 large eating apples
4 tablespoons chopped or
  grated hazel nuts or almonds

Serves 4

Put the condensed milk and lemon juice into a large bowl and mix them until they're smooth, then stir in the oats. Wash the apples and grate them fairly coarsely then add them to the bowl. If the mixture seems rather stiff add a little cold water or orange juice. Spoon the muesli into individual bowls and sprinkle the nuts over the top.

For a less sweet version of this pudding you can use natural

yoghurt instead of the condensed milk but the consistency will
not be quite the same.

GOOSEBERRY FOOL
ENGLAND

It's up to you whether you sieve or liquidize the gooseberries
for this fool. If you sieve them you'll get a very smooth mixture;
if you just liquidize them it will be more lumpy, but I think this
texture is rather nice. I like it best made with half yoghurt,
which gives a pleasant sharpness, and half cream, but you could
use all yoghurt for a more weight-conscious version. It's nice
made with other fruits, too; cooked rhubarb, apple, dried apricots
or blackberries, or fresh uncooked raspberries or strawberries.

450 g (1 lb) gooseberries
2 tablespoons water
125 g (4 oz) sugar
60 ml (2½ fl oz) natural yoghurt

60 ml (2½ fl oz) double cream
A little chocolate vermicelli
   or a few roasted hazel nuts

Serves 4

Wash the gooseberries then 'top and tail' them with a small
sharp knife. Put the gooseberries into a medium-sized heavy-
based saucepan with the water and cook them gently with a lid
on the saucepan until they're tender – 10–15 minutes – then
strain off the liquid which you won't need for this recipe. Sieve
or liquidize the gooseberries. Stir in the sugar, then leave them on
one side to cool.

Mix the yoghurt into the cooled gooseberry purée. Whisk the
cream until it's standing in soft peaks, then fold it gently but
thoroughly into the gooseberry mixture. Spoon the fool into
individual glass dishes and chill them in the refrigerator until
needed. Sprinkle a few strands of chocolate vermicelli or some
chopped nuts on top just before serving. This fool is nice with
macaroons.

Don't make the mistake I made while testing recipes for this book: on a hot July day I served chilled cucumber soup for a starter and gooseberry fool for a pudding – the two mixtures looked almost the same!

GROUND RICE AND ROSEWATER PUDDING   TURKEY

The traditional way of making this pudding involves simmering the milk for a long time to reduce it and thicken the mixture, so my method, using evaporated milk, is a shortcut, but it gives a lovely creamy result. I know the rosewater flavouring is not to everyone's taste, but I love it. This is a useful dish because it's rich with protein.

40 g (1½ oz) ground rice
1 large can evaporated milk
50 g (2 oz) sugar
2 tablespoons rosewater
A little red vegetable colouring

A few crystallized rose petals
  to serve
A few pistachio nuts, shelled –
  or a little chopped angelica,
  for economy

Serves 4–6

Put the ground rice into a small bowl and mix it to a paste with a little of the milk. Put the rest of the milk into a saucepan with the sugar and bring to the boil. Pour a little of the boiling milk into the ground rice paste and mix, then tip this into the saucepan of milk. Put the saucepan over a gentle heat and stir for 4–5 minutes until it has thickened and will coat the spoon fairly heavily.

Take the saucepan off the heat and stir in the rosewater and enough red colouring to tint the mixture a pale pink, then pour it into one large bowl or 4–6 individual dishes – glass ones are nice if you've got them. Leave the pudding to cool, then chill it in the refrigerator. Just before serving decorate the top with the rose petals and pistachio nuts or angelica.

LEMON WHIP   HOLLAND

This is a very light delicious pudding, just right for serving after a substantial main course that's filled you up. It's also useful because though it tastes so airy it's rich in protein. It sounds a bit fiddly to make, but really it isn't.

2 large lemons or 3–4 smaller   A few flaked almonds, toasted
  ones   under the grill until golden
125 g (4 oz) caster sugar   brown and cooled
4 eggs, separated

Serves 4–6

To make this pudding you will need a double saucepan or a china or glass basin set over a saucepan of water. Put the water to heat while you prepare the mixture. Scrub the lemons thoroughly in hot water to get rid of any residue from sprays with which they may have been treated, then grate the rind into the top of the double saucepan or the bowl. Halve the lemons, squeeze out the juice and put it in with the rind, together with the sugar. Add the egg yolks to the lemon mixture. Put the whites into a clean bowl and leave them on one side for the moment.

Stir the egg yolks, sugar and lemon over the simmering water. Gradually they will thicken to a shiny golden sauce (like lemon curd) which will coat the back of a spoon thickly. This takes about 10 minutes. Remove from the heat. Whisk the whites until they are stiff and standing in peaks, then gradually whisk in the lemon sauce. Spoon the whip into individual glasses and put it ˙nto the fridge to chill. Serve it sprinkled with the nuts.

Crisp biscuits are nice with this pudding.

MONT BLANC   FRANCE

Actually this pudding is found in both France and Italy. It's
very simple and I think very delicious, a 'mountain' of soft sieved
chestnut topped with a snowy cap of whipped cream. You could
use fresh chestnuts but I must admit I use canned chestnut purée.
Get the sweetened kind if you can; if not, beat unsweetened
purée with 125 g (4 oz) icing sugar, form it into a ball, wrap it
in foil and put it in the fridge for several hours to chill and firm up
then push it through the vegetable mill as described in the recipe.

440 g (15½ oz) can sweetened   150 ml (¼ pint) whipping cream
  chestnut purée   1 tablespoon kirsch or brandy

Serves 6

Put the chestnut purée into a vegetable mill (a Mouli-légumes)
fitted with a fairly fine blade; hold this over the flat dish from
which you intend to serve the pudding and push the chestnut
purée through. The sieved chestnut purée will fall into a mountain
shape; don't attempt to shape it at all, let the pudding stay as it is.

You can do this a few hours in advance and keep it carefully
in a cool place. Whip the cream with the kirsch or brandy until
it's in soft peaks, then spoon this gently on top of the chestnut
mountain just before serving.

This is quite a rich, filling pudding; lovely after something like
spinach *gnocchi*.

FRESH ORANGE SALAD   ITALY

This is one of the most refreshing puddings of all and I find it
very useful for serving after a more substantial main course.

| 6 large oranges | A little extra orange juice if |
| 25 g (1 oz) sugar or honey | necessary |

Serves 4

First of all wash one of the oranges and then shave off some thin slices of peel – I find a potato peeler good for this. Then using kitchen scissors snip the peel into shreds and put them into a large bowl. Next cut the peel and pith off all the oranges. Do this with a sharp knife and a round-and-round sawing action (like peeling a whole apple when you want to make a long curl of peel) and hold the oranges over the bowl as you do so to catch every drop of juice. Again with a sharp knife cut the individual sections of orange away from the white skin and add them to the bowl. When all the sections have been removed from the white skin, squeeze this over the bowl to extract the remaining juice. Add the sugar or honey to the bowl and chill.

For a Middle-eastern style orange salad, for serving after say *hummus* followed by stuffed vine leaves or pilaf, add a tablespoonful of orange flavoured water or rosewater to the mixture and garnish with a scattering of toasted almonds.

PASHKA
RUSSIA

This traditional Easter dish from Russia makes a beautiful pudding and it's useful when you're planning a cereal or vegetable meal because it's rich in protein. In Russia it's made in a special tall pyramid-shaped mould and decorated with the initials 'XB' for 'Christ is Risen'. I use a 15 cm (6 in) clay flower pot which I scrubbed and baked in a hot oven and now keep in my kitchen cupboard. *Pashka* needs to be prepared several hours before you want to eat it to allow time for the liquid to drain away through the hole in the flower pot leaving the mixture firm enough to turn out. It's nice served with macaroons, sponge fingers or slices of Madeira cake.

282

2 egg yolks

75 g (3 oz) vanilla sugar; or caster sugar and a drop or two of vanilla essence

4 tablespoons single cream or creamy milk

700 g (1½ lb) curd cheese, quark or cottage cheese

125 g (4 oz) unsalted butter, softened

50 g (2 oz) chopped candied fruits

50 g (2 oz) chopped blanched almonds

A little chopped glacé fruit

Serves 6

Beat the egg yolks and sugar together until they're pale and foamy. Put the cream or creamy milk into a small saucepan and bring it just to the boil, then pour it over the egg yolks and sugar. Tip the whole lot back into the saucepan and stir over a gentle heat until it has thickened – this won't take a moment, so watch it carefully. Leave on one side to cool.

Beat together the cheese and butter; add the candied fruits and nuts and finally the cooled custard. Line your 15 cm (6 in) flower pot with a double layer of dampened muslin or fine net curtain, spoon in the *pashka* mixture and smooth the top. Fold the ends of the muslin over the top, cover with a saucer and a weight and leave in a cool place or the fridge for several hours, preferably overnight. Some moisture will seep out of the hole in the base of the flower pot so stand it on a plate.

To serve the pudding invert the flower pot on to a serving dish, turn out the *pashka* and carefully peel off the muslin or net. Decorate with the glacé fruit.

FRESH PEACH SALAD   ITALY

A luscious salad that's very refreshing after a substantial main course. I make it with orange juice instead of a sugar syrup; this is healthier and also adds its own delicious flavour. It's lovely accompanied by crunchy macaroons.

8 large ripe peaches
150 ml (¼ pint) orange juice

Serves 6

Put the peaches into a bowl and cover them with boiling water. Leave the peaches for 1 minute, then drain and cover them with cold water. Strip the skins off using a small, sharp pointed knife. Cut the peaches in half, remove the stones, then slice the flesh fairly thinly. Put the slices into a serving dish – a pretty glass bowl is ideal – cover them with orange juice and chill until needed.

STUFFED PEACHES   ITALY

In this recipe peaches are stuffed with macaroon crumbs and baked until tender. It's a curiously pleasant blend of flavours and a good way of using peaches which are not quite as luscious as they might be.

4 large peaches
75 g (3 oz) macaroons (about 3)
1 egg yolk

Serves 4

Set the oven to 180°C (350°F), gas mark 4. Cut the peaches in half and carefully prise out the stones, then scoop out a little of the peach flesh to make a larger cavity for the stuffing. Crush the macaroons with a rolling pin; mix the macaroon crumbs with the chopped, scooped-out peach flesh and the egg yolk. Spoon the mixture into the peach cavities and place the two halves of the peach together again. Put the stuffed peaches into a buttered ovenproof dish – a nice one that you can take to the table is best – and bake them for 45–60 minutes until they're tender when pierced with a knife. They're good with single cream or chilled vanilla custard.

PEARS BAKED IN WINE   FRANCE

One of the nicest things about this dish is its appearance: shapely whole pears, richly and deeply stained and flavoured with wine. A large bowl of them always goes down well. The only trouble is that they take about 4 hours to cook in a lowish oven, so they're only really worth doing if you can justify the oven heat by baking a fruit cake, casserole or even meringues at the same time.

Serve the pears with a big bowl of light, fluffy whipped cream and some home-made shortbread or macaroons for a special occasion pudding.

900 g (2 lb) small, hard pears – l   400 ml ($\frac{3}{4}$ pint) cheap red wine
  like Conference   125 g (4 oz) granulated sugar

Serves 4

Set the oven to 160°C (325°F), gas mark 3. Peel the pears, keeping them whole and leaving their stalks on. Put them into a shallow ovenproof casserole and add the wine and sugar. Place the casserole in the oven and bake (uncovered) for about 4 hours, until the pears feel very tender when pierced with the point of a knife. Turn the pears over once or twice during the cooking time so that they bake evenly.

When the pears are ready pour the liquid off into a small saucepan and bubble it over a high heat for about 10 minutes until it has reduced in quantity and looks syrupy. Arrange the pears in a serving dish and pour the syrupy liquid over them. Serve them warm or chill them in the fridge.

PINEAPPLE SORBET
ITALY

If you've got a liquidizer this is very easy to make. It turns out a beautiful pale yellow and has a lovely sweet true pineapple flavour, very refreshing after a filling meal. Because the pineapple is naturally sweet you don't need to add much sugar.

1 large ripe pineapple
50 g (2 oz) sugar
2 egg whites

Serves 4–6

Turn the fridge to its coldest setting. Slice the pineapple into quarters then cut off the leafy top and all the prickly skin; also any hard core. Cut the pineapple into rough chunks, put them into the liquidizer with the sugar and blend them to a smooth creamy looking purée. Tip this purée into a container which will fit into the freezing part of your fridge and freeze until it's solid round the edges.

Whisk the egg whites until they stand in soft peaks. Break up the pineapple mixture with a fork then gradually add it to the egg whites, still whisking. Put the mixture back into the fridge and freeze until it's solid.

Turn the fridge back to its normal setting. The sorbet tastes best when it's not too cold and iced so it's a good idea to move it from the freezing part of the fridge on to one of the shelves about 30–45 minutes before you sit down for your first course. It's nice with crumbly shortbread fingers and I must admit I also like some whipped cream with it.

PRUNE DELIGHT

NORWAY

In Norway this is called *sviskeblancmange*, which means prune blancmange but if I call it this I find it tends to put people off and so I refer to it as prune delight which I think describes it better. I know that to some people the thought of prunes can never be delightful, but if you like them, as I do, then I think you will enjoy this pudding.

350 g (12 oz) prunes
2 tablespoons cornflour
Grated rind of ½ lemon
About 50 g (2 oz) sugar

Flaked almonds
Whipped cream
A little cinnamon powder

Serves 4–6

Put the prunes into a good-sized bowl, cover them with boiling water and leave them to soak for several hours if possible. Then transfer them to a saucepan and simmer them gently until they're tender. Drain the prunes but keep the liquid. Using a small sharp knife remove the stones. Put the prunes into the liquidizer with 400 ml (¾ pint) of the liquid in which they were cooked and blend until smooth; or put the prunes through a Mouli-légumes then mix them with the liquid.

Put the cornflour into a small bowl and mix it to a smooth paste with a little of the prune purée. Bring the remaining purée to the boil in a medium-sized saucepan and then add a little of it to the cornflour; when it is blended pour all of this cornflour mixture in with the rest in the saucepan and stir it over a gentle heat for a couple of minutes to cook the cornflour. Take the mixture off the the heat and let it cool slightly then add the lemon rind and sugar to taste. Pour into individual dishes and leave to cool, then chill in the fridge.

Scatter the top of each pudding thickly with almonds and serve with whipped cream, or pipe or spoon some cream on top of each portion and sprinkle with cinnamon powder. Crumbly short-bread fingers go well with this.

I haven't tried this yet but I think this pudding would be delicious for a special occasion if you soaked the prunes in sweet white wine or cider instead of water with maybe a dash of brandy added to the mixture after cooking.

PUMPKIN IN ORANGE SYRUP   SOUTH AMERICA

If you don't tell people what this is they may well think it's some exotic fruit they're eating!

1½ kilos (3½ lb) pumpkin,
    weighed in the shop with skin
    and pips

275 ml (½ pint) water
125 g (4 oz) sugar
1 orange

Serves 4

Remove the peel and seeds from the pumpkin and slice the flesh into pieces. Put the water and sugar into a medium-sized saucepan and bring to the boil over a gentle heat. Scrub the orange under hot water then cut off 3 thin ribbons of peel – a potato peeler is good for doing this. Add the peel and the pumpkin to the sugar syrup in the saucepan and let it all simmer gently for about 10 minutes, until the pumpkin is tender. Remove the pumpkin and orange peel with a draining spoon and put them into a bowl. Boil the syrup in which the pumpkin was cooked until it has reduced to just 2–3 tablespoonfuls and is very thick. This will take just a few minutes over a high heat without a lid on the saucepan. Pour the syrup over the pumpkin in the bowl and leave it to get cool.

Serve the pumpkin chilled. A tablespoonful of orange liqueur is lovely added to the syrup if you really want to be impressive. Another variation is to cover the cooked, drained pumpkin with orange juice instead of the syrup – this is a fresh-tasting, lower calorie version!

RED FRUIT PUDDING
DENMARK

I think this is one of the most delicious puddings and it makes a little fruit go a long way. My version is unusual in that I hardly cook the fruit; I think this gives a particularly fresh-tasting result. Serve the pudding in individual glass bowls if possible to show off its rich ruby red colouring.

225 g (8 oz) fresh ripe fruit –
    redcurrants, raspberries or
    strawberries, or a mixture
575 ml (1 pint) water
50 g (2 oz) cornflour

125 g (4 oz) caster sugar
A few flaked almonds
Whipped cream (optional)
Sponge fingers

Serves 4

Wash the fruit and remove any little bits of stalk. Put the fruit into the liquidizer goblet with all the other ingredients and blend to a purée. Tip this purée into a saucepan and stir over a gentle heat until it thickens. Cook for a couple of minutes, then take off the heat and pour into 1 large or 4 smaller dishes. Let the pudding cool, then chill it if you wish. Decorate the top with a sprinkling of flaked almonds and some cream if you like, and serve with sponge fingers.

RHUBARB COMPOTE
NORWAY

I think this pretty pink, slightly jellied compote is one of the nicest rhubarb puddings. It's light and refreshing, delicious with crisp crumbly shortbread biscuits or sponge fingers.

450 g (1 lb) rhubarb

275 ml (½ pint) water

125 g (4 oz) caster sugar

A vanilla pod or a few drops
of vanilla essence

2 tablespoons cornflour or
arrowroot

Shortbread biscuits or
sponge fingers

Lightly whipped cream
(optional)

Serves 4

Wash and trim the rhubarb, cutting off the leaves and scraping
off tough fibres if necessary, then cut the stalks in 2·5 cm (1 in)
lengths. Put the water, sugar and vanilla into a medium-sized
saucepan and bring to the boil. Add the rhubarb and simmer
very gently, with a lid on the saucepan, until the rhubarb is almost
tender. This takes from 5–15 minutes, depending on the age and
type of rhubarb. Remove the vanilla pod.

Mix the cornflour or arrowroot to a paste with a little cold
water and add to the rhubarb, stirring all the time. Simmer for 2
minutes, until thickened. Pour into 4 individual serving bowls;
cool, then chill. Serve with the crunchy biscuits or sponge fingers
and cream.

RICE AND ALMOND PUDDING   DENMARK

This is rich and luxurious-tasting and guaranteed to appeal even
to people who think they don't like rice pudding! In Denmark
it's served at Christmas time. You will notice that I use ordinary
white 'pudding' rice for this recipe. If you're very keen on whole
foods you might not approve of this but I haven't found brown
rice satisfactory, and the amount is so small anyway.

40 g (1½ oz) white 'pudding'
   rice
575 ml (1 pint) milk
40 g (1½ oz) sugar
50 g (2 oz) flaked almonds
1 teaspoon vanilla essence

150 ml (5 fl oz) whipping
   cream
225 g (8 oz) frozen raspberries
A little caster sugar
1 tablespoon cherry brandy
   or kirsch (optional)

Serves 4–6

Wash the rice and put it into a pie dish with the milk and sugar.
Bake in a lowish oven for 2–3 hours, to make a rice pudding. The
temperature isn't crucial: 150°–160°C (300–325°F), gas mark 2–3
is best but if necessary the pudding can cook near the bottom of
a hotter oven. As the skin forms stir it into the pudding – this gives
a nice creamy result. When the rice is soft and the pudding thick
take it out of the oven and leave it to get cold, then beat it and
add the almonds and vanilla. Whip the cream until it stands in
soft peaks, then fold into the rice mixture. Chill.

Next make the raspberry sauce. Sieve the raspberries, sweeten
them with just a little caster sugar and flavour with the cherry
brandy or kirsch if using it. Serve the pudding in small bowls and
spoon the sauce attractively over the top.

TRIFLE   ENGLAND

Proper trifle, made with egg custard and topped with whipped
cream, is a delicious pudding, light, not too sweet and excellent
served after a cereal or vegetable-based main course or to round
off a salady buffet meal.

1 small sponge cake or 1
   batch of sponge fingers
   (page 313)
3 tablespoons raspberry jam
4 tablespoons cheap sherry

For the custard:
3 eggs
50 g (2 oz) caster sugar –
   vanilla sugar if you have it,

otherwise add a few drops
   of vanilla essence
575 ml (1 pint) milk

To finish:
250 ml (10 fl oz) whipping
   cream
25 g (1 oz) toasted flaked
   almonds

Serves 6–8

Split the sponge cake and sandwich with the jam or sandwich the fingers together in pairs then cut them up into smaller pieces. Put the pieces of sponge into the base of a serving dish – a pretty glass one is nice – and pour the sherry over them. Leave on one side while you make the custard.

Whisk the eggs and sugar together in a bowl; put the milk into a saucepan and bring it just to the boil, then pour it over the egg mixture and whisk again. Strain the mixture back into the saucepan and stir over a gentle heat for just a minute or two until it thickens. Don't let it over-cook or it will separate. (If this does happen I've found if I put it in the liquidizer for a moment and blend it at a high speed, amazingly, it seems to be all right again.) Pour the custard over the sponge pieces and leave on one side to cool. To finish the trifle whisk the cream until it's softly thickened, then spoon it over the top of the trifle. Chill the trifle then sprinkle the almonds over the top just before you serve it, so that they're still crisp.

VANILLA ICE CREAM   ITALY

Home-made ice cream sounds like hard work but it isn't really all that much effort and the result is so delicate and creamy that it's well worth it. My recipe is a fairly modest economical one but I think you'll find the flavour and texture are good. Actually home-made ice cream isn't really extravagant when you consider what a useful source of protein it is and plan the meal accordingly. It's excellent, for instance, after a simple pasta, rice or vegetable-based meal.

2 eggs or 4 egg yolks
275 ml (½ pint) creamy milk
75 g (3 oz) vanilla sugar, or
   caster sugar plus a few

drops of vanilla essence
250 ml (10 fl oz) whipping
   cream

Serves 4

Turn the fridge to its coldest setting. Whisk the eggs in a medium-sized bowl. Put the milk and sugar into a heavy-based saucepan and bring just up to the boil, then slowly add it to the eggs, stirring all the time. Strain the eggs and milk back into the saucepan, put back on the heat and stir for just a minute or two until the mixture thickens – this happens very suddenly and the custard soon goes lumpy and curdled if you're not careful. Don't worry if it does; I've found that this doesn't affect the ice cream. Cool.

Whisk the cream until it has thickened and is standing in soft peaks, then fold this gently but thoroughly into the cooled egg custard. Pour the mixture into a suitable container (don't cover with a lid) and freeze until it's setting well round the edges. Then scrape the ice cream into a bowl and whisk it thoroughly. Put the ice cream back into the container and freeze it until it's firm

It's a good idea to put the ice cream into the main part of the refrigerator at the beginning of the meal so that it can soften a little. Don't forget to turn the fridge setting back to normal.

YOGHURT

MIDDLE EAST

Chilled and served in small bowls, yoghurt makes a delicious, refreshing pudding. It's particularly good for a special occasion if you use evaporated milk or even single cream or a proportion of single cream. It's also used in a number of other recipes in this book; I find it particularly useful in salad dressings. It's not difficult to make; all you need is a suitable warm place in which to put the yoghurt while it sets. I stand my yoghurt on the gas cooker by the pilot light; alternatively you can use an airing cupboard or find a corner near a radiator.

575 ml (1 pint) milk
2 rounded tablespoons skim
  milk powder
1 teaspoon fresh natural

yoghurt – from a carton or
  from your last batch
A little demerara sugar to
  serve

Serves 4–6

Put the milk into a saucepan and bring up to the boil, than leave it to simmer, without a lid on the saucepan, for 10 minutes. This reduces the milk a little and makes the yoghurt thick and creamy. Take the saucepan off the heat and leave it until it has cooled to lukewarm. While you are waiting for the milk to cool select a bowl or two jars big enough to take the milk and sterilize them by swishing them out with warm water with some household bleach added, then rinse them thoroughly again in hot water.

Whisk the milk powder and yoghurt into the milk then pour it into your clean sterilized bowl or jars, cover with foil and leave in a warm place for a few hours or overnight until it's firm. Cool, then put the yoghurt into the fridge where it will firm up even more and be thick and creamy to eat. To serve spoon the yoghurt out into individual dishes and sprinkle with sugar just before taking to the table.

If you prefer you can make the yoghurt directly into little individual dishes, as you would egg custards. I think it's particularly attractive done like this because you can dig your spoon into the firm, creamy mixture.

Sweet Pastries, Biscuits and Cakes

This is quite a varied collection of goodies. There are some mouthwatering pastries such as the apple tart from France, the cheese cake and raisin sour cream pie from the USA, the yoghurt tart from Greece and *linzertorte* from Austria, which all make delicious puddings after a light main course or salad. Then there are a few cakes, such as Madeira cake and Dundee cake which are probably mainly useful for tea-time, although a slice of Dundee cake can be nice after a salad instead of a pudding, and slices of Madeira cake are good with fools and fruit salads. Also good as accompaniments to puddings are the various biscuits which is the main reason I've included them: a little dish of crumbly home-made shortbread, crunchy coconut biscuits or crisp macaroons provide the final touch when you're serving a special fruit salad or compote and they're not difficult to make.

As you will have gathered by now I am keen on using wholewheat flour and some of the recipes are made entirely with wholewheat flour while in others I suggest using a mixture of wholewheat flour and white flour (try to get unbleached white flour from the health shop). You can of course use just wholewheat flour or just white flour if you prefer; but the proportions I've suggested in the recipes are the ones which I've found to work in practice, bearing in mind the sometimes conflicting aims of healthiness on the one hand and taste and appearance on the other!

APPLE TART
FRANCE

This tart looks so appetizing with its glossy golden rings of apple slices on a crisp pastry base. If you have time bake the pastry base before you put on the topping because the pastry is then lovely and crisp, a delicious contrast to the soft apple slices and moist golden apricot glaze. I make this tart on one of those big round ceramic pizza dishes measuring 30 cm (12 in) across but any big flat ovenproof plate or tin would do.

For the pastry base:
200 g (8 oz) plain wholewheat flour
2 teaspoons baking powder
50 g (2 oz) soft margarine
50 g (2 oz) white vegetable fat
2 tablespoons water

For the topping:
900 g (2 lb) apples – Bramleys or Golden Delicious

For the glaze:
350 g (12 oz) apricot jam
4 tablespoons water
2 teaspoons cornflour

Serves 6

First set the oven to 200°C (400°F), gas mark 6, then make the pastry. Sift the flour into a large bowl, adding also the residue of bran left in the sieve. With your fingertips rub the fats into the flour until the mixture looks like breadcrumbs, then add the cold water and mix a dough. Turn the dough on to a floured board and roll it out to fit your plate or tin. Turn under the edges of the pastry to make it fit the dish neatly then decorate the edge by pressing it with the prongs of a fork. Prick the pastry all over then bake it in the preheated oven for 15 minutes, until it's golden brown. Take the flan out but leave the oven on.

While the flan is cooking prepare the apples. Cut them into quarters, then remove the skin and core with a sharp knife and cut the apples into thin slices. Arrange these slices on the pastry base, overlapping them a bit to get a nice even pattern. When the apple is all arranged put the tart into the oven and bake it for 30 minutes, until the apple feels tender when pierced with the point of a knife.

Towards the end of the cooking time prepare the apricot glaze. Heat the apricot jam in a small saucepan with 2 tablespoons of the water. Mix the remaining 2 tablespoons with the cornflour in a small bowl or cup. When the jam is boiling, pour some of it over the cornflour mixture, stir, then return it to the saucepan and stir over the heat for about 2 minutes until it has thickened. Take the saucepan off the heat and pour the glaze evenly over the top of the hot tart; try to make sure that all the apple is covered with the lovely shiny apricot glaze, then leave it to cool slightly before serving. We like it best hot, but you could equally well serve it cold.

BRANDY SNAPS   GREAT BRITAIN

Crisp brandy snaps with their filling of brandy-flavoured whipped cream are really sheer indulgence and a very French-tasting British contribution. This is an easy recipe for brandy snaps because it doesn't contain golden syrup and so you have more time to get the brandy snaps off the baking tray and curl them up before they harden. They are really quite easy, and lovely for serving for a special occasion, perhaps to accompany a fruit salad or purée. You can also keep them flat and serve them without cream as crisp biscuits, or roll them up tightly into 'cigarettes'. Like this they're good with gooseberry fool.

50 g (2 oz) soft margarine
50 g (2 oz) soft brown sugar
50 g (2 oz) plain flour – I use
  white for these
¼ teaspoon ground ginger

To finish:
150 ml (5 fl oz) whipping
  cream
A little icing sugar
1–2 teaspoons brandy

Makes 12

Put the margarine and sugar into the bowl and cream them together, then sift in the flour and ginger and mix to a smooth dough. If you've got time to cover the bowl and leave it on one side for an hour or so before using, I've found this helps the brandy snaps to cook better.

When you're ready to cook them, set the oven to 190°C (375°F), gas mark 5. Grease a large baking sheet with butter. Roll teaspoons of the brandy snap mixture into balls and place them well apart on the baking sheet. You will probably have to cook them in two batches. Bake the brandy snaps for about 15 minutes, until they're golden brown in the middle, deeper brown at the edges. Take the baking sheet out of the oven and let it stand for 2 minutes, then ease the brandy snaps off the baking sheet with a palette knife. (As there is quite a lot of fat in the mixture it's not difficult to get them off the tray and I find I don't have to grease it again between batches.) Roll the brandy snaps around the handle of a wooden spoon and leave them to cool. As they cool they will get crisp. Keep them in an air-tight tin until you want them.

Whip the cream until it's standing in soft peaks. Stir in the icing sugar to taste and the brandy and whip again. Then spoon or pipe the cream into the brandy snaps. Serve them as soon as possible after this, while they're still crisp.

CHEESE CAKE   USA

This cheese cake looks most impressive if you make it in a small-ish, deep tin – an 18 cm (7 in) spring cake tin with removable base is ideal – so you get a good layer of the lovely white creamy mixture above the crumb base. Alternatively you can use a cake tin lined with foil or a fluted porcelain flan dish, but with the flan dish, of course, the sides of the cheese cake are hidden, and I think then a topping of fruit, such as strawberries with a shiny glaze of red-currant jelly, is a nice finish.

I've experimented a good deal to find the right combination of cream cheese and cream and I think this mixture of low-fat quark (or cottage cheese if you can't get it) and soured cream gives the best result – light but creamy. If you prefer a richer cheese cake you could use cream cheese or half cream cheese and

299

half quark or cottage cheese. On the other hand, you can make a very good low-fat cheese cake by using cottage cheese or skim milk quark with natural low-fat yoghurt instead of the soured cream.

125 g (4 oz) digestive biscuits	½ teaspoon vanilla extract
50 g (2 oz) butter, softened	or essence
225 g (8 oz) low-fat quark or	75 g (3 oz) caster sugar
cottage cheese	1 tablespoon lemon juice
2 eggs	150 ml (5 fl oz) soured cream

Serves 6–8

Set the oven to 150°C (300°F), gas mark 2. Put the digestive biscuits on a board and crush them with a rolling pin, then mix them with the butter. Press the biscuit mixture evenly into the base of your chosen container. Leave on one side while you make the filling. To do this, if you've got a liquidizer, just put everything into the goblet and blend for a minute until smooth. Alternatively, push the cottage cheese through a sieve into a large bowl, or just put the quark straight into the bowl, then add the eggs, vanilla, sugar, lemon juice and soured cream and beat thoroughly to a smooth creamy consistency. Pour the mixture into the tin or flan dish on top of the crumbs.

Bake the cheese cake towards the bottom of the oven for 1–1¼ hours (depending on the size of the tin) or until it looks set and feels firm to a very light touch. Cool, then chill. If you've used a cake tin with a removable base, slip a knife round the sides of the cheese cake and unclip the spring on the tin. Stand the tin on something like a jam jar and carefully slip the sides of the tin down, leaving the cheese cake standing clear. If you've used a foil-lined tin, lift the cheese cake out of the tin then flatten the edges of the foil and carefully lift the cheese cake off the foil using a fish slice.

If you want to top your cheese cake with fruit you'll need 350–450 g (12 oz–1 lb) strawberries and about 4 tablespoons of redcurrant jelly. Wash and dry the strawberries then arrange them on top of the chilled cheese cake. Melt the jelly in a small

saucepan then pour it evenly over the strawberries to glaze them.
Leave to set before serving.

HONEY CHEESE CAKE   GREECE

I think this cheese cake, like the one from the USA, is best made
in one of those deep spring cake tins, 18 cm (7 in) diameter, with
a loose base, because this gives a nice thick luscious layer of
filling. You can of course also use a cake tin with a layer of foil,
or a 20–23 cm (8–9 in) fluted china flan dish, although with the
flan dish the layer of filling will be thinner.

For the flan case:
150 g (6 oz) plain flour – use
   wholewheat or half wholewheat
   and half white
100 g (4 oz) butter
1 egg yolk

For the filling:
450 g (1 lb) low-fat quark or
   cottage cheese
125 g (4 oz) sugar
175 g (6 oz) honey
2 eggs
1 teaspoon powdered
   cinnamon
1 egg white

Serves 6

First set the oven to 190°C (375°F), gas mark 5, then prepare
your container by greasing it lightly with butter. Next make the
pastry. Sift the flour into a bowl (adding any residue of bran left
in the sieve), then rub in the butter until the mixture looks like
fine breadcrumbs. Add the egg yolk and knead the mixture
gently together to form a dough. Turn the dough out on to a
lightly floured board, knead it a little until it's smooth, then roll it
out and gently ease it into your baking tin or flan dish. I find the
best way to do this with the crumbly wholewheat pastry is to tip
the pastry straight from the board to the tin, hoiding the board
with one hand and easing the pastry into the tin with the other.
Leave on one side while you make the filling.

The easiest way to make the filling is to put everything into the liquidizer goblet except the egg white and blend until it's smooth. Alternatively, push the cottage cheese through a sieve (no need to sieve quark), then gradually beat in all the other ingredients except the egg white. Whisk the egg white until it's stiff and fold it in, then pour the mixture into the pastry case and smooth the top gently. If you're using the deep tin it may be necessary to trim the pastry a little so that it's practically level with the filling. Put the cheese cake into the oven to bake it for 30 minutes then turn the oven down to 160°C (325°F), gas mark 3 and cook for a further 50 minutes.

Let the cheese cake cool before serving. It can be served just warm or chilled – I think this is best as the chilling firms the cheese cake up and makes the filling luscious and creamy to eat. This is an ideal pudding to serve after one of the low-protein stuffed vegetable main courses, with perhaps *hummus* to start the meal.

CHOCOLATE BROWNIES

USA

These chocolate slices are quick and easy to make and don't need any icing as they're lovely and gooey. I like them particularly because you can use brown sugar and wholewheat flour to make them and they're all the better for it. You can use other nuts instead of pecans if you like – walnuts are probably the obvious substitute but I think hazel nuts are especially good because they make the brownies taste rather like nutty chocolate!

225 g (8 oz) butter or
  vegetable margarine
25 g (1 oz) cocoa
200 g (7 oz) brown sugar
2 eggs
75 g (3 oz) plain wholewheat
  flour

½ teaspoon baking powder
½ teaspoon vanilla extract
75 g (3 oz) roughly chopped
  pecan nuts – or use walnuts
  or hazel nuts

Makes 18

302

Set the oven to 180°C (350°F), gas mark 4. Lightly grease a Swiss roll tin. Put the butter or margarine into a saucepan with the cocoa and sugar and heat gently until melted. Remove from the heat and cool to lukewarm, then beat in the eggs one by one. Sift the flour and baking powder into the mixture, adding the bran left in the sieve as well, and mix well, then stir in the vanilla extract and nuts. Pour the mixture into the prepared tin, pushing it into the corners. Bake in the centre of the oven for about 30 minutes, until the mixture springs back when touched lightly in the centre.

Allow the brownies to cool in the tin, then cut them into 18 pieces.

COCONUT BISCUITS   SOUTH AMERICA

These crunchy coconut biscuits are lovely with creamy fools and fruit salads, especially the exotic fruit salad which comes from South America too.

50 g (2 oz) butter, softened
100 g (3½ oz) caster sugar
100 g (3½ oz) plain
  wholewheat flour

1 teaspoon baking powder
3 tablespoons beaten egg
25 g (1 oz) desiccated coconut
Extra coconut to finish

Makes 24

Set the oven to 180°C (350°F), gas mark 4. Put the butter and sugar into a bowl and sift the flour and baking powder on top. Also add the beaten egg and coconut then just mix everything together to a soft dough. Sprinkle a board with desiccated coconut and turn the dough out on to this; knead it lightly into a long sausage shape, then flatten the sausage a bit. Cut 6 mm (¼ in) slices off the sausage to make roughly finger-shaped biscuits and place these on a greased and floured baking sheet. Don't put them very close together as they will almost double in size.

Press a little more coconut on to the top of each biscuit and bake them for 15–20 minutes until they're golden brown. Let them cool for a few minutes on the baking sheet, then transfer them to a wire cooling rack.

DUNDEE CAKE SCOTLAND

You can make this traditional Scottish cake very quickly if you use the modern all-in-one method. I've included it partly because it's irresistible, with its luscious fruit inside and topping of crunchy almonds, and also because it makes a very acceptable 'pudding' after a salad lunch or supper.

275 g (10 oz) mixed dried fruit
125 g (4 oz) glacé cherries
150 g (5 oz) plain wholewheat
  flour
Pinch of salt
2 teaspoons baking powder
1 teaspoon mixed spice

125 g (4 oz) butter, softened
125 g (4 oz) soft brown sugar
2 eggs
1 teaspoon grated orange rind
2 tablespoons orange juice
25 g (1 oz) flaked almonds

Makes one 15 cm (6 in) cake

Prepare a 15 cm (6 in) round cake tin by lining it with a strip of greaseproof paper round the edge and a circle in the base. Set the oven to 160°C (325°F), gas mark 3.

Wash the dried fruit in warm water then dry it well in a clean cloth. Rinse the cherries under hot water to wash off the syrup, then halve them. Sift the flour, salt, baking powder and mixed spice into a bowl, adding also the residue of bran which will be left in the sieve. Add all the ingredients except the almonds and beat them until they're light – this is of course easily done with an electric mixer. The mixture should be light, thick and fluffy looking.

Spoon the mixture into the prepared tin, sprinkle the flaked almonds on top and bake in the centre of the oven for 2 hours or until a skewer pushed gently into the centre of the cake comes out clean. Remove the cake from the oven and cool it on a wire rack. Strip off the paper when the cake is cool.

LINZERTORTE

This light, crumbly tart is delicately flavoured with spices and lemon rind and melts in your mouth. I experimented many times with this recipe until I came up with this version which we think is just right. With one of my later efforts my husband said he liked the flavour but the tart wasn't thick enough to get his teeth into, so I increased the amount of pastry to the present quantity. If you'd like to make a thinner tart you could try using only 125 g (4 oz) of flour, almonds and butter and 25 g (1 oz) sugar or alternatively use a larger tin.

175 g (6 oz) plain wholewheat flour
1 teaspoon powdered cinnamon
Pinch of ground cloves
175 g (6 oz) ground almonds – or whole unbleached almonds pulverized in a liquidizer

Grated rind of ½ lemon
40 g (1½ oz) sugar
175 g (6 oz) butter
1 egg yolk
175–225 g (6–8 oz) raspberry, cherry or blackcurrant jam – the raw sugar conserves from health shops are ideal
A little icing sugar

Serves 6

Sift the flour, cinnamon and cloves into a bowl; add also the residue of bran left in the sieve. Mix in the almonds, lemon rind and sugar then rub the butter into the dry ingredients as if you were making pastry. Gently mix in the egg yolk to make a soft dough. If possible wrap the dough in a piece of foil or polythene and chill it in the refrigerator for 30 minutes or so. If you have time for this the dough will be easier to roll out but it isn't essential if you're in a hurry.

Set the oven to 200°C (400°F), gas mark 6. On a lightly floured board roll out three-quarters of the dough to fit a 20–23 cm (8–9 in) fluted flan dish – one of those pretty porcelain ones is ideal for this recipe. Spread the jam evenly over the pastry. Roll out the rest of the pastry and cut into long strips; arrange these strips in a lattice over the jam, then fold the edges of the pastry down and press them in to make a sort of rim round the edge of the tart. Bake the tart for 25–30 minutes, until it's slightly risen and golden brown.

You can serve the tart hot, cold or, my choice, warm. Sieve a little icing sugar over the top of the tart before taking it to the table; the red jam looks very appetizing glistening underneath this snowy topping. It's nice with single cream.

MACAROONS
FRANCE

Crisp macaroons are lovely for serving with cold, creamy puddings. Although they might seem a bit extravagant they are in fact rich in protein and so not completely frivolous.

1 egg white	Rice paper
125 g (4 oz) ground almonds	12 whole blanched almonds
125 g (4 oz) caster sugar	

Makes 12

Set the oven to 180°C (350°F), gas mark 4. Put the egg white into a good-sized bowl and whisk lightly, just to break it up. Stir in the ground almonds and caster sugar and mix to a paste. Lay the rice paper on baking sheets and put spoonfuls of the macaroon mixture on it, leaving room for them to spread a little. Smooth the macaroons with the back of a spoon dipped in cold water and place an almond in the centre of each. Bake for 15–25 minutes.

Transfer the macaroons to a wire rack, tearing the rice paper roughly; trim off the remaining paper when the macaroons have cooled.

MADEIRA CAKE
ENGLAND

This cake used to be served in England to accompany a glass of Madeira wine but I think it is useful for serving with some desserts, especially the Russian *pashka*. But really it's such a beautiful, delicately flavoured, smooth-textured cake that it's useful on all sorts of occasions. In my family it has formed the basis of a number of birthday cakes ranging from an enchanted house to a teddy bear which I literally carved out of an oblong block of cake. Normally I just bake the cake in a loaf tin and serve it unadorned except for the piece of peel baked into the top. I like to use a loaf tin as it is easier for cutting and you can arrange the peel all down the centre so that everyone gets some on top of their slice.

150 g (5 oz) plain flour – half wholewheat, half white is best for this
½ teaspoon baking powder
125 g (4 oz) butter, softened
125 g (4 oz) caster sugar

1 tablespoon grated lemon rind
2 eggs
2 tablespoons milk
Piece of citrus peel

Makes one 450 g (1 lb) cake

Set the oven to 160°C (325°F), gas mark 3. Line a 450 g (1 lb) loaf tin with a strip of greaseproof paper and brush with softened butter, then sprinkle with a little flour

Sift the flour and baking powder into a large bowl or the bowl of your mixer, adding also the residue of bran left in the sieve and all the other ingredients except the citrus peel. Beat everything well together to make a light, fluffy mixture. Spoon the mixture lightly into the prepared tin and level the top. Place in the oven and bake for 25 minutes, then without taking the cake out of the oven, very carefully lay the citrus peel along the top of the cake, and bake it for a further 35 minutes.

Cool the cake for a few minutes in the tin, then turn it out on to a wire rack to cool completely. Take off the greaseproof paper when it's cold.

BABY MERINGUES

Crisp little meringues make a very nice accompaniment to smooth
fools and ice creams. They're also a pretty garnish to use on a
pudding such as a trifle or an egg custard if you don't want to use
cream.

2 egg whites
125 g (4 oz) caster sugar

Makes about 24

First prepare a couple of baking sheets by covering them with
greaseproof paper then brushing the paper with cooking oil. Or
use non-stick baking paper.

Whisk the egg whites until they're very stiff. Add half the sugar,
and quickly whisk it into the mixture, then fold in the remaining
sugar using a metal spoon.

The best way to put the meringues on to the baking sheets is to
use a piping bag fitted with a 1 cm ($\frac{1}{2}$ in) shell nozzle, but if you
haven't got one a teaspoon will do. Pipe or spoon the mixture on
to the baking sheets, leaving a little space between the meringues,
as they will spread slightly and I find they bake best if they are not
too close together. Put the meringues into the oven and set it to
its lowest temperature – 110°C (225°F), gas mark $\frac{1}{4}$.

They will take about 1$\frac{1}{2}$ hours to dry out. Test one by taking it
off the tin and tapping it on the base to see if it feels and sounds
firm and dry. Let the meringues cool on the trays, then take them
off and store them in an air-tight tin. In theory they keep well in
a tin for a week or so but in practice I find they never get the
chance to do so!

PARKIN

This is one of those cakes in which you can use wholewheat flour,
brown sugar and black treacle without any problems at all and
the result is delicious as well as nutritious. It's moist and gooey,

particularly if you wrap it in foil and keep it for a few days before you eat it.

125 g (4 oz) butter or margarine	1 teaspoon baking powder
225 g (8 oz) black treacle	1 teaspoon ground ginger
125 g (4 oz) dark brown sugar	1 teaspoon mixed spice
125 g (4 oz) plain wholewheat flour	125 g (4 oz) medium oatmeal
	6 tablespoons milk
	1 egg

Makes 15–18 pieces

Preheat the oven to 160°C (325°F), gas mark 3. Put the butter or margarine into a small saucepan with the black treacle and sugar and heat gently until melted, but don't let the mixture boil. Cool. Sift the flour, baking powder and spices into a bowl and stir in the residue of bran left in the sieve and the oatmeal. Make a well in the centre of the dry ingredients and pour in the treacle mixture and the milk, then add the egg and mix everything until smooth. Brush an 18 cm (7 in) square tin with softened butter or margarine, then pour in the parkin and put it in the oven.

Bake it for 55–60 minutes, or until it has shrunk away from the edges of the tin and feels firm to the touch. Cool in the tin, then cut into slices when it's cold.

Note: As treacle is rather a nuisance to weigh out, if you like parkin you can get around this by making up a double batch of parkin at a time using a whole 450 g (1 lb) tin of treacle and keeping one lot of parkin either in the deep freeze, or if you want it to get all nice and gooey, wrapped in foil and stored in a tin until it's needed.

PUMPKIN PIE   USA

An American friend gave me this recipe which I've adapted to give the right quantity for a 20–22 cm (8–9 in) flan dish. It makes a lovely autumn pudding, smooth and warmly spiced. I think it's best when it's hot but you can also serve it cold; it's nicest with cream. Sometimes I scatter some roughly chopped walnuts over the top of the pie which makes it look specially interesting and is a pleasant variation.

For the flan case:
175 g (6 oz) plain wholewheat
   flour
1½ teaspoons baking powder
125 g (4 oz) white vegetable
   fat and margarine, mixed
1 tablespoon cold water

For the filling:
1 kilo (2¼ lb) pumpkin,
   weighed in the shop with
   skin and pips
4 tablespoons water
125 g (4 oz) soft brown sugar
½ teaspoon ground ginger
½ teaspoon powdered
   cinnamon
A little grated nutmeg
Pinch of cloves
150 ml (5 fl oz) single cream
2 eggs

Serves 6

Set the oven to 200°C (400°F), gas mark 6. Sift the flour and baking powder into a bowl and add the residue of bran left in the sieve. Rub in the fats until the mixture looks like fine bread-crumbs then add the water and mix to a dough. Roll the pastry out on a lightly floured board and put into a 20–23 cm (8–9 in) diameter flan dish. Prick the base, then bake the flan in the oven for about 15 minutes until it's browned and crisp. Take it out of the oven and let it cool slightly while you make the filling. Reduce the oven setting to 180°C (350°F), gas mark 4.

Peel the pumpkin and remove the pips. Cut the pumpkin into even-sized pieces, put them into a heavy-based saucepan with the water and cook gently, with a lid on the saucepan, until the pumpkin is tender – about 10 minutes. Put the pumpkin into a colander and drain it very well indeed, pressing gently with a spoon to extract as much water as possible. Put the pumpkin into a bowl and add the sugar, spices, cream and eggs. Mix well, then pour into the flan case and bake in the preheated oven for about 50 minutes, until it's set.

RAISIN SOUR CREAM PIE   USA

The friend in the USA who kindly gave me this recipe serves it as an alternative to pumpkin pie at Thanksgiving. I think it also makes an excellent alternative to mincemeat pie at Christmas because it's got a spicy, festive flavour. It's a nourishing, protein-rich pudding with the wholewheat flour, eggs and nuts. If you can't get pecan nuts you can use walnuts instead, or flaked almonds which I like best of all; and an alternative to the soured cream is natural yoghurt.

225 g (8 oz) seedless raisins –
  or use sultanas
150 ml (5 fl oz) soured cream
¼ teaspoon ground cloves
¼ teaspoon grated nutmeg
1 teaspoon powdered
  cinnamon
2 eggs
50 g (2 oz) soft brown sugar
50 g (2 oz) pecan nuts or

walnuts, chopped; or flaked
almonds

For the flan case:
100 g (4 oz) plain wholewheat
  flour
1 teaspoon baking powder
50 g (2 oz) butter or soft
  vegetable margarine
1 tablespoon cold water

Serves 6

First start making the filling by putting the raisins or sultanas into a bowl with the soured cream and the spices; mix well, then leave on one side while you make the flan case.

Set the oven to 200°C (400°F), gas mark 6. To make the pastry sift the flour and baking powder into a bowl and also add the residue of bran left in the sieve. Rub in the fat until the mixture looks like breadcrumbs, then mix in the water and gently press the mixture together to form a dough. Roll out the dough on a lightly floured board and use to line a 20–23 cm (8–9 in) flan dish. Trim the edges and prick the base of the flan, then bake it in the oven for about 15 minutes, until it is set and golden brown. Take the flan out of the oven and reduce the temperature to 180°C (350°F), gas mark 4.

Finish making the filling: beat the eggs, then add them to the

311

soured cream and fruit mixture, together with the sugar and nuts. Mix everything together well, then pour the filling evenly into the flan case – it doesn't matter if this is still warm – and smooth the top gently with a knife or the back of a spoon. Bake the flan in the oven for 35–40 minutes, until the filling is set. You can serve the flan hot or cold but I think it's nicest hot.

SHORTBREAD FINGERS   SCOTLAND

These crisp little biscuits melt in your mouth and are so useful for serving with fruit salads, fools and creamy puddings as well as being popular at tea-time.

125 g (4 oz) plain wholewheat flour
125 g (4 oz) plain white flour
2 teaspoons baking powder

75 g (3 oz) caster sugar
200 g (7 oz) butter, softened
Caster sugar

Makes 18–20

Set the oven to 160°C (325°F), gas mark 3. Sift the flours and baking powder into a large bowl or the bowl of your mixer, and tip in the bran from the sieve too. Add the sugar and butter, then beat everything together to a soft dough. Turn the dough out on to a floured board and knead it a little, then roll the dough out 6 mm ($\frac{1}{4}$ in) thick and cut it into fingers. Put these on a lightly floured baking sheet then prick them all over with a fork and bake them for about 20 minutes, until they're golden brown.

Let them cool on the baking sheet as they're fragile while they're still hot. Sprinkle them generously with caster sugar before serving them.

SPONGE FINGERS FRANCE

These are useful for serving with fools and creamy puddings where you want something crisp but not as rich as shortbread. You really do need an electric mixer for these and they're best made the day you want to eat them.

1 egg
40 g (1½ oz) granulated sugar
40 g (1½ oz) plain flour –
white is best for the small

quantity needed for this recipe
Extra granulated sugar to dredge

Makes 12–15

Set the oven to 190°C (375°F), gas mark 5. Prepare a baking sheet by covering it with a piece of greaseproof paper and brushing with oil. Put the egg and granulated sugar into the bowl of your mixer and whisk at top speed until it's very thick and pale and able to hold its shape. Gently sift the flour over the top of the egg mixture and carefully cut and fold it in with a metal spoon. Pipe or spoon thin fingers of the mixture on to the prepared baking sheet, allowing space for them to spread – they will roughly double in width. Sprinkle the tops of the fingers thickly with sugar, then bake them for about 12 minutes until they're golden brown and firm to a light touch. Let the fingers cool slightly, then carefully ease them off the baking sheet and put them on a wire rack to finish cooling.

STRAWBERRY TARTLETS FRANCE

The combination of crisp pastry, creamy filling and shiny strawberries makes these little tartlets very delicious. You can vary the flavour of the filling; I like it with rose essence or rosewater as a change from vanilla. The tartlets are also good made with other fruit toppings: I particularly like them with those little green seedless grapes or halved and seeded black grapes, with lemon-flavoured filling and apricot jam to glaze.

For the pastry cream:
25 g (1 oz) flour
1 egg yolk
200 ml (7 fl oz) milk
25 g (1 oz) sugar – vanilla
  sugar is best if you have it
15 g (1½ oz) butter

For the pastry:
175 g (6 oz) plain whole-
  wheat flour – or you could
  use a mixture of white and
  wholewheat

1½ teaspoons baking powder
75 g (3 oz) butter or vegetable
  margarine
1½ tablespoons cold water

For the topping:
225 g (8 oz) small ripe
  strawberries
125 g (4 oz) redcurrant jelly
2 tablespoons water
½ teaspoon cornflour

Makes 12

First make the pastry cream. You can do this a day or two
in advance if you like because it will keep perfectly in a covered
container in the fridge. Put the flour into a small bowl with the
egg yolk and enough milk to make a smooth paste. Put the rest
of the milk and the sugar into a small saucepan and bring to the
boil, then pour it over the egg and flour mixture, stirring. Tip
the mixture back into the saucepan and stir over a moderate
heat. It will go lumpy, but go on stirring hard and after a few
minutes you will have a thick, smooth sauce. Take the saucepan
off the heat, turn the mixture into a small bowl and add a little
vanilla essence or any other flavouring you fancy to tone with the
fruit. Dot the butter over the top of the mixture – this will prevent
a skin from forming – cover with a piece of foil and leave on one
side. When the pastry cream is cool, store it in the fridge until you
need it.

Next make the tartlet cases. Set the oven to 200°C (400°F),
gas mark 6. Sift the flour and baking powder into a bowl;
if you're using wholewheat flour add also the bran which will
be left in the sieve. Rub the fat into the flour using your fingertips, then mix to a dough with the cold water. Roll the dough
out on a lightly floured board then use it to line 12 tartlet tins.
Prick the base of each tartlet lightly with a fork, then bake them in
the preheated oven for about 15 minutes, until they're golden
brown. Leave on one side to cool.

When you're ready to fill the tartlet cases whisk the pastry cream to blend in the butter and make the mixture smooth and light, then put about a teaspoonful of pastry cream in each tartlet. The exact amount will depend on how deep the tartlets are and you may find you don't need quite all the pastry cream. Hull and wash the strawberries and halve or quarter them unless they're really small. Arrange the strawberries on top of the pastry cream.

To make the glaze melt the redcurrant jelly with 1 tablespoonful of the water. Mix the cornflour to a paste with another tablespoonful of water and add this to the redcurrant jelly in the saucepan, stirring until you have a smooth slightly thickened glaze. Spoon the glaze over the strawberries on the tartlets then leave them to cool. Eat them the same day.

YOGHURT TART   GREECE

In this tart the combination of creamy, fresh-tasting filling and crisp wholewheat pastry is delicious, and it couldn't be simpler to make as the filling is uncooked.

For the flan case:	*For the filling:*
100 g (4 oz) plain wholewheat flour	225 g (8 oz) low-fat quark or cream cheese
1 teaspoon baking powder	150 ml (5 fl oz) natural yoghurt
50 g (2 oz) butter	1 tablespoon honey
1 tablespoon cold water	1 tablespoon sugar
	A few chopped walnuts

Serves 6

Set the oven to 200°C (400°F), gas mark 6. Sift the flour and baking powder into a bowl, adding the bran in the sieve too. Rub the fat into the flour then mix to a dough with the cold water. Roll the pastry out on a lightly floured board then put the pastry into a 20–23 cm (8–9 in) flan dish; trim the edges and

315

prick the base. Bake the flan for about 15 minutes until it's set and golden brown. Leave on one side while you make the filling.

Put the quark or cream cheese into a bowl and break it up with a fork, then gradually beat in the yoghurt, honey and sugar until you've got a light, creamy mixture. Spoon the mixture into the flan case and smooth the top. Chill the flan for 1–2 hours, then scatter a few chopped nuts over the top just before serving. The filling will be fairly soft at first but it will firm up as it chills.

Breads, Scones and Sandwiches

You will see I suggest wholewheat flour for most of these recipes; as I'm convinced of the value of wholewheat flour I was determined to try to make good wholewheat versions of some of the traditional international breads and scones. I'm particularly pleased with the wholewheat version of pitta bread which we think is nicer than the type you can buy in the shops. If you want to use wheatmeal flour or white flour instead of some of the wholewheat flour you can of course do so. As wholewheat flour absorbs less water than white or wheatmeal you will probably need to add a little extra liquid to the recipe.

For the yeast recipes I suggest dried yeast because that's what I normally use – mainly because I can keep a large drum of it in my cupboard and it's one less thing to have to remember to buy, or, with me, forget to buy! You can certainly use fresh yeast for the recipes, though, if you prefer; simply use double the amount and crumble it into the liquid without adding the $\frac{1}{2}$ teaspoonful of sugar, then continue with the recipe as described.

These breads and scones can make the basis of very nourishing meals; a bowl of lentil soup and wholewheat rolls, or some lovely hunks of home-made wholewheat bread with cheese and fruit may be simple to prepare but they contain as many nutrients as a cooked meal and always seem to be popular.

CHAPATIS INDIA

These circles of unleavened bread are delicious with any curry dish; they can also be rolled round salad fillings or stuffed and baked in a similar way to the tortillas in the pasta and pancakes section of the book.

250 g (9 oz) plain wholewheat flour
1½ teaspoon oil, melted butter or *ghee*

1 teaspoon sea salt
About 150 ml (¼ pint) cold water

Makes 12

Sieve the flour into a bowl, adding also the bran which will be left in the sieve. Mix in the fat, salt and water to make a firm dough. When the dough has formed turn it out on to a very lightly floured board and knead it for about 5 minutes. Then if possible cover it with a damp cloth and leave it to rest for 2–3 hours before kneading it again.

Divide the dough into 12 pieces, form each into a ball with your hands, then roll them out with a rolling pin so that they are 15–20 cm (6–8 in) across. Fry the chapatis both sides in an ungreased frying pan. Pile them up on a plate as they're done and cover them with a piece of foil to prevent them from drying out.

If you like you can brush them over with a little oil, melted butter or *ghee* before serving them.

CHEESE SCONES SCOTLAND

Light and savoury, cheese scones are delicious both with creamy dips and with hot soups, especially if the scones have come straight from the oven. As they're quick and easy to make it's not difficult to mix up a batch while the soup is finishing cooking and they really make it into a meal, with just some fruit to follow.

319

225 g (8 oz) plain wholewheat flour, or use half wholewheat and half white if you prefer

2 teaspoons baking powder

½ teaspoon mustard powder

½ teaspoon sea salt

50 g (2 oz) softened butter or soft vegetable margarine

125 g (4 oz) finely grated cheese

75–100 ml (3–4 fl oz) milk

Makes about 12

Set the oven to 200°C (400°F), gas mark 6. Sift the flour, baking powder, mustard and salt into a large bowl adding also the residue of bran left in the sieve. Using your fingertips rub the fat into the flour until the mixture looks like fine breadcrumbs. Lightly mix in the grated cheese, then enough of the milk to make a soft but firm dough. Turn the dough on to a lightly floured board and knead briefly, then roll it or press it out to a thickness of about 1 cm (½ in). Use a plain 5 cm (2 in) pastry cutter to cut the dough into rounds. Place the rounds on a floured baking sheet and bake in the preheated oven for about 10 minutes until the scones are risen and golden brown.

VARIATION

Cheese and walnut scones are delicious. Add 50 g (2 oz) chopped walnuts to the mixture with the grated cheese.

CHRISTMAS FRUIT LOAF   DENMARK

The candied fruits make this a pretty, jewelled loaf. It's nice for Christmas because it's festive without being too rich. The best way to get the crushed cardamom is to buy some cardamom pods at a health shop or Indian shop and crush them in a pestle and mortar or with the back of a spoon – the seeds will come out of the pods as you crush them and you keep the seeds and discard the pods. If you can't get it leave it out, but it does give a beautiful flavour and cardamom is a useful flavouring for curries and spicy rice dishes, too.

100 ml (3½ fl oz) lukewarm
  milk
½ teaspoon caster sugar
2 teaspoons dried yeast
450 g (1 lb) plain flour – I
  use half wholewheat, half
  white for this recipe, or you
  could use wheatmeal
Pinch of salt
50 g (2 oz) soft brown sugar

125 g (4 oz) softened butter or
  soft margarine
½ teaspoon crushed cardamom
2 teaspoons vanilla essence
Rind of ½ lemon
225 g (8 oz) mixed candied
  fruits, chopped – try to get a
  nice variety of colours
2 eggs, beaten

Makes 1 large loaf

First grease a 1 kilo (2 lb) loaf tin with butter. Then put the milk
into a small bowl, stir in the caster sugar and yeast and leave on
one side to froth up. Meanwhile mix together the flour, salt and
sugar and rub in the butter or margarine; add the cardamom,
vanilla, lemon, fruit and eggs. Make a well in the centre and
pour in the yeast mixture. Mix to a soft dough, adding a little
more flour if necessary, then knead for 10 minutes. Put the dough
into an oiled bowl, cover with a clean damp cloth then with a
polythene carrier bag and leave it in a warm place until doubled
in bulk – about 1 hour.

Punch the dough down, knead it again lightly, form into a loaf
shape and put into the prepared tin. Cover the loaf with the cloth
and polythene bag again and leave in a warm place for about 30
minutes to rise. Set the oven to 180°C (350°F), gas mark 4. When
the loaf has come up to the top of the tin, bake it until it's golden
and crisp. The loaf should sound hollow when turned out of its
tin and tapped on the base. Leave on a wire rack to cool. It's nice
served with a rich pudding, like *pashka* or *crème brûlée*, or sliced
and buttered for tea.

DANISH PASTRIES

DENMARK

Light, crisp and not-too-sweet, Danish pastries are ideal for serving with coffee on a special occasion. They take time to make, but are not difficult; I found it particularly satisfying to produce a wheatmeal version that was light and delicious. They freeze well, but leave the final icing until just before serving.

150 g (5 oz) butter
225 ml (8 fl oz) warm water
1 teaspoon sugar
15 g ($\frac{1}{2}$ oz) dried yeast
40 g ($1\frac{1}{2}$ oz) butter
275 g (10 oz) plain wheatmeal
   flour
1 egg

For the fillings:
50 g (2 oz) mixed dried fruit

Makes 15

40 g ($1\frac{1}{2}$ oz) caster sugar
1 teaspoon mixed spice
125 g (4 oz) marzipan

To finish:
Beaten egg to glaze
Glacé icing made from 175 g
   (6 oz) icing sugar and a
   little water
50 g (2 oz) flaked almonds

Beat the 150 g (5 oz) of butter to make it soft then spread it out into a square about 20 cm × 20 cm (8 in × 8 in) and place it in the refrigerator to get really hard while you prepare the dough.

Put the water into a small bowl and stir in the sugar and dried yeast; leave on one side for 10 minutes to froth up. Rub the 40 g ($1\frac{1}{2}$ oz) of butter into the flour, then make a well in the centre, pour in the frothy yeast mixture and add the egg. Mix everything together to make a soft dough, then knead it until it feels smooth and pliable. Put the dough into a polythene bag and leave it in the fridge to rest for 15 minutes. Roll the dough 6 mm ($\frac{1}{4}$ in) thick into an oblong 30 cm × 20 cm (12 in × 8 in). Place the square of butter on the dough covering two-thirds of it. Fold the remaining third of the dough over the butter-covered part and then fold the remaining pieces of butter-covered dough over so that you have the un-buttered piece in the centre.

Seal the edges by pressing with a rolling pin, then chill the dough in the fridge for 15 minutes. Roll the dough into an oblong again and fold in three as before, then chill in the fridge for 15 minutes. Repeat the rolling and folding 3 or 4 times more, then roll the dough out 1 cm (½ in) thick and cut into 3 pieces.

Roll one of these pieces into an oblong about 30 cm × 20 cm (12 in × 8 in), sprinkle the dried fruit, caster sugar and spice over the top of the dough and press it in lightly with a rolling pin. Roll up the dough from the long side like a roly-poly pudding. Cut the roll into 6 even-sized pieces, then make two deep cuts in each piece and open them out slightly. Place them on a baking sheet.

Cut both the remaining pieces of dough into 6 pieces. Roll each piece into a square roughly 10 cm × 10 cm (4 in × 4 in). Cut the marzipan into 12 pieces. Form 6 of the pieces of marzipan into 2·5 cm × 10 cm (1 in × 4 in) strips. Place a strip of marzipan at the top edges of 6 of the squares of dough. Roll the dough over then make cuts all down the length, almost through to the edge, and curl the dough round to make a cock's comb. For the remaining pieces of dough fold the corners to the centre and press down. Form the remaining marzipan into rounds. Place one round in the centre of each piece of dough.

Brush all the pastries with beaten egg. Set the oven to 220°C (425°F), gas mark 7. Place the pastries on top of the cooker to get the heat of the oven as it warms up. When the pastries are puffy looking, after about 20 minutes or so, place them in the oven and bake for 20 minutes. Cool the pastries on a wire rack, then ice them and sprinkle with toasted flaked almonds. I think they're best warmed through before serving.

To freeze Danish pastries, open-freeze the cooled pastries. When they're firm store them in a polythene bag. To use them, put them on a wire rack to de-frost – allow about 2 hours for this – then ice them as usual.

GARLIC BREAD FRANCE

Hot bread oozing with melted butter and garlic is a wonderful accompaniment to soups and creamy dips, particularly those containing lentils and beans. French bread is of course the type that is normally used for garlic bread, and there's no doubt that this is delicious, with a crisp crust and tender crumb, but wholewheat bread can also be used very successfully. Although the loaf is a different shape you treat it in just the same way, but allow a little longer for it to heat through. For quick wholewheat garlic bread for just one or two people you can spread slices of wholewheat bread with garlic butter, lay them out individually on a baking sheet or grill pan without any foil covering and heat them in the oven or under the grill until the butter has melted and the bread is just crispy round the edges.

1 French loaf or 1 small wholewheat loaf
3–4 cloves of garlic

Salt
125 g (4 oz) butter, softened

Serves 4–6

Set the oven to 200°C (400°F), gas mark 6. Slice the French loaf almost through into chunky pieces – they should just hold together at the base. Cut the wholewheat loaf right through into slices – don't make them too thick. Make the garlic butter by peeling the garlic and crushing it in a little salt, then mixing it into the butter. Spread this butter on both sides of the slices of bread. Pile the wholewheat bread back into the loaf shape. Wrap the loaf in foil and place it on a baking sheet in the oven. Bake it for about 20 minutes, until it's heated right through and crisp on the outside. Serve at once.

MELBA TOAST   FRANCE

Wholewheat Melba toast is delicious, crisp and nutty-tasting.
This is the method I've found most successful for making Melba
toast with wholewheat bread.

8 thin slices wholewheat
  bread

Serves 4

Preheat the oven to 200°C (400°F), gas mark 6. Cut the slices
of bread as thin as you can; it helps if the bread is a couple of days
old. Lay the slices on baking sheets and place in the oven. After
about 7 minutes turn the bread over and bake it for a further 7–10
minutes, or until lightly browned. As soon as the bread comes out
of the oven cut it diagonally across, then cool the slices on a wire
rack – they'll crispen as they get cold. Melba toast is particularly
good with the creamy dips.

OATCAKES   SCOTLAND

Oatcakes are easy to make and crisp and nutty-tasting to eat.
Try them for breakfast or tea with butter and clear honey,
or serve them with a creamy dip or Scottish cream cheese.

225 g (8 oz) medium oatmeal   25 g (1 oz) butter or margarine,
½ teaspoon baking powder   melted
¼ teaspoon salt   6 teaspoons hot water
                                  A little extra oatmeal to finish

Makes 24–28

Set the oven to 200°C (400°F), gas mark 6. Put the oatmeal into
a bowl with the baking powder, salt and butter or margarine.

Mix them together lightly, then stir in enough warm water to make a dough – you'll need about 6 teaspoonsful.

Sprinkle some oatmeal on a board and turn the dough out on to this, kneading lightly, then roll it out to a thickness of about 3 mm ($\frac{1}{8}$ in), sprinkling the surface with a little extra oatmeal if necessary to prevent it from sticking. You can either roll the mixture into a circle and then cut it into wedges, or stamp it into rounds using a pastry cutter. Transfer the oatcakes to a baking sheet and bake them for about 15 minutes until firm and lightly coloured. Let them cool on the tin for a few minutes, then transfer them to a wire cooling rack. Or serve them straight from the oven, all warm and crumbly.

OPEN SANDWICHES   DENMARK

A tray of colourful open sandwiches looks really mouthwatering and is a surprisingly practical way of feeding a large group of people. If you want to make the meal more substantial serve mugs or bowls of soup as well with a choice of different puddings laid out on a separate table for people to help themselves. Medium-sized plates and forks will be needed for eating the sandwiches and plenty of paper napkins are advisable.

It's fun to make the open sandwiches and not difficult to make them look pretty. I think the easiest way to do them is to prepare a really good assortment of different ingredients and spread them all out in front of you so that you can create different combinations as you go along.

For the base:

Wholewheat bread, rye bread
  or pumpernickel
Butter
Crisp lettuce leaves

For the toppings:

Finely grated cheese mixed to a
  paste with mayonnaise,
  cream or milk
Sliced hardboiled egg
Chopped hardboiled egg mixed
  with mayonnaise or low-fat
  quark
Cold scrambled egg
Peanut butter
Cottage cheese
Quark or cream cheese
Any of the dips on pages 65–73
  (*hummus*, mock caviar, Liptauer
  cheese and avocado dip are
  particularly good)
Cold bean or lentil salads
  are also excellent

For the garnishes:

Slices of lemon, tomato,
  avocado (tossed in lemon
  juice) onion, red and green
  pepper, cooked beetroot,
  cucumber, radishes, spring
  onions
Sprigs of parsley, mint or
  watercress
Chopped chives
Pineapple cubes or rings
Chopped apple, sliced banana
  tossed in lemon juice
Raisins, dates, chopped dried
  apricots
Black or green grapes
Black or green olives
Chopped walnuts and flaked
  almonds
Chopped stem ginger
Mango chutney
Olive oil
Mayonnaise
Paprika pepper

Butter the bread fairly generously and place it on the tray from
which it will be served. Cover each piece of bread with a lettuce
leaf, pressing it down so that the butter sticks it on to the bread.
Now arrange your toppings and garnishes on the lettuce leaf,
covering each as generously as possible whilst making them
practical to eat. Here are some ideas for different combinations:

1. Avocado (dipped in lemon juice), watercress, a spoonful of
   mayonnaise, quark or cottage cheese, chopped walnuts.
2. Peanut butter, coarsely grated carrot, green pepper rings,
   sliced onion.
3. Quark or cottage cheese, pineapple rings, black grapes,
   toasted flaked almonds.

4. Sliced cooked beetroot, onion rings, chopped walnuts, cream cheese or quark.
5. Cold lentil salad, mango chutney, chopped apple, parsley.
6. *Hummus*, onion rings, paprika, sliced tomato, parsley,
7. Mock caviar or aubergine and sesame pâté, sliced tomato, onion rings, olive oil.
8. Liptauer cheese, tomato, black olives, parsley sprigs.
9. Goat cheese and herb spread, sliced cucumber and radishes.
10. Avocado dip, coarsely grated carrot, sliced tomato, chopped walnuts.
11. Cubes of cold spicy fritters, mango chutney, tomato, onion rings, garlic mayonnaise.
12. Quark or cream cheese, apple, chopped stem ginger, walnuts.

PEAR BREAD   SWITZERLAND

Slices of this pear bread, *birnbrot*, are lovely served warm with coffee, or if you serve it hot with single cream it makes a very good pudding. I think it goes rather well after a fondue because it's sweet without being rich. You can leave out the kirsch and wine but they do give a beautiful flavour for a special occasion. You will probably be able to get dried pears at a health shop; they're also nice in fruit compotes.

5 tablespoons lukewarm milk
¼ teaspoon caster sugar
1 teaspoon dried yeast
150 g (5 oz) plain wholewheat flour
150 g (5 oz) plain white flour
Pinch of salt
50 g (2 oz) butter or soft margarine
50 g (2 oz) soft brown sugar
1 egg, beaten

For the filling:
275 ml (½ pint) water
125 g (4 oz) dried stoned prunes
225 g (8 oz) dried pears
50 g (2 oz) seedless raisins
Rind and juice of ½ lemon
50 g (2 oz) soft brown sugar
A little ground cinnamon
Grated nutmeg

1 tablespoon each of dry red   *To glaze:*
   wine and kirsch (optional)   A little beaten egg

Makes 1 large loaf

Grease a large baking sheet with butter; leave on one side. First make the dough. Put the milk into a small bowl and stir in the caster sugar and yeast. Leave in a warm place for the yeast to froth up. Put the flours and salt into a large bowl; rub in the butter or margarine and add the sugar. Make a well in the centre and pour in the yeast and milk, together with the beaten egg. Mix everything together to make a smooth, soft dough, adding a little more flour if necessary. Turn the dough on to a floured board and knead it for 10 minutes, then put the dough into a clean, oiled bowl, cover it with a clean damp cloth then put the bowl inside a large polythene carrier bag and leave it in a warm place for about an hour or until it has doubled in bulk.

While this is happening make the filling. Put the water, prunes, pears and raisins into a small pan and heat gently until soft, thick and dry. Sieve, finely chop or liquidize the mixture, then add the lemon and sugar and some cinnamon and nutmeg to taste – about $\frac{1}{4}$ teaspoonful of each – and the wine and kirsch if you are using them. Don't make the mixture too liquid – it should hold it's shape.

To assemble the pear bread take the risen dough and knead it for a minute or two, then put it on to a lightly floured board and roll out into a large square, about 38 cm × 38 cm (15 in × 15 in) and not more than 6 mm ($\frac{1}{4}$ in) thick. Spread the fruity filling over the square to within about 2·5 cm (1 in) of the edges. Fold the edges over to enclose the filling, then roll it firmly like a Swiss roll and put it on to the prepared baking sheet. Prick the pear bread all over, cover it with a clean cloth and put it into a warm place for 30 minutes to rise. About 15 minutes before the pear bread is ready, set the oven to 180 °C (350°F), gas mark 4. Then brush the bread over with beaten egg and bake it in the centre of the oven, for about 35 minutes, or until it's golden brown and crisp. Serve warm.

PITTA BREAD   MIDDLE EAST

These long thin bread 'pockets' are very popular with my
children who irreverently refer to them as 'Arabs' feet' on account
of their shape! They're no more trouble to make than rolls and
fun to eat because you can fill them with lots of crunchy salad,
dips, cottage cheese etc., when they make a delectable lunch or
supper. The only problem is you do need one or two large baking
sheets to cook them on as they take up rather a lot of space.

300 ml (½ pint) hand-hot   2 teaspoons salt
   water   1 teaspoon sugar
½ teaspoon sugar   1 tablespoon oil
2 teaspoons dried yeast
450 g (1 lb) plain wholewheat
   flour

Makes 12

Put the water into a jug and stir in the yeast and the ½ teaspoon
of sugar; leave on one side to froth up. Meanwhile put the
flour, salt, the sugar and the olive oil into a bowl and mix together.
Add the yeast mixture and mix to a dough. Knead for 5 minutes
until smooth. Put the dough into an oiled bowl, cover with a
damp cloth, cover the bowl with a polythene carrier bag and leave
it in a warm place for 1 hour to rise. When the dough has doubled
in size, punch it down and knead it lightly. Set the oven to 230°C
(450°F), gas mark 8.

Divide the dough into 12 pieces and roll each into an oblong
about 18 cm (7 in) long and 7 cm (3 in) wide. Put the pieces on to
oiled baking sheets and leave them in a warm place or on top of
the cooker for 15 minutes to rise a bit.

Put them in the oven and bake them for 5 minutes, then turn
the oven heat down to 200°C (400°F), gas mark 6 and bake for a
further 10 minutes or so, until the pitta are golden brown.
When they come out of the oven they'll be light and puffed up;
cool them on a wire rack and make them into pouches by inserting

the point of a sharp knife into one of the long edges and sliding it along.

That's proper pitta bread, but when I was working out this recipe I made a batch which I rolled out rather longer and thinner and baked for a bit longer at the higher temperature and they came out thin and very crisp and that is how my children always ask me to make them now.

SODA BREAD   IRELAND

Soda bread is quick to make, an ideal standby when the bread-bin is empty and there is no time to make yeast bread. It only takes about 40 minutes from start to finish and is delicious served slightly warm. It's particularly good with runny honey. Although I'm very much a wholewheat bread fan, I think this particular recipe is best made with half wholewheat and half white flour, or with wheatmeal flour. Alternatively, an Irishman I met while writing this book told me that although no one ever made bread like his mother he thought the most authentic-tasting loaf was made with scofa flour and buttermilk.

450 g (1 lb) plain wholewheat
   and white flour mixed; or
   plain wheatmeal flour;
   or scofa flour
1 teaspoon salt
1 rounded teaspoon bicarbonate
   of soda
Makes 1 loaf

25 g (1 oz) butter or
   vegetable margarine
275 ml (½ pint) buttermilk,
sour milk or milk warmed
with a tablespoon of cider
vinegar or lemon juice to
sour it

Set the oven to 220°C (425°F), gas mark 7. Flour a baking sheet. Sift the flour, salt and bicarbonate of soda into a large bowl. With your fingertips, rub in the fat until the mixture resembles fine breadcrumbs. Make a well in the centre and pour in the

331

milk, then gradually mix everything together to make a dough. Turn the dough out on to a floured board and knead it lightly, then form it into a round loaf. Put the loaf on the prepared baking sheet and using a sharp knife cut a cross shape in the top. Bake the loaf for 30–35 minutes until it's risen, golden and crusty, then leave it to cool on a wire rack.

Soda bread doesn't keep well; it's really best eaten the same day.

TORTILLAS MEXICO

In Mexico tortillas are eaten as we would eat bread. They're easy to make and versatile. You can eat them as they are, with butter or other toppings; you can roll them round salad mixtures such as cottage cheese, lettuce and tomato or mixed bean salad, watercress and onion to make a kind of hearty rolled sandwich. If you fry them in hot oil they become crisp like poppadums and can be served with creamy salad dips. They can also be treated like pancakes, filled with savoury mixtures, covered with a well-flavoured sauce and baked there are two recipes for this in the pancakes and pasta section of this book.

100 g (4 oz) maize flour – you get this from health shops, or use plain wholewheat flour
150 g (5 oz) plain wholewheat flour

1 teaspoon sea salt
About 150 ml ($\frac{1}{4}$ pint) cold water

Makes 12

Sift the flours into a bowl, tipping in any extra bran left in the sieve, then stir in the salt and enough water to make a dough that's soft but not sticky – like a scone dough. Turn the dough on to a floured board and knead it slightly to make it smooth, then divide it into 12 pieces. Roll each piece into a ball, then use a rolling pin to roll each into a thin round – about 15–20 cm (6–8 in) diameter.

Heat a frying pan without any fat in it and fry the tortillas in this, one at a time: keep the heat fairly low. When the underside is set turn the tortilla over and cook the other side. Put them on a plate when they're ready and cover them with a piece of foil because they quickly become dry and brittle.

Serve the tortillas with salads instead of bread. A pile of freshly cooked tortillas and bowls of spicy avocado dip, sliced tomatoes, quarters of hardboiled egg, grated cheese, red bean salad and shredded lettuce makes a lovely easy-going buffet lunch or supper.

TOSTADAS   MEXICO

A *tostada* is a tortilla that has been fried in oil so that it becomes crisp, like a poppadum. *Tostadas* are particularly good with creamy dips and salads because their crispness is such a pleasant contrast.

12 tortillas – see page 332
Oil for shallow frying

Makes 12

Make the tortillas as described · this can be done in advance if more convenient. Heat a little oil in a frying pan and fry the tortillas until they're crisp on one side then turn them over and fry on the other side. Drain them well on kitchen paper.

Tostadas make an excellent 'edible plate' for a salad – allow a *tostada* for each person and arrange the salad on top, making it as colourful and mouthwatering as you can. Lettuce makes a good foundation – make sure it's well dried so that the *tostada* remains crisp – followed by some or all of the following: sliced tomato, grated carrot, red bean salad, grated cheese, cottage cheese or quark, watercress and spring onion, piled up well and finished off with a generous dollop of spicy avocado dip or mayonnaise.

WHOLEWHEAT BREAD   ENGLAND

So many recipes for bread-making start off 'bread-making is easy' – and it really is – but still many people say they find the prospect daunting! I must admit that what recipes should say is 'bread-making is easy when you do it often'. If you make bread twice a week or so you learn a lot about the behaviour of the yeast and the dough and the effect of heat on the mixture. But for everyone there has to be a first time and so I'm going to try and put down all the things I've discovered and I hope this will be helpful and make it as easy as possible for you.

If you're baking for a family, or have a deep freeze, I don't think it's worth making up less than a 1·5 kilo (3 lb 5 oz) bag of flour. You can use all wholewheat flour, or, if your family isn't used to wholewheat flour, you might find it best to use wheatmeal flour, which is flour which has been sieved once by the millers to remove the coarsest part of the grain, and contains 85–90% of the grain, whereas wholewheat flour consists of 100%. Or you might find it best to use wheatmeal flour or wholewheat flour with a proportion of strong white bread flour (preferably unbleached) – half and half is a good mixture to start with.

I use dried yeast, largely because it's handy – one of those large tubs lasts ages and so I don't have to keep remembering to buy it; also it's more predictable, and I think, easier when you're learning. But it is important that the dried yeast should be fresh, so buy it from a shop which has a quick turnover and, unless you know you're going to do a lot of breadmaking, it's best to buy a small quantity to start with.

If you've got a warm place like an airing cupboard you can put the bread to rise; I stand mine near the pilot light on my gas cooker. But the bread will rise just as well but more slowly standing on the working surface in the kitchen; you don't especially need to put it into a warm place, and it's important not to let it get too hot.

300 ml (½ pint) hand-hot water

½ teaspoon sugar

2 tablespoons dried yeast

1·5 kilo (3 lb 5 oz) bag of wheatmeal or wholewheat flour; or a mixture of

wholewheat flour and strong white bread flour

2 tablespoons sugar

4 teaspoons fine sea salt

50 g (2 oz) butter or margarine

600–700 ml (1–1½ pints) hand-hot water

Makes five 450 g (1 lb) loaves

Put the 300 ml (½ pint) of water into a small jug or bowl and stir in the ½ teaspoonful of sugar and the dried yeast. Leave on one side for 5–10 minutes to froth up. While this is happening grease your loaf tins by brushing them with a little oil or softened butter, then leave them on one side too, in a warm place if there's one handy, but this isn't essential.

Now put your flour into a large bowl – the bowl of your electric mixer if the mixer has a dough hook attachment – and add the 2 tablespoons of sugar and the salt. Rub in the butter with your fingers. By this time you should find that the yeast has frothed up quite dramatically into a lovely volcanic mass and you can add it to your flour, together with the water, but don't add quite all the water; start off with 600 ml (just over a pint), and leave the rest for a moment. Mix the flour, yeast and water together until the dough forms – add the remaining water now if the dough seems too stiff. It should be firm, but soft enough to handle pleasantly, rather like soft well-worked Plasticine. If you've got a dough hook on your mixer – and I must say it's since I got one that I've managed to make our bread regularly – you can now leave it to knead the dough for 5 minutes. Otherwise, turn the dough out and knead it by hand, pushing and pummelling, folding and refolding it, for 5 minutes or even 10 minutes if you can manage it. As you knead the dough you'll feel it change from a coarse, lumpy and slightly sticky texture to a beautiful smooth, supple, silky one.

Put the dough back in its bowl, cover it with a damp tea-towel then stand the bowl in a polythene carrier bag and leave it to double in size. I find this takes an hour in a warm place, perhaps slightly longer if the bowl is just standing on the working surface and up to 2 hours if the kitchen is cold.

Now punch down the dough with your fist and knead it again a little – just 1–2 minutes this time, to wake the yeast up again. Cut the dough into 5 equal-sized pieces and shape them to fit the tins. I find the best way to do this is to flatten each piece with the palm of my hand, then gently roll it up and pop it into the tin with the fold underneath. Then I press the sides and corners down so that the centre of the loaf is higher, coming up into a nice dome shape. Put the loaves on top of the cooker or in a warm place, cover with the damp cloth again and set the oven to 240°C (475°F), gas mark 9. (If you put the loaves on top of the cooker the heat of the oven as it warms up will help them to rise.)

They'll take about 30 minutes to rise: as soon as the dough is just peeping over the tops of the tins put them into the oven. Don't let them over-rise or they'll collapse in the oven: if there is still some rise left in them the heat from the oven will give them a final boost and they'll have a lovely domed crust.

After 10 minutes turn the heat down to 200°C (400°F), gas mark 6 and bake the loaves for a further 25 minutes. Turn the loaves out of their tins straight away – they should sound hollow when you tap them on the base with your knuckles – and leave them on a wire rack to cool.

You can of course make 2 large loaves and 1 small loaf if you'd prefer; large loaves take about 10 minutes longer to bake.

WHOLEWHEAT ROLLS ENGLAND

Warm home-made rolls are useful for serving with so many dishes and they're really not difficult to make. This recipe is based on half one of the new metric bags of flour containing 1·5 kilos, which is why the amount looks rather strange in the Imperial measurements.

200 ml (7 fl oz) hand-hot water
1 tablespoon dried yeast
½ teaspoon sugar
750 g (1 lb 10½ oz) wholewheat
  flour
2 teaspoons salt

1 tablespoon sugar
50 g (2 oz) butter
200 ml (7 fl oz) milk
1 egg, beaten
A little extra flour to finish

Makes 24

Put the water into a small bowl and stir in the yeast and the ½ teaspoon of sugar. Leave on one side for 10 minutes to froth up. Meanwhile put the flour, salt and the 1 tablespoon of sugar into a bowl and rub in the butter. Pour the frothed-up yeast into the centre of the flour and add the milk and egg; mix together to make a firm but pliable dough. Turn the dough out and knead it for 10 minutes, then put it back into the bowl, cover with a damp cloth, stand the bowl inside a polythene carrier bag and leave until it's doubled in size. This takes about an hour in a warm place, 1–2 hours just standing on a working surface, depending on how warm the room is.

When the dough has risen set the oven to 220°C (425°F), gas mark 7. Punch down the dough, knead it again lightly then divide it into 24 pieces. Form the pieces into rounds then flatten them with the palm of your hand and place them on greased baking trays, allowing room for them to spread. Cover them with a damp cloth and leave in a warm place for 20–30 minutes to double in size – I put mine on top of the cooker so that they get the benefit of the heat of the oven as it warms up. Sprinkle the rolls with a little flour then bake them for 15 minutes. Cool on a wire rack.

Recipes Classified under Countries

AUSTRIA
Beetroot and horseradish salad
Gnocchi in mushroom sauce
Linzertorte

BULGARIA
Chilled cucumber soup
Lentil and red pepper stew
Red kidney bean stew

CARIBBEAN – see also Jamaica
Banana fritters with lime
Courgettes stuffed with cheese
 and onion
Red bean rice

CHINA
Chop suey
Fried wheat protein with sweet and
 sour sauce
Mushrooms and tofu
Stir-fried Chinese cabbage

CZECHOSLOVAKIA
Yellow split pea soup

DENMARK
Christmas fruit loaf
Danish pastries
Open sandwiches
Red fruit pudding
Rice and almond pudding

ENGLAND
Crème brûlée

Gooseberry fool
Leek pie
Macaroni cheese
Madeira cake
Mint sauce
Parkin
Pouring custard
Trifle
Wholewheat bread
Wholewheat rolls

FINLAND
Apple snow
Mushroom salad
Mushrooms in soured cream

FRANCE
Aïoli with crudités
Apple tart
Baby meringues
Carrots *à la Vichy*
Celeriac salad
Cheese sauce (*sauce Mornay*)
Cheese soufflé
Chick peas and vegetable
 mayonnaise (*aigroissade*)
Coeurs à la crème
Cold *gougère* with cream cheese
 filling
Courgettes with fresh herbs
Crêpes suzette
Garlic bread
Gougère with mushrooms, onions
 and red wine
Green salad

338

FRANCE – *cont.*
Green salad with Gruyère cheese
Haricot bean salad
Individual asparagus tarts
Individual cheese soufflés
Leek flan
Leek soufflé
Lentil salad
Lettuce soup
Little coffee custards
Macaroons
Mayonnaise
Melba toast
Mont blanc
Mushroom flan
Mushroom soufflé
Mushrooms *à la Grecque*
Omelettes
Onion flan
Onion soup
Pancakes stuffed with mushrooms
   and artichoke hearts
Pears baked in wine
Peas braised with lettuce
Pipérade
Potato soup
Potatoes Anna
Potatoes baked with cream (*gratin
   dauphinoise*)
Pumpkin baked with butter and
   garlic
Ratatouille
Red cabbage and chestnut
   casserole
Red cabbage stuffed with
   chestnuts
Rice and artichoke heart salad
Salade Niçoise
Salsify with parsley and butter
Sponge fingers
Strawberry tartlets
Stuffed aubergines *à la duxelles*
Stuffed tomatoes à la Provençale
Sugar-glazed parsnips

Tian
Tomato, cheese and olive salad
Tomato salad
Tomato soup
Vinaigrette
Watercress soup
White sauce (*sauce Béchamel*)
Wine sauce

GERMANY
Carrots with apples
Dried fruit compote
Haricot beans with apples
Mushroom soup
Potato pancakes
Potatoes with apples
Rice and peas with tomato sauce
   (*Schoten*)
Stewed red cabbage
Yellow split pea purée with
   vegetables

GREAT BRITAIN
Apple sauce
Baked potatoes
Brandy snaps
Gravy
Pease pudding
Roast potatoes

GREECE – see also Middle East
Cauliflower in tomato sauce
Cheese pie
Honey cheese cake
Stuffed aubergines in béchamel
   sauce
Stuffed vine or cabbage leaves
Tomatoes stuffed with rice
Yoghurt tart

HOLLAND
Brussels sprouts with cheese
Green split pea soup
Lemon whip
Potato bake
Potato and watercress soufflé

HUNGARY
Chilled cherry soup
Green pepper and tomato stew
(*Lecso*)
Liptauer cheese
Potato and mushroom stew with
soured cream

INDIA
Biriani
Chapatis
Cheese curry
Curried stuffed eggs
Curry sauce
Fried rice
Ghee
Khitchari
Samosas
Spicy okra
Vegetable curry

IRELAND
Soda bread

ITALY
Asparagus pudding (*sformato*)
Aubergine bake (*parmigiana*)
Cheese and onion soup
Chestnut soup
Chick peas and vermicelli
Coffee *ricotta* pudding
Fennel baked with cheese
Fennel and cucumber salad
Fresh fruit salad
Fresh orange salad
Fresh peach salad
Fried *gnocchi*
Gnocchi alla Romana
Lasagne with spinach and cheese
Pasta and beans
Pasta with cream cheese and
walnuts
Pineapple sorbet
Pizza
Quick non-yeast pizza (*al tegame*)

Red peppers with tomatoes and
onions (*peperonata*)
Rice and peas (*risi e bisi*)
Rice croquettes
Ricotta gnocchi
Risotto bianco
Spaghetti with *pesto*
Spinach *gnocchi*
Stuffed cucumber salad
Stuffed onions
Stuffed peaches
Tomato sauce
Vanilla ice cream

JAMAICA – see also Caribbean
Pumpkin soup

MEXICO – see also South America
Avocado dip (*guacamole*)
Pancakes stuffed with cheese
and baked in spicy tomato sauce
Pancakes stuffed with spicy red
beans
Tortillas
Tostadas

MIDDLE EAST – see also Greece,
Turkey, North Africa and
Morocco
Avocado and carrot salad
Aubergine and sesame pâté
Bean pâté
Bulgur wheat pilaf
Bulgur wheat and cheese pilaf
Bulgur wheat, tomato and parsley
salad (*Tabbouleh*)
Butter bean salad
Cabbage salad with mint and
pomegranate
Cold cooked spinach salad
Cucumber and yoghurt salad
Hummus
Lentil soup
Pasta with lentils
Pitta bread

MIDDLE EAST – *cont.*
Spicy fritters
Spinach pie
Yoghurt

MOROCCO – see also Middle East
Couscous

NORTH AFRICA – see also Middle
East
Orange and radish salad

NORWAY
Cabbage with soured cream
New potatoes baked in butter
Prune delight
Rhubarb compote

POLAND
Red cabbage salad
Vegetable and bean salad (*salata mehania*)

PORTUGAL
Kidney beans with tomatoes, onions and cumin
Red kidney bean stew
Tomatoes stuffed with cheese

RUMANIA
Goat cheese and herb spread
Mixed vegetable stew (*ghiveci*)

RUSSIA
Baked stuffed eggs
Beetroot soup (borsch)
Blini
Cauliflower, egg and potato bake
Cucumber salad with soured cream and hardboiled eggs
Little cheese tartlets (*vatrushki*)
Mock caviar
Pashka

SCOTLAND
Cheese scones
Dundee cake
Oatcakes
Shortbread fingers

SOUTH AMERICA – see also Mexico
Chilled avocado soup
Coconut biscuits
Exotic fruit salad
Hot potato salad with peanut dressing
Pumpkin in orange syrup

SPAIN
Chick pea soup
Chocolate and orange mousse
Gazpacho
Green salad
Paella
Stuffed courgette bake
Stuffed peppers

SWEDEN
Apricot and almond pudding
Baked creamed swedes
Creamed spinach

SWITZERLAND
Cheese fondue
Cheese and onion tart
Fruity muesli
Pear bread (*birnbrot*)
Stuffed tomato salad
Swiss fried potato cake (*rösti*)

TURKEY – see also Middle East
Chilled cucumber soup
Ground rice and rosewater pudding

USA
Cauliflower and apple salad
Cheese cake

USA – *cont.*
Chocolate brownies
Coleslaw
Cranberry sauce
Cream cheese and soured
  cream dip
Creamed onions and peas
Glazed sweet potatoes
Potato salad
Pumpkin pie
Raisin sour cream pie
Red bean salad
Spinach salad

Sweetcorn fritters
Sweetcorn pudding
Three-bean salad
Vichyssoise
Waldorf salad

WALES
Bread and cheese pudding
Glamorgan sausage
Welsh rabbit

YUGOSLAVIA
Aubergines stuffed with cheese

Index

343

Ishbel Addyman was born in North Yorkshire in 1976. She was educated at Oxford University and Paul Valéry University in Montpellier. She took fencing lessons in preparation for writing about the legendary duellist Cyrano de Bergerac but is not yet up to fighting off one hundred assailants single-handedly.

Cyrano

Adventures in space and time
with the legendary French hero

ISHBEL ADDYMAN

POCKET
BOOKS

LONDON · SYDNEY · NEW YORK · TORONTO

First published in Great Britain by Simon & Schuster UK Ltd, 2008
This edition first published by Pocket Books, 2009
An imprint of Simon & Schuster UK Ltd
A CBS COMPANY

1 3 5 7 9 10 8 6 4 2

Simon & Schuster UK Ltd
1st Floor
222 Gray's Inn Road
London WC1X 8HB

www.simonsays.co.uk

Simon & Schuster Australia
Sydney

PICTURE CREDITS
1, 13, © RMN
2, 12, © Photos12
3, 11, 18, 24, © Bridgeman Art Library
4, 14b, © Alamy
5, 16, © Mary Evans
6, 7, © Getty
8, 17, 20, courtesy of author
9, courtesy of Collection David-Sertillanges, www.cyranodebergerac.fr
10, 15, 21, © Corbis
14a, © Wellcome
19, © Lebrecht
22, © Ronald Grant Archive
23, © Rex
25, © Advertising Archives
26, © Scala Archives

A CIP catalogue for this book is available
from the British Library.

ISBN: 978-1-41652-240-9

Typeset in Bembo by M Rules
Printed by CPI Cox & Wyman, Reading, Berkshire RG1 8EX

For my Mother
with love always

Contents

'The joy of a spirit is the measure of its power'

Ninon de Lenclos (1620–1705)

'Failure is always a proof of freedom'

Jacques Brel (1929–1978)

PROLOGUE

Lieutenant de Cavais to Marshal de Gassion – 1642

Honoured Sir,
I am given to understand that, after the report made to you by
Monsieur de Bourgogne, you wished to have further
information regarding the incident that took place at the de
Nesle gate, at which I was also present. I am sensible of the
honour you do me in requesting my account. I dare to hope
that the following will serve the purpose, it is as faithful and as
detailed a description as I could make it.

It was late afternoon when we eventually left the tavern. I
don't think anyone apart from me took his suggestion
seriously. As usual, he had drunk much less than the rest of us
and, while we spilt out into the sunshine, stumbling over one
another, he was a still point at the centre of the rabble. Most of
the others laughed off his invitation to come and watch what
would happen. In the end only four of us followed him
towards the de Nesle gate. It is an area I would normally avoid
but I was determined to witness his humiliation. He had
angered me that day with several clever witticisms at my

expense, and I admit that I was eager for revenge. Setting off, I was elated that his hour was finally come. I was praying for him to fail, to be silenced. As we got nearer and the sound of voices began to reach us, I felt the first squirt of fear through my guts. My fellow officers had insisted on accompanying him in order to protect him and I knew that I might also be expected to step in. When we caught the first sight of the crowd of villains waiting for us, there was no doubt in my mind that this was not a fight I wanted any part in; we were outnumbered at least ten to one and by a crowd of the most ungentlemanly ruffians. He turned and asked to us to wait behind him, and under no circumstances to attempt to interfere. It was a suicidally stupid thing to say and I almost laughed, but the sound died in my throat. One of the men hurled an obscene insult in our direction and I felt all their eyes on us, sizing us up. It was at that moment that I realized I had lost all my previous envy of him. My corrosive desire to be a spectator at the moment of his bloody and ignominious death had vanished.

He walked towards them and drew his sword. I remember that he spoke but not the words, which were quickly drowned out in any case by coarse mocking laughter and howls of almost hysterical derision. It was clear that the men had been drinking and one or two of them seemed to be finding the situation increasingly comic. That this single, lean figure should step forward to challenge them all was preposterous indeed. I no longer wished to witness the moment when they would sweep over him like a pack of wolves and tear him to shreds. But I was compelled to keep looking. He continued advancing towards them at an unhurried pace. The tension in this moment of calm while both sides waited to see what the other would do was making the hairs on the back of my neck itch and I felt my armpits and groin suddenly prickle with sweat. My former enemy, beckoned the nearest of the gang to come towards him. The ruffian responded with a sarcastic jibe and, laughing back over his shoulder to his companions, he swaggered forward. Most of them seemed to be armed with thick clubs or glinting knives but the first to fight was unsheathing a heavy sword. All the others watched hungrily as the two figures came within reach of one another. The next thing I saw was the impossible brightness of the blood arching from the lackey's neck and seeming almost to hang a moment in the air along with his suddenly awkward form, before both fell to earth together. The brilliant redness oozed all around the man's lifeless body, soaking through his grubby clothes and seeping into the ground. The reaction from the watching rabble was swift and varied; some rushed forward yelling furiously, others were already beginning to edge away. With extraordinary agility and speed, their opponent was already on the move, and had leapt across in order to position himself on the fallen rubble in such a way that the ditch protected him from attack from the rear and the masonry prevented his adversaries from being able to rush or crowd him. If they wanted to fight him, they would have to do so according to his rules, each man individually. What followed was a simply dazzling display of swordsmanship. There were moments when I was convinced he was lost. He received a powerful blow from a cudgel which ought to have felled him, but he recovered in time to deliver a swift slashing riposte. His assailant screamed and ran off cradling his arm. Shortly after, I saw his sword catch in one fellow's eye-socket and seem to stick there – it looked as though the extraordinary duellist would be disarmed and left defenceless in the face of the howling mob, but he calmly used his gloved left hand to dislodge the blade with a sharp downwards tug. Later, he almost fell amongst them, when, scrabbling for purchase, he slipped on the severed finger of one of the knife-wielding attackers, but he regained his balance just in time. Soon the unruly crowd had dwindled to almost nothing. Half-a-dozen inert forms were strewn about and others were limping and stumbling away, aided by their fellows. The most craven were already long gone, having fled at the sight of a man's throat being opened. My companions rushed over to tend to their exhausted hero, while I inspected the fallen men. Two were already corpses, rapidly cooling, and I counted another seven incapacitated and weeping or groaning in their agony. I have seen my share of such slow, lingering deaths on the battlefield and the sound of their suffering brought back insistent and terrible memories. I drew my dagger thinking to dispatch them to a swifter end. In an instant he was beside me, his hand was on mine and he said to me, 'No, leave them, they will tell the story.' I observed him bend to each of the wounded men in turn and say, 'We have not yet been introduced; my name is Monsieur de Cyrano de Bergerac.'

This is the true and faithful record of my observations and I hope that my humble testimony will prove useful to your honour. If I may serve you further in any way possible, I dare to hope that so noble a military leader will not disdain the unworthy but unfailing loyalty of one of his devoted subordinates. I remain your humble servant,

Monsieur de Cavais

Introduction

Over three and a half centuries ago, a lone swordsman stepped out of the shadows of obscurity and into the light of lasting legend. His 'duel with a hundred men', as it became known, was a defining moment in the career of a man whose insane daring made him a legend in French history. At the time, the story blazed through the taverns and back streets of seventeenth-century Paris and brought Cyrano de Bergerac to the attention of Marshal de Gassion, one of the highest military commanders in the land. As a result, Gassion attempted to hire the hero of the hour for his own company, but his offer came too late. The invincible swordsman had already decided to leave his military career behind.

The precise details of Cyrano's single-handed battle against a gang of hired thugs have been lost in the tide of admiration and exaggeration that such a feat naturally provoked. There is no surviving documentary evidence recording the incident directly: the letter with which this book opened is a fiction. But the eyewitness, Monsieur de Cavais, is not himself an invention. Although neither Cavais nor Bourgogne left a written account, their names are known to us (along with that of a third witness, a soldier named

Cuigy) thanks to another man, Cyrano's loyal friend and fellow officer, Henri Le Bret. Le Bret was by his side at the de Nesle gate, and in 1656 he published his version of the story. He only offers the barest outline of the tale, but it is one of the highlights of the first ever biography of Cyrano de Bergerac.

Today, the name Cyrano is known to most of us as that of a fictional character: the eponymous hero of a five-act tragi-comedy in verse, *Cyrano de Bergerac* by Edmond Rostand. The play has won over audiences around the globe and Rostand used the duel with one hundred men in order to establish his hero as a man of phenomenal courage and death-defying, swashbuckling talent. The story of the duel has to be the single element of the play that one would least expect to have any basis in historical fact, and yet it was not invented by the poet Rostand, but drawn from the life story of a real person, as recounted by one of his closest friends.

Before the hero there was a man, and before the legend there was a life. Born in Paris in 1619, the real Cyrano de Bergerac came from an inauspicious bourgeois background. He was uncompromising, unconventional and eccentric to the last, and yet the real Cyrano was also on some level a slave to the social conventions of his time. Determined to efface his comparatively humble origins, Cyrano worked hard to transform himself from Savinien de Cyrano, the grandson of a Sardinian fishmonger, into Cyrano de Bergerac, the supposed scion of a great family of Gascon noblemen. To this day, despite his well-documented Parisian immigrant roots, the Gascon town of Bergerac in the south-west of France proudly proclaims Cyrano as its most famous native son. The centre of this pretty, small town is graced by not one, but two statues of him. In the course of his life, Cyrano determinedly eclipsed his true history. His flamboyant manipulation of his own image was so successful that ultimately the legend blotted out the reality altogether. Like a shadow, his image is distorted and stretches far beyond its original source. He also inadvertently sparked off a chain reaction which has seen his extraordinary story told and re-told in the centuries since his death, in versions which range from the sublime to the ridiculous.

The phenomenal success of Rostand's fictionalized version of Cyrano's life has been so overwhelming that today it is a surprise to many to learn that Cyrano de Bergerac really existed. The play is full of inaccuracies and anachronisms but it undoubtedly captures the spirit of the original Cyrano. The real Cyrano de Bergerac and Rostand's hero share certain points of contact, but in the end the truth is infinitely more intriguing than the fiction. While the stage Cyrano is an undeniably appealing creation, the man himself was considerably more complex and more impressive. The scarcity of evidence in piecing together the biography of the real Cyrano has tended to favour those writers who use the absence of proof as an encouragement to invention. The tendency to want to fill in the mysterious gaps in Cyrano's life story with suitably dashing and romantic episodes is both natural and profoundly unhelpful. For the entire period 1641 to 1648 (almost the whole of Cyrano's twenties) only one document has so far been found relating to the great swordsman. Hard evidence about the life of the real Cyrano is scarce and in order to make the most of the fragments that we have, it is essential to consider each element with forensic caution. The illumination provided by setting each detail in its historical context is vital. An investigation of such scraps of proof as have survived the passage of time is perhaps the only way to finally unearth the untold story of this unsung hero. The fictional Cyrano looms large, and a process that attempts to reveal a little of the human weaknesses and complexity behind a heroic façade might have been one of increasing disillusionment and disappointment. Instead, the real Cyrano, source of a legend, stands revealed as a man who richly deserves the respect, the attention and the affection currently only given to his fictional counterpart.

The real Cyrano wrote letters, plays and poetry and his stylistic range covered satire, tragedy and comedy. His masterwork was an innovative science fiction novel, a delirious, fantastical adventure in outer space, in which he imagined the hot air balloon, talking books, rocket propulsion, the eerie sensations of zero gravity and the lunar landing years ahead of their time. His work served as an important inspiration to other illustrious writers: Molière, Voltaire, Jonathan Swift, Jules Verne and H. G. Wells all owe a debt to Cyrano. Yet attempts to define this extraordinarily talented and daring individual quickly run into difficulty: murderous pacifist, serious comedian, frivolous intellectual, honest deceiver. Cyrano de Bergerac has always been a profoundly paradoxical figure: in his lifetime the real Cyrano, a difficult, daring and dangerous individual, provoked extreme responses, he was much loved and much hated. As a result opposing accounts of the man struggled for dominance, no single version was strictly factual or entirely objective. In the writing of both Cyrano's detractors and his apologists fact and fiction are interwoven and the outlines of the man and the legend haze and blur. In the late nineteenth century, these confused elements of Cyrano's story suddenly crystallized into two distinct accounts: the first saw the unadorned facts presented by a diligent academic and in the second the romantic legend was blazoned abroad by a playwright at the height of his powers. A new division emerged, which has since grown and deepened.

Today there are two distinct figures who share the name Cyrano de Bergerac. One, a fictional character with an enormous nose is celebrated, admired, even adored, while the other, the original, is forgotten, dismissed or ignored. A fiery, fascinating individual is now remembered only as a romanticized burlesque figure. The story of Cyrano has appeared in poems, novels, plays, on film, as an opera and even as a ballet. There is, however, only one element of the story which is common to each of the myriad versions of the man and the legend – all accounts agree that Cyrano de Bergerac was an invincible duellist. In a letter written by the man himself, he made light of his extraordinary sword–fighting reputation and came up with a neat summary of the paradoxical polarization of opinion he provoked, declaring: 'In truth, it is a very great consolation to me to be hated because I am loved; to find enemies everywhere because I have friends everywhere.'

I

A grain of truth

The play *Cyrano de Bergerac* by Edmond Rostand premiered in Paris on 28 December 1897. Audience and actors alike were immediately caught up in the delirious storm of a *succès fou*. At two o'clock in the morning all the lights were still blazing in the Théâtre de la Porte St Martin, the auditorium was still packed to capacity and outside in the surrounding streets crowds of curious onlookers had gathered. The final ovation lasted over an hour and after the first forty curtain calls the stage manager gave in and simply left the curtain raised. An account of the night's events appears in the memoir of Rostand that his wife Rosemunde published after his death. She claims that the emotional impact of the play had been so overwhelming that friends who had been at each other's throats for years suddenly threw themselves into one another's arms. Whether the production really did put an end to decade-long feuds or not, its success was undeniably phenomenal and enduring. At the age of twenty-nine, the poet Edmond Rostand had produced his masterpiece.

Cyrano de Bergerac not only transformed its author overnight into the darling of literary Paris, winning him the prestigious Croix de la Légion d'honneur, it also endured beyond all expectation. The play has never really lost its original extraordinary popularity. Over one hundred years have passed since the extravagant success of that opening night and *Cyrano de Bergerac* has been translated into many different languages and continues to be performed all over the world. Cyrano made his first appearance on the silver screen in 1900 and since then a variety of films have featured the legendary swordsman. Recent adaptations range from the lavish French costume drama directed by Jean-Paul Rappeneau to Steve Martin's updated Hollywood comedy *Roxanne*, complete with happy ending. From the very first, admirers of the real Cyrano scented the danger that Rostand's work represented. As early as 1898, the academic Pierre Brun predicted that: 'The legendary Cyrano will absorb the real Cyrano over the centuries', adding rather sadly, 'I have ceased to fool myself about this.'

When Edmond Rostand wrote his box-office smash he didn't create the legend of Cyrano, he merely added new fuel to a fire that had already been burning fitfully for over two hundred and fifty years. Tales of some of Cyrano de Bergerac's more extreme exploits had filtered down through the generations, taking on greater and more heroic proportions as time passed. Much the same could be said of Cyrano's nose, which had also swollen to epic proportions, thanks to the operation of time and exaggeration. The increasing inaccuracy of the Cyrano legend was in direct proportion to the increasing length of Cyrano's nose – Pinocchio-like, the longer the nose, the bigger the lie. We may be fairly certain that few members of the audience who attended the opening night had more than a hazy notion of the reality behind the legend. In the late nineteenth century Cyrano de Bergerac had become a grotesque caricature. Two and a half centuries after his death he was still remembered, but was variously dismissed as a dangerous lunatic, or a laughable eccentric.

Edmond Rostand created his own moving version of Cyrano's

life, which echoed the fairy tale 'Beauty and the Beast'. Like the authors of all the best fairy tales, he didn't allow facts to stand in the way of romance. Rostand's father was a successful barrister who wrote poetry in his spare time and he seems to have envisaged a similar career for his son. He financed Edmond's law degree, keen to see his offspring suitably qualified for a respectable, lucrative career. However, Rostand junior abandoned his legal training to devote himself entirely to poetry. It is hardly surprising then that this headstrong young man was uninterested in establishing the truth behind the legend of Cyrano de Bergerac. He longed to write dramatic, inspirational verse, to 'give lessons of the soul', not to replicate the accuracy and precision of dry legal documents.[1]

The stage Cyrano is a burlesque figure, a man whose nose is so disproportionately vast that his hideousness renders him savage. He has fought countless duels, and is reputed to be capable of killing a man just for looking at him askance. However, this fearless, fero-cious Cyrano falls madly in love with his beautiful cousin Roxane. Cyrano's passionate devotion to Roxane exerts a powerful human-izing influence, rendering the bestial soldier vulnerable. Cyrano's desperation to be close to his beloved and his need to express his love (without risking her scorn) famously leads him to embrace an opportunity to woo her by proxy. He allows the Baron Christian de Neuvillette, an attractive, young cadet from his own regiment, who has caught his cousin's eye, to speak for him. Christian is so entranced by Roxane's beauty and wit that he cannot find the courage to speak to her himself and consequently he is happy to accept Cyrano's offer to write his love letters for him, and even allows Cyrano to make a moving speech on his behalf from the shadows beneath Roxane's balcony, pleading for a kiss. This bal-cony scene deliberately recalls Romeo and Juliet, and the action of the play unfolds in similarly tragic vein.

Directly after their hastily improvised wedding ceremony, Roxane's new husband, the Baron Christian de Neuvillette, is sent away from her to Arras on the orders of the Count de Guiche who is his jealous love rival. While they are besieged at Arras, Cyrano continues to write love letters to Roxane, braving enemy fire to cross the siege lines in order to send daily letters to his beloved. Roxane in turn risks her own life to follow her husband to the battlefield. Intoxicated by the letters, she determines to beg Christian to forgive her for having loved him at first just for his beauty. But her attempts to reassure Christian of the purity of her love for him backfire horribly. In her insistence that it is his soul, as revealed to her in his letters from the battlefield, that she loves so passionately, she unknowingly betrays to him the fact that it is Cyrano who has won her heart. Christian is killed by enemy fire before he can force Cyrano to admit the deception and ask Roxane to choose between them. The action of the play then skips forward fourteen years. The final act takes place in the courtyard of the convent where Roxane has shut herself away from the world to mourn the loss of her beloved husband. In the final scene a wounded and dying Cyrano arrives for his weekly visit to his 'old friend', he finally admits to Roxane that he was the one who wrote the letters but that he felt constrained to keep silent because although the tear stains on the final farewell letter were his own, the bloodstains were Christian's. The truth having finally been revealed to her too late Roxane laments,

> *I never loved but one man in my life.*
> *Now I must lose him twice.*[2]

The play itself is undeniably romantic and beautifully written, but its initial startling success was also underpinned by some extremely canny marketing. Rostand was fortunate that, as a charming and personable young poet, he had managed to find his way to the heart of the close-knit theatrical and literary community in *fin de siècle* Paris. He benefited from a close association with some of the

leading figures in French theatre. In particular Rostand was spec-
tacularly fortunate in his choice of leading man. Benoît-Constant
Coquelin would play the title role over four hundred times in the
course of the initial fourteen-month-long sell-out run of *Cyrano de
Bergerac*. Coquelin also played the role in London and in the United
States and was the first actor to play Cyrano on film. He was one
of the most celebrated and successful actors of his generation,
adored by the public and critics alike. Contemporary reviews of his
performance praise 'the extraordinary brilliancy of M. Coquelin's
action and delivery', giving a clear idea of the significance of
Coquelin's skill in creating the role of Cyrano.[3] The distinguished
English theatre critic C. E. Montague was unequivocal in his admiration of Coquelin's powers: 'the sheer comic force with which he
embraced and enjoyed the idea of what he was acting. The com-
municable energy of his joy in all the contents of human nature was
incomparable; no comedian in our time has glowed with a more
radiant heat of life and delight.'[4]

In 1897, Coquelin was fifty-six years old and a highly experienced actor. In the first published edition of the play Rostand
acknowledged the significant contribution that his talented lead had
made to the creation of the play in a characteristically lyrical dedication. 'I had intended to dedicate this poem to the spirit of
Cyrano. But since his soul has passed into you, Coquelin, I dedicate
it to you.'[5] Rostand owed an additional debt of thanks to Coquelin
for an open letter to the poet that the actor had written and which
had appeared on the front page of *Le Petit Parisien*:

In his work he does something that few men of today even
among the most illustrious know how to do, he writes with his
heart. Above all he is a sincere being . . . I am proud to have lived
to come into contact with such a man and I am happy to have
the chance to say so here: Cyrano has been the most wonderful
creation of my career and the greatest joy of my existence.[6]

Another imposing figure who offered Rostand crucial support and exposure was the legendarily talented and eccentric actress Sarah Bernhardt. Bernhardt, who was known as 'the eighth wonder of the world', dined regularly with Rostand and his beautiful young wife and the poet had penned an earlier play *La Princesse Lointaine* specifically for her. *La grande Sarah* was at the height of her powers in 1897. At the age of fifty-three she had a distinguished career behind her and was the proprietor of her own theatre. Her endorsement was an extremely important seal of approval for a new work. Bernhardt also had a genius for publicity; early on in her career as a tragedienne she had let it be known that, convinced she was destined to die young, she had ordered herself a beautiful silk-lined coffin that she kept in her bedroom and occasionally slept in. She was constantly surrounded by a court of admirers and a menagerie that included a wolf, a leopard and a monkey named Darwin. She dispensed her patronage with regal aplomb. *Cyrano de Bergerac* represented a collaboration between a poet she considered a charming protégé and a fellow thespian who was one of her oldest colleagues and dearest friends. Bernhardt recognized immediately that the combination of Rostand's sublime poetry and Coquelin's overwhelming charisma would make for theatrical magic. She gave the production her blessing in typically extravagant fashion. The following letter to Coquelin was published in *Le Figaro* on the day after the premiere.

I can't begin to tell you my joy for your triumph of yesterday and of this evening. What happiness, my Coq! What happiness! It is the triumph of Art, and of beauty. It's your immense talent! It's the genius of our Poet! I am so happy, oh! so! I send you my love, my heart beating with the purest joy and the sincerest friendship, Sarah.[7]

Sarah Bernhardt's ebullient lust for glory had enabled her to become an internationally recognized celebrity. Despite her dubious social status as an unapologetically unmarried mother she had embarked on successful tours of England and the United States; her trailblazing paved the way for a similar tour later undertaken by the cast of *Cyrano de Bergerac*.

Edmond Rostand was not just a dreamy romantic he was also an astute observer of the zeitgeist and he had recognized that the time was ripe for his swashbuckling sonneteer. The late nineteenth century was an uncomfortable period in French history, the economy was static, social welfare was failing, labour-management was increasingly problematic and the birth rate was falling. In 1870, Bismarck's Germany had defeated the French Army in the Franco-Prussian War, triggering the collapse of Napoleon III's Second Empire. In 1894, the nation was gripped by a profoundly divisive scandal, when the anti-Semitism underpinning the conviction of Captain Alfred Dreyfus for treason was revealed. Looking back, to an age when matters of honour were settled swiftly and decisively, sword in hand, allowed audiences to escape the uncertainties of the present and revel in a heroic past, when life was less complicated and heroes were unequivocally noble and dashing. This romantic fascination with the age of the musketeers had begun some fifty years earlier with a flowering of fictional re-creations of the seventeenth century. Most famously Alexandre Dumas had achieved enormous success with his series of novels detailing the daring escapades of d'Artagnan and the Three Musketeers: *Les Trois Mousquetaires* (1844), *Vingt Ans après* (1845) and *Le Vicomte de Bragelonne* (1848–50). Edmond Rostand shrewdly rewrote history and transformed Cyrano from an anti-establishment rebel into a national hero.

Just three years before the opening of the play, a rather different version of Cyrano's life story had appeared, with considerably less fanfare. In 1894, the academic Pierre Brun had published a complete edition of the works of Cyrano de Bergerac, accompanied by an account of his life. The work had begun as Brun's doctoral thesis at Montpellier University and the full title of the published version was *Savinien de Cyrano Bergerac – his Life and his Works drawn from previously unpublished documents*, which is admittedly a bit less snappy than Rostand's *Cyrano de Bergerac*. Brun's biography had been painstakingly pieced together from various sources that he had managed to unearth from the obscurity of parish records and the dark depths of the Bibliothèque Nationale. The aim of Brun's six years of dedicated research was to establish a clear, factual picture of the real Cyrano, unclouded by the exaggerations and rumour that his extraordinary career had always attracted. Ironically, Brun's new edition of Cyrano's life and works may very well have been a key element in drawing Rostand's attention to the subject.

Sadly, for the unassuming academic, his work was quickly overshadowed by Rostand's popular success and the adulation of enraptured critics who declared: 'We do not want realism we want fantasy.'[8] The reviewers also advised the public not to be disenchanted by Pierre Brun's book, but to go to the theatre and 'forget about Brun for an evening'.[9] Given the way in which the public readily embraced this advice, Brun could be forgiven for bitterly resenting Rostand and his creation. In fact, he remained remarkably calm and patient as six years of hard work, attempting to replace the legendary Cyrano with the real, were swept away on a tide of enthusiasm. Although clearly terribly disappointed, Brun refused to rage against Rostand. He understood and appreciated the powerful appeal of Rostand's lyrical distortion of the true story of Cyrano de Bergerac. An eager young academic named Émile Magne was quick to step into the breach, and shortly after the play opened Magne published a pamphlet in which he attacked the historical inaccuracies of Rostand's work. Brun refused to be drawn, however, affectionately dismissing Magne's study as unnecessary: 'With the bold intolerance of youth . . . he makes use of an enormous tome to crush a brilliant butterfly.'[10] Clearly the kindly old academic had a healthy sense of proportion.

Émile Magne may not have particularly impressed Brun with his account of the numerous factual errors to be found in the play, but his outspoken attack certainly succeeded in riling the playwright. The second edition of Magne's work contains a reproduction of Rostand's handwritten letter to the author furiously repudiating Magne's criticism. It seems that Edmond Rostand took great offence at his shaky grasp of history being highlighted in this way and promptly launched a misguided campaign to defend himself. However reluctant he was to criticize Rostand's work, which he greatly admired, Brun was not above enjoying a quiet revenge. He published a second academic study on the same theme as the first, and included a brief but cheerfully scathing reference to the poet's undignified response to Émile Magne's pamphlet. He also expressed disappointment that his own painstaking research would inevitably be overshadowed by the romantic appeal of Rostand's creation, and the works of the real Cyrano ignored by readers dazzled by the fictional hero: 'I had hoped that the real Cyrano would eventually replace the legendary Cyrano entirely. I had hoped – touching illusion – that I might have corrected various errors and approximations . . . It was not long before I was disenchanted.'[11]

Brun's second study of Cyrano was entitled *Savinien de Cyrano de Bergerac – Parisian Gentleman, the history and the legend*. His inclusion of the phrase 'Parisian Gentleman' in the title was significant, because one of the most basic errors about Cyrano, further propagated by Rostand's work, was the idea that the great swordsman was a Gascon nobleman from the Périgord region in the southwest of France. In fact the estate from which the family took their name was not the large prosperous Gascon town of Bergerac but a small rural estate just outside Paris. Far from belonging to the highest ranks of the Gascon nobility, the family were originally a pretty lowly bunch of Sardinian immigrants. The family name Cyrano was simply a French version of the Italian surname *Cirano*. Cyrano's first name, as Brun's title reveals, was Savinien. He was named after his paternal grandfather, who had begun life as a fish-monger.

The continued confusion over Cyrano's origins still persists today, despite the fact that Brun had published the parish records of Cyrano's baptism, proving incontrovertibly that he was born in the heart of Paris. This simple error is one of the most persistent and with good reason; it originated with that master of misinformation, Cyrano himself. If the family had owned the estate or *seigneurie* of Bergerac in Gascony, then they would necessarily also have been far richer and more influential than they were. It was no accident that Cyrano chose to join the most famous Gascon regiment of his day, the Cadets de Carbon de Castel-Jaloux. Not only did Cyrano join a Gascon regiment but he made quite sure to outdo them all in fulfilling the stereotype of a Gascon noble. He was fiercely independent and gained renown as a 'demon of bravery'. History is silent on the question of whether he also assumed the distinctive thick Gascon accent. Personally, I like to think he would have made that little extra effort. Despite Brun's attempts to situate his historical Cyrano in a detailed context the legend was too vigorous to be confined by the recitation of facts and dates. But it is to facts and dates that we must return in order to retrace the origins of the legend and understand its extraordinary vigour.

2

The time of games

In 1707 Abel-Pierre de Cyrano (the nephew of the great swords-man) ran into some legal trouble. In the course of his defence he confirmed the family's Sardinian origins. More recently, it has been discovered that on their arrival from Italy the family had originally settled in the provinces. The parish records of the town of Sens over 100 kilometres to the south-east of Paris, reveal details of a baptism in 1532 of one Savinien Cyrano, as well as later property transactions under the same name.[1] This is almost certainly Cyrano's grandfather, and it shows the dynamic head of the family selling up his interests in Sens and moving to the capital to seek his fortune. Cyrano's namesake, his grandfather Savinien greatly improved the family's lot by securing lucrative court appointments. It must have taken extraordinary amounts of confidence and charm to make the leap from the fish market to the royal court. Social mobility did exist in the seventeenth century but only in rare cases. Money talked, then as now, but on the whole if you were born a fishmonger you died a fishmonger and so did your children. Having seduced and married a nobleman's daughter, Savinien, the seafood-selling son of a Sardinian, had used her contacts to go on

21

to become *secrétaire du roi*. This was a minor administrative position in the court of Henri IV, and Savinien would have paid good money for the privilege. He negotiated the cut-throat world of the court with wit and aplomb. After just two years he secured another even more lucrative sinecure, becoming *auditeur à la cour des Comptes*. This was another role similar to the first, with responsibility for assisting in the administration of the king's income from the complex system of taxes and duties. The salary for such a post was minimal; it was tacitly understood that in going about their duties, courtly administrators would naturally have ample opportunities to line their own pockets. In addition, appointees were exempt from taxation.

Savinien had used his gains to purchase the estates of Mauvières and Soub-Forêts in the idyllic setting of the valley of Chevreuse just outside Paris. It was partly thanks to his father's dynamism that Savinien's eldest son, Abel, Cyrano's father, was able to make a very advantageous alliance. In 1612, at the comparatively advanced age of forty-five, Abel married Espérance Bellanger. Espérance was worth waiting for. She was a minor heiress (her parents and all her siblings having died before her marriage) who came from a wealthy family of financiers. Abel and Espérance were married on the 3rd of September at the church of Saint-Gervais in the heart of Paris. An inventory of all the goods belonging to each of them was made at this time, as part of the financial settlement between the two, and although Espérance's half is lost we have a detailed list of Abel's possessions. It provides an interesting glimpse into the household into which Cyrano was born. The inventory includes a library of over a hundred fine-bound volumes of works, mostly in French and Italian but featuring Greek and Latin texts as well. The high proportion of books in Italian would seem to confirm the Cyrano family's Sardinian roots. The books themselves also suggest a cultured and intelligent readership – they cover a diverse range of subjects from legal texts to Rabelais, to Pliny's *Natural History*. This library would have been the original source of Cyrano's lifelong love affair with the written word. An interesting range of *objets d'art* also lend weight to the picture of a family not indifferent to the arts. Several sculptures and paintings of mythological subjects are listed, along with more domestic subjects: a little boy, a flute-player, a villager and his wife, a horse, two dogs, a bull and a lion. It is also noted that Abel owned half a horse; he shared the animal with his brother Samuel. There was a fine pearl necklace which must have made a welcome wedding gift for Espérance. The list also includes a life-size bust of Henri IV and thirteen medallions featuring the king and his queen.

The inventory builds a picture of the Cyranos as successful, cultivated members of the minor gentry, with strong ties of loyalty to the king. However, the family's fortunes did not continue to thrive. The root cause may perhaps be connected to the dramatic assassination of King Henri IV in 1610. Henri was stabbed to death by a mad monk, who leapt into the royal carriage. At the time of the king's sudden death, his baby son was still too young to rule the country and a regency was established to govern during the new king's minority. Many of Henri IV's underlings would have found themselves abruptly displaced by favourites of the new regime. Abel had not inherited his father's forceful personality and gift for diplomacy and so he had to live off his small legal practice and the income from the family's estates, being either incapable of regaining his father's position in the vicious, precarious world of the court, or unwilling to try. He did, however, manage to marry very well indeed. Although Abel would not achieve any spectacular social ascension, some of the relations on his new wife's side of the family rose to lucrative positions of great prestige and responsibility.

Cyrano's parents had already been married six years by the time he was born on 6 March in 1619. Their eldest son, Denis, had been born on 13 March 1614. In vivid contrast to Cyrano, Denis was devout and serious. He showed an early propensity for theological study and eventually entered the priesthood. Two more sons followed in quick succession, Antoine born 11 February 1616, and Honoré born 3 July 1617; both Antoine and Honoré died very young. Cyrano also had a younger brother named Abel born around 1624. He had at least one sister, Catherine, whose date of birth is lost to us. Altogether, Espérance gave birth at least six times, but only four of her children lived into adulthood and only Abel II went on to have a family and children of his own. It is quite possible that Cyrano also had other siblings whose names and dates of birth are lost to us, the baptismal record is far from reliable and in the seventeenth century death in childbirth was terrifyingly commonplace and infant mortality rates were cruelly high. In an age before vaccination small children had virtually no protection against the virulent epidemics that regularly swept through the community and mothers often succumbed to deadly post-natal infections.

In the larger towns and cities such as Paris, where Cyrano spent the first three years of his life, living conditions were unsanitary and filthy. There were no proper drains and no organized method of rubbish disposal, so infectious diseases were readily transmitted. The greater population density exacerbated the problem and consequently epidemics were more frequent in urban areas. Leprosy, typhoid, cholera and diphtheria were all common and usually fatal. Throughout Cyrano's lifetime terrifying outbreaks of the plague would also periodically strike the city, leaving thousands dead. The historian J. L. Flandrin, having looked at the way in which levels of infant mortality began to fall in the eighteenth century, comes to a distinctly disturbing conclusion, arguing that since, 'it cannot be explained by reasons of medicine or hygiene; we had simply ceased to let children die or to help them to die when they were not wanted.'[2] Whether one accepts this allegation of seventeenth-century infanticide or not, it is at the very least vividly apparent that attitudes towards children and family life were significantly different from our own. In a work published in 1622, when Cyrano was three years old, a young mother about to give birth to her sixth child is offered the following consolation by a friendly female neighbour: 'Before they are old enough to give you much trouble you will have lost half of them, or maybe all.'[3]

A child's initial chances of survival were reduced still further by the bourgeois practice of sending new-born babies away to be looked after by a wet-nurse who would breast-feed them until they were weaned, at which point they would be returned to the family home. A professional wet-nurse would be a woman from the lowest rank of society, and as a result the living conditions in which the baby would spend its earliest weeks of life would be the poorest it might ever experience. Fortunately, Cyrano was a strong and healthy baby and it was perhaps to reflect this vigour that he had been named after the dynamic head of the family, his paternal grandfather Savinien.

Despite the fact that the loss of a young child was a far more common occurrence than today, for every tiny unmarked grave there were also significant memorials to these brief lives erected by those privileged enough to be able to afford to indulge their grief. In contrast to portraits from previous centuries, seventeenth-century family groups often included images of children who had died in infancy. These little phantoms were generally immortalized in such a way as to render them indistinguishable from their surviving siblings; such paintings give no hint that certain of the subjects had died years before the painting was executed. In spite of the resignation in the face of high infant-mortality rates expressed by authors such as the great philosopher Montaigne, who remarked, 'I lost two or three children in their infancy, not without regret but without fuss', it is natural to assume that privately many families experienced this harsh fact of seventeenth-century life with a grief that was no less agonizing for being commonplace.[4]

In his prose masterpiece *The Voyage to the Moon* (1656) Cyrano seems to rebel against his humble origins, reflecting bitterly on the fact that a man's birth is the only aspect of his destiny over which he has absolutely no control. One of his central characters launches a surprisingly vehement attack on the biblical commandment 'Honour thy father and thy mother'. The hero is also confronted with the first great injustice of existence – the fact that in the moment of conception the baby, who is after all the one for whom the occasion has the greatest importance, is also the one with the least say in the matter. 'Alas! In an affair in which you were the only one concerned, you were the only person whose opinion was not consulted!'[5] Cyrano introduces the novel idea that rather than gratitude for having been brought into existence, a son owes his father resentment for having denied him the possibility of a more impressive birthright in a more illustrious family. In the superior rational society of the moon, as Cyrano's imagination saw it, the inhabitants recognized that the traditional 'tyrannical authority' of fathers was both unjust and unreasonable. He conjures up a vision of a nation in which the young men rule the family and take all important decisions without consulting the wishes of their elders, treating their parents with disrespect that borders on disdain.

Cyrano deliberately took the argument to its extreme, and Dyrcona the space-travelling hero of *The Voyage to the Moon* is given the following disturbing advice by his lunar protector: 'Tread on the belly of the father who engendered you, trample on the bosom of the mother who conceived you.'[6] The shocked hero is later reassured by his mentor that some degree of exaggeration had been necessary in order to correct the wrong-headedness of the poor misguided earthling. He compares his technique to that of a gardener attempting to straighten out a tree that is growing twisted: 'I was obliged to act like one who wishes to straighten a crooked tree; twisting it to the other side so that between the two contortions it grows straight again.'[7] This vivid explanation is also the perfect metaphor for Cyrano's satirical writing; it serves as a useful warning to the reader not to take any of the ideas expressed too literally. The extreme nature of Cyrano's attack on the parent-child relationship is far from providing proof that Cyrano had an unhappy childhood or a troubled relationship with his parents, it is a typical moment of provocation. But some documentary evidence does suggest that, whatever may have been the case when Cyrano was a child, in later life his relationship with his father did degenerate alarmingly. It is impossible to recover the fine detail of Cyrano's boyhood but a minimum of investigation serves to cast doubt on the rosy vision of a cosseted aristocratic background which Edmond Rostand imagined for his hero.

In a poignant early scene between Cyrano and Roxane the two cousins evoke an idyllic picture of their shared childhood.

Roxane: But, for the confession I have come to make,
         I need to find in you my almost-brother
         With whom I played in the park, by the lake.
Cyrano: Yes, you came to Bergerac every summer.
Roxane: You used reeds for your swords in those days.
Cyrano: And you used corn-silk for your doll's hair.
Roxane: It was the time of games.[8]

The real Cyrano did have a cousin named Madeleine Robineau, who may have served as the model for Roxane, but she was ten years older than her swashbuckling relative; of course the pair may still have played together in their childhood, but not in the landscaped grounds of a stately chateau in Bergerac. As we have seen, Cyrano had lived in the heart of Paris until the age of three. In 1622, the family moved out to the manor house on the estate of Mauvières near Chevreuse, to the south-west of Paris on the road to Chartres. The house was beautifully situated beside a river in the thickly wooded splendour of the Valley of Chevreuse, an area currently protected for its outstanding natural beauty. The estates were not large; there was a working watermill and a few farm buildings attached, but no elegant park or ornamental lake in sight. The chateau was completely rebuilt in the eighteenth century so the only original traces of Cyrano's childhood home that survive today are the watermill and a very pretty dovecote. The name Bergerac had attached to the lands in the late fourteenth century when they were awarded as a gift from King Charles V to Ramond de la Rivière de la Martigne for his bravery in regaining that city from the invading English. La Rivière was originally from Bergerac and so renamed the meadows to the west of his land in honour of his home town and of his achievement, so that the seigneurie became known as de Mauvières et de Bergerac.

Rostand's duet of shared memories is perfectly pitched to serve the dramatic needs of the scene; it establishes the harmonious counterpoint of two voices which will then be abruptly broken. In the play Roxane has summoned Cyrano to a private rendezvous in order to confess to him her love for Christian. She hopes to enlist his help in protecting the young Baron (who has just joined Cyrano's own regiment) and also in passing on the flattering news of her interest in him. The exchange is cleverly constructed to reveal to the audience, but not to the embarrassed and oblivious Roxane, that a deeply smitten Cyrano is expecting her proposed avowal of a secret passion to concern him rather more directly. His heroic attempts to conceal the pain caused by the abrupt discovery of her feelings for Christian are subtly underplayed; only as Roxane leaves him with a parting compliment on his extraordinary bravery in fighting alone against one hundred armed men does he allow himself the sardonic reflection: 'I've done better than that since then.'[9]

As we have seen, Rostand's version of Cyrano's life was criticized in his lifetime for the inaccuracies and anachronisms which abound in the work. Émile Magne, the young academic who put

his criticisms into print, objected to the 'hybrid' nature of historical fiction. He highlighted the fact that Rostand's *Cyrano* was at
times appallingly inaccurate and at others a perfect reflection of the
original.[10] As the older and wiser academic Pierre Brun pointed
out, it is a pointless exercise to look for academic precision in a
work of fiction. Rather than focusing on the numerous occasions
when Rostand chose inspiration over historical investigation, it is
more interesting to consider the elements of the life of the real
Cyrano which did make it onto the stage.

Certain details in the play reveal that Rostand had paid close
attention to Cyrano's own writing. For example, when the fictional
Cyrano looks back with longing on a childhood spent in the countryside, climbing trees and eating unripe blackberries he voices a
deep attachment to the rural landscape, which appears time and
again in the writing of the real Cyrano. In a letter 'On a house in
the Country' the absent host is reproached for staying away from
his 'enchanted palace'. Cyrano waxes lyrical about the myriad
beauties of a landscape scented with violets and wild roses, where
a stream whispers the story of its journey to the pebbles, and the
trees towering above him seem to carry the whole world sus-
pended from their roots. Cyrano's delight in the countryside is
unequivocal, 'I have found the Garden of Eden, I have found the
golden age and the source of eternal youth . . . here one laughs
with one's whole heart.'[11] His unfailing fascination with animals,
birds and plants and his keen eye for the details of the natural
world were to provide some interesting highlights in his satirical
writing, not least in the moment in *The Voyage to the Sun* (1662)
when the hero, Dyrcona, is put on trial for the crime of being
human by an enlightened parliament of birds.

Since Cyrano's entire adult life was spent in the city of Paris
(with the obvious exception of his time on the battlefield) it seems
that his passionate relationship with the natural world must have
begun in childhood. Cyrano's family moved to the countryside

when he was three, just as he reached an age to be able to appreciate it. His increasing awareness of his surroundings coincided with a new-found freedom. Released from the confines of a town house in the heart of a bustling city, he would have been able to toddle about and explore this newly expanded world. Although the real Cyrano retained a lifelong affection for the scenes of his childhood, Rostand's nostalgic vision springs from a nineteenth-century romantic idea of childhood. The reality is likely to have been much darker.

In 1618, the year in which Cyrano's mother became pregnant, events were taking place elsewhere in Europe that would eventually impact on the destiny of her unborn child. On the morning of the 23rd of May, the power struggle between Catholic and Protestant factions in Northern Europe erupted in a small-scale violent confrontation that would have extremely wide-ranging consequences. Members of a Protestant assembly in Prague had come to the conclusion that a provocative confrontational act was required if their concerns were to be taken seriously. At around 9 a.m., a group of armed men forced their way into the Hradschin Castle and up to a council room where they found four of the ten regents appointed by the Catholic Habsburg Emperor Matthias to rule the kingdom of Bohemia. Two of the four, namely Vilém Slawata and Jaroslav Martinitz were known to support a plan to re-Catholicize Bohemia. First Martinitz and then Slawata were hurled bodily from a high castle window. Slawata managed to cling to the sill but his grip was loosened by a couple of vicious blows from a knife handle. Finally, a scribe was thrown out after the two regents. The dramatic events of 'the defenestration of Prague' (as the incident became known) precipitated Bohemia and the Habsburg Empire into a conflict that would gradually encompass most of Western Europe. The power struggle between Protestant and Catholic factions already smouldering away throughout Europe was ignited by this spark and raged on for thirty blood-soaked years. All three of the men thrown out of the window actually survived. Opinion was divided at the time as to what it was that saved them. The Catholics insisted that the men were rescued by ministering angels, whereas the Protestants offered the more prosaic explanation of a soft landing in a giant pile of manure. In Cyrano's lifetime, France would in turn be drawn into the Thirty Years War. He lived through a turbulent era when the nation was periodically ravaged by war and violence was endemic in society.

One particularly notable event in Cyrano's early childhood was the explosion of a dramatic scandal at court. The execution of the dashing young duellist, Comte de Montmorency-Bouteville, in 1627 caused a huge public outcry. Cyrano was only eight at the time but the execution was the culmination of a long-running, notorious controversy of the sort uniquely fitted to appeal to the imagination of a small boy. It certainly seems to have marked him strongly and may even have been instrumental in dictating certain elements of his future career. In February 1626, shortly before Cyrano's seventh birthday, King Louis XIII had issued an edict designed to reinforce the ban on duelling. Cardinal Richelieu, the king's ambitious advisor and the most powerful politician of the era, had hoped to eradicate the aristocratic practice of settling quarrels over matters of honour with bloody swordfights. The statesmen of France had been trying for years to wipe out this fatal craze but to no avail. Richelieu himself had personal experience of the damage a duel could inflict – his father had killed a man in a duel and his eldest brother died in another. Duelling was already illegal, having been banned by laws passed in 1566 and 1579. Nevertheless, the young nobles continued to slaughter one another.

The edict of February 1626 had imposed heavy penalties on duellists. The act of issuing the challenge to a duel was rendered punishable by the loss of offices, the confiscation of half of the challenger's property and his banishment for the period of three years. If the challenger or the defender did not die in the duel they could both be stripped of their noble status, or even executed. The illegal art of the duel therefore carried a double death penalty – if your opponent didn't kill you there was a chance that the king might. One man in particular bitterly resented this attempt at royal interference in what was deemed to be an established right of the nobility. Comte François de Montmorency-Bouteville was twenty-eight years old, and already the successful champion of twenty-two duels, when he determined to stage a dramatic public protest against the edict. On the 14th of May 1627, he arranged for duels to take place between six noblemen in the middle of the Place Royal in broad daylight. One well-known noble, Bussy d'Amboise, died in the duel and another man was gravely wounded. Comte de Montmorency-Bouteville and his cousin Comte des Chapelles, who had both survived the contest, fled Paris. They were soon hunted down and brought back to the capital, where they were imprisoned in the Bastille. Montmorency-Bouteville's family, the illustrious Montmorency-Luxembourg clan, were one of the highest in the land, and they attempted to close ranks to get Montmorency-Bouteville and des Chapelles pardoned.

At the trial, the influential Duc de Montmorency and the Prince de Condé appealed for clemency alongside the Comtesse de Montmorency-Bouteville and other aristocratic ladies. Despite the intercession of these influential figures and the emotional testimony given by the countess, Montmorency-Bouteville's young wife, who was pregnant at the time, the king remained unmoved. The two men were publicly executed in the Place de Grève on the 22nd of June 1627. The king's only comment was 'I pity the woman but I must defend my authority.'[12] Public opinion was outraged. The people of Paris had followed the details of the case avidly, from the first dramatic moment when the young count had publicly demonstrated his contempt for the anti-duelling law in such spectacular fashion. There were huge crowds present at his execution. It is unlikely, however, that he and des Chapelles gained much comfort from the fact that *le tout Paris* had gathered to register their anger at the king's harsh decision. Richelieu responded by producing propaganda pamphlets, designed to convince the people of the justice of the punishment and the iniquity of duelling.

To a young boy, the story must have been endlessly fascinating. Later in life, Cyrano paid homage to his boyhood hero in a letter, recounting a vivid dream about a journey through the afterlife in which he described hearing Montmorency-Bouteville's voice. The count's ghost is heard raging against his solitude. His isolation is explained as the result of the fear that his duelling prowess inspires in all those around him: 'I distinguished the voice of de Bouteville, who was thundering on about the fact that everyone refused his company; but his anger did him no service: no one dared to approach him for fear of a quarrel. That man carried solitude with him.'[13] Cyrano would eventually become as notorious and skilful a practitioner of the illegal duel as the flamboyant count himself. Another effect of the scandal would become apparent much earlier on, when the young Cyrano, tremendously impressed by Montmorency-Bouteville's fierce independence and flagrant disregard for authority, began to imitate his hero's determined defiance in his own private rebellion.

When he was about seven years old Cyrano was sent away from home to be taught alongside other boys his age by the local country curate. It was here that he first met Henri Le Bret. Their friendship would last a lifetime and Le Bret would prove to be Cyrano's most loyal and devoted ally. Cyrano's friend would also eventually become his first editor and biographer. It was common practice for families to send their sons away to be educated at around the age of seven or eight, and until that age Cyrano would have been taught the rudiments of reading and writing at home, spending all his time with his mother and siblings. At around seven years old, a boy was supposed to have left the earliest phase of childhood behind and had to be ready to assume the beginnings of an independent existence outside the nursery. Monsieur Héroard, the doctor who was in charge of supervising the education of the future King Louis XIII, kept a meticulous diary detailing his supervision of the prince's upbringing which makes for intriguing and occasionally disturbing reading. In the diary Héroard describes the moment when he informed the young prince that he must leave his nursery playthings behind and start behaving like an adult, 'You must not play with these little toys any more . . . you are big now, you are no longer a child.'[14] Louis was six years old.

Apart from a couple of lines penned by Le Bret in which he describes the curé with whom he and Cyrano lodged as 'a good country priest who took in little boarders', there is no surviving record of Cyrano's early education.[15] Rostand's vision of a high-spirited young Cyrano leaping around brandishing a reed for a sword may well be perfectly accurate, but it is also obviously incomplete. The curé who looked after the young Cyrano left no records but some years later a curé, in a similar country parish, began a journal in which he recounted the everyday details of his existence and that of his parishioners. The journal of Alexandre Dubois makes for eye-opening reading; rather than a rural paradise the parish is revealed as a decidedly dangerous place. Henri Platelle who edited a modern edition of the diary remarks on 'the spirit of violence which seems to reign in the village'.[16] The very first entry tells the story of a dangerous criminal who had burned down the vicarage several years earlier. The unnamed arsonist had also murdered one Hubert Couteau the censor from a nearby town and the parishioners took it upon themselves to ensure that vengeance was swift. 'He was killed himself in the most tragic manner, more than twenty villagers having dipped their hands in the blood of this murderer, immediately after he had bathed his own in the blood of the poor censor.'[17]

The priest's diary is packed with incident; some children spot a group of Spanish soldiers hiding in the wheatfields and the enemies are duly hunted down and killed. A brawl breaks out in front of the church which leads to blood being spilt in the graveyard. A pregnant girl and her unsuitable lover refuse to submit to the authority of her male relatives and the lover ends up shooting the girl's brother. The pair then run off to get married leaving the brother to die of his wounds. Inseparable friends both called Pierre destroy their friendship and themselves in a row over a woman which ends in another fatal shooting. Dubois also gives a particularly lively thumbnail sketch of a honey-tongued criminal who ends up being hanged, leaving behind a pregnant wife and three small children. 'He was a hypocrite who stole everyday, and who, when his curate admonished him, responded with such fine words that if you didn't know him you would take him for a saint.'[18] In another entry a marauding soldier (not an enemy but one of the French troops) was caught stealing a chicken and shot. We have no way of knowing whether similar events took place in the parish in which Cyrano's schoolmaster was curé, but none of the incidents inspires any degree of surprise or outrage in the priest and his resigned attitude gives some indication that such incidents were far from being isolated cases and the parish far from unusual. The boys would inevitably have seen and heard a great deal as the curé was the focal point of the community. The priest's responsibility for collecting the church tax, administering the last rites, and recording births and deaths made him a figure respected and resented in about equal measure.

Dubois complains frequently about the reluctance of his parishioners to attend divine services and even mutters darkly about the 'blackness of their souls'. Cyrano and Le Bret would have had no option about attendance and the inescapable close-up view which Cyrano had of the church as a small boy may well have contributed to his determined atheism in later life. An extract from a contemporary sermon written by one Father Lejeune and entitled 'On the duty of Fathers' gives an indication of the attitude towards education encouraged by the moral leaders of the community. Lejeune insists that regular beatings form an indispensable part of the correct upbringing of children and in particular of boys. His rationale is that any amount of physical suffering is far preferable to the spiritual agony which ultimately awaits youngsters who are left to their own devices. 'If you do not punish your children they profane the churches . . . when they form the habit of swearing, lying, cursing . . . when they haunt meetings of girls . . . if you knew the evil which would result for them you would prefer to break their arms and legs.'[19] It was hoped that the mortification of the flesh would lead to the purification of the soul. Educational discipline was often the result of an attempt to achieve, not just good conduct from pupils, but also moral and spiritual improvement. That the result of such practices was the raising of generations of devout and pure-minded young men seems decidedly unlikely. In Cyrano's case at least we may be certain that the theory was an abject failure. In such a context his provocative attack on paternal authority suddenly becomes rather more understandable.

Le Bret's account of the boys' early education leaves little doubt that the young Cyrano was simply too clever for his own good. He describes Cyrano's 'aversion' for the pedantic professor and his lack of respect for the curé's learning, which Le Bret admits was minimal. He reveals that Cyrano considered his first schoolmaster incapable of teaching him anything at all, and that he paid little attention to his lessons as a result and still less to his teacher's corrections. The precocious little troublemaker was not, however, as unremittingly obnoxious as his extravagant contempt for the curate might suggest. In fact, he won the love and admiration of at least one of the adults who knew him as a small boy. In 1628, when he was nine years old, Cyrano's godmother, Marie Feydeau, died. Her will made special provision to leave him a legacy of six hundred *livres*. This legacy was in the form of an annuity, which was to be used, initially, to help fund Cyrano's studious older brother Denis as he made his preparations for the priesthood, but was ultimately to be given to Cyrano in its entirety on his parents' death, with no restrictions as to its intended use. It was by no means a matter of course for a godparent to single out their god-child for a generous bequest of this nature and it seems to imply that the mischievous young Cyrano had won his godmother's heart. As a little boy Cyrano was already capable of inspiring great affection and loyalty in those closest to him.

Le Bret reveals that Cyrano's rebellion against the regime in the home of the country curate was ultimately successful. He managed to persuade his father to move him back to Paris.

> He paid so little attention to his lessons and to his corrections that his father, who was a good old gentleman but fairly indif-ferent to the education of his children, and too credulous of Cyrano's complaints suddenly took him away; and without ver-ifying whether his son would be better elsewhere he sent him to this town [Paris] where he left him to his own devices until the age of nineteen.[20]

The fact that Le Bret criticizes Cyrano's father for indulging his son and giving in to his request to leave the home of the curate suggests that he may have resented being left behind for a certain time to face the uninspiring lessons alone. This would have been particu-larly galling because Le Bret was a couple of years older than Cyrano. It seems probable given their enduring friendship that Cyrano and Le Bret were eventually reunited in one of the colleges in the centre of Paris where the sons of the gentry traditionally went to finish off their education. There is no surviving written record to prove Cyrano's attendance at a particular college but it seems likely that he would have followed the traditional educational path and his writing reveals a strong link with one college in par-ticular, the Collège de Beauvais.

Cyrano's first success as a professional writer was a comedy entitled *Le Pédant Joué*. This play was not performed in public until 1645, when Cyrano was twenty-six years old, but certain scenes seem to have been composed much earlier. It is entirely possible that Cyrano began work on the play while still at college. The central character is a pedantic college principal named Granger. The principal of the Collège de Beauvais was an erudite and pedantic professor of Rhetoric named Jean Grangier. The real Grangier was legendary for his avarice and for his vicious treatment of the young pupils in his charge. He had a longstanding affair with one of the college servants who had several children by him. When he reached an age where it became clear that no legitimate offspring were going to be forthcoming, thanks to the failure of various attempts on his part to find a respectable bride, he decided to legitimize his existing children, by marrying their mother. This sparked off something of a scandal, not because of the relationship, or the resulting children, such liaisons were commonplace and were accepted as such provided those concerned were vaguely discreet. Rather, it was the attempt to make such a relationship respectable and to change the status of the woman concerned that was seen to be perverse and dishonourable. Grangier had to apply for special dispensation from the church authorities for the marriage to be allowed.

During this time a rebellion broke out at the college. The students accused Grangier of enriching himself at their expense through the corrupt administration of college funds. The professor was famously miserly and certainly didn't use the money paid by the college parents to keep the boys in grand style. It is likely that the scandal of Grangier's wedding had played a significant part in igniting the student rebellion. However, the students were unable to prove that Grangier had been misappropriating college funds and the rebellion was soon quashed.

The plot of Cyrano's *Le Pédant Joué* reworks a familiar theme of seventeenth-century comedy, in which a profoundly unsympathetic central character is duped and outwitted by his subordinates, to the great delight of the audience. The title of the play, which translates as 'The Pedant Duped', highlights this theme and promises the audience the pleasure of seeing an authority figure brought down a peg or three. The basic plot concerns the attempts of the pedant of the title to win the hand of the beautiful young heroine Genevote de la Tremblaye. In the course of the action the professor is constantly outwitted and undermined by his own son; Granger junior is his rival for Genevote's affections and is aided by a particularly crafty manservant named Corbinelli. The heroine has no intention of allowing herself to be shackled to the repellent old man; she has fallen in love with his rebellious son. At the end of the play the young people triumph and the pedant is forced to agree to their marriage. At which point the son whisks his new bride off to bed, leaving the professor to the consolations of philosophy.

The pedant's hapless pursuit of the feisty Genevote may perhaps have been inspired by one of Grangier's own doomed attempts to find a respectable bride. Cyrano's play also depicts the professor as a miser, which recalls the suspicion of the students of Beauvais that the original Professor Grangier was hoarding their fees rather than spending them appropriately on the college and the students. In one notable scene Genevote launches into an exhaustive, insulting description of Granger senior to his face; she pretends to welcome the pedant's attentions, while simultaneously asking him to join her in laughing at a particularly horrible, old college professor that she claims to have heard about. Even when he recognizes himself in her insulting description the professor does not give up hope of winning her hand. The insults in question read exactly like the kind of scatological invective a vengeful fourteen-year-old might concoct, being rather laboured and heavily reliant on schoolboy humour. The pedant is likened to a legendary tree that, in its various parts, can provide all the necessities of life for an entire nation. A brief extract will be more than enough to give an idea of the whole,

> Genevote: . . . his sores provide the meal, his ears the sails of the windmill; his arse the wind to make the sails turn, his mouth the bread oven; and his person the donkey to carry the flour. As for his nose, well it's just asking for us to have a dig. This wonderful nose arrives everywhere a quarter of an hour before its master; ten reasonably fat cobblers could take shelter from the rain underneath it to do their work.[21]

Ironically, this impassioned outpouring of bile would come back to haunt its creator. Edmond Rostand borrowed the nose gags from this passage and had his fictional Cyrano use them against himself. In an early scene in Rostand's play, the stage Cyrano attacks a man who has insulted his nose. Deriding the other's pathetic lack of imagination, Cyrano promptly reels off a series of far more creative insults. Although Rostand may have played with the facts he caught the spirit of Cyrano; this was a man who, even in his teens, was already immensely proud of his satirical creativity, and who relished the challenge of devising increasingly elaborate and inventive insults. The teaching methods of the seventeenth century did not allow for the expression of imagination or individuality by pupils, and this may be the reason why Cyrano first began to write creatively. Cyrano's response to the repressive religious regime, which was standard educational practice at the time, was an unrelenting anti-authoritarian stance. He would retain an element of that adolescent rebelliousness throughout his adult life.

3

A dangerous tendency

In the legend of Cyrano, the rebelliousness that marks the hero's character and the fact that he 'carries solitude with him' (like the Comte de Montmorency-Bouteville) are attributed to his physical difference and the sense of isolation that this imposes. The single fact about Cyrano de Bergerac that most people remember is that he had a big nose. On stage Cyrano's hypersensitivity about his appearance is the axis around which almost all of the dramatic action turns. The historical Cyrano does not seem to have been plagued by any such morbid dissatisfaction with his own appearance. In fact, there is evidence to suggest rather the reverse. There is a portrait of Cyrano that was engraved in the year before his death. It shows him in three-quarter profile, his eyes soulfully downcast. This pose hardly seems the most likely to be adopted by a man who wished to minimize the impact of his supposed 'disfigurement' since it throws his considerable snout sharply into relief. The portrait reveals that the real Cyrano was not hideous and that, although he did have a fairly long beaky nose, he definitely didn't have a complex about it. If anything Cyrano was rather proud of this distinguishing feature and made various jokes about it being a sign of superiority to have a large nose. These same jokes would ultimately be turned against their creator in the process of his transformation into the legendary grotesque.

In *The Voyage to the Moon* the hero is surprised to learn that a big nose can be a particularly useful attribute. When he asks a lunarian to tell him the time he is bewildered that the man simply lifts his head a little and turns a broad fixed grin upon him. It is only later that he learns that the men in the moon tell the time in this manner, using the shadow cast by their noses on to the dial of their teeth as a rudimentary sundial. He is also later informed that on the moon small nosed people are not allowed to breed; his host explains the logic of this 'barbarity' by revealing that: 'We have observed over thirty centuries that a large nose is like a sign above the door of our corporal homes that says "Herein dwells a man who is witty, prudent, courteous, affable, generous and liberal".'[1]

Apart from the odd passing allusion to his supposed noble Gascon origins the fictional versions of the legendary Cyrano generally depict a mature man, whose story is taken up only at the height of his career, presupposing an unremarkable youth. In fact the real Cyrano died at the age of thirty-six, and at the high point of his swashbuckling heyday he was only twenty years old. This quirk of chronology in the transformation from life to legend springs from Rostand's original casting of the portly 56-year-old Coquelin in the lead role. Ever since, representations of Cyrano on stage and screen have all tended to take their cue from Rostand, and Cyrano is often played by a mature man, while Roxane and Christian are interpreted by younger actors. Rostand's decision to pass over Cyrano's youth in dignified silence was perhaps also inspired by his awareness that a mysterious shadow hung over Cyrano's adolescence. The end of the 1630s, when Cyrano was in his late teens, was a distinctly enigmatic point in his career. Despite his confident declaration in later life that, 'it would be better to allow young people to govern their families rather than the elderly',

Cyrano's own early youth seems at first glance to have been a far from illustrious time.[2] In Henri Le Bret's brief biography of his friend, the author expresses mild resentment on the subject of Cyrano senior's laissez-faire attitude to his son's education and his decision to allow Cyrano to spend his teenage years in Paris unsupervised. Le Bret's criticism seems to spring, not just from the fact that for a time he was left behind in the country without his friend, but also from the fact that eventually Cyrano's father seems to have regretted allowing his son such freedom.

The roots of the quarrel that would erupt between father and son lie not only in Cyrano's questionable conduct as a headstrong youth, but also in the fact that the pair had very different priorities and fundamentally different temperaments. Savinien the elder, Cyrano's grandfather, had never been content with his lot as a bourgeois tradesman and had worked hard to escape his humble origins. Cyrano inherited this desire to achieve nobility at any price. Abel on the other hand had none of his father's restless determination to improve the family's social standing. This indifference to aristocratic pretension was evident in Abel's decision to sell the family estates of Mauvières and Bergerac. In 1636, Cyrano's father signed over the land to Antoine Balestrier, seigneur d'Arbalestrière, for the princely sum of 17,200 livres. Abel had grown up in the city and was content with the comfortable existence of the urban bourgeoisie. He may have preferred the ready money that the sale provided to the surface appearance of gentility, which the possession of land could bestow. Abel de Cyrano was unusual in the family for his lack of pretension to nobility. When he sold off the family land and returned to the centre of Paris, the whole family should, by rights, have ceased using the names de Bergerac and de Mauvières and the associated crests, since they no longer had any legal claim to do so.

Despite his father's chosen course of action, Cyrano was not about to abandon his dignified title and return to the homely

Savinien de Cyrano. Not only did Cyrano continue to use the name de Bergerac throughout his life but he also occasionally assumed more heroic-sounding christian names: Alexandre, for the great warrior king Alexander the Great and Hercule for the invincible hero of Greek legend.

The practice of appropriating key signifiers of noble rank was to become increasingly common among the wealthy urban elites of Cyrano's time. In his comic epic *Francion*, first published in 1623, the novelist Charles Sorel jokes about a 'fat rogue' who calls himself *le Sieur de Guillaume* not realizing that the noble sounding 'de' needs to appear before the name of a seigneurie and not before a christian name and that calling himself the Lord of William is not going to convince anybody.[3] Significant tax exemptions made noble status all the more desirable and the numbers of the fraudulent nobility were so overwhelming that the king was eventually forced to take action. In 1666, Louis XIV ordered a nationwide investigation that lasted eight years. Those claiming noble rank were required to present documentary proof of their claims or cease all pretension to nobility and pay up on their outstanding taxes. The royal crackdown came into effect after Cyrano's death and his nephew was fined for continuing to use the name associated with the estates sold by Cyrano's father some forty years earlier. The sale took place when Cyrano was seventeen years old, at the high point of his carefree existence as a student in the capital. It has been alleged that the young Cyrano had run up gambling debts so great as to force his father's hand in the sale, but no documentary evidence exists to support this claim. The loss of the family's estates would have hit Cyrano particularly hard; he had always been happiest in the countryside and his later works reflect this passionate love of the natural world. Although as an adolescent he was intent on tasting all the indulgences that the city had to offer, in later years he would look back with regret to the lost Elysium of the countryside.

Cyrano's anger at his father's decision to sell off the country estates and his conviction that he could have handled the family's fortunes better himself, may help to explain the theme of father–son conflict which runs throughout his works. In *The Pedant Duped* the main orchestrator of the professor's downfall is his own son. Another contemporary example of a father–son dispute provides a vivid illustration of the high-handedness of parental authority in action. After an argument with his son and the exchange of angry letters on both sides, Henri de la Trémoille's son (a near contemporary of Cyrano) refused to apologize to his father and, as a result, he received the following letter.

Know then, ingrate, that you do not deserve to be treated like the least of my servants, who has not merited as you have, every sort of punishment . . . learn that except for my mercy you ought to demand nothing but leave to die . . . the parricide committed by Cromwell and his colonels is a lesser crime than the ingratitude of an unnatural son, since it touches a father more keenly than the executioner's axe.[4]

La Trémoille junior did not respond favourably to this fire and brimstone, and the two were never reconciled. The story represents a parallel to that of Cyrano and his father whose relationship could so easily have fractured in similar fashion. Cyrano, or more accurately Savinien junior, had inherited his paternal grandfather's restless spirit; at first this echo of his own father may well have been a source of pride to Abel. But once the sale of the land brought the two into direct conflict it is likely that Abel would have reacted with anger and resentment that his son should presume to criticize his decisions.

When Le Bret came to write his biography of Cyrano he passes over the period marked by this family dispute in haste, but not without dropping an intriguing veiled hint at unspecified debauchery: 'That age at which human nature is more easily corrupted and the great freedom he had to do whatever he pleased led him to a dangerous tendency . . .'[5] Le Bret goes on to say that having finished his own studies and resolved on joining up he decided to persuade Cyrano that they should join the king's army together. The decision to enlist was a stroke of genius on the part of Le Bret. The army was the perfect solution to Cyrano's crisis. Through deeds of military daring, a young man could earn himself the gratitude of his monarch, and in so doing ascend the dizzying heights of the nobility far more rapidly than by any other route. All new recruits at officer level were automatically ennobled and entitled to style themselves *écuyer* (squire). In the military, Cyrano would find, not only the discipline necessary to control a decidedly eccentric and wayward spirit, but also an outlet for his extraordinary energy and courage. As so often in his life, the dominant theme directing Cyrano's career was to be friendship. Without the steadying influence of his best friend, Cyrano could easily have found himself abandoned by his family, disinherited and disowned. If Le Bret had not been there to save him from himself, his writing career might never have been, and his star might have faltered and faded before he even reached adulthood.

Henri Le Bret's tantalizing hints of decadence and corruption have inspired the curiosity of almost all who have taken an interest in Cyrano. Le Bret gives no detail about the specific nature of the 'dangerous tendency' from which his friend needed rescuing. There is no way to conclusively ascertain what Le Bret is referring to and as a result the temptation is to allow the imagination to run riot. In 1834, Théophile Gautier wrote an article for the review *La France Littéraire*, ostensibly in order to rescue Cyrano's neglected literary reputation. Gautier succumbed to the temptation to fill in the gaps in Cyrano's intriguing biography. His interpretation of Cyrano's 'lost years' is particularly appealing and seems to have had a certain influence on Rostand. 'The good old days of beautiful, poetic courtesans, the time of balconies climbed, of silken rope-ladders, of ballets and masquerades, of that Spanish gallantry solemn and delirious at the same time, devoted to the point of inanity, ardent to the point of ferocity.'[6] His account of these 'beautiful adventuresses', the poetic courtesans, is tinged with both fear and lust; they were 'voluptuous and proud creatures loving gold, blood and perfumes with an equal love'.[7] In his imagination Gautier conjures up a heady mix of danger and desire. Then, carried away with his own invention, he declares it inevitable that Cyrano should have strayed awhile among such irresistible temptations. A survey of all the distractions on offer to a young man in seventeenth-century Paris may cast useful light on the mystery of Cyrano's time amid 'dangerous' temptations and lend a little more substance to Le Bret's veiled hint.

Thomas Overbury, an English traveller to France who published his *Observations* on his return, commented disdainfully on the common French tendency to abandon academic study at an early age. 'The Gentlemen are all good outward men, good Courtiers, good Soldiers, and knowing enough in Men and businesse, but meerly ignorant in matters of letters, because at fifteene they quit bookes and begin to live in the world.'[8] It is unclear at what stage Cyrano left the Collège de Beauvais, but it seems probable that he did so reasonably early on, being jealous of his freedom and determined to live the life of a young nobleman with appropriate abandon. A certain dalliance with the seamy underworld of the city was considered as something of a gentlemanly rite of passage. François Lhuillier, the father of one of Cyrano's closest friends (a young man known as La Chapelle) joked with an acquaintance who wished to arrange an appointment to visit him at home, 'No, don't come that day, it's my brothel day.' Lhuillier also took his son along with him on one notable 'brothel day', in order to arrange for the boy to lose his virginity. Which was either the *ne plus ultra* of adolescent parental embarrassment or the best birthday present ever. Above all it may have been the result of a bit of shrewd practical thinking on the part of Lhuillier senior – by introducing the boy to an establishment where he knew that he could trust the staff, he may in fact have been trying to protect his son and to prevent him from falling into the hands of some of the city's most dangerous and unscrupulous criminals.

Without the benefit of this paternal introduction a stranger in the city often found that the temptations of the flesh could prove fatal. An anonymous English author recounting his *New Journey* through France towards the close of the seventeenth century warned that the haunts of highwaymen and footpads were not the only parts of the city to be avoided on pain of death. 'It is as dangerous to pick up a whore, or go into a Bawdy-House; for they most commonly strip a man both of his money, clothes and life, giving him the House of Office for a grave.'[9] We can deduce from the indignant tone of this warning that our anonymous British traveller clearly expects his audience to consider the whore and the 'Bawdy-House' as standard conveniences of continental city life. Despite the overwhelming evidence that attitudes to prostitution and the sex-trade were decidedly flexible, the cynicism of Lhuillier senior's parenting technique can still seem slightly surprising. However, it should be noted that the whole idea of childhood as a sacred time set apart from the realities of adult life is a modern construct and would have been entirely foreign to the families of the time.

Consider the education of the king himself. Louis XIII was born in September 1601 and would rule France for a significant part of Cyrano's lifetime. At the age of three the future king was encouraged to take part in a joke whereby his father would ask him, 'Who is father's darling?' To which the prince would reply by pointing to his chest. Then his father would ask, 'And who is the infanta's darling?' (the infanta being the six-month-old Spanish princess to whom Louis was already formally engaged) to which

Louis would reply by pointing to his crotch, cue roars of laughter all round.[10] The modern isolation of children from adult sexuality is a relatively recent phenomenon. As the historian François de Dainville points out in his study of the Jesuit influence on education in Cyrano's time, the modern idea of the respect due to childish sensibilities was entirely unheard of at this time: 'In front of them nothing was forbidden: crude speech, lewd actions and situations; they heard and saw everything.'[11] This was not only true for families where the constraints of economic pressure meant that the whole family slept together in one room. Louis XIII shared his bed chamber with his nurse, and she shared her bed with her husband.

To some extent the foreignness of such attitudes may be explained by the contemporary conviction that very young children were naturally innocent and protected by their pre-pubescent ignorance of sexuality. The point where this issue becomes rather hazier is at the age of puberty; in the seventeenth century it was still common for girls to be married as young as eleven years of age, although the average age for wedlock was nearer to twenty-five. Equally revelatory of the sexual mores of Cyrano's adolescent years (and equally disturbing to a modern audience) is Montaigne's flippant remark that 'one hundred schoolboys will have caught the pox before having reached Aristotle's lesson on Chastity'.[12]

If the emotional landscape of Cyrano's time seems decidedly unfamiliar, the physical landscape was equally unrecognizable. Peter Heylyn, another British traveller who recorded his impressions of seventeenth-century France paints a delightful portrait of the streets of the most romantic city in the world:

As it is now the least rain maketh it very slippery and troublesome; and as little a continuance of warm weather, stinking and poisonous. But whether this noisomenesse proceed from the nature of the ground, the sluttishness of the people in their

houses, or the neglect of the Magistrates in not providing a suf-
ficiency of Scavengers, or all, I am not to determine. This I am
confident of, that the nastiest lane in London, is Frankincense
and Juniper, to the sweetest street in this city.[13]

Like Overbury's 'observation' of the ignorance of the average
Frenchman, Heylyn's prose is clearly coloured by jingoistic exaggeration but his account is by no means unusual. Another
seventeenth-century traveller, James Howell, recounts a saying current among the Parisians themselves, 'That an ill name is like the
Crot (the dirt) of Paris, which is indelible'; Howell leaves nothing
to the imagination, 'besides the stain this dirt leaves, it gives off also
so strong a scent that it may be smelt many miles off'.[14]

The filth and stench of poor sanitation was far from the worst
that the scenery of Cyrano's lifetime had to offer. That robbery and
murder were rife does not prove that the era was lawless – in fact,
just as in England, the authorities had vigorous and enthusiastic
recourse to judicial punishments ranging from torture to execution.
The death penalty was used on a grand scale. In order to serve the
double purpose of punishment and warning all such events took
place firmly in the public eye and the results were often kept on
display for a considerable length of time with predictably gory
results. The author of *A New Journey*, on passing through a peaceful woodland on the outskirts of Orléans 'perceived the Trees were
loaded with very ungrateful Fruit, so rotten that I was forced to
hold my nose from the confounded stink that proceeded from it;
the spectacle was very hideous, being above twenty Highwaymen,
that were hung to the branches of the trees *in Terrorem*.'[15]

The young Cyrano would have been used to such sights and
would almost certainly have frequented the *cabarets*, drinking joints,
haunted by many a future tenant of the scaffold. The cabarets were
the equivalent of English taverns and they were much despised by
the religious authorities for their destructive influence on the

parishioners. As one contemporary author put it: 'The debauched young person can see his chances of pleasing the Lord escaping out of the windows of the brothels and cabarets.'[16] A curate determined to help his flock, much against their wishes, often struggled in vain to limit the opening hours of the cabarets, in the hope of limiting the worldly distraction available to the less than high-minded customers. The bishops, who had the authority to enforce such measures, were reluctant to do so, recognizing that over-zealous interference from the local clergy should not be allowed to go too far, for fear of provoking outright revolt. The sons of the nobility delighted in the contrast between these rough places and their own pampered lives. Certain cabarets were also the haunt of literary men. In particular, the infamous taverns the Pomme de Pin (The Pine Cone) and the Chêne Vert (The Green Oak) may well have been where Cyrano first encountered the free-thinking poets, playwrights and authors who were to form his turbulent inner circle as he took his first steps towards a literary career.

Cyrano was the true heir of his talented grandfather, both Savinien senior and junior were vigorous social climbers, who placed great importance on striving to live nobly. In the seventeenth century, social mobility was not just a question of money, but also of codes of honourable or 'honest' behaviour. In 1630, when Cyrano was eleven years old, Nicolas Faret had published a handbook of aristocratic behaviour entitled *The Honest Gentleman*, subtitled 'the art of pleasing at court'. Faret's book was enormously popular with numerous sell-out editions appearing throughout Cyrano's lifetime. The book's extraordinary appeal is partly explained by that subtitle 'pleasing at court', the art at which Cyrano's grandfather had excelled, and the key to wealth and advancement. Faret gave his readers a detailed account of the essentials of noble conduct. Those who wished to achieve the aristocratic ideal would find invaluable instruction in its pages.

Living nobly was not solely a question of being born into the right family. This was made explicit in another, rather more radical book than Faret's entitled *Traité de la Sagesse* (On Wisdom). The author, Pierre Charron, drew a distinction between two different types of nobility. On the one hand, there was the 'natural' nobility, determined entirely by birth, but Charron also described a second category, 'personal and acquired' nobility which he saw as based on virtue. The most important of the noble virtues, as Faret's title revealed, was honesty. Of course, more often than not, it was money rather than virtue which allowed the successful bourgeois tradesman to aspire to the trappings of nobility and snobbish English travellers were particularly scathing about the ease with which the ranks of the aristocracy could be infiltrated by such upstarts. Peter Heylyn quips 'Heaven hath not more stars than France Nobles' and in his memoirs one John Reresby ends a sycophantic account of the impressiveness of the French dukes with the supercilious observation that, 'This title is the only one at this day considerable in France, those of earl, marquis, baron and knight being so common, a man needs not lands to acquire them; good clothes and a splendid equipage creates them daily.'[17]

Molière, the great comic writer (and plagiarist of Cyrano) satirized this contemporary trend in his comedy *Le Bourgeois Gentilhomme*. The play's humour is largely reliant on the comic ineptitude of the bourgeois gentleman of the title and his increasingly desperate attempts to pass himself off as a true aristocrat. The foremost signifier of social superiority was the lack of visible means of support. Trade was irredeemably bourgeois and incompatible with noble 'honesty'. This is probably a fairly shrewd assessment of the realities of seventeenth-century business practice. Although the 'honesty' of the parasitic alternative, namely living off the sweat of the peasants, is another question. One of the most obvious privileges of the aristocracy was being so unimaginably rich that money ceased to have any real meaning. The extravagance and excesses of the French aristocracy are legendary and we all know what they eventually led to. The downside of joining the ranks of the pseudo-aristocracy was the need to assume an indifference to excessive expenditure that many could ill afford.

The nineteenth-century novelist Alexandre Dumas vividly depicts the consequences of noble liberality in *The Three Musketeers*. The heroes live a hand-to-mouth existence, treating one another to sumptuous feasts with vast quantities of expensive wine when in funds and going hungry when fortune is less kind. In one scene Athos confirms his status as the most noble of all the musketeers by playing a high stakes game of dice with some grasping Englishmen and reacting with supreme courtly indifference when they successfully (albeit fraudulently) strip him of all his money and possessions and those of his friends as well. The accuracy of this presentation of gambling as a mark of high noble status may be judged by the words of the same contemporary author who warned against the debauchery of brothels and cabarets. The Maréchal de Caillière, in his own aristocratic handbook – which was specifically aimed at the aspiring class of *gentilhommes particuliers* to which Cyrano certainly belonged, comes to the following somewhat startling conclusion: 'I have always esteemed the love of gaming as one of nature's benefits, I have often recognised its usefulness . . . I would argue that it is natural to us to love gambling.' He goes on to explain this conviction with the argument that gaming gives access to the best company and can provide a reasonable living to a talented player, he also warns that rich people should avoid the temptation, since they have more to lose. Finally, he makes a suggestion, which to a modern reader is distinctly unexpected, coming from a determinedly devout and pious author: 'I advise a man who knows how to play and who enjoys games of chance, to risk his money there, since he has little to lose he doesn't risk much and he could win a great deal.'[18] In spite of Caillière's unmixed approval, gambling was officially illegal. Although largely tolerated by the authorities the cabarets which served as gambling dens were notoriously attractive not just to the idle rich and the hopeful poor, but also to thieves, beggars, prostitutes and loan-sharks.

Among this seething mass of temptation and debauchery it is small wonder if Cyrano lost his way for a time. The question remains, what exactly did Le Bret mean by a 'dangerous tendency'? It is possible that it was around this time that Cyrano first came into contact with the man who was to become his nemesis. Charles Coypeau Dassoucy, the self-styled 'emperor of the burlesque', was the son of a lawyer. His mother was a musician of Italian descent, a feisty and impulsive woman who was, according to Dassoucy's own account of her, so wildly unfaithful that he was not at all sure that he was his father's son. His parents separated early after a turbulent marriage that apparently included a duel fought over a passage in Justinian. Once separated, his father soon gave him a serving girl for a stepmother, a fact that he seems to have bitterly resented. Dassoucy was a successful composer, who would have made a handsome living from his musical talents were it not for his tendency to gamble. He frequently referred to music and gambling as the two central passions of his life, but his semi-autobiographical novel *Adventures of M. Dassoucy* reveals that his other main passion was a choirboy named Pierrotin, whom he labels the 'evil spirit' of his life. Having been forced to flee the court and the capital, in order to avoid prosecution and imprisonment for blasphemy and sexual offences, Dassoucy spent some years in the provinces and in Italy touring with his music and his choirboy performers. In 1673, he was imprisoned in Paris, but he won his release with an eloquent plea addressed to Pope Clement IX. He died in Paris in 1677 on the 29th October at the age of seventy-two.

Dassoucy was charming and intelligent with an endearing line in self-deprecating humour. He was also a poet, a talented composer and musician, who earned his living writing comic songs to entertain the king. Dassoucy was at the centre of a lively circle of musicians, poets and playwrights all struggling to make a living from their art. Such company would have been enormously appealing to the young Cyrano, but Dassoucy was not only charming and seductive, he was also an alcoholic and addicted to gambling. Above all, Dassoucy was a sexual predator, who preyed upon a succession of vulnerable young men and boys. The vexed question of Cyrano's tortured relationship with Dassoucy (whom he began by comparing to Orpheus and ended by threatening to murder) is one to which we will return later on. Whether Le Bret would really have congratulated himself on 'stopping' a homosexual Cyrano by taking him off to live in an all-male establishment seems rather doubtful. It may be that he saw the need to remove Cyrano from Dassoucy's pernicious sphere of influence and that he saw the beginnings of an abusive relationship developing between the two, observing the combination of manipulation and seduction that was the hallmark of all Dassoucy's involvements with impressionable young men.

Dassoucy's homosexuality may have been the least of Le Bret's worries, since he was also a notorious 'libertin', one of the godless group of intellectuals for whom sedition and blasphemy were the proofs of 'free thought', whose debauchery and disrespect of authority led more than one of their number to perish in prison or at the stake. The royal family had included more than one obviously gay member in the past and in Cyrano's lifetime the king's brother would surround himself with a coterie of 'mignons', gorgeous male companions who squabbled among themselves for the prince's favour. 'The Italian vice' as it was known was a commonplace and less dangerous tendency than the thought-crime of 'libertinage'. The contemporary moralists Father Garasse and Father Mersenne both write at length about libertinism as a terrible 'danger' to the youth of the country and if there was one thing that attracted the young Cyrano beyond any other it was danger.

4

The temptation of heroism

Henri Le Bret had chosen to enlist and he succeeded in persuading Cyrano to join him in this new adventure. For the young Cyrano, there was a specific appeal to such a potentially lethal step. In his bestselling book of useful advice for the aspiring noble, Nicolas Faret highlights the social advantages of a career in the armed forces. 'Since every man has to choose a profession . . ., it seems to me that there is none more honourable or more essential to a gentleman than that of arms . . . Nobility is acquired by arms.'[1] In an earlier, similar work, Olivier de la Marche had identified five possible paths to greatness. The first, the possession of 'an office appointed by the crown', was the route taken by Savinien senior, Cyrano's ambitious grandfather, whose purchase of court appointments secured the family both money and prestige.[2] No matter that in the early eighteenth century the types of court offices purchased by Savinien senior would become known as *savonnette à vilain* (soap for scum), in the early seventeenth century such appointments were a solid path to respectability.

If the offices bought by Savinien senior had been filled by the family for two generations or more, the Cyranos would have been

assured their place within the *noblesse de robe* (nobility of the gown).
Cyrano's father, however, had chosen the second option in de la
Marche's list, the deceptively simple sounding 'honest life of noble
gentlemen'.[3] Since the family owned the estates and the seigneurie
of Mauvières, Abel simply had to preside as lord of the manor and
this in itself would be all the proof needed of the family's standing.
Whether as a result of poor management, or distaste for the rural
life, Abel had abandoned this path, selling off the family estates and
returning to Paris. This left three other options theoretically open
to Cyrano, since a return to either of the first two would have
required significant investments of capital. The third and fourth
options, 'general service of the prince' and 'letters patent of nobility accorded by the monarch' both depended on gaining direct
access to the king. Such access was both limited and hotly contested
and, as an unknown adolescent of dubious social standing, Cyrano
had no hope of rubbing shoulders with Louis XIII. This left one
remaining path for him to try: 'the career of arms'.[4]

Cyrano's time as a member of the 'honourable profession' was
comparatively short-lived. He served as a member of the noble
corps of cadets under the aristocratic commander Carbon de
Castel-Jaloux for just short of two years between 1638 and 1640.
The name cadets derives from the tradition that it was the younger
brother or *cadet* who was destined for the army. The oldest son,
being the heir to the family fortune, was too precious to be risked
on the battlefield and was kept at home, where he would learn to
manage his estates and be groomed for a life as lord of the manor.
Younger sons, with no such glittering prospect to look forward to,
were expected to forge a path for themselves. The church and the
army were the two main career prospects open to the nobility.
Cyrano would not have got far as a priest. There was also the
option of studying law, as many of Cyrano's male relatives and
fellow authors chose to do; but poring over legal documents and
resolving the petty disputes of his neighbours was apparently not a

sufficiently enticing prospect. Whatever his initial enthusiasm for the military may have been, Cyrano's experience of the armed forces nearly killed him and would scar him for life in more ways than one.

In spite of the brevity of Cyrano's time as a soldier, today it is perhaps the best-known fact of his career. Naturally, this is largely due to Rostand's vision of the cadets. The playwright seems to have taken his cue from Henri Le Bret's depiction of Cyrano as the ultimate soldier-poet: 'I saw him one day, in the guardroom, working on an Elegy with as little distraction as if he had been in a study far removed from all the noise.'[5] Le Bret's brief biographical note may not be definitive, but it is at least the testimony of someone who was there. Not only that, but the evidence of Cyrano's works also seems to support Le Bret's vision of a poet whose passionate concentration allowed him to blot out the myriad distractions of a noisy crowd of guardsmen in order to focus on the work of creation. He was not the most polished wit of the era, nor, perhaps, the most talented, but an undeniable vein of high-voltage imaginative intensity is a consistent and distinctive feature of Cyrano's style. Le Bret's testimony in this instance has a ring of truth. The snapshot it affords us of the young Cyrano also serves to confirm that his compulsion to write was a lifelong trait and not solely a feature of his later years. The real Cyrano was only temporarily a soldier but he was always a poet.

Rostand took this brief glimpse of Cyrano, seen at the heart of his regiment, yet at the same time far removed from his fellow recruits, and fashioned from it the portrait of a fictional Cyrano, who is, at once, loved and feared by the other cadets. His distance from them is palpable throughout the play and it is this distance that both isolates and elevates him. Rostand's cadets are ostensibly Castel-Jaloux's men, but when the hardships of the siege of Arras force the men almost to the point of revolt, the commander is forced to call on Cyrano for help. Castel-Jaloux asks Cyrano to cheer the men up to calm their aggressive despair; instead Cyrano's successful strategy is to depress them still further. He asks the regimental piper to play an air from the old country and to the melancholy sound of the music he conjures up a poetic vision of Gascony. In this way he manages to pacify the men by transmuting their suffering into a 'nobler hunger', nostalgia. He reminds the men of the peaceful, edenic splendours of 'the green softness of evenings on the Dordogne' in terms which recall the real Cyrano's letter to his friend singing the praises of an 'enchanted palace' in the countryside. There is no evidence to support Rostand's view of Cyrano as the true leader of the regiment, in fact his distaste for following orders and his frustration with his subordinate position probably hastened his withdrawal from the army. But Rostand's departures from historical reality serve to infuse the real Cyrano's passion for the pastoral and the unexpected into the behaviour of his theatrical shadow.

It was at the point of his enrolment with Castel-Jaloux's men that Cyrano introduced the element of ambiguity about his origins that was to prove so enduring. Firstly, by his use of the name Cyrano de Bergerac, rather than the more accurate Savinien de Cyrano, and secondly, by his affiliation to an almost exclusively Gascon regiment. Le Bret specifically states that the guards were nearly all Gascons. It was not just the consequent convenient assumption that his family were a more significant land-owning presence than they really were that Cyrano stood to gain from this association with a company of Gascons. The region was famed for producing particularly courageous soldiers and Tréville, the captain of the king's personal regiment (known to us as the Musketeers) was himself a Gascon, who favoured the promotion of his fellow countrymen. Thanks to the popularity of the novels by Alexandre Dumas the term Musketeer has come to be indissolubly linked to the elite regiment captained by Tréville and later by d'Artagnan himself. In practice, at the time, it signified anyone armed with a musket and was thus applicable to many other troops. Cyrano and Le Bret were both musketeers in the cadets.

Tréville, the son of a merchant, was a page to the king at fourteen, then a cadet in the *regiment des gardes françaises*. He entered into the company of the king's musketeers as a second lieutenant and became captain in 1634. By joining the cadets Cyrano identified himself with men who revelled in a proud tradition of loyalty and courage. The Gascon soldiers were such a strong and charismatic presence in Paris that they too engendered a legend which would outlive them and ensure immortality to certain key figures. If Rostand chose to depict Cyrano as a Gascon, it was not because he didn't know any better – as he would protest angrily when challenged on this point. In fact Edmond Rostand had realized that a Gascon Cyrano made for a better story. A fashion for historical novels set in the seventeenth century and featuring heroic Gascon noblemen had swept the nation in the nineteenth century and Edmond Rostand understood and hoped to emulate the popularity of these evocations of a golden age of chivalry and adventure.

The most famous of the swashbuckling epics to feature a Gascon soldier as its hero is Alexandre Dumas' 1844 novel, *The Three Musketeers*. Dumas's book begins with a wily literary hoax intended to add spice to a tale of high adventure and intrigue. In his introduction Dumas describes how he had been working in the Bibliothèque Royale doing some research for his history of Louis XIV when he stumbled upon the 'Mémoires de M. d'Artagnan', which, he explains, had been printed in Amsterdam to avoid French censorship of the scandalous truths found within. Fascinated by the characters appearing in the memoir, Dumas pursued his researches further and discovered an unpublished manuscript, for which he even goes so far as to give the library code as 4772 or 4773. The manuscript is entitled *Memoirs of Monsieur the Count of La Fère, concerning certain events that took place in France towards the end of the reign of King Louis XIII*, and in its pages

Dumas is delighted to discover the names of the three Musketeers who feature in d'Artagnan's memoirs: Athos, Porthos and Aramis. With this wealth of factual material he is able to construct a historical novel which is directly drawn from the true confessions of the principal figures. The Count of La Fère being none other than the superbly aristocratic Musketeer, Athos himself. Sadly, manuscript 4772 (or 4773) was a pure invention, but the three-volume memoirs of d'Artagnan do actually exist and are still available in print today. These memoirs, which served as Dumas's most important source, were themselves a seventeenth-century literary hoax. They were written not by d'Artagnan but by one Gatien Courtilz de Sandras and first published in 1700, nearly thirty years after d'Artagnan's death. Dumas' claim that the memoirs were published in Amsterdam in order to avoid French censorship was entirely accurate. However, the 'truths' contained within the memoir are not so certain. Courtilz had served as a musketeer, and so was able to pass himself off as a member of d'Artagnan's inner circle. In reality, he was unlikely to have had any significant contact with d'Artagnan as he had actually served in a different troop from that commanded by the great Musketeer, and his 'memoirs' were simply a wildly racy and inventive collection of anecdotes, loosely intertwined with a few basic facts of d'Artagnan's actual career.

Having no personal fortune, the career soldier Courtilz had turned to his pen to make a living after being forced to abandon the sword when his regiment was disbanded following the peace of Nimègues in 1678. His new speciality was controversial historical pieces like the d'Artagnan memoirs – the incendiary political criticisms that Courtilz included in his work did not spring from a dedication to any particular cause. On seeing the success and the scandal surrounding the memoirs he promptly penned an anonymous pamphlet in which he attacked his own publication and contradicted every controversial opinion expressed in the original. This neat trick enabled him to cash in on both sides of the furore he had caused. Courtilz's impudence and imagination earned him two lengthy periods of imprisonment in the Bastille, the second and longer of which ultimately killed him. Courtilz and Cyrano were kindred spirits but sadly their paths almost certainly never crossed, since Cyrano died when Courtilz was just eleven years old. As for the three musketeers, Cyrano's membership of a Gascon regiment means that he may very well have come into contact with Isaac de Porthau, Henri d'Aramitz and Armand de Sillègue d'Athos d'Auteville. The three were almost his exact contemporaries and were all serving in the Musketeers by around 1641.

Cyrano and d'Artagnan fought side by side at the siege of Arras and were both wounded in the fray. Their paths may well have crossed, but it seems unlikely that they ever became close. The real d'Artagnan was actually about a decade older than Cyrano and the three musketeers. Born in 1611, his full name was Charles de Batz de Castelmore, but he chose to style himself Count d'Artagnan (a name taken from his mother's side of the family) when he left Gascony at the age of sixteen to seek his fortune in the army. Unlike Cyrano, d'Artagnan was a skilled courtier and rose rapidly to occupy a trusted position within the king's personal guard (the Musketeers). The real d'Artagnan was also sent on spying missions to republican England. He had two sons, both of whom he named Louis, after the king, in an act of blatant crawling that Cyrano would have been unlikely to admire.*

The author Théophile Gautier had helped to draw Rostand's attention to Cyrano as an interesting subject with an 1834 article that featured his imaginative vision of the young Cyrano dallying with perfumed courtesans, amid scenes which could have come straight from Courtilz's pages. Gautier also wrote a historical novel

---

* It was common in the seventeenth century to reuse a name when a child died young so it is unlikely that the two little boys, both called Louis, were alive at the same time.

set in the seventeenth century whose hero was (like Dumas' d'Artagnan) an impoverished Gascon noble. The story of *Le Capitaine Fracasse* follows the adventures of the Baron de Sigognac, who leaves his ruined chateau behind to follow a troupe of travelling players to Paris, where he becomes involved in a series of picaresque adventures. Gautier's portrait of the Baron owes much to the legend of the noble Gascon and not a little to Cyrano himself. Slightly cruelly, his only acknowledgement of this debt is in the portrait of Lampourde, an expert duellist who is hired by the villain of the piece to assassinate the Baron. Jacquemin Lampourde is a mercenary, not a nobleman, and his appearance is decidedly unprepossessing. He has long monkey arms, heron legs, a bony chest and worst of all, 'a prodigious nose that recalled that of Cyrano de Bergerac, the pretext for so many duels . . . Lampourde consoled himself with the popular axiom: "A face is never spoiled by a big nose."'[6] After further detailing Lampourde's excessive ugliness the description of his face ends with the reflection that 'nevertheless no one ever cared to mock him, his expression was too worrying, sardonic and ferocious'.[7] Gautier's portrayal of Lampourde seems to have been partly inspired by the attacks on Cyrano, which began to appear after his untimely death. Rostand had been familiar with Gautier's vision of Cyrano since childhood; when he was a schoolboy his teacher had read both *Le Capitaine Fracasse* and *Les Grotesques* to the class.

Cyrano's decision to join the cadets may have been partly prompted by a pragmatic desire to improve his lot in life, but it was above all a decision to seek death or glory. Jacques Prévot, the author of a critical study of the life and works of Cyrano de Bergerac published in the late 1970s, opens his discussion of the poet's life with the discouraging reflection that 'the biography of Cyrano evades all investigations'.[8] His thoughtful analysis of Cyrano's *oeuvre*, nevertheless, outlines a vision of the soldier-poet striving to surpass himself, to overcome the limitations of the world he inhabited. For Prévot, the real Cyrano was continually succumbing to 'the temptation of heroism'.[9] It is perhaps this distinctive feature of the man above all else that gave rise to a legend which would not only outlive him but grow and transform with extraordinary vigour for centuries after his death. At the beginning of his adult life, the evidence of Cyrano's surrender to the temptation of heroism is clear. In the seventeenth century, opportunities for reckless heroics abounded. Across Europe, taking into account both civil and international wars, only two years in the entire century could be counted as entirely peaceful: 1669 and 1670. In *The Courtiers Guide* of 1606 a similar (if less popular) book to Faret's *The Honest Gentleman*, the author reflects on the thoughtless enthusiasm of young nobles for the aristocratic rite of passage that was going to war. He describes young noblemen muttering resentfully about the peace and the fact that it prevents them from proving themselves on the battlefield.

Cyrano's opportunity to show what he was made of came with a conflict that had been raging throughout central Europe since before his birth. The Thirty Years War had begun in 1618, the year of Cyrano's conception. In 1635, France had finally become officially involved in the conflict, declaring war on the Spanish and on the Empire. By 1636 things were not going well for the French and an important defeat at Corbie-sur-la-Somme led to panic in the capital, as fears of invasion swept the city. The king (or perhaps more accurately his trusted advisor the brilliant politician Cardinal Richelieu) realized the crucial importance of strengthening France's military defences and an urgent recruitment drive was set in train.

In the course of Louis XIII's reign France's army would swell from around 30,000 men to around 250,000. The recruitment methods used in Cyrano's lifetime were both unsophisticated and ineffectual. In 1635 an official request was made for men to present themselves to the *prévôt de Paris* within twenty-four hours of the call in order to join up and receive in return 12 livres pay, of which 6 were to be paid in advance. Levels of desertion in the armed forces at the time have been estimated at 50 per cent rising to 75 per cent at the end of campaigns as winter approached. Richelieu commented in his memoirs that he always divided in half any numbers he was given for the size of France's troops for precisely this reason. The recruitment request was designed to be a sort of amnesty, aimed at luring back deserters and rounding up vagabonds and masterless men in the hope of transforming the layabouts and troublemakers of the realm into a useful commodity – cannon fodder. Of those that turned up, most sensibly took the money and ran. A profound discrepancy existed between the noble ideal of the soldier, as outlined in popular works of the time and the reality, which was that the greatest percentage of France's military forces were, of necessity, made up of violent and unreliable malcontents. In his time with the cadets Cyrano found himself confronted by this clash between the idealized fiction of warfare and the stark reality.

The year of Cyrano's enlistment had seen some exciting developments for the French nation and a new mood of optimism was the result. After twenty-three years of childless union, the king and queen had finally produced their first child, a baby boy. Until this 'miraculous' birth, the lack of a direct male descendant had meant that the threat of a disastrous power vacuum hung over the nation. King Louis XIII's health was never strong and his death would have seen the crown pass to his younger brother, who had already staged rebellions in an attempt to seize power prematurely, with the backing of his unpopular mother, Marie de Medici. Such a failure of the direct male line all too often triggered internal power struggles. A nation prey to the infighting of warring factions was a nation one step away from bloody civil war. As such, the celebrations that marked the birth of the Dauphin were both dramatic and heartfelt. The little boy came to be known as Louis Dieudonné in recognition of the seemingly miraculous nature of his arrival after more than two decades of disappointment. The birth of the future Sun King Louis XIV was hailed as quite literally 'a gift from God' and Parisians celebrated the gift in style. Fountains flowed with wine, fireworks and festivities were organized and the nation breathed a collective sigh of relief.

As it turned out, the collective rejoicing was somewhat precipitate, since Louis XIII's death just five years later would leave France subject to the violent unrest of the uprising known as the Fronde. This rebellion, or more accurately this series of rebellions was largely due to the unpopularity of a regency in which France was ruled by two foreigners: the Spanish queen mother Ann of Austria and Richelieu's replacement the Italian Cardinal-Minister Giulio Mazarini, known as Mazarin. In the meantime, the positive mood was unsullied by any indication of the storms to come and Cyrano must have experienced an initial rush of pride in the thought that he was going to risk his life for king and country. In order to join the regiment Cyrano's family would have had to pay for his commission as one of the cadets and also for his equipment. A contemporary text gives a list of the items he would have required: strong boots, stockings and breeches, two or preferably more thick shirts, a stout leather doublet, a waterproof greatcoat, a large felt hat. It was suggested that clothes should all be on the large size and feature a bare minimum of stitches, as seams were the favourite residence of fleas and lice. For the same reason the author advised against fur as too attractive to parasites. Cyrano would also have been expected to provide his own musket and sword and his own horse.

It was during the seventeenth century that military uniforms were first introduced and in certain regiments the commanding officer would gift his men with a uniform. There was an element of showmanship involved in dressing one's troops, just as in the expensive liveries worn by the servants of great lords. As such the king's Musketeers had a suitably flashy uniform, graced with the fleur de lys (which they had to hand back as property of the crown when Cardinal Mazarin disbanded the regiment in 1646). For troops who did not wear uniforms, it was traditional to include a colourful mark of some kind to aid mutual recognition.

At first, Cyrano would have spent some time with the unit in Paris undertaking some basic training before beginning the long march to the campaign grounds. Pierre Charron's comment on military training gives a hint of the challenge facing the young Cyrano, unaccustomed to serious physical hardship. Charron reflects that training should harden the men against suffering, sweat and dust. Charron was concerned that recruits ought to be selected on the basis of a predisposition to withstand the hardships of warfare. In his *Treatise on Wisdom* Charron suggests to the king that certain environments are more likely to produce men hardy enough for the horrors of war. 'They should be taken from the fields, the mountains, sterile places, nourished on all kinds of hardship . . . Because those from the towns, nourished in the shade on pleasure and gain are more cowardly and insolent, effeminate.'[10] Cyrano had joined a troop in which most of his fellow cadets came from the mountainous regions of the Pyrenees and who therefore fulfilled Charron's criteria. Despite being an indolent, spoilt Parisian and therefore liable to abandon himself to 'to delights and to women' at any minute, Cyrano would belie this accusation of the cowardice of city dwellers. He may very well have proved the point about insolence though.

On joining the cadets Cyrano found himself plunged into a world very different from anything he had ever known before and surrounded by men, many of them as young as him, but all of whom must have seemed more assured and more at ease. The Gascons shared a common heritage, common ideals and common experience. In order to survive in this new environment Cyrano had to choose between keeping a low profile and trying to surpass the courageous Gascons – predictably, he went for the latter option.

Faret's invaluable book offers a word of advice as to what are the legitimate ambitions of a young nobleman: 'It seems to me, therefore, that the greatest ambition of he who carries a sword is to be considered a man of boldness and courage.'[11] The simplest way to fulfil this ambition was to fight duels and within his first few days with the company Cyrano was to throw himself headlong into the fray.

The call of adventure and the desire to mark oneself out by individual acts of courage was a noble French tradition with roots in the age of chivalry. An edict of 1600 had even ratified the link between military prowess and aristocratic distinction. Above all the warrior-hero was a literary staple and one of the biggest successes to sweep the capital in Cyrano's youth was a play based entirely on this notion of bravery and military success as indicators of nobility of soul. *Le Cid* by Pierre Corneille was first performed in 1637; Louis XIII, not normally a great patron of the theatre, commanded three private performances at the Louvre. In his enthusiasm for the piece, the king ennobled Corneille (a demonstration of the fourth of Olivier de la Marche's paths to greatness in action). In fact it was Corneille's father who was accorded the letters patent of ennoblement so that the playwright's honour should not be sullied by nobility too freshly acquired. Richelieu, who was a passionate devotee of the arts, also personally accorded the playwright a stipend. This worldly success provoked jealousy and a vicious flurry of pamphlets known as *La querelle du Cid* in which both the play and the author were attacked. The most important crime Corneille had committed was that of innovation. *Le Cid* was denigrated for failing to conform to the Aristotelian rules of tragedy, notably in its failure to conform to the three unities and to the norms of the genre. It was further alleged that Corneille had stolen the work outright from a Spanish author, Guillen de Castro whose play *Las Mocedades del Cid*, based on the life of the eleventh-century Castilian knight Rodrigo of Vavar, first appeared around 1599.

Corneille had freely admitted taking his inspiration from de Castro's text and termed his play a tragicomedy because despite its tragic register (there aren't any jokes) the action ends happily with a marriage, the traditional conclusion of a comedy. Richelieu himself was eventually forced to step in to defend his protégé personally.

In *Le Cid* Corneille depicts the dilemma faced by the various protagonists forced to choose between honour and love. The heroine, Chimène, finds herself in a similarly unenviable position to Shakespeare's Ophelia, her father having been killed by her beloved. Chimène refuses to be broken by her predicament. Her unhesitating response to the news that her fiancé Don Rodrigue has slaughtered her father in a duel is to choose duty over love. She is unwavering in her conviction that Don Rodrigue must die to avenge her family honour. In spite of the pain it causes her, she appeals to the king for the execution of the man she loves. This leads to the central dilemma of the play since the king refuses to execute Don Rodrigue as by rights he ought to do. The king's decision is based on a pragmatic realization that he cannot afford to punish the courageous Don Rodrigue, because, in the interim, the young hero has taken the place of the murdered count and saved the city from the threat of invasion. The king cannot afford to execute so talented a military commander, the safety of his kingdom depends on it.

This was the image of the very real dilemma faced by Louis XIII. His edicts against duelling all too often went unenforced because the duellists were the military heroes of the nation. Louis could not afford to sacrifice his rebellious nobles to the scaffold. He needed them to spill their blood for him on the battlefield rather than in fighting duels amongst themselves. Corneille's play vividly illustrates the problem faced by the monarch: how to distinguish between the courage required for military success, and the courage required to settle personal differences 'honourably' by duelling, when the two are inextricably linked in the minds of the heroes themselves? Another contemporary text, the *Catéchisme royal* by Pierre Fortin de la Hoguette, attempts to provide a model for the king to follow, but conspicuously fails to address the issue of the intrinsic link between the two forms of courage. In the dialogue it is the monarch himself who recognizes the duel as an honourable proof of noble courage:

> The King: But if we take away the duels how will the nobility prove their courage?
>
> The Governor: In your armies, Sire.
>
> The King: And if there is no war?
>
> The Governor: If there is no war is it reasonable to suffer civil war to rage between them in order to satisfy this curious itch for honour?[12]

The governor's dismissal of the 'curious itch for honour' is both glib and facile, clearly an attempt to minimize and ridicule the duel, in order to lessen its power and, despite emphasizing the rebellious nature of the act by likening the duellists' encounters to 'civil war', the governor has not really answered the king's question. Pierre Corneille's phenomenal success with *Le Cid* did not arise because he was able to present the king with a solution to the problem of the duel but rather because he observed and reflected back to the society of the time one of its most fascinating and complex preoccupations.

Pierre Corneille was just thirteen years older than Cyrano, but his glittering career provides a stark contrast to that of our hero. Setting aside the question of their respective artistic merits, it remains undeniable that an unbridgeable gulf existed between Cyrano de Bergerac, whose writing gained him neither honours nor worldly success and whose two plays would languish unperformed and unpublished for many years and Pierre Corneille, who knew how to court royal favour and who was ennobled and richly rewarded as a result. A key moment from *Le Cid* may serve to illustrate this. As the venerable old man Don Diègue attempts to calm the anger of the hot-headed count, he evokes the absolutist nature of Royal authority:

> Don Diègue: But we owe this respect to absolute power,
> To question nothing that is the King's desire.[13]

These lines are interesting in that they highlight a central problem which would later confront Cyrano in his attempts to make his way in the world – the need to subject oneself 'unquestioningly' to the authority of one's superiors was to prove an insurmountable barrier for him. Cyrano's constant struggle was to submit to no superiors of any kind and thus he would never pay the necessary respect to those who could have assisted his advancement.

As an adolescent Cyrano could hardly have avoided seeing at least one performance of *Le Cid*, if not more; it was the most celebrated and controversial play of his youth. He would certainly have been attracted by its theme of duelling and family honour and he may well have been inspired by the high ideals of courage and duty depicted on stage. In particular, as a headstrong nineteen-year-old, keen to make his mark in the world he may have been struck by the character of Don Rodrigue: the young hero of the play, a historical figure who demonstrates his greatness on the battlefield and in two dramatic duels. No doubt Don Rodrigue's proud reflection that 'Valour does not wait upon the number of years' chimed with the fearless youth. Cyrano's next step would not see him sagely attempting to emulate the concrete successes of his fellow author, but rather risking life and limb to defend his nation and his honour in emulation of the theatrical hero whom all Paris was talking about. *Le Cid* was an inspirational example of the way in which a life could become the stuff of legend.

5

A demon of bravery

On first joining his new regiment, Cyrano was a nobody. As we know, he had no influential connections and no conspicuous personal wealth. In order to distinguish himself as a hero, he first needed to overcome his own insignificance. In Corneille's later comedy *Le Menteur* (1643) the character Dorante, the 'Liar' of the title, confronts the same problem: how to make the most of a less than impressive background? Dorante is desperately anxious to transcend his inexperience and lack of importance in order to convince those around him that he is nothing less than the model nobleman.

> Dorante: Tell me, do you think I make a good cavalier?
> You don't see anything about me that smacks of the
> schoolboy do you?[1]

Fresh from school, dressing up as a soldier for the first time Cyrano must have worried, like Dorante, that his inexperience would shine through and his new clothes be shown up as just a costume. In his determination not to seem like a provincial nobody, Dorante spins an elaborate web of lies that draws him to the brink of catastrophe.

Cyrano opted for a much simpler method to compensate for his lack of money or social standing. Le Bret describes how in Cyrano's first few days with the guards, rather than hoping to impress his fellow recruits with invented glories he decided to win their respect on their own terms. He would fight his way into their approval: 'Duels which in those days seemed the single, fastest way to make oneself known rendered him so famous in so few days that the Gascons, of whom the regiment was almost exclusively made up, considered him as a demon of bravery, and reckoned him as many duels as he had spent days in the company.'[2]

Cyrano's ambition to 'make himself known' took the simplest and the most extreme form possible: every single day he fought a new duel and, within a very short time, his fearsome reputation was established. Fencing would have been a part of Cyrano's education at the Collège de Beauvais – the art of swordplay being considered an essential gentlemanly accomplishment. The right to carry a sword was in itself a noble privilege. Books of the period, outlining the details of a gentlemanly education, are insistent on the importance, not just of fencing, but also of the fundamentals of military training. In Cyrano's lifetime, the terms *gentilhomme* (gentleman) and *homme d'épée* (swordsman) were synonymous. From the mid-sixteenth century to the mid-seventeenth century the fury of duelling had grown and grown. With the inexorable rise of the bourgeoisie, rich and successful tradesmen were often capable of living more nobly than the nobles, at least in terms of outward show. A new social instability had crept into French society. As the definition of a gentleman became hazier, so the duel became ever more popular and widespread. While the country was rapidly leaving its feudal past behind, the aristocracy found itself pressured by a successful and expanding bourgeoisie, consequently the old marks of nobility became suspect. As Le Bret's comment makes explicit, duelling was not just the fastest way to make oneself known, but also the only truly certain way. By the time Cyrano entered into the world of the cadets, the literature of the time was unequivocal in attributing to the duel the status of an unquestionable proof of nobility or *marque de noblesse*.

Despite ancient roots that can be traced back to gladiatorial Rome, via the age of knightly chivalry and the medieval trial by combat, the phenomenon of the duel had come to represent a thoroughly modern affirmation of individuality. The duellist, who chose to risk death, not for king and country, but for the individual issue of a personal quarrel or point of honour, showed proof of a dangerous independence that the authorities were determined to suppress at any cost. As a duellist, Cyrano was firmly on the side of the rebels. Richelieu expressed his determination to put an end to duelling while at the same time admitting the magnitude of the task: 'It is difficult to find a sure way to stop the course of this fury.'[3] In his memoirs, he reflected on the extraordinary proliferation of combats and there is a despairing poetry to his remark that, 'duels have become so commonplace that the streets have begun to serve as battlefields and, as if the day were not long enough for them to vent all their fury, the duellists continue to fight under the stars or by the light of torches that serve as deadly suns.'[4]

In the twenty years between 1588 and 1608, 7,000 nobles died in duels. There was an urgent need to put an end to this bloody insubordination. This urgency was the reason why Count Montmorency-Bouteville served as an example and ended his days on the scaffold. Montmorency-Bouteville's execution evidently did not suffice in itself to ensure the shift of public opinion away from adulation of the heroic duellist. The popular outcry at the time, and the success of *Le Cid* over a decade later, demonstrate that. Attitudes to duelling were complex and shifting; *Le Cid* was both tremendously successful and marked by controversy. Corneille's genius was in capturing the complexity of the subject.

Back in the mid-sixteenth century, the council of Trent had pronounced a condemnation of the duel, which established the excommunication, not only of the duellists themselves, but also of any prince who allowed the practice to continue unpunished within his realm. The irreligious aspect of the duel was therefore an important argument urged against it by the various reformers of the period. As, for example, in the 1617 religious text *Revelations of the Solitary Hermit* by J. Chenel de la Chapperonaye, in which the author rages against the profoundly immoral, suicidal impulse which drives duellists to their demonic encounters. 'It is the action of an atheist, since all sorts of religions condemn it. It is the action of a man in despair, possessed by the devil, hurling himself into perdition in cold blood, like the man who hangs himself and brings about his own death.'[5] Duelling was inextricably linked to blasphemy and the ruling of the council of Trent had made this explicit. When Montmorency-Bouteville was executed for duelling in 1627, it was actually as the result of his second royal death sentence.

Three years earlier, the troublesome noble had fought a duel on Easter Sunday after a drunken quarrel in a tavern. The added outrage of the date on which the duel took place had provoked the genuinely pious King Louis into pronouncing Montmorency-Bouteville's death sentence. The nobleman was, however, given sufficient warning to allow him to go into exile and in the event it was only his effigy which was strung up – and even that symbolic act was to be a fleeting gesture as the effigy was swiftly cut down again by Montmorency-Bouteville's supporters. This first offence was duly pardoned and Montmorency-Bouteville soon returned to court. The account of his crime provided by a contemporary gazette, the *Mercure français*, insists on the gravity of the offence but at the same time reveals an overwhelming fascination with the taboo subject:

We will not relate here the subject of the quarrel that took place between Sir Bouteville de Montmorency, & the Count de Pontgibault, nor how the challenge was made, nor how they each sent to look for a second, nor how they took knives from the tavern to serve as daggers, nor the wicked and despicable words that it is reported one of them said as he went to fight, nor what happened in the course of their fight which took place on Easter day itself . . .

The strategy of reporting the controversial affair in this bizarre negative fashion springs from the need to avoid censorship. All Paris was clearly dying to hear the details and although forced to disappoint its public the *Mercure* was not going to go so far as to miss out altogether on such a story. When the massive outcry against Montmorency-Bouteville's second and fatal condemnation broke out, the *Mercure* even went as far as to publish a 'Reproof from Lady Bouteville to the King'. Richelieu was forced to confront the problem using subtler measures. In order to combat the enormous popular support for the doomed duellist, the cardinal shifted to a different tactic – propaganda. He published a series of pamphlets which presented duelling as an offence against God, the king and the nation itself. The pamphlets were carefully imagined and inventive. They ranged from a straight address to the nobility, *Les Paroles de la France à la noblesse française*; to a letter from a fictional Dutchman, arguing that while French duellists were slaughtering each other their enemies the Spanish were preparing to profit from the resulting chaos; to a dramatic monologue in which Montmorency-Bouteville himself addressed his fellow duellists from beyond the grave, urging them not to make the same mistake as him: 'Be wise at my expense, take advantage of my loss and renounce this unfortunate custom of duelling which a Fury has brought into France out of Hell to destroy souls and bodies and to weaken the Kingdom in the interests of its foes.'[6]

At the point when Cyrano began his duelling career in earnest among the cadets, the authorities were attempting the new tactic of clemency. In 1638 and again in 1640 royal pardons had been issued in the face of too many duels for the king to be able to punish. As Corneille points out, the dilemma facing the monarch who wished to control the murderous fury of the duellists was that, not only were they often too valuable to sacrifice, but their much vaunted indifference in the face of death meant that expecting the threat of capital punishment to dissuade them was woefully optimistic.

> The Count: No threats can daunt me, I've no fear of death.
> I'll weather any storms while I have breath.
> I might be forced to live in misery,
> But without honour life is death for me.[7]

Alternative solutions were required and during Cyrano's lifetime the authorities experimented with a system whereby, after a quarrel between two noblemen, one of the potential duellists would be put under guard in order to prevent the fight. Obviously, this arrangement relied on the relevant authorities being warned of the initial quarrel in time to intervene. This flaw in the system gave rise to a perception of this preventative measure as one only likely to be put in place with the cowardly cooperation of one of the duellists. Cyrano makes exactly that satirical point in his comedy *The Pedant Tricked* — a play, elements of whose composition he may well have been working on at this time. The duellist under guard in Cyrano's comedy is called Captain Chateaufort. He is a coward who brags about his courage but who is totally terrified by the prospect of a duel. His careful connivance with his guard '*le soin de bien garder mon Garde*' is made all too clear when he realizes that he is no longer accompanied and starts to panic at the horrifying prospect of suddenly being called upon actually to fight.

> Chateaufort: Hey! Oh My God, Sirs, I have lost my guard, has none of you met with him? . . . He's a guard that the Marshals of

France sent me in order to prevent me from fighting the bloodiest duel ever to redden the grass in the Clerks Meadow. Heavens above, what will the nobles say when they learn that I have not taken care to guard my guard?[8]

Cyrano was not alone in considering that the only way the state would successfully prevent a duel was with the cowardly connivance of one of the potential combatants. In 1650, Louis XIV introduced a pledge against duelling that the nobility were pressured to sign. The notion was very slow to take root and the vow to abstain from duelling, and to further undertake to dissuade others from the practice, remained largely ineffectual, despite the apparent reasonableness of the proposition: the idea being that if all the nobles jointly renounced the duel, then questions of honour would no longer be resolved by bloodshed. The text of the pledge emphasized the irreligious and irrational nature of the duel, as well as its illegality. Signatories were formalizing a promise: 'not to fight a duel for any conceivable cause, and to give all possible testimony of the hatred they have of the duel as of a thing that is against reason and the laws of the State and incompatible with salvation and the Christian religion.'[9] Not only did the nobles prove reluctant to sign, but the courtiers openly mocked the idea and dismissed those who had signed, as presumably infirm and therefore grateful for the excuse.

The idea that one could refuse a duel was simply not taken seriously at first, the practice having become so ingrained in the noble consciousness. The importance of demonstrating one's courage was paramount. The resolution of conflict through discussion was hardly in keeping with years of warrior tradition and an apology for an offence was considered worse than useless. Corneille had initially included lines to this purpose in the text of *Le Cid*, but had suppressed them as too provocative. They were well known throughout courtly circles nonetheless, and spread throughout fashionable Paris as a witty summary of the necessity of the duel.

> These satisfactions do not calm the soul
> Who accepts them has nothing, who makes them defames himself,
> And of all such agreements the most common effect
> Is to make two men lose their honour instead of one.[10]

The logic of this conviction that an apology fails to 'satisfy' the honour of either party, but rather dishonours both still further is unexpected but insistent. The language of duelling frequently refers to the need to remove the 'stain' of dishonour from the family name and the only effective method was to resort to violence and bloodshed. In 1606, the colourfully named English author Lodowick Bryskett wrote *A Discourse of Civill Life*, a work advertised as being, 'fit to instruct a Gentleman in the course of a virtuous life'. Bryskett explained the importance of the idea of 'honesty' to the mechanics of the duel. Essentially, he underlines the fact that it is so much more shameful to be accused of lying than it is to be insulted, that in an angry exchange any initial insulting comment is reduced to nothing by the response 'thou liest', and it is therefore the honour of the man who finds himself accused of lying that is at stake rather than the man who was initially insulted. Bryskett goes on to state 'it standeth so charged in his honor and reputation, that he can not disburden himselfe of that imputation, but by striking of him that hath so given it, or by challenging him to combat'.[11] According to the logic of the duel, any initial insult may be neutralized by an accusation of dishonesty; it was the response to an insult which provoked the duel not usually the insult or argument directly. The *démenti* or 'giving the lie' was the spark that began the conflagration. It was common practice for the demand for satisfaction to be formalized and written down in the form of a *cartel*.

In the 1640s, Cyrano penned a series of satirical letters; these were initially circulated in manuscript form to a select readership, then collected together and published in 1654. In one witty tirade, that has come to be known as 'Le Duelliste', Cyrano joked that he had no time to read anything else because he was so inundated by written requests to fight. Theoretically, this could lend support to the claims of Cyrano's enemies, who wrote (after his death) that all his duels came about as a result of his reaction to insults about the size of his nose. Such accusations are implausible but impossible to disprove since none of the *cartels* survive.

Although the duel had its origins in the judicial practice of settling disputes through trial by combat, and although many duels were fought in order to avenge private grievances (a notorious and clichéd example would be the cuckolded husbands who resorted to the duel to restore their honour) the enormous variety of motivation for the fights was naturally as diverse as human nature. Not only that, but as the practice gained in popularity the question of motivation became increasingly secondary. The duellists were fighting in order to demonstrate their courage and their nobility and the less reason they had to take up arms against one another the greater the prestige in doing so. This gives us a clue to the contradiction between the posthumous allegations of Cyrano's enemies and Le Bret's version. Cyrano's friend never gives a specific reason for any of the fights, mentioning only Cyrano's invincible reputation attracting challengers to him, and emphasizing the fact that he fought as a second and not on his own behalf. Therefore depending on who you choose to believe – and given the lack of proof it can only ever be a matter of belief – Cyrano was either vicious and morbidly sensitive, constantly giving the lie to his tormentors and fighting duels as a doomed attempt to stave off the humiliation of being constantly insulted, or he was the dashing and reckless young hero who fought for his friends and risked his life, purely for the principal of the thing. The truth presumably falls somewhere between the two.

In his play *Le Bourgeois Gentilhomme* Molière included a reference to the practice of duelling as a codification of 'true nobility' in keeping with the practice of fellow playwrights Corneille and Cyrano. The 'bourgeois gentleman' of the title is determined to act the nobleman convincingly and one of the steps he takes towards fulfilling this ambition is to engage a fencing master, although his innate cowardice wins through in the end. On creating a ballet for the court Molière was forced to negotiate the shift in attitudes to the duel which Louis XIV was attempting to institute. In *Les Fâcheux* (as in *Le coucou imaginaire, Le mariage forcé* and *Les fourberies de Scapin*) Molière links the duel to irrationality and dangerous hotheadedness. In the course of the action, the noble hero Eraste is constantly assailed by irritating interruptions as he attempts to arrange a romantic tryst with his beloved. One of these interruptions takes the form of another noble who has heard that Eraste has been called out to fight a duel and is determined to act as his second. Even when Eraste explains that he is on his way to a romantic rendezvous the second tries to insist on accompanying him. The sensible and witty hero does not wish to fight and Molière gratified his royal audience with a long speech supporting the king's authority and his anti-duelling campaigns.

> Eraste: I was a soldier before I was a courtier. I served fourteen years, and I think I may fairly refrain from such a step with propriety, not fearing that the refusal of my sword can be imputed to cowardice. A duel puts one in an awkward light, and our King is not the mere shadow of a monarch. He knows how to make the highest in the state obey him, and I think he acts like a wise Prince. When he needs my service, I have courage enough to perform it; but I have none to displease him. His commands are a supreme law to me; seek someone else to disobey him.[12]

Eraste's insistence that it is perfectly noble and brave to refuse a duel is pure propaganda and the inclusion of this speech in the play is evidence that, although the current of public opinion may have been beginning to change, there was far to go before a war hero who bravely scorns duelling would be anything more than a decidedly far-fetched work of fiction. The reality was that, unlike Eraste, most of the king's army did not make his order 'a supreme law' – at least not where duelling was concerned.

Since Le Bret's account of Cyrano's duels with the cadets gives no details of the combats themselves we have no way of knowing for certain what the causes of the fights were, nor whether lives were lost, nor if Cyrano sustained any injuries in the course of the fights. It is possible that the duels remained amongst the cadets and that the fights were therefore stopped at the point when the first blood was spilt. It is also perfectly possible that one or more of the duels in which Cyrano fought may have been a fight to the death. Throughout his biography of Cyrano, Le Bret emphasizes his friend's good humour and insists that he never fought on his own account but always as a second. The honour to be accrued from the position of second was all the greater because the second risked his life without any real personal motivation apart from friendship, thus the danger and the thrill were all the purer. The accounts that paint the clearest picture of such combats are those found in the reminiscences of some of the memorialists of the age. Roger de Rabutin, Comte de Bussy was a courtier and soldier who wrote prolifically throughout his career and whose memoirs provide several descriptions of the experience of a duel told from the point of view of the combatant.

Bussy-Rabutin was just one year older than Cyrano but his high birth guaranteed him a far more illustrious career. Like Cyrano, Bussy-Rabutin had determined early on to join the military: 'As soon as I entered into society my first and my strongest inclination was to become an honest gentleman and to achieve great military honours.' He was present at his first siege at the age of sixteen and four years later was commanding his father's infantry regiment.

On his father's death in 1645, Bussy succeeded him as lieutenant general of the king's armies in Nivernais and state counsellor. Alongside his military career, Bussy was a prolific letter writer, who also composed songs, poetry and witty bons mots to amuse his friends. His most successful work was the scandalous *Histoire Amoureuse des Gaules* (*Amorous History of the Gauls*), a hugely popular, salacious romp through all the sexual liaisons of the various prominent figures at court, the publication of which earned him a thirteen-month residence in the Bastille. Bussy's account of his duel with a Gascon called Busc is unusual, in that for once the story is being told by the losing party, and the author admits to his fear and to the panic that causes him to grab his opponent's sword by the blade in a last desperate attempt to save himself.

> On the second blow that I struck I pierced his lung; and because I had advanced close to him I tried to break, but without thinking of the curtain behind me, such that I fell over backwards. Busc who felt himself gravely injured threw himself on me; and screaming at me to beg for my life, he tried at the same time to plunge his sword into my body but I dodged the blow and the sword just scraped my ribs and entered the ground. My fear increased twofold and made me grab his sword by the blade; but in tearing it away he cut my fingers and particularly my thumb then putting his weapon to my throat he forced me to give up my own.[13]

Count de Forbin was another high-born military man who wrote his memoirs and included the stories of duels he had fought. Unlike Bussy, he does not choose to recount any defeats and the duel is presented as an essential part of his noble advancement. He describes how, on fighting his first-ever duel, he wins the approval of his uncle, who, proud of the courage he has displayed, proceeds to arrange his promotion to a higher military rank. Although

Forbin's promotion was probably a matter of course, springing as it did from his influential family connections, he presents the duel as pivotal in the decision being taken at that time. Later in the memoir, he describes a duel with Le Chevalier de Gourdon which makes for horrifying reading:

We fought in front of the bishop's palace; I struck him in the stomach and then again in the throat where, in parrying, my sword got stuck. Finding myself without my weapon, I received a wound in the ribs, which forced me back several paces; at that moment, my sword, which had been sticking out of the cavalier's throat fell to the ground: he picked it up. I wanted to throw myself at him, but he presented me with the points of the two swords and said: 'Stop there, you are disarmed! Here, take your sword! You have murdered me but I am an honest man.' So saying he fell stone dead.[14]

The sheer violence of the phenomenon should not be underestimated, and the writers who claimed after Cyrano's death that he was disfigured by duelling scars may not have been relying entirely on their imaginations. Naturally, it was precisely this violence which attracted so many young men of the era to the duel, the extreme sport of the age. In 1645 René de Ceriziers published a book in which he analysed the essentials of military glory. He writes that courage is the single most essential quality in a great captain: 'One of the most necessary parts of those who command is courage; since courage is as much the making of a Hero as reason is the making of a man.' Despite the illegality of the duel he clearly approves wholeheartedly of the practice and contents himself with the following equivocation: 'Since I cannot name it a worthy act of courage; I will call it the most beautiful error and the most forgivable sin of youth.'[15]

Ceriziers is just one in a long line of admirers of this 'most forgivable sin'; the heroic aspect appealed not just to the reckless young men themselves and to contemporary dramatists but to generations to follow. In the nineteenth century, Alexandre Dumas, Théophile Gautier and Charles Nodier not only chose to write about swashbuckling adventurers but they aspired to emulate then. Along with fellow author Paul Féval, who contented himself with being an attentive spectator, they frequented the fencing school of Maître Augustin Grisier at number 4 rue du Faubourg Montmartre, where they undertook intensive training in the art of swordplay. Dumas even gained the reputation as an excellent duellist, although, much to his vociferous disgust, he was more often called out to duel with pistols, the more modern and infinitely less noble weapon of choice at the time. In spite of their fascination with the duel, the authors who described the swashbuckling legends of the seventeenth century recognized that the historical reality of the practice needed a little modification in order to be acceptable to their readership. Thus they tended to situate their combats in contexts where the hero's motivation for fighting was clear, and to cast the fights in the simple terms of good versus evil. Of the countless duels fought in the seventeenth century, precious few would be found to fit such a pattern. The author of an anti-duelling text of the era entitled *Notable Discourse on Duels* laments this element of thoughtlessness in the combats and the fact that the duellists were not even concerned whether they were fighting for a just cause or not. 'Today no one looks more closely [at motives]. As soon as one is called, one must fight, at any cost, whether for right or wrong.'[16] The reason for the fights was relatively unimportant and this insouciance was not in keeping with the rules of fiction, where honour and danger needed to be placed in a clear context of right and wrong.

The duellist as reckless thrill-seeker is not a model that appears in any of the story-book versions of the phenomenon, and yet it is undeniably an important element in explaining the attraction of this extraordinarily dangerous craze. In reality, when Cyrano fought his duels, right and wrong were not the issues at stake; however he was not purely motivated by the lure of the forbidden and the heady rush of dicing with death. There was an expectation among the duellists that their exploits deserved a degree of recognition. The need to 'make himself known' is the reason that Le Bret gives for Cyrano's combats. To some extent, this search for recognition is reflected in the fictional representations of the duel, and the combat is frequently shown as the catalyst which leads to the revelation of the 'true worth' of the hero, and a consequent dramatic transformation of his situation. Sadly as Cyrano was to discover, in real life, without powerful friends or the leverage of significant wealth, the recognition of one's extraordinary courage did not necessarily lead on to the transformation of one's situation.

Rostand had read enough of the real Cyrano's writing to realize that an added dimension to the caricature would save his dramatic hero from being a pathetic or petulant figure. Like Prévot, Rostand saw in Cyrano a personality infused with a determination to surpass his own limitations and those that society would attempt to impose on him. The stage Cyrano declares: 'I've decided to excel in everything' and the original is suddenly vividly present.[17] Rostand clearly saw the dramatic potential of Cyrano's duels as a priceless opportunity and gifted the great actor Coquelin with the inspired scene of a duel in verse, in which Cyrano fences and improvises a ballad at the same time; thereby simultaneously demonstrating his intellectual and physical superiority to his opponent. The repetition of the line with the promise, or rather the threat, '*à la fin de l'envoi je touche!*' is a particularly memorable device. The stage Cyrano is as good as his word and vanquishes the enemy to the admiring applause of the surrounding onlookers (and the theatrical audience). At which point, Rostand neatly worked in a graceful nod to Alexandre Dumas; a soldier steps forward out of the crowd to congratulate Cyrano, and is then revealed to be none other than the great d'Artagnan.

Once his period of training with the cadets in Paris was complete, the real Cyrano left for Mouzon and the front line of the war with Germany. The city was under siege and the young man would face the hardships of a military campaign and either confirm or disprove the opinion expressed later by Napoleon Bonaparte, the most successful French military leader of all time, that: 'Good duellists make bad soldiers.'

6

Make love not war

In Cyrano's mature work reflections on the futility of war abound. He goes to some length to develop the theory that it is ultimately more honourable to make love and create new life than to make war and destroy it. Or as he puts it, 'It is much more honest to sweat at the construction than the destruction of one's species.'[1] It seems paradoxical that the soldier who had thrown himself so wholeheartedly into the bloody violence of the duel should turn pacifist, and declare the enterprise of warfare 'a channel for every injustice' but that was the eventual result of Cyrano's time in the army. His first experience of a military engagement was at the siege of Mouzon in 1639. This was just one of the many battles that formed part of the ongoing Thirty Years War. Mouzon is not far from the French border with Luxembourg and the Germans were besieging the French inhabitants with the intention of extending their reach further into Louis XIII's kingdom.

Siege warfare was perhaps the most important element of military strategy in the seventeenth century. In his account of the fundamentals of a gentlemanly education Cardinal Richelieu included the study of fortifications as an essential subject. In another text of the period by the Italian Montecuccoli, the author felt sufficiently sure of his readership's familiarity with the art of the siege to be able to introduce the subject with an almost comic brevity: 'They must set up camp, open the trench, construct the approaches, place the cannons, force the exterior, open the counterscarp, pass the ditch with the tunnels, secure the sapper, make a breach and launch the attack.'[2] The simplicity of this list belies a messy and uncertain reality in which the outcome of any engagement was far from sure.

In the real world, the military textbook ceases to have much meaning. Instead we can turn to a fragment of autobiographical information about the siege of Mouzon to be found in Cyrano's letter 'Sur le blocus d'une ville' (On the blockade of a town). This letter, which recounts the author's experience of being under siege with his fellow officers, is only an unfinished fragment. In contrast to the majority of his published letters where Cyrano's imagination overflows with an abundance of burlesque witticisms, here inspiration was clearly absent and, although he attempts to make light of a terrible situation, the jokes fall rather flat. The letter draws a flippant parallel between the slow starvation inflicted on a besieged city and the lenten fasting of Catholic tradition. 'We have no reason at all to complain, we are in another sort of Heaven, since we neither drink nor eat; they want to bring us to Paradise through starvation; and for fear that we might take nourishment in at the ears they even forbid us words in bad taste.'[3]

The image of the commanding officers refusing the men even the sustenance of *paroles grasses* – that is coarse phrases or literally 'greasy words' – affords a brief glimpse of the undisciplined soldiers indulging in the minor rebellion of vulgarity. Cyrano demonstrates his solidarity with the men and he notes mockingly that attempting to forbid miserable, hungry soldiers from expressing themselves crudely is as pointless as hoping they can survive on the nourishment of a dirty joke. The gallows humour of the letter, and in particular the fact that it simply tails off, as if the author lacked the energy to continue, speak volumes for the demoralizing effect of the siege.

On 21 June 1639, Marshal de Châtillon arrived with reinforcements to relieve the besieged soldiers. The French army were victorious, the enemy were forced to withdraw. Supply lines could be opened once again and the men were saved from a slow death from starvation. Meanwhile, Cyrano had been wounded in one of the attacks; a musket ball had passed right through his side. The unfinished state of the letter may even be testament to this unexpected end to Cyrano's famous ability to focus and write even in the midst of military chaos. Such an injury could easily have been fatal in a time when surgical procedures were approximate at best and the importance of basic hygiene practically unknown. The wound may well have been cauterized to aid healing: a brand applied to the flesh to sear the wound, a practice which acted as a very rudimentary method of sterilization. The pain of such a procedure would have been horrific but Cyrano was fortunate enough – if the musket ball had lodged in his flesh, it is possible that he would have survived the operation to remove it, but probably not the inevitable post-operative infection.

Bussy-Rabutin, who fell gravely ill while on campaign, was a close friend of the Prince de Condé and, as such, earned the dubious privilege of being treated by the prince's personal physician. He sums up the skill of his medical attendant with admirable brevity: 'Luckily he fell ill himself and died; if not he would have killed me.' Cyrano, whose health was always poor, from the time of his first injury onwards, came up with a blasphemous version of the same joke. In his satirical letter 'Contre les médecins' (Against Doctors), he compares doctors to Christ because their deaths are mankind's salvation: 'they die as well as God for the salvation of man'.[4] The letter is a comic masterpiece, in which Cyrano goes into great detail about the horrors and indignities inflicted on him by the 'torturers' of the medical profession. It ends with a paroxysm of hilarity as the letter suddenly shifts to the present tense, when the patient, seeing his doctor approaching, screeches at him, '*Vade retro Satanas*' (Get thee behind me Satan), as if hoping to exorcize the terrible demon.

Cyrano's second military campaign saw him taking part in the siege of Arras. The recapture of Arras from the occupying Spanish forces was of critical importance for the king due to France's deepening involvement in the power struggles of the Thirty Years War. The town's strategic position close to the border with the Low Countries gave it military significance in Cyrano's time and many years later when the trenches of the First World War saw the nearby landscape soaked with blood. Towards the end of April 1640, French forces arrived at Arras. The initial difficulty facing the French troops was how even to set up camp near enough to the target without drawing devastating Spanish fire. As a result, a diversionary attack was launched on the nearby towns of Aire-sur-la-Lys and Béthune, north of Arras itself. A significant section of the Spanish garrison left Arras to deal with the situation, and the French were able to set up camp.

In June, the king himself visited the encampment to inspect his troops. However, the tables were rapidly turned on the French troops when the Spanish forces encircled their encampment and the besieging French found themselves under siege. The troops were trapped for two weeks without provisions, water was scarce and sanitary conditions appalling. Epidemics seized the weakened men and the dead and dying piled up in the trenches; no one dared to brave the Spanish fire to collect the corpses. As the heat of summer added further discomforts to the dire conditions in the encampment, battles raged, unceasing and murderous. The Spanish lines were broken on the 2nd of August and by the 9th the French were victorious, reclaiming Arras for their own.

There is some controversy as to whether Cyrano had gained

promotion into the guards of the Prince de Conti at this point, which springs largely from the evidence of Cyrano's friendship with various key figures who were Conti's men. It seems unlikely that Cyrano had changed regiments, particularly since no reference to such a change is to be found. The friendships cited as proof only really show that Cyrano knew members of this regiment, which included Le Bret's younger brother, but nothing more. The controversy is founded on an anachronism, since the prince was only eleven years old at the time when Cyrano was in the army and his company was not created until 1649.

Although we know that d'Artagnan and Cyrano both fought in the siege of Arras there is no surviving documentary evidence of an encounter between the two heroes. However, since both were serving with Gascon regiments it seems at least possible that such an encounter did take place. Paul Féval *fils*, son of the creator of the legendary Lagardère, decided that such an encounter was not just possible but inevitable. His imaginative vision of the adventures of the two heroes in his popular serial novels *D'Artagnan contre Cyrano de Bergerac* (1925) and *D'Artagnan et Cyrano réconciliés* (1928) was even accompanied by a preface in which he claimed to have discovered yet another 'lost manuscript', number 4772, from which the events of the two books are drawn. On the whole Féval follows Rostand's vision of Cyrano and relates the adventures of the courageous but eccentric poet as he befriends the dashing young *Chevalier Mystère*, the love child of Anne of Austria and the Duke of Buckingham. In *D'Artagnan et Cyrano réconciliés*, Cyrano is given a happy ending for once and is married off to the beautiful Roxane. Whether that was the sort of happy ending that the real Cyrano would have chosen for himself is another question.

The occupying Spaniards taunted the French soldiers that they would only succeed in taking the city of Arras 'when rats eat cats'. In fact the French did eventually retake Arras giving rise to bizarre celebratory engravings depicting cats in full Spanish armour defeated by giant soldier rats. In the fray Cyrano had suffered another serious injury, a sword wound to the throat. In his biography, Le Bret refers to Cyrano's war wounds as an important element in his decision to leave the army, remarking with admirable understatement that the 'inconvenience' they caused him would affect him for the rest of his life. Cyrano's time in the army had also exposed him to other less concrete but more insidious dangers. His youthful vision of the world was threatened, and there can be little doubt that it was his time in the army, which, more than anything, instilled in him the bitter cynicism and unshakeable atheism that would only sharpen with age. Theoretically, joining the army was supposed to be the pinnacle of the heroic destiny of a nobleman, and as such, the young Cyrano had probably expected to encounter inspiring examples of courage and self-sacrifice in the arena of war. The reality was infinitely more prosaic, more brutal, and years later Cyrano would still be struggling with the memories of his army years, trying to make sense of the lessons he learnt about humanity in that time. Not least of which was the truth of Montaigne's maxim that: 'there is no beast so greatly to be feared by man as man'.[5]

In 1669 a novel was published which unmasked the everyday reality of life in the armed forces during the Thirty Years War. *The Adventures of Simplicius Simplicissimus* described the day-to-day occupations of the members of the so-called 'honourable profession' in the following revealing terms;

. . . for their entire activity consisted of hard drinking, suffering hunger and thirst, whoring and pederasty, rattling dice and gambling, overeating and overdrinking, killing and being killed, harassing and being harassed, hunting down and being hunted, being afraid and causing fear, robbing and being robbed, mugging and being mugged, inflicting misery and suffering it, beating and being beaten – in a few words, spoiling and harming, and being despoiled and harmed in turn.[6]

And after such a life the future that awaited the men was without hope of respite or improvement.

> . . . they continued eagerly in their works until after a while they finally gave up the ghost, died and croaked in battles, sieges, storms, campaigns, and even in their quarters . . . except only a few oldsters who (unless they had stashed away stolen or extorted goods) made the very best panhandlers and beggars.[7]

The hero of the novel is named Simplicius as a reference to the fact that he is a simple peasant and not a nobleman, but his name is also ironic. Simplicius's wily vagabond ways and his damning view of the armed forces as seen from the bottom up are anything but simple. As well as denouncing the rape, pillage and other outrages committed by the foot soldiers the story also satirizes the corruption and brutality of the aristocrats. In between campaigns and on the marches, moving from one battleground to another, troops were quartered on local villages (larger towns were exempted from this trial) and horrendous abuses were all too frequently the result. A proverb of the time asked how many peasants were required to support a single soldier and the reply was three: one to lend him his house, a second to lend him his wife and a third to go to hell in his stead.

In 1633, Jacques Callot published a series of eighteen engravings entitled 'Miseries and Misfortunes of War'. The engravings depict soldiers on the rampage: the devastation of an inn, the pillage of a peasant dwelling, the sacking of a church and the burning of a village. The series also shows the guilty soldiers arrested and the gory punishments meted out by their superior officers and local justice. A tree is transformed into a gibbet, the firing squad is put in place and an executioner breaks the arms and legs of a torture victim strapped to the wheel. Finally, in the seventeenth engraving the peasants are shown massacring the soldiers, and the title explains the legitimacy of their revenge: 'These unfortunates revenge themselves thus for the loss of their goods, for which they [the soldiers] are solely responsible.' This penultimate scene which shows beatings and stabbings is strikingly similar to a passage in the adventures of Simplicius in which Grimmelshausen depicts the sack of a village and the reaction of the peasants. The village is in flames having been pillaged and then set alight by soldiers, some peasants have run off, others are taken prisoner, including the village pastor who gets trampled by a horse and receives a blow to the head from the rider. While the soldiers are exercising this 'tyrannous cruelty' seemingly in the grip of madness, suddenly armed peasants emerge from the forest and Grimmelshausen compares the ensuing, ferocious battle to the effect of shaking a wasps' nest.

Although Grimmelshausen was German his satirical exposé of the reality of the Thirty Years War is equally relevant to the French army. In the public archives of the town of Artois a collection of more than 3,000 letters of complaint against the army testify to the accuracy of his fictional description and to the frequency with which such outrages were occurring.

The experiences related by English travellers in France also highlight the threat that the soldiers posed to law and order. Sir Philip Perceval's tutor wrote to him from Angers in 1677 with a tale of the criminal behaviour of French troops. 'The soldiers quartered here have been very troublesome with their robberies and abuses at night til one of them, who killed a townsman, hath been hanged, so that now they are quiet enough within the gates, but without they rob people of what they are bringing to market.'[8] Lady Fanshawe, a royalist in exile, described in her memoirs her journey from Calais to Paris to join her husband. On reaching the town of Abbeville she was informed that because of the danger of highway robbery she should take a guard of garrison soldiers with her on the next stage of her journey.

The next morning they sent me ten troopers well armed, and when I had gone about four leagues, as we ascended a hill, says some of these, 'Madame, look out but fear nothing'. They rid all up to a hill and met a well mounted troop of horse, about fifty or more, which after some parly wheeled about in the woods again. When we came upon the hill I asked how it was possible so many men so well armed should turne, having so few to oppose them; at which they laugh'd and say'd 'Madame, we are all of a company and quarter in this town. The truth is our pay is short, and we are forced to help ourselves this way, but we have this rule, that if we in a party guard any company, the rest never molest them, but let them pass free.' I having past all danger, as they said, gave them a pistole each, and so left them.[9]

These eyewitness accounts help to explain the rapacious behaviour of the troops, as well as the inevitability of their choosing the soft target of the local peasants, who could not bribe their way to protection. The peasants, bringing food to market, are set upon by soldiers who face an alternative of starvation. As Lady Fanshawe's guard informs her, 'pay is short, and we are forced to help ourselves in this way'. The ordinary soldiers were left with little choice but to use their professional skills – violence and intimidation – to extract the means to live from the most vulnerable members of society.

The question of how to pay and supply the vast armies mustered to fight in the various battles of the Thirty Years War proved to be an insurmountable logistical problem for the government. From 1635 onwards, as numbers of troops swelled, many of the French army's defeats were caused by the financial burden of keeping the forces in the field. Across Europe, the same difficulties confronted leaders determined to attain military dominance at any price. In *The Voyage to the Moon*, Cyrano's hero encounters a kind and gentle lunar noblewoman who pronounces judgement on the callousness of the generals laughingly sending millions to their deaths: 'And while they send more than four million better men than they off to get their heads broken, they are in their studies laughing at the cir-cumstances of the massacre of these poor simpletons.'[10]

Despite being far from suffering, like their subordinates, from the painful uncertainty as to where the next meal might be coming from, even the most privileged of the king's soldiers were capable of extraordinarily aberrant behaviour in wartime. Bussy-Rabutin's memoirs provide us with the story of the truly bizarre way in which certain officers chose to amuse themselves while serving under the Prince de Condé at the ill-fated siege of Lérida in Spain. Bussy had been invited to a dinner with fellow officers La Vallière, Le Bretèche, Jumeaux and Barbentane. The friends decided to dine in a ruined church by the ramparts of the town; Barbentane went off into the nearby cemetery where he prised the lid off a tomb and brought out a cadaver, which he dragged back to the group. Then with the assistance of Le Bretèche they made the corpse dance to the music of the prince's violins. Bussy-Rabutin was, according to his own account, both disgusted and terrified and insisted that they take the corpse away and return it to its coffin. The dinner continued with bawdy songs and further revelry until an officer named La Trousse arrived to take guard duty with La Vallière. Seeing the state of the men, La Trousse volunteered to leave La Vallière to stay and finish his enjoyment but the drunken La Vallière chose to accompany La Trousse in order to fill him in on operations.

As the two walked along the edge of the trench, La Vallière was shot in the head and killed instantly. The revellers were informed, but chose to carry on regardless, and Jumeaux even went as far as to hurry to the prince to ask for the government of the town, pre-viously held by his friend La Vallière. Bussy-Rabutin, meanwhile, began to convince himself that divine retribution was responsible for this sudden death and became increasingly superstitious and scared. Rumours started to fly around the camp that the corpse was the body of a saint miraculously preserved from decay. Bussy

Rabutin made a deal with Jumeaux that whichever of the two died first would come to the other with news of the afterlife. When Jumeaux died suddenly a few days later Bussy-Rabutin was gripped with terror each night, fearing that his ghost would soon return. Bussy-Rabutin became convinced that the men who had been present at the supper were all cursed and that they would all die off one by one. He ended up running away from Spain and returning home to Burgundy. The prince eventually had to abandon the siege and the name of the town, Lérida, became synonymous with failure and many satirical rhymes were made about the defeat.

Aristocratic officers like Bussy-Rabutin and his friends rose in rank using money and influence and, at the top of the hierarchy, the supreme commander-in-chief of the French army was the king himself. Both Louis XIII and his son after him were groomed from childhood to be warrior princes who led by example. Having taken part in drilling exercises and war games from a very young age, the monarch was expected to command his troops from the front line of battle to the extent that the French king occasionally found himself in the very thick of the action. In one notorious incident at a siege of 1654 a soldier had his hand blown off by a cannon ball just metres away from the young Louis XIV. It was reported that the unfortunate casualty staggered to where his severed hand lay in the mud and 'nobly picking it up again he came to present it to the King, whom he told that he was proud to have lost the limb in his service'. This little anecdote is related by Michel de Marroles in his *History of the Kings of France*, as an example of the extremes of willing self-sacrifice to which the king's loyal subjects were prepared to go. Whether the account is accurate or not, the fact that Marroles presents it as such is sufficient evidence of the strength of devotion which was expected of the king's men. Louis's reaction is not recorded in the anecdote and one is naturally left wondering: what exactly is the correct royal etiquette for the reception of bloody severed limbs? The king visited his troops at the siege of Arras but we have no record of Cyrano's reaction to this close-up view of the head of state. The right to command was seen as a privilege of birth as much in military terms as in politics. This was partly a throwback to feudalism and partly due to the venality of offices as the ever observant (and ever critical) John Reresby noted in his *Memoirs and Travels*,

> The gentry are well bred, but no scholars, being usually taken from their studies at about fourteen, then put into the academy to learn their exercises, as fencing, dancing, music, riding the great horse, and the like, and then sent into the army, where if they purchase not some command, after a campaign or two (for the stoutest must pay as well as the rest) they return to such employments as their friends prepare for them elsewhere.[11]

Reresby also provides a further clue as to the brevity of Cyrano's military career with his parenthetical remark that 'the stoutest must pay as well as the rest'. It was not enough to gain a reputation as a demon of courage – no amount of heroics could compensate the lack of cold hard cash. As, for example, in the case of the Gascon Captain Tréville (of Musketeer fame) who served for twenty years as the acting commander of his regiment with neither the official title nor the pay commensurate to the post because the position nominally belonged to the king's favourite Luynes. Appointed when he was just fifteen, Luynes was never expected to assume any of the responsibilities of the position or do any work. Tréville was there for that and it would only take two decades of this thankless toil in the shadow of an overprivileged child before Tréville would gain his due recognition only to have the honour snatched away again when Cardinal Mazarin disbanded the regiment. After a campaign or two Cyrano was in no position to purchase a command and was faced with the alternative of time-serving, like the loyal Tréville, or cutting his losses and returning to Paris while still in possession of all his limbs. Cyrano's choice was soon made.

The estimated death toll for the Thirty Years War is 2,071,000 and this figure does not even include those on the fringes of the combat who found themselves preyed upon by their own national troops. One of the most tragic and telling testimonies to the miseries of the Thirty Years War is that provided by a few lines scrawled in a family Bible in the final year of the war: 'They say that the terrible war is over now. But there is still no sign of peace. Envy, hatred and greed are everywhere; they are all the war has taught us [. . .] We live like animals eating bark and grass. No one could ever have imagined that such things would happen to us. Many people say that there is no God.' Astonishingly, the writer ends with a frail ray of hope, evidence of the extraordinary strength and dignity that are sometimes kindled in the human heart by terrible suffering: 'But we still believe that God has not abandoned us. We must unite and help one another.'[12]

The consolation of faith would not have reassured Cyrano, he was not susceptible to the idea that the horrific scenes he witnessed as a soldier were part of some divine plan. He was all too aware of the resolutely human origins of the conflict. After all, the French were fighting on the side of the Protestant Dutch and Swedes (despite being themselves a Catholic nation) due to the political necessity of supporting resistance to their dangerously powerful Catholic rivals, Spain and the Holy Roman Empire. Any argument for the religious justification of the conflict was on decidedly shaky ground. In *The Voyage to the Moon*, Cyrano talks about the use of military music as a means to distract and betray the men, preventing them from reflecting on the importance of their lives by whipping them up into a fury of bloodlust and fear. In order to communicate his shame and disappointment in mankind, Cyrano invented an escape voyage into outer space, where he imagined the possibility of more humane civilizations. Only in this way could his criticism of the myriad failings of the human race be voiced with impunity. The lunar noblewoman, 'the prettiest of the queen's ladies-in-waiting', who had condemned the barbarity of generals sending their men to die in the wars was equally unsparing of the victims of the slaughter. She acknowledges the courage shown by the men who fight for their country, but undercuts the remark with a sarcastic reflection on the flimsiness of their motivation: 'But I am wrong to blame the valour of your brave subjects: they do well to die for their country; the affair is important, since it means the difference between being the subject of a king who wears a ruff or one who wears bands.'[13]

Elsewhere, Cyrano would express the heartfelt conviction that 'a true gentleman is neither French, nor German nor Spanish; he is a citizen of the world and his homeland is everywhere'.[14] Cyrano's insistence that sex is nobler than killing is further developed when his lunar-voyaging hero sniggeringly remarks the fact that the noblemen in the moon wear something other than a sword to symbolize their rank and honour. Eventually, having first made sure there are no ladies present, he plucks up the courage to ask whether the object hanging from the belts of the courtiers really is what he thinks it is. The response is dignified and determined: 'Know then that the sash with which this man is honoured and whereby hangs a form of medal in the shape of a virile member is the symbol of a gentleman and the mark that distinguishes a nobleman from a commoner.'[15] The space traveller is unable to contain his amusement at this and bursts out laughing. He then condescendingly reveals the superior terrestrial tradition of wearing a sword as the mark of nobility. The lunar gentleman is unperturbed and calmly explains why this is yet another proof of the moral inferiority of the terrestrial viewpoint.

He was not moved by this but exclaimed: 'My little man, the nobles in your world are mad to parade an instrument which is the mark of a hangman, which is only forged for our destruction and is indeed the sworn enemy of everything that lives! And just as mad to hide a member without which we should be in the category of things that are not . . . Woe to the country where the marks of generation are ignominious and those of destruction are honourable! You call that member "the parts of shame" as if there were anything more glorious than to give life and anything more infamous than to take it away.'[16]

In Cyrano's imagination, warfare on the moon was strictly regulated in order to prevent any combat between unequally matched enemies, and preference given to the settlement of disputes by peaceful arbitration. The mature Cyrano also denounced the duel; in a spirit of humorous perversity the great duellist took pleasure in proving that all victories in single combat were, ultimately, a matter of luck. During his time with the cadets, Cyrano seems to have been forced to accept the truth of the statement, found in an anti-duelling text by the archbishop of Embrun, that: 'The most famous duellists have never been our most illustrious captains.'[17] This truism would be enshrined in the annals of military history thanks to its repetition by Napoleon. Although left with no choice but to abandon his hopes of winning glory on the battlefield, Cyrano did not immediately give up on the idea that honour may be acquired by arms. The hour of his greatest martial achievement was still to come.

7

The itch for glory

It would be anachronistic to picture the young Cyrano leaving the army in 1641 as some kind of seventeenth-century conscientious objector. His decision was essentially pragmatic and, although he abandoned the career of arms, he continued to fight duels and his disenchantment with violence and bloodshed was to be a slow and gradual process. He always retained a profound admiration for the military heroics of figures like Alexander the Great, Achilles and Hercules. When Le Bret describes this period in Cyrano's life, he does not oversimplify his friend's situation. Various factors had combined to bring Cyrano's military career to an abrupt halt and Le Bret is honest enough to include them all. Firstly, in his typically calm and understated manner, he describes the two major wounds that Cyrano had received in the thick of battle. Cyrano's health was dramatically compromised, but not to an extent that would have seen him invalided out of the army. One of the most successful and revered military leaders of Cyrano's time lost an arm, a leg, an eye and an ear in battle; Marshal Jean de Gassion was a decade older than Cyrano and a gifted military strategist. He was appointed to one of the highest military dignities in the land in 1643 when he was named a marshal of France. In his spirited defence of Cardinal Mazarin, Cyrano mentions this appointment approvingly as a proof of the cardinal's ability to recognize and reward military talent. He obviously respected and admired Gassion but not enough to want to follow in his footsteps.

Le Bret also remarks on his friend's 'small hope of consideration'.[1] This was a less tangible but considerably more significant handicap than Cyrano's injuries. After a couple of campaigns a soldier from a noble background had served his apprenticeship and it was expected that he would purchase a captaincy and start to advance in rank. It was essential to progress to higher military dignities in keeping with one's social standing. To stay as a lowly subordinate would have jarred not only with Cyrano's independent spirit but also with his strong sense of his own importance. If he had remained in the army without advancing he would have destroyed his own myth in the process. Le Bret, as the keeper of the flame, does not allow that Cyrano's 'small hope of consideration' was due to the fact that his family were neither wealthy nor influential enough to secure the next step up in his military career, because (at least on his mother's side) they were.

Instead he focuses on a less degrading obstacle to success – Cyrano's own free-spirited refusal to accept the help of an influential patron who could have ensured his advancement. This is a neat sleight of hand, concealing Cyrano's relatively humble position behind a mask of haughty independence. Such a claim would seem a ludicrous bluff were it not that Le Bret is able to back up his suggestion that Cyrano proudly refused to attach himself to a noble patron with a concrete example. Early in the 1640s, not long after leaving the army, Cyrano apparently rejected an offer of patronage from none other than Marshal de Gassion himself. Despite his obvious admiration for the military commander, the soldier-poet was not tempted to rejoin the ranks of the king's army and, when the one-legged hero died at the siege of Lens in 1647, Cyrano was not by his side.

Le Bret cites the frequency with which Cyrano was called upon by his fellow soldiers to fight in duels as another of the reasons why he wished to leave the army. Cyrano's reputation, as a skilled and courageous duellist, made him the ideal choice as a second and consequently he was apparently permanently in demand. Le Bret's insistence that Cyrano fought over a hundred duels as a second and none at all on his own account seems highly improbable, but it's not impossible. Elsewhere, Le Bret stresses his friend's great good humour and the sweetness of his disposition, although, given the vituperative nature of some of the satirical letters that Cyrano wrote, it is rather hard to believe that he was always as conciliatory as Le Bret implies. The letters he wrote on the subject reveal that Cyrano himself learned not to take his reputation as an invincible duellist too seriously. In the letter 'Against a coward', Cyrano takes his usual contrary stance and, assuming the character of a craven coward, he proceeds to outline a hilarious series of excuses for not fighting a duel. He even quotes the famous Cornelian maxim from *Le Cid* that 'Stained honour may be washed clean only with blood', purely in order to turn it to ridicule. Although the letter is written in the first person and, despite Cyrano's obvious delight in confounding expectations, the piece is, above all, a comic fiction and the persona of the coward owes a great deal to the stock theatrical buffoon the *matamore*.

In *Le Pédant Joué* Cyrano had also taken pleasure in inventing ridiculous posturing speeches for Chateaufort who is a perfect example of this type, a braggart whose excessive boasts about his courage and his powers of seduction cannot conceal his innate cowardice or his amorous failures. Cyrano's legend has suffered from the gleeful pleasure with which he imagined the ranting and humiliation of this fictional character. After his death Cyrano's enemies cast him in the role of cowardly braggart and attributed to him all the grotesqueness of his own fictional creations. Even Rostand's Cyrano is a descendant of the matamore, sharing his ranting and bluster and his humiliating rejection by a beautiful young woman. The shadow of Cyrano's swashbuckling prowess looms large and his decision to put such things behind him at a relatively young age is all but eclipsed by the flamboyance of the legend.

In late 1640 or early 1641, Cyrano enrolled himself as a student at the Collège de Lisieux. He had never completed his original degree at the Collège de Beauvais and he did not last long at this new institution either. He was strongly attracted to the newest fields of enquiry and these were not studied in the stuffy confines of the Jesuit-run colleges. One of the writers Cyrano most admired wrote that it was their excess of virtue which led to the *libertins* being marginalized. In his *Heroic Verses*, Tristan L'Hermite declared that virtue was his 'high mistress' and that this caused him to shun worldly success. In Cyrano's two-volume masterpiece *The Voyages to the Sun and the Moon*, he refers to various contemporary figures in order to pay homage to their erudition and originality, but none receives more heartfelt, unequivocal praise than Tristan. The passage in question begins with a trademark piece of verbal trickery as Tristan is denounced as 'the disgrace of his nation'. This is then revealed to be one of Cyrano's typical paradoxes because the disgrace referred to is the failure of the great and the good of France to honour such a worthy individual: 'the disgrace of his nation; since it is certainly a disgrace to the great nobles of your State to recognise in him without worshipping it, the virtue that he enshrines'.[2] Cyrano follows Tristan's lead in identifying the poet's defining characteristic as virtue. He goes on: 'He is thoroughly witty, thoroughly brave [. . .] In short I can add nothing to the praise of this great man, except to say that he is the sole poet, the sole philosopher, and the sole free man that you have.'[3]

There are certain interesting parallels between the biographies of the two authors. Tristan's real name was François but he adopted the name Tristan in order to increase his own personal prestige by highlighting his connection to an illustrious ancestor of the same name, who was grand provost at the court of Louis XI in the late Middle Ages. In his poem entitled 'La Servitude', Tristan reflects on the humiliation of dependence. The rhetorical question he poses could almost have been the inspiration for Rostand's tirade:

> *Should I go about to abase myself in a thousand, thousand different*
> *   ways*
> *And lay siege to twenty houses,*
> *In order to snatch the bread that is not offered to me?*[4]

Tristan was reasonably well connected but not personally wealthy, and his life was plagued by ill health. Neither his poverty, nor his poor health was much helped by his self-confessed addictions to drinking and gambling. He was also a redoubtable duellist and had to flee from his position as a page in the court of Henri IV after killing an opponent when he was only in his early teens. He recounts his ensuing adventures in England, Poland and Spain in the semi-autobiographical novel *The Disgraced Page*.

It has been suggested that Cyrano may also have travelled to Poland and to England and that the strong friendship between the two men may have been forged in part from these common experiences. But apart from fictional references to these destinations, no proof for such a theory has yet been uncovered. Cyrano and Tristan shared a fascination with alchemy and Cyrano makes explicit reference to this fact in an aside in which the character who praises Tristan is revealed to be an escapee from Tristan's own novel *The Disgraced Page*, an ancient sage, who had so mastered the alchemical arts as to succeed in creating the philosopher's stone.

If the testimony of contemporary authors such as the Italian diplomat Primi Visconti are to be believed then a preference for study over slaughter was a far from fashionable choice. Rather it was a decision which from a worldly point of view must inevitably bring Cyrano down in the estimation of his peers. 'Indeed, in France none but military honours are held in esteem, those of literature and of all other professions are despised and a man of quality who knows how to write is considered vile.'[5] Still more explicitly, Guez de Balzac, in a letter of 1637, ridicules the very idea that anyone should be prepared to sink so low. 'Is it possible that a man . . . who has not received a commandment from the King on pain of death to go to his books could wish to abandon the rank of honest gentleman that he holds in the world in order to go and take up that of ridiculous and impertinent child amidst teachers and schoolboys?'[6] Balzac's mockery helps to explain why Théophile de Viau, Tristan and Cyrano all wrote about being poor and disregarded. Choosing to be a poet, who wrote, not for the delight of the king and his courtiers or for a wealthy patron, but simply to be true to himself, was choosing to fail in worldly terms.

And yet, in the same year as he entered the Collège de Lisieux, Cyrano also entered into two contracts, which reveal that he had not entirely abandoned all ideas of mixing in fashionable society. Papers survive which reveal that, on 8 October 1641, Cyrano entered into a contract with Pierre Moussard, a fencing master with a studio on rue Saint Jacques. The agreement was that Moussard would provide regular lessons for the period of two years for the price of 10 livres a month. On the 23rd of the same month Cyrano also entered into an identical arrangement with one David Dupron, a dancing master based in the same street. This biographical fragment recalls Molière's play in which the social-climbing bourgeois gentleman also engages himself dancing and fencing masters, in order to ape the accomplishments of the nobility. Sadly, no further trace of Cyrano's lessons survive, so we have no way of knowing whether Maître Dupron considered him a miracle of grace or a clodhopping idiot. Maître Moussard on the other hand must have been proud to call Cyrano his pupil, since he carried off a swashbuckling feat of such bravado as to capture the attention even of the great Gassion himself: the duel with one hundred men.

Le Bret gives the names of at least three eye witnesses to Cyrano's most momentous exploit. He describes how Monsieur de Bourgogne, who was the *maître de camp* of the Prince de Conti's infantry regiment, had been responsible for informing Marshal de Gassion and further notes that two other soldiers, Monsieur de Cavais and Monsieur de Cuigy, were also witnesses to the scene. Le Bret's version of events briefly states that the men felled by Cyrano deserved their fate and that 'two of them paid with their lives and seven others with serious injuries for their malicious plot'. Le Bret readily admits that the story is unconvincing and that it would be dismissed as pure fiction, were it not that the scene was witnessed by these 'several persons of quality', who made it their business to spread the word widely enough to eliminate the possibility of doubt. Le Bret refers to the assailants as intending to 'insult' one of Cyrano's friends, and this may be a clue as to the true nature of this extraordinary ambush in broad daylight at the de Nesle gate. It seems most probable that the men were lackeys, armed with a motley selection of swords, knives and clubs, paid to administer a *bastonnade* (a severe beating with clubs) perhaps to silence one of Cyrano's controversial circle once and for all. The bastonnade was a fate traditionally reserved for poets and writers, who, by virtue of their profession, were considered to have descended too far below the rank of the nobility to merit an exchange of swordplay, and the codes of duelling strictly stated that a duel could only be fought between combatants of equal rank. Hence the bastonnade was the fate reserved for those who were not important enough to merit a true duel. The very fact of administering such a beating was a terrible insult because it implied that the subject was far beneath the dignity of their attacker.

Who ordered this attack and whether the intended victim was Lignières, another poet friend, or even Cyrano himself, remains a mystery – Rostand's identification of the Duc de Guise as the culprit has no more basis in historical fact than his vision of Lignières as the intended victim. Le Bret's reference to 'a friend' as the target of this attack is very vague; no doubt he wanted to gloss over the question of what the person singled out for this excessive punishment had done to merit the 'insult' of an armed ambush. Here we find ourselves in territory that is dark and difficult to negotiate, with very good reason. Le Bret's biography bears the traces of the rigorous censorship that was the norm at the time and, as we will see later, there are still murkier aspects of Cyrano's tragic destiny that he tried to talk about, only to be rapidly silenced.

Considering the circles in which Cyrano moved, and his close association with the thought-crime of libertinism, there can have been no shortage of threatening presences desperate to see him and his like taught a violent lesson. If Le Bret's account passes over this last paroxysm of Cyrano's passion for physical combat rather quickly, that may point to the fact that the incident was still dangerous to discuss even at a distance of some twelve or thirteen years. Le Bret places the events of the fight with one hundred men at the period in Cyrano's life when he had left the army in order to devote himself full time to study. As he puts it, Cyrano 'had abandoned Mars in order to devote himself to Minerva'. Cyrano soon strayed out of the realms of straightforward martial devotion to the monarch and the state and was to become deeply engaged in a programme of study that was radical in the extreme. It is entirely possible that, having already begun to exercise his considerable talents as a satirist, Cyrano had himself offended someone highly placed and wealthy enough to command a crushing retribution.

We have a few shreds of evidence regarding Cyrano's activities in the years 1640–2, such as the contracts he entered into with Dupron and Moussard and these make it seem likely that the incident took place in 1642–3, but without further proof any date is necessarily purely speculative. Le Bret's unfailing loyalty to Cyrano saw him tell the story in such a way as to minimize the question of why the ambush happened in the first place and to focus attention instead on Cyrano's skill and daring, but it may well have been an early, unsuccessful attempt to silence the turbulent poet or intimidate him into submission and greater circumspection. The attack (just like all the beatings Cyrano had received in the course of his schooling) had the exact opposite result, confirming Cyrano in a lifelong determination to resist intimidation and to defy authority at any cost.

Despite Le Bret's unassuming tone, the story of the duel with one hundred men smacks of the publicity stunt. There is an element of theatricality to the tale, which suggests that Cyrano knew all too well the importance of the spectacle that he was engineering. He made sure to have witnesses and he made sure to fight alone against overwhelming odds. Cyrano had turned his back on a military career but he railed against the exclusion from the ranks of honourable gentlemen supposedly implicit in such a step. The climate of popular opinion at the time saw intellectual engagement as suspect, set against the unthinking loyalty and unquestioning obedience that characterized the greatest 'honour' of the military ideal. Cyrano determined to stand up for the honour of the poet, the courage of the intellectual. The bastonnade, an inglorious ambush by mercenary thugs, was a powerful symbol of a poet's demotion from the ranks of polite society, marking him out as it did as one undeserving of the gentlemanly ritual of the duel. Cyrano refused to play by the rules and transformed what should have been a potentially deadly rite of humiliation and defeat into a flamboyant life-affirming triumph.

Perhaps more than any other element of his biography, the story of the duel with one hundred men sealed Cyrano's posthumous reputation as a reckless, hot-headed, dare-devil. Here again we see the paradox of Cyrano's apotheosis from man to legend: what was in truth an act of considered rebellion against the status quo became characterized as little more than an aggressive whim. In Rostand's play, Cyrano's infamous duel with one hundred men takes place at night and is introduced with a lyrical description of Paris by moonlight whose air of mystery seems entirely appropriate to an encounter that Le Bret terms a 'superhuman combat'.

> *Ah! Paris, swimming through nocturnal mist,*
> *The rooftops draped in azure, shyly kissed*
> *By an uncertain moon – proscenium*
> *All dressed and ready for the scene to come,*
> *Or like a magic mirror, breathes the Seine,*
> *Trembling, compact of myth and mystery –*
> *You're going to see now what you're going to see.*[7]

Despite the closing promise 'You're going to see now what you're going to see', the original audience of 1897 did not in fact witness the fight itself as the first act ends just after this speech. Later film versions, like that starring Gérard Depardieu, have since taken on the challenge of choreographing the extraordinary swordplay required to re-enact a battle featuring one man against a hundred opponents. Much is made of the element of surprise and the fear induced in Cyrano's antagonists by his sudden appearance out of the darkness, but in Le Bret's account of the fight the scene actually takes place in broad daylight. The duel with one hundred men has become an integral part of the myth of Cyrano and it doesn't much matter whether there is an element of exaggeration in the telling. Of course it is unlikely there were really as many as one hundred assailants lying in wait for Cyrano, but Le Bret lists two deaths and seven seriously wounded which puts the lowest possible figure at nine against one. If we accept that at least some others must have escaped unhurt, having run away at the first sign that things were not going as expected, the odds lengthen still further. Any way you look at it, it was an impressive feat of skill and daring.

It was perhaps the fact of having pulled off such a Herculean escapade that gave Cyrano the confidence to poke fun at his own redoubtable reputation. In a letter entitled 'Le Duelliste' Cyrano expresses the same idea that Le Bret would touch on in his biography, jokingly referring to the fact that his reputation attracted constant calls for him to fight. 'I sometimes imagine that I have become a porcupine, seeing that no one can approach me without pricking himself.'[8] Cyrano's comic vision of himself as a porcupine stems from a play on the word 'piquer' which can mean both anger and prick. In depicting himself as the hapless porcupine who does not set out to quarrel but who inadvertently spikes anyone who comes near, Cyrano also neatly characterized himself as the only true gentleman amid a crowd of hotheads who unlike the porcupine-hero have failed to recognize the truth of La Rochefoucauld's maxim: *Le vrai honnête homme est celui qui ne se pique de rien* (The true gentleman never allows himself to be angered). Underneath the laughter there is also a melancholy echo of the picture Cyrano had drawn of the lost soul of Montmorency-Bouteville, lamenting his isolation; a human porcupine was necessarily also 'a man who carried solitude with him'.

An air of injured innocence and apparent indifference to the world was a favourite comic stance of Cyrano's in his satirical letters and in the 'Lettre contre un faux brave' (Against a cowardly braggart) he neatly combines menace and mockery, as he remonstrates with his 'dear friend' for dishonestly bragging that the great Cyrano intends to kill him: 'It has been reported to me from various sources that you have been bragging that I planned to murder you. Alas! My dear friend, do you think me so crazy as to attempt the impossible? Ha! For pity's sake, where can one strike a man in order to kill him instantly when he has neither a heart nor a brain?'[9]

Elsewhere, he creates a witty play on words, inspired by the constant requests for him to fight as a second: 'Really you would be very wrong to call me now the first of men; because I protest that for over a month now I have been everybody's second.'[10] The unwritten double meaning to this particular paradox is that the modesty of the protest belies a cunning bit of self-promotion, because in terms of honour the 'second' is actually 'first'. By far the most irreverent of all Cyrano's duelling jokes is the one ending the letter 'The Duellist'. He begs Le Bret to return to Paris to exercise his calming influence and return Cyrano to philosophical mood before the 'itch for glory' pushes him to fatal extremes: 'I am afraid that this itch for glory may invite me to carry my name as far as Heaven itself. That is why I beg you to come back soon, because it would anger terribly me if on your return instead of finding me in my study you were to find me in a church . . .'[11] Cyrano's anger, at being in church for his own funeral, rather than at his books in his study, is obvious and comically incongruous, but the lines also contain a typical libertine double meaning. He also implies that he would be furious should his friend find him worshipping or praying in church instead of studying or writing.

Legend has it that Cyrano's fight with the crowd of hired assassins was undertaken in defence of his friend Lignières, thereby lending greater substance to the paradoxical claim made in Cyrano's letter on duelling: 'In truth, it is a very great consolation to me to be hated because I am loved; to find enemies everywhere because I have friends everywhere and to see that my unhappiness stems from my good fortune.'[12] Le Bret's biography does not confirm this theory; Lignières is briefly referred to as someone who was a good friend of Cyrano's, but not in the context of the fight at the de Nesle gate.

Émile Magne, the academic who had attacked Rostand so vociferously on the subject of the anachronisms and inaccuracies to be found in his play, wrote an entire book devoted to the subject of

Cyrano's friendship with the Chevalier de Lignières. The book is surprisingly playful and presents Magne's own version of events drawn from his wide reading. Magne follows Rostand in attributing the fight with one hundred men to a defence of Lignières but without providing any additional evidence. Rather surprisingly, given his fury at Rostand for making such a caricature of Cyrano he introduces the idea that the friendship between the two men was in part based on the length of their noses. He quotes some lines of Lignières's as decisive proof of this affinity.

> *When they laugh at my nose, I never get angry*
> *I hold that large noses are not without their charms*
> *And that a big nose never made a face less attractive.*[13]

Strangely Magne is also guilty of putting the words of one of Cyrano's comic creations into the mouth of his hero. At the moment when he is poised to begin his Herculean attack, Magne's Cyrano suddenly launches into an absurd overblown series of boasts, taken directly from one of the satirical letters. Magne apparently didn't consider the spectacular inappropriateness of giving his hero lines which the real Cyrano penned revelling in the stupidity of their bombast and bluff. Cyrano becomes the victim of his own success and is made the target of his own comic buffoonery. Cyrano's fictions have sufficient life that they often vie with and overcome the truth. It is Cyrano's propensity to construct his own myth that makes this process inevitable; he constantly tempts his readers to try to reach the truth behind the fiction. Every book, play, film, opera, poem or piece of music ever written about Cyrano (this one included) inevitably has its roots in this skilled manipulation of his own image in which the original so delighted.

Edmond Rostand took the idea of this free-spirited, almost self-destructively independent character and spun from it one of the finest speeches of his playwriting career. In the second act of the play, a penniless Cyrano refuses an offer of patronage from the Duc de Guise, determined to retain his liberty at any cost. When Le Bret accuses him of taking an exaggerated stance, he replies;

> *Well then yes, I exaggerate! . . .*
> *But for the principle of the thing and as an example*
> *I think that it's good to exaggerate.*

Rostand then proceeds to outline this 'principle' and 'example' in a long speech which is known as *Le tirade de Non Merci*. The tirade is one of the most superb moments of the whole play. It is very cleverly constructed: Cyrano begins by asking 'So what should I do?' and then makes a series of suggestions of suitably cringing, self-serving behaviour. These are sarcastically framed as questions and Cyrano answers himself with a sardonic rejection of such servility, always repeating the same simple response: *Non, merci*.

> Cyrano: *What would you have me do?*
> *Seek out a powerful protector, pursue*
> *A potent patron? Cling like a leeching vine*
> *To a tree? Crawl my way up? Fawn, whine*
> *For all that sticky candy called success?*
> *No, thank you. Be a sycophant and dress*
> *In sickly rhymes a prayer to a moneylender?*
> *Play the buffoon, desperate to engender*
> *A smirk on a refrigerated jowl?*
> *No, thank you. Slake my morning mouth with foul*
> *Lees and leavings, breakfast off a toad?*
> *Wriggle and grovel on the dirty road*
> *To advancement and wear the skin of my belly through?*
> *Get grimy calluses on my kneecaps? Do*
> *A daily dozen to soften up my spine?*
> *No, thank you . . .*[14]

The use of repetition and the increasing vehemence of the speech allow the actor to build to a crescendo and then suddenly switch registers to end with an idealized vision of the alternative destiny which Cyrano desires for himself and his fellow freethinkers.

> *No, no, no,*
> *Thank you, no. No, thank you. But to go*
> *Free of the filthy world, to sing, to be*
> *Blessed with a voice vibrating virility,*
> *Blessed with an eye equipped for looking at*
> *Things as they really are, cocking my hat*
> *Where I please, at a word, at a deed, at a yes or no,*
> *Fighting or writing; this is the true life. So*
> *I go along any road under my moon,*
> *Careless of glory, indifferent to the boon*
> *Or bane of fortune, without hope, without fear,*
> *Writing only the words down that I hear*
> *Here – and saying, with a sort of modesty,*
> *'My heart, be satisfied with what you see*
> *And smell and taste in your own garden – weeds,*
> *As much as fruit and flowers.' [. . .]*
> *I myself am a tree,*
> *Not high perhaps, not beautiful, but free –*
> *My flesh deciduous, but the enduring bone*
> *Of spirit, tough, indifferent, and alone!*[15]

The passionate force of this outburst and the powerful images in which Rostand cloaks Cyrano's 'exaggeration' serve to elevate the 'principle' above the mundane level of everyday reality. This is Rostand's dream of what a poet should be and naturally has only the faintest corresponding echo in real life. In reality neither Cyrano nor Rostand could ever have been said to have been totally

Careless of glory, indifferent to the boon
Or bane of fortune.

After all, Rostand was not starving in a garret when he wrote these lines, he was the pampered darling of French high society, and the real Cyrano was not above penning a lucrative defence of Cardinal Mazarin, nor of eventually accepting the intervention of a patron in order to see his works make it into print.

The reality of Cyrano's writing career may have been more prosaic and less exalted than Rostand's dream of it, but the underlying principle remains the same. Le Bret makes this explicit, when he reiterates his remarks about Cyrano's reluctance to accept help for fear of compromising his artistic freedom. Le Bret explains that the notion of personal freedom was so essential to his friend's nature that even conformity to accepted opinion seemed a constraint to Cyrano:

> He did not limit his hatred of subjection to that which a great nobleman to whom one might attach oneself would demand; he extended it still further, and even as far as any thing that seemed to him to constrain thought itself and his opinions in which he wished to remain as free as in his most indifferent actions.[16]

This little passage provides a neat summary of the literary movement to which Cyrano's works have been allied. He is known as one of the *libertins* or the freethinkers. At the time their intellectual nonconformity was viewed with deep suspicion and the freethinkers were often marginal, their place in society precarious at best, criminal at worst. In 1623, the Jesuit priest Father Garasse published a lengthy and virulent attack on the freethinkers, entitled *La Doctrine Curieuse des Beaux Esprits de ce temps* (The Curious Doctrine of the fine wits of our age). The title was darkly sarcastic; Garasse considered the provocative young wits of his age as agents of the Antichrist. 'The devil instructs and trains certain wicked minds, who are more damned than devils incarnate [. . .] When a mind abandons itself to evildoing it is like an unstoppable gangrene one must cut, sever and burn otherwise the affair is desperate.'[17]

The writer against whom Garasse's most vitriolic outbursts were directed was one of Cyrano's most important influences, the satirical poet Théophile de Viau. Garasse had not succeeded in seeing Théophile burned at the stake, but the poet perished in exile in 1625, his health having been fatally undermined by a long period of imprisonment. Garasse's work had precipitated his downfall and it was only due to the intervention of Théophile's influential supporters that he managed to escape the death sentence that had been pronounced on him at his trial. Théophile's work was an important model for Cyrano's own forays into the world of letters and it was often outrageously blasphemous and offensive. He deliberately courted controversy with his obscene and irreverent writing and there is no question that his influence was very significant in creating a new way of thinking about what it meant to be a writer. Théophile and the libertins who followed him considered their intellectual and artistic freedom as paramount, and this was a dangerous precedent to set. In his 'Ode' Théophile painted a vivid (self-)portrait of the libertin:

> *He never envies others,*
> *When all those happier than him*
> *Mock his misery*
> *Laughter is his only retort.*
> *[. . .]*
> *The sparkle of golden rooms,*
> *Where princes are worshipped,*
> *Appeal less to him than the fresh face*
> *Of the countryside or the clouds.*
> *[. . .]*

He has never pretended to
Either fortune or poverty;
He is neither servant nor master
He is nought but what he would be.[18]

In our time the word *libertine* has become synonomous with immorality and sexual licence but, as Théophile's lines reveal, the original sense of the word was that of freedom to be true to oneself, to be 'neither servant nor master'. In the eighteenth century the figure of the libertine was typified by that amoral, lascivious rake the Vicomte de Valmont, the charismatic anti-hero of Choderlos de Laclos's scandalous novel *Les Liaisons Dangereuses*. This shift in meaning was in part due to scare-mongering works like Garasse's and was also influenced by Molière's popular comedy *Dom Juan*, in which the eponymous hero is an exaggerated burlesque caricature of a *libertin*. Molière's Dom Juan is an unrepentant atheist and a serial womanizer and it has been suggested that the character was modelled in part on that of the real Cyrano. Dom Juan's epitaph is pronounced by his impudent manservant Sganarelle who declares that his master's death is a cause of rejoicing for the whole world except him, but he mourns his master's death purely for the sake of his lost wages:

Sganarelle: Alas! My wages! My wages! Everyone is satisfied by his death. Offended heaven, violated laws, maids seduced, families dishonoured, parents outraged, wives ruined, husbands driven to despair, all are satisfied. I alone am unhappy. My wages, my wages, my wages![19]

Molière took the idea of the libertine to its extreme for comic effect, but the reality was that, in Cyrano's time, the true free-thinkers were not necessarily hedonistic pleasure-seekers – they were intellectual rebels. This is why Le Bret stresses the importance of Cyrano's intellectual enthusiasm as the deciding factor in his decision to leave the army: 'And finally, the great love that he had for study made him renounce entirely the career of war, which demands all of a man and renders him as much an enemy of literature as literature makes him the friend of peace.'[20] Cyrano was a 'friend of peace' then, but no pacifist. If he were also a womanizer, like Dom Juan (or any other kind of hedonist), Le Bret would have been the last to say so. Ever the loyal defender of his friend's choices, Le Bret was as open about Cyrano's passion for study as he was reticent about other passions that may have flamed his blood.

8

Far from having lost my heart

O n 14 July 1642, Cyrano's family were assembled to attend the wedding of his cousin Marie de Cyrano. Marie married a man named Honoré Morel and it is thanks to Baron Frédy de Coubertin, a descendant of their union, that we have a description of the Cyrano coat of arms. It was azure blue and featured a silver chevron and two gold stars, as well as a rampant lion with a brilliant red tongue. Cyrano may have made liberal use of this coat of arms to further bolster his pretensions to nobility. While his cousin Marie was publicly celebrating her summer wedding surrounded by family and friends, Cyrano's own romantic involvements remained a closely guarded secret. It is rather ironic that the stage Cyrano should protest (untruthfully) that the passionate love letters, which he provides for Christian to send to Roxane, are nothing more than exercises of style, written on a whim and with no genuine feeling behind them: 'the more eloquent for being insincere', since this is exactly how the critics interpret the love letters of the real Cyrano.[1] Jacques Prévot states baldly 'woman is absent from them' alleging that: 'Cyrano tells nothing of his heart; literary creation here [. . .] rests on no power of real emotion, no nostalgia, it is nourished by no passion, present or past, it expresses no experiences and does not spring from any spontaneity.'[2]

Whether one accepts Prévot's sweeping dismissal of Cyrano's letters or not, his magisterial pronouncement usefully underlines the fact that any interrogation of Cyrano's published love letters for details of his private life is a futile exercise. The title phrase of this chapter, a typical equivocation from one of Cyrano's love letters, echoes the question asked by so many curious admirers of the great swordsman – did the real Cyrano ever lose his heart? The fact is that such a question must remain unanswered. In the absence of any concrete proof, critics and historians may speculate about Cyrano's feelings and the intimate details of his love life, but the truth will remain as mysterious as Cyrano intended. Le Bret waxes lyrical about Cyrano's many friendships but barely mentions his love life. He restricts himself to a phrase whose very discretion has only served to inflame further curiosity. Le Bret states, somewhat enigmatically, that Cyrano showed 'so great a reticence towards the fair sex that one could say that he never overstepped the bounds of the respect owed to them.'[3] Recent critics have seen in this phrase a covert avowal of Cyrano's homosexuality, particularly when allied to the mysterious hint of a 'dangerous tendency' in Cyrano's behaviour in late adolescence.

Aside from the interpretation of certain homoerotic passages in his work, the most conclusive evidence offered to support the idea is Cyrano's close connection to two men who were almost certainly lovers and his virulent dispute with one of them, which has been construed as the result of a tortured love affair. The two men, identified as forming this unhappy gay love triangle with Cyrano, were the poet Dassoucy (who was repeatedly prosecuted and imprisoned for his homosexuality) and a young man named Chapelle. Cyrano's association with them probably dates from the early 1640s, when he had left the army and was studying at the Collège de Lisieux and taking those dancing and fencing lessons.

Claude-Emmanuel Lhuillier de la Chapelle, usually known as Chapelle, was born in 1626. Seven years younger than Cyrano, he was the bastard child of a young noblewoman named Marie Chanut. Marie was the sister of the French ambassador to Sweden and having been seduced and abandoned by Lhuillier she married one Hector Musnier, who was perhaps not altogether thrilled by her shady history, although he may well have agreed to take Marie as his wife precisely because her notorious connection with Lhuillier enabled him to demand an inflated dowry. Such payments went a long way towards reconciling a man to a certain moral flexibility in his bride. Perhaps unsurprisingly, the marriage was not a success and Hector and Marie seem to have separated after a short time.

Chapelle was extremely fortunate to be his father's only son, ordinarily the fate of a bastard son supplanted by a legitimate heir was not a happy one – that familiar conflict is played out in Shakespeare's *King Lear* between the half-brothers Edgar, the legitimate and dutiful son, and Edmund, the intelligent and manipulative schemer who turns out to be an evil bastard. As his father's legitimate heir, Chapelle had access to a world of privilege and ease. In 1642 Lhuillier senior took steps to have his child legitimized. He had not only introduced his son to his favoured brothel to complete his education, but rather more helpfully had also taken the trouble to secure the philosopher and mathematician Pierre Gassendi, one of the greatest minds of the age, as a tutor for him. Lhuillier had first been introduced to Gassendi in 1628 by a mutual friend and the two men had embarked on a lengthy tour of Holland together in December of the same year.

Born 22 January 1592, Gassendi was nearly fifty years old when Cyrano first came into his orbit. He was a great philosopher and an enthusiastic proponent of experimental science. His contribution to science is commemorated by the fact that there is a crater on the moon named after him. Gassendi was a sincere Christian but he centred his teaching around the scepticism of the classical philosopher Epicurus. He was not a radical but a deeply modest individual and a natural teacher. He was to play a pivotal role in Cyrano's career.

Cyrano seems to have been a student of Gassendi in the period 1641–3. Writing in 1707, an early biographer of Molière describes Cyrano infiltrating the circle of like-minded young friends that Chapelle had gathered around him to profit from Gassendi's teaching. According to Grimarest (who got most of his information from Molière's daughter and his protégé, a young actor named Baron) the group included both Molière and Cyrano, but the biographer alleges that Cyrano was accepted only with 'reluctance' due to his 'turbulent spirit'. He does acknowledge that Cyrano was apparently gifted with an excellent memory and was clearly 'very eager for knowledge'. His vision of how the group's initially unwelcoming attitude to Cyrano was overcome takes the form of a rhetorical question: 'how to be rid of a young man as ingratiating, as lively, as Gascon as Cyrano?'[4] This is the second mention he makes of Cyrano's supposed Gascon origins; the great swordsman had apparently early established, not just his reputation for flamboyant vivacity and wit, but his fictional background as well. A later version of the same story, as retold by Father Niceron, sees an interesting variant creeping in. Where Grimarest had Cyrano being reluctantly accepted into a group, where his excitable temperament was at odds with the studious atmosphere, Niceron has Cyrano effecting his entry sword in hand and intimidating the students and their master with his threats. This is a good example of the way that exaggeration was to blacken Cyrano's reputation and set his story off down the path of caricature.

Cyrano's later work reveals that however turbulent he may have been, he was certainly also an enthusiastic and talented student. He was passionate about communicating and exploring the ideas of the new philosophy and he is careful to cite Gassendi by name and note the importance of the great man's work. Cyrano never completed his studies at the Collège de Lisieux, his name does not figure on the list of those taking their degrees and it seems probable that, having found a richer and far more modern curriculum being taught by Gassendi, he soon abandoned the more traditional educational model as a result. It was to Chapelle, as much as to Gassendi himself, that Cyrano owed the favour of his acceptance into this erudite company and, according to the bitter comments made in later life by an aged Dassoucy, he was also beholden to Chapelle for lodging, food and drink and probably for more besides.

In his semi-autobiographical work *The Adventures of M. Dassoucy*, the author describes being introduced to the sixteen-year-old Chapelle by Cyrano and talks about having shared Chapelle's bed. Dassoucy's version of events is naturally clouded by the fact that he could not write openly about homosexual relationships but he strongly implies that Cyrano and Chapelle were lovers. The simple fact is that, without clearer evidence, the exact details of the enmity that later erupted between Cyrano and Dassoucy will remain a matter of speculation. Literary quarrel or lovers' tiff? Romantic or intellectual rivalry? Either is possible and, although Cyrano's outpouring of angry vitriol against his former friend has been read as, either the excoriating fury of a betrayed lover, or the righteous anger of a plagiarized author, perhaps the most likely answer is that it was a little of both. The quarrel is one to which we will return, but at this stage in the early 1640s, whatever romantic entanglements there may have been between the three men, they seem to have been frequent companions and good friends, and to have remained so for the best part of the decade.

The love letters are the works for which the fictional Cyrano is best known and a vitally important plot device in Rostand's play. And yet, although the real Cyrano was not above using his literary talent to engage in passionate and playful games of seduction, he was always more interested in subversion than sentiment and was not a man to concentrate his energies solely on the pursuit of romance, or to spill his deepest feelings on to the page for public consumption. The very elusiveness of Cyrano's secret emotions has stimulated legions of later authors to proclaim their own inventions as the key to the mystery.

In 1927 Louis-Raymond Lefèvre published a *Life of Cyrano de Bergerac* in which he dedicated a chapter to revealing the secrets of Cyrano's love life. He claims to have been scrupulously exact in his research but admits to having 'taken the liberty' in the absence of any documentary evidence to the contrary, of supposing that all Cyrano's love letters were addressed to one woman. Lefèvre weaves together various details from the letters such as the encounter at a fishing party and the gift of bracelets woven from the beloved's hair and from these disparate elements he constructs a vivid and unhappy tale. Lefèvre's Cyrano is clearly a descendant of Rostand's creation sharing the stage Cyrano's romantic soul. He has waited in vain for an encounter with the perfectly beautiful and noble creature who will live up to his soaring ideals: 'a woman worthy of his spirit, and capable of enjoying not just sensual pleasures but the refined passion which the "*précieuses*" had celebrated. He sighed in anticipation as he waited for fate to bring him this dream woman.'[5] Rather cruelly fate (or rather L.-R. Lefèvre) sends Cyrano, not his soulmate, but a red-haired temptress named Alexie, who is the polar opposite of the virtuous and idealistic Roxane. The avaricious Alexie nearly bankrupts her naive admirer, mercilessly exploiting his generosity and then, when he can no longer continue paying her many debts, she heartlessly casts him aside. The day after their split the desolate Cyrano wakes up to the realization that his dream woman has infected him with the pox. Whatever the reality behind its creation, Cyrano's letter 'For a red-haired lady', is one of the gems of his early work. Thanks to its combination of playfulness and sensuality, it remains one of the most effective and touching of all the published love letters. Reading the closing lines one can scarcely blame Lefèvre for his extravagant flights of fancy:

> Therefore, since we must all become slaves to beauty, would it not be better to lose our freedom in chains of gold, than chains of hemp, or iron? For myself all that I desire, o my beautiful M . . ., is that in wandering at liberty amongst these little labyrinths of gold that you have for hair, I should soon lose myself there; and all that I wish for is never to recover my freedom once lost, if you would but promise me that my life will not last longer than my servitude; and that you will not be angry if I declare myself, until death,
>
> Madame,
>
> Your I know not what?[6]

Cyrano's love letters may conceal as much as they reveal but there are undeniably moments in them that do seem to suggest the inspiration of genuine feeling, especially in the letters that were not published during his lifetime. The shortest of all the unpublished letters describes the writer's desperation after a day's separation from his beloved with an anguished simplicity that is worlds away from the studied imagery and convoluted witticisms to be found elsewhere. This little unsigned note is also the only letter which uses the familiar 'tu' form of address; this was not common in seventeenth-century correspondence. Even in letters between spouses it is more usual to find the 'vous' form, and so the note has an additional urgency and tenderness. The note is also unusual because it bears no signature and no formal opening; the addressee is indicated only by the initial M. The letter 'For a red-haired lady' is also addressed to the mysterious M.

As a writer, Cyrano always revelled in the possibilities of double meaning and paradox and seems to have found the love letter a particularly rich field for his inventive, playful wit. Love letter IV opens with declaration, 'Far from having lost my heart when I rendered you the homage of my freedom, on the contrary, I find that, since that day, my heart has grown much larger.'[7] He confounds his reader's expectation by announcing the exact opposite of a traditional lover's plaint. It is vital to recognize that the 'love letters' written by the real Cyrano are not private documents. They were written for the amusement of a select public and circulated in manuscript copies. They first appeared collected together in print in 1654 when the Duc d'Arpajon arranged for the editor Charles de Sercy to publish a selection of Cyrano's works under the title *Oeuvres Diverses*. Other similar collections of love letters also appeared around the same time, such as the *Lettres de Babet* which were promoted as the authentic correspondence between Babet and her suitor, but which are clearly a fictional construction with playful set pieces and a carefully constructed plot. Another collection, the *Lettres Portugaises*, were ostensibly translated from the original Portuguese and consist of the increasingly desperate pleas of a young Portuguese woman named Mariane who had been seduced and abandoned by a French knight. Critics agree that there may well have been a genuine relationship behind these letters, convincing historical counterparts for the real Mariane and her knight having been identified in Mariana Alcoforada and the Comte de Chamilly. But the published version is a literary piece, a fictional work by the letters' 'translator' the Comte de Guilleragues.

The notable exception to the rule that love letters which made it into the public domain did so because their composition owed more to art than to emotion was the work of Marie-Catherine Desjardins whose *Lettres et billets galants* were published in 1667 despite her attempts to prevent their disclosure. Marie-Catherine was something of a literary celebrity, a successful authoress celebrated for her wit. The letters had been written to her lover Antoine Boësset, Sieur de Villedieu and they reveal the painful (for her at least) disintegration of the relationship. It seems that these letters became well known because the loathsome Villedieu, in spite of his growing indifference and infidelity, was encouraging Marie-Catherine to write to him in order to have the cachet of showing off her letters to his friends and acquaintances. Marie-Catherine seems to have struggled with her growing awareness of Villedieu's true character and the strength of her infatuation with him. In spite of significant periods of cohabitation, two signed promises of marriage and once having made it as far as the altar, where an ecclesiastical technicality prevented the ceremony from going ahead as planned, Villedieu and Marie-Catherine never married.

He eventually succeeded in persuading her to formally renounce her two signed marriage promises in order to let him marry someone else. Marie-Catherine seems to have accepted this final humiliation thanks to reassurances from Villedieu that she would remain his mistress and his one true love. It would have been perfectly credible to her that Villedieu's marriage was not a matter of the heart. But sadly the worst was yet to come. Just a few months after Villedieu's wedding France declared war on Spain and Villedieu, who was the captain of a regiment, found himself urgently needing to raise money. He borrowed from his brother and secured the rest by selling Marie-Catherine's love letters to the printer Barbin.

At first Marie-Catherine refused to believe that Villedieu would stoop so low and convinced herself that a thief must have been responsible for bringing her inmost thoughts and sufferings into the public domain. She asked friends to institute an investigation and to start legal proceedings against the thief, but her instructions included a proviso to protect Villedieu if he turned out to be the guilty party: 'If you can not defend me except by ruining him entirely, do not defend me at all I beg you.'[8] It is fairly clear that she knew what the truth of the situation would be and although her intermediaries succeeded in gettting her name removed from the letters they were unable to stop the publication. Just three months later Villedieu was killed on the battlefield at Lille. After his death his official widow quickly remarried and Marie-Catherine was thus free to continue calling herself Mme de Villedieu. Which she did for another decade until she finally married and started a family.

Marie-Catherine's letters ended up in the public domain in spite of her ardent desire to suppress them and their sincerity is further underlined by the circumstances of their publication. In contrast, Cyrano's letters do not form a coherent whole, nor can they be read as part of a recognizable dynamic of courtship or betrayal and their appearance in print was controlled and supervised by their author. Contradictory though it may seem after dismissing the letters as a source of information about Cyrano's life, it has recently been argued that a manuscript copy of one of Cyrano's letters holds the key to his disputed sexuality. Scholars have unearthed a version of the letter which is addressed to 'Monsieur', rather than 'Madame' as in all the other versions. This particular letter is one of the most irreverent and salacious that Cyrano ever penned and Jacques Prévot, working on the hint given by a reference to Saint Denis, identifies a possible masculine recipient in Charles de Marguetel de Saint Denis, seigneur de Saint-Evremond, a libertine five years Cyrano's senior. Charles de Saint-Evremond was a life-long friend of the fabulously free-spirited courtesan Ninon de Lenclos and a writer who pleaded for religious toleration and temperate hedonism. A man after Cyrano's own heart, perhaps literally. The distinguished Cyrano critic Madeleine Alcover also points out that the dancing and fencing lessons which Cyrano undertook may also point to his homosexuality. She compares the premises of these all-male establishments to ancient Greek gymnasia. Whatever Cyrano's sexuality, it is unlikely that this was his primary reason for undertaking the lessons, and Alcover herself has unearthed documentary evidence that Cyrano may have felt a need to refresh his sword arm.

Four months before signing the contract with Masters Dupron

and Moussard, Cyrano and a young friend, named Louis Prévost de Dimier, had been involved in a fight with a student from another college. The manuscript of the agreement, reached to settle the matter, reveals certain details which reflect rather badly on our young hero. In a notarized document, dated 18 June 1641, Cyrano's mother signed her agreement to pay 15 livres in damages to the student named Le Heurteur, who had been assaulted by her son and his 'accomplice', as well as 15 livres to the surgeon, who treated Le Heurteur, and an unspecified amount to the college authorities to guarantee that the matter would go no further. She also testified that her son's épée and his friend's cloak had been returned to them at the same time. This is an important detail in a legal case of the time since both were valuable possessions, cloaks in particular were often the object of street robberies. The tumultuous chain of events that led to the two young men attacking another and then fleeing the scene leaving their possessions behind them is probably best left to the imagination. This is not an episode that Le Bret saw fit to include in his biography and it is a little difficult to reconcile the role of invincible duellist which Cyrano fashioned for himself, with this aperçu into the humiliation of an unruly student, who not only apparently breaks the code of the duel by fighting two against one, but also loses his sword in the brawl and ends up called to order by the college authorities and bailed out by his own mother. Here is the reverse image of the duel with one hundred men and a weaker, more human side to the legendary figure.

In Rostand's play the true motivation for Cyrano's Herculean battle is that his extraordinary courage has been further bolstered by an unexpected ray of hope in his love for Roxane. Having been informed by her maid that she wishes to see him in private, the next day he cannot control his excitement and leaps at the chance to dissipate his energies in a feat of extraordinary bravery. He drags the reluctant Lignières to his feet and insists on escorting him home himself in order to confront the armed ambush at the de

Nesle gate. Above all else, Rostand's play is a love story. The heart of the plot is Cyrano's doomed passion for his beautiful cousin Madeleine Robin, known as Roxane.

The real Madeleine was born on 24 August 1609, making her a decade older than Cyrano. Her actual surname was Robineau and she was a distant cousin of Cyrano's on his mother's side of the family. Their maternal grandmothers were cousins, both named Catherine. The lowliness of Cyrano's origins has been rather exaggerated; as we have seen, his mother's side of the family were wealthy financiers. The real-life Roxane married Christophe de Champagne, Baron de Neuvillette on 20 February 1635. In keeping with her riches and position her husband was a nobleman, but the match also seems to have had an important romantic element.

Sadly, a few years later, the unfortunate baron was killed at the siege of Arras, just as in the play, leaving a devastated and heart-broken widow to mourn his loss. On losing her husband, Rostand's Roxane retires from the world to live in a convent and spend the rest of her life mourning the death of a man whom she had never really got to know, having only just married him in a hurriedly improvised ceremony when he is sent off to fight. The real Madeleine, who had been married for five years when she lost her husband, reacted even more dramatically. When the news came, she had only recently lost her mother and she was heavily pregnant; she soon suffered a third bereavement as the child was stillborn. She must have felt terribly alone. On hearing of her husband's death in battle, she became obsessed with the fact that he had not had the chance to make a final confession and was thus condemned to the sufferings of purgatory. As the ghost of Hamlet's father eloquently puts it:

> *Cut off even in the blossoms of my sin,*
> *Unhouseled, dis-appointed, unaneled,*

No reck'ning made, but sent to my account
With all my imperfections on my head.
O horrible, O horrible, most horrible!

It was not in Madeleine's power to release her husband's spirit from the horrors of purgatory by avenging his murder as the ghost begs Hamlet to do, but in her desperation, tormented by visions of his suffering, she beseeched her confessor whether it might not be possible for her to ransom her husband's soul with her own. She declared herself ready to go to hell in his stead if only his soul could be guaranteed eternal life in Paradise. Madeleine's spiritual advisor assured her that such a pact was impossible and that all she could do was to devote the rest of her life to piety and good works and pray regularly for the soul of her departed husband. This was exactly what the distraught widow decided to do but rather than entering a convent she dedicated her time to visiting the condemned prisoners in the hideous, stinking cells of the Conciergerie prison. She would bring food and drink to the doomed criminals, pleading with the lost souls to confess their sins and repent before it was too late. She would even accompany them to the foot of the scaffold, determined not to abandon her self-appointed mission until all hope was definitively lost.

Madeleine's piety impressed one Father Cyprien de la Nativité so much that on her death in 1660, he published a biography entitled *Compendium of the virtues and the writings of Madame the Baroness of Neuvillette recently deceased in the city of Paris*. In her youth Madeleine had been a beautiful girl dedicated to luxury and pleasure. Before losing her husband she was high-spirited, witty and slightly spoilt. Father Cyprien notes that she was not just lovely to look at but also intelligent, possessed of a 'brilliant mind'. He also admits that Madeleine lost her looks relatively young, suggesting that her over-indulgence in the finer things of life had rapidly transformed her into a considerably less attractive figure. He reveals that in her later years it was no longer obvious that she had once been a beauty. He notes that even so she retained a certain something which singled her out among her sex as someone out of the ordinary. There was no tragic love affair between Cyrano and his cousin, but they were united in possessing equally headstrong and individualistic characters. In their very different ways both found themselves attracting the attention of their peers and standing out from the crowd in their determination to follow their own conception of what was right, rather than what society expected.

Madeleine's determination to make a difference in the lives of those around her is tremendously admirable, all the more so in an age when it took uncommon courage for a woman to act for herself and attempt to retain some degree of autonomy. Madeleine's spiritual advisor had expected her to confine herself to a convent, praying quietly and allowing him to take care of administering her fortune for the benefit of selected good causes. Her wilful independence and personal ministrations to dying criminals were considered vaguely scandalous. Madeleine's biographer notes the hostility of her neighbours, who dismissed her as 'insane and laughable', irritated perhaps by her habit of borrowing money in order to make charitable donations. Even her friends were to dismiss her fervour as 'madness' and 'hypochondria', as Madeleine took to wearing a hair shirt and a *cilice*, the spiked belt that cuts into the skin, in order to mortify the flesh and purify the soul.

The possibilities for women in Cyrano's day were strictly limited and those who stood out against the overwhelming pressure to conform were all the more notable. The celebrated courtesan Ninon de Lenclos reacted to the constraints and unfairness of a woman's lot by deciding that the rules simply did not apply to her. She famously declared: 'men enjoy thousands of freedoms that women do not taste. Therefore I will be a man.'[9] Ninon's extraordinary career and those of the two peasant women who went to war disguised as men and calling themselves Antoine de

L'Espérance and Pierre de la Jeunesse, were the startling exceptions to a general rule of obedience, repression and an oppressive lack of freedom. Witness the heartfelt cry of Montaigne's adopted daughter Mlle de Gournay in her 1622 work *Égalité des hommes et des femmes*: 'Blessed are you, reader, if you are not of that sex to whom all property is forbidden, depriving them of freedom,[. . .] in order to allow for their sole felicity for their only sovereign virtues: ignorance, servitude and the ability to play the fool if that game should appeal.'[10]

Her frustration is understandable; not only were women forced into dependence and subordination but misogyny was rife. In Cyrano's lifetime, books were published with titles like *The Purgatory of Married Men*, *The Foolish Antics of the Women of Today* and the bestselling *Alphabet of the Imperfection and Malice of Women* that went through twelve sell-out editions in thirty years. Young girls received no formal education of the sort available to their brothers. The century did see the beginning of a big shift in popular literacy as basic schooling was slowly extended to include female children, and the expansion of parish schools meant that even the poorest families increasingly had access (at least theoretically) to the basics of reading and writing. But further education was not an option for girls, however intelligent, and the best they could hope for, aside from initiation into domestic management, was to be sent to a convent for purely religious instruction. Despite this distinct lack of opportunity, many seventeenth-century young women contrived to become cultured, intellectual beings in their own right. Just at the point when many boys were gratefully closing their books on leaving school behind, the girls leaving their convents were opening them with equal eagerness.

Cyrano never married and an air of mystery surrounds his relations with the fairer sex. He was probably gay, rather than simply biding his time, waiting to meet the right woman, as his nineteenth-century biographers have suggested. We will return to

Cyrano's emotional entanglements later, but for now suffice to say that homosexuality would not necessarily have been a bar to a shrewd matrimonial alliance, as the marriages of the flamboyantly gay King Henri III, or that in Cyrano's own lifetime of the Prince de Condé demonstrated. In Cyrano's era, marriage as an institution was seldom regarded as the sanctification of a romantic or sexual liaison, it was essentially a dynastic and financial arrangement. The total lack of cupidity in Cyrano's nature may therefore partly explain his failure to secure himself an advantageous alliance with the aid of those rich maternal relations. In the seventeenth century, women were all too often considered as little more than a useful commodity to be shrewdly traded. The author of the *Entretiens spirituels* revealingly advises that in marriage, as in any contract, the choice of partner should be considered most carefully, with as much assiduous attention to detail as for 'the purchase of a horse, a house or an annuity'.[11] The celebrated Mlle de Scudéry expressed a decidedly pessimistic view of the married state which is perhaps unsurprising in an era when a woman's own views on her future marriage were the last to be consulted. 'One marries in order to hate. It is for that reason that no true lover should ever speak of marriage, because to be a lover is to want to be loved and to want to be a husband is to want to be hated.'[12] This attitude is echoed by one of the characters in the novel *La Prétieuse* by the Abbé de Pure. 'I was an innocent victim sacrificed to unknown motives and to the obscure interests of the family, but sacrificed like a slave bound and gagged [. . .] I was entombed or rather I was buried alive in my shroud in Evandre's son's bed.'[13]

In certain instances the metaphor of the reluctant bride delivered bound and gagged as a slave to her husband's family took on a horrifying reality. It was not uncommon for heiresses, as young as ten or eleven, to be kidnapped and married against their will and even against that of their own family. In his memoirs, Cyrano's contemporary Bussy-Rabutin claims to have been tricked into kidnapping a young, recently widowed heiress, having been wrongly assured that she was willing to marry him. Luckily for the young woman, Bussy was not an entirely unscrupulous fortune hunter and, as he attempted to extricate himself from this messy situation, the incident veered into the realms of farce rather than those of tragedy. Bussy found himself pursued on and off in the courts for compensation in the lengthy legal battle which followed. The heiress's outraged family refused to give in to the pressure exerted by Bussy's protector the Prince de Condé. Condé was a great general who famously had numerous camp followers; Bussy was one of the few straight men to form part of his inner circle. Widowhood could prove a boon, greatly increasing a woman's personal freedom and it seems that Bussy's heiress, Mme de Miramion, was far from keen to abandon the state. Instead, she chose, like Madeleine, to devote the rest of her life and fortune to good works. She founded a refuge for fallen women. Charitable works of this sort were the one sphere of activity in which women could exercise some degree of autonomy, although as Madeleine's example demonstrates even such selfless activity was deemed irrational and suspicious.

Rostand's Roxane is described as one of the *précieuses*, and Christian is all the more intimidated by her on discovering that she belongs to this fashionable group of female intellectuals, whose objections to the manifold inconveniences of the married state were well known. These objections were undoubtedly well founded in a justifiable dissatisfaction. They were not expressed as such, but rather as the celebration of a platonic alternative, a sort of chivalric ideal of loving friendship. In fact, Rostand's identification of Madeleine Robineau as one of the précieuses was probably based on a case of mistaken identity. The woman who featured, as the beautiful Roxane, in the pages of the *Dictionnaire Précieuses*, was actually Marie Robineau, no relation.

The real women who dedicated themselves to the précieuse ideal of cultivated refinement were soon overshadowed by their exaggerated fictional counterparts. Their excessive linguistic refinements and their fascination with gallantry and with lengthy, highly idealized romantic novels made these witty and cultivated women an easy target for ridicule. Never one to miss the opportunity for a good laugh, Molière penned *Les Précieuses ridicules* which premièred in 1659. This satire, aimed squarely at the pretensions of the female salon wits, caused a scandal on its first appearance and Molière attempted to mollify the important female members of his courtly audience, who considered themselves personally targeted by the play, by specifying that his heroines were only ignorant provincials, aping the nobility and making fools of themselves in the process. After the tremendous popular success of *Les Précieuses ridicules*, Molière went on to target female intellectuals more directly in *Les Femmes Savantes* (1672). In this play, one of the characters betrays the hypocrisy of the male response to female learning. Essentially he says that it is all right for women to be intelligent and knowledgeable as long as they hide it well:

> *In short, if she must study I don't want her to show it,*
> *She should have knowledge without wanting everyone to know it.*[14]

The writer Guez de Balzac was even less polite than Molière, declaring robustly: 'I would as lief endure a woman with a beard as one of these women who try to be savante.'[15]

Cyrano moved in more enlightened circles; his good friend the mathematician Jacques Rouhault gave weekly lectures on physics to the nobility at which the front row was always reserved for ladies. Cyrano's lifetime saw growing numbers of learned women making up for the deficiencies of their early instruction with wide reading. This trend was made possible by the increasing numbers of savants, like Descartes, choosing to publish in the vernacular rather than in Latin. Cyrano's mentor Gassendi, on the other hand, was one of those who stuck to the old scholarly tradition and who published all his scientific writings in Latin. This has been suggested as one of the reasons that his importance and the modernity of many of his ideas were long overlooked.

Towards the end of the century, another author, Bernard de Bovier la Fontenelle, published a vernacular discussion of the new ideas in astronomy, framed as a series of conversations between the author and an intelligent and well-informed young woman. In the preface to his book, *On the Plurality of Worlds* (1686), he explained that he hoped that the example of the young woman in his work would inspire and 'encourage' other young women to an appreciation of his subject matter and to the recognition that following the ideas of the new science required no greater effort than following the plot of the popular romantic novel *La Princesse de Clèves*.* From the testimony of Madame de Sévigné it seems that women were indeed increasingly at the forefront in the enthusiastic reception of new ideas. On 17 December 1664 she noted how the enthusiasm of her female friends ultimately convinced even blasé courtiers like d'Artagnan to show an interest in the appearance of a notable astronomical phenomenon. 'For four days now a comet has appeared. At first it was only talked about by women and no one cared, but now everyone has seen it. M. d'Artagnan stayed up last night to see it much to his satisfaction.'[16]

In Cyrano's lifetime things were changing for female intellectuals, but slowly. Cyrano played with the still scandalous notion of an intelligent and well-informed female when he cast the prettiest and sweetest woman in the court of the moon as an acute social commentator. This is a deliberate equivocation allowing for a double reading: Cyrano puts his most telling criticisms of the futility of war into the mouth of this charming and gentle lunar noblewoman and, in doing so, he neatly evades criticism. His

---

* Fittingly, the first English translation of this text published in 1688, was the work of Aphra Behn, one of the first women to make a living from her pen.

provocative dismissal of soldiers and generals alike can be over-looked as laughable and harmless, coming from the mouth of a beautiful young woman, whose words no one on earth would take seriously. This was a clever tactic, because a reader, who was suffi-ciently forward thinking to accept that a woman might have an intelligent and pertinent point to make, would consequently also be one unlikely to object to the radical opinions she expresses, and vice versa. The real Cyrano openly ridiculed the exaggerated gal-lantry that the précieuses so admired and which Rostand's Roxane demands of her hybrid lover.

In the *Voyage to the Sun*, Cyrano's hero meets a woman who is a native of 'the Republic of Truth'. She has come to live in 'the Nation of Lovers' and her literal interpretations of the traditional overly refined and metaphorical language used by her suitors (a pas-tiche of the literary style affected by the précieuses) highlight their inanity. She is so disturbed and terrified by the protestations of her lovers, that they 'cry seas and floods of tears for her sake' and that her 'merest glance can cause a mortal wound', that she determines to commit suicide. The most absurd and vehement of her admir-ers, known only as *Le Jaloux* (the jealous one), persuades the unfortunate young woman to this extreme course of action and assures her that her best escape route from the world will be to tear out her own heart to use as a vessel to carry her away. He declares that she need not fear that it can hold her, since it can hold so many others, nor that it will sink since it is so light, and that the 'favourable wind of his sighs will carry [her] safe to port in spite of the tempest of his rivals'. Fortunately, the young woman is inter-rupted by another of her admirers as she is attempting to cut out her own heart. The rival saves the young woman and the jealous lover is brought to justice for his crime: '. . . condemned to ban-ishment for life and to end his days as a slave in the territories of the Republic of Truth with a prohibition to all his descendants down to the fourth generation to set foot in the Province of the Lovers;

moreover, he was enjoined never to use hyperboles on pain of death.'[17]

Cyrano's satisfaction with a world where a man could be banned from using hyperbole, on pain of death, is evident, and perhaps reveals a further gap between the fictional Cyrano and his historical counterpart. The stage Cyrano masterminds an elaborate poetic deception that wins him the heart (if not the hand) of his beloved mistress – the real Cyrano was above all a proud citizen of the Republic of Truth. He questioned the honesty of lovers' eloquence and wrote a series of love letters which were more satirical than sentimental and seem designed to mock the very protestations they contain. The real Cyrano was particularly alert to the rich source of comedy provided by the convoluted sexual politics of his time. Fans of the fictional Cyrano may be disappointed to learn that there is no corresponding tragic love story to be told about the real Cyrano. Perhaps they may also allow that his outspoken defence of individuality, passion and personal freedom, his devotion to ideals of sincerity and loyalty are a more important legacy than any gossipy account of his love life could ever be.

9

Paternoster of the wolf

Cyrano's family background was one of religious conformity and even devotion. By the time Cyrano returned from the war, his older brother Denis had entered the priesthood. This is rather unusual because Denis was the eldest son. He stood to inherit his father's entire estate and would therefore normally have been expected to make a good marriage and carry on the family name. Cyrano's sister Catherine also chose religion rather than marriage and a family. She had entered the Parisian convent of the Daughters of the Cross, in rue de Charonne, in 1637. In 1641, the year of Cyrano's return to Paris, she made her final vows and changed her name to Sister Hyacinthe. Her parents had to pay for her board and lodging during her probationary year and then provide her with a dowry which represented a significant investment. Abel's will reveals that he also owned several expensive works of religious art.

Cyrano's unorthodox opinions were clearly not just a reaction against mainstream society but also a more personal rebellion against a more than usually devout family. Although the real Cyrano may have been somewhat reticent about revealing the details of his private, emotional life, when it came to his intellectual convictions he was determinedly outspoken and never more so than when his opinions went against the norm. He was not afraid to confront the very darkest aspects of the society in which he lived. Having abandoned his military career for the intellectual life, Cyrano seems to have quickly discovered that his boundless imagination and dark wit were best suited to satire. His writing career encompassed a range of styles and over a period of a decade he was to produce two plays (a tragedy and a comedy), some verse (of which the surviving examples are mainly those written in praise of his writer friends and published in their works), various letters and a two-volume science fiction novel. We will come to the story of how his works finally made it into print later. At this stage in his career, Cyrano seems to have settled quietly in Paris and lived a fairly simple life. He had a private income from his family that was not large enough to allow him any great extravagances, but enough money to live off and so he was able to devote all his time to studying the subjects that interested him. He does not seem to have actively pursued commercial publication at this stage and so he also had total freedom to write about whatever he chose.

Often he chose the most controversial and difficult subjects possible. His determination to provoke is constantly in evidence. Even in the love letters he maintained a deliberately irreverent and occasionally downright blasphemous levity. Certain details are not without unexpected significance; the mysterious red-haired 'M' who features in the letter already mentioned is not purely a romantic figure. It is no accident that the letter focuses on the glory of the beloved's flaming red hair; at the time red hair was linked to witchcraft and devilry and was considered as something of a curse. Cyrano begins his letter by stating his intention to defy such superstitious nonsense and to admire M's hair 'like a man of sense'. In Cyrano's lifetime, belief in the Devil was as fundamental a part of Catholic orthodoxy as belief in God. As a result, belief in witchcraft and demonic possession as tangible works of the Devil was considered a firm proof of piety. A strong link had been forged between freethinking and sorcery; the refusal to believe in the terrifying hysteria of the witch-hunt was considered tantamount to denying the existence of God. The English philosopher Joseph Glanvill makes this explicit in his book *Philosophical Considerations touching Witches and Witchcraft*: 'Those that dare not bluntly say, "There is no God" content themselves (for a fair step and introduction) to deny that there are spirits and witches.'[1] Glanvill prided himself on being a deeply rational man and was an enthusiastic founding member of the Royal Society of London for the Improvement of Natural Knowledge; he would not have dreamt of putting forward a proposition such as the existence of witches and demons without strong evidence. Thus he assembled a series of thirty-five detailed accounts of incidents of demonic possession, haunting and sorcery which, when advertised as 'Proof of Apparitions, Spirits and Witches from a choice collection of modern Relations', went a long way to assuring the book's popular success.

Cyrano de Bergerac, on the other hand, remained magnificently scornful of the whole phenomenon. He dedicated two of his published letters to the subject, ostensibly writing the cases for and against the existence of witches. In fact both letters argue forcibly against. In the seventeenth century, to suggest, as Cyrano did, that witchcraft was nothing more than a pitiful mass of peasant superstition and popular credulity was to court serious controversy. Serious scientific thinkers such as Francis Bacon, René Descartes and Johannes Kepler all accepted witchcraft as an obvious part of life – why then was Cyrano so determined to swim against the tide?

The letter 'Against Witches' contains the most passionate, spontaneous outpouring of Cyrano's particular brand of individualistic idealism to be found anywhere in his works:

No, I do not remotely believe in Witches, even though many great Persons have not been of my opinion, and I defer to no one's authority, unless accompanied by reason . . . Neither the name of Aristotle, more learned than me, nor that of Plato, nor that of Socrates persuade me one jot, if my judgement is not convinced by the reason of what they say. Reason alone is my queen . . .

For Cyrano, as the product of a profoundly conformist background, there was more at stake in a consideration of the subject of witchcraft than the supposed crimes committed by some toothless crone in a remote, forgotten village. He chose the subject to be a test case for his challenge to the supremacy of dogma over deduction, of belief over reason. Cyrano's letters on witchcraft also reveal his fascination with the sheer imaginative scope provided by the supernatural. In the letter 'For Witches', he recounts a series of delirious visions culminating in a dramatic encounter with an aged sorcerer. With typical perversity, this damnable subject matter inspired Cyrano to passages of breathtaking lyrical beauty. Cyrano opens the letter by setting the scene; he observes with careful precision the way the natural world offers eerie presages of the strange adventure to follow:

I saw the stars shimmering in the sky with a sparkling fire; the moon was full, but much paler than normal: there were three eclipses and three times the moon seemed to hurtle down out of her sphere; the winds were paralysed, the fountains were silent, birds forgot their song, fish seemed encased in glass; not an animal moved except for the small movement of their trembling; the horror of a terrifying silence reigned throughout and everywhere Nature seemed to be in suspense awaiting some great adventure.[2]

Despite entitling the letter 'For Witches', Cyrano was actually intent, not on proving the existence of witches, but on parodying 'the dark and ridiculous imaginings' of traditional accounts of demons and sorcerers. The scene takes place at midnight by the light of a full moon; Cyrano describes being abducted and flown to the middle of a wood on an enchanted broomstick. These were familiar elements in accounts of witchcraft given by those accused and facing the stake. The mysterious sorcerer that Cyrano encounters in the dark wood also behaves in a way which Cyrano's readership would have recognized from the popular printed accounts of famous cases of demonic possession; at one point the old man falls to the ground and contorts his body into strange shapes and throughout the mysterious ceremony that he performs to summon a demon he issues strange cries and invocations. Contortions, fits and speaking in tongues were considered clear symptoms of demonic possession. Occasionally, the more sceptical observers present at public exorcisms noted that the demons possessing the victims seemed to have a surprisingly shaky grasp of Latin and no knowledge at all of Greek.

Cyrano's magician betrays no such weaknesses. Sporting a flowing beard and long white robes with a half-dead bat pinned over his heart, he performs a complex and mysterious ceremony. Still more impressively, his performance of these arcane rites is accompanied by whirlwinds, blood-red hail, thunderstorms and a rain of fire. Natural special effects of this sort were far from a consistent feature of the cases of demonic possession with which Cyrano's audience would have been so familiar. They add enormously to the theatricality and dreamlike atmosphere that Cyrano required to make his point about the difference between reality and 'ridiculous imaginings'. The magic ceremony which the old man then performs before Cyrano's very eyes involves the evisceration of a fox, a mole and a screech owl. The old man devours their hearts and mixes up a concoction of their blood with fresh dew. He spouts bizarre incantations and draws various mystic circles on the ground.

These latter, less noxious aspects of his practice recall the magical antics of another old man who appears performing a mysterious secret ceremony. The opening of Charles Sorel's 1623 novel *The Comical History of Francion* features the conjurations of the character Valentin. Unlike the terrifying sorcerer Agrippa who features in Cyrano's letter, Valentin turns out to be just a harmless old fool whom the hero Francion has tricked into performing an elaborate series of 'conjurations' in order to summon up a demon to cure his impotence. Francion takes full advantage of the old man's credulity, sending his valet to perform the role of the demon and tie the terrified old man to a tree, leaving Francion free to set off for his prearranged rendezvous for a night of passion with Valentin's beautiful (and frustrated) young wife, Laurette. Like Cyrano, Sorel was a sceptic and a libertin and he makes a vivid point about the possibility that 'magic' is all too often little more than the means for an unscrupulous swindler to take advantage of a gullible mark. Ben Jonson explored the same idea in his 1610 play *The Alchemist*.

Cyrano's Agrippa, on the other hand, is apparently no confidence trickster but the genuine article. Born in Cologne in 1486, Henry Cornelius Agrippa von Nettesheim was reputed (largely due to his own exorbitant claims) to be a fearsome sorcerer. Despite his claims to have discovered the philosopher's stone, the real Agrippa died a pauper's death in 1535. Cyrano's tall tale in the letter 'For Witches' playfully resurrects him and in doing so vindicates the old man's claim to have discovered the elixir of eternal life. At the climax of their encounter Agrippa addresses a long speech to Cyrano in which he describes in loving detail the scope of his magic powers and the evil uses to which he puts them.

According to his own account this all-powerful magician can start wars, influence the harvests, drown unwary travellers, make fairies dance in the moonlight, inspire gamblers to search under the gibbet for a lucky four-leafed clover. He describes how he liberates spirits from their graves at midnight and sends them, garbed in the obligatory sheet that no self-respecting phantom would be without, to demand that their heirs fulfil their dying wishes. He also explains that he is responsible for causing demons to haunt abandoned castles, lurking in readiness to slit the throat of any unwary peasant who might attempt to seek shelter there, guarding the secret of the treasure buried in the ruins. He claims to have taught shepherds to recite 'the Paternoster of the wolf'. It was common in contemporary witch trials for the accused to describe the demonic ceremonies of the 'sabbath' as reversed or perverted versions of traditional elements of Catholic worship. Hence the 'Paternoster of the wolf' is an unholy counterpart to the Lord's prayer. This is just one example of the ways in which demonology was dependent on orthodoxy for its very existence.

Cyrano's sorcerer also claims to be able to bestow the magical mandragore or 'hand of glory' on any pauper he should wish to enrich. He prompts thieves to burn candles made of the fat of a hanged man in order to enchant unwitting householders to sleep soundly while they are burgled. He knows the secret of enchanted coins which will keep flying back to the owner's pocket every time they are used in payment for something and of magic rings which can transport a person across the country in a single day. He claims responsibility for the appearance of poltergeists and for showing old women how to cure fevers with only words. He explains that he teaches other sorcerers how to turn themselves into werewolves, forcing them to eat any children they should encounter once they are transformed and then abandoning them when some brave soul cuts off their wolf's paw which then mysteriously turns into a human hand, leading to them being recognized and brought to justice. He also claims to be able to cure werewolves with a pitchfork wound between the eyes. He sends a tall dark man to trick fools into signing away their souls in a pact with the Devil. He blinds people crossing witches on their way to the Sabbath into seeing nothing but a group of cats. He orchestrates the obscene ceremonies of the witches' Sabbath. He sends incubi to the beds of lustful women and succubi to the beds of lecherous men. He teaches sadistic subjects how to make wax voodoo images of an enemy and then to inflict harm on them by sticking pins into the model or throwing it in the fire. He prevents butter from forming in the churn. He instructs vengeful peasants to put a knot of hair or a toad under the sheepfold belonging to the farmer they wish to ruin, with the result that all the sheep who cross over the hidden talisman inevitably fall down dead. He imparts the secret of the much dreaded curse which caused impotence to strike a man on his wedding night. He can conjure up money which once spent reveals itself to be nothing more than a handful of enchanted leaves. He knows the secrets of ghosts, magic mirrors, charms and talismans of every sort.

This extraordinary and exhausting list of achievements represents nothing less than a catalogue of popular superstitions current in Cyrano's time. The average peasant (or even educated man of science like Joseph Glanvill) would see nothing to contradict in any of the individual elements of this list, but by putting them all together and attributing them all to one great sorcerer, Cyrano highlights the implausibility and ridiculousness of these superstitions. Separately, each claim has a certain eerie power but heaped together in this way their improbability is manifest. As a true son of the scientific revolution, Cyrano is assembling the evidence in order to consider the likelihood or possibility of witchcraft. As Glanvill's work demonstrates, both those who believed and those who doubted the existence of witches felt that their cause would be best served by careful study of all the evidence. It was essential, therefore, to ascertain what could be reasonably accepted as 'evidence'. In the letter 'Against Witches' Cyrano points out that hearsay ought not to be admissible and that just because superstitious peasants recount stories of ghouls and goblins that should not influence the rigorous standard of 'proof'. His response to tales of moonlit flights through the air and other superhuman feats of witchcraft is short and to the point: 'one should not believe anything of a man but that which is human'.[3] No doubt his sister and brother would have been utterly horrified by such an assertion, since it not only casts doubt on the antics of demons and witches but also on all the saintly miracles, which were the object of devout Catholic worship.

Elsewhere, Cyrano states baldly that he does not believe in miracles, but is convinced that there is always a natural explanation for apparently supernatural events. This helps to explain something that to modern eyes can seem contradictory: the fact that it was his insistence on reason, doubt and scepticism which marked Cyrano out to his contemporaries as dangerous and possibly mad. That he should refuse to accept what everyone believed is what causes modern critics to praise his 'eminently sane and courageous mind', but at the time, his nonconformism was deeply suspect. The existence of demons and witches was not just approved by the church but also by royalty. Louis XIII's devoutly religious wife, Queen Anne, took a keen interest in witchcraft and possession, and in England James I was a fervent believer in sorcery. He even penned a learned treatise on demonology which was published in 1597. Shakespeare's shrewd decision to present three 'secret, black and midnight hags', on stage in *Macbeth*, was a direct appeal to the king's well-known fascination with witches. Cyrano's lifetime saw the beginning of a widespread popular debate on the subject of witchcraft, comparable to the modern fascination with aliens and alien abduction. Carl Sagan has produced some fascinating research detailing the extraordinary similarities between the two phenomena. Just as those on trial for witchcraft faithfully reproduced the details recorded in popular demonology texts, so alien abductees unfailingly claim to have encountered aliens whose spaceships and personal appearance correspond very closely to whatever representation has most recently appeared on film. Not only that, but striking similarities emerge between the actual accounts of victims of 'possession' and of 'abduction', for which Sagan gives eminently rational physiological and psychological explanations, with no need for the intervention of creatures from hell or the heavens. Cyrano would be delighted.

Throughout the 1630s and 1640s, intermittent poor harvests and recurring outbreaks of the plague had led to terrible hardship for rural communities across France. From time to time a natural occurrence, such as a devastating hailstorm, would unleash a paroxysm of terror in the beleaguered communities of the rural poor. This climate of fear and uncertainty triggered off widespread popular witch-hunts. In Burgundy, Champagne and Gascony travelling witchfinders were active and hundreds of suspects were sent for trial. Others were almost certainly dealt with in a more direct and deadly manner. Retributive killings were not uncommon in rural communities when a flashpoint was reached as the result of the loss of vital crops or livestock. The local people would take it upon themselves to bring the suspected 'evildoers' to justice.

In the village of Rouze in 1643 a witchfinder assembled all the inhabitants of the area in order to identify those responsible for the poor harvests, hardship and general misery which blighted the region. He picked out thirty-five women, charging 100 écus for the privilege of his services. The women were saved from the flames thanks to the timely arrival of the local bishop who interrogated the 'witchfinder' and forced him to admit that he was a charlatan. The thirty-five pseudo-witches were released and the pseudo-witchfinder was fined and imprisoned. In the mountains of the Languedoc region in September a court order had to be issued to force the lord of the manor of Rombret and Rouergue to release six prisoners (five women and one man) from the dungeons of his castle. The order came too late to save two of the six who had not survived the horrifying torture inflicted on them in order to extract their confessions. The *parlements* of Dijon and Toulouse reacted to the 'witch-craze' by ordering the arrest of all witchfinders, some of whom were summarily executed and hundreds of accused were set free. It was almost equally common, however, for murderers who claimed their crimes were committed against witches to be pardoned. In December 1630 in a village in the Franche Comté region, a woman suspected of witchcraft was beaten by a group of villagers and left to die in the snow.

Such horrors help to explain why Cyrano felt the need to engage in this particular debate and why he was convinced that witchcraft was an illusion. The letter 'Against Witches' gives a still clearer explanation of why Cyrano was so keen to expose popular superstitions about witches and demons as unfounded nonsense. He cites the examples of three famously scandalous witchcraft cases: the sorcery of Louis Gaufridy, the demons of Loudun and the bewitching of Madeleine Bavent.

These three cases in particular took the public imagination by storm, because in each instance there was something more to the story than the all-too-common scapegoating of a harmless, marginal individual by a troubled, rural community. The scandals which exploded in Aix, Loudun and Louviers became national sensations, partly because they concerned the apparent insurgence of Satan and his minions into the very heart of the religious mainstream, igniting as they all did within the confines of a nunnery. But they also generated such intense interest because key members of the church chose to disseminate the shocking details as widely as possible. Priests, who were supposed to be responsible for calming these explosive situations determined instead to add fuel to the fire, staging showy public exorcisms and allowing the publication of the salacious 'confessions' of the victims. The theory was that, the greater publicity given to the mysteries of demonic possession and witchcraft, the greater the public's consequent fear of the devil. The reality was not so simple.

In Aix in the summer of 1609, a young girl named Madeleine Demandolx de la Palud complained to the mother superior at the Ursuline convent, in which she was staying, that she had been suffering from night terrors and hallucinations. A series of exorcisms was set under way. In the spring of 1610, the 'devil' in Madeleine denounced a curé from Marseille as the source of her suffering. The priest whose name was Louis Gaufridy had been her family's confessor and a close friend of her mother's. The exorcisms continued attracting large crowds and two more girls also fell victim to 'possession'. One of them, Louise Capeau, accused Madeleine of having bewitched her.

By early 1611, Gaufridy had been incarcerated and subjected to torture sessions designed to elicit a full confession. After a couple of months Gaufridy broke down and admitted to having signed a pact with the Devil in order to be able to seduce any woman he wanted. He claimed to have chosen to sell his soul in order to satisfy his overwhelming lust for certain young girls, including Madeleine. The Devil had then apparently granted Gaufridy the power to seduce any woman he desired just by blowing into her nostrils. The priests in charge of the case stage-managed the exorcisms to the terror and fascination of large crowds, with the intention of 'converting' as many unbelievers as possible and instilling a healthy fear of the Devil into the masses. In a spectacular *coup de théâtre* which would later be repeated in Loudun, Gaufridy was brought out to stand before his accuser. On seeing him again Madeleine lost the power of speech. Stripping away the 'supernatural' elements of Gaufridy's crime a skeleton of sexual obsession and abuse is revealed, an all too common element in witchcraft confessions. Gaufridy describes how he won the trust of Madeleine's family in order to get close to her, seducing her mother in order to have free access to the young girl. On 30 April 1611, Gaufridy was burned at the stake. His confession was printed and sold like hot cakes.

Although the Gaufridy case took place before Cyrano was born its notoriety was such that it was far from forgotten in his lifetime; an account of his trial, condemnation and execution had been published in 1611 and a salacious 'biography' entitled *The horrible and appalling witchcraft of Louis Goffredy* appeared later in the century. In Cyrano's teens another possession scandal erupted in the town of Loudun and it is hard to believe that he would not have followed the progression of the affair as breathlessly as anyone else. This time, the accused was another priest and the 'victim' was Jeanne des Anges, the prioress of the Ursuline convent in Loudun. The town had been struck by the plague in 1632, and later the same year, perhaps influenced by the resulting climate of fear and horror, Jeanne des Anges had declared herself possessed by the Devil and subject to disturbing erotic hallucinations.

When the exorcisms began, she eventually pointed the finger at the handsome young priest named Urbain Grandier, whom she had previously attempted to engage as the convent's confessor and spiritual director. Jeanne seems to have fixed on Grandier as the focus of an erotic obsession fuelled by the town gossip about his many sexual conquests among female parishioners that she had eagerly garnered at the gates of the convent. At the time of her accusation Jeanne des Anges had never even met Grandier. She had been keen to meet him and had gone as far as to write to him, offering him the position of confessor to the convent. Grandier's high-handed refusal probably sealed his fate. Urbain Grandier's crimes were rather more mundane than demonic. He was an intelligent, handsome and successful individual, essentially guilty of nothing worse than arrogance and womanizing. His quarrelsome nature and his unshakeable conviction of his own superiority had made him various important enemies in the town, enemies who were quick to seize on the excuse offered by the accusations made by the mentally unstable Jeanne des Anges. Urbain Grandier had been foolish enough to behave as if the rules didn't apply to him – even going so far as to pen a learned treatise against the celibacy of priests in order to reassure his pregnant lover. This weighed heavily against him at his trial. Just after his execution, one of his acquaintances summed him up in a letter to the great Pierre Gassendi as a man who 'had great virtues but who also had great vices'.[4]

The 'possession' did not abate after Grandier's execution and soon a large number of the nuns and a whole roster of the legions of hell were involved. Cracks appeared in the show exorcisms even at their height and dissenting voices were heard in the crowd casting doubt on the whole performance. One doubting nobleman, the Comte de Lude, even went so far as to trick the priest into letting him test whether some holy relics he possessed were really genuine by seeing how the Devil in Jeanne reacted to contact with them. The box containing the precious burden was duly pressed to Jeanne's head and she went into a more than usually dramatic round of howling and convulsing. When the priest handed back the box, he remarked how pleased the count must be with such a confirmation of the holy nature of his precious relics and asked to be permitted to see such a precious treasure. The count happily complied, opening the box to reveal that there were no relics within and that he had engineered the occasion to expose the 'possession' as a fraud. The exorcisms were popular theatrical events which attracted large crowds, most of whom were much more easily convinced than the count. The celebrity of the prioress reached such a pitch that Queen Anne summoned her to a royal audience in Paris.

Some years earlier, while awaiting the execution of his sentence Grandier had penned an urgent appeal to the king himself. The eloquent desperation with which he pointed out the numerous flaws in the accusations against him and the impossible catch-22 in which the priests had caught him, was sadly not enough to save him. It is doubtful that the king ever even read the letter. As Grandier pointed out in his plea, his trial was a farce and the accusations made against him by Jeanne and her fellow nuns were inconsistent and contradictory. The women had withdrawn their identification of him as their tormentor on more than one occasion but this was discounted on the grounds that Satan was the prince of deceit. When the 'demons' named Grandier they told the truth but when they pronounced him innocent they were lying. A similar paradox was used to deal with the results of interrogation under torture, confession was proof of guilt but refusal to confess under torture was also proof of guilt since only the devil could be responsible for such inhuman resistance.

The great philosopher Montaigne, an important influence on Cyrano's own thinking about the subject, had pointed out the terrible flaw in the use of judicial torture: 'What would one not say, what would one not do to flee such terrible pains? [. . .] Suffering forces even innocents to lie.'[5] Montaigne had even undertaken to research the whole issue of witchcraft and possession personally. He went to see some prisoners accused of witchcraft to examine them for himself. He was unconvinced by what he saw and argued strongly in favour of scepticism and tolerance, suggesting that it is putting too great a faith in conjecture and hearsay to see a man burned alive on the strength of them. It was the terrible arrogance of the priests standing in judgement over their fellow man that Cyrano objected to so virulently and in the letter 'Against Witchcraft', he states categorically that he does not believe that any of the three famous possession cases were genuine.

The third outbreak of satanic interference in a nunnery took place in Louviers, a small town with a previous history of demonic possession. In 1591 a young serving girl named Françoise Fontaine, who was being wooed by a rich merchant of the town, convinced herself that she was possessed by a demon and the ecclesiastical authorities arranged an exorcism. Her story was well known in the town and had even been published in the local chronicle in the early 1600s. A local priest had attended some of the earliest exorcism attempts at Loudun in 1633–4 and brought back with him terrifying tales that ran like wildfire through the town. Whispered accounts even filtered into the confines of the Convent des Hospitalières de Saint Louis et Sainte Elisabeth where Madeleine Bavent was a nun. It was at this point that the first problems began in the convent with isolated incidents of a similar nature to the events at Loudun. At first the spiritual director of the convent, Mathurin Picard, a calm and moderate man succeeded in controlling the situation. Recognizing the link between the manifestation of 'satanic' attacks on the nuns in his care and the news from Loudun, he suppressed the affair and refused to hold exorcisms or to inform the religious authorities. In this way peace reigned in the nunnery until Picard's death at the close of the year 1642.

With the calming presence of Picard removed Madeleine's 'possession' broke out once more and six other nuns were also afflicted. Exorcisms were arranged and after ten days of investigation Madeleine was condemned for witchcraft and locked up in the town dungeons. The affair dragged on for three more years as Madeleine's various accusations were investigated. This led to the distressing battle over the disinterment of Picard's body; his family had to fight through the courts to prevent him from being burned posthumously on a pyre in the town square. Eventually the convent was disbanded and the building sold.

In Cyrano's lifetime the burning of witches was generally regarded as a just punishment, in keeping with biblical commandment and with God's will. As Henri Boguet put it in response for calls for moderation,

No, no, witches are walking abroad in their thousands, multiplying on the earth like the caterpillars in our gardens, it is a disgrace to the Magistrates to whom the punishment of crimes and misdemeanours belongs; because when we have no less than the express commandment from God to put them to death as his greatest enemies why do we continue to endure them any longer, rendering ourselves disobedient to his most high Majesty?[6]

Boguet was a witchfinder reputedly responsible for as many as 600 deaths. Although documentary evidence of only twenty-eight of his cases has survived, these include the harrowing account of the 'witches' who committed suicide rather than face Boguet and the trial process.

Cyrano's stance against the ignorant superstition and hideous violence of the witch-hunts stems from his awareness of human fallibility. In the letter 'Against Witchcraft' he writes, 'our fathers were wrong in times past, their descendants are wrong now; ours will be wrong one day.'[7] Given Cyrano's family background, his decision to highlight the three highly controversial possession cases can be seen as doubly provocative, and his comment about the errors of fathers and their offspring seems to take on a particularly personal significance. Thanks to the intervention of humane individuals like Cyrano the tide of opinion would eventually turn against witchcraft, although the last case in rural France occurred as recently as the 1950s. Looking back over the events of the century, Voltaire remarked that philosophy had ultimately prevailed and cured the judges of 'this abominable illusion', teaching them that 'one should not burn imbeciles'.[8]

IO

A madman named Cyrano

In 1647, nine-year-old King Louis XIII was gravely ill with smallpox, his younger brother Philippe was also very sick, and, as a result, the throne looked to be in serious danger. Around this time, Cyrano had begun work on a blood-soaked classical tragedy in five acts. He entitled the play *La Mort d'Agrippine* (*The Death of Agrippina*) and in it he explored ideas about power and corruption and expressed ideas that were a direct challenge to the Catholic hegemony. The work is very dark and extremely violent, but critics have commended its 'strange and savage beauty'.[1] The plot revolves around the devices and desires of Agrippina, widow of the Germanicus Caesar and mother of the depraved future Emperor Caligula. Agrippina is at the heart of a failed revolt against the tyrant Tiberius, along with the tyrant's traitorous favourite, Sejanus, and Sejanus's murderously bitter former mistress Livilla. Sejanus is an unrepentant atheist anti-hero, who declares that man created the gods, and not the other way around. He argues, as did other creations of Cyrano's, that life after death is a figment of the imagination – that what awaits us after death is just the same as what we experienced before birth: nothingness. Cyrano put a

typically double-edged bit of provocation into the mouth of his
hero:

> *These lovely nothings that we worship without knowing why,*
> *These creatures athirst for the blood of our slaughtered beasts,*
> *These gods that man created, who did not create man,*
> *Even the most solid State rests upon this absurd fantasy,*
> *Fie, fie, Térentius, who fears them, fears nothing.*

The final line is deliberately ambiguous and, in isolation, could be
read as a harmless homily; that the godfearing man need fear nothing. The context of the speech reveals a far more radical argument:
that he who fears the gods is afraid of a figment of his own imagination. There are no definite records of the play in performance so
we have no indication when it might have been staged or where. It
seems likely that it was withdrawn early in its first run and it has
been largely neglected ever since.

According to an anecdote, which may be apocryphal since it is
first recorded as late as 1715, the play attracted large audiences at
first, due to its controversial theme. The writer La Monnoye
describes large numbers of uncultured playgoers enthusiastically
determined to attend and be scandalized, knowing that there were
'dangerous' passages in the *The Death of Agrippina* but failing, in
their simplicity, to notice the real blasphemy and instead finally
seizing on a perfectly innocent use of the word 'hostie' (a poetic
synonym for 'victim' but also coincidentally the word for the
sacramental host). Thus when Sejanus declared his intention to
strike his victim, he was apparently greeted with cries from the
audience of 'Oh! The wicked fellow! Oh! The atheist! Listen to
how he speaks of the holy sacrament.' Another anecdote, told by
Tallemant des Reaux, relates that, once the play was printed, it
sold out almost immediately precisely because of its scandalous
notoriety.

horrifying events. Six days after the ceremony, on the eve of the feast of St Bartholomew, Admiral de Coligny, the leader of the French Protestant faction, and a number of other leading Huguenot nobles were murdered outside Coligny's Parisian home by royal troops. The violence spread throughout the city, whole families were slaughtered and, when the news reached the provincial towns of Lyons, Rouen, Toulouse and Bordeaux, they followed suit with massacres of their own. It is undeniable, and perhaps unsurprising that, with the end of overt religious conflict, when the converted Protestant King Henri IV began to impose a series of measures promoting religious tolerance, came a noticeable rise in blasphemy and irreligion. Prosecutions for the crime of heresy rose steadily from 1599 onwards.

A verdict of 'lèse-majesté divine' – that is atheism or heresy – was not always indicative of the repression of religious dissension. In a number of cases, an allegation of blasphemy was added to the charges against a criminal, as a means of highlighting the gravity of their offence. Of the sixty-three convictions in the first half of the century, at least sixteen fall into this category, where atheism was a secondary charge. Specifically, seven were found guilty of false testimony, three were accused of being sorcerers, one was an assassin, another had been caught stealing church silver, one was a woman found guilty of infanticide, two were robbers who had made the mistake of choosing Christmas Eve for their heist, and finally two were men who had been convicted of kidnapping and assault in a monastery. Although this catalogue of misdeeds reveals no common link and no direct evidence of religious dissension, damnable conduct was seen as the natural corollary of suspect ideology. In Cyrano's time the punishment of blasphemy followed a set series of stages with the penalties escalating according to the persistence of the offender. A rigorous system had been worked out over the years to establish the gravity of an offence of blasphemy and the nature of the punishment merited.

Jean-Benoît Constant Coquelin was the first stage Cyrano. Rostand's play was dedicated to him with the words: 'I had intended to dedicate this poem to the spirit of Cyrano. But since his soul has passed into you, Coquelin, I dedicate it to you.'

Edmond Rostand trained as a lawyer but chose to become a writer instead. In order to fulfil his ambition to 'give lessons of the soul', he deliberately turned away from the historical Cyrano towards the creation of a romantic legend.

The flamboyant actress and theatre owner Sarah Bernhardt was instrumental in orchestrating crucial publicity for Rostand's sell-out play *Cyrano de Bergerac*.

Jean Paul Rappeneau's lavish film version of *Cyrano de Bergerac* (1990) starred Gérard Depardieu as Cyrano and Anne Brochet as Roxane. It was rumoured at the time that Depardieu even went so far as to sleep in his false nose to get into character for the multi-award-winning film.

The real Cyrano was proud of his large nose and posed for this soulful portrait by his friend the engraver Zachary Heince (c.1654).

Printed for Henry Rhodes, next the swan Tavern. in Fleet street

F. H. Van. Hove. sculp.

Illustration from an English edition (1687) of Cyrano's deliriously funny and inventive space travel satire.

Opposite page: Cyrano tried hard to counteract popular superstition about witches. This was a controversial position to take at a time when refusal to believe in the terrifying hysteria of the witch-hunt was considered tantamount to denying the existence of God.

In this illustration from an eighteenth-century edition of Cyrano's *Voyages to the Moon and Sun* the hero is being carried up into the air thanks to the bottles of dew strapped round his waist. Cyrano intended his hero's adventures in outer space to offer a defence of Galileo's new ideas about the universe.

Cyrano's satirical science-fiction flight of fantasy was his masterpiece. In this illustration his hero/alter-ego 'Dyrcona' is on trial in the Republic of the Birds for the crime of being human.

The fat actor Montfleury, with whom Cyrano quarrelled and wrote a scurrilous attack, lambasting him for his size and his lack of wit.

Robert Parker danced the title role in the ballet of *Cyrano de Bergerac.*

Mauro Corda's new statue of Cyrano in Bergerac town centre gazes up to the heavens, in recognition of the original Cyrano's preoccupation with outer space.

Varoqueaux's statue of Cyrano in the town of Bergerac is quite badly damaged and keeps having its nose stolen.

"Bringing crowds to the Carlton. Haymarket and drawing them from all classes."

Joan Rowan
KINE WEEKLY
18th Oct 1951

JOSÉ
FERRER

1951 ACADEMY
AWARD WINNER

IN

STANLEY
KRAMER'S
Production

'Londoners are crowding to enjoy the fiery acting of 'Cyrano de Bergerac' – and to pay the unusual tribute of applause at the end of each performance.'
Sunday Dispatch 28th Oct 1951

Cyrano
de Bergerac

CO - STARRING
MALA POWERS

WITH
WILLIAM PRINCE - MORRIS CARNOVSKY
RALPH CLANTON - LLOYD CORRIGAN
VIRGINIA FARMER

Produced by STANLEY KRAMER-Directed by MICHAEL GORDON

UNITED
ARTISTS

George Clooney's uncle, José Ferrer, starred as Cyrano de Bergerac on stage and on film. He won an Oscar and a Tony for the same role – a rare distinction.

Below: Steve Martin's romantic comedy *Roxanne* (1987) was inspired by the play *Cyrano de Bergerac*. Like Rostand before him, Martin included a joke in his script that was originally penned by the real Cyrano centuries before: 'Your nose was on time but you were fifteen minutes late'.

Louis Gallet's serialisation of *Cyrano de Bergerac* acknowledged the hero's provocative nature. His version was entitled *Captain Satan*.

Cyrano's adventures have been retold in myriad different forms, even as a comic book.

Ce buste a été réalisé en 1998 par *Dan ROBERT*, artiste Sannoisien
et inauguré le 29 avril 2000 par Yanick PATERNOTTE,
Maire de SANNOIS

In 1655, Cyrano died at the house of his cousin Pierre in Sannois, he was only 36
years old. Today, the small Parisian suburb is proud of its connection to the real
Cyrano. This bronze bust is to be found in 'Place Cyrano'.

The French anti-blasphemy laws have their origins in a ruling pronounced by King Philippe VI on 22 February 1347, which established punishments for heresy ranging from public humiliation in shackles or the pillory, to incision of the lips and removal of the tongue. On 6 April 1594, Henri IV had issued a declaration establishing a system whereby the first two offences of blasphemy were punishable by a fine and the third by an unspecified corporal punishment. On 10 November 1617, the blasphemy laws were further refined by the sixteen-year-old King Louis XIII. The fines were increased and were to be reinforced by imprisonment, however recourse to corporal punishment was put back from the third to the fourth offence and the nature of the physical chastisements remained unspecified, allowing judges the freedom to maintain a degree of clemency. However, in 1636 when Cyrano was seventeen years of age and on the brink of his military career the laws were considerably altered in response to pressure from senior Catholic clergy to protect the sanctity of 'the century of saints' from the rising tide of impiety and irreligion.

On 19 May 1636 a new proclamation brought a new degree of order and rigidity to the punishment of heretics. The first four offences were punishable by fines which were doubled, then tripled and then quadrupled; on the fifth offence the fine not only rose to five times the original sum but was accompanied by an unspecified period of confinement in shackles. This would involve the victim being imprisoned in a sort of wooden neck brace linked by chains to the hands and feet and then secured in a public place. The assembled masses would then have the opportunity to pelt the criminal with rotten fruit or vegetables or even with stones. The rigour of this public retribution would depend on the notoriety of the offender and the description of their crime, hung on a placard around their neck. By the sixth offence the prescribed punishment had escalated to a deliberate and permanent disfigurement. The upper lip would be seared with a branding iron and the unfortunate victim would then be confined in the pillory (or stocks) to display their ignominious brand to the world. The pillory offered a still more painful confinement than the shackles and the same possibility of public retribution. On the seventh offence the lower lip was to be slit and on the eighth the tongue was to be torn out. Given this escalating scale of dire reprisals, one might imagine that incidences of persistent irreligious behaviour would simply not occur. The extraordinary career of the Chevalier de Roquelaure provides flamboyant proof to the contrary.

Roquelaure's numerous outrages against the holy church ran to a long and colourful list. He sang obscene rhymes in church, he was frequently heard to utter blasphemous oaths and phrases, he arranged mock baptisms and weddings for his dogs, he attempted to bribe a mendicant priest into denying God by a lavish donation of alms and he even conducted a parody of communion as the finale of his frequent orgies. The chevalier was arrested in Toulouse but within four days of his arrest he had escaped from prison and fled. The chevalier's father was a marshal of France and this may help to explain the fact that Roquelaure's flight was apparently aided by eight officials who included lawyers, members of the council and even prosecutors from the *Parlement* itself. The chevalier was consequently tried *in absentia*. He was convicted by default and condemned to be beheaded. Roquelaure was recaptured in Paris and imprisoned for a further twenty months, during which time the Parlement of Paris failed to reach a decision on whether to confirm the original sentence pronounced in Toulouse. Before they could decide, Roquelaure escaped again and this time he made sure not to reappear.

Roquelaure's egregious escapades took place in the mid-1640s just at the time when Cyrano was composing his own heretical masterpiece and the laughing atheist may have served as some degree of inspiration for Dyrcona, the hero of Cyrano's *Voyages to the Moon and Sun*, who is also condemned by the Parlement of

Toulouse and who also escapes from prison on more than one occasion. Not all those found guilty of blasphemy were lucky enough to have influential friends strategically placed to aid a daring prison breakout. The case of the Chevalier de Roquelaure was exceptional but it serves to highlight a commonly acknowledged fact of the times. 'Libertine behaviour was a luxury for gentlemen . . . before attacking God it was prudent to assure that one had protectors among men.'[9] Cyrano as a lowly writer was far from enjoying the extraordinary freedoms that Roquelaure had so abused. As a result Cyrano's rebellion was considerably more cerebral and initially more private; this may give some clue as to why, unlike Roquelaure, he was not to receive an official death sentence.

When Cyrano was still a child two very significant heresy trials took place, both of which resulted in the deaths of the accused. The two very different condemned men were both to provide models for Cyrano's own subsequent career of free thought and irreligion. The first was Giulio Vanini who died at the stake in 1619, the year of Cyrano's birth. While Cyrano was a newborn baby mewling out his first faint cries in Paris Vanini's howls were dying away in distant Toulouse. Vanini, a disgraced Carmelite monk was burned at the stake in the town square. In a letter written to a friend at the time of the trial the chief prosecutor who had been responsible for conducting extensive interviews with the condemned man described him as 'the finest and the wickedest mind I have ever known'.[10] As well as this ambivalent accolade, numerous other manuscript accounts of Vanini's notorious fate have survived, among them the following graphic description of the condemned man's final agonies:

At the last moment his face was wild and horrible, his soul tormented, his speech confused and, though he frequently proclaimed that he would die like a philosopher, he died like a beast. Before the fire was lit, being ordered to submit his tongue to the knife, he refused and pincers were used to drag it out; having seized it the executioner sliced it off. Never was heard a more horrible cry; one would have said the bellow of a stricken ox. The fire consuming the remains; the ashes were scattered to the winds.[11]

The motivation for recording these hideous details can be deduced from the description itself. There is no shred of pity for the victim's horrible fate expressed by the writer, just a grim satisfaction that the dangerous radical got what he deserved. This harrowing description is, in fact, an early example of gutter-press journalism. It was written to flog to a bloodthirsty population keen to devour the latest gory details of someone else's private tragedy. This lucrative business ultimately served the same purpose as the public spectacle of execution itself. Firstly, it offered a horrible warning to other nonconformists and secondly it served as propaganda, confirming the justice of the sentence. In spite of the obvious bias in the telling of the story it is nonetheless very revealing.

We learn, for example, that Vanini's tongue was cut out before he was put to death. The surgical removal of the tongue and the burning or slitting of the lips was seen as a symbolic and fitting reward for blasphemy, hence its permanent enshrinement in the stricter blasphemy laws of 1636. The operation also conveniently prevented the victims from addressing any dangerously inspired or eloquent last words to the crowd. In an age before mass communication had become an everyday reality the opportunity to address the assembled hordes at an execution was one of the few instances in which a wide and varied audience could be reached directly. Our eyewitness account also reveals that Vanini saw himself as a 'philosopher' but that his torturers deliberately relegated him to the level of a 'beast' by denying him mankind's defining characteristic: speech. The decision to execute such determined sinners by immolation was also deeply significant since it brought vividly to life the imagined future of the damned, burning in a lake of hell-fire. In this way the authorities stage-managed a live-action, tangible vision of hell for the masses. Why leave the horrors of damnation to the imagination when you can bring the real thing to the town square of your choice? This also explains why the eye-witness account speaks of Vanini's horrifying pain in metaphysical terms, insisting that not just his flesh but 'his soul was tormented'.

A second outrageous dissident was famously condemned for blasphemy in Cyrano's childhood. Théophile de Viau perished in exile in 1625 when Cyrano was six years old, his health having been fatally undermined by a long period of imprisonment. Cyrano certainly read Viau's works and would have been vividly aware of the fate of his predecessor. It was the shocking content of the provocative verses collected in the *Parnasse des Poètes Satyriques* that had brought Théophile and his fellow authors to the attention of the authorities. The four main writers behind the collection were lucky enough to benefit from the patronage and protection of the powerful Duc de Montmorency and as such all of them succeeded in escaping Paris when the inevitable storm broke. They were tried *in absentia*, Théophile was identified as the ringleader and was the only one of the four to be condemned to be burned at the stake. In the absence of the man himself an effigy was hanged and then burned.

In September 1623 Théophile was arrested in Saint Quentin and brought back to Paris. In March 1624 the Parisian Parlement began the lengthy process of interrogation, in the course of which the chief prosecutor Mathieu Molé recorded his conviction of a strong connection between Théophile and Vanini. Among the allegations against the poet was that of considering nature as 'the sovereign power over men and all that is mortal, just as much as over animals, in accordance with the doctrine of his master Vanini'.[12] For over a year and a half Théophile was held in a dungeon and periodically interrogated. He held out against this ordeal and made no damning admissions, nor could anyone be found to testify against him; as a result his sentence was reduced to perpetual banishment and he was eventually released in September 1625. However, the horrific conditions in which he had been held had totally destroyed Théophile's health and he died shortly after his release.

In 1736 Voltaire wrote to a friend asking him to send copies of Vanini's works expecting to find within them the outrageous blasphemies which had led to Vanini's considerable notoriety as 'such a depraved character'. On reading the works he was extremely disappointed. 'I am annoyed that they fried that poor Neapolitan but I would gladly burn his boring books.'[13] This reaction gives a clue as to a paradoxical divergence of fortune between Vanini and Cyrano. Vanini's works were heretical but Cyrano's were flamboyantly atheistic. Although Vanini's works were considerably less provocative, his life was one of precarious exile and his conduct was occasionally decidedly questionable, which left him vulnerable to official reprisals. Cyrano's outspoken condemnation of the practice of burning dissidents at the stake draws attention to the fact that in a case where the question of guilt or innocence is a subject of ideological debate the practice of setting the accused alight renders the debate null and void. 'Although their accusation is ridiculous, doubtless the result of their stupidity, I shall be none the less dead when a dozen men of wit who have seen me grilled observe that my judges are fools. All their arguments proving my innocence will not resuscitate me.'[14]

In *The Voyage to the Sun* Cyrano dramatized the enthusiastic reception of *The Voyage to the Moon* and the public hunger for the challenging ideas it contained. His hero/alter-ego Dyrcona is accused of sorcery, and although this is a fictional work it is not too far-fetched to assume that there were important autobiographical elements in the account. It was long supposed that the imprisonment for the crime of sorcery which Cyrano describes in such graphic detail was a pure invention, but new evidence has recently come to light which suggests that Cyrano probably was incarcerated at a late stage in his career. Cyrano wrote his novel in the first person and christened his intrepid space traveller *Dyrcona*, an anagram of D. Cyrano. In choosing a thinly veiled version of his own name for his space-travelling hero he identified his protagonist's riotous interplanetary progress with his own terrestrial explorations and adventures.

Cyrano was always acutely aware of the image-making process. From an early age he showed a fascination with the possibilities for self-publicity that the right name could offer. Throughout his duelling career and his later incarnation as a mordant satirist, he retained a sense of theatre that contributed to the creation of a legend that would outgrow him and take on a life of its own after his death. At different times in his lifetime he signed himself in each of the following ways: Alexandre de Cyrano Bergerac, Hercule de Bergerac, de Bergerac, de Bergerac Cyrano, De Cyrano de Bergerac, Savinien de Cyrano, the last being the only name that was officially his by right. Cyrano was no respecter of officialdom and he refused to give up the name de Bergerac just because he no longer had a legal claim to it. He also decided to appropriate more dashing forenames: Alexandre (as in Alexander the Great) and Hercules both having obvious connotations of power and military might that Savinien did not. Savinien was a popular Christian name in the small provincial town of Sens where the Cyrano family had first established itself on arrival from Sardinia. Cyrano may have shrugged off the name as a way to prevent anyone from making the connection.

In the manner of modern-day spin doctors and publicists Cyrano recognized the importance of presentation. As such he was happy for his readers to identify Dyrcona, the inventor and philosopher whose travels explore some of the most controversial ideas of his time with himself. In keeping with Naudé's analysis, Cyrano realized that an accusation of witchcraft was the sign of a great mind and was therefore something to be flaunted and celebrated. In typical, iconoclastic fashion he also found in the subject an inexhaustible source of comedy. He gleefully mocks the ignorance and superstition of the unenlightened. The fearful suspense and tension created by the arrival of town officials to hunt down Dyrcona and lead him off to the stake are swiftly undercut by hilarity. Colignac, the hero's noble friend and host is unable to control his amusement when one of the officials, failing to understand Colignac's reluctance to denounce his friend, offers the following friendly consolation as an incentive for him to reveal the sorcerer's whereabouts: 'The magician is a person you love; but you have nothing to fear; things will go easily with respect to you: you just need to deliver him into our hands and for love of you we will engage upon our honour to get him burnt without a scandal.'[15] The rest of the officials' arguments are drowned out by Colignac's peals of laughter. Dyrcona's friend does not betray him but the hero is separated from his friends when they decide to leave the area, and finds himself cornered by a fanatical priest and some angry peasants. A superbly knockabout chase sequence ensues in which he is captured, escapes, is captured again, escapes a second time and then is finally recaptured. His influential friends succeed in getting him moved out of his slimy dungeon into a comfortable cell in a high tower and they insist on him being allowed all the books and materials he requires. As a result the adventurer succeeds in constructing a flying machine which, rather than simply aiding his escape as he had intended, carries him off into the skies and all the way to the sun. In this way a second adventure in outer space unfolds.

In reality of course a visit from the ecclesiastical authorities was no laughing matter. In Italy the career of the great Galileo Galilei, one of Cyrano's heroes, was famously dogged by many such unwelcome visits and in 1633 after having published his *Dialogue concerning the two chief World Systems* (1632) he ended up on trial and facing a death sentence. Galileo had presented his controversial scientific findings in the form of a fictional debate between invented characters. In spite of these precautions he still fell foul of the Catholic authorities and ended up seeing his works banned and living out his days under house arrest. Galileo was an extraordinarily talented, visionary man of science who risked his life to publish his astronomical findings for the benefit of the growing community of natural philosophers. Cyrano de Bergerac was a science popularizer, a writer who used his abundant imagination to try to communicate the excitement of the scientific revolution. While Galileo worked on analysing the raw data of his astronomical observations and drawing fascinating and startling conclusions therefrom, Cyrano and others like him enthusiastically attempted to assimilate some of the implications of the new science and to analyse the imaginative possibilities of this extraordinary broadening of mankind's perspective on the universe. Unlike Dyrcona, who had powerful friends and a spaceship to aid his escape, the real Cyrano was to find himself abruptly abandoned by those who might have been able to shield him when the storm clouds of sectarian disapproval started to gather threateningly above.

Even today the act of publishing a book, albeit a work of purest fiction can potentially be fraught with danger, as the novelist Salman Rushdie can attest. Books are powerful. Books are dangerous. Books can get a person into a lot of trouble. Small wonder that Cyrano, a lifelong devotee of rebellion and troublemaking, would grow to love them so dearly. Dyrcona is nearly torn to pieces by a group of yokels for possessing a book. It is a copy of Descartes' *Physics* but the peasants, who can't read and, lacking the ability to recognize the work for what it really is, assume that the diagrams it contains must have occult significance and the owner of the book is therefore condemned as a witch. They are preparing to execute him when he makes his escape. The incident is deliberately farcical, but this does not undermine the satirical intent with which it was conceived.

Even in our own increasingly secular age, examples abound which teach us that the absolute certainty of the zealot can unleash unspeakable evil. Cyrano was born into a society in which religious extremism occupied a position not at the marginalized terrorist fringes but at the very heart of the ruling classes. As such, his free-thinking stance was all the more heroic and inspirational. Religious conviction can strike like lightning; one moment the sky is lit with divine brilliance, the next a smoking corpse lies cooling on the ground. Throughout history belief has been a dangerous business with a determined few prepared to die for their faith and an even larger number happy to kill for it. As Cyrano points out in *The Voyage to the Moon*, it is a little too late to argue the rights and wrongs of ideological execution once the accused has been set alight.

I fell from the moon

On 20 July 1969 Neil Armstrong and his fellow astronaut Buzz Aldrin revealed to a fascinated public their first-hand observations of the surface of the moon. Television screens across the globe relayed images of a barren, rocky landscape marked by gigantic craters, the vivid scars of ancient asteroid strikes. Over three centuries earlier Cyrano de Bergerac had revealed to an equally fascinated public that the lunar landscape was lush and verdant and extraordinarily similar to that of the earth. He entranced readers with the revelation that the moon was inhabited by intelligent extraterrestrials, who were superbly scornful of humanity. Although Cyrano's imaginative exploration of the moon may have been a long way from scientifically accurate there was one common element between Cyrano's journey to the moon and that of *Apollo* 11. Both Cyrano and the American astronauts had taken the opportunity to look back at the earth from above and to reflect on the insights to be gained from this extraordinary new perspective.

As the great seventeenth-century astronomer Johannes Kepler realized, there has never been any shortage of people whose reaction to the spectacular panorama of the night sky is to look up at the stars and imagine heading off out into the vast interstellar emptiness to explore, leaving the earth spinning below. As early as 1610 Kepler wrote: 'Let us create vessels and sails adjusted to the heavenly ether and there will be plenty of people unafraid of the empty wastes.'[1] Astronomers like Kepler and Galileo Galilei had given the world more detail than ever before to enhance such imaginings. Today the thirst to get out there among the 'empty wastes' is so great that a certain privileged few are prepared to pay enormous sums of money to the chronically underfunded Russian space programme and in doing so secure themselves a seat on a vessel which can take them out of this world. Space tourism has recently become a reality. In 2004, Richard Branson announced his intention to launch the first purely commercial space flights. Over 350 years earlier several men possessed only of the vast wealth of their imaginations set off on space tourism's earliest missions. It is fair to ask the question why. Exactly what was it that inspired Cyrano de Bergerac to write about a trip through the 'heavenly ether', so many years before the possibility of such a trip could be realized?

Despite writing a fantastical description of rocket propulsion three centuries ahead of its time, Cyrano was no rocket scientist. The best efforts of the talented philosopher-mathematician Pierre Gassendi infused Cyrano with a passionate enthusiasm for the ideas of the new science, but failed to introduce any kind of scientific rigour into Cyrano's 'turbulent mind'. He may not have had any great technical or mathematical abilities but Cyrano had a riotous imagination and so it was that his work saw the first description of a hot air balloon, over 130 years before the Montgolfier brothers would develop the first workable prototype. He dreamt up the concept of the mobile home, pleased with the idea of whole cities being transported under their own power, with each house on wheels travelling great distances, allowing the inhabitants an enjoyable sense of freedom. He also described the peculiar sensation of weightlessness in zero gravity in terms that were echoed by the first astronauts some 300 years later. He even imagined personal stereos, although his vision of the device that lunarians carried about with them might not be immediately recognizable to the MP3 generation. Its primary purpose was not to play music but rather talking books; it was the fantasy of a voracious reader. Cyrano came up with the idea as a way for the super-intelligent people of the moon to read and do other things at the same time, thus considerably expanding the amount of time in the day that could be devoted to this uniquely enriching activity.

Cyrano amused himself dreaming up elaborate ways to escape the confines of the earth, which range from the sublime (a solar-powered spaceship complete with a small sail for steering, whose rectangular box-like form echoes that of Doctor Who's *Tardis*) to the ridiculous (smearing his naked body with marrowbone jelly, as a remedy for the bruises sustained in a previous unsuccessful lift-off and then, having escaped the earth's atmosphere by rocket power, discovering that the moon's influence operating on the marrowbone draws him into a lunar landing softened by a fall through the branches of a tree). Given the endearingly high level of confusion and misapprehension in Cyrano's 'scientific' writings, one might wonder why it was that he chose subjects for which he was so manifestly ill-qualified. He was attracted to such subjects because he sensed both their phenomenal potential and their tremendous scope for provocation. Cyrano recognized that the vehemence of popular hostility to the controversial themes of natural philosophy was a good indicator of its seminal importance. There is no doubt that the scientific discoveries of the era precipitated one of the most dramatic paradigm shifts in the history of human understanding.

The late sixteenth and early seventeenth centuries witnessed a flowering of new ideas about the world. Ancient methods of enquiry inherited from diverse disciplines from philosophy to natural magic and alchemy began to coalesce and transform into a rational system. This system was known as natural philosophy and is recognizable as the root of all modern science, from astrophysics to zoology. Natural philosophy represented an entirely new way of looking at the world; the most important characteristic of a natural philosopher was a tendency to ask questions, lots of questions. Previously, European conceptions of knowledge had largely been defined by biblical insistence on the authority of 'the Word'. Essentially, all knowledge had to derive in some way from an existing written source, preferably the Holy Scriptures or failing that the works of Aristotle. The great minds of the Renaissance had started to challenge this extremely limiting notion. Various flamboyant characters had embraced natural philosophy: they were beginning to recognize the value of poking things with sticks, setting things on fire, and generally having more fun than was to be had in merely accepting whatever conclusions were reached in ancient texts, solely on the basis that 'it is written'.

In the early sixteenth century Leonardo da Vinci had been one of the first thinkers to advocate this essential shift in scientific methodology. Leonardo writes scathingly in his notebooks about the misguided masses who fail to ask searching questions, who look to books instead of to the real world for knowledge and understanding. Perhaps the greatest of all Leonardo's inventions was his invention of the scientific experiment. He recognized that the true scientist must seek knowledge through direct investigation of the natural world. This innovation was to become increasingly popular over the following decades. In Cyrano's fantastic voyages, the hero Dyrcona succeeds in inventing a spaceship through a lengthy process of trial and error. Such investigations were not without risk however; natural philosophers who turned away from written authority and chose instead to look to the real world and the deductions of human reasoning in their search for truth all too often came into violent conflict with the religious authorities. Galileo's clashes with the Holy Inquisition are well known. Less familiar is the fate of Giordano Bruno, one of Galileo's most important influences. Cyrano was probably first introduced to Bruno's works by Gassendi and he seems to have studied them thoroughly. Bruno's thinking runs through Cyrano's science fiction like an underground stream, providing a wellspring of inspiration.

Giordano Bruno was a disgraced ex-monk and a talented scientist. As a young man, his insatiable fascination for natural philosophy led to his expulsion from a Dominican monastery in Naples. Having fallen foul of the religious authorities, Bruno was a wanted man. Rather than face the potentially fatal consequences of a heresy trial, he fled the country. In the course of a life spent on the run, Bruno's extravagant intelligence secured him access to the royal courts of Henri IV in France and Elizabeth I in England, where he showed off the power of his phenomenal memory and fascinated and aggravated courtiers and royalty alike. Bruno eventually returned to his native Italy where the Inquisition finally caught up with him. His published works reveal that he was unequivocal in embracing the new methodology: 'Arguments are presented in the name of tradition; but the truth is far more often to be found in the present and the future than in the past.'[2]

This rebellious rejection of the authority of the ancients appealed enormously to Cyrano. Early in his career Bruno had published a satirical comedy for the stage, entitled *Il Candelaio*. The play enjoyed considerable popular success, largely thanks to the fact that it was a lively knockabout farce with an incredible number of absolutely filthy jokes, penned by an ex-monk. *Il Candelaio* was an important influence on Cyrano. The French translation had appeared in 1633 under the title *Le Pédant Joué* – it was no coincidence that Cyrano chose to give his own first satirical comedy the exact same title. The two plays share a common theme – in which an unappealing central character is mercilessly tricked and outwitted by his social inferiors. Cyrano did not plagiarize *Il Candelaio*, but in using the same title he scrupulously acknowledged Bruno's influence.

Bruno's works on natural philosophy reveal his overpowering confidence in his conclusions. Throughout his lifetime, in addition to performing stunts to show off his prodigious memory to courtly audiences and working as a freelance tutor for aristocratic pupils, Bruno devoted himself to a rigorous programme of study and calculation. His enthusiasm for natural philosophical investigation had led him to place an innovative focus on 'evidence' and 'reason' in his quest for knowledge and understanding. A key statement in which he explains this focus also holds the key to his ultimate decision to face death rather than renounce his convictions: 'If the evidence is missing, if reason and the senses are mute, we should know to doubt and wait. Authority is not outside of ourselves, but within us. A divine light shines in the depths of the soul to inspire us and guide our thoughts. That is the true authority.'[3]

Bruno's faith in the illumination of this 'divine light' was total. Ultimately, he was condemned for his adherence to a new scientific theory which the Inquisition considered atheistic and dangerous, a theory which emerged as a direct result of the new form of scientific investigation, with earth-shattering consequences.

The ancient Ptolemaic model of the universe described the earth as the still point around which the entire universe rotated. This was in strict accordance with the Holy Scripture, and, having been outlined by Ptolemy in AD150 in an impenetrably complicated work entitled *Almagest*, it was also acceptably ancient. The essence of Bruno's heresy was his rejection of Ptolemy. Bruno's earliest conflicts with his religious superiors had sprung, not from a lack of faith, but rather from an excess of faith. Specifically, Bruno was convinced that since God's power was infinite he had naturally created an infinite universe, within which there would naturally be an infinite number of habited worlds. His studies led him to the conviction that Ptolemy's closed system with its seven spheres and rigid boundaries was unworkable and inaccurate. Bruno rejected outright Ptolemy's convoluted system of epicycles and, in doing so, found himself overwhelmed by the awe-inspiring possibilities of an infinitely expanded horizon.

A radical alternative to the geocentric system had been suggested by a mathematician named Nicolaus Copernicus in 1543. Copernicus taught that the sun was the centre of the solar system and that the earth was just one of several astronomical objects rotating on its own axis and proceeding in an orbit around the sun. Copernicus had published his new heliocentric system in a work entitled *De revolutionibus orbum coelestium*. This was a ferociously technical work, which came stamped with the discouraging warning 'For Mathematicians Only' on the title page. Hardly surprisingly therefore that the Copernican system had been largely ignored until the explosive events of the early seventeenth century brought this astronomical controversy vividly to life. Bruno's vociferous support for the Copernican system had awakened the attention of the European intelligentsia to the debate.

In 1592, at the age of forty-eight, Bruno had begun to tire of his nomadic existence and he gave in to the repeated requests for a private tutor made to him by the nobleman Giovanni Mocenigo. Sadly the job offer turned out to be a trap designed to lure Bruno back to Italy where he could stand trial for crimes against the faith. Mocenigo was almost certainly in the pay of the Inquisition and he spent months convincing Bruno to take up his offer of a well-paid post, only then to testify against Bruno to the Venetian Inquisition. Once Bruno was back on Italian soil and Mocenigo had had some time to gather as much incriminating evidence as possible, the reaction was swift and decisive. Bruno was arrested and imprisoned. Had he stood trial in the comparatively liberal state of Venice, he might have been spared but Bruno had been a wanted man ever since his initial flight years before and in 1593 he was transferred to Rome and imprisoned at the headquarters of the Holy Inquisition. His trial dragged on for a further seven years; the methods of the Inquisition are well known and Bruno was certainly tortured during his incarceration. Nevertheless, he refused to capitulate. Instead on the 21 December 1599, just two months before his execution, Bruno's tormentors noted the following statement which reveals his overwhelming obstinacy in the face of years of violence and oppression; the prisoner declares that 'he does not wish to repent and that it is not for him to repent, that he has nothing to repent, and that he is unaware what he is supposed to repent of.'[4] On 17 February 1600, Giordano Bruno was burned at the stake.

Cyrano's work reveals a keen engagement with Bruno's ideas about the universe, and he would certainly have admired Bruno's extraordinary courage and extravagant style. The cruel irony of Bruno's fate was that it was his absolute devotion to his faith which killed him. He was by no means an atheist or an enemy of the faith. He had been so inspired by the revelations of the new cosmology that he formed the conviction that it was to the greater glory of God to have created a universe which far exceeded the scope of mankind's previous petty imaginings. Bruno was an enthusiast and a profoundly religious man. If he had cared less about the glory of God, he would have been able to recant his statement and save his life. It was just eleven years after Bruno's murder that Galileo published a book detailing findings which seemed to support the controversial Copernican system. Naturally, the example of Bruno's hideous fiery death loomed large in the minds of those engaged in astronomical studies. Hardly surprising then that Galileo chose to make no mention of Bruno in his work.

At the beginning of the seventeenth century, the moon had become the focus of an impassioned debate. Galileo's telescope had revealed mountains and lakes and other geographical features on the lunar landscape, which seemed to suggest that the moon was a planet like the earth. In fact, these mountains and lakes were actually impact craters and the moon is a satellite rather than a planet. The importance of Galileo's work was that, in accordance with the new methodology, he had used applied mathematics and observational proofs to support and underpin his scientific reasoning. All of Galileo's discoveries, from the mountains on the moon, to Jupiter's satellites, to the phases of Saturn were crucial bits of evidence in a much bigger argument. Galileo was looking at the concrete mathematical proofs that had been previously been lacking to confirm that the earth was in motion and not the centre of the universe. Essentially the question of whether the moon was a world like the earth was of vital significance because it seemed to hold the key to the triumph of the Copernican world-view.

Cyrano was not the first author to dream of travelling into space to resolve the argument first-hand. An English author, Bishop Francis Godwin, had written a book entitled *The Man in the Moon*, describing the adventures of a cocky Spaniard, Domingo Gonsales, who hitches a lift to the moon by ensnaring a flock of geese. Godwin had been a student at the University of Oxford during the period when Giordano Bruno tried with customary bravado, but without success, to convert the professors of that institution to Copernicanism. Although Bruno failed to win over the professors, it seems he found some sympathy among the students. Francis Godwin's work had appeared a good decade before Cyrano's and was an important source of inspiration to the Frenchman, a fact which Cyrano acknowledged with characteristic flair.* In the course of Cyrano's *Voyage to the Moon*, his hero encounters the hero of Godwin's work and the two are imprisoned together by the lunar inhabitants who have mistaken them for monkeys. Cyrano gives the following revealing explanation for the Spaniard's presence on the moon: 'In reality what had forced him to flee across the whole Earth, and eventually to abandon it for the Moon, was the

---

* *The Man in the Moon* was first published in 1638 and a French translation was published in Paris in 1648. We do not know for certain if Cyrano understood English; if he did not, then he had perhaps already begun his own moon voyage story before he read Godwin's work. Either way, he made no secret of his admiration for Godwin's work.

fact that he had been unable to find a single country where the imagination itself was free.'[5] Rather than try to hide the debt he owed to Godwin, Cyrano used it as a source of comedy. Cyrano's hero jokingly reproaches Gonsales for having preceded him, complaining that in looking for a way to reach the moon he had been forced to take the trouble of building a flying machine because Gonsales had already taken the easy option of flying there by harnessing migrating geese.

These poetic exiles had fled to the moon to discuss radical natural philosophy ideas with freedom. Unfortunately, for them lunar society turns out to have restrictions of its own and Dyrcona is eventually put on trial for insisting that he comes from earth. In a neat reversal of the terrestrial controversy, Dyrcona insists that their moon (the earth) is a world to his people and vice versa; this throws the religious authorities of the moon into confusion. Dyrcona is forced to recant, but the form of the address which Cyrano's man in the moon makes to his assembled public is steeped in irony and underlines the futility of a forced capitulation of this kind. 'People, I declare to you that this moon here is not a moon, but a world; and that that world down there is not a world but a moon. That is what the priests think it good you should believe.'[6]

These lines and the situation of Dyrcona's trial on the moon not only present an eloquent argument in favour of freedom of the imagination, they also have a very specific contemporary significance. Cyrano's readership would instantly have recognized the reference to a dramatic event in which one of the most renowned and respected thinkers of the age had been compelled, on pain of death, to pronounce a disavowal of his most firmly held convictions. In 1633, when Cyrano was a rebellious student at the Collège de Beauvais, Galileo Galilei had been put on trial by the Papal Inquisition. It was the second time that the great scientist had faced the wrath of the Holy Office and this time he would not escape unscathed. One of the key elements of Galileo's work to which the inquisitors objected was his contention that the geography of the moon, observable through his famous telescope revealed striking similarities to the geography of the earth.

Not only does Cyrano's account echo the fact of Galileo's forced renunciation, it also recalls the popular belief that, after pronouncing his formal statement that the earth was the unmoving centre of the universe, in strict accordance with biblical tradition, the great scientist muttered, '*Eppur si muove!*'★ As Cyrano wisely pointed out, however repressive the regime, however dire the threatened punishments, the state could still only control the ideas that its people expressed, it could never control their private beliefs. In the course of Dyrcona's trial on the moon, his defence is led by an erudite extraterrestrial who has taken pity on the hopelessness of the poor human and who does his best to convince the lunar authorities of the unreasonableness of attempting to control the private convictions of its people: 'Since every man is free, is he not also free to imagine whatever he wishes? What? Can you compel him to have no visions but your own? You can certainly force him to say that the moon is not a world, however he won't believe it for all that.'[7]

To a modern readership this defence of free thought seems rational and just, and consequently unremarkable. However, in the contemporary context this emphasis on the freedom of the individual imagination was dynamite. The Jesuit priest Father Garasse, who wrote numerous attacks on the freethinkers, highlights this very idea as 'the quintessence of atheism': 'The first moronic doctrine of these supposed wits: that there is nothing more free than belief and that no one should be forced or compelled to believe this or that.'[8] Although Cyrano had put his argument into the mouth of an extraterrestrial his polemical intention is clear.

Cyrano repeatedly emphasized the overwhelming and entirely unjustified arrogance of humanity. The aliens, encountered by his

★ 'But it does move.'

hero, serve to highlight the numerous failings of the human race. Cyrano shows humanity to be unbearably self-satisfied, he constantly decries 'the insufferable pride of human beings'.[9] This appeal for humility springs from the teaching of the new science. Just as Bruno tried to argue that sometimes it can be better to doubt and wait, than to leap precipitately to a wrong conclusion, Cyrano tries again and again to suggest that human understanding is all too often flawed and unreliable. These reflections form the most heretical aspect of the new cosmology. The papacy was not against the act of modelling a saner solar system mathematically. In fact, the notion of a heliocentric universe predated Christianity. The real controversy lay in the perceived implications of the heliocentric model. The public imagination was not likely to be gripped by Copernicus's complex series of mathematical workings, but as more accessible texts began to appear, exploring the implications of the new cosmology, the church had to fight a rising tide of speculation about mankind's place in the universe, not to mention the shock of a direct contradiction of biblical authority.

The scientific revolution that so enthralled Cyrano was not solely the result of a new conception of methodology. A series of factors combined to produce a tremendously fertile climate for scientific discovery. For example, optical instrumentation had become increasingly sophisticated and this enabled early modern astronomers to work with more detailed mathematical information than ever before in making their calculations. One technological advance in particular was crucial: the 'perspective glass' (or telescope as it came to be called) was invented by a Dutchman in the late sixteenth century. When Galileo trained his telescope on the stars and realized that the Copernican model of the universe came much closer to offering an explanation of the observations he made, that revelation produced a profoundly important epistemological shift towards a new humility and awareness that mankind's perception was actually extremely limited and his role as lord of creation perhaps not so assured. For rebellious radicals like Cyrano the sun-centred universe was an electrifying place of possibility and wonder.

Johannes Kepler, a younger man than Galileo and a citizen of Protestant Germany was inspired by his greater distance from the horrors of the Papal Inquisition to take the new cosmology a stage further than Galileo could have risked doing. In his letter written in reply to Galileo's work and published as *Conversations With Galileo's Sidereal Messenger*, he admits the possibility of a plurality of inhabited worlds, but is careful to maintain the earth's privileged position as the home of mankind, deducing 'that this world of ours is the most excellent of them all if there should happen to be plurality of worlds'. In the same letter he also refers directly to the fate of the devout monk Giordano Bruno. He does so in order to underline the extent of his commitment to the truth of Galileo's observations. He implies that he would die to defend Galileo's results. 'If you had discovered any planets revolving around one of the fixed stars there would now be waiting for me chains and a prison amid Bruno's innumerabilities, I should rather say exile to his infinite space.'[10]

Privately, Kepler was less circumspect, becoming one of the earliest of many authors to succumb to the allure of an imaginative exploration of the moon. His *Somnium* (*The Dream*) is another of Cyrano's important influences; it was one of the earliest texts to combine serious scientific thought with vivid speculation about the possibility of life on the moon. Unlike Cyrano, Kepler scrupulously avoids any challenge to mankind's position as 'lord of creation' from the lunar inhabitants. They are depicted as an unprepossessing bunch of giant, slimy monsters. Kepler did not publish this work in his lifetime but it did circulate fairly widely in manuscript and despite his precautions it almost certainly contributed to his mother being put on trial for witchcraft. She narrowly escaped being condemned to death. It took all of Kepler's ingenuity and influence to save the eccentric but harmless old lady.

In its early years scientific enquiry was fraught with very real danger. Those who became involved with the new cosmology were men whose impressive intellect was equalled by their great courage. Small wonder then that the new cosmological ideas were so appealing to Cyrano. One of the most inflammatory aspects of Galileo's work was his observation of distinct similarities between the observed surface of the moon and the familiar geography of the earth, because this gave rise to speculation that the moon might very well prove to be an inhabited planet like our own. This idea, which directly contradicted biblical authority, was to prove enormously seductive, but it was left to the next generation, and radical authors such as Cyrano, to question the received wisdom that revelations about the moon could not challenge mankind's position as the 'primary rational creature' and dead centre of the turning universe.[11]

The secret illness

Aside from the works themselves, for which we have no definite composition dates, there is a lone surviving shred of
concrete evidence relating to the period 1641 to 1648. The document, an IOU dated 1 April 1645, has been particularly
inflammatory despite its relative brevity. The paper is an acknowledgement of a debt owed to the barber surgeon Elie Pigou by a
patient, who signs himself Alexandre de Cyrano Bergerac.
According to the document, Cyrano was lodged, fed and treated by
Pigou for a period of four months and the resulting debt amounted
to 400 livres. According to the terms of the contract, Pigou had
'treated, dressed, medicated and cured him of the secret illness
with which he was afflicted'.[1]

The phrase 'secret illness' has naturally attracted a great deal of
speculation as to what exactly may have been wrong with Cyrano.
The nineteenth-century scholar Frédéric Lachèvre who first published this document assumed that a secret illness must imply
venereal disease. He extrapolated out from this clue and described
Cyrano as a rake: a lecherous womanizer, who drank, gambled and
whored away his inheritance and ended up catching the pox. For

Lachèvre the 'secret illness' had to be a sexually transmitted disease and the sexually transmitted disease had to be syphilis. Lachèvre shores up this chain of reasoning with a further 'proof': the existence of a poem entitled 'Le Pauvre Malade' signed with an initial C. This poem was initially attributed to Cyrano by another academic, Lacroix, who had seen in it the description of Cyrano's fatal wounding of 1654 and dated it accordingly. Lachèvre decided that the poem was about the pox and dated it to 1645. The opening line of 'Le Pauvre Malade': 'Magdelon, I am very ill' does offer a vague echo of the first line of Théophile de Viau's poem about the pox, albeit in a far less aggressive register. Théophile's poem begins with the unambiguous statement: 'Phylis, It's all fucked, I am dying of the pox', and ends with a deliberately inverted and obscene parody of a repentant prayer for forgiveness. Lachèvre's interpretation of 'Le Pauvre Malade' is seriously undermined by the lines

> *People who see me in the street . . .*
> *. . . Imagine that it must be the pox*

This phrase clearly implies that an added humiliation and increase of the poet's sufferings is that his weakness and fever cause him to be mistaken for a syphilitic. The signature C. does not appear in all volumes in which the poem appears and in 1901 the poem was attributed to the Abbot Testu who was suffering not from the pox but from diseased lungs.[2]

The contract with Pigou is not proof that Cyrano was suffering from syphilis and 'Le Pauvre Malade' even less so.

There are two other possible explanations of the contract: Cyrano may have been receiving treatment for a disease other than syphilis or his illness may have been linked to lingering health problems caused by the severe injuries he had sustained in the army, as suggested by Le Bret in his biography. Certain critics have read the document as a proof that Cyrano's 'secret parts' had been damaged by the musket shot he received in the war; they trace themes of castration through the work and speculate that he may have been rendered impotent by the injury. Ultimately, the contract with Pigou does not contain sufficient information to resolve the question but the 'secrecy' of the illness may well imply that it was of a sexual nature.

A key link in the chain of inference that eventually saw Cyrano labelled a syphilitic is the fact that a common and devastating symptom of tertiary syphilis is insanity. In the late stages of the disease, once neurosyphilis sets in, the patient experiences bewildering mood swings, delusions of grandeur, paranoia and eventually dementia. There were no references to Cyrano's madness during his lifetime, perhaps because no one wanted to risk reprisals from the great swordsman, and the first reference to Cyrano as a syphilitic was not to appear until over two centuries after his death. The first accusation of insanity dates from sometime between 1657 and 1659. In his *Historiettes*, composed between these dates, but not published until the early eighteenth century, Tallemant des Reaux referred to the scandal caused by *The Death of Agrippina* and described the author as 'a madman named Cyrano'. Given the context it is clear that Tallemant's remark was chiefly intended as a comment on the outrageousness of Cyrano's work and the provocation it contained. In his attempt to get himself released from the clutches of the Inquisition, Charles Dassoucy had written an attack on the atheists of his time in which he described Cyrano as having 'died insane'.[3] However, Dassoucy's evidence was obtained by the Inquisition whose techniques are well known, and in any case the man is the very definition of an unreliable witness. There is no shred of evidence to suggest that Cyrano was either syphilitic or suffering from any kind of mental illness, if anything he was only too lucid.

While certain minds recoiled in horror from the new science and its devastation of the old certainties, Cyrano was one of the few truly adventurous thinkers who considered the idea of mankind cast adrift in an infinite void as an extraordinary liberation. As the fictional lunar explorer Domingo Gonsales tells Cyrano's hero – outer space was the only remaining refuge for the freethinker. Cyrano has the Spaniard lament the impossibility of finding a country on earth where the imagination is truly free. Gonsales explains that his scientific interests had nearly landed him in the clutches of the Spanish Inquisition. He remarks that if an outsider (i.e. not a member of church or university) expresses any interesting ideas he will instantly be dismissed as 'an idiot, a madman or an atheist'.[4] Cyrano was accused at various times of being all three and yet he found a way to use such accusations to his advantage. If only a madman, a fool or an atheist would uphold and explore the possibilities of the new science then the solution was to try to make the repressive censorship of the time work in the author's favour – by penning a text so foolish, crazy and atheistical that the very excesses of his provocation would serve to protect him. It is not for nothing that the first edition of *The Voyage to the Moon* published by Le Bret was retitled *A Comical History* – it was essential to underline the humorous nature of the text in order that the authorities might be tricked into dismissing Cyrano's imaginings as too outrageous to be taken seriously.

Le Bret includes a detailed list of all the authors from Lucian to Gassendi who have supported the idea of a world in the moon in order to legitimize his friend's work and even goes so far as to insist that out of all the illustrious company to have considered the idea he is 'all the more to be praised because he treated in an amusing way a chimaera which they handled all too seriously'.[5] This is disingenuous in the extreme – for, although the overall tone of Cyrano's madcap adventures in outer space is playful, the burlesque buffoonery of the voyages conceals a serious purpose: a determined and provocative iconoclasm. His imaginary exploration of the newly expanded universe afforded Cyrano not only an opportunity to contribute to the ongoing debate about Copernicanism, but also a vehicle for some biting satirical comment on a society with which he found himself increasingly at odds.

If further testimony, aside from the passionate hilarity of Cyrano's science-fiction masterpiece, is needed, we may turn to a text written by Charles Dassoucy. Dassoucy had been a vivid presence in Cyrano's youth but a bitter quarrel divided them. After Cyrano's death Dassoucy penned a number of mocking attacks on his erstwhile friend and in particular, whilst languishing in the dungeons of the Holy Inquisition in Rome, he wrote an address to the Pope entitled *The Thoughts of Monsieur Dassoucy in the Holy Office in Rome* in which he admitted to having been connected to some notorious free thinkers but detailed at length the sharp contrast between their dubious ideas and his own strict adherence to the principles of the true faith. Allowances must be made for the desperation of a man on death row. Dassoucy's betrayal of Cyrano (who was already dead in any case) and others was of little consequence since he was careful not to name names. His description of Cyrano is interesting because he dismisses him as a madman, and in order to prove this insanity he details the extent of Cyrano's Copernican convictions:

He had such a powerful imagination that there was nothing neither so ridiculous nor so extravagant that he would not consider as an unassailable truth; and he was not content with being entirely convinced if others were not also as convinced as him. He wanted everyone to believe that each star is a world and that on top of that there were an infinity of others, and that there were numerous suns and no matter what I fed him he would quarrel with me and would not have thought twice about breaking off with me if I did not agree to allow that there was a world in the moon.[6]

This vision of Cyrano's aggressive commitment to the new science contrasts sharply with Le Bret's deliberate attempt to tone down the controversial nature of his friend's work by describing it as having been written without serious intent, purely in order to 'amuse'. Religious opposition to the new cosmology was only part of the battle; ancient convictions about the nature of knowledge itself also needed to be overturned before the new science could begin to grow into a truly creative enterprise. Writers like Cyrano and Francis Godwin (the original creator of Domingo Gonsales) deliberately blurred the boundaries between truth and fiction in order to open up a space within which the essential new scientific concept of 'probability' could be explored.

In his *Novum Organum*, published in 1620 when Cyrano was only a year old, Francis Bacon had reflected on the inadequacies of the old optical technology and of the old conceptions of knowledge, 'the human understanding is like a false mirror, which, receiving rays irregularly distorts and discolours the nature of things by mingling its own nature with it'.[7] Bacon's acute perception of the limitations of the human perspective led to his dream of a coordinated programme of utilitarian cooperation and discovery. In *The Voyage to the Moon* Cyrano's befuddled space traveller is told that his attempts to comprehend the mysteries of the universe using his woefully limited sense perception are like a blind man's attempts to describe colour or the beauty of a landscape. Despite his identification of 'vain imaginations' as one of the 'distempers of learning' Francis Bacon was unable to resist the temptation to pen his own 'science fiction' fantasy. In the *New Atlantis*, published posthumously in 1627, Bacon outlined his utopian vision of a devout Christian society dedicated to progress through scientific research and experimentation. The story describes the wonders achieved by the men of 'Bensalem', a remote island community in the South Pacific, thanks to their adherence to Bacon's own scientific ideas. Ironically, despite his extraordinarily perceptive theories on scientific development, Bacon, like Cyrano, was far from possessing a truly scientific mind and the 'false mirror' of his own perceptions led him into a misguided dismissal of the central importance of mathematics. Bacon was profoundly hostile to the work of mathematicians, regarding it as divorced from the reality of natural philosophical investigation. Furthermore, Bacon considered the attainment of certain absolute principles as the true aim of such investigations. In contrast with practitioners, such as Robert Hooke, who had begun to recognize that approximation and probabilistic ideas were the key to scientific development, Bacon refused to accept that absolute certainty was a concept of little or no value to the natural philosopher. The authors of fictional accounts of the world in the moon were engaged in the development of a conception of knowledge reliant on intelligent, imaginative speculation.

Johannes Kepler acknowledged the comical works of the classical author Lucian as the literary source which first inspired the composition of his own account of exile to the freedom of the world in the moon, *The Dream*. 'Later I came across the two books of Lucian's *True Hisory* written in Greek, which I chose as my means of mastering the language . . . These were my first traces of a trip to the moon, which was my aspiration in later times.'[8] The application of satirical techniques to the new science was a radical achievement of early modern authors and formed the earliest roots of the 'thought experiment', an essential tool of modern-day astrophysics. Lucian's *True History* plays with notions of truth and lies, and many of the readers of early science fiction must have anticipated precisely the same pleasure which Lucian promises his readers: 'to heare so many notorious lies perswasively set down'.[9]

The decision to treat urgent scientific inquiry in a lighthearted manner sprang not just from the necessity imposed by censorship but seems also to be the result of a determination to disseminate the radical ideas of the new science as widely as possible. The work of Bernard le Bovier de Fontenelle was perhaps the first text to openly declare its intention to popularize scientific ideas. By choosing to address a specifically female audience in the person of the Noble Lady with whom the discussions take place, Fontenelle aimed to demonstrate that a specialized education (of the sort unavailable to women) was not essential to an understanding of the new ideas about the universe. Furthermore, Fontenelle recognized the value of a blending of fictional and factual elements in the explication of scientific theory. He acknowledged that such a method was central to his endeavour without being able to explain adequately why this should be the case. 'The visions themselves that I have added, have something of a real Foundation in them; the True and the False are here mixed . . . I do not undertake to justifie a Composure so fantastical: This is the most important Point of this Work, and 'tis only this that I cannot give a Reason for.'[10]

His description of his method recalls that of Kepler, who was called to account for allowing his imagination too free a rein in his writing. He acknowledges this fact at the start of a letter written in response to Galileo's *Sidereus Nuncius*, 'my friends cautioned me that it seemed a little too unconventional in conception'.[11] The astronomer was unapologetic about his extravagant, irreverent style and defended the importance of humour to the discussion of serious scientific subjects: 'Whereas most debaters get all heated up, I regard humour as a more pleasant tone in discussions. Other authors strive for impressiveness in the exposition of philosophy by the weightiness of their assertions; yet they often prove amusing, unintentionally. I seem by nature cut out to lighten the hard work and difficulty of a subject by mental relaxation, conveyed by the style.'[12]

Cyrano's work was nothing if not 'unconventional in conception' and he recognized that humour could prove a powerful means of persuasion. Just as Cyrano's hero frequently reveals his own limited 'earthbound' perspective in his inappropriate mocking laughter, so he is in turn the butt of the joke to the superior beings he encounters. Cyrano dared to imagine that seen from space, mankind was not much more than a cosmic joke. In the world of *The Voyages to the Moon and Sun* (just as in Douglas Adams's *A Hitchhiker's Guide to the Galaxy* in our own time) the rest of the universe is shown to be laughing at the puny race of upstarts who have the colossal ignorance and arrogance to imagine that they are the centre of the universe. While conversing with the lunar courtiers about the physics of the universe, Dyrcona disingenuously admits that, were it not for the fact that their ideas are contrary to the teachings of the Catholic faith, he would consider their explanations 'far more reasonable than our own'. He then gamely tries to use a biblical reference to contradict their rationalistic account of the origins of the universe to little effect: 'I asked him what he could reply to the authority of Moses and that this great patriarch expressly declares that God created the world in six days. Instead of answering me the ignorant fellow only laughed.'[13] Laughter in this instance is used to signal the flimsiness of the church's arguments against the new science. Paradoxically the intent is at once polemical and self-mocking.

The one subject that Cyrano consistently refused to take seriously was that of the terrible risk involved in contradicting the teachings of the church. Cyrano clearly took great pleasure in using the freedom of fiction to laugh in the face of his opposition. As for example, when Dyrcona finds himself surrounded by threatening hordes who look set to tear him limb from limb, or at the very least deliver him into the hands of the religious authorities who have vowed to burn him at the stake. The peasants' suspicion and fear of the cornered 'magician' and his demonic black horse mount to fever pitch, the priest leading them screams a garbled exorcism that ends in a threat to eviscerate Dyrcona if he moves a muscle. The hero cannot flee for his life, not because he is intimidated by the priest's vehemence, but because he is laughing too hard. Weak with hilarity at the ignorance and superstition of his enemies, he is easy prey and is quickly caught and bound hand and foot. Meanwhile, in a revealing little background vignette the priest's servant secures Dyrcona's black horse for the vicarage stable, the peasants being too frightened to stake their own claim on the valuable animal that the priest has convinced them is satanic. It was not only Cyrano's fictional hero who would set laughter above his own safety. The serious comedian himself would eventually pay the ultimate price in the real world as a result of his comical irreverence.

Cyrano's frequent laughter is occasionally edged with bitterness and like many a modern stand-up comedian he is often at his funniest when he is at his angriest or most exasperated. In particular, one episode which occurs during *The Voyage to the Sun* allows Cyrano to elaborate his most comprehensive attack on the 'presumptuous stupidity' of mankind. In a comic reversal of fortune man is for once in the power of the beasts. In a direct contradiction of the Old Testament the 'fowl of the air' rule over mankind, whose God-given dominion over the natural world suddenly starts to look rather shaky. The birds who capture Dyrcona have a democratically elected leader, a sophisticated judiciary and an unrelenting contempt for mankind. He is put on trial for the crime of 'being human' and his only hope of reprieve is to convince them that he is in fact a monkey. Throughout *Voyage to the Sun* references to the Old Testament account of creation abound only to be swiftly subverted and turned to ridicule.

Dyrcona's confrontation with the republic of the birds serves partly as a satirical comment on the human tendency to dismiss difference as a sure sign of inferiority. The less enlightened birds condemn the captive purely on the basis that he doesn't look like them declaring: 'That it was horrible to believe that a beast who did not have a face made like their own could be in possession of reason. "Ha! What," they murmured to one another, "he has no beak, no feathers, no claws and yet his soul should be spiritual? O gods! What impertinence!'"[14] But there is another deeper purpose to the encounter. Here is yet another example of Cyrano using comedy in order to address issues of contemporary philosophical debate. In the late sixteenth century Montaigne had made the controversial assertion that animals were not only rational and moral beings but that their morality and reason were superior to that of humans. In Cyrano's lifetime this idea became the focus of a vivid controversy sparked by the great philosopher René Descartes. Descartes dismissed Montaigne's ideas and asserted that not only were animals neither rational nor moral but that they were not even conscious. Cyrano was an admirer of Descartes and mentions him in *The Voyage to the Sun* as 'this famous philosopher of our time'.[15] But when the hotly contested dispute about animal consciousness and the nature of the soul arose, setting Descartes at odds with his old mentor Pierre Gassendi, Cyrano naturally sided firmly with Gassendi and the animals.

In 1641 Descartes had published a book entitled *Méditations métaphysiques* in which he argued that the soul and the body were entirely separate and that only mankind was possessed of an immortal soul while animals were no more than automata or machines. Gassendi wrote a detailed response in his *Disquisitio metaphysica* in 1644. Among other objections he offers up the charming example (that he had personally witnessed) of a dog that had learnt to bark along in imitation of a trumpet. He points out that just because animals do not possess human reasoning it does not follow that they possess no form of reasoning at all – just as the fact that they are unable to speak human languages (despite occasional feats of imitation like that of the musical dog) does not preclude their communicating in languages of their own, which we in turn cannot speak nor understand. Cyrano takes this process of argument a stage further. He highlights the absurdity of some of Descartes's propositions by putting them into the mouths of the birds who condemn his hero Dyrcona to death for the crime of being human. They reverse Descartes's own argument, insisting that although a man may imitate birdsong he doesn't understand it and is therefore not a rational creature and certainly not possessed of an immortal soul. Dassoucy also mentions this debate in his document written to get him out of the claws of the Inquisition. With his characteristic humour he pokes fun at the libertines for their affection for the natural world: 'As they do not believe in God or the Devil. They do not believe in the the immortality of the soul either; and what is amusing about them is that there is no man so vile or stupid but he believes himself above all the animals, but these men, with all their haughtiness and their wit do not draw any distinction between their own souls and those of their horses.'[16]

Dassoucy was certainly not a partisan of the animal faction at any time and his choice of a horse as an example is not without significance. In his semi-autobiographical novel he laughs at himself for the 'cowardice' which meant that he never rode if he could possibly avoid it. In one instance he congratulates himself on wisely refusing to take to the saddle after having spotted the nasty look on the horse's face. In contrast Cyrano's overwhelming affection for the natural world is a strong theme throughout his work and one is left in no doubt as to his allegiance in the debate. When the birds encountered in *The Voyage to the Sun* sit in judgement on the 'monster' that is man, some focus on Dyrcona's unfortunate lack of a beak and feathers and this serves as a satirical comment on humanity's tendency to react badly to physical difference. However, the more intelligent members of this avian community despise his self-appointed (biblical) role as lord of creation and this gives rise to a sophisticated critique of mankind's engagement with the natural world:

> Man . . . so stupid and so vain, that he convinces himself that we were all created for him; man, so clear-sighted that he can not even distinguish between sugar and arsenic, and who would swallow

hemlock that his fine judgement would have him take for parsley; man who insists that we reason only through the senses and yet who has the weakest, the slowest and the falsest senses of all creatures; man in short, whom nature created for the sake of variety like other freaks, but in whom she nevertheless instilled an ambition to rule over all other animals and to destroy them all.[17]

This is a determinedly non-Christian viewpoint, attributing the creation of humanity to 'nature' not to God and thereby directly contradicting more than one biblical teaching. According to the Bible man was made in God's image, here he is seen as an aberration of nature, a monstrous freak. The Bible teaches that man is given dominion over the animals by divine right, the birds, however, see mankind as abusing his natural (not divine) strength and intelligence, striving to dominate and destroy the rest of the natural world. The passage also highlights man's flawed sense perception, a central preoccupation of the new science.

The environmentalist focus of this passage seems extraordinarily modern even if Cyrano could never have anticipated the extent to which his criticisms of mankind's ignorant destruction of the natural world would become relevant on a global scale. His denunciation of 'the insufferable pride of human beings which persuades them that nature was created only for them' is all the more starkly relevant in our own time when technological advances have only increased mankind's devastating power to ravage and destroy the environment.[18] Cyrano could never have predicted the horrors we have inflicted on the planet and yet he was not only ahead of his own time in his criticisms but ahead of ours too.

Cyrano's search for a naturalistic, irreligious explanation to replace the biblical account of creation leads him elsewhere in *The Voyage to the Sun* to an imaginative vision of the creative power of 'chance', which could almost have been written by Darwin himself:

But, you will say, how could chance have assembled in one place all the things that were necessary to produce this oak tree? I reply that it is no marvel that the material should be assembled in such a way as to form an oak, but rather that the material being so assembled the marvel would have been great indeed if the oak had not been formed. A little less of certain forms and it could have been an elm, a poplar, a willow, an elder, some heather or some moss; a few more of certain other forms and it had been a sensitive plant, an oyster, a worm, a fly, a frog, a sparrow, a monkey, a man.[19]

Cyrano may not have been a talented physicist, but his profound love of nature and his careful observation of the natural world and the intricate connections between all forms of life made him a truly excellent naturalist. He may not have anticipated Darwin but it cannot be denied that this is an eerie precursor of the theory of natural selection. He contrasts the infinite variety of possible forms with the relatively small number of actual forms seen in nature, one of the favoured arguments of the renowned evolutionary theorist Richard Dawkins:

You are surprised that this matter, mixed up pell-mell by chance, should have built up a man, since so many things are necessary to the construction of his being. But you do not know that this matter moving towards the design of a man has stopped a hundred million times on the way to form, some-times a stone, sometimes lead, sometimes coral, sometimes a flower, sometimes a comet, for the excess or the lack of cer-tain forms which were necessary or superfluous to the design of a man. It is not marvellous that an infinite quantity of matter changing and moving continually should have met together to form the few animals, vegetables and minerals that we see.[20]

Dyrcona's trial is delayed at first because according to the rules of the avian court he cannot be judged in case the miserable weather influences the jury to be harsher than they might be otherwise. This impressive ideal of impartiality is ever so slightly undermined though by the choice of advocates in his case. The prosecution is led by a partridge who has recently escaped from earth where an encounter with a hunter has left him with a vicious throat wound. It is interesting that Cyrano chose to gift the prosecutor with the exact same injury that he himself had suffered. Meanwhile the defence is undertaken by a starling, an apparently anodyne choice except that 'starling' was a synonym for chatterbox or 'bird brain'. Despite the pronouncement of a death sentence Dyrcona is ultimately reprieved by the last-minute intervention of a parakeet whom he had previously released from captivity on earth. Here again Cyrano reveres 'freedom' as the highest moral ideal and also shows the birds to be more 'humane' than humans – no last-minute reprieve had been forthcoming for Vanini or for Giordano Bruno.

It is Cyrano's endless inventiveness and wit that save his satire from becoming morose. His dark vision of mankind may occasionally recall that of the pitiful figure of the card sharp who appears in Dassoucy's 'adventures'. Having been found cheating and badly beaten, the card sharp defends the dishonesty of his profession on the basis that 'The world is nothing but a great forest where men, a hundred times more dangerous than wild beasts, devour each other like wolves.'[21] The negative view taken by the lowly criminal reflects that of one of the greatest philosophers of the time. In *Leviathan* (1651), Thomas Hobbes had argued that 'without government, human life is solitary, poor, mean, nasty, brutish, and short'.[22]

Of the three imprisonments to which Cyrano's hero is subjected, it is at the hands of men that he suffers the most injustice and it is only the parliament of birds who show mercy, tolerance and understanding. Although Cyrano constantly compares humanity to a variety of beasts and although his hero is mistaken at various times for a monkey, an ostrich and even a monster, he retains a faith in nature which seems to provide him with the same inspiration and reassurance as other men found in religion. Cyrano's letter, 'On the reflections of the trees in the water' is a delirious prose poem, a hymn to an upside-down world, where 'the fishes stroll through the woods'.[23] In the letter 'On a house in the country' he not only laughingly refers to the rejuvenating power of the countryside (a theme he returned to in *The Voyage to the Moon*) but also to its ennobling effect, such that 'a rural gentleman is an unknown prince'.[24] In order to underline the superiority of lunar society Cyrano chose to describe the delicious luxury of a bedchamber, not draped with the silk and velvet that might have been expected, but where the beds are made from deep piles of jasmine and orange blossom and the room is lit by glow-worm-filled lanterns. This preference of the 'natural' to the artificial was a characteristic feature of the freethinkers whose extensive classical reading caused them to dream of a golden age of Arcadian simplicity before the corruption of court and city could pervert the 'natural' virtue of mankind. In Théophile de Viau's 'Elegy to a Lady' he paints a vivid portrait of this naturalistic libertine ideal,

> *I wish to write verses that are not forced,*
> *Let my mind wander through little pathways,*
> *To seek out secret spots where nothing bothers me,*
> *To spend an hour staring at my reflection in the water,*
> *Listen in a dream to the course of a stream,*
> *Write in the woods, break off, be silent,*
> *Compose a quatrain without thinking about it.*[25]

The solitude and isolation essential to the libertine ideal of creation and virtue seem to have been the rule by which Cyrano chose to guide his own writing life. Just as Le Bret had described him in the guardhouse voluntarily isolating himself from his companions to work on a sonnet, so Cyrano's own letter 'On a house in the country' asks the absent lord of the manor: 'O Gods! Is it possible that a philosopher like you should prefer the vanity, sorrows and trouble of the court to the peace and quiet of such an agreeable retreat?'[26] Despite having initially tried hard to live up to the standards of courtly life, following the traditional 'gentlemanly' path of a career in the armed forces and disguising his humble origins under a self-created myth of noble Gascon lineage, Cyrano ultimately turned his back on 'worldly' success and chose to revel in the independence and freedom the decision offered him. No surprise then that in his fantasy world dressing luxuriously in the latest fashions was a mark of ignominy nor that in his ideal society no poet ever starves as long as his inspiration lasts because original thought is a currency worth more than gold. Nor that he should dream of a superior alien society in outer space where, rather than recommending each other to the care of God (*Adieu*), Lunarians bid one another farewell using the phrase 'Remember to live free.'[27]

13

A profane brotherhood

To a certain extent Cyrano's status as a marginal member of society was fixed even before his birth. His grandfather's Protestantism had cast the family into the heart of a repressed and hated minority. Certain members of the younger generation (notably Cyrano's father and siblings) seem to have rejected this alienation and striven to eradicate the stain of difference by an intense devotion to the Catholic norm, but Cyrano displayed a 'dangerous tendency' to isolate and differentiate himself still further. Refusing to define his beliefs, his sexuality or even his biography, he embraced and exaggerated the role of outsider. As Le Bret would put it, 'as he had nought but exceptional sentiments, so none of his works were ever commonplace'.[1]

On occasion, Cyrano seems to have gone out of his way to be as outrageous and offensive as possible, almost as if he were determined to test the limits of his audience. He repeatedly made jokes which defied even the most sacred teachings of the church. In their condemnation of Dyrcona the parliament of birds reveal their conviction that the human belief in life after death springs from the fundamentally servile nature of mankind. The birds suggest that humanity's 'false hopes of immortality' spring less from the 'horror which un-being inspires in them than from the fear of having no one to order them around after death'.[2] The birds of paradise sent to console Dyrcona on his deathbed express the same atheistic notion as the character Sejanus in Cyrano's tragedy *The Death of Agrippina*. They whisper that Dyrcona should liberate himself from his fear of death by accepting that: 'in the blink of an eye after your life ends you will become that which you were a blink of an eye before it began'.[3] This is an idea that in our own time many might find disquieting, but that in Cyrano's lifetime could have led to its author being tortured, having his tongue cut out or being burned at the stake.

Cyrano's desire to think the unthinkable sometimes led him into very dark imaginings indeed. His account of the funeral rites on the world of the moon is a perfect example. At first his introduction of the pagan idea that cremation is a pure and noble end and that only criminals should be buried in the earth seems to be a simple reversal of expectations, intended to vindicate the heretics whose death by fire was supposed to be the proof of their damnation. This alternative viewpoint also neatly undermines the triumph of the religious authorities. Cyrano even includes a nightmarish vision of Christian burial designed to call the notion of 'resting in peace' sharply into question: 'Can you imagine anything more hideous than a corpse crawling with swarms of worms, at the mercy of toads that gnaw at its cheeks; in short, the plague dressed in a man's body?'[4] As a battle-hardened soldier Cyrano would have been all too familiar with the horrific reality of a putrefying corpse.

And yet this is not the last of the provocation; not only does Cyrano deliberately dwell on the physicality of death but he even dreams up a vision of vampirism to rival Bram Stoker's wildest imaginings. He explains that while cremation was the usual funeral rite on the moon another fate awaited the mortal remains of the most noble. The friends of a moribund philosopher would gather round his deathbed and his closest friend would watch for the moment when the dying man was on the brink of death in order to plunge a dagger into the failing heart and drink his friend's life blood. A ritual would then take place during which all the dearest friends of the departed would partake in an orgy of lovemaking and cannibalistic feasting in an attempt to see the dead reborn in the form of a child conceived during one of the ritual couplings. This is a grim, literal rereading of the Catholic doctrine of the holy sacrament of communion – with the friends of the dead man consuming his body and his blood in order to guarantee a 'resurrection'. Perhaps the choice of an attack on the doctrine of transubstantiation also reveals the traces of Cyrano's Protestant roots.

It is possible that this morbid focus on the rituals of death and decay may have been inspired by the death of Cyrano's father on 18 January 1648. Although the exact composition dates of *The Voyages to the Moon and Sun* are unknown, the most likely periods are 1642–3 and 1648–9 for the *Moon* and 1648–54 for the *Sun*; no doubt the loss of a father with whom he had never enjoyed an easy relationship must have been a spur to Cyrano's creativity. Grief is all the more devastating when mixed with anger and self-reproach. It is impossible to reconstruct the complex nature of Cyrano's feelings for his father but the hints in his work seem to imply a strong element of conflict. A codicil in Abel senior's will mentions a theft from his house that took place during his final illness and states that the victim wished to conceal the identities of the two culprits. The discovery of this document has led to accusations that Cyrano and his brother Abel II were guilty of taking advantage of their father's weakened state. No concrete evidence can be found to support this interpretation of the mysterious document but its existence casts a dark shadow over the family. Cyrano's mother had died at an earlier unknown date and he and his brother Abel were the sole beneficiaries of their father's will. Their two other siblings, Denis and Catherine, were both members of religious orders and therefore ineligible to inherit any part of the estate.

Cyrano chose to sign his first published work, a short introductory piece for his friend Dassoucy's poetic work *The Judgment of Paris*, not with his family name but with a pen name that he had chosen for himself for its combination of a Gascon surname and a truly heroic forename. He set down in black and white his rejection of the homely Savinien de Cyrano in favour of a name to conjure with – *Hercule de Bergerac*. The letter is addressed 'To the stupid reader and not to the wise' and in it Cyrano explains that only idiots will not appreciate Dassoucy's work and recommends therefore that they leave it well alone, rather than risk revealing their ignorance in misguided criticism of his friend's talents. Cyrano jokingly concludes with a wish that all idiots could be lumped together to form a single monster that he might slay in true Herculean fashion.

Although this was Cyrano's first printed work it is extremely unlikely that it was his first composition. By 1648 he had already begun to establish a reputation for himself due to the circulation of his works in manuscript form. The preface was also the first concrete link tying him to Charles Dassoucy. His close association with Dassoucy is one of the keystones of the argument for his homosexuality. Certain references and jokes within Cyrano's works, as well as the comments of some of his contemporaries, do seem to point to his having been involved in one or more passionate same-sex relationships. The anecdote most often cited to support the idea of Cyrano's involvement in a gay love triangle with Dassoucy and Chapelle is the 'Chapon' incident, as related by Dassoucy himself in his semi-autobiographical novel *The Adventures*. To explain the bitter enmity between himself and Cyrano and the duellist's frequent threats to kill him (which he admits to taking seriously enough to flee the country) Dassoucy describes an obscure practical joke:

The late B[ergerac] had good reason to wish to kill me, since in
his worst fit of famine I was inhuman enough to hide away from
his need a de Mans capon straight from the spit, that I hid under
my bed in vain since the steam that roused his appetite and at the
same time hardened his heart made him well enough aware that
he had in me nothing more than a cruel and barbarous friend.[5]

The fact that the word *chapon* meaning capon could also be used to
signify a young man combined with the alliterative link
Chapelle/chapon has led to this anecdote being read, not just as a
fling at Cyrano's poverty and near starvation – humiliating accusations in themselves which would be taken up by other enemies of
Cyrano after his death – but as the key to the relationship linking
the three men. According to this interpretation the clash between
Cyrano and Dassoucy would have as its origin their rivalry for
Chapelle's favours.

As further corroboration of Cyrano's disappointed love for
Chapelle a literary portrait of the young man has been identified in
the character known only as the 'son of the host' who appears
towards the end of *The Voyage to the Moon*. There does seem to be
a parallel between the situation of the fictional young man who
entertains Dyrcona at a dinner with an elderly sage and that of
Chapelle, the son of François Lhuillier who played host to the
philosopher Gassendi and his circle. The glamorous and intelligent
youth described in Cyrano's prose rules his household with a rod of
iron, he takes precedence over his ageing father and the elderly
philosophers who discourse wisely with the space traveller. The
author's admiration for his good looks, vitality and outstanding
promise is clear. He is also by far the most irreverent and provocative character encountered by the hero, and it is the 'son of the
host' who offers the most daring challenges to religious orthodoxy.
In the uncensored original ending of *The Voyage to the Moon* a particularly blasphemous exchange between Dyrcona and the young

man is brought to a sudden and dramatic end. In response to Dyrcona's half-hearted evocation of the word of God the young man retorts, 'Not so fast . . . you are still at "God has said"; you must first prove there is a God, which for my part I wholly deny.'[6] This prompts the hero to consider his interlocutor more closely and to reflect that he is not so attractive as he had seemed at first, and the dramatic tension is built up as Dyrcona starts to become thoroughly alarmed by the young man's 'devilish opinions'. He is torn between fear and admiration and threatens the young man with 'a bad end' only to be interrupted by the arrival of the Devil himself who seizes the atheistic young man in his claws and flies off with him to hell. Dyrcona can't bear to let his friend be carried away and so seizes him by the waist in an attempt to save him from the Devil's clutches but only succeeds in being carried off along with him. In reality, the monster that was to seize Chapelle in an unbreakable hold was that of alcoholism.

The real Chapelle was certainly an attractive and witty young man who inspired profound attachments. Dassoucy wrote of their relationship 'I could not live without him and he had trouble living without me' and this passionate phrase echoes that used by Bernier in his description of Chapelle's friendship with Molière: 'the illustrious Molière could not live without Chapelle'.[7] In later life Chapelle became an embittered alcoholic whose notorious excesses were to spoil his early promise. There is a story that while attending a banquet at Molière's house in the country Chapelle had stayed up drinking into the early hours with a group of friends. When Molière was woken at four in the morning and went down to check on them, Chapelle informed him that since the world was such a terrible place and life such a burden the group were all determined to drown themselves in the river. He begged Molière to join them in their noble plan. Molière diplomatically agreed that it was an excellent idea but managed to persuade them that it would be as well to retire for the night and put off the group suicide until the next day, since it would be easier to get to the river in the light. When the revellers eventually resurfaced the trip to the river was mercifully forgotten.

Cyrano's intimacy with Chapelle and Dassoucy dates from the early 1640s to 1651. The end of their friendship is fairly clearly defined. Early in 1650 Cyrano penned another contribution to support one of Dassoucy's publications. This time an eight-line poem signed simply *de Bergerac*, but in 1651 manuscript versions of Cyrano's letters appeared, including bitter attacks on both Dassoucy and Chapelle. We will return to the nature of their falling out, for now it will suffice to note that in 1653 Chapelle wrote a poem for another of Dassoucy's publications, and so the initial rupture clearly involved Cyrano alone. A few years later Chapelle also fell out with Dassoucy and wrote a travelogue with his friend Beaumont in which he ridiculed Dassoucy for his misadventures in Montpellier. Dassoucy had been forced to leave Paris and tour the provinces having fallen out of favour at court and having been imprisoned for sodomy on more than one occasion. In Montpellier his notoriety had reached fever pitch and the townspeople were baying for his blood. He was saved from death at the stake at the last minute by the intervention of his noble patron. In *The Adventures*, Dassoucy refers to this incident, as well as to Chapelle's betrayal, in terms which do nothing to dispel the rumours of his forbidden sexuality, but rather serve to draw his two friends into the controversy with him:

Friend C[hapelle] was not yet seventeen when the late B[erg-erac] who was already eating his bread and using his sheets gave me the honour of an introduction. That is why no one should be astonished if I made the most of the situation. Since at that time he was very generous, when he had kept me late supping at his house and the hour being unsuitable for me to return home he gave up very liberally half of his bed to me. This is why after having long had proofs of the nature of my desires and having several times deigned to honour me with his bed, it seems to me that it's rather for him to justify me than for the magistrates of Montpellier with whom I have never slept. But what! One must pardon something to one's friends; we are not always in our right minds, the brain does not always enjoy an even temperature; my friend C. has like others, good and bad moments.[8]

It should be noted that Dassoucy is anything but a reliable witness and the 'capon' anecdote was written at a time when he was at odds with Chapell and Cyrano; Chapelle he dismissed as a 'spoilt child', mocking his cowardice and his 'inextinguishable thirst'.[9] The attacks were all written after Cyrano had died and he could therefore make no objections or corrections to the story. The style is typically flippant and forms part of a fictional work. It cannot be considered much more than circumstantial evidence of a personal element to the dispute. Cyrano's own works offer another possible explanation in the form of a bitter professional rivalry.

Cyrano's determined refusal to conform and his passionate longing for freedom possibly lend weight to the theory that he was homosexual. If he were gay or bisexual this additional element of difference would in some degree help to account for his lifelong isolation and rebellion. In seventeenth-century France 'sodomy' was a capital offence, although power and influence could buy a level of immunity as Dassoucy's repeated escapes from death row demonstrate. That anyone should dream of a legitimate alternative to heterosexual relationships was heretical in the extreme. In outer space of course anything was possible and at one point in the world on the moon Cyrano's hero finds himself ordered by royal command to enter into a gay relationship. Having been mistaken for monkeys, both he and the Spaniard Gonsales are being kept as pets by the royal court. Dyrcona is taken for the female and the Spaniard for the male and the king orders that they should they share a cage in the hope that they will breed:

> . . . the King commanded his monkey-keeper to take us away, with strict orders to make the Spaniard and me lie together to multiply our species in his kingdom. The Prince's command was carried out in every point and I was very glad of it for the pleasure I took in having someone with whom to converse during the solitude of my brutification.[10]

Love cannot be legislated against and, despite the official repression of homosexuality, the Collège de Lisieux, which Cyrano attended in his early twenties, was notorious for the numerous affairs which flourished among its all-male population.

Another element in identifying Cyrano as a member of a group of homosexual friends and lovers was a letter written by Montigny in 1656 which was aimed at disgracing the notorious womanizer Lignières by identifying him as an acolyte of the dangerous pervert Cyrano. 'It is an irregular way of life unknown to our fathers [. . .] and a sort of profane brotherhood, of which Cyrano had been the founder.'[11] The reference to a monk-like brotherhood (*moinerie*) conjures up ideas of celibacy and poverty both of which Le Bret refers to in his preface. Montigny's attack is clearly not intended to suggest self-denial however, rather it is the rejection of worldly success coupled to the frank enjoyment of male friendship and probably love that cast Cyrano beyond the pale. Cyrano's decision to turn his back on courtly success and to refuse early offers of patronage had laid him open to allegations of failure and penury and even paradoxically of parasitism. In *Menagiana*, Gilles Ménage stated that Cyrano was penniless and mad at his death and there was even an allegation that he ended his days in the poor house. Much has been written about Cyrano's poverty and his dilapidation of his inheritance but there is in fact little evidence to support these allegations.

That Cyrano quickly frittered away his share of his inheritance leaving his brother Abel saddled with extensive debts has been a persistent element of his legend but this is easily refuted. A legal document in which Abel gifts two of his children with money from the family inheritance shows that the rents were undiminished in 1680. This means that on Cyrano's death his share of their inheritance must have been returned to his brother (sole beneficiary of Cyrano's will) largely untouched. To some extent evidence of payments made by Cyrano towards large debts seems to have clouded the issue. In fact, the irregularity of the payment of rents from the family estate would mean that on occasion debts would build up. Therefore it would sometimes be necessary for Cyrano to deal with other agents. This was commonplace in an era when much banking and many financial transactions were the province of individuals acting as moneylenders rather than a modern banking system as we would understand it. Professor Madeleine Alcover has examined in detail the various surviving shreds of Cyrano's accounts, including bills for lodging and food, and she concludes that the evidence proves that Le Bret's following remarks about Cyrano's frugal habits were entirely accurate:

He was always considered a man with a rare mind: nature had also gifted him with a happy control over his senses such that he was always able to submit his appetites as much as he wanted to his will, with the result that he drank wine but rarely, because as he said, in excess it stupefies the mind, and one needs to take the same precautions as one would with arsenic (that was what he compared it to) since one should fear poison in whatever form it might appear.[12]

Le Bret also noted that Cyrano was 'no less moderate in his eating habits' and in particular remarks on his avoidance of 'stews' and preference for simpler dishes, a sensible move in an era when heavily

spiced or strongly flavoured dishes were often the means of concealing food which had gone bad. These ascetic habits do not sit easily
with the caricatured image of the hedonistic libertine. That Cyrano
should have been rather serious and self-denying is a contradiction of
the various accusations that have been thrown at him.

The forms of greeting used by the inhabitants of the moon offer
an insight into the two guiding principles of Cyrano's existence. To
say 'Hello' the lunarians say 'Love me sage as I love you' and to say
'Goodbye' they say 'Remember to live free'.[13] Neither affection
nor freedom were ever simple and in Cyrano's case devotion to
freedom cost him firstly his liberty and ultimately his life, while
devotion to friendship (as he himself boasted) was to gain him
bitter enemies. Cyrano's friendships were, according to Le Bret's
account of him, the most important thing in his life and a close
reading of his works entirely supports this idea. Whereas references to romantic love of the sort celebrated by Rostand's play are
rare, references to friendship are both frequent and insistent. In the
enlightened republic of birds one of their number is condemned for
a crime described as 'the most serious that can blacken any bird. He
is accused . . . but good gods! Even to think of it makes my head-
feathers stand on end . . . he is accused of having not deserved to
have a friend for the last six years.'[14] In Cyrano's ideal society such
a heinous crime would carry a suitably harsh penalty. In his pro-
logue Le Bret names twenty-five different people whose friendship
and support of Cyrano he wishes to acknowledge publicly. Among
these names some are familiar – the poet Lignières, Cyrano's patron
the Duc d'Arpajon, his cousin Madeleine de Neuvillette, the war
hero Maréchal de Gassion, and Monsieur de Bourgogne the eyewitness of Cyrano's famous duel with one hundred men. Certain
other names are notable by their absence, in particular those of
Chapelle and Dassoucy.

It is possible and even probable that some of Cyrano's celebrations of masculine friendship are the outpourings of his repressed

homosexual romanticism. If he could not write openly in support of gay relationships at a time when to do so would cost him his life, he still included enough elements in his fictional works to reveal a profound conviction that whether gay, straight or bisexual what matters most in the relationships we form is honesty, courage and selflessness. Le Bret describes Cyrano's selflessness as being carried to such a pitch that he cared nothing for personal possessions and considered that whatever belonged to him was less his than it was the property of whichever of his friends (or lovers) might happen to have need of it. His generosity was, according to the testimony of his oldest friend, his most noteworthy characteristic. Le Bret paints a picture of a warm-hearted, intrepid and thoroughly noble individual, respected, admired and held in great affection by all who knew him. There is no reason to disbelieve any of Le Bret's complimentary references to his friend's kindness and wit but naturally the elegy composed by Cyrano's grieving friend is only half the story.

Cyrano certainly seems to have been a loyal and much cherished friend to many people but he could also be an extremely venomous enemy when he chose, a fact which Le Bret naturally leaves out of his eulogy. Cyrano's works include a certain number of virulent attacks on those he considered beneath contempt: among them the coward, the plagiarist, the ingrate and the pedant. Like the love letters these were compositions written for public consumption and do not represent an individual correspondence, but rather the carefully crafted expression of Cyrano's values, or at least those values by which he wished to be known. On the whole the letters are the expression of a general idea and no specific target can be identified for their towering wrath but there are notable exceptions to this rule.

The letter 'Against a fat man' is generally considered to be aimed at the famously corpulent actor Zacharie Jacob de Montfleury. In 1694, Gilles Ménage had alleged that Cyrano had taken a dislike to the actor Montfleury and forbidden him to appear on stage for a month. When the ban was disregarded two days later, he apparently interrupted a performance to threaten Montfleury with violence if he didn't leave the stage. Rostand dramatizes the confrontation between Cyrano and the fat actor in the opening scene of his play and identifies the source of their enmity as partly due to Cyrano's indignation at Montfleury's spectacular lack of talent and partly due to a jealous reaction to Montfleury having dared to rest his lascivious gaze on Roxane.

In reality Montfleury was a very successful and talented actor who was praised by contemporaries for having the rare ability to shine in both tragic and comic roles. Born in Anjou in 1600 he had joined the theatre of the Hôtel de Bourgogne in Paris around 1638. This would put him in the right place at the right time for a clash with Cyrano that is likely to have been professional rather than personal. Cyrano had composed two plays, a comedy and a tragedy, and it seems probable that he may have attempted to interest the illustrious players of the Hôtel de Bourgogne in staging one or both of them. If Montfleury were instrumental in rejecting Cyrano's work and if in doing so the celebrated actor treated the unknown fiery young playwright with disdain then the sublimely comical letter 'Against a fat man' with its inventive insults and its dire threats of a bastonnade or worse, may well have been the natural result. In the course of the letter Cyrano also reproaches Montfleury with having written a play which is nothing but an anthology of ideas and incidents stolen from other authors. That the fat actor should have succeeded with a second-rate, unoriginal work while his own compositions languished unperformed would have been a bitter pill indeed for Cyrano.

Cyrano's epistolary rants also include examples where the targets are identified still more directly. His quarrel with fellow burlesque author Paul Scarron remains obscure. There is no reference to Cyrano anywhere in Scarron's works but in the manuscript version of the letter 'Against Scarron' Cyrano states that Scarron had accused him of writing works which 'stank of the moneybag'.[15] Scarron was a lifelong invalid whose infirmity was believed to have originated with an ill-advised midnight swim. The story is excellent and it is characteristic of Scarron's self-deprecating humour; he describes how he had decided to disguise himself as a bird for the carnival of Le Mans in 1638 and so had smeared himself in honey and then rolled in some feathers. Later in the evening the worse for drink he was set upon by thieves and in order to escape and to remove his embarrassing costume he plunged into the River Huisne. He blamed the chill that he caught for his debilitating condition. In reality his disability was far more likely to have been the result of a genetic disorder. Cyrano's vicious mockery of Scarron's physical disability does not reflect at all well on the author and reveals that his much-vaunted generosity did not extend to his enemies. He was not one to forgive and forget. Scarron remains the only subject where the published version of Cyrano's satirical letter against him proves harsher than the manuscript original. The legendary hero was only human after all, and although he was capable of greatness he was equally capable of petty meanness.

Cyrano reserved the lion's share of his spite for his former friend Dassoucy. They had begun on excellent terms and Cyrano had written congratulatory verse for him. Yet Cyrano chose to attack Dassoucy again and again. The key to his hatred of Dassoucy seems to lie in the phrase with which he opens the letter 'Against an ungrateful person': 'By the affection in which I held you of which you are unworthy, I have made you deserve to be my enemy.'[16] The bitterness of Cyrano's hatred was, as he states it here, the curdled remains of love and respect. Dassoucy was an accomplished seducer. He had a gift for self-deprecation and wit that causes the reader of his works to laugh and pity the hapless protagonist even at the same time as an element of disquiet is sounded by the presence of Dassoucy's 'evil spirit' Pierrotin. The boy was the star of Dassoucy's retinue of choirboys, young men and boys who worked for him performing the music he composed and whom he 'adopted'. Thankfully Pierrotin was able to exact a degree of revenge on the man in whose power he found himself – he was personally responsible for seeing Dassoucy jailed on numerous occasions and were it not for the intervention of noble patrons might even have seen him condemned to death. Both Pierrotin and Cyrano seem to have experienced the sickening disillusionment that follows the initial seduction in an abusive relationship. There is certainly an element of terrible indignation, anger and an overwhelming sense of betrayal in the climax of the letter in which Cyrano promises to see Dassoucy punished even if it means being judge, jury and executioner himself:

> And yet you boast of my friendship. O heavens! Punisher of heresies, punish this one with thunder! I loved you then? I brought you my heart as an offering? [. . .] you will have in me alone,
>> Your prosecutor, Your judge
>> And your executioner[17]

Having seen the capacity for human beings to do each other terrible harm it is perhaps not surprising that Cyrano felt greater companionship with animals. The birds on the sun dismiss humans as 'those vile beasts' and the most touching love story Cyrano ever created featured a bird and an alien prince rather than human lovers.[18] It is the tale of a nightingale who defies death to follow his beloved. However, the nightingale he has fallen so hopelessly in love with turns out to be a shape-changing alien prince who tries to explain that their love is impossible. The nightingale simply refuses to accept this rejection and ultimately his stubborn devotion wins through. It seems certain that whatever the emotional connection between

Cyrano, Dassoucy and Chapelle, the letters against plagiarism reveal an important intellectual rivalry that exploded into accusations and fury. Given the real Cyrano's incandescent reaction to the idea or the fact of plagiarism it is all the more ironic that his legend was to become so hopelessly entangled with recurring literary thefts.

14

'What the devil was he doing in that galley?'

In 2002, when Evan Mark Katz decided to leave his job in the customer service department of an Internet dating site and set up on his own, he chose to name his new company e-Cyrano.com. Katz had spotted a gap in the Internet dating market. His daily conversations with dissatisfied customers had made him realize that although there were many sites offering hopeful singles the chance to find true love online, none of them gave advice on how best to present oneself and one's expectations in the process. The idea of e-Cyrano was not to write fake descriptions of clients enabling them to hoodwink unwitting strangers into going on doomed dates, but rather to provide them with an honest but infinitely more eloquent account of themselves to send out into the ether: 'Making personal ads more personal' as their strapline puts it. The prevalence of e-mail and the extraordinary growth of online communication has seen something of a renaissance in the lost art of the love letter and Katz sees his role as that of a latter-day Cyrano de Bergerac.

In Rostand's play Cyrano offers to help Christian express his true feelings for Roxane – the complication is that his own emotion colours his intermediary role and he strays from helping Christian to open his heart into the more dangerous territory of revealing his own deepest feelings. The plot of Rostand's play revolves around an unwitting act of plagiarism as Christian passes off Cyrano's passionately sincere declarations of love as his own, with the result that Roxane falls deeply in love. Rostand had chosen to present his fictional version of Cyrano as a man prepared to connive in plagiarism and deception. Audiences are easily reconciled to this fact since the act of deception is motivated by a poetic ideal of self-sacrificing greatness. Cyrano's deceit is paradoxically honourable and generous as well as beautifully unrealistic.

There is a further paradox in the fact that the real Cyrano abhorred plagiarism above all things. In a satirical letter 'Against a plagiarist of thoughts' he once wrote that plagiarism should be considered a mark of esteem since the thief wouldn't make off with stolen ideas unless he saw value in them but he then went on to develop a virulently scathing attack. There was no legal notion of copyright in Cyrano's time and consequently plagiarism was commonplace. As an author who always placed the highest value on originality Cyrano considered the plagiarist as the lowest of the low. Le Bret's biography echoes the famous line from *Othello* 'who steals my purse steals trash', in order to explain that Cyrano felt strongly that there are worse crimes than the tangible, concluding that 'since glory is a more precious possession than a cloak, a horse or even than gold',[1] then plagiarists who attempt to steal that glory should be punished with harsher penalties than highway robbers.*

In contrast, at the end of Rostand's play the fictional Cyrano is informed of Molière's theft of an entire scene from his comedy *The Pedant Tricked* and responds that he approves of the plagiarism, asking only if the scene went down well and humbly acknowledging Molière's superior talent as a playwright. At the play's tragic

---

*The punishment for highway robbery was hanging. Apparently Cyrano envisaged a fate worse than death for the 'thief of thoughts'.

climax the fictional Cyrano sums up his entire lifetime as having been spent patiently waiting in the shadows while others thrust themselves into the sunlight realms of love and recognition.

> Cyrano: *My life – all of a piece – a shaft*
> *Of sun, a puff of air, and then not even*
> *A memory. Roxane – do you recall*
> *That night – the balcony, the ivied wall,*
> *Christian? I stood in the shadows, underneath,*
> *And left it to another to climb and claim*
> *The kiss of glory. It happened again and again –*
> *The shadow for me, for others the applause, the fame.*
> *There's a kind of justice somewhere. Even in the teeth*
> *Of what's to come I can say: Gentlemen,*
> *Take down this truism in your commonplace books:*
> *Molière had genius; Christian had good looks.*[2]

The regrets expressed by the real Cyrano on his deathbed were of an entirely different nature. In retelling Cyrano's story Rostand was engaged in rescuing a neglected author from literary oblivion. As the above lines from Cyrano's death scene are spoken the audience inwardly protest against the hero's gloomy vision of himself. Rostand skilfully manipulates his audience into recognition of his hero's greatness precisely by having him deny and reject that greatness. Moments later, as death finally overpowers Cyrano he rebels one last time and, refusing to go quietly, he launches into one last poetic tirade, raging against the dying of the light. He is established as an unforgettable hero even as he anticipates his own oblivion. Rostand's ending is sublime but profoundly anachronistic. Molière's act of plagiarism really did take place, but not until sixteen years after Cyrano's death. Rostand's deliberate decision to ignore this historical detail was the result of his determination to throw the contrast between the two writers into sharp relief. It was natural that Rostand should focus on the contrast between Molière the 'genius' and popular favourite and Cyrano the neglected, heroic failure. In the nineteenth century at the time of writing, Cyrano was an obscure author, a quirky footnote in literary history, whereas Molière was a mainstream popular success.

Today this balance is being slowly redressed, Cyrano's genius is now more generally recognized and his innovative and provocative writing is more and more widely read. The difference between his and Molière's positions in the literary canon are no longer considered to be a simple question of superior and inferior talent. Molière was a comic genius and his brilliantly observed characters remain as popular and as funny on the modern stage as when he wrote them. This extraordinary achievement is in no way diminished by the revelation that he was a frequent plagiarist and a court toady. The two men may well have been friends, they certainly frequented the same circles and had friends in common, but they had very different literary careers. Molière started out as an actor and he learned his art through a long apprenticeship touring the provinces. He was a determined and ambitious individual who rose to lead his own theatre troupe. He became a wealthy celebrity, a favourite with royalty and the populace alike. The king commissioned Molière to write for court entertainments and the royal family subsidized his Parisian theatre. Molière always wrote with the reaction of his audience very clearly in mind. As a leading actor in his own plays he was able to judge and refine the nuances of dialogue, and his version of the stolen scene is consequently the superior in polish. Cyrano worked in isolation and rebellion; hardly surprising then that his provocative and uncompromising works should slide slowly into near-oblivion while Molière's crowd-pleasing witticisms would go on delighting audiences for centuries to come.

Even today, despite the revival of interest in Cyrano's writing, his artistic reputation is utterly eclipsed by that of Molière. The latter's works are a standard at both school and university and very few people are aware of the various clever thefts dotted throughout Molière's *oeuvre*, still less that a frequently quoted line from one of his plays was actually originally written by Cyrano de Bergerac. The scene stolen from Cyrano appears in *The Schemings of Scapin*, which was written and performed in 1671. Sixteen years had elapsed since Cyrano's death, not only allowing audiences sufficient time to have forgotten the original – *The Pedant Tricked* premiered some twenty-six years earlier – but also showing that Molière had the sense to realize that if you are going to steal from the greatest swordsman of the day, you wait until he is safely dead and buried first. Molière's biographers have attempted to save the great playwright's reputation by inventing the unconvincing theory of a collaboration with Cyrano, which they date to the time when the young men were studying with Gassendi in the early 1640s. According to this theory, first suggested in the early eighteenth century by Grimarest, Cyrano used the scene first but it was written by Molière and thus he did no more than reclaim it for his own later play.[3] That Molière should have 'esteemed' Cyrano's works highly enough to steal from him was a difficult pill to swallow for those who chose to see in Molière the flourishing genius and in Cyrano the dangerous outsider, penniless and probably insane. Nowadays critics are prepared to acknowledge Molière's numerous thefts and to recognize that like Shakespeare, who also relied heavily on earlier works for his inspiration, his luminous talent remains undimmed by such revelations.

The central character of Cyrano's play and the hero of the stolen scene is the cantankerous, selfish and miserly college professor Granger. In the scene that caught Molière's fancy, Granger junior has staged an elaborate hoax in order to trick his tight-fisted father into handing over some money. He achieves this by sending his crafty servant Corbinelli to his father to recount the story of his terrible abduction by bloodthirsty Turks and to demand a ransom to free him from their clutches. The colourful story that the two conspirators concoct hinges on the fact that galleys or slave ships were a common phenomenon at the time. Corbinelli tells Granger senior that he and his master had both been captured and taken prisoner, condemned to serve out the rest of their lives as galley slaves. Corbinelli explains that he owes his own escape to his suggestion that he should be set free in order to go to Granger to obtain an impressive ransom.

In spite of the fact that his son's life apparently hangs in the balance, Granger senior displays great reluctance to part with any cash, as well as comic incredulity at finding *himself* in such a terrible position, repeatedly asking how his son could have let such a thing happen: '*Que Diable, aller faire en cette galère?*'★ This phrase as reformulated by Molière '*Que Diable allait-il faire en cette galère?*' has become proverbial and is still in current usage in France to express incredulity at someone who allows themselves to get caught up in any particularly disastrous situation. The word '*galère*' on its own has become convenient shorthand for misfortune and difficulty.

And so a joke written by a supposedly 'forgotten' author survives and flourishes over three and a half centuries later. Molière also plagiarized a comic type that Cyrano had invented for the play, a wily old peasant called Mathieu Gareau who speaks in a tortuously thick accent and creates much hilarity with his combination of idiocy and impenetrable self-confidence. Cyrano's name for this character also came to be proverbial in his lifetime, denoting a sly or cunning peasant.

Just like Molière, Cyrano read widely and was not above taking his inspiration from his reading. The difference was that Cyrano was always scrupulous in acknowledging his debts. Determined never to commit the crime that he considered worse than highway robbery, Cyrano came up with a range of inventive solutions to the problem of citing his influences and most often he chose to do so

★ 'What the devil was he doing in that galley?'

through a comic device. Where he did repeat an idea, he was also ready to joke about it. In the *Comical History of Francion* by Charles Sorel the idea of using poetry as an alternative form of currency appears as one of the many crack-brained notions of the character Hortensius. Cyrano liked the idea so much he included it as one of the idiosyncrasies of the civilization on the moon. Somewhat cheekily, he refers to his original source by having Dyrcona speculate that Sorel must have got the idea from the lunarians – 'O really!' I said to myself, 'that's just the money that Sorel makes Hortensius use in *Francion*, as I recall. This must be where he stole the idea from; but who the devil could he have learnt it from? It must have been from his mother, because I have heard it said that she was something of a lunatic.'[4]

Le Bret informs us that although Cyrano abhorred all instances of intellectual theft he never blamed a work too much if he found one original thing in it. Cyrano also seems to have understood that following in the path of a literary predecessor could sometimes be a spur to creativity, forcing an author to be more inventive in order not simply to repeat what has gone before. In spite of Cyrano's own feelings about the subject, his legend remains hopelessly entangled with instances of plagiarism both real and imagined. The central conceit of Rostand's play, Christian passing off Cyrano's words as his own, is one of the most familiar aspects of the Cyrano legend and yet it is also one of the most striking divergences between the real and the fictional Cyrano.

At one time, critics could have pointed to the existence of the *Mazarinades* poems and letters as proof that the real Cyrano was prepared to lend his voice to another, in this instance to the political interests hoping to dislodge the all-powerful Cardinal Mazarin, chief advisor to the regent Anne of Austria. These works have always been somewhat controversial since they directly contradict another letter that Cyrano wrote in defence of the cardinal. As a result, Cyrano has been accused of opportunism and being a political turncoat. No definitively convincing case has ever been made to support their inclusion in the canon of Cyrano's work (beyond the flimsy coincidence of their being signed with the initials B.D. and D.B.). The attribution of these works to Cyrano (always dubious), may now be dismissed out of hand.[5]

The real Cyrano reacted with characteristic wit to the real or imagined thefts from his work made by Beaulieu and Chapelle (the two men named as the targets of his two letters 'Against a thief of thoughts'). The highlight of the letter against Chapelle is a spectacular tirade in which Cyrano declares that Chapelle is compelled to plagiarize because he lacks the intelligence, the inspiration or the wit to do otherwise. 'He never opens his mouth but you'll find a theft, and he has become so accustomed to this pillage that, even when he doesn't speak, it is in order to steal the silence from some poor mute.'[6]

Cyrano's former friends Beaulieu and Chapelle were not the only ones who had good reason to be grateful that France never did take up Cyrano's suggestion that plagiarists should be subject to a punishment worse than hanging. In 1902, an international scandal erupted as the hugely successful play *Cyrano de Bergerac* became the focus of a plagiarism trial. Edmond Rostand stood accused of having stolen the essentials of his hit play from an American work entitled *The Merchant Prince of Cornville*. The trial took place in Chicago and under advice from his lawyers the complainant had finally decided not to bring his action against Rostand himself but against the American actor Richard Mansfield, who had bought the rights to stage a production of the play in New York, in which he played the starring role. Mansfield's moment of glory was short-lived, as he found himself threatened with a huge damages claim by the author of *The Merchant Prince*, a successful Chicago businessman named Samuel Eberly Gross. Gross, as rich men will, employed some clever and unscrupulous lawyers who duly pointed out to Mansfield that if he agreed to put forward no defence to the charges they would drop the original astronomical damages claim down to a single cent. Mansfield, as an impecunious actor, had no choice but to agree and the case was therefore decided in Gross's favour and Rostand's play was consequently banned from the American stage for twenty years.

Unlike *Cyrano de Bergerac*, *The Merchant Prince of Cornville* is a terrible play and had quite naturally been rejected by all the theatre producers who ever had the misfortune to have it thrust under their noses by the irrepressible Samuel Gross. And yet the plagiarism accusation has a grain of truth in it. A close analysis of the two texts reveals that Rostand almost certainly did take a few scraps of straw from *The Merchant Prince of Cornville* and spin them into the box-office gold of *Cyrano de Bergerac*. Possibly the similarities between the two plays are nothing more than coincidence, and Rosemunde Rostand's charming tale of her husband's intervention in the floundering love-life of a tongue-tied young friend may be the true origins of his play, but the evidence against Rostand is compelling.

Having failed to interest theatre producers in Chicago and New York of the merits of his play, Samuel Gross had decided that his work was simply too subtle for his fellow Americans and that it would certainly have a better reception from the more sophisticated Europeans. In 1889 he took the opportunity of a business trip to Paris to leave a manuscript copy of *The Merchant Prince* at the very playhouse which would later see the spectacular success of *Cyrano de Bergerac*, the Théâtre de la Porte St Martin, whose director Coquelin would create the role of Cyrano. Gross never heard back from Coquelin and a few years later he took matters into his own hands. In 1896 Gross travelled to London, rented a theatre, hired some actors and produced his play himself. The reception it received was sufficiently dire to convince Gross to close after one night. He paid for the play to be printed and distributed copies to various friends and acquaintances. There the matter might have rested but for the fact that when *Cyrano de Bergerac* hit the New York stage, two of Gross's friends who had read his play wrote independently to draw his attention to the similarity between the hit French play and his own work.

When the scandal first erupted, Rostand went to some lengths to disprove Gross's claims. He argued that he didn't speak a word of English. This seems distinctly implausible given that he had attended an English kindergarten for three years as a child and employed an English au pair in his own family to ensure that his children would be fluent in the language. He also misquoted the date that Gross had left the manuscript at the theatre, and asked for a copy in translation to be provided offering to recommend it to his own publisher. The facts remains that the play had been waiting at the theatre for a translation and there is no great leap of faith required to imagine that Rostand may have picked it up and flicked through it. He would then no doubt have cast it aside as worthless but he may also have retained the odd good idea that he could improve upon and use in the context of his own work. At worst Rostand took a few ideas and the odd phrase from Gross's work and these he transformed so utterly that Gross's lawsuit should by rights have been thrown out immediately as laughable and pointless.

When the twenty-year ban was nearly up the case was retried in New York and on a closer examination of the evidence the judgement in favour of Gross was reversed. After the initial flurry of excitement caused by the scandal the press were unanimous in deciding in favour of Rostand. One London journalist even remarked 'It wants a bit of believing, Eh? Presently we may hear that Cyrano himself has arisen to ask for an injunction against Rostand.'[7] Once the initial anxiety had died down Rostand gained the necessary confidence to dismiss the case as laughable and prepare a light-hearted and witty response to the controversy. In a letter published in *Le Temps* he wrote:

In the four years which this affair has lasted, I have always refused and I still refuse to take it seriously . . . In the meantime I am ready to admit that I have taken Cyrano de Bergerac, his name, the panache, the Hôtel de Bourgogne, Montfleury, the Rôtisserie de Ragueneau, the soul of *préciosité*, Roxane kissing Cyrano's words on Christian's lips, the trip to the moon, the siege of Arras, the Gascon cadets, in fact our whole seventeenth century from Mr Eberly Gross of Chicago.[8]

If nothing else the controversy certainly puts a new spin on Rostand's decision to have the dying Cyrano accept Molière's plagiarism with such angelic grace. He was to learn from his own experience with Gross just how unlikely a scenario this was.

In the memoirs that Rosemunde Rostand wrote about her husband, she included her own artful defence against the accusations of plagiarism. She gives her own version of the play's genesis, insisting that the painful love triangle at its heart was actually inspired by a far from tragic incident in Rostand's own life. A young friend named Amédée had apparently confided in the great poet his despair over a hopeless love affair. He explained that he was madly in love with an intelligent and spirited young woman, but that he was failing miserably in his attempts to win her heart. Rostand taking pity on the young man asked him for more detail.

'Alas!' cried the young man, 'I talk, I plead all in vain, she doesn't even listen to me.' What do you say to her? asked Rostand who found himself acknowledging the young girl's cruelty.

'I tell her that I love her.'

'Then what?

'I repeat the same thing!'

'And then what?'

'That's it.'

'When she loves you that will be enough,' concluded the poet. 'But for now she needs something else. I know her; she is pedantic, affected, she is even snobbish. She requires flowery language, paradoxes. When she is simplified by her love for you she will only require a single word but for now she needs lots of them.'[9]

And so began a collaboration in which Amédée returned every day to consult the poet for his lesson in the art of wooing, leaving with his head stuffed full of witty remarks and poetic speculations. A little while later, the poet encountered the young woman and overheard her confiding to a friend that the admirer whom she had originally considered so dull and uninteresting had turned out to have wonderful hidden depths – Amédée was a poet, a thinker and a prodigious talent. Rosemunde does not describe what happened next to the young lovers. We are left to wonder whether they lived happily ever after, or whether, once the lessons were over, Amédée reverted to type and his sweetheart got bored and ran off with a cavalry officer. Instead, Rosemunde concludes her story with the triumphant, but probably disingenuous declaration: 'The first idea for "Cyrano" had been found!!'

Whatever the truth of the play's origins and, aside from his own feelings about the ethics of the situation, there was another more compelling reason for Rostand to include the story of Molière's plagiarism in his play. As his biographer Sue Lloyd reveals in her book *The Man Who Was Cyrano*, Rostand was obsessed with what he termed *'les ratés'* – life's failures. For Rostand, Cyrano was an excellent example of such a failure and the comparison with Molière served as additional confirmation of this 'fact'. Throughout his life Edmond Rostand was haunted by bouts of depression and a crippling fear of failure. The poet fêted by an entire nation and beloved of high society and ordinary folk alike, always aspired to be the champion of the underdog, the lost cause, the failure. For this reason Rostand's works were to provide comfort and inspiration to many a doomed soldier amidst the horrors of the First World War. Rostand was not eligible for military service because of his poor health, but he wrote hundreds of letters of support and encouragement to the men in the trenches. Lloyd recounts how Cyrano was to become an important symbol of French heroism and courage during the war. Rostand received letters from men at the front describing how they carried his works in their backpacks and drew strength from the example of the legendary hero.

Two infantrymen composed a parody entitled *Cyronac de Bergerot* to entertain the troops and in 1918 Joseph Suberville published a one-act drama entitled *Cyrano de Bergerac in the Trenches*. The play was performed at the front and published in the review *The Ideal* in March 1918. The action dramatizes a conversation between Cyrano (freshly arrived from the moon) and a French infantryman. There is a terrible poignancy to Cyrano's initial bewilderment at the scene of devastation he sees around him as he wonders aloud, 'perhaps I have landed on the wrong planet . . .' The two military men discuss heroism and warfare and conclude that although battles in the modern age may have become a bloodier and still more horrifying business than in the age of the musketeers the innate heroism of the soldiers fighting for freedom remains the same. There is no room in such a context for the real Cyrano's complex feelings about the life of a soldier and his ultimate rejection of codes of chivalry and honour as a fraud designed to send men willingly to the slaughter for the sake of a political futility. In such a historical moment it is the hero of Rostand's play who must step forward to represent the self-sacrifice and the courage of those lost young men dying in their millions for the sake of freedom. In a time of universal tragedy the power of such an emblem is significant but it should not be forgotten that Rostand's noble hero has his origins in the life of a real man. While the fictional hero of *Cyrano de Bergerac in the Trenches* is confounded by the cynical battlefield humour of the infantryman the real Cyrano would have understood only too well, the real Cyrano would have had no difficulty in relating to exactly what those young men were going through.

In the play, when asked the cause of the war the infantryman replies by evoking a patriotic vision of the pastoral beauty of his beloved homeland.

> *. . . Because*
> *Our fields were too green and our sky too blue,*
> *Because too intoxicating blood flowed from our vines*
> *And because for the French the earth was benign*
> *While she sulked on the other side of the Rhine!*

This recalls the speech made by Rostand's Cyrano when he needs to calm and encourage the troops on the eve of their last desperate assault at Arras. The words of the fictional infantryman chime with those of the fictional Cyrano but if we turn to the words of a real First World War soldier we find a more accurate echo of the real Cyrano. An English journalist named A. M. Burrage wrote a memoir of his time fighting in the trenches in France entitled *War is War*. At one point he asks,

> Who will ever forget Arras who saw her then in the middle days of the war? The whole rows of houses with their façades torn off so that one could see into every room, as in an architect's sectional drawing; pictures hanging askew, beds with the clothes dragged aside and left just as when their occupants leaped up and ran for safety, perhaps more than a year since; open wardrobes and garments still hanging on the pegs; intimate medical appliances left ruthlessly exposed [. . .] Arras was a more poignant sight than Ypres. Ypres was a bleeding corpse and Arras was still writhing in her death agony.[10]

Cyrano's own experiences in the same place underline the tragic fact that three centuries on nothing has changed. Cyrano's reflections on the futility of war, his plea for the recognition of this fact, his insistence that true nobility in mankind would be for us to understand that we are all citizens of the world rather than citizens of one nation or another, remain sadly as urgent and as little heeded as ever. Time moves on and the technology of war advances horribly but the individuals caught up in the fighting can no more hope to understand or accept their situation now than they could in Cyrano's day.

Burrage's experience of war forced him to take refuge in cynicism and black humour notably similar to Cyrano's own. Burrage explains how essential it was to maintain this protective barrier of mockery and wit in order not to break one's heart with anguish. Both men also join in denying that courage exists in warfare, stating that abject terror is more natural and more current on the battlefield. Burrage published his account anonymously under the pseudonym 'Ex-Private X' and explained that he did so in order to be free to tell the truth about his experiences. 'If any young man should ask an old soldier, "Was it really like this?" and the old soldier answers, "Yes, it's all true," this book will have served its purpose. And I shall not mind if the young man exclaims, "What a very unpleasant fellow the author must be!" Perhaps I am.'[11] Just like Cyrano, Burrage was a man who put his duty to tell the hard, painful truths that society might not want to hear above the fear that he might be considered an 'unpleasant fellow'.

15

An ambush vile

It was in the period leading up to his untimely death that Cyrano's literary career began to take off. In 1653, he had finally accepted the assistance of a noble patron, the Duc d'Arpajon, and was preparing his work for print publication. Two volumes duly went before the censor for official approval in late 1653, and in early 1654 Cyrano's *Diverse Works* and *The Death of Agrippina* were published by the bookseller Charles de Sercy. The finished products were elegant quarto editions featuring the duke's coat of arms and, in the case of the *Works*, a specially commissioned portrait engraving of the author by his friend Zachary Heince. *The Death of Agrippina* was a great success thanks to rumours about its scandalous atheistic content lending it sinful notoriety. The volume of letters, accompanied by *The Pedant Tricked*, also found favour.

An English edition was published in 1658 by the bookseller Henry Herringman under the title *Satyrical Characters, and Handsome Descriptions in letters, written to severall persons of quality . . . Translated by a person of honour*. The accompanying translator's note 'To the Reader' promises plentiful wit 'in these essayes, cloathed by the Author, in smooth and significant expressions, and such high and unthought-of raptures you'll meet with . . . for like Pliny's fish he carries teeth in his tongue', as well as concluding on the plaintive note that 'Those that can judge of the Originall will I believe grant, that 'tis almost as hard a Book to translate well, as any in prose that is extant in that Language.'[1] This is not just a final self-congratulatory flourish but also an important acknowledgement of the complexity and intricacy of Cyrano's writing.

Cyrano's new patron, the Duc d'Arpajon, was an ex-soldier who had fought valiantly in Turkey and earned himself the dignities of Knight of the Grand Cross and Knight of the Order of Malta. One of his contemporaries described d'Arpajon as the slow but steady type: 'of easy relations with his superiors, never compromising them, more tenacious than enterprising, prudent, cunning even, self-centred, painstaking; he was one of those men who barely shine, and yet who, marching with a firm tread from degree to degree, without great leaps but without pause, finish by accumulating favours, rank and dignities'.[2] In short, he was the exact temperamental opposite of Cyrano.

Tallemant des Réaux also recorded a less than flattering story about the duke in his *Historiettes*. One evening d'Arpajon invited Sarasin and Pellisson, two well-known authors to dinner. The duke complimented Sarasin on a recent work entitled *Springtime*, only to be told indignantly that it was the work of a different author, the poet Montplaisir. He tried again, praising *The Temple of Death* (by Habert) with the same result, and it was only with a whispered hint from Pellisson that he was able finally to come up with praise for the *Sonnet for Eve*, a piece that Sarasin had actually written. It was a common enough phenomenon for great men to frequent authors, since it was considered gentlemanly to take a certain interest in literary matters. John Evelyn's *Diary* contains a sarcastic passage in which he bemoans the fact that all too often the great noblemen were content to construct libraries purely for show, paying no attention at all to the content of the books as long as their bindings were acceptable and they filled up the space becomingly: 'He doth not much amuse himself in the particular elections of either Authors or Impressions; but having erected his cases & measured them, accords with a Stationer to furnish him with so many gilded Folioes, so many yard of quarto's and octavo's by the great, till his Bibliotheke be full of Volumes.'[3] It seems fair to suspect that d'Arpajon might have been one of those who bought his books by the yard. He clearly wished to appear cultured, but he seems to have contented himself with patronizing impecunious writers without necessarily taking the trouble of actually reading their work. Such a man was ideal for Cyrano's purposes; what could be more apposite for the provocateur than a patron who would not read his works too closely (if at all) and would therefore be unlikely to raise any objections, or worse, suggest any modifications. Also, Cyrano's friend, the poet Tristan L'Hermite whom he greatly admired, had previously accepted d'Arpajon's patronage; Tristan dedicated *Heroic Verses* to d'Arpajon in 1648. This precedent must have been important to Cyrano and significantly he once described Tristan as 'the only free man' in France.[4]

For Cyrano a patron was a necessary evil; d'Arpajon took him on as a part of his household. As a '*domestique*' Cyrano lived in d'Arpajon's home but was neither servant nor honoured guest – his was an intermediary and subordinate position. In such circumstances an author was expected to earn the generosity of his noble sponsor. One way in which to do so was by writing a suitably fawning letter to the patron to be printed at the start of the works. In return for these dedications, nobles would then show their gratitude in the form of a 'gift' of hard cash. Cyrano had been living with d'Arpajon and his family for nearly a year at the point when he composed his *Dedicatory Epistle* to the duke. In his dedication, Cyrano dismissed his own works as a haphazard collection of 'caprices', the product of his youthful folly. This was a fairly standard stance for the author to take in a dedication. The necessary combination of grovelling and false modesty led to the very common ploy of dismissing the work, as nowhere near good enough to recompense the extraordinary honour paid by the distinguished patron in accepting the dedication. In Cyrano's case, there is a ring of truth to his rejection of the letters and plays.

By the time he came to publish them, he had progressed enormously in his art and was working on a far more original and daring project – his science fiction novels. In the second volume of these novels, Cyrano writes about the experience of being a well-known author, whose portrait has been circulated and whose works have caused a controversy that has overtaken the whole town. He is rather scathing about his readership, complaining that certain ignorant souls initially praised the work to the skies without understanding a word of it, purely in order to seem intelligent and cultivated. He describes how these 'idiots' then grew to resent the author's success and their own ignorance and consequently performed a spectacular U-turn dismissing the work as ridiculous and the author as a madman. It is tempting to read an indirect reference to d'Arpajon in this little vignette because, from having been Cyrano's champion, albeit one who undoubtedly had little affinity with his protégé's work, d'Arpajon had eventually reversed his allegiance and thrown a gravely injured Cyrano out of his house.

Cyrano's disgrace and expulsion from the house of d'Arpajon seems to have been the direct result of a dramatic incident that took place in early 1654, right at the point when his works had finally made it into print. Until the discovery of the uncensored version of Le Bret's biography, d'Arpajon's decision to kick the dying Cyrano out of his house was extremely difficult to account for. According to the facts as related in outline, Cyrano had suffered a blow to the head that had left him seriously ill, and it was in this condition that he was suddenly sent away from the duke's household in disgrace. How a terrible accident could prejudice Cyrano's patron against him was a vexed question and one to which no satisfactory answer had been found. The syphilis theory was one way of explaining the facts away differently but this directly contradicted Le Bret's assertion that the cause of *both* Cyrano's illness and his disgrace was a serious head injury. Those who chose to accept the slightly confusing version of events offered by Le Bret's censored account duly dreamt up the theory of the falling beam or roof tile. According to that theory, a beam was dislodged in the course of either renovations or a fire (depending on whose account one favours) and Cyrano had the misfortune to walk underneath at just the wrong moment. It is thoroughly appropriate that in Rostand's play this fictional falling beam also fells the fictional Cyrano, but Rostand also understood enough about the real Cyrano to guess at the real cause of his death, and in the play the beam did not fall but was pushed. Cyrano's death is the result of an ambush, as the hero himself declares:

> *Monsieur de Bergerac*
> *Was foully, ignobly*
> *Murdered.*[5]

The uncensored version of Le Bret's biography cast a stronger doubt than ever before on the theories of Cyrano's death by disease or accident. Further documents, recently come to light, add convincing detail to corroborate the theory of a botched assassination attempt. It had always seemed significant that after the 'accident' which destroyed Cyrano's health he was no longer welcome in d'Arpajon's home. Le Bret states quite explicitly that the incident 'caused his disgrace'. The timing alone of Cyrano's injury and subsequent ejection from the d'Arpajon household seemed to imply that the source of his serious injuries was known and feared – since a genuine accident would surely have inspired sympathy and a greater degree of support rather than this summary dismissal. A shred of rhymed gossip recorded by the poet Loret in his *Gazette*

paints a picture of a late-night attack on the duke's carriage that
ended in death and disarray.

> *Sir d'Arpajou* [sic.] *by simple chance*
> *Heading rather late to his residence,*
> *Encountered some armed men*
> *Who caused him pandemonium*
> *As they dared his coach to attack.*
> *But on a sudden he forced them back.*
> *Four horsemen of his retinue*
> *Made the ten men flee without ado,*
> *Excepting, of their number, two;*
> *One of whom, a reckless fool,*
> *Was overthrown, left dead in the mud*
> *Wearing a most miserable expression;*
> *The Other, like a night prowler,*
> *Straight to Prison was led further.*
> *But in this same war as well,*
> *One of his own men also fell,*
> *Mortally wounded, they said,*
> *By a bloody blow, a musket shot.*
> *And even, a valuable horse*
> *Shared in the misfortune of their sort*
> *It was the one (so I heard)*
> *On which the duke's equerry rode.*
> *Whether such an unfortunate fight,*
> *Taking place under bright moonlight,*
> *Was madness or an ambush vile,*
> *The suspense continues yet awhile.*[6]

The horse-drawn vehicles of the aristocracy were cumbersome
and not easily manoeuvrable in the narrow streets of Paris; carriages
were therefore vulnerable to attack. The lack of street lighting and

the myriad, interconnecting crossroads and alleyways formed the perfect setting for a clandestine attack. As the poem reveals, the underhand plot involved the waylaying of the duke's carriage in the dark streets and the result was not a robbery, as might have been anticipated in such circumstances, but a single member of the duke's retinue shot at close range. That wounded man was almost certainly Cyrano. There was a well-known royal precedent for a murderous ambush of this kind in the streets of Paris. On 14 May 1610, King Henri IV's carriage had been held up in a narrow lane and the fanatical monk Ravaillac leapt into the carriage and repeatedly stabbed the king and then gave himself up to the guards. James Howell, writing in 1619, remarked on the frequency of traffic jams in Paris and the resulting potential for murderous ambush:

> A world of coaches, carts and Horses of all sorts that go to and fro perpetually, so that sometimes one shall meet with a stop half a mile long of those coaches, carts and Horses, that can move neither forward nor backward by reason of some sudden encounter of others coming a crosse-way; so that oftentimes it will be an hour or two before they can disintangle: In such a stop the great Henry was so fatally slain by Ravillac.

In Le Bret's biography, he describes Cyrano's injury as a gunshot wound, the timing and his description are in accordance with the account given by Loret: ten men sent to surround and stop the carriage and one of them to take the opportunity to fire the fatal bullet at close range – this is clearly testament to the great swordsman's fearsome reputation. After his extraordinary feat of bravery at the de Nesle gate, there could be no question of engaging him in swordplay; instead this dastardly method of eliminating him was chosen. The moment when the attack on the carriage happened, it must have become unpleasantly clear to d'Arpajon that supporting Cyrano was a risky undertaking with consequences far beyond those of literary scandal. Possibly the loss of his 'valuable horse' weighed more heavily with d'Arpajon than the loss of the troublesome poet. It is not clear from Loret's account whether the duke was in the carriage himself at the time of the attack, but if he was, then his precipitate haste in ridding himself of the seriously injured Cyrano is, perhaps, the more easily understood. Exactly who ordered the attack on Cyrano will probably never be known. When a criminal has escaped justice he is unlikely to be brought to book over 350 years later. But before the attack happened, Cyrano had already voiced his own suspicions that an attempt would be made on his life.

An extraordinary letter, that features in the manuscript collections but not in the printed editions of Cyrano's works, is entitled 'Against a murderous and slandering Jesuit'. This letter foreshadows the disaster to come in chillingly accurate detail – in the opening line Cyrano jokes that the murderous priest clearly takes him for a king since he is attempting to incite his acolytes to follow the example of Ravaillac. He goes on to suggest that one failed attempt has already been made on his life. He describes the priest having succeeded in convincing a 'savage', already guilty of one murder, that the key to his salvation was the assassination of Cyrano. The proposed 'ambush' apparently missed Cyrano as he provokingly reminds his enemy 'by one day' and so failed to 'redden the streets with my blood'.[7] He points out that if the Jesuit had been less tight-fisted and had seen fit to embolden his hired killer with ready money instead of with sermons, 'indulgences and medallions', then perhaps his chosen assassin would have been rather more dedicated to his task. Cyrano also points out the notable hypocrisy in the Jesuit's preaching this doctrine of justifiable homicide to his followers. If the priest really believed that Cyrano's death were for the greater good of Christianity, he should personally attempt to take Cyrano's life. If he dare not, for fear of eternal damnation, then he should not encourage others to run that risk on his behalf.

Another of Cyrano's accusations against the priest is that he is guilty of sexually abusing the pupils in his charge. Cyrano's vision of authority was that it was inseparable from abuse of power and he seems to have particularly distrusted the hypocrisy of those whose power was divinely sanctioned. In the 1640s in France, there were indeed Jesuit priests (such as Niccolo Baldelli, who may or may not be the same Nicholas B. to whom Cyrano's harangue is addressed) openly preaching the astonishing doctrine that murder was acceptable in certain circumstances to save one's honour.

The evidence is circumstantial, Cyrano's letter to the murderous priest is a damning indictment of the Jesuit brotherhood but it does not prove in itself that the Jesuits were responsible for Cyrano's death. It does prove that he felt that certain members of the brotherhood represented a very real threat and maybe even that he believed one attempt on his life had already been made, before the incident in which the duke's carriage was attacked.

One of the nineteenth-century editors of Cyrano's work, Paul Lacroix, investigated the bibliographical history of Cyrano's works. In particular, he was intrigued by the scarcity of surviving copies. Given Cyrano's popularity (there were at least twelve reprints of the complete works and numerous editions of individual works) Lacroix expected to find far more extant copies. His explanation for the disappearance of so many books was that it could not be an accident. He was convinced that editions of Cyrano's works had been 'systematically destroyed by the tireless efforts of the mysterious brotherhood of the Index'. If Lacroix is to be believed, the brotherhood pursued their vendetta against Cyrano beyond the grave. There is certainly compelling evidence that such campaigns against 'heretical' authors did take place. Even with a concerted campaign to consign Cyrano to oblivion in full force, his name at least lived on. But the impact on his readership was dramatic. In 1858, Lacroix wrote that: 'everyone knows the name Cyrano; but no one, or hardly anyone, reads his books'. After the explosion of

Rostand's Cyrano on to the stage nearly forty years later, this situation would only become the more acute. Despite the familiarity of Cyrano's name, his works were to languish under a cloud of oppression and censorship. It was not until 1977, when Jacques Prévot published an edition of the *Complete Works* based on precious manuscript sources, that Cyrano's fractured texts were finally fully reconstituted, uncensored and entire. Cyrano seems to have been the victim of a double assassination attempt, in which his enemies had chosen to act in the most cowardly and underhand manner imaginable, seeking to extinguish not just his life but also his literary legacy.

He was almost certainly the target of the d'Arpajon ambush, but in the darkness and confusion of the fray the ten men sent to destroy this rebellious spirit were not enough to totally silence him. Although his attackers left him drenched in his own blood and with a life-threatening head injury, he was still alive. Cyrano stubbornly fought for life for several crowded months more, during which a fresh catastrophe overtook him before he finally surrendered to the darkness. In his biography of Cyrano, Le Bret refers to the head injury his friend had sustained and a following period of serious illness caused by 'a long captivity', but the full account he made of these terrifying events was rapidly censored and lost to view for centuries to come. As a result, biographers chose to believe that Cyrano was either the victim of a tragic accident or of the deadly neurosyphilis. Perhaps madness is in the eye of beholder and Cyrano was labelled a lunatic because he consistently went out of his way to defy convention. Despite Cyrano's obvious allegiance to a notorious line of heretics who had died fiery deaths before him, he was never prosecuted for blasphemy. It is significant to note, though, that such prosecutions were in fact becoming increasingly rare from 1653 onwards, as a new, more insidious response to nonconformity had emerged. Blasphemy was beginning to be categorized as a mental disorder and therefore treated as illness more frequently than crime. Similarly, witchcraft was grad-ually becoming more the affair of the asylum than the stake. Cyrano's case may well have been on the cusp of this wave.

The experience of the author Bonaventure Forcroy, who wrote a *Life of Apollonius of Thyane*, offers a strong parallel with Cyrano. Forcroy's work was essentially a learned attack on the Christian idea of the miracle, an idea that Cyrano also disputed in his late works. Forcroy then wrote a thesis addressed to the doctors of the Sorbonne setting out seventeen 'doubts on religion' in which he asked the question whether natural law were not the 'sole veritable religion'.[8] In return for his provocative challenges to religious doc-trine Forcroy was neither burnt at the stake nor thrown in prison. Nor was he left in peace to express his radical views. Instead, he was locked away in the lunatic asylum of St Lazare for six years until he showed himself docile and started taking the sacrament regularly. When he was eventually released he was banished from Paris back to his home town of Noyon.

Forcroy's case is relevant to Cyrano because it shows the author-ities reacting to dissidence in a new way. Imprisonment and the label of insanity were as effective, if not more so, than the previous strategy – the criminalization of such individuals. Not least because the troublesome, rebellious elements of society were more effec-tively silenced shut away in a lunatic asylum, than when offered the oxygen of publicity. Criminal prosecution attracted the attention of the public, particularly when it ended in a big showy execution. Once the public's curiosity was aroused, a fascinated determination to read the scandalous works of the 'demonic' miscreants was all too often the result. Even years later, the lingering whiff of fire and damnation could lend a forbidden glamour to certain works. Voltaire acknowledged that his desire to read Vanini's writings sprang from his fascination with their author's notorious fate. Cyrano's own bookseller suggested that it was precisely the reputa-tion of blasphemy and scandal attached to *The Death of Agrippina* that guaranteed its success. By the time Cyrano had published his own dissident writings, the authorities had perhaps begun to appreciate the fact that it was better to make such seditious subjects silently disappear, than to risk whipping up a frenzy of public interest in them – interest, which despite being nominally disapproving would only serve to draw attention to the criticisms and challenges to be found in the works of these passionate rebels.

Conditions inside the lunatic asylums of the seventeenth century were little different than those in the prisons. Dark, damp and disease-ridden, the cells in which the inmates were confined were occasionally little better than dungeons. In the opening of *The Voyage to the Sun* Cyrano recounts his hero's imprisonment in a 'black dungeon'; the experience has the vivid quality of a waking nightmare. The description of his imprisonment, as it emerges in Cyrano's fiction, is at once a wellspring of irrepressible black humour and a harrowing insight into the harsh reality of a society where freedom of expression did not exist; where corruption and oppression masqueraded as authority and justice. In the novel, the events that lead up to the imprisonment of Cyrano's protagonist Dyrcona are depicted with a combination of high drama and slapstick humour. A high-voltage chase sequence sees Dyrcona on the run from his jailers. He manages to trick his gullible guard into taking him to say a prayer in a local church with an elaborate story of angelic visitation (and the promise of a hefty bribe). Once outside the confines of the prison, he quickly gives his guard the slip and goes on the run through the streets of Toulouse. Although Cyrano had probably completed much of *Voyage to the Sun* before the date of his incarceration, it seems likely that he rewrote this opening section in order to include the new material inspired by his recent experiences. Dyrcona is not an autobiographical portrait of the author, yet comparisons between the two are unavoidable; both identify themselves as notorious due to their authorship of a text entitled *Voyage to the Moon*, whose accompanying portrait engraving has launched a degree of celebrity that is both uncomfortable and clearly a source of pride, and both were wrongly imprisoned. The first public portrait of the real Cyrano was that engraved by his friend Zachary Heince in 1653, to accompany the publication of the *Oeuvres Diverses*. In *The Voyage to the Sun*, Cyrano reflects that *The Voyage to the Moon* has sparked such controversy that the debate touches every household, dividing families and crossing social divides: 'From the gentleman to the monk . . . even women took their part'; all enthusiastically joining in the debate about the intriguing possibility of a world in the moon.[9]

Dyrcona discovers the downside to this sudden celebrity; he becomes aware that he is dangerously well known, thanks to the circulation of his portrait on the publication of his *Voyage to the Moon*. He is forced to disguise himself to escape detection: first of all as a peasant, then as a mute beggar and finally as a plague victim. His outlaw career is short-lived despite his quick thinking and terrified headlong flight. He has the ill luck to run straight into the head jailer but manages to escape once again, by tricking the crowd of onlookers into misinterpreting the jailer's initial consternation at the sight of his escaped prisoner and thereby neatly reversing their roles. He makes a quick-witted appeal to the crowd and various young hot-heads, eager for the reward that he tells them has been offered for the jailer's capture, seize on the unfortunate official and start beating him soundly. Meanwhile, Dyrcona sneaks away to seek refuge from the riot that he has set in motion. It is at this point that his good fortune utterly abandons him; he finds that in following a group of people, all trying to escape from the street fight into a nearby building, he has inadvertently returned himself to captivity. Dyrcona collapses, fainting with horror at this turn of misfortune. His fellow refugees from the brawl rush to his aid and the first to reach him is one of the town guards, who instantly recognizes him and arrests him on the spot. So ends his first prison break. The second, definitive escape takes place after his friends have discovered him in prison and paid for him to be transferred out of the dungeon and into a large well-appointed tower room, where he is allowed to have all his mathematical books and instruments with him. He orders materials delivered to his cell and manages to construct a spaceship (relying on a form of rudimentary rocket propulsion), which takes him on his second unintentional flight into outer space, this time on a voyage to the sun.

These elaborate escape fantasies probably reflect no more of the real Cyrano's actual experience of incarceration than the spur to his comical and fantastical imagination provided by isolation and deprivation. It is to be hoped that the description of his confinement in a rat-infested dungeon, where he is crawled over by lizards and snakes, where slugs and toads drip their slime in his hair and leeches suck his blood also owes more to imagination than reality. There is, perhaps, an element of wish-fulfilment in his portrait of an insouciant hero who reacts to the nightmarish horrors of this rancid prison with an unfailing stream of cheeky quips to his jailer and a witty refusal to be downcast. But there is one moment when it seems clear that the real Cyrano's experience of imprisonment intrudes on this fictionalizing process. He interrupts the description of Dyrcona's dungeon with the reflection that: 'to describe the rest is more than I can bear: it is beyond all belief; and I don't dare attempt to remember, I am too afraid that my conviction that I have escaped from my prison should prove to be no more than a dream from which I might be about to wake up'.[10]

Cyrano's description includes no elements of the trial that would naturally loom large in an instance of criminal imprisonment: this would not be part of the experience of incarceration in an asylum. The focus on visible punishment is the central difference between a blasphemy prosecution and imprisonment in an asylum. There was no programme of treatment for asylum inmates – beyond the regular ministrations of a priest – but at least there was, as Forcroy's case shows, the possibility of a 'cure' and consequent release. The living conditions may have been every bit as dirty, disease-ridden and dangerous as in the prisons, but the threat of torture or the stake was at least withheld. The inmates of asylums like St Lazare were an extremely varied population. Manuscript sources, detailing the proceedings that led to their incarceration, offer an interesting sample list of unfortunates: 'a persistent litigant', 'the most litigious man', 'a very wicked and argumentative man', 'a man who spends his days and nights deafening other people with his songs and uttering the most terrible blasphemies', 'a great liar', 'an anxious, melancholy and surly spirit', 'a billposter'.[11] With the possible exception of the troublesome singer or the melancholy soul, it is hard to see in these descriptions any elements recognizable to a modern conception of mental illness.

The asylums were perhaps becoming a convenient dumping ground for the disposal of those thorns in the side of the civil authorities whose conduct was not strictly illegal. As such, individuals who had the requisite money and influence could also use the asylums to settle private disputes. Such seems to have been Cyrano's case, although exactly who was responsible for arranging his incarceration remains a vexed question. The conditions in the asylums were undoubtedly unsanitary and appallingly grim. It must have been torture for the devotee of the woods and rivers of the beautiful valley of Chevreuse to be locked away from all light and hint of green, surrounded only by filth, decay and infestation.

16

Towards the sky

In order to retrace Cyrano's final months of life one can only rely on inference and the various hints strewn through the text of his final, posthumously published masterpiece *The Voyage to the Sun*. The shreds of documentary evidence that have survived are sadly few and far between. Censorship of Le Bret's biography has proved quite extraordinarily effective, shrouding Cyrano's death in a mystery that has endured to the present day. The rediscovery of the censored section of Le Bret's work reveals not only a clearer explanation of Cyrano's injury and illness, but also an accusation. Le Bret charges Abel II with having had Cyrano locked up in pretence that it was for his own good and as a result of his 'illness' but in reality as a low trick motivated by 'cowardly covetousness'.[1]

Essentially then, Cyrano seems to have gained his reputation as a madman, not because he was suffering from the dementia caused by neurosyphilis, but because his own brother apparently had him locked away in a lunatic asylum. The details were never entirely clear because of the rapid censorship of Le Bret's accusation, but now that the uncensored version has been recovered, it becomes possible to retrace the events with a little more clarity. In the suppressed section of Le Bret's preface, he states that Cyrano's close friend Jacques Rouhault had been 'the first to discover the ill-treatment that his brother had subjected him to, and the one who, with all his friends, painstakingly sought the means to shield him from the cruelties of that barbarian'.[2] Le Bret also thanks Cyrano's benefactor Tanneguy Renault des Boisclairs, the man responsible for 'breaking the iron-fetters in which his barbarous brother was keeping him prisoner', and with whom Cyrano was then to lodge for the next fourteen months.[3] Tanneguy was distantly related to Cyrano through his uncle Samuel; he was also something of a philanthropist, and it is to be assumed that he broke those iron fetters with the help of a substantial sum of money, paid to free Cyrano from the asylum. Le Bret never specifies that Cyrano's 'captivity' was within the walls of an asylum, rather than a prison – hardly surprising that he would not wish to record such an ignominious fact. The balance of probability is nevertheless in favour of a mental institution, rather than a prison, as this would also fit with the later reputation of insanity that attached to Cyrano's legend, as well as with the apparent ease with which his friends succeeded in releasing him from his 'fetters'. If he had been facing criminal prosecution this would have been considerably more difficult.[4]

Le Bret's condemnation of Abel is extremely damning, but it is possible that he may have been mistaken. At first glance, Cyrano's case seems to fall into the fairly common category of families who despaired of a troublesome member, whose outrageous conduct was likely to bring disgrace and possibly prosecution upon them if not checked in time. In such circumstances, one solution was to turn to the asylums in the hope of a 'cure'. Chapelle's aunts apparently had him locked away in St Lazare for a time in an attempt to curb his worst excesses. Another family tried to arrange a transfer for their son when a dangerous prison fever swept the asylum of St Lazare because they didn't want to risk losing him. Contrary to what one might imagine, they genuinely believed they were acting for his good in having him locked away, as their plea for his transfer affirms: 'having no design to cause their son's death when they had solicited the order to have him imprisoned but only to correct and recover his wits that were almost completely lost'.[5]

Le Bret's accusation is that Abel acted maliciously and avariciously, under pretence of a similar concern for his brother's good. This feigned concern lends significant weight to the theory that Cyrano's nightmare in the 'black dungeon' took place within an asylum rather than a prison. In the censored section of his published letter to Tanneguy des Boisclairs, Le Bret draws a direct contrast between the selflessness of the philanthropist and the selfishness of Abel de Cyrano. He also suggests that Cyrano was devastated by his brother's betrayal and that this accelerated the course of his illness: 'Your generous care had stayed the swift course of his illness, that his vexation at the inhumanity of this wicked brother alone had rendered so violent, I consider you as a miracle of our time, and I console myself, amid the hard-heartedness of a century when men are generally so self-serving, when I see a friend so kind and so generous.'[6]

Le Bret's identification of Abel as the author of Cyrano's downfall was published in 1656, in his preface to the edited version of *The Voyage to the Moon* that he had seen through the press. Within a very short space of time, the offending sections of the preface had been cut out of copies of the work and replaced with a confusing shortened version, in which vague references to Cyrano's head injury and illness replaced the description of his captivity and Abel's barbarity. Only one surviving copy of the uncensored version has come to light since, and that only very recently. In 1662, Cyrano's bookseller (publisher) Charles de Sercy published a new edition of Cyrano's works, in which *The Voyage to the Sun* appeared for the first time. Sercy opened the volume with a letter addressed to Abel de Cyrano in which he speaks to him of his brother's numerous enemies, who cruelly persecuted him with their 'envy and malicious gossip'.[7] Sercy alludes to a plot against the two brothers, but he declares the failure of the 'deception' to harm a fraternal friendship that endures beyond death.

If the bookseller's comments are accurate, they suggest that the accusation against Abel was the result of a conspiracy against the family. It is perfectly possible that Le Bret's condemnation of Abel was unfounded, and that he had been presumed upon by enemies of the family, who had deliberately hidden their own involvement by casting the blame on Abel. If it wasn't Abel who was responsible for Cyrano's imprisonment, then these same shadowy enemies somehow managed to orchestrate Cyrano's commitment to an asylum under Abel's name, without Abel having genuinely given his consent. This would probably not have been a particularly difficult task and would only have required money and the knowledge of the right palms to grease. Cyrano's own suspects of choice, the Jesuit brotherhood, certainly had the funds and connections to pull off such a thing. Sercy argues that Cyrano's brother was no more than an unknowing scapegoat. Abel could have been complicit in the plot to silence his troublesome brother and rival for the family fortune. Sercy explicitly states that Abel was his brother's heir, inheriting not only Cyrano's half of the estate but all of his literary production too, and there is some indication that Sercy was unsure what Abel's reaction to the publication of the *New Works* would be.

In the course of his letter, Sercy makes his own contribution to the Cyrano legend. Following in the path laid down by Cyrano himself, he draws a comparison with Alexander the Great and points out the fact that, like his hero, Cyrano was not the sort to live to a quiet old age. In a sad presentiment of his own fate, Cyrano had written in celebration of legendary heroes such as Hercules, Achilles, Alexander and Caesar, who had lived fast and died young. All of them, he noted approvingly, died before the age of forty. Sercy conjures up a vision of Cyrano as an 'incomparable genius', who, having exhausted the limitations of the earth, the moon and the sun, was forced to flee to the 'palace of the gods' in order to escape from these worlds 'too narrow for his ambition'.[8]

Whether Abel was an ally or an enemy, his situation could not have been further removed from that of his brother. Cyrano may already have been on the run from the late 1640s onwards (the date of the initial manuscript circulation of *The Voyage to the Moon*). Records show that Abel married a certain Michelle de Marcy on 1 July 1649, and settled with her in his father's house, living the rest of his life in the same faubourg as his parents before him. The family home was in rue Saint-Jacques in the parish of Saint-Jacques du Haut-Pas. Abel fathered a son Abel-Pierre and a daughter Marie-Catherine, whose births Cyrano did not live long enough to see. Cyrano's life, unlike his brother's, was far from settled, and what few clues remain to his domestic situation in the last few years of his life speak of upheaval and instability. In August 1650, he was staying with Monsieur Barat in the main street of the Faubourg Saint-Jacques. During the winter of 1651, he was in a different parish, Saint-Nicolas-des-Champs, in the inauspiciously named Cemetery Street. The spring of 1653 found him still in the same parish, but in a different street, the rather more appealing sounding Fountain Street.

In Le Bret's preface, he goes to some lengths to establish the broad network of supporters and friends that Cyrano had succeeded in building up. He mentions some twenty-five of them by name. This is naturally, a testament to the great swordsman's dual nature; while he could be antagonistic, angry and difficult he could also be charming, funny and loyal. He had endeared himself to many of his contemporaries and the image of his friends' desperate search for him after his mysterious disappearance is a touching one, but not all of those who were involved in taking care of Cyrano in the final months of his life were motivated purely by affection.

Tanneguy des Boisclair's involvement with the dying rebel is at first glance somewhat difficult to explain. Temperamentally, the two men had little in common and, unlike Rouhault, Le Bret or Le Royer de Prade, Tanneguy did not have a long-standing close, personal relationship with the poet. Instead, Tanneguy was part of the circle of devout Catholics centred around the charismatic Mother Superior of the Convent of the Daughters of the Cross, in which Cyrano's sister and cousin were both nuns. La Mère Marguerite de Jésus was rumoured to be so persuasive and appealing that young women were afraid to pay a visit to her nunnery, for fear of being 'charmed' by her into giving up their chances of matrimony and a family by taking the veil. Le Bret refers to the Mother Superior as someone who took a particular interest in Cyrano, and mentions that she attempted to introduce him to various useful acquaintances. This determined and energetic old lady seems to have made full use of the privilege of her position to involve herself in the lives of those around her, in a fashion that verged on the managerial. She lends a crucial note of solid respectability to Le Bret's epitaph and the list of Cyrano's friends, but the devoted biographer has to tread a fine line between praising her involvement with his friend's destiny, and admitting that Cyrano resisted her interference and neglected to cultivate the improving acquaintances she had hoped to procure for him. Cyrano's patron the Duc d'Arpajon was a benefactor of the convent and, given that the works were still going through the press at the time of the attack on Cyrano and his subsequent imprisonment, it may be that Mère Marguerite had a hand in preventing him from cancelling publication altogether.

Le Bret also notes the presence of the real Roxane at Cyrano's side in the final months of his life and he eulogizes her as a supremely pious and charitable woman. He credits Mme de Neuvillette with effecting such a change in his friend that he began to see free thought as monstrous, and to be sufficiently disgusted with the world to be ready for the next. Le Bret's depiction of a penitent Cyrano, meekly responding to the insistent appeals for repentance made by this circle of devout Catholics, is not entirely convincing. He also seems to have engaged in a little censorship of his own, as the edition of Cyrano's works that he supervised through the presses has gaps left in the text where the most outrageous and blasphemous passages should be. Le Bret explains away these gaps with an implausible tale of a break in that had entailed the loss of some of Cyrano's papers. Le Bret was ordained in 1656, and it is hard not to see the timing as significant. Finally free of his friend's powerful anti-establishment influence, Le Bret returned to the Catholic fold. There is one simple fact that emerges in his account of Cyrano's supposed deathbed conversion that he cannot disguise, however hard he tries to lessen its significance. Just five days before he died, Cyrano had fled from Tanneguy's house and the ministrations of his cousin and her Mother Superior, in order to return to the peace and tranquillity of the countryside.

Cyrano breathed his last on 28 July 1655, at the age of thirty-six. The parish records show that he died at the house of his cousin Pierre, in Sannois, a small village just outside Paris, on the fringes of his beloved valley of Chevreuse. This last-minute flight from repentance and respectability speaks volumes, casting significant doubt on the accuracy of Le Bret's assurance that Cyrano died a truly Christian death, regretting his freethinking, rebellious past. Father Garasse once wrote that: 'True freedom of the spirit consists in simply and sensibly believing all that the Church proposes, indifferently and without distinction.'[9] It is difficult to imagine Cyrano renouncing everything he ever believed in and fought for to accept a position of such unthinking conformity. Le Bret attempts to shore up his vision of a repentant Cyrano by recounting an exchange that passed between them near the end. Cyrano apparently quoted the classical author Tibullus on wasted youth, adding: 'no one has ever regretted as deeply as I do, so many beautiful days

squandered'. As evidence of Cyrano's supposed Christian resignation this is decidedly flimsy. Tibullus was a pagan philosopher-poet
whose four books of Elegies deal with his turbulent love affairs and
his profound attachment to the natural world. He longed for tran-
quility but lived a passionate and occasionally violent existence.
Like Cyrano, Tibullus died in his mid-thirties and he wrote with
anguished lyricism about the fleeting nature of human existance.
Rather than repenting his sins and focusing on the afterlife
Cyrano's thoughts seem to have been playing on the intellectual
achivements he had left unfinished, as for example, his scientific
treatise, 'the fragment of physics' that would never be completed,
the third volume of his interstellar adventures, *The Voyage to the
Stars*, that would never see the light of day, and the countless works
of his overflowing imagination that he had not yet even begun to
frame or capture.

Despite the terrible melancholy that seems to have gripped
Cyrano as he felt his hold on life weakening, he continued to
make jokes about death and Le Bret's preface opens with a comical vision of Cyrano's ghost, that he hints was directly inspired
(possibly even dictated) by the man himself. Even in the afterlife,
Cyrano is shown refusing to fall in with expectations. Rather than
tormenting superstitious mortals with any of the classic ghostly
activities like rattling his chains in an attic or knocking over furni-
ture, his ghost is described as being 'in excellent humour as always'.
Paradoxical to the last, the ghostly Cyrano attacks the sort of cred-
ulous fools who believe in ghosts.

Cyrano's attitude to death in his earlier works had always been
deliberately prosaic and fearlessly flippant. In the letter 'On a
Coward', his fictional coward makes a paradoxical boast: 'But does
he think he will have beaten me when he has taken away my life?
On the contrary, I will become all the more terrible and I am convinced that he will not be able to look upon me fifteen days later
without being frightened by me.'[10] In the same letter, the coward

contradicts the popular, gentlemanly notion that a glorious death is worth more than a long but insignificant life, remarking that, 'the least flea still living is worth more than Alexander the Great deceased'. This was written for comic effect but, by the time of his death, Cyrano was no longer the headstrong, reckless youth in pursuit of death or glory, who laughed at such cowardice. He had become a more mature and disillusioned man, who had seen the grim reality of such sacrifices and felt their tragic futility. Perhaps he also came to see the sense of lines that he had written originally in jest: that a man may risk his life before the age of thirty, because he does not know much of life, and so does not know what he stands to lose, but that to do so after that age, 'he would be crazy to risk it having known it'. Cyrano must surely have been aware that, if his life was ebbing away day by day, he had the freethinking rebellious stance that he had taken against the church to thank for it. Thus, it is hard to imagine that he would have found much comfort in the absolution promised by that same institution. It has been suggested that Molière modelled his atheistic anti-hero Dom Juan in part on Cyrano, and there is certainly an echo of Cyrano's provocative wit in the following exchange between Dom Juan and his manservant Sganarelle:

Sganarelle:	People must believe in something in this world. What do you believe?
Dom Juan:	What do I believe?
Sganarelle:	Yes.
Dom Juan:	I believe that two and two are four, Sganarelle, and that twice four are eight.[11]

In his short lifetime, Cyrano had succeeded in assuring that, for better or for worse, he would not soon be forgotten. He was a virtuoso of spin and the fact that he was known as a Gascon noble within his own lifetime is testament to the success of his image-making. Ultimately, that very success was to see him eclipsed by his own glory. Although he managed to project his flamboyant legend into the future, he could not control the direction it would take. But even in his lifetime, it already seemed clear that this was a man whose story would never die. Cyrano's good-humoured ghost has taken on many guises. His death was only the beginning of another story, a haunting that has so far lasted for three and a half centuries and counting.

In the immediate aftermath of his death more voices emerged praising his extraordinary, 'generous audacity', and admiring the brilliance of his 'uncommon mind', and the 'noble path to the heavens' that he had chosen to take. In the end, his independence and determined rejection of all authority and all conformity had led to his death. From Rostand's perspective, some two hundred years later, this made him the ideal symbol for every failure, every forgotten man who had ever struggled in vain against the vagaries of existence. But perhaps a more appropriate representation of Cyrano's 'failure' is that offered by the rebellious monk Giordano Bruno, who wrote, in anticipation of his own spectacular fall from grace: 'I am satisfied with my lofty enterprise; if the soul does not attain the desired target of its ardent zeal, what does that matter? It is enough to burn with such a noble fire; it is enough that I will have escaped towards the sky and delivered myself from the base multitude.'

Cyrano's own escape towards the sky did not prevent more earth-bound spirits from trying to drag his memory through the mud. A pamphlet circulated after his death, describing his apocryphal battle with a performing monkey. The first printed version of the pamphlet dates from 1704; it has been suggested that it may have circulated earlier in manuscript form and that the authorship may therefore be attributed to Dassoucy, who died in 1677. There is no proof to support this supposition. The pamphlet included a ridiculous description of Cyrano's appearance drawn for maximum comic effect: 'His head was almost entirely bereft of hair, one could count every strand from ten paces away. His eyes were lost under his eyebrows; his nose, wide at the stem and hooked, was rather like those of the green and yellow chatterboxes [parakeets] that they bring back from the Americas.'

According to the pamphlet, Cyrano found himself accosted by a crowd of lackeys gathered to watch the performing monkey on the Pont Neuf. One young man knocked off his hat while another flicked him on the nose and cried out: 'Is that really your everyday nose? What a devil of a nose! Back off a couple of steps won't you it's preventing me from seeing the show.' At which point, Cyrano prepared to fight single-handedly against his 'twenty or thirty aggressors' and found himself, in the confusion, stabbing to death the little monkey who was dressed as a cavalier. Sadly, such venomous attacks on Cyrano had as vigorous a life as the positive image-building he had achieved through his life and works. Théophile Gautier clearly used this parody as a source when writing his portrait of Cyrano in his *Grotesques*, and Rostand's Cyrano is a direct descendant from this distorted image. It is said that, in order to create just the right false nose for the actor Coquelin (the first ever incarnation of the stage Cyrano) the costume department tried and rejected over fifty different wax noses. In a letter published in *The Times* newspaper on 2 June 1931, a response is offered to a previously published letter that had posed the question 'Did Cyrano have a big nose?' The writer describes the 1654 portrait engraving of Cyrano, and reveals that he had personally demanded of Coquelin why he wore a big bulbous 'snout' rather than a high arched nose like that belonging to the real Cyrano – the answer given was that the arched version had made Coquelin squint.

The identification of Dassoucy as the author responsible for the tale of Cyrano's ignominious battle with the performing monkey is debatable, particularly since the pamphlet was first published some twenty-seven years after Dassoucy's death. There is no doubt, however, that Dassoucy was responsible for instigating the very first public criticisms of Cyrano after the great swordsman's death. In his memoirs, Dassoucy's references to Cyrano are designed to suggest that the great freethinker was little more than a dangerous madman. Dassoucy picks up on the idea of Cyrano's ghost continuing to haunt the land of the living and refers to 'the vengeful shade of that furious soldier'. The word 'furious' is weighted with significance since, at the time, it implied insanity as well as anger – it is the word that recurs most often in the descriptions of asylum inmates. In the context in which this reference appears, Dassoucy ridicules his own craven cowardice with his characteristic self-deprecating humour:

> But you also do not know how the late Mr D[e] B[ergerac], angry at having angered me, came to my abode to be reconciled with me. I was terribly afraid on seeing the pistol holster that he had brought with him because he was taking it to be repaired and this caused me to flee France for Italy; and even after his death, travelling from Paris to Turin by the light of the moon, my fear of my own shadow caused me to throw myself in a river, convinced that it was the vengeful shade of that furious soldier, terror of the living, and nightmare of the brave, who was at my heels in order to avenge himself for the capon affair.

Dassoucy's comical 'confession', that he fled the country out of fear of Cyrano, neatly conceals the fact that he was really forced to flee because of his conduct towards the retinue of small boys he kept as pages and trained as choirboys. Dassoucy's abuse of the young men he had in his power led to his imprisonment on more than one occasion and, if he left France, it was not to escape from Cyrano but from the scandal. He was pursued not by one vengeful shade but by many.

In the *Menagiana* of 1693, Dassoucy's suggestions were further embroidered upon in a fanciful account of Cyrano's death:

I believe that when he wrote his *Voyage to the Moon*, he already had the first quarter in his head. He died mad. The first public sign he gave of his madness was to go to midday Mass at la Mercy in breeches and a nightcap without a doublet. He hadn't a penny when he fell into a severe illness from which he died; and without M. Sainthe-Marthe, who had the charity to provide for his necessity he would have been obliged to go to the poor house.[12]

A year later, on publishing a new edition of the *Menagiana*, the author had added a further inaccuracy: 'He died at the Hôtel d'Arpajon where the duke of that name had given him refuge.'[13] This is a neat illustration of the obfuscating powers of unbridled gossip in action. We have already seen that Cyrano was far from bankrupt when he died, the registers of the parish prove that he died at his cousin's house in Sannois, not at d'Arpajon's home in central Paris, and the picture of him attending mass in a nightcap is an amusing, but not particularly relevant or convincing detail. As for the statement that Cyrano was slowly falling under the influence of the moon in the course of his writing and died a full-blown lunatic, nothing could be further from the truth.

Thankfully, Dassoucy's merry spite was far from Cyrano's only epitaph. In 1703, an Englishman named David Russen published a book-length review of Cyrano's *Voyage to the Moon*, entitled *Iter Lunare*. Russen was an enthusiastic admirer of Cyrano, who declared it impossible to read *Voyage to the Moon*, 'without abundance of delight'. He also took issue with the work being labelled as 'a comical history', insisting that, since it contained 'many discourses worth the observation of the most learned', that 'though it be interlaced with much matter of mirth, wit and invention . . . yet it is throughout carried on with that strength of argument, force of reason and solidity of judgement', that instead of comical it 'may deserve the Epithete of the *most Rational History of the Government of the Moon'.*[14] Here was someone who would vigorously deny those allegations of insanity levelled at Cyrano. Even with the support of dedicated admirers from Russen to Rostand, and despite his important influence on writers of genius like Molière, Voltaire and Jonathan Swift, Cyrano's literary heritage has been obscured for a long time. He penned an experimental and successful comedy, an audacious and powerful tragedy, letters that ranged from the passionately seductive, through lyrical description and sparkling wit to the bitterest invective and a novel that pushed back the boundaries of inventiveness and hilarity. And yet none of this was enough to rival his most creative work of all – his life story. As often as Cyrano is misrepresented as a person, he is also undervalued as a writer.

After Russen, Cyrano's posthumous reputation continued to fluctuate for the next two hundred years; those who actually read his work were inspired and delighted, while those who contented themselves with repeating stale slanders continued to exaggerate his failings and to denigrate his talent. It was not until the advent of Rostand's play that the two extremes were reconciled. Rostand crafted a compelling story from the disparate elements of Cyrano's life and legend and, in doing so, unleashed an avalanche of renewed interest in his hero. In 1908, a decade on from the opening of the play, a reviewer for *The Times* declared that: 'Not to have seen Coquelin's Cyrano is to have failed in life.' There have been many more unmissably wonderful incarnations of the swashbuckling hero since then. In 1992, Robert Lindsay's wonderfully funny and touching performance was perfectly pitched between bravado and tenderness. Derek Jacobi's storming performance in the RSC's 1983 production inspired choreographer David Bintley to go away and create *Cyrano* the ballet.

Bintley's first attempt in 1991 was a costly flop for the Royal Ballet. However in February 2007 the Birmingham Royal Ballet staged his new version with a new score and an amended choreography. The new production was well reviewed, with particular praise being heaped on Robert Parker in the title role. In a neat little twist to the tale, this was to be Parker's last performance before leaving ballet to become a pilot. David Bintley explained his persistence in attempting to retell the story through dance, with a reference to the overwhelming appeal of Cyrano's legend: 'He's a magnificent character; he's endlessly fascinating.' It has been suggested that the failure of Bintley's first production stemmed partly from the importance of language to the play – it is after all a story about eloquence and poetry, written by a supremely eloquent poet.

In 1936, Franco Alfano staged an opera of *Cyrano de Bergerac* which struggled, to a lesser extent with the same fundamental difficulty. The work has endured all the same; Montpellier Opera's lively 2003 production, starring Roberto Alagna, was given a second run in 2006. Although Alagna and Parker both gave charismatic and appealing performances, both productions, whatever their successes, also inevitably highlighted this innate problem with all adaptations of Rostand. The original work is so flawless that, however rapturous the singing, however expressive the dancing, the necessary cuts and alterations diminish the piece.

On film, two interpretations in particular loom large. In 1950, George Clooney's uncle, the actor José Ferrer gained the extremely rare distinction of winning an Oscar and a Tony for the same part – Cyrano de Bergerac. He also reprised the role in 1964 for the French film adaptation of *Cyrano and D'Artagnan*. More recently, in 1990, Jean Paul Rappeneau directed a lavish production starring Gérard Depardieu in the title role. Depardieu excels in the scenes of bombast and fury but also offers a genuinely moving and nuanced portrayal. He is well supported by Anne Brochet, who manages to bring an appealing mixture of fragility and courage to the part of Roxane, and by Vincent Perez, whose Christian is no mere foil for Cyrano's blazing wit but a courageous and noble individual in his own right.

The comedian Steve Martin had long contemplated modernizing

the play, but it was a friend's suggestion that he give Cyrano a happy ending that finally triggered him to sit down and write a screenplay. The resulting romantic comedy *Roxanne* (1987) is an outstanding example of the genre. Cyrano is metamorphosed into the small-town fire-chief C. D. Bales (played by Martin at his mercurial best), and Roxane becomes an astrophysicist named Roxanne Kowalski (played by a radiant Darryl Hannah). In an even looser adaptation, the 1996 romantic comedy *The Truth about Cats and Dogs* by Audrey Wells, took Cyrano's crippling insecurity about his appearance and transposed it to a charming, wisecracking female lead, Janeane Garofalo. The most unusual film adaptation of them all has to be *Samurai Saga* (1960) starring Toshiro Mifune. The Cyrano character has transformed again, this time into a Samurai warrior, and his story is retold with all the passion and humour of the original. The autumn leaves that fall in the final scene are transformed into a dying fall of cherry blossom, and the Samurai code of courage, honour and self-sacrifice forms a fascinating reflection of Cyrano's own lofty ideals. It is an unexpected, but appropriate direction for the legend to have taken in its progress ever onwards and always 'towards the sky'.

Epilogue

On arriving in Bergerac by train, the first thing the traveller sees is a large hoarding advertising the local radio station Cyrano FM. The town centre is a short stroll away and other Cyrano-related distractions are on offer at every turn; see a film at the local Le Cyrano cinema, go for a drink in the Cyrano Hotel Bar, stay a night in the pretty Cyrano and Roxane-themed guest house, or just simply go for a wander down Cyrano Street. The fictional Cyrano's face is everywhere, and his name is used to sell everything from foie gras to window blinds. Local businesses are proud to identify themselves with a national hero; the 'Crémerie Cyrano' sells a variety of cheeses; 'Alu Cyrano' offers aluminium guttering; the 'Allo Cyrano' taxi company takes locals and tourists from A to B; 'Cyrano Colis' provides courier services, and so on and so forth. At the tourist office, the friendly staff are well used to enquiries about the city's adopted son. Visitor numbers are on the increase, particularly since the huge, international success of the film starring Gérard Depardieu. Every year, enthusiasts travel thousands of miles from all over the world to pay homage to their swashbuckling hero. In the tourist office, these pilgrims are gently disabused of the notion that they can see the house where Cyrano lived or Roxane's balcony, and then directed towards the two statues of Cyrano that grace the picturesque old town.

The first statue, by the contemporary artist Mauro Corda, is a recent addition, having been unveiled in July 2005. Cast in polychrome bronze, it stands 2.4 metres high and dominates the small square beside the Church of St Jacques, at the top of a hill. The square is surrounded by quaint half-timbered houses, and constantly circled by an ever-shifting tide of admiring, camera-wielding tourists. Cyrano's eyes are turned heavenward, reflecting his preoccupation with outer space, but also in order to give him a suitable dreamy, romantic air. His right hand rests lightly on the hilt of his gleaming sword and his large floppy hat is held loosely in his left. Corda used a model for Cyrano's imposing frame but created the face from his imagination; as he put it – 'there was no question of just sticking a Pinocchio nose on him'. A little further down the hill, in a quieter, flower-strewn, leafy square, the older statue is in a slightly sorry state. Cyrano's nose has been broken off and stolen (once again) and someone has attempted corrective surgery with a gigantic blob of chewing gum. This statue of Cyrano, the work of the sculptor Varoqueaux, has been a feature in the town since November 1977, and it would seem that familiarity has bred a degree of contempt.

In a little antique store opposite the statue there was a bundle of sentimental postcards from the 1920s for sale when I visited. Flicking through them, it became clear that they were all addressed to one man by a variety of different female admirers. When I remarked on the adoring tone of the letters and asked about buying the collection – the gentleman who had been engaged in a long haggling debate about rent with the owner of the shop asked me with a wink if I were planning on using them to get some tips, and 'doing a Cyrano'. The final paradox of Cyrano's story is that the real Cyrano is so totally overshadowed by his fictional counterpart, that the place where he is most vividly present in modern-day France is Bergerac – a city that the real Cyrano probably never even visited.

On leaving the town, I picked up a copy of French *Marie Claire* only to find an article about five female Cyranos, or 'Cyranettes', as the author dubbed them. The women had agreed to be photographed in profile showing off their dramatic features, for an article entitled 'I've got a big nose, so what?' All were attractive and successful, and unanimous in celebrating their large noses as a sign of their individuality. This inheritance from the original Cyrano has at least filtered down the ages intact. As for Roxane, it would not be until 1997 that the French novelist Amélie Nothomb would deliver her post-feminist revenge. In a reworking of the Cyrano legend, Nothomb tells the story of the hideously ugly anti-hero Epiphane Otos, and his murderous love for the deliriously beautiful Ethel. Nothomb's heroine soundly rejects Otos and, in doing so, points out the double standard he attempts to impose on her. He expects her to love him for his soul and to overlook his outward appearance, but he himself is capable of no such greatness since he has chosen her, with all her beauty for his adoration, rather than an ugly girl with a pure soul. The real Cyrano would have delighted in the searing honesty of Nothomb's vicious little satire.

Ever since Rostand, Cyrano has become a sort of shorthand for an endearing incompetence in affairs of the heart. Witness an episode of the radio comedy *Hancock's Half Hour*, entitled 'Cyrano de Hancock', in which Sid falls in love with Hancock's forbidding secretary, Miss Pugh. Hancock's attempts to help him win her nearly end in catastrophe, as he finds himself unwillingly led to the altar in Sid's place. Only the benign incompetence of the registrar, played by Kenneth Williams, can save him, and in the confusion Hancock is granted an eleventh-hour reprieve of sorts, when he finds himself married to the registrar instead of Miss Pugh.

There are myriad modern references to Cyrano: from the

Filipino mobile phone ad featuring 'Cyrano de Bitoy', to the frenetic *Sesame Street* character, who stars in the 'Cyranose de Bergerac' edition of Monsterpiece Theatre. American high-school students post Cyrano-inspired videos on the Internet – these range from a spoof history channel documentary to the re-enactment of a duel, with Cyrano played by a stuffed penguin and his opponent by a toy frog, to a delirious three-part sequel to the play. My personal favourite of all the numerous references to Cyrano that occur in other texts is probably the exchange between Madeleine 'the stars are God's daisy chain' Bassett and Bertie Wooster in P. G. Wodehouse's *Right Ho, Jeeves*, in which Madeleine tells Bertie that he is like a modern-day Cyrano. Bertie has been desperately trying to promote the cause of Madeleine's sweetheart, his rather hopeless newt-loving friend, Gussie Fink-Nottle, largely because if their engagement fails he will be forced to marry her himself.

> 'You have a splendid, chivalrous soul.'
> 'Oh, no.'
> 'Yes, you have. You remind me of Cyrano.'
> 'Who?'
> 'Cyrano de Bergerac.'
> 'The chap with the nose?'
> 'Yes.'
> I can't say I was too pleased. I felt the old beak furtively. It was a bit on the prominent side, perhaps, but, dash it, not in the Cyrano class.

Cyrano himself was a big fan of the nose gag, but it is still a little disheartening to realize that the man who was once a wild adventurer, explorer of the known and unknown universe, is now seen only as a funny-looking romantic failure. Father Garasse, nemesis of the freethinkers, wrote angrily about their need not to follow the expected path: 'never judging according to common understanding but always going off at tangent, swerving and forging a new path'. This refusal of the norm was the very quality that Cyrano's admirers most prized in him, a man who found the wide world too narrow for his lavish imagination:

> *The fire of his mind and his selfless daring,*
> *Roamed through the vast deserts of earth and sky,*
> *But finding them always of too narrow compass,*
> *He broke open their ramparts to pass into the universe.*

Audiences love the fictional Cyrano because he's a heroic failure, noble but cursed. The original Cyrano is sharper, funnier and, ironically, more modern than the romantic hero whose creation he inspired. The tragedy of the real Cyrano is that, despite his extraordinary independence of mind, his heroic courage, his sharp wit, his unfailing good humour and his riotous creativity, he is generally only remembered as 'the chap with the nose'. The combined extravagances of Cyrano's life and works can ultimately be refined to a single overriding message to humanity, paradoxical perhaps, coming from the dangerous duellist, but no less heartfelt for that. After condemning the hero of *The Voyage to the Sun* to death, for the crime of being human, the leader of the republic of birds (a dove) hears evidence that he once set free a caged bird. His liberation of a fellow creature redeems the condemned man. The judgement is reversed and he is sent on his way with the following blessing:

'Go in peace then and live joyfully.'

Notes

CHAPTER ONE

1. Rostand, quoted in Jean Suberville, *Edmond Rostand*, Paris, 1921, p.iii.
2. Edmond Rostand, *Cyrano de Bergerac*, trans. A. Burgess, Hutchinson, 1985, p.171.
3. William Archer, *Study and Stage: A Year-Book of Criticism*, London, 1899, p.50.
4. C. E. Montague, *Dramatic Values*, London, 1911, p.46.
5. Edmond Rostand, *Cyrano de Bergerac*, Paris, 1897.
6. Coquelin, Letter to Edmond Rostand, *Le Petit Parisien*, 1897.
7. Sarah Bernhardt, Letter to Constant Coquelin, *Le Figaro*, 29 December 1897.
8. William Archer, *Study and Stage: A Year-Book of Criticism*, London, 1899, p.50.
9. Quoted in Pierre Brun, *Cyrano de Bergerac – Gentilhomme Parisien, l'histoire et la légende*, p.6.
10. Pierre Brun, *Cyrano de Bergerac – Gentilhomme Parisien, l'histoire et la légende*, 1909, p.7.
11. Pierre Brun, *Savinien de Cyrano Bergerac – Gentilhomme Parisien, l'histoire et la légende d'après des documents inédits*, Paris, 1893, p.4.

CHAPTER TWO

1. First published by Professor M. Alcover in her article 'Le grand-père de Cyrano était-il sénonais?' in *La Lettre Clandestine*, no.13, Paris: Presses de l'Université de Paris-Sorbonne, 2005, pp.261–78
2. J. L. Flandrin, *La revue XVII siecle, Conference 1972–3*, quoted in P. Ariès, *L'enfant et la vie familiale sous L'Ancien Régime*, Editions du Seuil, 1973, p.15.
3. Anonymous, *Le Caquet de l'Accouchée*, 1622.
4. See Michel de Montaigne, 'De l'Affection des Pères aux enfants', *Essays*, II, Gallimard, 1965, pp.77–98.
5. Cyrano de Bergerac, *Les Etats et Empire de la Lune et du Soleil*, Paris: Folio, 2004, p.117.
   NB Cyrano's two-volume novel *The Other World* was published in two sections and is known by various titles. The title that Cyrano gave the work

The States and Empires of the Moon and Sun was a deliberate parody of a contemporary work of travel writing but this title was not used in the first posthumous publications. For the sake of simplicity the work will be referred to by the title of each volume as *The Voyage to the Moon* and *The Voyage to the Sun*, these being the names by which the works were most familiar to Cyrano's contemporaries.

6. Cyrano de Bergerac, *Les Etats et Empire de la Lune et du Soleil*, Paris: Folio, 2004, p.115.

7. Cyrano de Bergerac, *Les Etats et Empire de la Lune et du Soleil*, Paris: Folio, 2004, p.118.

8. Edmond Rostand, *Cyrano de Bergerac*, Flammarion, 1989, pp.116–17.

9. Edmond Rostand, *Cyrano de Bergerac*, trans. A. Burgess, Hutchinson, 1985, p.61.

10. See E. Magne, *Les Erreurs de documentation de Cyrano de Bergerac*, Paris, 1898.

11. Cyrano de Bergerac, Letter XI 'D'une Maison de Campagne' in *Les Oeuvres Comiques Galantes et Littéraires*, Paris, 1962, p.40.

12. King Louis XIII, quoted in M. Monestier, *Duels*, Paris, 1991, p.152.

13. Cyrano de Bergerac, Letter XVII 'D'un Songe', *Les Oeuvres Comiques Galantes et Littéraires*, Paris, 1962, p.80.

14. Héroard, *Journal sur L'Enfance et la Jeunesse de Louis XIII*, quoted in P. Ariès, *L'enfant et la vie familiale sous L'Ancien Régime* Editions du Seuil, 1973, p.79.

15. Henri Le Bret, 'Préface' (1657) In *Les Etats et Empire de la Lune et du Soleil*, Honoré Champion, 2004, p.483

16. Alexandre Dubois, *Journal d'un Curé de Campagne au XVIIe siècle*, Henri Platelle (ed.) Paris, 1965, p.29.

17. Alexandre Dubois, *Journal d'un Curé de Campagne au XVIIe siècle*, Paris, 1965, p.71.

18. Alexandre Dubois, *Journal d'un Curé de Campagne au XVIIe siècle*, Paris, 1965, p.130.

19. Père Lejeune, *Du devoir des pères*, 1620. Quoted in R. Briggs, *Communities of Belief*, Oxford: Clarendon Press, 1989.

20. Henri Le Bret, 'Préface' (1657) In *Les Etats et Empire de la Lune et du Soleil*, Honoré Champion, 2004, p.483

21. Cyrano de Bergerac, *Le Pédant Joué* in *Oeuvres Comiques, Galantes et Littéraires*, Paris, 1962, p.285.

CHAPTER THREE

1. Cyrano de Bergerac, *Les Etats et Empire de la Lune et du Soleil*, Paris: Folio, 2004, p.146.

2. Cyrano de Bergerac, *Les Etats et Empire de la Lune et du Soleil*, Paris: Folio, 2004, p.115.

3. Charles Sorel, *Histoire Comique de Francion*, Editions Gallimard, 1996, p.551.

4. Henri de la Trémoille, *Letter to his son*, 1662, quoted in J. Dewald, *Aristocratic*

experience and the origins of Modern Culture, University of California Press, 1993, p. 73.

5. Henri Le Bret, 'Préface' in *Les Etats et Empires de la Lune et du Soleil*, Honoré Champion, 2004, p.490

6. Théophile Gautier, *La France Littéraire* (1834): quoted in *Cyrano dans tous ses Etats*, ed. L. Calvié, Toulouse Anacharsis Editions, 2004, p.126.

7. Ibid., p.125.

8. Thomas Overbury, *Observations*, 1609, quoted in *France Observed in the 17th Century by British Travellers*, ed. J. Lough, Oriel Press, 1985, p.95.

9. Anonymous, *A New Journey*, 1715, quoted in *France Observed in the 17th Century by British Travellers*, ed. J. Lough, Oriel Press, 1985, p.106.

10. See Héroard, *Journal sur L'Enfance et la Jeunesse de Louis XIII*, 1868.

11. F. de Dainville, *La Naissance de L'Humanisme Moderne*, Paris, 1940, p.160.

12. Michel de Montaigne, *Essais* I, Gallimard, 1965, p.238.

13. Peter Heylyn, *Travels*, 1656, quoted in *France Observed in the 17th Century by British Travellers*, ed. J. Lough, Oriel Press, 1985, p.53.

14. James Howell, *Letters*, 1619, quoted in *France Observed in the 17th Century by British Travellers*, ed. J. Lough, Oriel Press, 1985, p.54.

15. Anonymous, *A New Journey*, 1715, quoted in *France Observed in the 17th Century by British Travellers*, ed. J. Lough, Oriel Press, 1985, p.107.

16. Maréchal de Caillière, *Les Fortunes de gens de qualité et des gentilhommes particuliers*, 1661, p.72.

17. Peter Heylyn, *Travels*, 1656. and J. Reresby, *Memoirs and Travels* quoted in *France Observed in the 17th Century by British Travellers*, ed. J. Lough, Oriel Press, 1985, p.92.

18. Maréchal de Caillière, *Les Fortunes de gens de qualité et des gentilhommes particuliers*, 1661, quoted in P. Ariès, *L'enfant et la vie familiale sous l'Ancien Régime*, Editions du Seuil, 1973, p.117.

CHAPTER FOUR

1. Nicolas Faret, *L'Honnête Homme ou l'art de plaire à la court*, 1630, quoted in J. Dewald, *Aristocratic experience and the origins of Modern Culture*, University of California Press, 1993, p.45.

2. Olivier de la Marche, *Traité de Duel*, 1436, quoted in Jean-Marie Constant, *La Noblesse française aux XVIe et XVIIe siècles*, Hachette, 1985, p.98

3. Ibid.

4. Ibid.

5. Henri Le Bret, 'Préface', in *Les Etats et Empires de la Lune et du Soleil*, Honoré Champion, 2004, p.484.

6. Théophile Gautier, *Le Capitaine Fracasse*, Paris, 1863, p.320.

7. Théophile Gautier, *Le Capitaine Fracasse*, Paris, 1863, p.320.

8. Jacques Prévot, *Cyrano de Bergerac Poète et Dramaturge*, 1978, p.7.

9. Jacques Prévot, *Cyrano de Bergerac Poète et Dramaturge*, 1978, p.7.

10. Pierre Charron, *Traité de la Sagesse*, Bk.III ch.iii, (1601) quoted in J. Cornette, *Le Roi de Guerre*, Paris, 1993, p.52.

11. Nicolas Faret, *L'Honnête Homme ou l'art de plaire à la court*, Paris, 1630, quoted in E. Schalk, *From Valor to Pedigree*, Princeton, 1986, p.145.

12. Pierre Fortin de la Hoguette, *Catéchisme royal*, Paris, 1650, p.16.

13. Corneille, *Le Cid*, ed. Eve, Cambridge University Press, 1924, p.10.

CHAPTER FIVE

1. Pierre Corneille, *Le Menteur*, 1643, Act I, sc.i, Magnard, 2002, p.21.

2. Le Bret, 'Préface' in *Les Etats et Empires de la Lune et du Soleil*, Honoré Champion, 2004, p.484.

3. Cardinal Richelieu, *Testament Politique*, quoted in F. Bluche, *Richelieu*, 2003, p.125.

4. Richelieu, *Mémoires*, quoted in M. Monestier, *Duels*, Paris, 1991, p.145.

5. J. Chenel de la Chapperonaye, *Revelations of the Solitary Hermit* (1617), quoted in F. Billacois, *The Duel: its Rise and Fall in Early Modern France*, Yale, 1990, p.83.

6. Quoted in R. J. Knecht, *Richelieu*, Longman, 1991, p.52.

7. Corneille, *Le Cid* (a translation in Rhymed Couplets by V. Cheng), University of Delaware Press, 1987, p.57.

8. Cyrano de Bergerac, *le Pédant Joué* in *Oeuvres Comiques, Galantes et Littéraires*, Paris, 1962, pp.278-9.

9. Quoted in M. Cuenin, *Le Duel sous L'Ancien Régime*, Paris, 1982, p.132.

10. Corneille, *Le Cid*, quoted in M. Cuenin, *Le Duel sous L'Ancien Régime*, Paris, 1982, p.115.

11. Lodowick Bryskett, *A Discourse of Civill Life*, New York: Da Capo Press, 1971, pp.64-5.

12. Molière, *Les Fâcheux (1661)* in *Oeuvres Complètes*, vol.1, Gallimard, 1983, p.378.
    Eraste: *On m'a vu soldat avant que courtisan;*
    J'ai servi quatorze ans, et je crois être en passe
    De pouvoir d'un tel pas me tirer avec grâce,
    Et de ne craindre point qu'a quelque lâcheté
    Le refus de mon bras me puisse être imputé.
    Un duel met les gens en mauvaise posture,
    Et notre roi n'est pas un monarque en peinture:
    Il sait faire obéir les plus grands de l'État,
    Et je trouve qu'il fait en digne potentat.
    Quand il faut le servir, j'ai du coeur pour le faire;
    Mais je ne m'en sens point quand il faut lui déplaire;
    Je me fais de son ordre une suprême loi:
    Pour lui déobéir cherche un autre que moi.

    Translation by H. van Laun, *The Works of Molière*,
    Edinburgh, 1875, p.107

13. Bussy-Rabutin, *Les Mémoires de Messire Roger de Rabutin, Comte de Bussy, Lieutenant Général des Armées du Roy et mestre de camp général de la cavalerie légère*, Paris, 1696, pp.27-8.

14. Comte de Forbin, *Mémoires du Comte de Forbin*, Paris, 1993, p.40.

15. René de Ceriziers, *Le Héros français ou l'idée du grand capitaine* (1645), quoted

in Briost, Drevillon, Serna, *Croiser le Fer – Violence et culture de l'épée dans la France Moderne*, 2002, p.270.

16. Jean de La Taille, *Discours Notable sur les Duels* (1607) quoted in M. Cuenin, *Le Duel sous L'Ancien Régime*, Paris, 1982, p.27.

17. Rostand, *Cyrano de Bergerac*, trans. A. Burgess, Hutchinson, 1985, p.37.

CHAPTER SIX

1. Cyrano de Bergerac, 'Lettre à M. Gerzan, sur son *Triomphe des Dames*' in *Oeuvres Comiques, Galantes et Littéraires*, Paris, 1962, p.65.

2. Quoted in F. Bluche, *Richelieu*, Paris, 2003, p.140.

3. Cyrano de Bergerac, Lettre 'Sur le Blocus d'une Ville' in *Oeuvres Comiques, Galantes et Littéraires*, Paris, 1962, p.114. NB. Professor M. Alcover makes a compelling case for a reading of this work as an account of the siege of Paris but Mouzon is the more traditionally accepted interpretation.

4. Cyrano de Bergerac, Lettre 'Contre les médecins' in *Oeuvres Comiques, Galantes et Littéraires*, Paris, 1962, p.171.

5. Michel de Montaigne, 'De la Liberté de Conscience', *Essais II*, Gallimard, 1965, p.434.

6. H. J. C. von Grimmelshausen, *The Adventures of Simplicius Simplicissimus* (translated by G. Schulz-Behrend), Camden House, Columbia, 1993, p.26.

7. H. J. C. von Grimmelshausen, *The Adventures of Simplicius Simplicissimus* (translated by G. Schulz-Behrend), Camden House, Columbia, 1993, p.26.

8. Quoted in *France Observed in the 17th Century by British Travellers*, ed. John Lough, Oriel Press, 1985, p.168.

9. Lady Fanshawe, *Memoirs*, quoted in *France Observed in the 17th Century by British Travellers*, ed. J. Lough, Oriel Press, 1985, p.167.

10. Cyrano de Bergerac, *Les Etats et Empire de la Lune et du Soleil*, Paris: Folio, 2004, p.106.

11. Quoted in *France Observed in the 17th Century by British Travellers*, ed. J. Lough, Oriel Press, 1985, p.95.

12. Quoted in G. Parker, *The Thirty Years War*, Routledge, 1997, p.270.

13. Cyrano de Bergerac, *Les Etats et Empire de la Lune et du Soleil*, Paris: Folio, 2004, p.106.

14. Cyrano de Bergerac, 'Contre les Frondeurs', *Oeuvres Comiques, Galantes et Littéraires*, Paris, 1962, pp.83–4.

15. Cyrano de Bergerac, *Les Etats et Empire de la Lune et du Soleil*, Paris, Folio, 2004, p.147.

16. Cyrano de Bergerac, *Les Etats et Empire de la Lune et du Soleil*, Paris, Folio, 2004, pp.147–8.

17. Archevêque d'Embrun, quoted in M. Cuenin, *Le Duel sous L'Ancien Régime*, Paris, 1982, p.165.

CHAPTER SEVEN

1. Le Bret, 'Préface' in *Les Etats et Empires de la Lune et du Soleil*, Honoré Champion, 2004. p.484.

2. Cyrano de Bergerac, *Les Etats et Empire de la Lune et du Soleil*, Paris: Folio, 2004, p.79.

3. Cyrano de Bergerac, *Les Etats et Empire de la Lune et du Soleil*, Paris: Folio, 2004, p.79.

4. Tristan L'Hermite, 'La Servitude' in *Le Page Disgracié*, ed. J. Serroy, Presse Universitaire de Grenoble, 1980, p.9.

5. Primi Visconti, quoted in W. D. Howarth, *Molière – A Playwright and his Audience*, Cambridge University Press, 1982, p.50.

6. Guez de Balzac, Letter (1637) quoted in W. D. Howarth, *Molière – A Playwright and his Audience*, Cambridge University Press, 1982, p.50.

7. Rostand, *Cyrano de Bergerac*, trans. A. Burgess, Hutchinson, 1985, p.44.

8. Cyrano de Bergerac, Lettre 'Le Duelliste' in *Oeuvres Comiques, Galantes et Littéraires*, Paris, 1962, p.68.

9. Cyrano de Bergerac, Lettre 'Contre un faux brave' in *Oeuvres Comiques, Galantes et Littéraires*, Paris, 1962, p.172.

10. Cyrano de Bergerac, Lettre 'Le Duelliste' in *Oeuvres Comiques, Galantes et Littéraires*, Paris, 1962, p.67.

11. Cyrano de Bergerac, Lettre 'Le Duelliste' in *Oeuvres Comiques, Galantes et Littéraires*, Paris, 1962, p.68.

12. Cyrano de Bergerac, Lettre 'Le Duelliste' in *Oeuvres Comiques, Galantes et Littéraires*, Paris, 1962, p.68.

13. E. Magne, *Le Chevalier de Lignières*, Paris, 1920, p.27.

14. Rostand, *Cyrano de Bergerac*, trans. A. Burgess, Hutchinson, 1985, pp.69–70.

15. Rostand, *Cyrano de Bergerac*, trans. A. Burgess, Hutchinson, 1985, pp.70–1.

16. Le Bret, 'Préface' in *Les Etats et Empires de la Lune et du Soleil*, Honoré Champion, 2004. p.485.

17. Fr. Garasse, *La Doctrine Curieuse des Beaux Esprits de ce temps*, Paris, 1624, p.5.

18. Théophile de Viau, *Théophile de Viau: un poète rebelle*, Paris: Guido Saba, 1999, p.18.

19. Molière, *Dom Juan*, translated by H. van Laun, *Dramatic Works of Molière*, Edinburgh, 1876, p.168.

20. Le Bret, 'Préface' in *Les Etats et Empires de la Lune et du Soleil*, Honoré Champion, 2004, p.484.

CHAPTER EIGHT

1. Rostand, *Cyrano de Bergerac*, trans A. Burgess, Hutchinson, 1985, p.79.

2. J. Prévot, *Cyrano de Bergerac – Poète et Dramaturge*, Paris, 1978, p.46.

3. Le Bret, 'Préface' in *Les Etats et Empires de la Lune et du Soleil*, Honoré Champion, 2004, p.491.

4. Le Sieur de Grimarest, *La vie de M. de Molière* (1707), Paris, 1955, p.39.

5. L.-R. Lefèvre, *La Vie de Cyrano de Bergerac*, Paris, 1927, p.139.

6. Cyrano de Bergerac, Lettre 'Pour une Dame Rousse', *Oeuvres Comiques, Galantes et Littéraires*, Paris, 1962, p.39

7. Cyrano de Bergerac, 'Lettre IV' in *Oeuvres Comiques, Galantes et Littéraires*, Paris, 1962, p.178.

Notes

8. Marie-Catherine Desjardins, Lettre, quoted in *Lettres d'Amour du XVIIe siècle*, ed. Rohou, Paris, 1994, p.288.

9. E. Magne, *Ninon de Lenclos*, Paris, 1925, p.40.

10. Marie de Gournay, *Égalité des hommes et des femmes* (1622), Paris, 1989, pp.108–9.

11. Quoted in C. Dulong, *La Vie Quotidienne des femmes au Grand Siècle*, Hachette, 1984, p.48.

12. Mlle de Scudéry, Lettre, quoted in C. Dulong, *La Vie Quotidienne des femmes au Grand Siècle*, Hachette, 1984, p.146.

13. L'Abbé de Pure, *La Prétieuse ou le mystère des ruelles*, ed. Magne, Paris, 1939, see also 'des remèdes aux maux de mariage' pp.13–113.

14. Molière, *Les Femmes Savantes*, Hachette, 1920, p.68.

15. Guez de Balzac, quoted in D. Maland, *Culture and Society in Seventeenth Century France*, London, 1970, p.48.

16 Mme de Sévigné, quoted in C. Dulong, *La Vie Quotidienne des femmes au Grand Siècle*, Hachette, 1984, p.153.

17. Cyrano de Bergerac, *Les Etats et Empire de la Lune et du Soleil*, Paris: Folio, 2004, p.303.

CHAPTER NINE

1. J. Glanvill, *Sadducismus Triumphatus or Philosophical Considerations touching Witches and Witchcraft*, London, 1682, p.2.

2. Cyrano de Bergerac, *Oeuvres Comiques, Galantes et Littéraires*, Paris, 1962, p.44.

3. Ibid, p.54.

4. Bouillau letter to Gassendi, quoted in M. Carmona, *Les Diables de Loudun*, Paris, 1988, p.71.

5. Montaigne, 'De la Conscience', *Essais II*, Gallimard, 1965, p.57.

6. H. Boguet, *Discours execrable des sorciers, Lyon*, 1605 [unpaginated].

7. Cyrano de Bergerac, Lettre 'Contre les Sorciers', *Oeuvres Comiques, Galantes et Littéraires*, Paris, 1962, p.53.

8. Voltaire, quoted in Robert Muchembled, *Le Roi et la Sorcière*, Paris, 1993, p.15.

CHAPTER TEN

1. Susan Read Baker, 'Permutations of Parricide: Cyrano de Bergerac's *La Mort d'Agrippine* (1647)', *The French Review*, Vol. 65, No. 3 (Feb 1992), pp. 375–84.

2. Tallemant des Réaux, *Historiettes*, Paris, 1960, pp.886–7.

3. Father Garasse, quoted in J. S. Spink, *French Free Thought*, Toronto, 1960, p.9.

4. G. Naudé, *Apologie pour tous les grands hommes qui ont été faussement soupçonnés de magie*, in *Libertins du XVIIe siècle*, ed. Prévot, Gallimard, 1998, pp.169–71.

5. Cyrano de Bergerac, 'Entretiens Pointus', *Oeuvres Comiques, Galantes et Littéraires*, Paris, 1962, p.202.

6. Cyrano de Bergerac, *Les Etats et Empire de la Lune et du Soleil*, Paris: Folio, 2004, p.168.

7. Thomas Browne, *Hydriotaphia*, 1620, p.51.

8. Cyrano de Bergerac, *Les Etats et Empire de la Lune et du Soleil*, Paris: Folio, 2004, p.157.

9. René Pintard, *Le Libertinage Erudit*, Paris, 1943, p.26.

10. Guillaume de Catel, Lettre Catel à Peyresc, Feb 1619.

11. *Historiarium Galliae ab excessu Henrici IV*, libri XVIII, 1643.

12. *Interrogatoire de Mathieu Molé*, MS 1623-a.

13. Voltaire, *Lettre à l'Abbé d'Olivet*, 6 Jan 1736.

14. Cyrano de Bergerac, *Les Etats et Empire de la Lune et du Soleil*, Paris: Folio, 2004, p.167.

15. Cyrano de Bergerac, *Les Etats et Empire de la Lune et du Soleil*, Paris: Folio, 2004, p.167.

CHAPTER ELEVEN

1. Johannes Kepler, Letter to Galileo, April 1610.

2. Giordano Bruno, *The Ash-Wednesday Supper*, 1584, dialogue III.

3. Ibid.

4. Quoted in Jean Rocchi, *L'Errance et l'hérésie ou le destin de Giordano Bruno*, Paris, 1989, p.261.

5. Cyrano de Bergerac, *Les Etats et Empires de la Lune et du Soleil*, Folio, 2004, p.92.

6. Cyrano de Bergerac, *Les Etats et Empires de la Lune et du Soleil*, Folio, 2004, p.112.

7. Cyrano de Bergerac, *Les Etats et Empires de la Lune et du Soleil*, Folio, 2004, p.110.

8. Fr. Garasse, *La Doctrine Curieuse des beaux esprits de ce temps*, Paris, 1650, pp.229-30.

9. Cyrano de Bergerac, *Les Etats et Empires de la Lune et du Soleil*, Folio, 2004, p.53.

10. Johannes Kepler, *Conversations with Galileo's Sidereal Messenger*, trans. Rosen, New York, 1965, p.36.

11. Johannes Kepler, *Conversations with Galileo's Sidereal Messenger*, trans. Rosen, New York, 1965, p.43.

CHAPTER TWELVE

1. Quoted in Cyrano de Bergerac, *Les Etats et Empires de la Lune et du Soleil*, ed. M. Alcover, Champion, 2004, p.xxxvi.

2. See discussion of the attribution in M. Alcover, *Cyrano relu et corrigé*, Genève: Droz, 1990.

3. *Les Pensées de M. Dassoucy dans le Saint Office de Rome*, quoted in *Les Libertins du XVIIe siecle*, ed. Jacques Prévot, Gallimard, 1998.

4. Cyrano de Bergerac, *Les Etats et Empires de la Lune et du Soleil*, Folio, 2004, p.92.

5. Le Bret, 'Préface', in *Les Etats et Empire de la Lune et du Soleil*, Honoré Champion, 2004, p.483.

6. Charles Dassoucy, *Les Pensées de Monsieur Dassoucy dans le S. Office de Rome*, in *Les Libertins du XVIIe siècle*, ed. Prévot, Gallimard, 1998, p.899.

7. Francis Bacon, *Novum Organum*, London, 1905, p.54.

8. Johannes Kepler, *Somnium*, trans. E. Rosen, University of Wisconsin, 1967, p.33.

9. Lucian, *Certain Select Dialogues of Lucian together with his True History*, 1634, p.107. This quotation is taken from an English translation by Francis Hickes which appeared in 1634, in itself a significant indication of the contemporary enthusiasm for texts which were blurring the boundaries between truth and fiction.

10. Bernard de Bovier de Fontenelle, *A Discovery of New Worlds*, trans, A. Behn, London, 1688, b5r–b5v.

11. Kepler, *Conversations with Galileo's Sidereal Messenger*, trans Rosen, New York, 1965, p.5.

12. Ibid, p.5.

13. Cyrano de Bergerac, *Les Etats et Empires de la Lune et du Soleil*, Folio, 2004, p.109.

14. Cyrano de Bergerac, *Les Etats et Empires de la Lune et du Soleil*, Folio, 2004, p.235.

15. Cyrano de Bergerac, *Les Etats et Empires de la Lune et du Soleil*, Folio, 2004, p.282.

16. Dassoucy, 'Les Pensées de M. Dassoucy dans le S. Office de Rome' (1676) in *Les Etats et Empires de la Lune et du Soleil*, ed. Alcover, Honoré Champion, 2004, pp.528–9.

17. Cyrano de Bergerac, *Les Etats et Empires de la Lune et du Soleil*, Folio, 2004, p.235

18. Cyrano de Bergerac, *Les Etats et Empires de la Lune et du Soleil*, Folio, 2004, p.53.

19. Cyrano de Bergerac, *Les Etats et Empires de la Lune et du Soleil*, Folio, 2004, p.134.

20. Cyrano de Bergerac, *Les Etats et Empires de la Lune et du Soleil*, Folio, 2004, pp.134–5.

21. Dassoucy, 'Les Aventures de M. Dassoucy', in *Les Libertins du XVIIe siècle*, ed. Prévot, Gallimard, 1998, p.765.

22. Thomas Hobbes, *Leviathan*, Amsterdam, 1670, p.65.

23. Cyrano de Bergerac, *Oeuvres Comiques, Galantes et Littéraires*, Paris, 1962, p.29.

24. Cyrano de Bergerac, *Oeuvres Comiques, Galantes et Littéraires*, Paris, 1962, p.40.

25. *Je veux faire des vers qui ne soient pas contraints,*
    Promener mon esprit par de petits desseins,
    Chercher des lieux secrets où rien ne me déplaise,
    Employer tout une heure à me mirer dans l'eau,
    Ouïr comme en songeant la course d'un ruisseau,

Écrire dans les bois, m'interrompre, me taire,
Composer un quatrain sans songer à le faire.

          Théophile de Viau, 'l'Elegie à une Dame' in
          G. Saba, *Théophile de Viau: un poète rebelle*, Paris, 1999, p.6

26. Cyrano de Bergerac, Lettre 'D'une Maison de Campagne', *Oeuvres Comiques, Galantes et Littéraires*, Paris, 1962, p.40.
27. Cyrano de Bergerac, *Les Etats et Empires de la Lune et du Soleil*, Folio, 2004, p.141. This phrase was initially censored and therefore did not appear in the 1657 edition of the text.

CHAPTER THIRTEEN

1. Henri Le Bret, 'Préface' in *Les Etats et Empire de la Lune et du Soleil*, Honoré Champion, 2004, p.483
2. Cyrano de Bergerac, *Les Etats et Empires de la Lune et du Soleil*, Folio, 2004, p.109.
3. Cyrano de Bergerac, *Les Etats et Empires de la Lune et du Soleil*, Folio, 2004, p.249.
4. Cyrano de Bergerac, *Les Etats et Empires de la Lune et du Soleil*, Folio, 2004, p.143.
5. Dassoucy, in *Les Libertins du XVIIe siècle*, vol I, ed. Prévot, Gallimard, 1998, p.880.
6. Cyrano de Bergerac, *Les Etats et Empires de la Lune et du Soleil*, Folio, 2004, p.156.
7. *Les Libertins de XVIIe siècle*, ed. Prévot, Gallimard, 1998, p.880.
8. Dassoucy, in *Les Libertins de XVIIe siècle*, ed. Prévot, Gallimard, 1998, p.885.
9. Dassoucy, in *Les Libertins de XVIIe siècle*, ed. Prévot, Gallimard, 1998, p.879.
10. Cyrano de Bergerac, *Les Etats et Empires de la Lune et du Soleil*, Folio, 2004, p.92.
11. Montigny, 'Lettre à Eraste', quoted in 'Introduction' to *Les Etats et Empires de la Lune et du Soleil*, ed. M. Alcover, Honoré Champion, 2004, p.xxxiv.
12. Le Bret, 'Préface' in *Les Etats et Empire de la Lune et du Soleil*, Honoré Champion, 2004, p.487.
13. Cyrano de Bergerac, *Les Etats et Empires de la Lune et du Soleil*, Folio, 2004, p.141.
14. Cyrano de Bergerac, *Les Etats et Empires de la Lune et du Soleil*, Folio, 2004, p.239.
15. Cyrano de Bergerac, quoted in 'Introduction' to *Les Etats et Empires de la Lune et du Soleil*, ed. M. Alcover, Honoré Champion, 2004, p.liv.
16. Cyrano de Bergerac, Lettre 'Contre un Ingrat', *Oeuvres Comiques, Galantes et Littéraires*, Paris, 1962, p.122
17. Cyrano de Bergerac, Lettre 'Contre un Ingrat', *Oeuvres Comiques, Galantes et Littéraires*, Paris, 1962, pp.123–4.
18. Cyrano de Bergerac, *Les Etats et Empires de la Lune et du Soleil*, Folio, 2004, p.236.

CHAPTER FOURTEEN

1. Le Bret, 'Préface' in *Les Etats et Empires de la Lune et du Soleil*, Honoré Champion, 2004, p.485.
2. Edmond Rostand, *Cyrano de Bergerac*, trans. A. Burgess, Hutchinson, 1985, p.170.

Notes

3. Le Sieur de Grimarest, *La vie de M. de Molière* (1705), ed. Mongredien, 1955, Paris, p.39

4. Cyrano de Bergerac, *Les Etats et Empires de la Lune et du Soleil*, Folio, 2004, p.89.

5. Professor Madeleine Alcover's detailed analysis of the texts proves the attribution baseless. See M. Alcover, 'Stylistique et critique d'attribution: Requiem pour les mazarinades défuntes de Cyrano', *La Lettre Clandestine*, no.13 (pp.233–59) Paris: Presses de l'Université de Paris-Sorbonne, 2004.

6. Cyrano de Bergerac, *Oeuvres Comiques, Galantes et Littéraires*, Paris, 1962, p.137.

7. *The Referee*, London, 25 May 1902, quoted in Hobart Ryland, *The Sources of the Play Cyrano de Bergerac*, Institut des Etudes Françaises, vol. 70–1, 1936. p.83.

8. Quoted in Hobart Ryland, *The Sources of the Play Cyrano de Bergerac*, Institut des Etudes Françaises, vol. 70–1, 1936. p.83.

9. Rosemunde Gérard, *Edmond Rostand*, Paris: Bibliothèque-Charpentier, 1935, p.11.

10. A. M. Burrage, *War is War*, by Ex-Private X, London, 1930, pp.57–8.

11. Burrage, *War is War*, by Ex-Private X, London, 1930, p.7.

CHAPTER FIFTEEN

1. M. de Cyrano Bergerac, *Satyrical Characters and handsome descriptions in Letters written to severall Persons of Quality*, London, 1658, A3r.

2. Quoted in M. Alcover, 'Cyrano *In Carcere*', *Papers on French Seventeenth Century Literature*, XXI, 41, 1994, p.402.

3. John Evelyn, *Diaries*, quoted in *France Observed in the 17th Century by British Travellers*, ed. Lough, Oriel Press, 1985, p.95.

4. Cyrano de Bergerac, *Les Etats et Empires de la Lune et du Soleil*, Paris, Folio, 2004, p.79.

5. Edmond Rostand, *Cyrano de Bergerac*, trans. A. Burgess, Hutchinson, 1985, p.169.

6. Quoted in Cyrano de Bergerac, *Les Etats et Empires de la Lune et du Soleil*. ed. M. Alcover, Champion, 2004. p.lxii [translation by Julie Labay].

7. Cyrano de Bergerac, 'Contre un jésuite assassin et médisant', *Lettres d'amour et d'humeur*, Librio, 2004, p.88.

8. Quoted in Michel Foucault, *L'Histoire de la Folie à l'âge classique*, Gallimard, 1972, p.112

9. Cyrano de Bergerac, *Les Etats et Empires de la Lune et du Soleil*, Honoré Champion, 2004. p.168.

10. Cyrano de Bergerac, *Les Etats et Empires de la Lune et du Soleil*, Honoré Champion, 2004. p.198.

11. Michel Foucault, *L'Histoire de la Folie à l'âge classique*, Gallimard, 1972, p.150.

CHAPTER SIXTEEN

1. Rediscovered thanks to the painstaking research of Professor Madeleine Alcover and published in her edition of *Les Etats et Empires de la Lune et du Soleil*, Honoré Champion, 2004, pp.477–93.

2. Le Bret, 'Préface' in *Les Etats et Empires de la Lune et du Soleil*, Honoré Champion, 2004, p.490.

3. Le Bret, 'Epître à Messire Tanneguy Renault des Boisclairs' in *Les Etats et Empires de la Lune et du Soleil*, Honoré Champion, 2004, p.478.

4. Although not impossible as the example of the Chevalier de Roquelaure demonstrates. However, Roquelaure also benefited from the fact that he was closely related to several of his prosecutors. A notable exception to the difficulty in obtaining a release from prison would be in the case of imprisonment for debt, but as we have seen there is no reason to suppose that Cyrano's finances were in that grievous a state.

5. M. S. Arsenal quoted in Michel Foucault, *L'Histoire de la Folie à l'âge classique*, Gallimard, 1972, p.129.

6. Le Bret, 'Epître à Messire Tanneguy Renault des Boisclairs' in *Les Etats et Empires de la Lune et du Soleil*, Honoré Champion, 2004, p.478.

7. Charles de Sercy, 'Epître à M. de Cyrano de Mauvières', in *Les Etats et Empires de la Lune et du Soleil*, Honoré Champion, 2004, p.494.

8. Charles de Sercy, 'Epître à M. de Cyrano de Mauvières', in *Les Etats et Empires de la Lune et du Soleil*, Honoré Champion, 2004, p.495.

9. Fr. Garasse, *La Doctrine Curieuse*, Paris, 1624, p.209.

10. Cyrano de Bergerac, 'Contre un Poltron', *Oeuvres Comiques, Galantes et Littéraires*, Paris, 1962, p.117.

11. Molière, *Dom Juan*, translated by H. van Laun, *The Dramatic Works of Molière*, Edinburgh, 1876, p.134.

12. Gilles Ménage, *Menagiana*, Paris, 1693, quoted in M. Alcover, 'Cyrano *In Carcere*', *Papers on French Seventeenth Century Literature*, XXI, 41, 1994, p.403.

13. Ibid.

14. D. Russen, *Iter Lunare*, London, 1703, p.3.

Select Bibliography

Alcover, M., 'Cyrano *In Carcere*', *Papers on French Seventeenth Century Literature*, XXI, 41, 1994.

Alcover, M., *Cyrano relu et corrigé*, Genève, 1990.

Alcover, M., *La Pensée Philosophique et scientifique de Cyrano de Bergerac*, Paris, 1970.

Alcover, M., 'Le grand-père de Cyrano était-il sénonais?', *La Lettre Clandestine*, no.14, (pp.261–78) Paris: Presses de l'Université de Paris-Sorbonne, 2005.

Alcover, M., 'Sisyphe au Parnasse: La réception des oeuvres de Cyrano aux XVIIe et XVIIIe siècles, *Oeuvres et Critiques*, XX, 3 (pp.219–50) Tübingen, 1995.

Alcover, M., 'Stylistique et critique d'attribution: Requiem pour les mazarinades défuntes de Cyrano', *La Lettre Clandestine*, no.13 (pp.233–59) Paris: Presses de l'Université de Paris-Sorbonne, 2004.

Alcover, M., 'Un gay trio: Cyrano, Chapelle, Dassoucy', *Actes du 4e colloque du Centre International de Rencontres sur le XVIIe siècle, Université de Miami, Biblio*, 17 (117), (pp.265–75) Tübingen, 1999.

Anonymous, *Le Caquet de l'Accouchée*, Paris, 1622.

Anonymous, *Le Combat de Cirano de Bergerac avec le singe de Brioché Au bout du Pont Neuf*, Paris, 1704.

Apostolides, J-M., *Cyrano qui fut tout et qui fut rien*, Paris, 2006.

Archer, W., *Study and Stage: a year-book of criticism*, London, 1899.

Aries, P., *L'enfant et la vie familiale sous L'Ancien Régime*, Editions du Seuil, 1973.

Bacon, F., *Novum Organum*, London, 1905.

Barrière-Flavy, C., *La Chronique Criminelle d'une Grande Province sous Louis XIV: les drames et les désordres les plus sensationnels du Languedoc au XVIIIe siècle d'après les archives du Parlemet de Toulouse*, Paris: Editions Occitania, 1926.

Billacois, F., *The Duel: its Rise and Fall in Early Modern France*, Yale UP, 1990.

Bireley, R., *The Jesuits and the Thirty Years War: Kings, Courts and Confessors*, Cambridge University Press, 2003.

Bluche, F., *Richelieu*, Paris, 2003.

Boguet, H., *Discours execrable des sorciers*, Lyon, 1605.

Briggs, R., *Communities of Belief*, Oxford: Clarendon, 1989.

Briggs, R., *Early Modern France 1560–1715*, Oxford: OUP, 1998.

Briost, Drevillon, Serna, *Croiser le Fer – Violence et culture de l'épée dans la France Moderne*, 2002.

Brissette, P., *La malediction littéraire – Du poète crotté au génie malheureux*, Montreal, 2005.

Browne, T., *Hydriotaphia*, 1620.

Brun, P., *Savinien de Cyrano Bergerac – Gentilhomme Parisien, l'histoire et la légende d'après des documents inédits*, Paris, 1893.

Bruno, G., *Oeuvres Complètes* (trans. Yves Hersaut) Paris, 1993.

Bryskett, L., *A Discourse of Civill Life*, New York: Da Capo Press, 1970.

Burrage, A. M., *War is War*, London, 1930.

Bussy-Rabutin, *Les Mémoires de Messire Roger de Rabutin, Comte de Bussy, Lieutenant Général des Armées du Roy et mestre de camp général de la cavalerie légère*, Paris, 1696.

Caillière, Maréchal de, *Les Fortunes de gens de qualité et des gentilhommes particuliers*, 1661.

Calvié, L., *Cyrano dans tous ses Etats*, Toulouse: Anacharsis Editions, 2004.

Carmona, M., *Les Diables de Loudun*, Paris, 1988.

Charron, P., *Traité de la Sagesse*, Paris, 1601.

Constant, J-M., *La noblesse Française aux XVIe et XVIIe siècles*, Hachette, 1985.

Corneille, P., *Le Cid*, Cambridge: CUP, 1924.

Corneille, P., *Le Cid (a translation in Rhymed Couplets* by V. Cheng), University of Delaware Press, 1987.

Corneille, P., *Le Menteur*, Magnard, 2002.

Cornette, J., *Le Roi de Guerre*, Paris, 1993.

Cuenin, M., *Le Duel sous L'Ancien Régime*, Paris, 1982.

Cyrano de Bergerac, S., *L'Autre Monde ou Les Estats et Empires de la Lune*, ed. M. Alcover, Paris: Champion, 1977.

Cyrano de Bergerac, S., *Les Etats et Empires de la Lune et du Soleil*, ed. M. Alcover, Paris: Honoré Champion, 2004.

Cyrano de Bergerac, S., *Les Etats et Empire de la Lune et du Soleil*, ed. Prévot, Paris: Folio, 2004.

Cyrano de Bergerac, S., *Les Etats et Empires du Soleil*, ed. B. Parmentier, Flammarion, 2003.

Cyrano de Bergerac, S., *Les Oeuvres Comiques Galantes et Littéraires*, Paris, 1962.

Cyrano de Bergerac, S., *Lettres d'amour et d'humeur*, Librio, 2004.

Cyrano de Bergerac, S., *Oeuvres*, ed. Lacroix, Paris, 1858.

Cyrano de Bergerac, S., *Oeuvres Complètes*, ed. Erba, Paris: Honoré Champion, 2001.

Cyrano de Bergerac, S., *Satyrical Characters and handsome descriptions in Letters written to severall Persons of Qualilty*, London, 1658.

Cyrano de Bergerac, S., *Selenarchia* (trans. St Serf) London, 1659.

Cyrano de Bergerac, S., *Voyages to the Moon and the Sun*, trans. Aldington, London: Folio Society, 1991.

Dainville, F. de, *La Naissance de l'Humanisme Moderne*, Paris, 1940.

Dewald, J., *Aristocratic experience and the origins of Modern Culture*, University of California Press, 1993.

Dubois, A., *Journal d'un Curé de Campagne au XVIIe siècle*, ed. Platelle, Paris, 1965.

Dulong, C., *La Vie Quotidienne des femmes au Grand Siècle*, Hachette, 1984.

Faret, N., *L'Honnête Homme ou l'art de plaire à la court*, Paris, 1630.

Fontenelle, B. le B. de, *A Discovery of New Worlds*, trans. A. Behn, London, 1688.

Forbin, Comte de, *Mémoires du Comte de Forbin*, Paris, 1993.

Fortin de la Hoguette, P., *Catéchisme royal*, Paris, 1650.

Foucault, D., *Giulio Cesare Vanini – Un Philosophe Libertin dans l'Europe Baroque*, Paris, 2003.

Foucault, M., *L'Histoire de la Folie à l'âge classique*, Gallimard, 1972.

Garasse, Fr., *La Doctrine Curieuse des beaux esprits de ce temps*, Paris, 1624.

Gautier, T., *Le Capitaine Fracasse*, Paris, 1863.

Gérard, R., *Edmond Rostand*, Paris: Bibliothèque–Charpentier, 1935.

Glanvill, J., *Sadducismus Triumphatus or Philosophical Considerations touching Witches and Witchcraft*, London, 1682.

Godwin, F., *The Man in the Moon*, London, 1638.

Gournay, M. de, *Égalité des hommes et des femmes*, Paris, 1989.

Grimarest, le sieur de, *La vie de M. de Molière*, Paris, 1955.

Grimmelshausen, H. J. C. von, *The Adventures of Simplicius Simplicissimus* (trans Schulz-Behrend), Camden House, Columbia, 1993.

Hayden, D., *Pox, Genius, Madness and the Mysteries of Syphilis*, Oxford, 2003.

Héroard, *Journal sur l'Enfance et la Jeunesse de Louis XIII*, 1868.

Hobbes, T., *Leviathan*, Amsterdam, 1670.

Howarth, W. D., *Molière – A Playwright and his Audience*, Cambridge University Press, 1982.

Jones, H., *Pierre Gassendi 1592–1655 – An Intellectual Biography*, Nieuwkoop, 1981.

Kepler, J., *Conversations with Galileo's Sidereal Messenger* (trans. Rosen), New York, 1965.

Kepler, J., *Somnium* (trans. Rosen), University of Wisconsin, 1967.

Knecht, R. J., *Richelieu*, Longman, 1991.

Koyré, A., *Du monde clos à l'univers infini*, Gallimard, 1988.

Lachèvre, F., *Cyrano de Bergerac – Notice Biographique*, Paris: Honoré Champion, 1920.

Lefèvre, L.-R., *La Vie de Cyrano de Bergerac*, Paris, 1927.

Lejeune, *Du devoir des pères*, 1620.

L'Hermite, T., *Le Page Disgracié*, Presse Universitaire de Grenoble, 1980.

Lloyd, S., *The Man Who Was Cyrano*, Indiana: Unlimited, 2002.

Lough, J. (ed.), *France Observed in the 17th Century by British Travellers*, Oriel Press, 1985.

Lucian, *Certain Select Dialogues of Lucian together with his True History* (trans. Hickes), 1634.

Magne, E., *Le Chevalier de Lignières*, Paris, 1920.

Magne, E., *Les Erreurs de documentation de Cyrano de Bergerac*, Paris, 1898.

Magne, E., *Ninon de Lenclos*, Paris, 1925.

Maland, D., *Culture and Society in Seventeenth Century France*, London, 1970.

Mandrou, R., *Magistrats et Sorciers en France au XVIIe siècle*, Paris: Seuil, 1980.

Marche, O. de la, *Traité de Duel*, 1436.

Maurel-Indart, H., *Du Plagiat*, Paris, 1999.

Ménage, G., *Menagiana*, Paris, 1715.

Michaut, G., *La Jeunesse de Molière*, Paris, 1922.

Molière, *Les Femmes Savantes*, Hachette, 1920.

Molière, *Oeuvres Complètes*, Gallimard, 1983.

Molière, *The Works of Molière* (trans. H. van Laun) Edinburgh, 1875.

Monestier, M., *Duels*, Paris, 1991.

Mongrédien, G., *Cyrano de Bergerac*, Paris, 1964.

Montague, C. E., *Dramatic Values*, London, 1911.

Montaigne, M. de, *Essays*, Gallimard, 1965.

Muchembled, R., *Le Roi et la Sorcière*, Paris, 1993.

Naudé, G., *Apologie pour tous les grands hommes qui ont été faussement soupçonnés de magie*, Paris, 1625.

Parker, G., *The Thirty Years War*, Routledge, 1997.

Petitfils, J-C., *Le véritable d'Artagnan*, Paris, 2002.

Pintard, R., *Le Libertinage Erudit*, Paris, 1943.

Prévot, J., *Cyrano de Bergerac – Poète et dramaturge*, Paris, 1978.

Prévot, J., *Cyrano de Bergerac romancier*, Paris, 1977.

Prévot, J., (ed.) *Les Libertins du XVIIe siècle*, Gallimard, 1998.

Pure, L'Abbé de, *La Prétieuse ou le mystère des ruelles*, Paris, 1939.

Quétel, C., *Le Mal de Naples – Histoire de la Syphilis*, Paris, 1986.

Ranum, O., *La Fronde*, Seuil, Paris, 1995.

Read Baker, S., 'Permutations of Parricide: Cyrano de Bergerac's *La Mort d'Agrippine*', *The French Review*, Vol. 65, No. 3 (Feb 1992), pp. 375–84.

Réaux, T. des, *Historiettes*, Paris, 1960.

Rizza, C., *Libertinage et Littérature*, Schena, 1996.

Rocchi, J., *L'Errance et l'hérésie ou le destin de Giordano Bruno*, Paris, 1989.

Rochester, J. Wilmot Earl of, *Rochester's Poems*, Shakespeare Head Press, 1984.

Rohou, *Lettres d'Amour du XVIIe siècle*, Paris, 1994.

Rostand, E., *Cyrano de Bergerac*, Flammarion, 1989.

Rostand E., *Cyrano de Bergerac*, trans. A. Burgess, Hutchinson, 1985.

Russen, D., *Iter Lunare*, London, 1703.

Ryland, H., *The sources of the play Cyrano de Bergerac*, Institut des Etudes Françaises, vol. 70–1, 1936.

Saba, G., *Théophile de Viau: un poète rebelle*, Paris, 1999.

Sacchi, H., *La Guerre des Trente Ans*, Paris: L'Harmattan, 1999.

Schalk, E., *From Valor to Pedigree*, Princeton UP, 1986.

Sorel, C., *Histoire Comique de Francion*, Editions Gallimard, 1996.

Spink, J. S. *French Free Thought*, Toronto, 1960.

Suberville, J., *Edmond Rostand*, Paris, 1921.

Verciani, L., *Le moi et ses diables*, Paris, 2001.

Wilkins, J., *A Discovery of a New World, or A Discourse tending to prove that 'tis Probable there may be another Habitable World in the Moon*, London, 1638.

Acknowledgments

My heartfelt thanks to: Sarah Reece for being my first reader and best source of encouragement; Jim Gill my wonderful agent for his invaluable help in the early stages and continued support; Andrew Gordon my editor for his insightful comments, his precision and his patience; Professor Alcover for her prompt and detailed response to my questions and for the vital archival research she has undertaken in order to establish a clearer, more detailed picture of the real Cyrano; Sophie Trouilhet pour Mauvières, Paris et pour son amitié précieuse; Dr Christian Belin and Dr Charles Whitworth for their kind help and support; Dr Robin Robbins for telling me to look for the gap on my shelf; M. Le Comte et Mme La Comtesse de Bryas merci pour votre accueil; Julie Labaye warmest thanks for invaluable translation assistance – tu es un ange; Lisa Mathieu for her excellent Master's thesis on the Chevalier de Roquelaure; Rob Bartlett for his belief in happy endings; thanks to Max Addyman for finding that elusive quotation for me; Mrs Jane Menon for always being there; Nandita Menon for her kind hospitality at La Trufière; Aliye and Nicole for New York; Delilah Seale for her invaluable help and kindness; Bruno for tea and sympathy; Olivier L'Hôte merci pour la musique et l'audace; Dr Nick Hughes – thanks for research assistance and for drinking those cappuccinos so that I didn't have to. Grateful thanks to the talented Kate Garnett for her lovely photo. Thanks to Karen and Joseph for their kind hospitality. Fabien Gaillard, merci pour la très belle coloration de gravure. Maître Fredairgues, mon maître d'escrime, merci pour vos conseils et votre enthousiasme pour ce projet.

Many thanks to the wonderful staff of the British Library reading rooms in London and Boston Spa. Merci également aux bibliothécaires à la Bibliothèque Nationale et à la Bibliothèque Mazarine à Paris, ainsi que ceux de la Bibliothèque de l'Université Paul Valéry III et de la Médiathèque Emile Zola à Montpellier.

I have been lucky enough to be taught by lots of brilliant and dedicated women over the years and would therefore like to thank all my teachers. Special mention must go to Mrs Hughes who worked so hard for us and whose efforts I didn't appreciate at the time. Also in fond memory of Mrs Small, a brilliant history teacher and Dr Avril Bruten, a true original. Special thanks also to Professor Isabel Rivers for attempting to instil discipline and academic rigour into me at an important early stage and to Ann Wordsworth for her inspirational teaching. Love and thanks to all my family and friends not already singled out above. But above all else, infinite, grovelling thanks to my parents for their unfailing support and generosity.

Index

Index